Practical Ajax Projects with Java™ Technology

Frank W. Zammetti

Apress®

Practical Ajax Projects with Java™ Technology

ISBN-13 (pbk): 987-1-59059-695-1

ISBN-10 (pbk): 1-59059-695-1

Printed and bound in the United States of America 9 8 7 6 5 4 3 2 1

Lead Editor: Chris Mills
Technical Reviewer: Herman van Rosmalen
Editorial Board: Steve Anglin, Ewan Buckingham, Gary Cornell, Jason Gilmore, Jonathan Gennick, Jonathan Hassell, James Huddleston, Chris Mills, Matthew Moodie, Dominic Shakeshaft, Jim Sumser, Keir Thomas, Matt Wade
Project Manager: Richard Dal Porto
Copy Edit Manager: Nicole LeClerc
Copy Editor: Liz Welch
Assistant Production Director: Kari Brooks-Copony
Production Editor: Kelly Gunther
Compositor: Lynn L'Heureux
Proofreader: Linda Seifert
Indexer: Brenda Miller
Cover Designer: Kurt Krames
Manufacturing Director: Tom Debolski

Distributed to the book trade worldwide by Springer-Verlag New York, Inc., 233 Spring Street, 6th Floor, New York, NY 10013. Phone 1-800-SPRINGER, fax 201-348-4505, e-mail orders-ny@springer-sbm.com, or visit http://www.springeronline.com.

For information on translations, please contact Apress directly at 2560 Ninth Street, Suite 219, Berkeley, CA 94710. Phone 510-549-5930, fax 510-549-5939, e-mail info@apress.com, or visit http://www.apress.com.

The source code for this book is available to readers at http://www.apress.com in the Source Code section.

For my wife Traci, who probably does not understand a single thing in this book, but who reminded me why I love her by being more excited for me than I was for myself about my first book.

For my two children, Andrew and Ashley, for whom I gladly worked all those long hours. Thanks for leaving Daddy alone (usually) long enough to get this done; I owe you each a pony. (I hope you both know about sarcasm by the time you read this!)

For Mom and Dad, who started it all with the seemingly innocuous purchase of a Timex Sinclair 1000 computer for Christmas 1982 (or 1983—my memory's a bit flaky 20+ years later!).

For John J. Sheridan, for keeping the Shadows off our backs.

Contents at a Glance

Contents

About the Author

FRANK W. ZAMMETTI is a web architecture specialist for a leading worldwide financial company by day, and a PocketPC and open source developer by night. He is the founder and chief software architect of Omnytex Technologies, a PocketPC development house.

He has more than 12 years of "professional" experience in the IT field, and 12 more of "amateur" experience. He began his nearly lifelong love of computers at age 7 when he became one of four students chosen to take part in the school district's pilot computer program. A year later, he was the only participant left! The first computer Frank owned (around 1982) was a Timex Sinclair 1000, on which he wrote a program to look up movie times for all of Long Island (and without the 16k expansion module!). After that, he moved on to an Atari computer, and then a Commodore 64, where he spent about 4 years doing nothing but assembly programming (games mostly). He finally got his first IBM-compatible PC in 1987, and began learning the finer points of programming (as they existed at that time!).

Frank has primarily developed web-based applications for about 8 years. Before that, he developed Windows-based client-server applications in a variety of languages. Frank holds numerous certifications, including SCJP, MCSD, CNA, i-Net+, A+, CIW Associate, MCP, and numerous BrainBench certifications. He is a contributor to a number of open source projects, including DataVision, Struts, PocketFrog, and Jakarta Commons. In addition, Frank has started two projects: Java Web Parts and The Struts Web Services Enablement Project. He also was one of the founding members of a project that created the first fully functioning Commodore 64 emulator for PocketPC devices (PocketHobbit).

Frank has authored various articles on topics that range from integrating DataVision into web apps to using Ajax in Struts-based applications. He is currently working on a new application framework specifically geared to creating next-generation web applications.

About the Technical Reviewer

HERMAN VAN ROSMALEN works as a developer/software architect for De Nederlandsche Bank N.V., the central bank of the Netherlands. He has more than 20 years of experience in developing software applications in a variety of programming languages. Herman has been involved in building mainframe, PC, and client-server applications. The past 6 years, however, he has been involved mainly in building J2EE web-based applications. After working with Struts for years (pre-1.0), he got interested in Ajax and joined the Java Web Parts open source project in 2005.

Herman lives in a small town, Pijnacker, in the Netherlands with his wife Liesbeth and their children, Barbara, Leonie, and Ramon.

About the Illustrator

ANTHONY VOLPE did the illustrations for this book and the AJAX Warrior video game. He has worked on several video games with author Frank Zammetti, including Invasion Trivia, Io Lander, and Krelmac, and Gentoo Arcade. Anthony lives in Collegeville, PA, and works as a graphic designer and front-end web developer. His hobbies include recording music, writing fiction, making video games, and going to karaoke bars to make a spectacle of himself.

Acknowledgments

Many people helped make this book a reality in one form or another, and some of them may not even realize it! I'll try and remember them all here, but chances are I haven't, and I apologize in advance!

First and foremost, I would like to thank everyone at Apress Publishing who made this book a reality, and for taking a chance on an essentially unknown quantity. I have nothing but kind words to say about everyone I interacted with and the whole process in general. Thank you for making it such a smooth, rewarding ride!

I would like to especially thank my editor, Chris Mills, and my project manager, Richard Dal Porto. Both of you guided me through an entirely unfamiliar territory and made it a pleasure, and I can't thank either of you enough for it! I know you were both just doing your jobs, and that makes it all that much more impressive. And besides, I turned Chris on to Shadow Gallery, so in a sense he owes me a big thanks!

A great deal of thanks goes to Herman van Rosmalen, one of my partners in crime on the Java Web Parts (`http://javawebparts.sourceforge.net`) project, and technical reviewer for this book. I know you put in a lot of time and effort in keeping me honest, and I can't tell you how much I appreciate it! Even when we perhaps didn't agree on things, you always made me think and consider alternatives, and that makes you truly worth your weight in gold. Now let's get to some of the items on the JWP to-do list!

A big thanks must also go to Anthony Volpe, the fine artist who did the illustrations for this book. He and I have been friends for about 10 years now, and we have collaborated on a number of projects, including three PocketPC games (check 'em out: `www.omnytex.com`) as well as a couple of Flash games (`www.planetvolpe.com/crackhead`) and some web cartoons (`www.planetvolpe.com/du`). He is a fantastic artist and, as I'm sure you can see for yourself, an incredibly creative person—and a good friend to boot.

I would like to thank Wendy Smoak, who put up with many rants from me during the course of writing this book. Believe it or not, you even helped solve a technical problem or two along the way, which certainly is very much appreciated, but having the ear there to yell into when the going got tough was even more appreciated!

I would also like to thank those who built some of the libraries used in this book, including Joe Walker (DWR), all the folks working on Dojo, and Sam Stephenson (Prototype).

Last but most definitely not least, I would like to thank everyone who buys this book! I sincerely hope you have as much fun reading it as I did writing it, and I hope that you find it to be worth your hard-earned dollars and that it proves to be an educational and eye-opening experience.

As I said, I know I am almost certainly forgetting a boatload of people, so how about I just thank the entire world and be done with it? In fact, if I had the technology, I'd be like Wowbagger the Infinitely Prolonged, only with "Thanks!" instead of insults.

And on that note, let's get to some code!

Introduction

Who would have imagined that someone cleverly applying the name of a popular cleaning agent to a programming technique would change the world? That's exactly what is happening right now!

Ajax, Asynchronous JavaScript and XML, has taken the web development world by storm, and for good reason. It not only ushers in a new era of potential for web applications to "grow up," so to speak, in terms of the user interface they provide their human users, but also allows for a fundamental paradigm shift in the way people approach web development. No longer are we bound to the document/page model of things, but the world of user-driven events, in a much more real way than was possible before, can now become a reality. Web *applications* can now be developed, perhaps for the first time—at least the first time in terms of developer mindshare (because, as you will learn, Ajax is not really anything new!). Cool!

Ajax has enjoyed a somewhat extended "hype bubble," as I like to call it. Usually, things like this come and go in the blink of an eye in Internet time. But we're going on over a year now since that fateful day when someone smarter than the rest of us, at least in terms of nifty naming, came up with a name that described something many of us had been doing for a long time. You know what they say: it's not so much the idea that matters, it's who names it first that does.

The fact that the hype is still going strong shows that Ajax may in fact be something different. And really, it isn't so much hype any more as it is people coming to grips with the reality of it, wanting to get past the marketing and the initial "wow" factor, and realizing that there is a lot of good there to be harnessed. Maybe it isn't just a pretty name—maybe there is some meat there. Indeed, there is!

A big part of the reason I wrote this book is because in order for many of us programmers to see why Ajax may be more than a temporary fad and much more of a paradigm shift, we have to see it in action. We can read all the white papers we want, we can ingest all the introductory articles on it that we can find, and we still will be scratching our heads and saying, "OK, I understand the mechanics of it, but how can it be applied in the real world?" My goal with this book is to give programmers real demonstrations of how Ajax can be used in real applications in cool ways, and explain how Ajax can reduce our dependency on fossil fuels and result in world peace.

OK, you got me. It can't replace gasoline—*yet*. Gimme another week.

Seriously though, this book is for the programmers out there who learn better when they are seeing real code in action, code they can dissect and play with. It isn't written for the theorists among us, or those who no longer twiddle bits on a regular basis. That isn't to say architects, of which I am one (I am just fortunate enough to still be able to write code too!), can't get anything from this book. Of course they can! But those in the trenches making the glorious designs a reality are the ones who will benefit most, I believe.

So, why should you read this book? Well, for starters, there's a game in it! And I'm not talking a hidden Easter egg game… flip to Chapter 10 right now… go ahead, I'll wait.

See? I wasn't kidding!

Aside from that, six other projects await you, each different from the others, and each showcasing how Ajax can make web development better, richer, and ultimately more dynamic. You will be introduced to a number of approaches, a number of different libraries, so that as you move forward in your own Ajax work you will be able to decide what approach suits you and the situation best, and you will have ready examples to get you started.

On a personal note, I have to say that I had a great deal of fun writing this book. It was my first, so it really could have been a bad experience, but it simply was the exact opposite. Sure, it was quite a lot of hard work, and I can tell you that my sleep habits have been pretty seriously messed up over the course of writing it! But it was well worth it. I truly believe that any developer who reads this book and explores the applications described within will gain a great deal of knowledge and experience, and I think have a good time doing it too. If you have a good time reading it *and* learn something in the process, then my mission has been accomplished.

An Overview of This Book

Chapter 1 is an introduction to the progression of web development in general and to Ajax in particular.

Chapter 2 covers the basics required to make sense of all this Ajax stuff: JavaScript, CSS, DOM scripting, and XML are all touched upon at an introductory level.

Chapter 3 talks about the server side of things, including a brief introduction to Ant, Apache Tomcat, webapps, servlets, JSPs, and a little more on XML.

Chapter 4 begins the projects, starting with Karnak, a concept very roughly, slightly, sort of, maybe, borrowed from Google Suggest. This chapter introduces AjaxTags in Java Web Parts (don't worry if you don't know what this, or anything else mentioned here, is… we'll get to that!).

Chapter 5 is a webmail client, similar to Google's Gmail. With this project you will be introduced to a cool Ajax library named DWR.

Chapter 6 presents a fairly typical Ajax application: an RSS feed reader. This project again demonstrates the usage of AjaxTags in Java Web Parts.

Chapter 7 is an application named PhotoShare, which allows you to build collections of photographs and share them with your friends and family. This application demonstrates some nifty animation techniques, and introduces another library: Dojo.

Chapter 8 is a project called The Organizer, which is intended to be a basic PIM application (i.e., notes, tasks, appointments, and contacts). With this project you will learn about a popular application framework named WebWork, as well as Spring a little bit, and Prototype, one of the most popular Ajax libraries.

Chapter 9 is an Ajax-based chat application named, unimaginatively, AjaxChat. This application is built on what may be the most famous framework of them all, Struts, and uses "naked" Ajax, that is, no library at all.

Chapter 10, finally, is the game! AJAX Warrior is its name, and it too is built using "naked" Ajax, and introduces a popular data format frequently seen in Ajax applications called JSON.

Obtaining This Book's Source Code

All the examples in this book are freely available from the Source Code section of the Apress website. In fact, due to the nature of this book, you will absolutely *have* to download the source before you begin Chapter 4. To do so, visit `www.apress.com`, click the Source Code link, and find *Practical Ajax Projects with Java™ Technology* in the list. From this book's home page you can download the source code as a zip file. The source code is organized by chapter.

Obtaining Updates for This Book

Writing a book is a big endeavor, quite a bit bigger than I thought it would be initially! Contrary to what I claim in private to my friends, I am not perfect. I make mistakes like everyone else. Not in this book, of course. Oh no, none at all.

AHEM.

Let me apologize in advance for any errors you may find in this book. Rest assured that everyone involved has gone to extremes to ensure there are none—but let's be real here, we've all read technical books before, and we know that the cold, sharp teeth of reality bite every now and again. I'm sorry, I'm sorry, I'm sorry!

A current errata list is available from this book's home page on the Apress website (`www.apress.com`), along with information about how to notify us of any errors you may find. This will usually involve some sort of telepathy, but we hear Windows Vista is being pushed back a few months so that feature can be added.

Contacting the Author

I very much would like to hear your questions and comments regarding this book's content and source code examples. Please feel free to e-mail me directly at `fzammetti@omnytex.com` (spammers *will* be hunted down by Sentinels and disposed of). I will reply to your inquiries as soon as I can, but please remember, I do have a life (ha, ha! I'm funny!), so I may not be able to reply immediately.

PART 1

■ ■ ■

Programming Using Ajax and Java

I never think of the future—it comes soon enough.

—Albert Einstein

We've heard that a million monkeys at a million keyboards could produce the complete works of Shakespeare; now, thanks to the Internet, we know that is not true.

—Robert Wilensky

The computing field is always in need of new clichés.

—Alan Perlis

The 'Net is a waste of time, and that's exactly what's right about it.

—William Gibson

The most overlooked advantage to owning a computer is that if they foul up there's no law against whacking them around a little.

—Joe Martin

The most likely way for the world to be destroyed, most experts agree, is by accident. That's where we come in; we're computer professionals. We cause accidents.

—Nathaniel Borenstein

CHAPTER 1

Ajax: The Brave New World

If this is your first experience with Ajax, and even web development in general, this chapter will serve as a good introduction to get you up to speed for what is to come. If, however, you are a relatively experienced developer, and especially if Ajax is not new to you, feel free to skip this chapter, as it will likely be just a review for you. This chapter begins our exploration of Ajax by examining how applications in general, and web applications in particular, have been developed over the past decade and a half or so. You'll discover an interesting cycle in terms of the basic structure of appli-cations. We'll look at some great examples of Ajax in action and talk about why Ajax is important and how it can fundamentally alter how you develop applications. You'll encounter your first code sample demonstrating Ajax in a very simple, basic way. We'll also briefly touch on some of the alternatives to Ajax, and some of the existing libraries and toolkits that make Ajax easier.

A Brief History of Web Development: The "Classic" Model

In the beginning, there was the Web. And it was good. All manner of catchy new words, phrases, and terms entered the lexicon, and we felt all the more cooler saying them (come on, admit it, you felt like Spock the first couple of times you used the word "hypertext" in conversation, didn't you?). "Webapps," as our work came to be known, were born. These apps were in a sense a throwback to years gone by when applications were hosted on "big iron" and were accessed in a timeshare fashion. They were in no way, shape, or form as "flashy" as the Visual Basic, PowerBuilder, and C++ "fat clients" that followed them (which are still used today, although less so with the advent of webapps.) But those fat clients did, and still do in many cases, get the job done, just like those timeshare systems of old.

In fact, if you really think about it, application development has followed a very up-and-down pattern, and if you walk down the timeline carefully and examine it, this pattern begins to emerge.

Starting with what I term the "modern" era, that is, the era in which applications took a form that most of us would basically recognize, we first encounter simple terminal emulation devices (for the sake of this argument, we'll skip the actual terminal period!) used to access remotely running processes. Screens like the one shown in Figure 1-1 were typical of those types of applications.

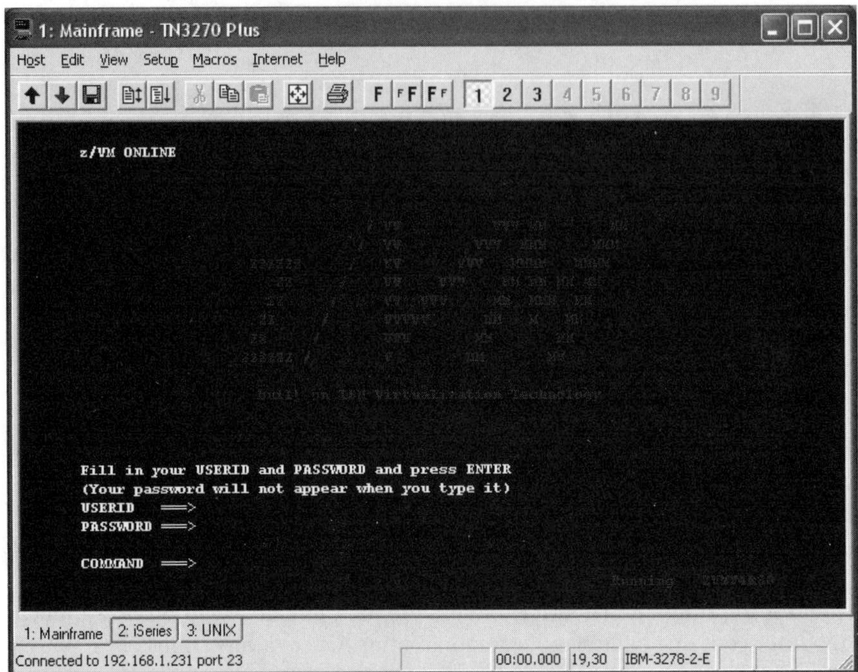

Figure 1-1. *TN3270 mainframe "green-screen" terminal display*

TN3270 screens are, of course, completely relevant in the sense that they are still used quite a bit, especially in the business world, as anyone who has done any sort of mainframe work can attest to. There are two interesting things to note, for the sake of this discussion. First, notice the simple nature of the user interfaces (UIs) back then—they were text-only, usually limited to 80 columns by 25 lines of text, with extremely limited data entry capabilities—essentially just editable mapped regions. Things like dropdowns, checkboxes, and grids were completely unknown in this domain. If it was a well-written application, you would be fortunate and have a real menu like so:

C. Create Record

D. Delete Record

E. Edit record

If you were unlucky, you would just have something like this:

..... 01A7C0D9ABABAC00

..... 89A6B3E34D79E998

If you have never worked on a mainframe, let me briefly explain what that is. For editing files (called data sets) on a mainframe, you usually use a tool called TSO/ISPF. This is just a form of text editor. This editor can be flipped between textual display and hex display, and the above is the hex display version. The dots that precede each line make up the command area. For instance, to insert a line above the line that begins with 89, you would go to the first dot in that line and replace it with i, then press the Enter key. If you wanted to delete that line, plus the line that starts with 01, you would go to the line that starts with 01, type dd over the first two dots, then go to the line you just inserted and put dd there as well, then press Enter (dd is for deleting a block of lines, you can use a single d to delete a single line).

Second, and more important here, is the question of what happens when the user performs an action that requires the application to do something. In many cases, what would happen is that the mainframe would redraw the entire screen, even the parts that would not change as a result of the operation. Every single operation occurred on the mainframe, and there was no local processing to speak of. Not even simple input validation was performed on the client; it was simply a view of a remote application's state, nothing more.

With the advent of the PC, when the amount of local processing power advanced orders of magnitude, a new trend emerged. At this point we began to see applications hosted locally instead of on central mainframes where at least some portion of the application actually executed locally. Many times, the entire application itself was running on the machine that the user was using. With the growth in popularity of Microsoft Windows more than anything else, "fat clients," as they came to be known, were suddenly the de facto standard in application development. The UI available in this paradigm was immensely more powerful and user-friendly, but the central hardware faded in importance for the most part (things like database servers notwithstanding). Screens like the one in Figure 1-2 became the norm.

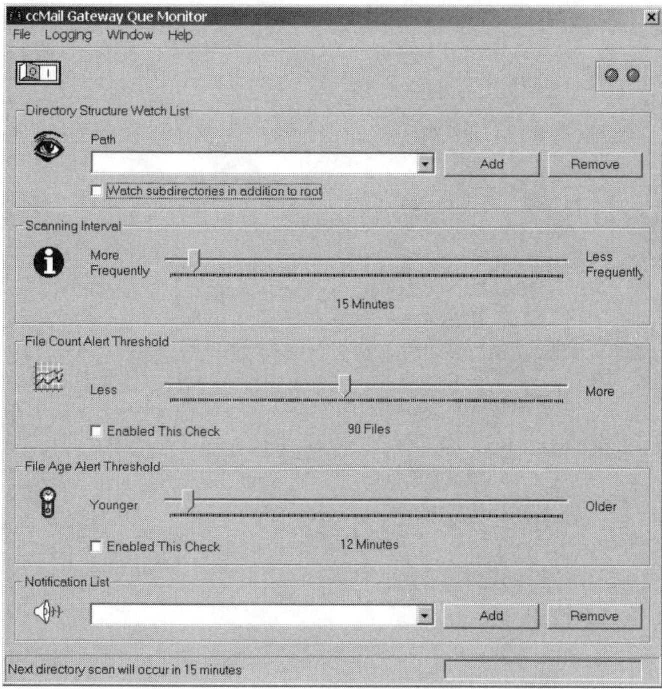

Figure 1-2. *A typical "fat-client" application*

Note how much richer the available UI metaphors are. It should come as no surprise to you and the rest of the user community out there that this is universally seen as "better" (you do see this as better, don't you?). Better is, of course, a relative term, and in some cases it is not better. You would think that people doing heads-down data entry all day might actually prefer those old green screens more because they lend themselves to more efficient keyboard-based data entry efficiency. No fussing with a mouse. No pointing and clicking. No need to take their eyes off the document they are keying off of to save a record. While all of that is true, it cannot be denied that, by and large, people will choose a fat-client version of a given application over a text-only version of it any day of the week! Go ahead, I dare you! Take an existing mainframe application and put it side by side with a fat-client version of the same application and see how many users actually want the mainframe version. I'll give you a hint: it will be less than 1, but not negative.

Thinking about how the application actually functions, though, what happens here when the user clicks a button, for example, or slides a slider, or clicks on a menu item? In most cases, only some region of the screen will be updated, and no external system is interacted with (usually). This is obviously more efficient and in all likelihood more user-friendly as well.

But what happened next in our timeline? A bit of a monkey wrench got thrown in the works with the rise of the Internet, and more specifically, the World Wide Web component, or just the Web for short (remember, the Web is *not*, in and of itself, the Internet!). With the emergence of the Web, screens like the one in Figure 1-3 became commonplace.

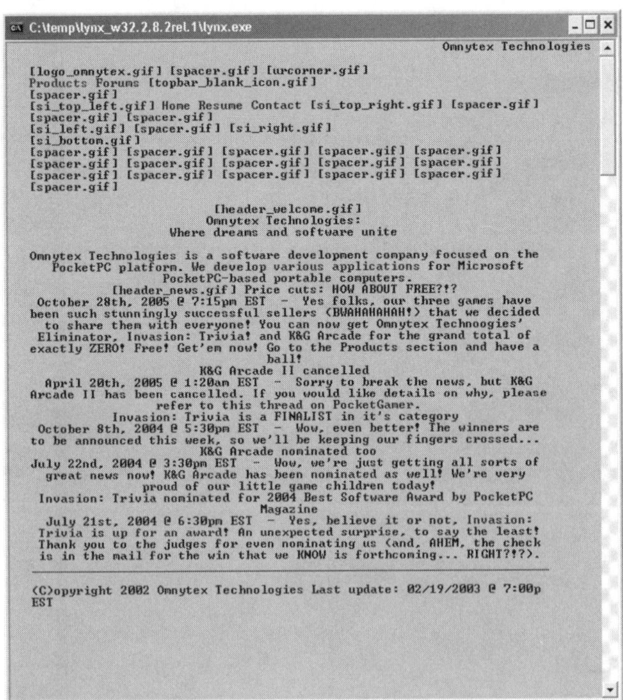

Figure 1-3. *omnytex.com as seen in Lynx, a text-based browser*

Wait a second, what happened? Where did all our fancy radio buttons, 3D buttons, list boxes, and all that go? The first iteration of the Web looked a heck of a lot, visually, like the old mainframe world. More important, though, is what was happening under the hood: we went back to the old way of doing things in terms of centralized machines actually running the applications, and entire screens at a time being redrawn for virtually every user interaction.

In a very real sense, we took a big step backward. The screen is redrawn by the server and returned to the user with each operation. Each and every user interaction (ignoring client-side scripting for the moment because it was not immediately available to the first web developers) required a call to a server to do the heavy lifting. See, we are back to the mainframe way of doing things, more or less! We didn't all just lose our minds overnight, of course; there were some good reasons for doing this. Avoidance of "DLL Hell," the phenomenon in the Windows world where library versions conflict and cause all sorts of headaches, was certainly one of them. Another reason was the need to distribute applications. When an application runs on a centralized server, it can be accessed from any PC with a web browser without having to first install it. Another good reason was the relative ease of application development. At least in the beginning when webapps were fairly simple things done with little more than HTML and simple back-end CGI programs, almost anyone could quickly and easily pick it up. The learning curve was not all that high, even for those who had not done much application development before.

Of course, the Web grew up mighty quick! In what seemed like the blink of an eye, we moved from Figure 1-3 to Figure 1-4.

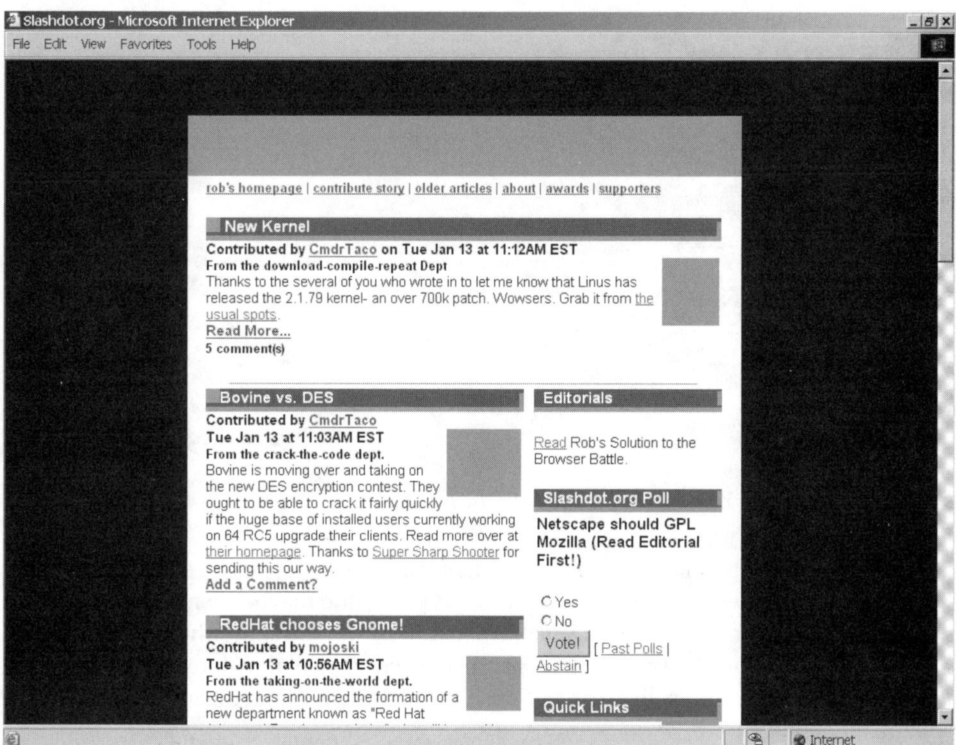

Figure 1-4. *Slashdot, circa 1998*

Now, that certainly looks a bit better, from a visual standpoint for sure. In addition to just the visual quality, we had a more robust palette of UI widgets available like dropdowns, radio buttons, checkboxes, and so forth. In many ways it was even better than the fat clients that preceded the rise of the Web because "multimedia" presentation was now becoming the norm. Graphics started to become a big part of what we were doing, so visually things were looking a lot better.

What about those pesky user interactions, though? Yes, you guessed it: we were still redrawing the entire screen each time at this point. The beginnings of client-side scripting emerged though, and this allowed at least some functionality to occur without the server, but by and large it was still two-tier architecture: a view tier and, well, the rest! For a while we had frames too, which alleviated that problem to some degree, but that was really more a minor divergence on the path than a contributor to the underlying pattern.

Before you could say "Internet time," though, we found ourselves in the "modern" era of the Web, or what we affectionately call "today" (see Figure 1-5).

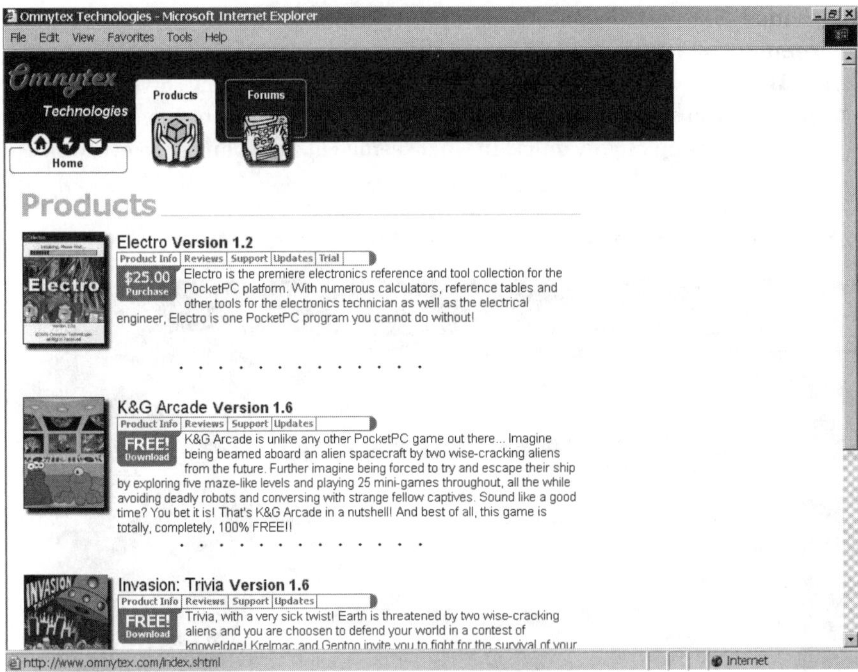

Figure 1-5. *The "modern" Web—omnytex.com as the example*

So, at least visually, as compared to the fat clients we were largely using throughout the late '80s and early '90s, we are now at about the same point, and maybe even a bit beyond that arguably. What about the UI elements available to us? Well, they are somewhere in the middle.

We have radio buttons and checkboxes and dropdowns and all that, but they are not quite as powerful as their fat-client counterparts. Still, it is clearly better than the text regions we had before the Web.

But the underlying problem that we have been talking about all along remains: we are still asking the server to redraw entire screens for virtually every little user event and still asking the server to do the vast majority of the work of our application. We have evolved slightly from the earlier incarnations of the Web to the extent that client-side scripting is now available. So in fact, in contrast to how it was just a few years ago, not *every* user event requires a server call. Simple things like trivial data entry validations and such are now commonly performed on the client machine, independent of the server. Still, the fact remains that most events do require intervention by the server, whether or not that is ideal. Also, where a user has scripting disabled, good design dictates that the site should "degrade" gracefully, which means the server again takes on most of the work.

At this point I would like to introduce a term I am fond of that I may or may not have invented (I had never heard anyone use it before me, but I cannot imagine I was the first). The term is the "classic" Web. The "classic" Web to me means the paradigm where the server, for nearly every user event, redraws the entire screen. This is how webapps have been built for about 15 years now, since the Web first began to be known in a broad sense. We will be talking about the classic Web versus the modern Web for the remainder of this chapter.

Before that, though, going back to our timeline, do you see the pattern? We started with centralized applications and complete redrawing of the screen in response to every single user action. Then we went to fat clients that largely ran locally and only updated the relevant portion of the screen. Then we went *back* to centralized applications, and also *back* to the central machine redrawing the entire screen.

So, what comes next? Well, simply put, the pendulum is beginning to swing right back the other way again, and in a big way!

What Is "Wrong" with the Classic Web?

In many ways, absolutely nothing! In fact, there is still a great deal of value to that way of designing webapps. The classic Web is great for largely linear application flows, and is also a wonderful medium for delivering information in an accessible way. It is easy for most people to publish information and to even create rudimentary applications with basic user interactions. The classic Web is efficient, simple, ubiquitous, and accessible to most people. It is not, however, an ideal environment for developing complex applications. The fact that people have been able to do so to this point is a testament to the ingenuity of engineers rather than an endorsement of the Web as an application distribution medium!

It makes sense to differentiate now between a "webapp" and a "web site," as summarized in Table 1-1.

Table 1-1. *Summary Comparison of "Webapps" vs. "Websites"*

Webapps	Websites
Designed with much greater user interaction in mind	Very little user interaction aside from navigation from document to document
Main purpose is to perform some function or functions, usually in real time, based on user inputs	Main purpose is to deliver information, period.
Uses techniques that require a lot more of the clients accessing them	Tends to be created for the lowest common denominator in terms of client capabilities
Accessibility tends to take a back seat to functionality out of necessity and the simple fact that it's hard to do complex and yet accessible webapps	Accessibility is usually considered and implemented to allow for the widest possible audience.
Tends to be more event-based and nonlinear	Tends to be somewhat linear with a path the user is generally expected to follow with only minor deviations

There are really two different purposes served by the Web at large. One is to deliver information. In this scenario, it is very important that the information be delivered in a manner that is readily accessible to the widest possible audience. This means not only people with disabilities who are using screen readers and such devices, but also those using more limited capability devices like cell phones, PocketPCs, and kiosk terminals. In such situations, there tends to be no user interactions aside from jumping from static document to static document, or at most very little interaction via simple fill-out forms. This mode of operation for the Web, if you will, can be classified as websites.

The webapps, on the other hand, have a wholly different focus. They are not concerned with simply presenting information, but in performing some function based on what the user does and what data the user provides. The user can be another automated system in many cases, but usually we are talking about real flesh-and-blood human beings. Webapps tend to be more complex and much more demanding of the clients that access them. In this case, "clients" refer to web browsers.

This does not have to be true. There are indeed some very complex webapps out there that do not require any more capability of clients than a website does. While it clearly is not impossible to build complex applications in the "website" mode, it is limiting and more difficult to do well in terms of user-friendliness, and it tends to require sacrifices in terms of capabilities or robustness of the capabilities provided.

This is the problem with the classic model: you generally have to design to the lowest common denominator, which severely limits what you can do.

Let's think a moment about what the lowest common denominator means in this context. Consider what you could and could not use to reach the absolute widest possible audience out there today. Here is a list of what comes to mind:

- Client-side scripting: Nope, you could not use this because many mobile devices do not yet have scripting support, or are severely limited. This does not even consider those people on full-blown PCs who simply choose to disable scripting for security or other reasons.

- Cascading Stylesheets (CSS): You could use it, but you would have to be very careful to use an older specification to ensure most browsers would render it properly—none of the fancier CSS 2.0 capabilities for instance.

- Frames: No, frames are not universally supported, especially on many portable devices. Even when they are supported you need to be careful because a frame is essentially like having another browser instance in terms of memory (and in some cases it very literally *is* another browser instance), and this can be a major factor in mobile devices.

- Graphics: Graphics can be tricky in terms of accessibility because they tend to convey more information than an `ALT` attribute can. So, some of the meaning of the graphic can easily be lost for those with disabilities, no matter how vigilant you are to help them.

- Newer HTML specs: There are still many people out there using older browsers that may not even support HTML 4.01, so to be safe you will probably want to code to HTML 3.0. You will lose some capabilities obviously in doing so.

Probably the most important element here is the lack of client-side scripting. Without client-side scripting, there are simply so many possibilities that are not available to you as a developer. Most important in the context of this book is the fact that you have virtually no choice but to have the server handle every single user interaction. You may be able to get away with some meta-refreshes in frames in some cases, or perhaps other tricks of the trade, but frames too are on the list, so you might not even have that option!

You may be wondering, "What is the problem with the server rendering entire pages?" Certainly there are benefits, and the inherent security of being in complete control of the runtime state of the application (i.e., the user can't hack the code) is a big one. Not having to incur the delay of downloading the code to the client is another. However, there are indeed some problems that in many cases overshadow the benefits. Perhaps the most obvious is the load on the server. Asking a server to do all this work on behalf of the client many times over across a number of simultaneous requests means that the server needs to be more robust and capable than it might otherwise need to be. This all translates to dollars and cents in the long run because you will have to purchase more server power to handle the load. Now, many people have the "just throw more hardware at it" mentality, and we are indeed in an age where that works most of the time. But that is much like saying that because we can throw bigger and bigger engines in cars to make them go faster then that's exactly what we should always do when we need or want more speed. In fact, we can make cars go faster by making a smaller engine more efficient in design and execution, which in many ways is much more desirable—that is, if you like clean, fresh air to breathe!

Perhaps an even better metaphor would be to say it is like taking a mid-sized car and continually adding seats tied to it around the outside to allow for more people to ride "in" the car rather than trying to find a more efficient way for them to get where they are going. While this duct-tape solution might work for a while, eventually someone is going to fall off and get crushed by the 18-wheeler driving behind us!

Another problem with the server-does-it-all approach is that of network traffic. Network technology continues to grow in leaps and bounds at a fantastic rate. Many of us now have broadband connections in our homes that we could not fully saturate if we tried (and I for one have tried!). However, that does not mean we should have applications that are sending far more information per request than they need to. We should still strive for thriftiness, should we not?

The other big problem is simply how the user perceives the application. When the server has to redraw the entire screen, it generally results in a longer wait time to see the results, not to mention the visual redrawing that many times occurs in webapps, flickering, and things of that nature. These are things users universally dislike in a big way. They also do not like losing everything they entered when something goes wrong, which is another common failing of the classic model.

At the end of the day, the classic model still works well on a small scale, and for delivering mostly static information, but it doesn't scale very well and it doesn't deal with the dynamic nature of the Web today nearly as well. In this context, "scale" refers to added functionality in the application, not simultaneous request handling capability (although it is quite possible that is in play, too). If things do not work as smoothly, or if breakages result in too much lost, or if perceived speed is diminished, then the approach didn't scale well.

The classic model will continue to serve us well for some time to come in the realm of websites, but in the realm of webapps—the realm you are likely interested in if you are reading this book—its demise is at hand, and its slayer is the hero of our tale: Ajax!

Enter Ajax

Ajax (see Figure 1-6...now you'll always know what code and architectures would look like personified as a super hero!) came to life, so to speak, at the hands of one Jesse James Garrett of Adaptive Path (`www.adaptivepath.com`). I am fighting my natural urge to make the obvious outlaw jokes here! Mr. Garrett wrote an essay in February 2005 (you can see it here: `www.adaptivepath.com/publications/essays/archives/000385.php`) in which he coined the term *Ajax*. Figures 1-7 through 1-9 show examples of Ajax-enabled applications.

Figure 1-6. *Ajax to the rescue!*

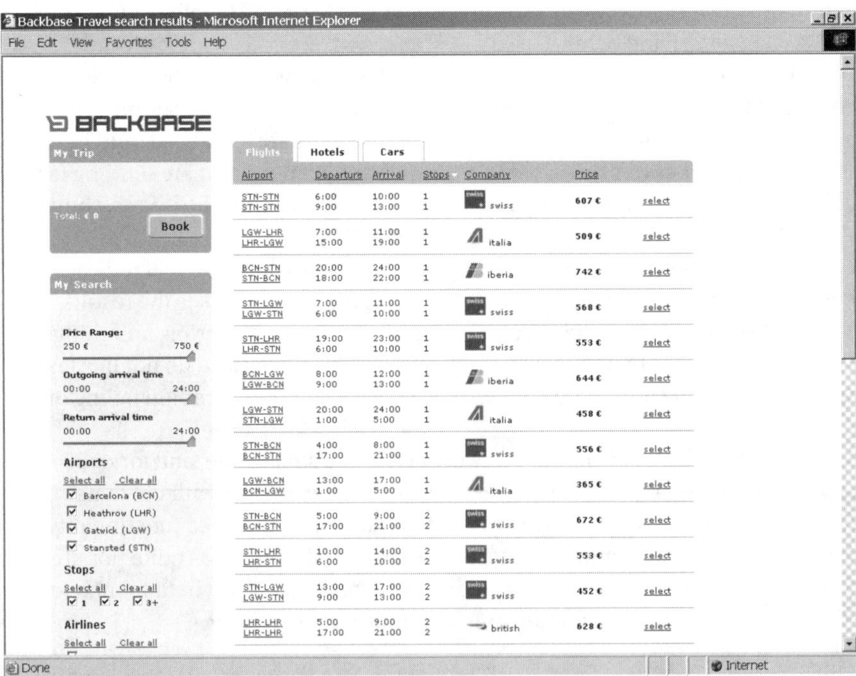

Figure 1-7. *Backbase, a commercial product for creating Ajax applications, shows off their product in this flight-booking application.*

Ajax, as I'd be willing to bet my dog you know already (I don't have a dog, but I will buy one and give it to you if you don't know what Ajax stands for! OK, not really) stands for Asynchronous JavaScript and XML. The interesting thing about Ajax, though, is that it doesn't have to be asynchronous (but virtually always is), doesn't have to involve JavaScript (but virtually always does), and doesn't need to use XML at all (but probably does half the time). In fact, one of the most famous Ajax examples, Google Suggest, doesn't pass back XML at all! The fact is that it does not even pass back data per se; it passes back JavaScript that contains data! Don't worry if that doesn't make much sense, because it will by the end of this book.

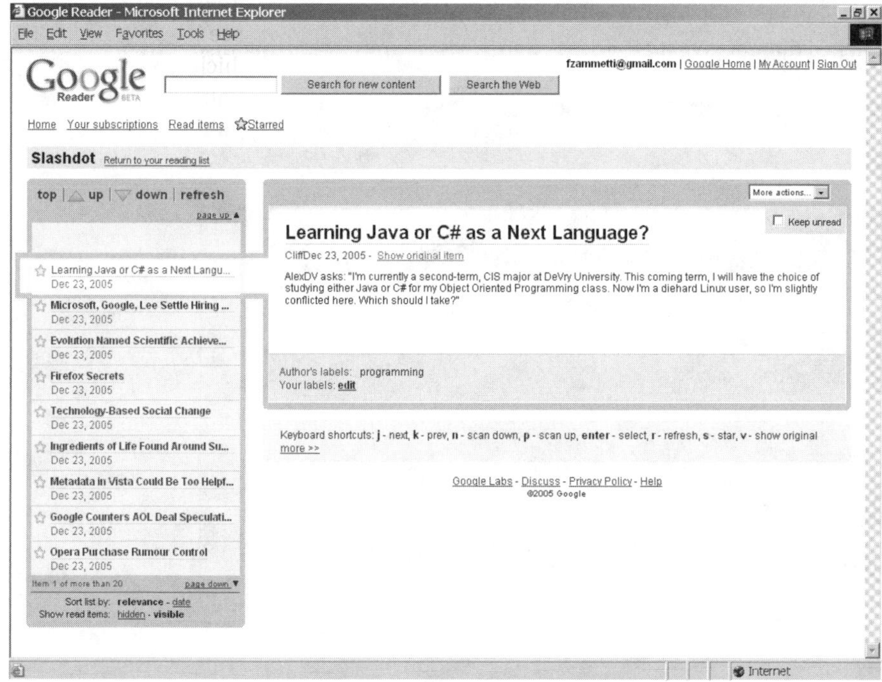

Figure 1-8. *Google Reader, now in beta, is a rather good Ajax-enabled RSS reader.*

Ajax is, at its core, an exceedingly simple, and by no stretch of the imagination original, concept: it is not necessary to refresh the entire contents of a web page for each user interaction, or each "event," if you will. When the user clicks a button, it is no longer necessary to ask the server to render an entirely new page, as is the case with the classic Web. Instead, you can define regions on the page to be updated, and have much more fine-grained control over user events as well. No longer are you limited to simply submitting a form or navigating to a new page when a link is clicked. You can now do something in direct response to a non-submit button being clicked, a key being pressed in a text box—in fact, to any event happening! The server is no longer completely responsible for rendering what the user sees; some of this logic is now performed in the user's browser. In fact, in a great many cases it is considerably better to simply return a set of data and not a bunch of markup for the browser to display. As we traced along our admittedly rough history of application development, we saw that the classic model of web development is in a sense an aberration to the extent that we actually had it right before then!

Ajax is a return to that thinking. Notice I said "thinking." That should be a very big clue to you about what Ajax really is. It is not a specific technology, and it is not the myriad toolkits available for doing Ajax, and it is not the `XMLHttpRequest` object (which we will get to in a moment). It is a way of thinking, an approach to application development, a mind-set.

The interesting thing about Ajax is that it is in no way, shape, or form *new*; only the term used to describe it is. I was recently reminded of this fact at the Philadelphia Java Users Group. A speaker by the name of Steve Banfield was talking about Ajax, and he said (paraphrasing from memory): "You can always tell someone who has actually done Ajax because they are pissed that it is all of a sudden popular." This could not be more true! I was one of those people doing Ajax years and years ago; I just never thought what I was doing was anything special and hence did not give it a "proper" name. Mr. Garrett holds that distinction.

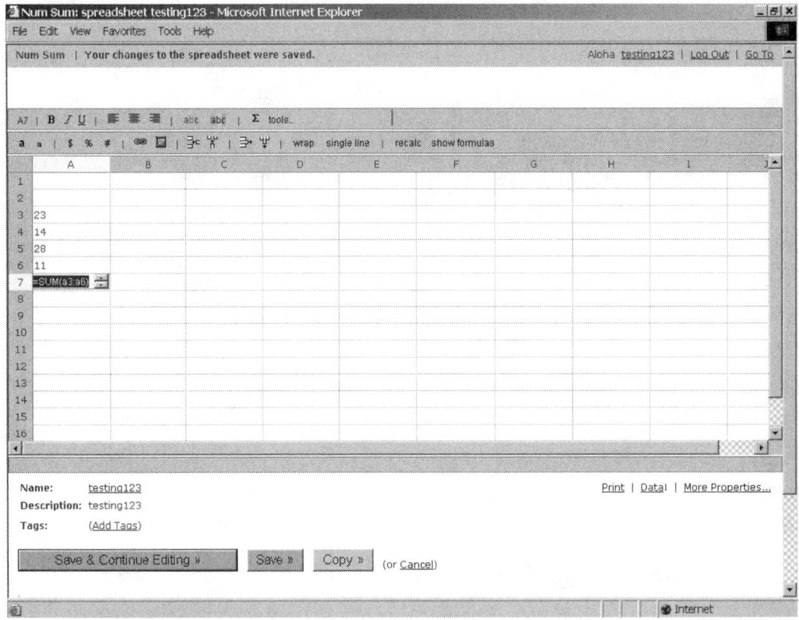

Figure 1-9. *Num Sum is an Ajax-based spreadsheet application.*

I mentioned that I personally have been doing Ajax for a number of years, and that is true. What I did not say, however, is that I have been using XML or that I have been using the `XMLHttpRequest` object. I will reveal what I was using all those years ago when we discuss alternatives to Ajax, but the important point here is that the approach that is at the heart of Ajax is nothing new as it does not, contrary to its very own name, require any specific technologies (aside from client-side scripting, which is, with few exceptions, required of an Ajax or Ajax-like solution).

When you get into the Ajax frame of mind, which is what we are really talking about, you are no longer bound by the rules of the classic Web. You can now take back at least some of the power the fat clients offered, while still keeping the benefits of the Web in place. Those benefits begin, most important perhaps, with the ubiquity of the web browser.

Have you ever been at work and had to give a demo of some new fat client app, for example, a Visual Basic app, that you ran on a machine you have never touched before? Ever have to do it in the boardroom in front of top company executives? Ever had that demo fail miserably because of some DLL conflict you couldn't possibly anticipate (Figure 1-10)! You are a developer, so the answer to all of those questions is likely yes (unless you work in the public sector, and then it probably was not corporate executives, but you get the point). If you have never done Windows development, you may not have had these experiences. You will have to take my word for it when I say that such situations were, for a long time, much more common than any of us would have liked. With a web-based application, this is generally not a concern. Ensure the PC has the correct browser and version, and off you go 98 percent of the time.

The other major benefit of a webapp is distribution. No longer do you need a 3-month shakedown period to ensure your new application does not conflict with the existing suite of corporate applications. An app running in a web browser, security issues aside, will not affect, or be affected, by any other application on the PC (and I am sure we all have war stories about exceptions to that, but they are just that: exceptions!).

Figure 1-10. *We've all been there. Live demos and engineers do not mix!*

Of course, you probably knew those benefits already, or you probably wouldn't be interested in web development in the first place.

The Flip Side of the Coin

Sounding good so far, huh? It is not all roses in Ajax land, however, and Ajax is not without its problems. Some of them are arguably only perceived problems, but others are concrete.

First and foremost, in my mind at least, is accessibility. You will lose at least some accessibility in your work by using Ajax because devices like screen readers are designed to read an entire page, and since you will no longer be sending back entire pages, screen readers will have trouble. My understanding is that some screen readers can deal with Ajax to some degree, largely depending on how Ajax is used (if the content is literally inserted into the Document Object Model, or DOM, makes a big difference). In any case, extreme caution should be used if you know people with disabilities are a target audience for your application, and you will seriously want to consider (and test!) whether Ajax will work in your situation. I am certain this problem will be addressed better as time goes on, but for now it is definitely a concern. Even still, there are some things you can do to improve accessibility:

- Put a note at the top of the page that says the page will be updated dynamically. This will give the user the knowledge that they may need to periodically request a reread of the page from the screen reader to hear the dynamic updates.
- Depending on the nature of the Ajax you are using on a page, use `alert()` pop-ups when possible as these are read by a screen reader. This is a reasonable enough suggestion for things like Ajax-based form submission that will not be happening too frequently, but obviously if you have a timed, repeating Ajax event, this suggestion would not be a good one.
- Remember that it is not only the blind who have accessibility needs; it can be sighted people as well. For them, try to use visual cues whenever possible. For instance, briefly highlighting items that have changed can be a big help. Some people call this the "Yellow Fade Effect,"[1] whereby you highlight the changed item in yellow and then slowly fade it back to the nonhighlighted state. Of course, it does not have to be yellow, and it does not have to fade, but the underlying concept is the same: highlight changed information to provide a visual cue that something has happened. Remember that changes caused by Ajax can sometimes be very subtle, so anything you can do to help people notice them will be appreciated.

Another disadvantage to many people is added complexity. Many shops do not have in-house the client-side coding expertise Ajax requires (the use of toolkits that make it easier notwithstanding). The fact is, errors that occur client-side are still, by and large, harder to track down than server-side problems, and Ajax does not make this any simpler. For example, View Source does not reflect changes made to the DOM (there are some tools available for Firefox that actually do allow this). Another issue is that Ajax applications will many times do away with some time-honored web concepts, most specifically back and forward buttons and bookmarking. Since there are no longer entire pages, but instead fragments of pages being returned, the browser cannot bookmark things in many cases. Moreover, the back and forward buttons cease to have the same meanings because they still refer to the last URL that was requested, and Ajax requests almost never are included (requests made through the `XMLHttpRequest` are not added to history, for example, because the URL generally does not change, especially when the method used is POST).

All of these disadvantages, except for perhaps accessibility to a somewhat lesser extent, have solutions, and we will see some of them later in the example apps. They do, however, represent differences in how webapps are developed for most developers, and they cause angst for many people. So they are things you should absolutely be aware of as you move forward with your Ajax work.

Why Is Ajax a Paradigm Shift? On the Road to RIAs

Ajax does in fact represent a paradigm shift for some people (even most people, given what most webapps are today) because it can fundamentally change the way you develop a webapp. More important perhaps is that it represents a paradigm shift for the *user*, and in fact it is the users who will drive the adoption of Ajax. Believe me; you will not long be able to ignore Ajax as a weapon in your toolbox.

[1] The term "Yellow Fade Effect" seems to have originated with a company called 37signals, as seen in this article: `www.37signals.com/svn/archives/000558.php`.

Put a non-Ajax webapp in front of a user, and then put that same app using Ajax techniques in front of them, and guess which one they are going to want to use all day nine times out of ten? The Ajax version! They will immediately see the increased responsiveness of the application and will notice that they no longer need to wait for a response from the server while they stare at a spinning browser logo wondering if anything is actually happening. They will see that the application alerts them on the fly of error conditions they would have to wait for the server to tell them about in the non-Ajax webapp. They will see functionality like type-ahead suggestions and instantly sortable tables and master-detail displays that update in real time—things that they would *not* see in a non-Ajax webapp. They will see maps that they can drag around like they can in the full-blown mapping applications they spent $80 on before. All of these things will be obvious advantages to the user. Users have become accustomed to the classic webapp model, but when confronted with something that harkens back to those fat-client days in terms of user-friendliness and responsiveness, there is almost an instantaneous realization that the Web as they knew it is dead, or at least should be!

If you think about many of the big technologies to come down the pipe in recent years, it should occur to you that we technology folks rather than the users were driving many of them. Do you think a user ever asked for an Enterprise JavaBean (EJB)-based application? No, we just all thought it was a good idea (how wrong we were there!). What about web services? Remember when they were going to fundamentally change the way the world of application construction worked? Sure, we are using them today, but are they, by and large, much more than an interface between cooperating systems? Not usually. Whatever happened to Universal Description, Discovery, and Integration (UDDI) directories and giving an application the ability to find, dynamically link to, and use a registered service on the fly? How good did that sound? To us geeks it was the next coming, but it didn't even register with users.

Ajax is different, though. Users can see the benefits. They are very real and very tangible to them. In fact, we as technology people, especially those of us doing Java web development, may even recoil at Ajax at first because more is being done on the client, which is contrary to what we have been drilling into our brains all these years. After all, we all believe scriptlets in JavaServer Pages (JSPs) are bad, eschewing them in favor of custom tags. The users do not care about elegant architectures and separation of concerns and abstractions allowing for code reuse. Users just want to be able to drag the map around in Google Maps (Figure 1-11) and have it happen real time without waiting for the whole page to refresh like they do (or did anyway) when using Yahoo!'s mapping solution.

The difference is clear. They want it, and they want it now (come on, we're adults here!)

Ajax is not the only new term floating around these days that essentially refers to the same thing. You may have also heard of Web 2.0 and RIAs. RIA is a term I particularly like, and I will discuss it a bit.

RIA stands for Rich Internet Application. Although there is no formal definition with which I am familiar, most people get the gist of its meaning without having to Google for it.

In short, the goal of an RIA is to create an application that is web based—that is, it runs in a web browser but looks, feels, and functions more like a typical fat-client application than a "typical" website. Things like partial-page updates are taken for granted, and hence Ajax is always involved in RIAs (although what form of Ajax is involved can vary; indeed you may not find the `XMLHttpRequest` object, the prototypical Ajax solution, lurking about at all!). These types of applications are always more user-friendly and better received by the user community they service. In fact, your goal in building RIAs should be for users to say, "I didn't even know it was a webapp!"

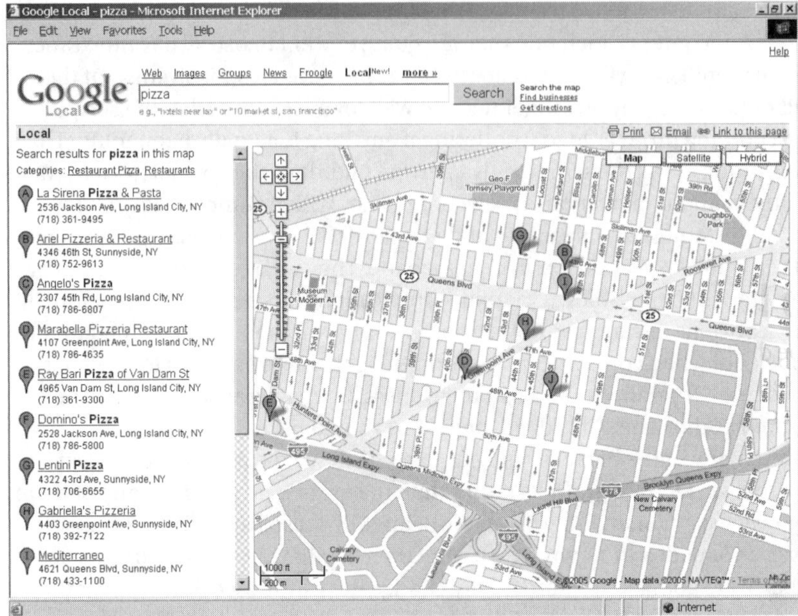

Figure 1-11. *Google Maps*

Gmail (Figure 1-12) is a good example of an RIA, although even it isn't perfect because while it has definite advantages over a typical website, it still looks and feels very much like a web page. Microsoft's Hotmail is another good example.

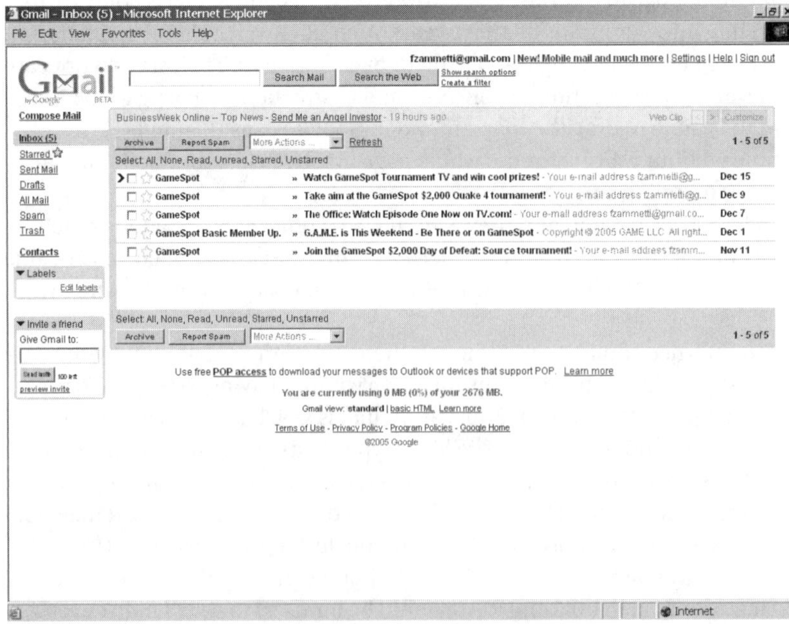

Figure 1-12. *Gmail, an Ajax webmail application from Google*

You may have noticed that many of the Ajax examples shown thus far have been from Google. That is not a coincidence. Google has done more to bring Ajax to the forefront of people's minds than anyone else. They were not the first to do it, or even the best necessarily, but they certainly have been some of the most visible examples and have really shown people what possibilities Ajax opens up.

Enough of the theory, definitions, history, and philosophy behind Ajax and RIAs and all that. Let's go get our hands dirty with some actual code!

Let's Get to It: Our First Ajax Example

This book aims to be different from most Ajax books in that it is based around the concept of giving you concrete examples to learn from, explaining them, explaining the decisions behind them (even the debatable ones), and letting you get your hands dirty with code. We are not going to spend a whole lot of time looking at UML diagrams, sequence diagrams, use case diagrams, and the like. You are more than welcome to pick up any of the fine UML books out there for that.

With that in mind, we are not going to waste any more time telling you what Ajax is, why it is the greatest thing since sliced bread, where the name came from, or any of that. Instead, we are going to jump right into some code!

This first example is somewhat unique in that it doesn't require Java. In fact, it does not require a server at all. Rest assured that all the other examples in this book do, as the title suggests. But we want to cover a simple Ajax app without server interaction first, just to get some of the basics covered, so here goes (Listing 1-1).

Listing 1-1. *Our First Real Ajax Application!*

```
<html>

  <head>

    <title>Simple Non-Server AJAX Example</title>

    <script>

      // This is a reference to an XMLHttpRequest object.
      xhr = null;

      // This function is called any time a selection is made in the first
      // <select> element.
      function updateCharacters() {
        // Instantiate an XMLHttpRequest object.
        if (window.XMLHttpRequest) {
          // Non-IE.
          xhr = new XMLHttpRequest();
        } else {
          // IE.
          xhr = new ActiveXObject("Microsoft.XMLHTTP");
        }
```

```
      xhr.onreadystatechange = callbackHandler;
      url = document.getElementById("selShow").value + ".htm";
      xhr.open("post", url, true);
      xhr.send(null);
    }

    // This is the function that will repeatedly be called by our
    // XMLHttpRequest object during the lifecycle of the request.
    function callbackHandler() {
      if (xhr.readyState == 4) {
        document.getElementById("divCharacters").innerHTML =
          xhr.responseText;
      }
    }

  </script>

</head>

<body>

  Our first simple AJAX example
  <br><br>

  Make a selection here:
  <br>
  <select onChange="updateCharacters();" id="selShow">
    <option value=""></option>
    <option value="b5">Babylon 5</option>
    <option value="bsg">Battlestar Galactica</option>
    <option value="sg1">Stargate SG-1</option>
    <option value="sttng">Star Trek The Next Generation</option>
  </select>
  <br><br>

  In response, a list of characters will appear here:
  <br>
  <div id="divCharacters">
    <select></select>
  </div>

 </body>
</html>
```

Figure 1-13 shows what it looks like on the screen (don't expect much here, folks!).

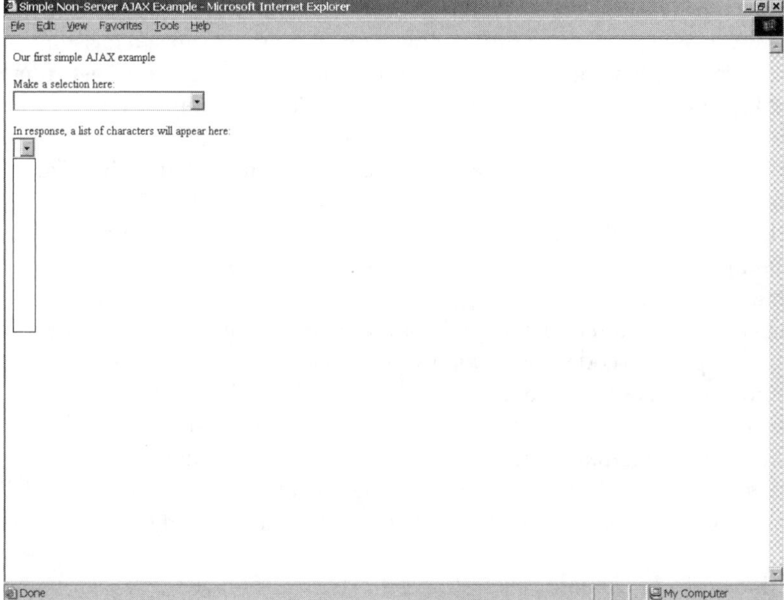

Figure 1-13. *Note that there is no content in the second dropdown because nothing has been selected yet in the first.*

As you can see, there is no content in the second dropdown initially. This will be dynamically populated once a selection is made in the first, as shown in Figure 1-14.

Figure 1-14. *A selection has been made in the first dropdown, and the contents of the second have been dynamically created from what was returned by the "server."*

Figure 1-14 shows that when a selection is made in the first dropdown, the contents of the second are dynamically updated. In this case we see characters from the greatest television show ever, "Babylon 5" (don't bother arguing, you know I'm right! And besides, you'll get your chance to put in your favorites later!). Now let's see how this "magic" is accomplished.

Listing 1-1 shows the first page of our simple Ajax example, which performs a fairly typical Ajax-type function: populate one `<select>` box based on the selection made in another. This comes up all the time in web development, and the "classic" way of doing it is to submit a form, whether by virtue of a button the user has to click or by a JavaScript event handler, to the server and let it render the page anew with the updated contents for the second `<select>`. With Ajax, none of that is necessary.

Let's walk through the code and see what is going on. Note that this is not meant to be a robust, production-quality piece of code. It is meant to give you an understanding of basic Ajax techniques, nothing more. There is no need to write in with all the flaws you find!

First things first: the markup itself. In our `<body>` we have little more than some text and two `<select>` elements. Notice that they are not part of a `<form>`. You will find that forms tend to have less meaning in the world of Ajax. You will many times begin to treat all your form UI elements as top-level objects along with all the other elements on your page (in the `<body>` anyway).

Let's look at the first `<select>` element (see Listing 1-2). This `<select>` element is given the ID `selShow`. This becomes a node in the DOM of the page. If you are not familiar with DOM, don't worry; we will get into it a bit in the next chapter. For now I will simply tell you that it stands for Document Object Model, and it is nothing more than a tree structure where each of the elements on your page can be found. In this case, we have a branch on our tree that is our `<select>` element, and we are naming it `selShow` so we can easily get at it later.

Listing 1-2. *The First <select> Element, Where You Choose a Show*

```
<select onChange="updateCharacters();" id="selShow">
  <option value=""></option>
  <option value="b5">Babylon 5</option>
  <option value="bsg">Battlestar Galactica</option>
  <option value="sg1">Stargate SG-1</option>
  <option value="sttng">Star Trek The Next Generation</option>
</select>
```

You will notice the JavaScript event handler attached to this element. Any time the value of the `<select>` changes, we will be calling the JavaScript function named `updateCharacters()`. This is where all the "magic" will happen. The rest of the element is nothing unusual. I have simply created an `<option>` for some of my favorite shows. After that we find another `<select>` element... sort of (Listing 1-3).

Listing 1-3. *The <div> Where the New <select> Will Be Drawn with Our Character List*

```
<div id="divCharacters">
  <select>
  </select>
</div>
```

It is indeed an empty <select> element, but wrapped in a <div>. You will find that probably the most commonly performed Ajax function is to replace the contents of some <div>. That is exactly what we will be doing here. In this case, what will be returned by the "server" (more on that in a minute) is the markup for our <select> element, complete with <option>'s listing characters from the selected show. So, when you make a show selection, the list of characters will be appropriately populated, and in true Ajax form, the whole page will not be redrawn, but only the portion that has changed—the second <select> element in this case (or more precisely, the <div> that wraps it) will be.

Let's quickly look at our mock server. Each of the shows in the first <select> has its own HTML file that in essence represents a server process. You have to take a leap of faith here and pretend a server was rendering the response that is those HTML pages. They all look virtually the same, so we will only show one as an example (Listing 1-4).

Listing 1-4. *Sample Response Listing Characters from the Greatest Show Ever, "Babylon 5"!*

```
<select>
  <option>Delenn</option>
  <option>Dr. Stephen Franklin</option>
  <option>G'Kar</option>
  <option>John Sheridan</option>
  <option>Kosh</option>
  <option>Lita Alexander</option>
  <option>Londo Mollari</option>
  <option>Marcus Cole</option>
  <option>Michael Garibaldi</option>
  <option>Mr. Morden</option>
</select>
```

As expected, it really is nothing but the markup for our second <select> element.

So, now we come to the part that does all the work here, our JavaScript function(s). First is the updateCharacters() function, shown in Listing 1-5.

Listing 1-5. *The updateCharacters() onChange() Event Handler*

```
// This function is called any time a selection is made in the first
// <select> element.
function updateCharacters() {

  // Instantiate an XMLHttpRequest object.
  if (window.XMLHttpRequest) {
    // Non-IE.
    xhr = new XMLHttpRequest();
  } else {
    // IE.
    xhr = new ActiveXObject("Microsoft.XMLHTTP");
  }
```

```
  xhr.onreadystatechange = callbackHandler;
  url = document.getElementById("selShow").value + ".htm";
  xhr.open("post", url, true);
  xhr.send(null);

}
```

This basic code will very soon be imprinted on the insides of your eyelids. This is the prototypical Ajax function. Let's tear it apart, shall we?

The first thing we need, as one would expect, is an XMLHttpRequest object. This object, a creation of Microsoft (believe it or not!) is nothing more than a proxy to a socket. It has a few (very few) methods and properties, but that is one of the benefits: it really is a very simple beast. The members of this object will be introduced as needed, but a complete reference can be found in Appendix A.

Notice the branching logic here. It turns out that getting an instance of the XMLHttpRequest object is different in Internet Explorer than in any other browser. Now, before you get your knickers in a knot and get your anti-Microsoft ire up, note that they invented this object, and it was the rest of the world that followed. So, while it would be nice if Microsoft updated their API to match everyone else's, it isn't their fault we need this branching logic! The others could just as easily have duplicated what Microsoft did exactly too, so let's not throw stones here—we're all in glass houses on this one!

This is probably a good time to point out that XMLHttpRequest is pretty much a de facto standard at this point. It is also being made a true W3C standard, but for now it is not. It is safe to assume that any "modern" browser—that is, a desktop web browser that is no more than a few versions old—will have this object available. More limited devices, like PocketPCs, cell phones, and the like will many times not have it, but by and large it is a pretty ubiquitous little piece of code.

Continuing on in our code review... once we have an XMLHttpRequest object instance, we assign the reference to it to the variable xhr in the global page scope. Think about this for just a min-ute; what happens if more than one onChange event fires at close to the same time? Essentially, the first will be lost because a new XMLHttpRequest object is spawned, and xhr will point to it. Worse still, because of the asynchronous nature of XMLHttpRequest, a situation can arise where the callback function for the first request is executing when the reference is null, which means that callback would throw errors due to trying to reference a null object. If that was not bad enough, this will be the case only in some browsers, but not all (although my research indicates most would throw errors), so it might not even be a consistent problem. Remember, I said this was not robust, production-quality code! This is a good example of why. That being said, it is actually many times perfectly acceptable to simply instantiate a new instance and start a new request. Think about a fat client that you use frequently. Can you spot instances where you can kick off an event that in essence cancels a previous event that was in the process of executing? For example, in your web browser, can you click the Home button while a page is loading, thereby causing the page load to be prematurely ended and the new page to begin loading? Yes you can, and that is what in essence happens by starting a new Ajax request using the same reference variable. It is not an unusual way for an application to work, and sometimes is downright desirable. That being said, though, you do need to keep it in mind and be sure it is how you want and need things to work. There are ways around the problem, and we will see that in later chapters.

The next step we need to accomplish is telling the XMLHttpRequest instance what callback handler function to use. An Ajax request has a well-defined and specific lifecycle, just like any HTTP request (and remember that is all an Ajax request is at the end of the day!). This cycle is defined as the transitions between ready states (hence the property name, onreadystatechange). At specific intervals in this lifecycle, the JavaScript function you name as the callback handler will be called. For instance, when the request begins, your function will be called. As the request is chunked back to the browser, in most browsers at least (IE being the unfortunate exception), you will get a call for each chunk returned (think about those cool status bars you can finally do with no complex queuing and callback code on the server!). Most important for us in this case, the function will be called when the request completes. We will see this function in just a moment.

The next step is probably pretty obvious: we have to tell the object what URL we want to call. We do this by calling the open() method of the object. This method takes three parameters: the HTTP method to perform, the URL to contact, and whether we want the call to be performed asynchronously (true) or not (false). Because this is a simple example, each television show gets its own HTML file pretending to be the server. The name of the HTML file is simply the value from the <select> element with .htm appended to the end. So, for each selection the user makes, a different URL is called. This is obviously not how a real solution would work—the real thing would likely call the same URL with some sort of parameter to specify the selected show—but some sacrifices were necessary to keep the example both simple and not needing anything on the server side of things.

The HTTP method can be any of the standard HTTP methods: GET POST, HEAD, etc. Ninety-eight percent of the time you will likely be passing GET or POST. The URL is self-explanatory, except for one detail: if you are doing a GET, you must construct the query string yourself and append it to the URL. That is one of the drawbacks of XMLHttpRequest: you take full responsibility for marshalling and unmarshalling data sent and received. Remember, it is in essence just a very thin wrapper around a socket. This is where any of the numerous Ajax toolkits can come in quite handy, but we will talk about that later.

Once we have the callback registered with the object and we have told it what we're going to connect to and how, we simply call the send() method. In this case, we are not actually sending anything, so we pass null. One thing to be aware of is that at least when I tested it, you can call send() with no arguments in IE and it will work, but Firefox will not. null works in both, though, so null it is.

Of course, if you actually had some content to send, you would do so here. You can pass a string of data into this method, and the data will be sent in the body of the HTTP request. Many times you will want to send actual parameters, and you do so by constructing essentially a query string in the typical form var1=val1&var1=val1 and so forth, but without the leading question mark. Alternatively, you can pass in an XML DOM object, and it will be serialized to a string and sent. Lastly, you could send any arbitrary data you want. If a comma-separated list does the trick, you can send that. Anything other than a parameter string will require you to deal with it; the parameter string will result in request parameters as expected.

So far we've described how a request is sent. It is pretty trivial, right? Well, the next part is what can be even more trivial, or much more complex. In our example, it is the former. I am referring to the callback handler function (Listing 1-6).

Listing 1-6. *Ajax Callback Lifecycle Handler*

```
// This is the function that will repeatedly be called by our
// XMLHttpRequest object during the lifecycle of the request.
function callbackHandler() {
  if (xhr.readyState == 4) {
    document.getElementById("divCharacters").innerHTML = xhr.responseText;
  }
}
```

Our callback handler function this time around does very little. First, it checks the `readystate` of the `XMLHttpRequest` object. Remember I said this callback will be called multiple times during the lifecycle of the request? Well, the `readystate` code you will see will vary with each lifecycle event. The full list of codes (and there is only a handful) can be found in Appendix A, but for the purposes of this example we are only interested in code 4, which indicates the request has completed. Notice that I didn't say completely *successfully*! Regardless of the response from the server, the `readystate` will be 4. Since this is a simple example, we don't care what the server returns. If an HTTP 404 error (page not found) is received, we don't care in this case. If an HTTP 500 error (server processing error), we still do not care. The function will do its thing in any of these cases. I repeat my refrain: this is not an industrial-strength example!

When the callback is called as a result of the request completing, we simply set the `innerHTML` property of the `<div>` on the page with the ID `divCharacters` to the text that was returned. In this case, the text returned is the markup for the populated `<select>`, and the end result is the second `<select>` is populated by characters from the selected show.

Now, that wasn't so bad, was it?

■ **Note** For a fun little exercise, and just to convince yourself of what is really going on, I suggest adding one or two of your own favorite shows in the first `<select>`, and creating the appropriately named HTML file to render the markup for the second `<select>`.

Choices in Ajax Toolkits

At this point you are probably thinking, "OK, Ajax is no big deal," and you would be right. At least in its more basic form, there is not much code to it, and it is pretty easy to follow.

However, if this is your first exposure to JavaScript and client-side development in general, it may seem like a lot of work. Or, if you intend to be doing more complex Ajax work, you may not want to be hand-coding handlers and functions all over the place. It is in these cases where a good Ajax library can come into play.

As you might imagine with all the hype surrounding Ajax recently, there are a ton of libraries and toolkits to choose from. Some are fairly blunt, general-purpose tools that make doing Ajax only a bit simpler, whereas others are rather robust libraries that seek to fill all your JavaScript and Ajax needs. Some provide powerful and fancy GUI widgets that use Ajax behind the scenes; others leave the widget building to you, but make it a lot easier.

In this book, I will be showing you how to use a number of the most popular libraries in the examples to come. You will see that they all shame some common ideas, but at their core they aren't doing anything different than what we saw in the previous example. They are all more robust and flexible, but they had better be!

The libraries I will be covering are Dojo (`http://dojotoolkit.org`), DWR (`http://getahead.ltd.uk/dwr`), Prototype (`http://prototype.conio.net`), and the AjaxTags component of the Java Web Parts project (`http://javawebparts.sourceforge.net`). All of these are free, open source toolkits that people are finding very useful in their Ajax work. This is only a very small subset of the libraries and toolkits available, but they probably represent the most popular.

At the end of the day, though, keep in mind that "naked" Ajax, as seen in the example from this chapter, is also extremely common and has many of its own benefits, some of which are control over what is happening at the most fundamental level and more opportunity to tune for performance and overall robustness. It is also never a bad idea to know exactly what is going on in your own applications! The balance of the examples in this book that are not using any particular library will be done in this fashion. If you are comfortable with JavaScript and client-side development in general, you may never need or want to touch any of these toolkits (I personally lean that way), but if you are just coming to the client-side party, these libraries can indeed make your life a lot easier.

Alternatives to Ajax

No discussion of Ajax would be complete without pointing out that it is not the only game in town. There are other ways to accomplish the goals of building RIAs than using Ajax.

Have you ever heard of Flash? Of course you have! Who hasn't been annoyed by all those animations all over some of the most popular websites around?

Flash can be very annoying at times, but when used properly it can provide what Ajax provides. One good example is Mappr (`www.mappr.com`), which is a Flash-based application for exploring places based on pictures people take and submit for them (Figure 1-15).

This is an example of how Flash, used properly, can truly enhance the web users' experience. Flash is a more "proper" development environment as well, complete with its own highly evolved integrated development environment (IDE), debugging facilities, and all that good stuff. It is also a tool that graphic designers can readily use to create some truly awe-inspiring multimedia presentations.

Flash is also fairly ubiquitous at this point. Virtually all browsers come with a Flash player bundled, or one can be added on with virtually no difficulty. Flash does, however, require a browser plug-in, whereas Ajax doesn't, and that is one advantage Ajax has. On the other hand, there are versions of Flash available for many mobile devices like PocketPCs and some cell phones, even those where `XMLHttpRequest` may not yet be available.

What are the negatives about Flash? First, it has a bit of a bad reputation because it is so easy to abuse. Many people choose to not install it or block all Flash content from their browser. Second, it is not completely "typical" programming; it is a little more like creating a presentation in the sense that you have to deal with the concept of a "timeline," so there can be a bit of a learning curve for "traditional" developers. Third, it can be somewhat heavyweight for users not on broadband connections, and even for those *with* broadband connections it can sometimes take longer than is ideal to start up. Lastly, Flash is owned by Adobe, and is not open source, which is something more and more people are shying away from. I personally would not discount Flash for this particular reason, but it is not something to be ignorant of either.

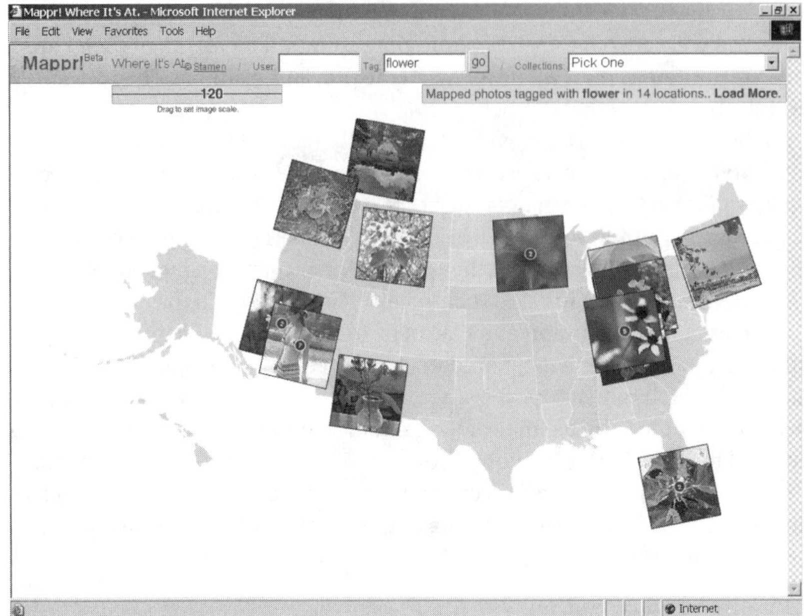

Figure 1-15. *Mappr, an excellent use of Flash*

All in all, Flash is a worthy alternative for building RIAs. It will sometimes even be a better choice, sometimes not, but it is always worth at least considering.

Flex, another product from Adobe, is certainly worth a look as well. Flex is a more full-stack solution in that it is a server-side solution as well as a client-side solution. It isn't just an extension to what you do and use today; it is pretty much a replacement for it.

Another alternative to Ajax that people sometimes miss is much older HTML tricks like hidden frames (be they iFrames or normal frames). You can, for instance, target a form submission to a hidden frame. You can then return to that hidden frame nothing but JavaScript that updates the display. You get the same effect as Ajax but without `XMLHttpRequest` and all the code that goes into that.

In 1999, I built an application for my employer that was a back-office type of application. It was to be intranet-based only, so I could do some fancier things than usual because I didn't have to worry about all sorts of different clients accessing the application. I was also able to target IE exclusively, which saved a lot of time and effort (but really only as far as cross-browser rendering issues go; the code itself would run cross-browser). This application took a fairly novel approach, even today. When you accessed the application's URL, you downloaded about 300K of HTML into a number of different frames. Most important, there was a single "main" frame that contained the markup for every screen of the application.

Each of those "screens" was enclosed in a `<div>`, and at any given time only a single `<div>` was visible. One of the frames was hidden and contained the application's API, a collection of JavaScript functions used throughout. Likewise, another hidden frame was termed the "target" frame, and as I mentioned earlier, all form submissions were targeted to this frame.

Any time the user performed a function that required the server, a form was submitted, and the server would respond with an HTML page something like the one shown in Listing 1-7.

Listing 1-7. *"Page" Returned by Server with JavaScript That Executes in Hidden Frame upon Load*

```
<html>
  <head>
    <title></title>
    <script>
      acctNum = "1234";
      firstName = "Frank";
      lastName = "Zammetti"
      ssn = "111-22-3333";
      function loadHandler() {
        document.getElementById("summaryPage.acctNum").value = acctNum;
        document.getElementById("summaryPage. firstName").value = firstName;
        document.getElementById("summaryPage. lastName").value = lastName;
        document.getElementById("summaryPage. ssn").value = ssn;
        window.top.fraAPI.currentScreen.style.display = "none";
        p = document.getElementById("summaryPage");
        p.style.display = "block";
        window.top.fraAPI.currentScreen = p;
      }
    </script>
  </head>
  <body onLoad="loadHandler();"></body>
</html>
```

So, all that happens is that once the server's response is received, the `loadHandler()` function fires. The data, which was passed back in JavaScript variables, is inserted into the appropriate elements on the page. Then, the current screen `<div>` is hidden and the new screen `<div>` is shown, and we record what the current screen `<div>` is so we can hide that, if applicable, on the next request.

The result of all of this is an application that is amazingly snappy and responsive and that takes the whole "do not refresh the entire screen each request" to an extreme. I generally would not recommend this approach as it relies a little too much on the client side of things (finding people capable of maintaining it has been a little challenging, not to mention the security implications, which in our case were not a concern but in general should be), but it does illustrate the underlying concept exceptionally well. It is very much Ajax in a philosophical sense, which as I mentioned earlier is what truly matters.

Yet another alternative is actually something that was intended originally to fulfill the niche that Ajax is now trying to fill: Java applets. Applets were intended to bring fat-client-like features to the Web by running, more or less, a full Java application in the browser. Applets are still used today, although certainly not to the extent originally envisioned. Applets have the benefit of giving you access to nearly the entire Java platform, with some security restrictions limiting certain things (like local file system I/O, for instance). Applets are also relatively easy to write for most Java developers. They also remove almost all of the cross-browser concerns that web development in general has by in a sense running "on top" of the browser. The applet is abstracted from any browser peculiarities by the Java Runtime Environment (JRE). Some of the concerns with applets, which for many people outweigh the benefits, are slow start-up time (I am sure we have all seen how relatively slow the Java Virtual Machine [JVM] starts up in a browser), overall slow UI performance (still to this day a concern of Java GUIs, although certainly far less than in the past), and the simple fact that many people choose to disable applets, be it for security reasons or for speed reasons. Still, for some things, applets are quite appropriate. As just one example, imagine a banded report writer. While this can (and has) been done in pure browser technologies, when you compare an applet version of the same report written, it tends to be perceived as more powerful.

Lastly, there is one alternative to Ajax that is almost always ignored: fat clients. You many times will hear Ajax proponents, including myself, talking about building webapps that look, feel, and work like fat clients. So, the logical question to ask in the face of such a proposition is "why not just build fat clients?" Indeed, that is a perfectly valid alternative!

Fat clients have gotten a bad rap because it is very easy to architect them poorly. Have you ever had to maintain a Visual Basic (VB) app that has all sorts of business logic embedded directly in button click handlers? Of course you have—well, if you have ever developed a VB app, that is. If you have not, just take my word for it that such a thing is, unfortunately, all too common! This is not the fault of the fat-client approach, nor is it the fault of Visual Basic. It is the fault of developers not understanding how to build applications with proper separation of concerns and a proper tiering model in the fat-client world. It is also a side effect of business drivers pushing deadlines and hence developers in unreasonable ways, but I am not trying to solve that age-old problem here!

If you have an application where a fat-client approach makes sense, then build a fat client. You will lose the benefits of web development that we discussed earlier, but you do gain some significant advantages, including more powerful UI widgets, full native execution speed, and less restricted access to system and possibly network resources.

In short, if a business need is better filled by a fat client, then build a fat client. Of course, if you are reading this, then you are likely a web developer, but do not let that cloud your judgment about what the best answer is.

Summary

If this chapter has seemed like an attempt to brainwash you, that is because in a sense, it was! Ajax can seem to some people like a really bad idea, but those people tend to only see the problems and completely ignore the benefits. Because of my belief that Ajax is more about philosophy and thought process than it is about specific technologies, it is important to sell you on the ideas underlying it. It is not enough to simply show you some code and hope you agree!

In this chapter we have looked at the evolution of web development over the past decade and a half or so. We have been introduced to Ajax, learned what it means, and seen how it is accomplished. We have discovered the term RIA and talked about why all of this really is a significant development for many people.

We have also discussed how the most important thing about Ajax is not the technologies in use but the mind-set and approach to application development that are its underpinnings.

We have seen and played with our first Ajax-based application and have discovered that the code involved is ultimately pretty trivial. We have discussed some alternatives to Ajax and have learned that Ajax has been done for years, but with different techniques and technologies.

We have also discussed how Ajax is more user-driven than developer-driven, which is a significant difference from many advances in the past (and also one good reason why Ajax isn't as likely to go away as easily).

I will close with just a few take-away points that succinctly summarize this chapter:

- Ajax is more about a mind-set, an approach to developing webapps, than it is about any specific technologies or programming techniques.
- Ajax does in fact represent a fundamental shift in how webapps are built, at least for many people.
- Ajax, at its core, is a pretty simple thing. What we build on top of it may get complex, but the basics are not a big deal.
- RIAs may or may not represent the future of application development in general, but almost certainly do in terms of web development.
- There are a number of alternatives to Ajax that you should not dismiss out-of-hand. Consider the problem you are trying to solve and choose the best solution. Ajax will be it in a great many (and a growing number) of cases, but may not always be.

CHAPTER 2

The Pillars of Ajax

As I mentioned in Chapter 1, if you are already a JavaScript, CSS, DOM, and XML guru, you will miss very little by skipping this chapter. However, if you are new to any of these, or do not feel you have a strong grasp of the concepts, then this chapter may serve you very well. In this chapter, we will look at the primary technologies you'll encounter when doing Ajax: JavaScript, DOM, XML, and CSS (Figure 2-1). This should be review for most readers, but can serve as a lightweight introduction for those with little experience in these topics. Note that the four areas covered here are expansive topics in and of themselves, worthy of whole books on their own. We will not necessarily cover them in as great a depth as they could be. My intention is to cover them in a level of detail that will give you the tools you need to work through the projects in this book and get as much out of them as possible. You are encouraged to grab one of the fine books available on each of these topics to get into them in far greater depth than we can here.

Figure 2-1. *Ajax the mighty! Yet, he could not do it alone: CSS, XML, DOM, and JavaScript are his "hero support."*

JavaScript Basics

Although the aim of this book is not to serve as an introduction to Ajax, I feel I would be remiss if I did not have what is essentially an introductory chapter to the technologies and techniques that underpin Ajax. If that makes it so that this book can in fact introduce someone who does not now possess a great deal of prior development experience, be it client side or server side, then so be it; that is an added bonus! Really, though, this particular chapter, along with the previous chapter and the next one as well, are meant to ensure there are no substantial holes in your knowledge and that you have the requisite understanding to move forward in examining the Ajax applications to come. If you are completely new to JavaScript, or client-side development in general, I highly recommend you pick up a book on the subject and read it before diving into the projects in this book.

All that being said, let's get to it!

JavaScript is one of those things that, much like Keanu Reeves, got a bad rap early on and has been fighting to overcome it ever since (although it is this writer's opinion that JavaScript has succeeded far more than Keanu has, but that is a debate for an entirely different book!). JavaScript has for a number of years now had the stigma of being a "child's" language. This is a typical attitude about any scripting language, but JavaScript has for a while now been the most-used scripting language out there, and therefore the one that tends to get abused the most. JavaScript is quite a bit different from a full-fledged programming language like Java, C, or C# in that it is a very polymorphic language, very pliable. It makes many things extremely easy, some things which would not be possible in something like Java at all, or at least not without a tremendous amount of effort and code on your part. All this power comes at a price, though: it is pretty easy to get things wrong. That is exactly what happened for many years, and that has resulted in the negative feelings about JavaScript.

JavaScript, from a syntactical standpoint, is clearly descended from the C family of languages, but the similarity largely stops with similar syntax. There is a common misconception about JavaScript that it is a simple language, especially for those already familiar with C-like languages, including C++ and Java, and at first glance this is true. Peel away a few layers of the onion, though, and you find something else lurking beneath. JavaScript is a powerful language that can be virtually as complex as you want to make it.

Some of the features that make JavaScript so powerful are summarized in Table 2-1. This table compares JavaScript to Java, since those are the two technologies this book is concerned with. However, it should be noted that JavaScript and Java share virtually nothing aside from a similar name, syntax, and a few concepts here and there. You should not make the mistake of thinking JavaScript is a subset of Java; that is not at all true.

Table 2-1. *Differences Between JavaScript and Java*

JavaScript	Java
Variables do not have defined types. It is referred to as a "loosely typed" language.	Variables have definitive types and cannot represent other types (ignoring casting and interfaces and such). This is called a "strongly typed" language.
There is no true object orientation in the sense that Java has it, i.e., there are no true classes, no interfaces, no inheritance as it exists in Java, etc. In JavaScript, every object is its own class in essence.	Objects are always of a specific type and inherit most attributes of the parent. Interfaces allow for polymorphism and multiple inheritance. This is the big league of object-oriented programming (OOP)!

JavaScript	Java
JavaScript is a lightweight, fully interpreted language.	Java is a pseudocompiled language, closer to native code than to interpreted code, and requires a fairly substantial infrastructure to run (the Java Virtual Machine, or JVM).
JavaScript has the concept of a "global" namespace.	Everything in Java belongs to some class, and even though you can view class members as global within that class, there is no global scope above classes.
Functions in JavaScript are just like objects. No, in fact, they *are* objects!	Since there is no global scope in Java, you could never have a stand-alone function, and therefore functions are not treated like objects (reflection notwithstanding).

Perhaps the key item in Table 2-1 is that JavaScript functions are just like objects, and in point of fact they actually are full-fledged objects as far as the JavaScript interpreter is concerned. This seemingly simple fact allows you to play some tricks that you just never could in Java. For instance, look at the code in Listing 2-1 and try to guess what it does, then actually give it a shot and see if you were right.

Listing 2-1. *An Example of the Flexibility of JavaScript*

```
function demo () {
  this.text = "Not set yet";
}

demo.prototype.setText = function(inText) {
  this.text = inText;
}

demo.prototype.showMe = function() {
  alert(this.text);
}

obj = new demo();
alert(obj.text);
obj["setText"]("Hello!");
obj["showMe"]();
```

In this example, we create a function called `demo()`. Inside it we create a "property" called `text` and set a default string. You can now think of this `demo()` function as a "class" in essence, although it is not quite the same as a class in Java of C++. Classes usually have methods too, but in JavaScript you do not define methods within the function; you attach them after the fact. That is what the next two blocks do. Notice the use of `prototype` here. I will go into this in just a bit in more detail, but for now simply think of it as a way to say "add the following member to the class preceding me." It is, in effect, equivalent to creating a class in Java and adding a method to it in the sense that a class is a blueprint from which to create objects, just as a prototype is a blueprint from which to create objects in JavaScript. The first attaches a "method" called setText() to the "class." This is used to set the text member to the parameter passed in. The next block simply attaches a "method" called showMe() that displays the current value of the text member. Lastly, the code that follows makes use of this "class" by first creating a new instance of it, displaying the default text, then setting the text and finally displaying the text again.

The part that is of interest here is actually the very last two lines. See the way we call the setText() and showMe() methods? If you're thinking that looks an awful lot like an array, you are completely correct! Classes, so to speak, in JavaScript, are really thinly veiled associative arrays (an array in which you can access any element by name). This allows us to do some pretty interesting things, and it also in essence gives us polymorphism because the variable obj could point to any kind of object, and as long as it has setText() and showMe() as member methods, the same code works. This of course is not true polymorphism, but it is about as close as you are going to get in an interpreted language!

All of that was just meant as an example of a small part of the flexibility JavaScript offers. We will get a bit more into the whole object-oriented approach to JavaScript in a bit. For now, we need to touch on some of the more basic concepts.

Variables, Scope, and Functions

Recall in the beginning of this chapter I said that variables in JavaScript are loosely typed. This means that first, you do not have to declare a variable to be of a given type, and second, you can store any value in the variable you want at any time. For example, look at Listing 2-2.

Listing 2-2. *Some JavaScript Variable Fun*

```
<html>
  <head>
    <title></title>

    <script>

      var v = 123;
      v = 6;
      v = document.getElementById("someDiv");
      v = "hello";

      function test() {
        a = "a set";
        var b = "b set";
      }

      function showVars(dummyVar) {
        test();
        alert(v);
        alert(a);
        alert(b);
      }
```

```
    </script>

  </head>
  <body onLoad="showVars();">
    <div id="someDiv"></div>
  </body>
</html>
```

All JavaScript on a web page, except when found in an event handler (more on this later) must appear within an enclosing pair of `<script>` tags. This forms, unsurprisingly, a script block. In the script block we see in this code, the first line declares a variable named `v`. Note the keyword `var` that precedes it. When you are declaring a variable in global scope, that is, outside of any function as is shown in Listing 2-2, the `var` keyword is completely optional, it has no effect either way. However, if you declare a variable inside a function as is done for the variables `a` and `b` in the `test()` function, is has a definite effect (as you will see in a bit).

Speaking of functions, we can see one named `showVars()` defined. It looks much like defining a function (or method in an object-oriented language) in any other C-like language. The differences to note are first that there are no modifiers before the function keyword; there are no scope keywords, etc. You always simply start with the function keyword. Next, in the parameter list, you never specify a type. In this case we have a single parameter named `dummyVar`. Why do we not declare a type? Because JavaScript is typeless! This is another example of the power of JavaScript: because any kind of data can be passed in that parameter, number, string, object reference, and so forth, you can do some fantastic things with this. It also means you have to be careful what you try to do before you determine what you actually received!

If you execute this code, you will see three things. First, you will get an alert that says "hello". You will then get another alert that says "a set". Lastly, you will get a JavaScript error telling you that `b` is undefined. That is the difference between using `var` and not: any variable within a function defined using `var` remains local to that function, while any defined without it continues to exist outside the function. This is clearly something to be cognizant of! It can be the source of much trouble if you are not careful.

Also note that JavaScript does not support the notion of block-level scope. In other words, if you define a variable inside a `for` loop, the variable will act as if you defined it outside the loop, with the same rules about its scope after the function ends in effect.

When naming your variables and functions, JavaScript takes its cues from Java; the same rules that apply there apply to JavaScript as well. Specifically, the first character must be a letter (lowercase or uppercase is fine; just remember there is a difference!), an underscore character (_), or a dollar sign ($). Note that numbers *are not* allowed as the first character. Any characters after that are allowed. Also, only ASCII characters are allowed by the ECMA specification; no Unicode characters may be used. As with any programming language, you should try to make your variable names make sense and describe what they are, but you also should not make them too long as to be unwieldy. Short, one-letter variables are generally OK inside loops and such, or when they are only used in a very small scope like a block. Of course, remember the rules about lifetime outside blocks!

Keywords

JavaScript is a fairly simple language in terms of the core language itself. For instance, there are not a whole lot of keywords in JavaScript. In fact, here they all are:

- `break`
- `do`
- `function`
- `null`
- `typeof`
- `case`
- `else`
- `if`
- `return`
- `var`
- `continue`
- `export`
- `import`
- `switch`
- `void`
- `default`
- `false`
- `in`
- `this`
- `while`
- `delete`
- `for`
- `new`
- `true`
- `with`

There are additionally a number of reserved words in the ECMAScript spec that, while not currently used, you should avoid using in your own code. These are

- `catch`
- `const`
- `enum`
- `finally`
- `throw`
- `class`
- `debugger`
- `extends`
- `super`
- `try`

Finally, there are a few further keywords taken from the Java language, which are reserved for future extensions. They are

- `abstract`
- `final`
- `int`
- `private`
- `synchronized`
- `boolean`
- `float`
- `interface`

- protected
- throws
- byte
- goto
- long
- public
- transient
- char
- implements
- native
- short
- double
- instanceof
- package
- static

I feel confident in saying that the native keyword will never be implemented, at least not in any browser-based JavaScript interpreter (think of all the security nightmares that would unleash!), and as far as the rest goes, you should avoid using them in your code to ensure forward compatibility.

Notice that all of the listed keywords in all three groups are in lowercase. This is not arbitrary. JavaScript will not understand `For` as being a keyword; only `for` will do the trick. JavaScript is an inherently case-sensitive language, not just for keywords but for everything. For example, look at this code:

```
var myvar = "Bill";
var myVar = "Ted";
alert(myvar);
alert(myVar);
```

If you were to put this, inside a `<script/>` block in the `<head>` of an HTML page and load it in your browser (hint: do that!), you would see that you get two alert pop-ups when the page is loaded, one that says "Bill", the other saying "Ted". This is because `myvar` and `myVar` are two different variables.

Whitespace

Note that JavaScript is, by and large, ignorant of whitespace. Spaces, tabs, and newlines all are considered whitespace, as in most other languages, and will be ignored.

Further, you can generally break lines up however you wish to. There are some exceptions, which will be mentioned shortly. Generally, though, as long as you do not break up a keyword, the interpreter will have no problem with it.

You should take advantage of this ignorance of whitespace and organize your code cleanly. Making your code "pretty" is an often-overlooked and yet very valuable habit to get into. It makes understanding the overall structure of the code, and its general flow, easier to comprehend and follow. As you would in any other language, try to group statements in a logical way, wrap long lines where appropriate, and generally try to make your code look nice, regardless of what the actual code is or does.

Again, it should be noted that there are a few exceptions to the rule about breaking lines, but again, those will be mentioned shortly.

Semicolons

Yes, a single character gets its own section heading!

Something else you may have noticed in the last snippet of code is that the first two lines do not have semicolons at the end, whereas the last two do. Semicolons, unlike in Java, are completely optional, as long as the statements appear on separate lines. What this means is, if you try to do

```
var myvar = "Bill" var myVar = "Ted"
```

the JavaScript interpreter will complain about that. If you instead do

```
Var myVar = "Bill"; var myVar = "Ted";
```

this will work just fine. You could even omit the semicolon after "Ted" and still have it work.

It is important to realize that what the JavaScript interpreter is doing behind-the-scenes is actually inserting an implicit semicolon after each full statement that it recognizes. This can lead to some difficult-to-track down bugs. For example, if you type

```
return
true;
```

what will happen is that JavaScript will interpret this as if you wrote

```
return;
true;
```

This is obviously not what you intended. Because the latter is technically valid from a syntactical standpoint, the interpreter will not flag it as an error, but certainly it really is an error of sorts since whatever called the function that this code is presumably a part of will not work as expected (i.e., the return value will be `undefined`, rather than true, as was probably expected). This is a situation where the ability to break up lines where you want and JavaScript's implicit semicolon insertion can bite you. There are, fortunately, very few situations where this can realistically occur.

It is my suggestion, as well as my own personal habit, as you will see in the code throughout this book, to always put semicolons in, even when you do not have to.

Comments

Comments in JavaScript, like in C, C++, and Java, come in three basic forms. The first is the // combination. Any text following // until the end of the line is considered a comment and will be ignored by the interpreter. The second type is the /* */ combination. The interpreter will ignore any text between these combinations. This represents two subtypes because /* */ can exist on a single line or can span lines. Here are some examples of valid comments:

```
var a = 3; // This is a comment
var /* One comment */ a = 3; // Another comment
/*
  This is a comment
 */
/*
 * This is another comment
 */
```

Note that comments may not be nested, that is, `/* This is // a comment */` *is not* valid. Also note that JavaScript also recognizes the HTML `<!--` comment opening marker, but it *does not* recognize the closing `-->` marker. It will treat `<!--` just like it does `//`.

Also note that you can use Unicode characters in comments, as per the ECMAScript specification.

Literal Values, Arrays, and Object Initializers

Literal values in JavaScript are, by and large, just like any other language and probably do not need much discussion. Here are some examples of literals in the JavaScript language:

```
a = "Frank"; // Frank is the literal
a = true; // true is the literal
a = 1.2; // 1.2 is the literal
```

Two additions that we will want to be aware of are object initializers and array initializers. For array initializers, the following syntax is recognized:

```
var a = [ "Tim", "Berners", "Lee" ];
```

Speaking of arrays, just like in Java, arrays in JavaScript are actually objects. They always have a property `length` that returns the number of elements in the array. They always have a `concat()` method to add elements and a `toString()` method to get a string representation of the array, and many more.

Each element in an array is referenced by an index number, where the first element is index 0. For instance, to retrieve the value "Berners" from the above array, we would do

```
var s = a[1];
```

There is another type of array in JavaScript called the associative array. This will come into play when we discuss object-oriented JavaScript.

Finally, object initializers allow us to initialize the members of an object quickly and easily. Listing 2-3 shows this concept.

Listing 2-3. *Using an Object Initializer*

```
<html>
  <head>
    <title></title>

    <script>

      function myObj() {
        this.myVal1 = 1;
        this.myVal2 = 2;
      }

      var m = new myObj();
      m = { myVal1:10, myVal2:20 };
      alert(m.myVal1 + " - " + m.myVal2);
```

```
    </script>

  </head>
  <body> </body>
</html>
```

This code begins by creating an object (a class in essence) called `myObj`. It then instantiates an instance of it referenced by the variable `m`. The line preceding the `alert()` call is the object initializer. Note that the members of the object are referenced by name, followed by the new value, in a comma-separated list. Pretty handy, huh?

Data Types

"Data types? I thought you said JavaScript was a typeless language?" Yes, I can hear your exclamation from here! In point of fact, JavaScript is a loosely typed language, meaning a variable can point to an object of any type. Unlike Java or other languages, JavaScript offers a very small pallet of underlying data types, namely numbers, strings, booleans, and objects.

Numbers

Numbers are pretty straightforward, with a few facts being important:

- All numbers in JavaScript are floating-point values; JavaScript does not have a separate integer type. In addition, if you are a Java programmer, you will recognize that all numbers in JavaScript are of type `double`, which corresponds to the 8-byte IEEE floating-point format. This means they can represent numbers up to +–1.7976931348623157x10^308 and down to +–5x10^–324.
- JavaScript supports numeric values in integer form (from –9007199254740992 to +9007199254740992), octal form (represented by any number, other than 0 by itself, beginning with a 0), and hexadecimal (represented by any number beginning with 0x).
- Floating-point values may use scientific notation.
- You can convert from between the different radix's by using the `toString()` method. So, you can do

  ```
  var a = 32;
  var b = a.toString(16);
  ```

  This will convert the value of `a`, 32, to its hexadecimal equivalent, 0x20. Likewise, if you call `toString(8)`, you will get the octal value, 40.
- There are a few special values associated with numbers in JavaScript. These include positive infinity (when a floating-point value is larger than can be represented), negative infinity (when a floating-point value is smaller than can be represented), not a number (represents mathematical error conditions, like the result of dividing 0 by 0), maximum value (the largest number that can be represented), and minimum value (the smallest number that can be represented).

In reference to the special values mentioned, there is an implicit object in JavaScript named `Number`. This contains constants that represent each of those special values. You can use them to determine outcomes of operations. One interesting point is that the special not a number value will not equate to any other number, not even to itself! For this situation, there is a special `isNaN()` function that can be used. To illustrate these points, try the code shown in Listing 2-4. When executed, it will show, via JavaScript `alert()`, the value of the `MIN_VALUE` and `MAX_VALUE` constants of `Number`. Lastly, it will show that dividing zero by zero yields a result that is not a number; hence calling `isNaN()` on it returns true.

Listing 2-4. *Demonstration of Special Numeric Values in JavaScript*

```
<html>
  <head>
    <title></title>

    <script>

      alert("Number.MIN_VALUE = " + Number.MIN_VALUE);
      alert("Number.MAX_VALUE = " + Number.MAX_VALUE);

      var a = 0 / 0;

      if (a == Number.NaN) {
        alert("a == Number.NaN");
      }

      if (isNaN(a)) {
        alert("isNaN(a)");
      }

    </script>

  </head>
  <body> </body>
</html>
```

Strings

Strings in JavaScript are about as simple as numbers. Just like in Java, they are an object, with a number of properties and methods.

Strings can contain Unicode characters, just as comments can.

The + operator is overloaded to perform string concatenation by default. The concatenation operator is actually quite a bit more than that in Java, though, owing to the loosely typed nature of the language. Have a look at Listing 2-5.

Listing 2-5. *The Concatenation Operator in a Loosely Typed Language*

```
<html>
  <head>
    <title></title>

    <script>

      var a = 10;
      var s = "20";

      alert(a + s);

    </script>

  </head>
  <body> </body>
</html>
```

What is the value shown in the alert pop-up here? Does an error occur? It would in a language like Java, but in JavaScript it is valid. What you will see is shown in Figure 2-2.

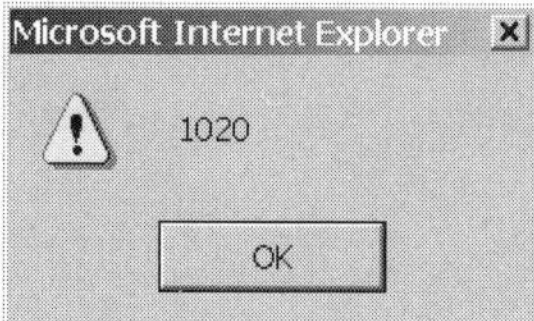

Figure 2-2. *Alert pop-up*

JavaScript essentially performs an implicit cast of the variable a to a string and concatenates them. This is analogous to what happens in Java if you do this:

```
int a = 123;
System.out.println("Testing " + a);
```

To get around this in JavaScript, you use one of the built-in parse functions. Change the line of code with the alert in it to the following and try it again:

```
alert(a + parseInt(s));
```

You will find that the alert now has the value 30, just as you would expect. This will sometimes come into play as well when you have a function that might receive a number and you need to get a string from it. Simply concatenate an empty string with the number, like so:

```
var a = 10;
myFunction(a);
function myFunction(inA) {
  var s = "" + inA;
  alert(20 + inA);
  alert(20 + s);
}
```

This first alert will result in 30, because we are adding a literal number to a variable holding a number, and the second alert will result in "2010" because 20 is "cast" to a string and concatenated with the value of s, which is our number "cast" to a string.

One last point about how strings relate to escape sequences: just like in Java or C, the backslash (\) character begins an escape sequence. Most of the same escape sequences you are likely already familiar with are present, with a few additions (for C programmers anyway). Table 2-2 summarizes the available escape sequences. Also note that if the escape sequence is not recognized, the interpreter will ignore the backslash. In other words, if you have a string "abc\def", the actual value will be "abcdef".

Table 2-2. *JavaScript String Escape Sequences*

Escape Sequence	Meaning
\b	Backspace
\f	Form feed
\n	Newline (frequently used as part of the combination \r\n, which is a common end-of-line indicator on most systems)
\r	Carriage return
\t	Tab
\'	Single-quote (apostrophe—this will be used frequently when you are inserting JavaScript dynamically into a page)
\"	Double quote (quotation mark—this too will be used frequently, perhaps even more so than \ ')
\\	Backslash (allows you to insert a backslash character into a string, which otherwise would not be possible)
\NNN	Allows you to insert a Unicode character into the string where the Unicode value is represented by an octal number. The number must be between 0 and 377.
\nNN	Allows you to insert a Unicode character into the string where the Unicode value is represented by a hexadecimal number. The number must be between 00 and ff.
\uNNNN	Allows you to insert a Unicode character into the string where the Unicode value is represented by a hexadecimal number, but always a four-digit hexadecimal number.

Booleans

Booleans are the typical yes/no, true/false variables they are in any other language. If you have ever worked with C, you probably know that the bool type in C is really not much more than an alias for the values 1 and 0. If you have ever worked with Java, you know that there is a real boolean type that is not just a mask of an integer value. In JavaScript, booleans are something of a hybrid. An interesting proof of this is shown in Listing 2-6; Figure 2-3 shows the result.

Listing 2-6. *The Dual Nature of the JavaScript Boolean Type*

```
<html>
  <head>
    <title></title>

 <script>

      var a = true;
      var b = 1;
      var c = a + b;

      alert(a + "\n" + b + "\n" + c);

    </script>

  </head>
  <body> </body>
</html>
```

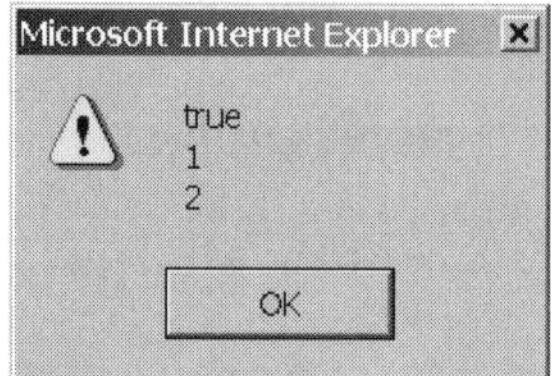

Figure 2-3. *The result of executing the code demonstrating the dual nature of JavaScript booleans*

It may seem like JavaScript is in fact treating the boolean like an integer, and in effect that is exactly what it is doing. In fact, it is not. What is happening is that when we hit var c = a + b; the interpreter is implicitly casting the boolean value true to 1 and performing the arithmetic operation. Looks can be deceiving! For all intents and purposes, you can go ahead and think like you would in C about booleans, but bear in mind that, under the covers, it is in fact more like Java.

null and undefined

null can be considered another data type, but only peripherally. Like boolean, JavaScript can do implicit casts from null to 0 when necessary. In general, though, they are not identical, just like true and false are not really the same as 1 and 0, even though it may seem like it. Note that `null` is always all lowercase in JavaScript.

`undefined` is a special type, like `null`, which comes up quite often, actually, more than `null` tends to. `undefined` is a value returned when you attempt to reference an object that does not exist, a variable that has never had a value assigned to it (although it could have been declared), or an object property that cannot be found. `null` and `undefined` are not the same thing, although in many cases you can treat them as if they were because if you do a comparison between an `undefined` object and `null`, the result will be true. Listing 2-7 demonstrates these concepts.

Listing 2-7. *null and undefined Special Values*

```
<html>
  <head>
    <title></title>

    <script>

      var a;

      alert(a);

      if (a == null) {
        alert("a is null");
      }

      if (typeof a == "undefined") {
        alert("a is undefined");
      }

      a = null;

      if (typeof a == "undefined") {
        alert("a is undefined again");
      }

    </script>

  </head>
  <body> </body>
</html>
```

In this code, the first alert will show `a` as undefined because no value was ever assigned to it. You will then see an alert that says `a` is `null`, because `undefined == null`. Lastly, you will see a third alert saying `a` is undefined. Here, we use the `typeof` keyword to make that determination. Notice that `typeof` returns a string, not a type (unlike `instanceOf` in Java). Finally, to drive the point home, notice that the last alert, the one that would say "a is undefined again", does not appear. This proves that `null` is not really the same as `undefined`.

In short, undefined will usually denote some error, either a typo on your part, or some code that did not execute that you expected to, while null is a generally valid value. There are of course exceptions to this, but in general that is the way you can approach it. In that regard, you should, most of the time, not treat null and undefined the same because they probably have a semantically (and subtly) different meaning, most of the time.

Anonymous Functions

Earlier, I briefly touched on the concept of functions being very flexible in JavaScript because they are true object types. To fully illustrate this, we need to look at the anonymous function concept. Let's jump right into it and show it in code in Listing 2-8.

Listing 2-8. *Anonymous Functions and a Form of Polymorphism*

```
<html>
  <head>
    <title></title>

    <script>

      var myFunction1 = new Function("name", "alert(name);");
      var myFunction2 = function(name) { alert(name); }
      var myFunction3 = function() {
        var i;
        for (i = 0; i < arguments.length; i++) {
          var property = arguments[i];
          alert(property);
        }
      }

      myFunction1("Frank");
      myFunction2("Zammetti");
      myFunction1 = myFunction3;
      myFunction1("a", 1, "b", 2);

    </script>

  </head>
  <body> </body>
</html>
```

Here we actually see two different ways of declaring an anonymous function. The first method, which the variable myFunction1 points to, using the new Function() approach, is not used much because the function definition needs to be enclosed in quotes, which makes it difficult many times to define a function with many lines of code (some are likely to have quotes, which you would need to escape). The second approach, which the variable myFunction2 points to, is by far more common. Additionally, with the first approach, the entire function would have to appear on a single line; otherwise an unterminated string constant error would occur. The second approach does not suffer from that shortcoming; you can break the function down across as many lines as you like.

For both, though, the code assigns the function to a variable, much like a pointer to a method in C++. You can then call the function by using the variable, just as if the function itself were named what the variables are. This portends a form of polymorphism in that you can change the function reference of either of the variables at any time and still call them the same (assuming the signatures are the same, and even that is not absolutely necessary in JavaScript!). Think about the reflection code you would have to write to do this in Java! Or think about the pointers you would have to mess around with in C. That is what `myFunction3` demonstrates. Here we create another function with a completely different signature than that which `myFunction1` points to. After we call on the first two functions to display my first name and last name, we point the variable `myFunction1` to the function that `myFunction3` points to. We then call it, passing it four parameters. It then uses the `arguments` array, which is an implicit object that all functions have access to that contains the arguments passed to the function, and displays the value of each. Did you notice what happened? Blink and you may have missed it: the variable `myFunction1` was changed to point to a different function than it started with, but we called it exactly the same, but with the added ability that we could have whatever signature we wanted for it. Again, if you try to replicate that example in Java, you will quickly realize that you will be knee-deep in reflection code to get anywhere near this. JavaScript, being much more dynamic, makes it a trivial exercise.

Memory Management

JavaScript, like Java, is a fully automatic memory-managed language, meaning that you never need to worry about freeing up memory you may have allocated by virtue of object instantiations and such. Most modern implementations of JavaScript use a mark-and-sweep algorithm for their garbage collection, and these algorithms are generally fairly efficient so that you should not notice any slowdowns as a result of garbage collection under most circumstances.

Note that there is a `delete` keyword in JavaScript, but it does not work like the `delete` keyword in C. In JavaScript, this keyword is used to remove properties from an object or elements from an array. You cannot delete an object reference as you can in C (doing so will fail silently).

This is all mostly a curiosity, though. JavaScript has automatic garbage collection, and that is about as far as you generally need to think about it!

Object-Oriented JavaScript, or Making JavaScript "Non-Kiddie-Like"

If what we have seen up to this point was all there was to JavaScript, then the perception of it being a "toy" language might not be far from the truth. To be sure, it would still be a very useful tool, but it would not lend itself to what we typically think of as "professional-level" coding. Thankfully, JavaScript still has quite a bit more to offer.

As I mentioned earlier, JavaScript is not Java, not by a long shot. But it does have some capabilities that make it fairly similar. One of those is the ability to quickly and easily create classes, objects, or custom data types, or whichever other similar term you would like to use. I tend to use the term "classes" and "objects" in the usual way, that is, classes are blueprints for objects, which are instances of a class. I do this for no other reason than to enforce the object-oriented mind-set. In point of fact, though, classes and objects in JavaScript bear only a passing resemblance to their big brothers in Java or C++ or other full-blown OOP languages. They are missing some very important OOP concepts, but in doing so they actually gain some flexibility.

In its simplest form, an object in JavaScript can actually exist without a class, in a sense. For instance, you can do the following:

```
var o = new Object();
```

The variable `o` now points to an object of type `Object`. `Object` is actually the class that is instantiated, and just like in Java, `Object` has some methods and properties and default implementations. `Object` has a `toString()` method, for example, so all objects created in JavaScript will also have that method, although the default implementation tends to be even less useful than the Java default implementation! What is important, though, is that you can now do the following:

```
o.name = "Michael Jordan";
```

Unlike Java, JavaScript allows you to add elements to an object on the fly. Here, we are adding a property named `name` to the object and giving it the value "Michael Jordan". In this way, objects in JavaScript are very much like a custom data type, a holder for just about anything you would like to stuff in them.

And yes, this means methods too! Let us say we have a function defined like so:

```
function sayName() {
  alert this.name;
}
```

The following is now perfectly valid:

```
o.sayMyName = sayName;
```

Try it! Load the code shown in Listing 2-9 in your browser and see what you get!

Listing 2-9. *The Flexibility of JavaScript Objects*

```
<html>
  <head>
    <title></title>

    <script>

      var o = new Object();

      o.name = "Michael Jordan";

      function sayName() {
        alert(this.name);
      }
```

```
      o.sayMyName = sayName;
      o.sayMyName();

    </script>

  </head>
  <body> </body>
</html>
```

Recall earlier when we said that functions in JavaScript are real objects? Now you can see where that bit of information comes back to help us. By being able to assign a reference to a function to a member of a class, we can add methods on the fly with ease.

Another important detail here is the usage of the `this` keyword in the `sayName()` function. The `this` keyword is common enough in OOP languages, but its usage here can seem a little bizarre because the function is not declared within any object. You may ask how it works in this case, and that would be a smart question. The answer is that the `this` keyword is given meaning at runtime, as in other languages, based on the object that is executing it. An important consequence is that you can attach the same function to as many objects as you like! In that case, whichever object calls the function is what `this` will point to at runtime.

By the way, `Object` is a built-in type in JavaScript. There are other built-in types that you can create, such as `Date()` or `Function()`. All of them allow the extensibility you have seen here. In fact, some Ajax libraries work by extending fundamental types in a similar manner as you have seen here, `Object` most often. Since, like in Java, all objects in JavaScript ultimately descend from `Object`, you can add the Ajax functionality to everything in one place. Very nifty, but also somewhat controversial because some people feel this is "polluting" JavaScript. In some cases, what you add to these fundamental types can have unforeseen consequences and should therefore be done with caution.

In fact, let's talk about how you might extend `Object`. Try the code seen in Listing 2-10 and see what is revealed.

Listing 2-10. *Extending Intrinsic JavaScript Types*

```
<html>
  <head>
    <title></title>

    <script>

      function sayName() {
        alert(this.name);
      }

      Object.prototype.sayMyName = sayName;
      Object.prototype.name = "test";

      var m = new Object();
      m.sayMyName();
```

```
    </script>

  </head>
  <body> </body>
</html>
```

You should see an alert that says "test" when you load this page. Now, go ahead and instantiate some other instances of `Object` and call its `sayMyName()` method. You will see that they all say "test". We have modified `Object` itself!

Every object in JavaScript has what is known as a "prototype" associated with it. This is most easily understood as the class the object inherits from. This is not strictly true, as JavaScript does not in fact have true inheritance. What JavaScript has is arguably more powerful. Every object in JavaScript is an instance of some "base" class. The object then has members bound to it using its prototype. This allows you to create objects that share some characteristics, but that then have their own, just like inheritance in Java allows for. It is a little odd in the case of `Object` because it is, in effect, its own prototype. This is not generally the case, though, as we will see shortly. To reference the prototype of any given class, we simply access its prototype property. The line of code from earlier

```
Object.prototype.sayMyName = sayName;
```

is essentially saying "add the `sayMyName` member to the parent of the `Object` class and set its value to point to the `sayName()` function." Again, since `Object` is really its own prototype in this class, it means that every `Object` created from this point on will have the `sayMyName` member, and will point to the `sayName()` function.

Let's create a slightly less confusing example. To do so we will have to learn about creating our own classes in JavaScript. It may seem odd, but all it takes is this:

```
function MyClass() {
}
```

You could now do

```
var m = new MyClass();
```

Inside this `MyClass` function, you would have an implicit reference to `this`. You can use that reference to further construct the class. For instance, try the example shown in Listing 2-11.

Listing 2-11. *Creating Your Own Class in JavaScript*

```
<html>
  <head>
    <title></title>

    <script>

      function sayName() {
        alert(this.name);
      }
```

```
      function MyClass(inName) {
        this.name = inName;
        this.sayMyName = sayName;
      }

      var m = new MyClass("Babe Ruth");
      m.sayMyName();

    </script>

  </head>
  <body> </body>
</html>
```

What we have done here is create a class called `MyClass`, and within it we have done two things. First, we set the value of the `name` property, which is new and would be dynamically attached, to the value passed in. What we have in effect done is create a constructor. In fact, to state things simply: whenever you create a custom class in JavaScript, you are implicitly creating a constructor for it as well. You can choose whether or not you need to pass in parameters. The consequence here is that if you need to overload constructors, you really cannot. Every constructor function you write is in fact its own class. This is not usually a problem, but you need to be aware of it.

The second thing we are doing is attaching the `sayName()` function to every instance of the `MyClass` class under the member name `sayMyName`. That is why when we create an instance of `MyClass`, and pass in "Babe Ruth" to the constructor, the call to `sayMyName()` results in an alert saying "Babe Ruth".

I can hear you asking now "what about inheritance?" It surprises many to learn that JavaScript does in fact support a kind of inheritance. The prototype again is how this is achieved. Let's look at an example, shown in Listing 2-12.

Listing 2-12. *Inheritance Example*

```
<html>
  <head>
    <title></title>

    <script>

      function MySuperclass() { }
      MySuperclass.prototype.name = "";
      MySuperclass.prototype.sayMyName = function() { alert(this.name); }

      function MySubclass() {
        this.name = "I am a subclass";
      }
      MySubclass.prototype = MySuperclass.prototype;
```

```
            var m = new MySubclass();
            m.sayMyName();

        </script>

    </head>
    <body> </body>
</html>
```

The first thing this code does is create an object called MySuperclass. Here, we simply want a prototype created with that name, which JavaScript will automatically do upon encountering a new object type. Next, we add a property to the MySuperclass prototype named name and give it what is essentially a default value. Next, we attach a function named sayMyName() to the prototype, which happens to be just like the previous examples, nothing but an alert of the name property of the object it is attached to.

Here is where it gets interesting. We now create another object named MySubclass, and in its constructor we set the value "I am a subclass" to the name property (I admit, I am not being terribly creative with the value here!). After that is done, we see the line

```
MySubclass.prototype = MySuperclass.prototype;
```

This is the line that literally makes the inheritance happen. What we are saying here is that we want the prototype of the MySubclass object to be the prototype of the MySuperclass object. This has the effect of taking all the members of MySuperclass and attaching them to MySubclass. In other words, MySubclass has inherited all the members of MySuperclass. That is why the call to m.sayMyName(); results in the alert shown in Figure 2-4.

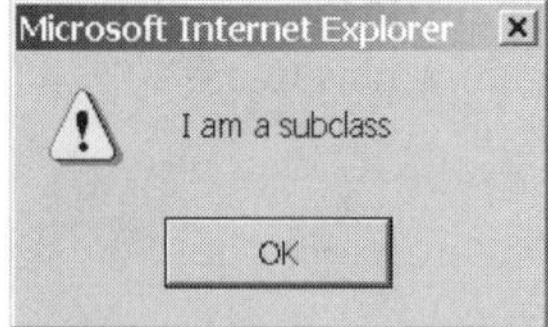

Figure 2-4. *Alert from MySubclass*

As you would expect, you can extend MySubclass however you wish, adding new members to it all you want. Note that the inherited properties are not copied from the parent to the child; instead the child merely references the members in the parent. This has two importance consequences. First, you can change the members after the fact, and the next time the child uses that member, it will be using the new version. Related to this, the second point is that you can add members to a child at any time by adding them to the parent, even after the prototype of the child has been assigned. It acts as if inheritance is redone with every member access in an object. That is not strictly speaking what is happening, but that is precisely how it appears, and that is exactly how you can treat it.

JavaScript also has the notion of instance and class members. Instance members are any members that are created (and optionally initialized) in a constructor. To illustrate the difference, look at the code in Listing 2-13.

Listing 2-13. *Example of Class and Instance Members*

```
<html>
  <head>
    <title></title>

    <script>

      function MyClass() {
        this.firstName = "George";
      }
      MyClass.lastName = "Washington";

      c1 = new MyClass();
      c2 = new MyClass();
      c2.firstName = "Bill";

      alert(c1.firstName);
      alert(c2.firstName);
      alert(MyClass.lastName);

    </script>

  </head>
  <body> </body>
</html>
```

When this code is executed, we see three alerts, the first saying "George", the second saying "Bill", and the last saying "Washington". The key to understanding it is actually in the difference between the three alert calls. The first is displaying an instance variable of the `c1` instance of `MyClass`. In this case, the instance variable `firstName` is set in the constructor to the value "George". The second alert displays the `firstName` members of the `c2` instance of `MyClass`. After the `c2` instance is instantiated, we change the value of the `firstName` members to "Bill". Because we see two different first names when the first two alerts are executed, we can see that each instance of `MyClass` has a different version of `firstName` associated with it, just as we would expect.

Class members, on the other hand, are accessed with a slightly different syntax. They look very much like accessing static fields in Java, and indeed that is an apt analogy. Likewise, when we set the value of the `lastName` field, we do so using the reference to `MyClass`, because using either `c1` or `c2` would make it an instance member.

Now that we have seen that JavaScript has fairly good support for many of the common object-oriented techniques we are used to, even if the syntax is a bit different, we now need to discuss the shortcomings, and there is really one that stands above any others: information hiding, or perhaps more specifically, encapsulation. Simply put, there is no such thing in JavaScript!

There is no notion of public and private because every member you add to an object is in effect public. When inheritance is involved, therefore, there is no way to have a member not be inheritable as there is in Java by declaring it private. Further, there is no concept of packages in JavaScript, and hence no protected access. We have no way to "hide" information inside an object; in other words, there is no such thing as encapsulation as is typically meant in the OOP world. Any object can access the members of any other object at any time, regardless of their relationship, or lack thereof. In the C++ world, this would be akin to every single class being a friend of every other!

This one simple shortcoming will tend to change the way you do things to some degree. For instance, while writing getters and setters for an object still makes sense, you have to understand that if someone comes along and bypasses them, you can't do a thing about it, so in some cases you may not even bother writing those methods (especially if they are the typical `this.field = field;` kind of method). You also have to keep it in mind when inheritance is involved. Since all members will be inherited, this could change how you architect your class hierarchy somewhat.

Overall, though, the level of support for object-oriented techniques in JavaScript is actually more robust than many people give it credit for. However, by its nature as a relatively simple scripting language, many people still tend to not do things in an object-oriented way. In fact, many of the examples in this book will actually not do things in an object-oriented way (some will of course). Part of that is my desire to demonstrate both ways of doing things, but part of it is that sometimes OOP in JavaScript makes a lot of sense, and sometimes it turns out to just be (arguably) superfluous coding. As with most things, there is a balancing act in play, and you will have to determine as you go which way makes more sense. My advice is to look at the problem you're trying to solve and pick the approach that makes the most sense. However, I *would* lean toward the object-oriented way if for no other reason than to make it more similar to the Java back-end you will likely be writing. Why shift your brain between two different gears if you can avoid it?

The Document Object Model and Scripting: Manipulating Content on the Fly

When we work with Ajax, we are interested in essentially three things:

- Making an out-of-band request, that is, a request that does not correspond to the normal transition between pages associated with a web application
- Performing a function on the server that generates some sort of response
- Actually doing something with that response back on the client

Although there are no hard-and-fast rules about what you should do when the response is received, one function is done far more often than anything else: updating the document object model.

As is usually the case in computer science, we love to come up with impressive-sounding phrases, and then run them through what I like to call the "alphabet soup filter." So, in this case, document object model becomes DOM.

A DOM, be it in the context of Ajax or elsewhere, is most often a tree structure that contains nodes representing each element of a document. For example, take the following simple HTML:

```
<html>
  <head>
    <title>Sample DOM</title>
  </head>
  <body>
    <table id="accountTable">
      <tr id="tableHeaders">
        <td id="accountBalanceHeader">Account Balance</td>
      </tr>
      <tr id="account1">
        <td id="accountBalanceValue1">$1,000,000,000,000,000.00</td>
      </tr>
    </table>
  </body>
</html>
```

(Oh, how I wish that account balance was real!) If we were to construct a DOM of this, it would look something like Figure 2-5.

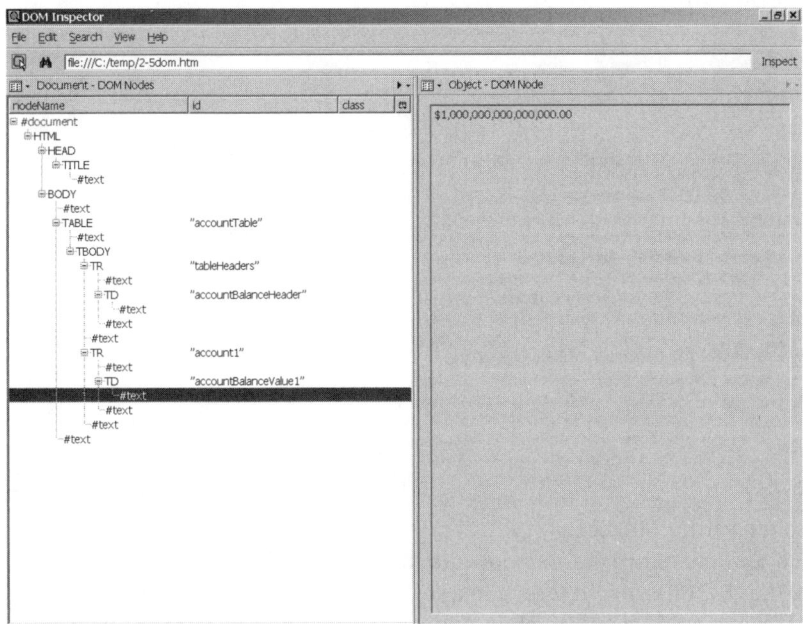

Figure 2-5. *DOM of a simple HTML page*

The most important things to note are first, the tree-like structure of the DOM, and second, that most of the elements are given a unique ID to identify them with. The structure corresponds to the layout of the HTML itself, and all the elements within it. This will sometimes matter when you want to get a reference to a particular element in a particular branch.

Something else interesting to note is that the text contained within an element is itself a text node. In other words, when you see

```
<div>Hello!</div>
```

that may seem like just one DOM node, but in fact it is two: the <div> itself (the combination of the opening and closing tags technically) and the text "Hello!" within it. You can determine whether you have a reference to a tag node or a text node by interrogating the nodeType attribute of the node object, which is what getElementById() is really returning.

By and large, though, and 95 percent of the time in this book, the really important detail is that elements have an ID assigned to them. This allows you to use the getElementById() method of the document object. In short, any element in the DOM with a unique ID can be retrieved, that is, you can get a reference to it, simply by doing

```
o = document.getElementById("accountBalanceValue1");
```

Note that the ID you reference *must* be unique! In other words, you could not do this:

```
<html>
  <head>
    <title>Sample DOM</title>
  </head>
  <body>
    <table id="accountTable">
      <tr id="tableHeaders">
        <td id="accountBalanceHeader">Account Balance</td>
      </tr>
      <tr id="account1">
        <td id="accountBalanceValue">$10</td>
      </tr>
      <tr id="account2">
        <td id="accountBalanceValue">$20</td>
      </tr>
    </table>
  </body>
</html>
```

You might reasonably expect that calling document.getElementById("account2.accountBalanceValue") would return the element with the value $20, but in fact it would return null because the DOM IDs do not form a tree structure, so you cannot address them with dot notation like you would access members of a class in Java. Also, if there are elements with the same ID on a page, getElementById() will return only the first element it encounters with the ID, so for instance, doing document.getElementById("accountBalanceValue") would return the <td> with the value $10 here all the time. So, take care, especially when rendering pages dynamically, to provide a unique ID for all elements you wish to address (you can in fact still address them by iterating over DOM nodes, but getElementById() will be of little use, and that is the most direct, and usually simplest, way to get access to an element, so unique IDs will make your life easier!).

You may be familiar with the name attribute many HTML tags have. Note that this is *not* the same as the id attribute! If we changed the id attributes to name attributes in our previous example and then tried to use `getElementById()`, as you can probably guess from the function name, we would get nothing back. It is, however, perfectly acceptable to have an element with both a `name` and an `id` attribute, and further, the value of both can be the same. You can think of this in terms of name being the "old world," i.e., plain HTML, and `id` being the "new world," that is, DOM, XML, and CSS. Both are still valid and have their places, but you need to be aware of the differences.

The DOM provides what is referred to as a "scriptable interface" to the structure of a document. In terms of HTML, this allows us to make changes to the document after it has been rendered via scripting. Whenever you get a reference to an element using `getElementById()`, you now have access to any methods or properties it exposes. Further, although you cannot access nested elements via dot notation as described earlier, what you can do is use the `getElementsByTagName()` method, which is a method of every node in the DOM, and it returns a collection of all the tags of the given type it contains. Listing 2-14 demonstrates various ways of manipulating the DOM and of using `getElementsByTagName()`. For the purposes of this book, this code demonstrates everything you should need to know, so I highly recommend playing with it and understanding it before continuing on. To go into this topic in more detail, I recommend the book *DOM Scripting: Web Design with JavaScript and the Document Object Model*, by Jeremy Keith (friends of ED, 2005).

Listing 2-14. *A Number of Examples of DOM Manipulation*

```
<html>
  <head>
    <title>DOM manipulation examples</title>

    <script>

      // These will be used by the moving text example.
      textTimer = null;
      textLeft = 0;
      textMoveDir = 1;

      // This function makes the someText visible.
      function showSomeText() {
        document.getElementById("someText").style.visibility = "visible";
      }

      // This function will start a timer that will fire and move
      // the text in the movingText div back and forth;
      function moveText() {
        if (textTimer == null) {
          textTimer = setTimeout("moveIt()", 0);
        } else {
          textTimer = null;
        }
      }

      // This is the function the timer will call periodically to update
```

```
    // the position of the moving text.
    function moveIt() {
      // Moving right.
      if (textMoveDir == 1) {
        textLeft++;
        if (textLeft > 300) {
          textMoveDir = 0;
        }
      // Moving left.
      } else {
        textLeft--;
        if (textLeft < 1) {
          textMoveDir = 1;
        }
      }
      // Show the current position.
      document.getElementById("showLeft").innerHTML = textLeft;
      // Update the position of the text.
      document.getElementById("movingText").style.left = textLeft;
      // Start the next iteration.
      textTimer = setTimeout("moveIt()", 0);
    }

    // This is called to change the background color of the page.
    function changeBGColor() {
      document.getElementById("thePage").style.backgroundColor = "#ff0000";
    }

    // This function gets a collection of child elements under a given
    // element, then changes each of their values.
    function changeDivVals() {
      o = document.getElementById("divCollection");
      c = o.getElementsByTagName("div");
      c[0].innerHTML = "20";
      c[1].innerHTML = "30";
      c[2].innerHTML = "10";

    }

  </script>

</head>

<body id="thePage">

  <hr>
  This shows how you can make this visible that were formerly invisible
  via DOM manipulation (and it works the other way around too of course!)
```

```
    <br><br>
    <div id="someText" style="visibility:hidden;">Now you can see me!</div>
    <br>
    <input type="button" onClick="showSomeText();"
      value="Click to show some text">

    <hr><br><br>

    <hr>
    This shows how you can do simple animation via DOM manipulation
    <br><br>
    <div id="movingText" style="position:absolute;left:0;">
      This text moves!
    </div>
    <br><br>
    <input type="button" onClick="moveText();"
      value="Click to move some text">
    <br><br>
    <div id="showLeft"> </div>

    <hr><br><br>

    <hr>
    This shows how you can change style attributes on the fly.
    <br><br>
    <input type="button" onClick="changeBGColor();"
      value="Click to change the background color of the page">

    <hr><br><br>

    This shows how you can get a collection of elements under a given element
    and access members of the collection to change their text.
    <br><br>
    <div id="divCollection">
      <b>First value:</b><br>
      <div>10</div>
      <b>Second value:</b><br>
      <div>20</div>
      <b>Third value:</b><br>
      <div>30</div>
    </div>
    <br>
    <input type="button" onClick="changeDivVals();"
      value="Click to change order of the above values">
    <hr>

  </body>

</html>
```

XML: The Language of Languages

Anyone who has spent any time at all in the computer field is familiar with the acronym CSV, which stands for comma-separated value. This is a very common file format where each element of data is separated by… wait for it… a *comma*!

Think about a CSV file for a moment, perhaps one like this:

```
18987445,Rothlesberry,Michael,212 Kiner,092387464
```

The data items here are

- 1898744511101
- Rothlesberry
- Michael
- 212 Kiner
- 092387464

Now, looking at that, you can make some reasonable deductions about what each item actually is. The 1898744511101 we really cannot say, although it could be an account number based on its size. Rothlesberry is obviously a name of some sort. Maybe a first name, maybe a last name, maybe a middle name, but probably a name for sure. The Michael following that is a typical first name, though, so we can reasonably guess that Rothlesberry is a last name. 212 Kiner looks a bit like a street address (at least here in the United States), so that too is a reasonable guess. The 092387464 is also tough to determine, but it does happen to have exactly the right number of digits to be a Social Security number, which might make some sense if we were examining this file in a financial context, especially if we guess that the first number is an account number.

You see the problem: we are making guesses, educated as they may be. This is clearly not an optimal way to store data if humans need to be able to read it.

More important, though, think about the exercise we just did. What were we really doing in trying to deduce the data elements' true natures? We were in effect using language to describe another language. We were using metalanguage, in other words, and that is precisely what XML is.

Extensible Markup Language (XML) should be quite familiar if you have ever clicked the View Source option on a web page. What you were looking at, the HTML, is essentially a specialized form of XML.

Historically, XML's forefather was something called Generalized Markup Language (GML). Charles Goldfarb, Ed Losher, and Ray Lorie, engineers at IBM, invented GML in 1969. Later on, Goldfarb continued development of GML and eventually produced Standardized Generalized Markup Language (SGML) in 1974. Both of these are ways of "marking up" content to bestow on them some contextual meaning. Both GML and SGML had the failing of being overly complex for most usages, although they did find some use in publishing documents at IBM and elsewhere.

Around this time, Tim Berners-Lee and Anders Berglund created what we now know as HTML. HTML took the general concept of SGML, that of marking up content, to give it meaning, and made it simpler. Probably the biggest difference between SGML and HTML is that HTML has a fixed set of tags, whereas SGML allows you to create your own.

Both of these were recognized as being valuable attributes, but neither "language" on its own was really sufficient. So, in roughly the mid-1990s, the World Wide Web Consortium (W3C) took the two, fused them, and created the first version of XML. XML is designed to be simpler than SGML, and much more flexible than HTML. Although it was not designed specifically with the Web in mind, clearly that is the place it has wound up being used the most.

OK, that's enough, history lesson over!

XML is the *x* in Ajax, and it will serve two purposes in various instances. First, it will serve as a configuration file format. In Java, developers have been storing configurations in properties files for a long time, similar to the following:

```
server=www.myserver.com
username=mike123
password=testpw
```

In XML, the following might be seen as

```
<configuration>
  <server>www.myserver.com</server>
  <username>mike123</username>
  <password>testpw</password>
</configuration>
```

In a situation like this, the difference is not that extreme, and the benefit of XML is not readily apparent. You could argue that being more verbose makes it a little clearer what things are in it. You could say that the XML version delineates the data elements better because you cannot only see where they begin but also where they end. But really, the difference is not that extreme here.

In the second use case, though, it might be. Imagine if you wanted to have a collection of items—let's say a bunch of usernames. In the properties file, since each element has to have its own unique identifier, your only choice is something like this:

```
server=www.myserver.com
username1=mike123
username2=mike456
username3=mike789
password=testpw
```

Clearly, this will be an inefficient, inflexible, and pedantic way to store this information. In XML, though, you could do this:

```
<configuration>
  <server>www.myserver.com</server>
  <users>
    <username>mike123</username>
    <username>mike456</username>
    <username>mike789</username>
  </users>
  <password>testpw</password>
</configuration>
```

Now, while it is true there are more characters used to describe the same general information, the XML version is far more flexible, especially when you try to read in this XML and correlate it to some data structure (think a `Map` here).

When XML first came to light for many developers, it was hailed as the be-all and end-all of data interchange. No more CSV files that have to have a layout map accompanying them. No more fixed-width data files that likewise need a fairly complex document to describe them. Best of all, no more proprietary data formats of any sort; everyone would use a standard, simple, generally obvious format, and the world would be a better place.

People began to realize, though, that XML was just another tool in the toolbox, not something to be used in every single situation. Indeed, one of the biggest problems with XML, which we can clearly see from our discussion thus far, is that expressing information in XML takes more space, and sometimes quite a bit more, than other formats. After all, our configuration file could be expressed like this:

```
www.myserver.com,mike123,mike456,mike789,testpw
```

Which can be transmitted faster and more efficiently over a network? Clearly, the CSV version can. The point here is that you should not have the mind-set of cramming XML into every data interchange situation; many times it will be counterproductive. You will see a number of examples in this book that do not use XML at all. XML is not required by Ajax, although it is frequently used. I will explain why I chose XML (or not) in each case, even if sometimes the answer is simply to demonstrate one or the other!

Parsing XML in JavaScript

XML is not of a whole lot of use unless you parse it and create structures in JavaScript or Java to manipulate and work with. Actually, depending on your use case, you may not create structures at all; you may simply read through the XML linearly once and react to each element encountered as appropriate. In fact, this is exactly what virtually all the examples in this book that use XML will be doing. In this section, we will look at how this is done, as well as some other parsing techniques for doing more complex things with XML. We will deal with parsing XML in Java in the next chapter; for now we are concerned only with how to do it on the client in JavaScript.

As an example, let's assume we have the following XML we want to parse:

```
<messages>
  <message text="Hello!" />
  <message text="I hope all is well with you!" />
</messages>
```

All we want to do is parse this and display the text attribute of each `<message>` element we encounter. The code in Listing 2-15 shows this, along with some other things that we will discuss.

Listing 2-15. *Simple XML Parsing Example in JavaScript*

```
<html>
  <head>
    <title></title>
```

```
    <script>

      if (window.XMLHttpRequest) {
        // Create an XML DOM object in non-IE browsers.  Set the root element
        // <messages> and add it to the DOM.
        create_xmlDoc =
          document.implementation.createDocument("", "messages", null);
      } else {
        // Create an XML DOM object in IE.
        create_xmlDoc = new ActiveXObject("Microsoft.XMLDOM");
        // Create the root element and add it to the DOM.
        create_root = create_xmlDoc.createElement("messages");
        create_xmlDoc.documentElement = create_root;
      }

      // Create a <message> node, set the text attribute and add it to the DOM.
      create_msg = create_xmlDoc.createElement("message");
      create_msg.setAttribute("text", "Hello!");
      create_xmlDoc.documentElement.appendChild(create_msg);

      // Create a <message> node, set the text attribute and add it to the DOM.
      create_msg = create_xmlDoc.createElement("message");
      create_msg.setAttribute("text", "I hope all is well with you!");
      create_xmlDoc.documentElement.appendChild(create_msg);

      // Just to prove it's really an object reference.
      xmlDoc = create_xmlDoc;

      // Parse the XML.  For each <message> element, display its text attribute.
      root = xmlDoc.getElementsByTagName("messages")[0];
      messages = root.getElementsByTagName("message");
      for (i = 0; i < messages.length; i++) {
        alert(messages[i].getAttribute("text"));
      }

    </script>

  </head>
  <body></body>
</html>
```

This first thing to notice is that not only are we parsing XML in this example, but we also can see how to create it. The first thing that happens when the page loads is the check to see if the `XMLHttpRequest` object is present in the window object. This should look familiar because it is the same check we use to determine how to instantiate the `XMLHttpRequest` object, as we saw in the first chapter. This again serves us well because creating a new XML DOM object is different in IE than it is in other browsers. So we branch as appropriate and get ourselves a new XML DOM object referenced by the variable `create_xmlDoc`. Note that in the case of browsers other than IE, the function call that constructs this object includes the root element <messages>, while the IE branch needs to add this element separately after the document object is instantiated.

For the sake of completeness, you can see that in the case of non-IE browsers, the function `createDocument()` takes three parameters. The first is the XML namespace, which we simply make nothing here; the second is the name of the root element, and the third is an object representing the document type being created. This third parameter does not yet seem to do anything in Mozilla-based browsers. You can basically ignore it and just pass `null` for it until such time as it is given some purpose other than being a placeholder for future enhancement.

Continuing on, we now have an actual DOM object that we can manipulate using DOM methods. Table 2-3 summarizes the methods available for manipulating the DOM.

Table 2-3. *Available DOM Manipulation Methods*

Method	Prototype	Description
`appendChild`	`parentNode.appendChild (childNode)`	Appends `childNode` to the specified `parentNode`. Returns the appended node object.
`applyElement`	`applyElement (parentNode)`	Applies the `childeNode` to the specified `parentNode`. This is essentially the same as `appendChild`, with a different syntax. Returns the appended node object.
`clearAttributes`	`targetNode.clearAttributes()`	Removes all attributes from the specified `targetNode`. Returns the node object after the attributes have been cleared.
`cloneNode`	`newNode = originalNode. cloneNode(deep)`	Creates a `newNode` object based on the `originalNode` object. The `deep` parameter determines whether a "deep" copy is done. When set to true, the object will be identical to the original in every respect; when set to false only the root will be copied. Returns the `newNode` object.
`createElement`	`newNode = document. createElement("???")`	Creates a `newNode` object with the specified name. Returns the `newNode` object.
`createTextNode`	`newNode = document. createTextNode("???")`	Creates a `newNode` object that has body text as specified. Returns the `newNode` object.
`hasChildNodes`	`hasChildren = testNode. hasChildNodes()`	Returns true if the specified `testNode` has children, false if not.
`insertBefore`	`parentNode.insertBefore (childNode, siblingNode)`	Inserts the specified `childNode` object as a child of the specified `parentNode` object just before the specified `siblingNode` object. Returns true if the insertion was successful, `null` if it was not.
`mergeAttributes`	`targetNode.mergeAttributes (sourceNode)`	Copies all of the attribute from the specified `sourceNode` object to the `targetNode` object. Returns the `targetNode` after the merge is completed.

Method	Prototype	Description
removeNode	deletedNode.removeNode(deep)	When deep is true, the entire deletedNode's subtree is removed from the DOM; when false only the deletedNode is deleted. Returns the deletedNode object.
replaceNode	oldNode.replaceNode(newNode)	Replaces an existing oldNode with a new newObj. Returns the replaced node object.
setAttribute	targetNode.setAttribute ("XXX", "YYY")	Sets the attribute XXX to the value YYY. If the attribute is not already present, it is added.
swapNode	firstNode.swapNode(secondNode)	Swaps the positions of firstNode and swapNode. Returns the firstNode object.

We use three methods in this example: createElement(), setAttribute(), and appendChild(). First we ask the document object to create a new element named <message>. We then set the text attribute of that new object. Finally, we ask the document object to append that node as a child of the root node <messages>. We do this twice, and the result at the end is an XML document with our desired structure.

Next, the variable xmlDoc is pointed at the DOM we just created. This is done simply to prove that we are really dealing with a true object here, an object that we can reference just like any other. Finally, the code to display the messages is executed:

```
// Parse the XML.  For each <message> element, display its text attribute.
root = xmlDoc.getElementsByTagName("messages")[0];
messages = root.getElementsByTagName("message");
for (i = 0; i < messages.length; i++) {
  alert(messages[i].getAttribute("text"));
}
```

The first line of code after the comment is responsible for getting the root element of our document. Since we know that the <messages> element is our root, we ask the document to give us the first element with that name using array notation, since the elements form an array in memory that we can traverse that way if we want. Once we have the root, we get the collection of elements with the name "message" (note that in fact you could call getElementsByTagName("message") on the xmlDoc variable rather than the root; they are functionally equivalent in this case). In other words, the variable messages now points to an array of <message> elements. Once we have that, we loop through that array, and for each element in it we request the text attribute, and display it. Simple!

As you probably have guessed, this method of parsing XML documents, while perfectly suitable in many instances, will sometimes not suffice. Sometimes you need more power and flexibility. Unfortunately, modern browsers do not provide much beyond what we have seen. To get the extra capabilities you need, it will become necessary to look for a JavaScript library.

One such library is called JSLib from the Mozilla project (http://jslib.mozdev.org/). This library contains a number of useful functions, but most important to us is contained in the sax.js file that is part of the library. This is a Simple API for XML (SAX) implementation. SAX is basically an event-driven model of XML parsing. You tell the SAX parser what events you are interested in by handing it function references. You then give the parser the XML to parse, and the parser will call the functions you told it about in response to various events, such as the document beginning, a new element being encountered, the body text of an element having been read, and ending events for these.

Although this is useful, it is not in and of itself ideal. It can take a fair amount of effort on your part to properly respond to the events you are really interested in, and if you happen to want to create objects based on the XML, which is not at all unusual, it will not help there. What we need is something on top of the SAX parser.

Such a tool exists! It is the `JSDigester` tag in the JSLib taglib component of the Java Web Parts project (`http://javawebparts.sourceforge.net`). Wow, that sounded like a mouthful! If you have ever used the Commons Digester component, then simply put, `JSDigester` is a JavaScript implementation of that (trimmed down quite a bit, but the same underlying concept).

If you have never used it before, Digester is a Java component that allows you to set up a collection of "rules" that will fire based on various events during the parsing of an XML document. If that sounds a lot like SAX, that is because Digester is actually built on top of SAX; in fact, Digester would not work without SAX at all. The difference is in the abstraction level you work at. With SAX, the events you receive are very fine-grained. You will receive an event callback for every element encountered for instance. With Digester, you can formally name the elements in the XML document that should fire an event, and you will only get a callback when that element is encountered.

Digester goes a step further in that it was explicitly created to deal with creating and populating objects from an XML document.

An example should very much bring this all together. Listing 2-16 is a complete example of using JSDigester.

Listing 2-16. *Example of Using JSDigester*

```
<jstags:jsDigester renderScriptTags="true" />

<script>

  function Actor() { this.gender = null; this.name   = null; }
  function Movie() { this.title  = null; this.actors = new Array(); }
  function Movies() { this.movieList = new Array(); this.numMovies = null; }

  Actor.prototype.setGender = function(inGender) { this.gender = inGender; }
  Actor.prototype.getGender = function() { return this.gender; }
  Actor.prototype.setName = function(inName) { this.name = inName; }
  Actor.prototype.getName = function() { return this.name; }
  Actor.prototype.toString = function() { return "Actor=[name=" +
    this.name + ",gender=" + this.gender + "]"; }

  Movie.prototype.setTitle = function(inTitle) { this.title = inTitle; }
  Movie.prototype.getTitle = function() { return this.title; }
  Movie.prototype.addActor = function(inActor) { this.actors.push(inActor); }
  Movie.prototype.getActors = function() { return this.actors; }
  Movie.prototype.toString = function() { return "Movie=[title=" + this.title +
    ",actors={" + this.actors + "}]"; }
```

```
  Movies.prototype.setNumMovies =
    function(inNumMovies) { this.numMovies = inNumMovies; }
  Movies.prototype.getNumMovies = function() { return this.numMovies; }
  Movies.prototype.addMovie = function(inMovie) { this.movieList.push(inMovie); }
  Movies.prototype.getMovieList = function() { return this.movieList; }
  Movies.prototype.toString = function() { return "Movies=[numMovies=" +
    this.numMovies + ",movieList={" + this.movieList + "}]"; }

sampleXML  = "<movies numMovies=\"2\">\n";
sampleXML += "  <movie>\n";
sampleXML += "    <title>Star Wars</title>\n";
sampleXML += "    <actor gender=\"male\">Harrison Ford</actor>\n";
sampleXML += "    <actor gender=\"female\">Carrie Fisher</actor>\n";
sampleXML += "  </movie>\n";
sampleXML += "  <movie>\n";
sampleXML += "    <title>Real Genius</title>\n";
sampleXML += "    <actor gender=\"male\">Val Kilmer</actor>\n";
sampleXML += "  </movie>\n";
sampleXML += "</movies>";
jsDigester = new JSDigester();
jsDigester.addObjectCreate("movies", "Movies");
jsDigester.addSetProperties("movies");
jsDigester.addObjectCreate("movies/movie", "Movie");
jsDigester.addBeanPropertySetter("movies/movie/title", "setTitle");
jsDigester.addObjectCreate("movies/movie/actor", "Actor");
jsDigester.addSetProperties("movies/movie/actor");
jsDigester.addBeanPropertySetter("movies/movie/actor", "setName");
jsDigester.addSetNext("movies/movie/actor", "addActor");
jsDigester.addSetNext("movies/movie", "addMovie");
myMovies = jsDigester.parse(sampleXML);
alert("JSDigester processed the following XML:\n\n" + sampleXML +
  "\n\nIt created an object graph consisting of a Movies object, " +
  "with a numMovies property, and containing a collection of " +
  "Movie objects.\n\nEach Movie object has a title property, and " +
  "contains a collection of Actor objects.\n\nEach Actor object has " +
  "two fields, name and gender.\n\n" +
  "Here's the final Movies object JSDigester returned: \n\n" +
  myMovies);

</script>
```

Executing this code results in the pop-up shown in Figure 2-6.

The first thing we encounter is a custom tag:

```
<jstags:jsDigester renderScriptTags="true" />
```

This is literally all the setup that is required to use JSDigester, aside from declaring the jstags taglib, of course. The Java Web Parts project, which you will be more formally introduced to in Chapter 4, has numerous highly useful little "parts" like this for you to use.

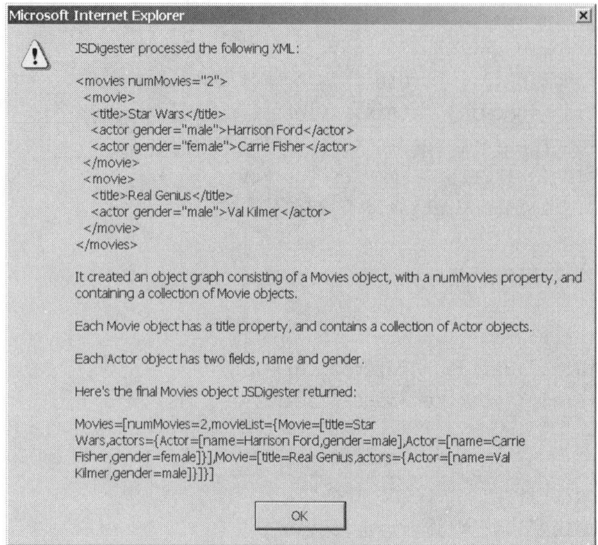

Figure 2-6. *The result of executing the JSDigester test*

After the `<jstags:jsDigester>` tag three functions are declared: `Actor()`, `Movie()`, and `Movies()`. These are essentially custom types that we will use. As JSDigester works, it will create instances of these objects and populate them. After the functions are declared, you can see that a number of methods are attached to them. Each has some accessors and mutators for various properties contained within, as well as a `toString()` method to give us a textual representation of the object.

Next up is the construction of a string of XML. This is simpler than constructing a whole XML DOM, and in many cases will be quite sufficient, as is the case here.

After that is where we start working with JSDigester:

```
jsDigester = new JSDigester();
jsDigester.addObjectCreate("movies", "Movies");
jsDigester.addSetProperties("movies");
jsDigester.addObjectCreate("movies/movie", "Movie");
jsDigester.addBeanPropertySetter("movies/movie/title", "setTitle");
jsDigester.addObjectCreate("movies/movie/actor", "Actor");
jsDigester.addSetProperties("movies/movie/actor");
jsDigester.addBeanPropertySetter("movies/movie/actor", "setName");
jsDigester.addSetNext("movies/movie/actor", "addActor");
jsDigester.addSetNext("movies/movie", "addMovie");
myMovies = jsDigester.parse(sampleXML);
```

The first line of code instantiates a JSDigester instance. The second line adds an `ObjectCreate` rule. What this rule says is that when the `<movies>` element in the XML is encountered, create an instance of the `Movies` class and push it onto the stack. JSDigester is a stack-based mechanism, which means that internally, created objects are pushed and popped from a stack, and rules work, for the most part, with the object on the top of the stack. JSDigester uses a first in, last out (FILO) stack, and therefore the order of rules can sometimes be very important.

The third line of code adds a SetProperty rule. This rule says that when the <movies> element is encountered, take whatever attributes it may have and set the corresponding properties on the object on the top of the stack. In this case, because of the previous rule, it would set the properties on our new Movies object.

The fourth line of code adds another ObjectCreate rule, this time creating a Movie object whenever the <movie> element, if it is a child of the <movies> element, is encountered. As you can see, we build up a "path" to a given element with the rules, starting at the top of the hierarchy, that is, the document's root node. Note that when this rule fires for our test XML, the Movies object will then become the second object on the stack, with the new Movie object on top of it.

The fifth line of code sets up a BeanPropertySetter rule. This rule will take the body text of a given element and call the named function on the object on the top of the stack. So, for example, when the <title> element is encountered, if it is a child of a <movie> element, which is itself a child of a <movies> element (hence the path "movies/movie/title") is encountered, the method setTitle() will be called on the object on the top of the stack (a Movie object, based on the previous rule) and will be passed the text between <title> and </title>. So, from our sample XML, the first movie created would be given the title "Star Wars".

The sixth line of code sets up another ObjectCreate rule to create Actor objects as children of a <movie> element.

The seventh line of code sets up another SetProperties rule to set the properties of the Actor created, which would be the gender attribute in this case.

The eighth line of code adds another PropertySetter rule to call the setName() method of the Actor object on the top of the stack to set the actor's name.

The ninth line of code adds a SetNext rule. The SetNext rule is used to take the object at the top of the stack and "add" it to the next object on the stack. This is used to create hierarchies of objects. In other words, each Movie object will have a collection of Actor objects in it. Likewise, the Movies object will have a collection of Movie objects in it. This is a pretty typical object hierarchy, with nothing unusual or unreasonable about it. The first SetNext rule will essentially add an Actor to the Movie it belongs to. Imagine what the state of the stack is at the point those rules would fire in parsing our XML. It would essentially look like Figure 2-7.

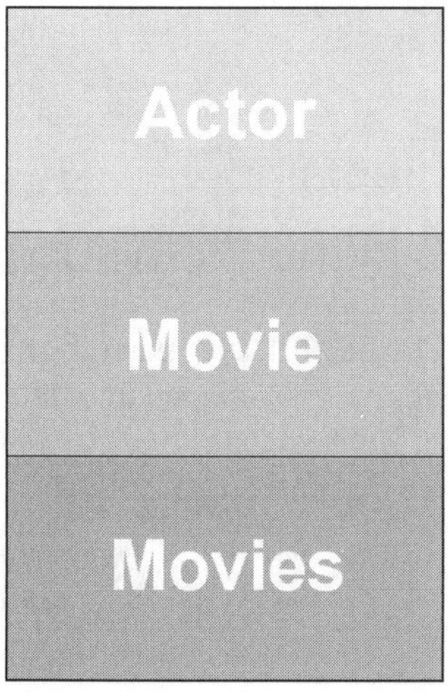

Figure 2-7. *The state of the stack at the point where the SetNext rules would fire*

So, the SetNext rule would take the object at the top of the stack, an Actor object, and call the addActor() method on the next object on the stack, a Movie object, passing it the Actor object. In addition, the object on the top of the stack, the Actor object, is now popped, so that the new top object is Movie. Then, when the SetNext rule on the tenth line fires, the Movie object on the top of the stack is passed to the addMovie() method of the next object on the stack, the Movies object, and the Movie object is popped off the stack, leaving the Movies object.

Since we have two <movie> elements in our XML, this process would happen again, minus the creation of the Movies object, because that would only occur once in this XML document.

The line

```
myMovies = jsDigester.parse(sampleXML);
```

is what actually starts this ball rolling. After all the rules are added to the JSDigester instance, the parse() method is called, passing it the XML to be parsed. What it returns is the last object to be popped off the stack, which in this case is our Movies object, precisely what we want! If you now did an alert() on the Movies object returned by JSDigester, you would be able to see all the data from the XML document present, in various objects, in the Movie object. Pretty neat, is it not?

If JSDigester seems a little confusing or overwhelming, do not despair! Many people, including me frankly, found it a little tricky at first. We will encounter it, both this client-side version and its big brother, the real Commons Digester component, a few more times in this book. It is my hope that you will come to see it as an invaluable tool that makes your life considerably easier, once you get the hang of it.

There are other ways to parse XML in JavaScript using other libraries, but in this book we will either be doing the straight-through approach or using JSDigester. The options are numerous, and I leave it as an exercise for you the reader to explore the other options. Just to get you started, though, here are a few popular options:

- Sarissa (http://sourceforge.net/projects/sarissa/): Sarissa is a very popular choice, and it does more than just parse XML. It is billed as a general-purpose XML processing tool for JavaScript and includes XSLT processing and much more.

- XML4Script (http://xmljs.sourceforge.net/website/documentation-w3cdom.html): Another popular choice.

Cascading Stylesheets

Consider for a moment the XML we looked at earlier. It seemed very nice for marking up bits of data to convey meaning on them. Imagine for a moment if you wanted to write a program to display that XML. Further assume that you did not want to just list the XML as it exists, but wanted to draw some elements in red, maybe some in bold type and maybe some in larger letters. You might imagine an easy way to do that would be to have attributes on various elements that would tell this program how to render the data a given tag marked up. Maybe you would have something like this:

```
<person fontStyle="bold">
  <firstName>Harrison</firstName>
  <lastName fontColor="red">Ford</lastName>
  <age fontSize="18pt">64 (I'm guessing!)</age>
</person>
```

That does not seem at all unreasonable. It would be easy to parse and easy to determine what characteristics the text that is displayed should have, and it's pretty clear and obvious what is going on at a glance.

This is essentially what HTML is, except that rather than just using element attributes, it many times uses specialized tags. For instance, here is essentially the same document snippet in HTML form:

```
<b>
  Harrison<br>
  <font color="#ff0000">Ford</font><br>
  <font size="18pt">66 (I'm guessing!)</font>
</b>
```

Ask yourself this question: what do the font tags convey about the information they are marking up? Do they tell you anything further about Harrison and Ford? No, they do not. They are something completely separate from the information they mark up, yet there it is, mixed in with the information itself. What would happen if you had a number of pages across a website that displayed similar information like this and you needed to change the display characteristics of the first name on all of them? That would be a very time-consuming chore!

Further, imagine you pass this HTML through a screen reader used by disabled individuals. What meaning does the `<font>` tag have in that case? Absolutely none! The `<b>` tag may have a meaning, perhaps to speak the enclosed information more forcefully, but even that is not certain.

This is where Cascading Stylesheets, or CSS, come in. CSS allows you to separate the presentation of information from the information itself, thereby making it easier to make changes. It also makes marked-up documents easier to follow by simply not having as much to look at. How many times have you looked at the source for a web page and spent longer than you probably should have had to just to make sense of all the formatting going on? Would it not have been easier if the formatting rules were separate from the data? Of course!

For example, we could change our example HTML to this:

```
<div class="person">
  Harrison<br>
  <div class="lastName">Ford</div><br>
  <div class="age">66 (I'm guessing!)</divt>
</div>
```

All we need now is to define a stylesheet, that is, the collection of styles a given page will use. This one might look something like this:

```
.person { font-weight:bold; }
.lastName { color:#ff0000; }
.age {font-size:18pt; }
```

This code is defining three CSS selectors named `person`, `lastName`, and `age`, which I will go into in just a moment, but for now you can simply think of it as a named group of style attributes. The `font-weight` style attribute corresponds to the `<b>` tag. The `color` attribute corresponds to the `<font>` tag with the `color` attribute, and the `font-size` attribute corresponds to the `<font>` tag with the `size` attribute. So, if you look at the HTML from before that had the font characteristics embedded in the tags, and then see how the selectors here map to the

HTML via the class attribute, you should see that the font characteristics of the text in the markup will be exactly the same as before, but now the markup itself is separated from the specifications of the font characteristics.

Now admittedly, that may not look like much of an improvement, until you realize two things. First, look at the modified HTML... there are no longer any directives about how elements should be displayed—not directly anyway. Since stylesheets can be external, meaning they do not have to be packaged along with the data, we have effectively separated the data from the presentation. Second, think about what happens if you have a lot of XML in a batch of files, and you want to change how the age in each will be displayed. All you need to do is modify the stylesheet, and the changes cascade across all the files (the acronym CSS should start to make some sense now).

CSS also has another advantage over the HTML styling components: it allows for more robust control of presentation and richer displays. CSS has more capabilities built into it than HTML alone does, giving you more control over how your pages are presented. For instance, in HTML you can do this:

```
<font face="arial" size="12pt" color="#ff0000">Hello!</font>
```

In CSS, however, you can do all of this:

```
.myFont {
  font-family : arial;
  font-size : 12pt;
  color : #ff0000;
  font-size-adjust : .23;
  font-stretch : ultra-expanded;
  font-variant : small-caps;
  font-weight : bolder;
}
<div class="myFont">Hello!</div>
```

Note how much more control you have over font characteristics, and this is not even all of them!

CSS is also fairly simple. In the previous example, we have used a concept called a CSS selector. Think of a selector as you would a base class in Java: it has a set of characteristics, and any class that extends it inherits those characteristics. In this case, any element in the HTML document that specifies it as its class will inherit its characteristics. So, any text within the <div> tag, "Hello!" in this case, will have the characteristics of the CSS selector named myFont.

A moment ago I mentioned that stylesheets can be "external." Let me explain what this means more fully. You can define stylesheets in a number of ways. They can be "inline" with the elements they style, like so:

```
<div style="font-color:#00ff00;">Green text</div>
```

Styles can also be defined somewhere in an HTML document and referenced later via the class attribute, as we have previously seen. Usually, you will see a document in this form:

```
<html>
  <head>
    <title>Stylesheet defined in the same document</title>
    <style>
      .cssGreenText {
       font-color : #00ff00;
      }
    </style>
  </head>
  <body>
    <div class="cssGreenText">My green text</div>
  </body>
</html>
```

This is generally considered preferable because the document is organized a little better and it will be easier to find a style to change it if you need to, rather than hunting through the markup to find it.

However, the penultimate usage of stylesheets is to make it completely separate from the HTML document by "linking" it in. You do that like this:

```
<html>
  <head>
    <title>Stylesheet defined in the same document</title>
    <link rel="stylesheet" href="styles.css" type="text/css">
  </head>
  <body>
    <div class="cssGreenText">My green text</div>
  </body>
</html>
```

Then, you create a separate file named `styles.css` (you can use whatever name you like) that looks simply like this:

```
.cssGreenText {
 font-color : #00ff00;
}
```

This makes finding the style you need to change even easier, but it has a more important consequence: you can change the look of a website simply by changing the `styles.css` file. Imagine that everything in a document had some style selector applied to it, and all the selectors were defined in an external stylesheet file that you linked in. Now imagine that your boss asked you to change all the fonts from Arial to Helvetica, and asked you to change all the text sizes from 10pt to 12pt, and also change the color of headings from green to red. Now further imagine that you were not dealing with just a single HTML document, but 50 of them across an entire website. As long as they all use the same stylesheet and you were diligent in applying the correct selectors to everything, you would only need to change the external stylesheet and in the blink of an eye your boss's changes would be applied across the entire site! I think you will agree that, from a maintenance perspective, this is clearly a desirable approach to use.

In this book, this is by and large how CSS will be used. You will also see some instances where styles are specified inline, like so:

```
<input type="text" style="color:#ff0000;">
```

This would result in a text box form element whose text color was red. This approach is usually not recommended as it still embeds style information within the structure of the document, and as we have been discussing, a big point of CSS is to externalize the presentation rules from the data to be presented. That being said, there are some instances where this is acceptable, usually when only a single style attribute needs to be set. Also, an important point here is that you can also do this:

```
<input type="text" class="myInputStyle" style="color:#ff0000;">
```

This code will apply the styles specified by the `myInputStyle` selector to the text box, but will then apply the color style specified by the inline style. This inline style will override any setting in the selector, so that if you want all your text boxes to look the same, but perhaps highlight in red those that contain an invalid entry, you can do so by simply specifying the inline style.

A note on text colors in CSS: you can define them as #rrggbb (red, green, and blue, where each value is a hex value from 00 to ff), as you will most frequently see me do. You can also use any of a number of plain-text equivalents. For instance, "blue" is equivalent to #0000ff, "red" is equivalent to #ff0000, "yellow" is equivalent to #ffff00, and "teal" is equivalent to #008080. Arguably, using the text versions is clearer and better for maintenance, and I would tend to agree. That being said, if you are comfortable with RGB values, as I am, you will likely be fine either way.

One of the most important aspects of CSS is that, in conjunction with JavaScript and COM manipulation, you can alter the style a given element uses on the fly. For example, look at Listing 2-17.

Listing 2-17. *A Simple Example of Switching Styles of an Element*

```
<html>
  <head>
    <title>Style switch example</title>

    <style>
      .style1 {
        color : #000000;
        font-weight : normal;
        font-size : 12pt;
      }
      .style2 {
        color : #ff0000;
        font-weight : bold;
        font-size : 20pt;
      }
    </style>
```

```
    <script>
      function switchStyle() {
        o = document.getElementById("myText");
        if (o.className == "style1") {
          o.className = "style2";
        } else {
          o.className = "style1";
        }
      }
    </script>
  </head>

  <body>
    <div class="style1" id="myText">Some text</div>
    <br>
    <input type="button" value="Click to switch styles"
     onClick="switchStyle();">
  </body>

</html>
```

The first thing to look at is the typical use of styles, that is, applying a selector to a `<div>` element. A `<div>` is basically just a container into which you can put anything you want that you will later want to address by ID. A `<div>` can include further markup, perhaps very complex markup, or anything else you could put on a web page. The underlying point is to be able to work with the contents of that `<div>` as a whole by referencing some DOM ID. In this example, we have a `<div>` that we assign the ID "myText". Initially, this `<div>` has the selector style1 applied to it. When the button is clicked, the `switchStyle()` function is called. This gets a reference to the `<div>` using the `getElementById()` method of the document object. This is the typical (and W3C-standard) way to get a reference to a DOM element. The variable `o` is now a reference to that DOM object. We can then manipulate it via its methods and properties, and in this case that means working with the `className` property. This property is analogous to the `class` attribute on the `<div>` tag. All we do is look at the value that property currently has, and switch to the opposite style selector. This is a very typical thing to do in Ajax applications, and you will see it throughout this book.

One other point I would like to mention is that some CSS style attributes can be a URL, most usually to an image. For instance, the `background-image` attribute, which makes a specified image the background for an element (think about a page that shows some light image behind everything else, for example) accepts a URL like so:

```
.cssMyBackground { background-image : url(pageBackground.gif); }
```

As you can see, you use the `url()` paradigm, which looks like a function call but really is not, to reference the URL. If you now attach the `cssMyBackground` selector to the `<body>` element of a page, it will have the image `pageBackground.gif` as its background.

CSS, at this point in time, is relatively cross-browser. There are currently two "levels" of CSS, termed simply CSS1 and CSS2. You can feel confident that anything that is CSS1-compliant will work much the same in all browsers. A large part of CSS2 will as well, but a bit less than CSS1. In this book I will strive to only use CSS1 attributes.

Perhaps the best example of the power and flexibility of CSS out there that I am aware of is a website called CSS Zen Garden (`www.csszengarden.com`). This site is dedicated to showing how you can change the entire face of a website simply by swapping in a new stylesheet. In Figures 2-8 through 2-10, you can see that the data contained on the pages are all identical. The only thing that is changed is what stylesheet each uses. Notice how the entire look and feel of the site can be changed in this way.

One thing to notice about the way CSS Zen Garden works is that it is not a table-based design. Look at the source for any of the example pages and note that there is not a single `<table>` tag to be found! By using CSS, you can rearrange a page in various ways without resorting to tables. Many CSS enthusiasts tout this as a big advantage because they view table-based layouts as overly complex and not separating presentation from content well. It is not unfortunately a clear-cut decision, though, because there are still layouts that are difficult to achieve with CSS that are not a big deal with tables.

Still, a site like CSS Zen Garden makes a fantastic case for pure CSS-based sites!

Before we are finished here, I would like to summarize the style attributes that you will most commonly see used throughout this book (Table 2-4). There are certainly many more that will not be used at all, and I highly recommend checking out the book *Beginning CSS Web Development: From Novice to Professional* by Simon Collison (Apress, 2006).

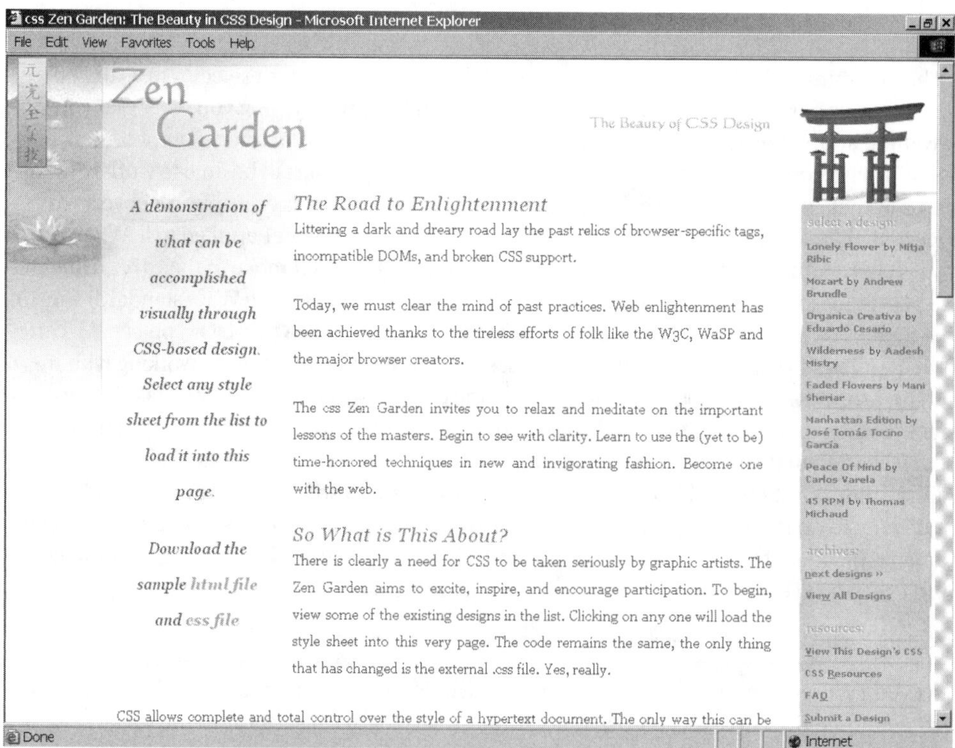

Figure 2-8. *CSS Zen Garden example, an oriental styling*

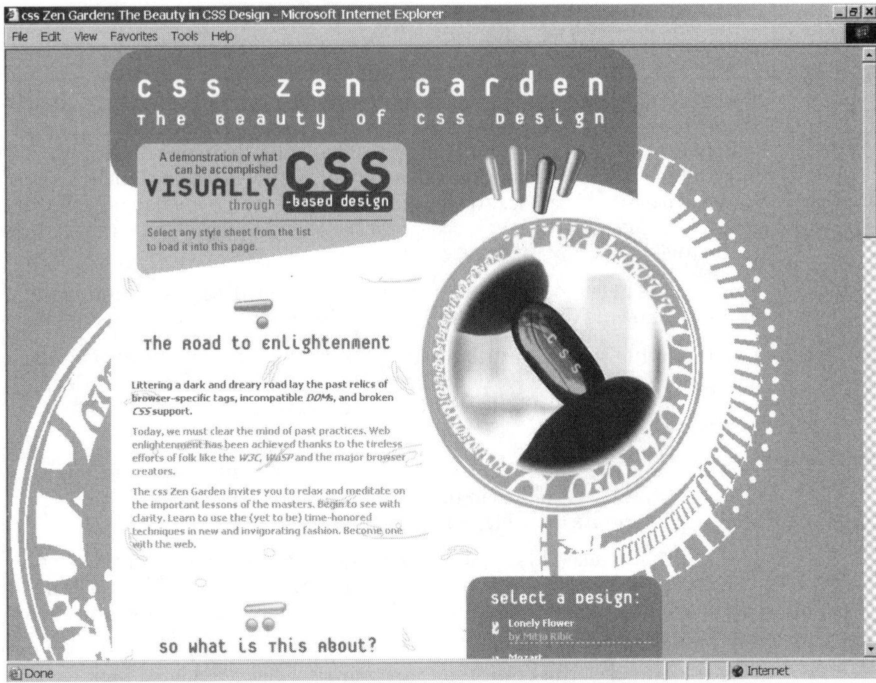

Figure 2-9. *CSS Zen Garden example, a more modern styling*

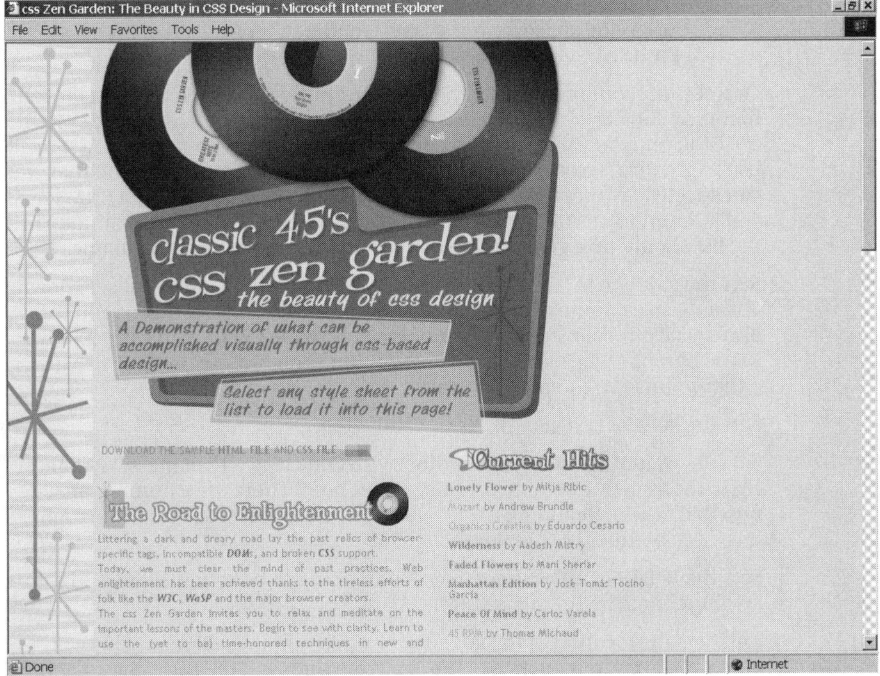

Figure 2-10. *CSS Zen Garden example, an old-fashioned styling*

Table 2-4. *Style Attributes Most Commonly Used in This Book*

Attribute	Description
`background`	There are actually a number of attributes that deal with the background of an element, but this one allows you to set a number of them at once. For instance, to set the background of a page to display an image tiled across it that will remain stationary (fixed) when the page scrolls, you could do `BODY { background: url(myBackground.gif) repeat fixed }` instead of having to set `background-image`, `background-attachment` and `background-repeat` individually.
`background-color`	This sets the background color of an element. You will see this a number of times for showing the active text field on a form, for instance, in InstaMail.
`border`	This is another shortcut attribute that allows you to set a number of border-related attributes at once. For instance, you could set a color red border 5 pixels wide on a `<div>` like this: `<div style="border:solid #ff0000 5px;">MyDiv</div>`.
`color`	This attribute is used to set the text color of an element. Note that some elements that are graphical in nature, like some form controls, may also apply this attribute to an element's edges or other parts of it.
`cursor`	This attribute is used to set the shape of the cursor for an element when the pointer on the screen hovers over it. For instance, if you would like a hand to appear over an element (in Internet Explorer at least), you can set the `cursor` attribute to the value `hand`.
`display`	This attribute describes how (or if) an element will be rendered in the document. Most usually, you will see two values set for this attribute: `block` or `none`. `none` simply means the element will not be rendered at all, and space will not be reserved in the document for it, and `block` indicates it should be rendered as a block, which is how elements are normally rendered. In other words, you can use this to show and hide elements without reserving space for it if it is not rendered (contrast this to the `visibility` attribute, described later).
`font-family`	This sets the font that text will be rendered in. You can specify a specific font name, or you can specify a generic family like `serif`. Note that if the system the browser is running on does not have the requested font, the browser will use a font that is as close as possible to the requested font. Note too that you can specify a comma-separated list of fonts and families, and the browser will attempt to use them in the order specified. Therefore, the final value in the list should be a generic as possible, hence a common family name.
`font-size`	Sets the size of text. You can specify one of a list of constants that set known absolute sizes, some of which are `xx-small`, `medium`, and `xx-large`. You can also specify the constants `larger` or `smaller`, which will set the size relative to the parent of the element. Lastly, you can specify a precise font size in either points (pt) or ems (em) units.
`font-style`	Sets the style of text, `normal`, `italic`, or `oblique`.
`font-weight`	Sets the weight of text, which is otherwise known as its boldness. Yes, that's right, there are more than just bold or not bold! There are a number of possible values, including `bold`, `bolder`, `lighter`, `100`, `500`. Usually, though, the value is either `bold` or `normal`.
`height`	Sets the height of an element. For this attribute to be settable, the `position` attribute must be set to `absolute`.
`left`	This sets the location of the left edge of a positionable element. This will either be measured relative to the browser window if the `position` attribute is set to `absolute`, or relative to the location the element would normally appear in the document when set to `relative`.

Attribute	Description
margin-bottom	Sets the amount of space that extends beyond an element's bottom border and that is not taken into account when calculating the height of the element.
margin-left	Sets the amount of space that extends beyond an element's left border and that is not taken into account when calculating the width of the element.
margin-right	Sets the amount of space that extends beyond an element's right border and that is not taken into account when calculating the width of the element.
margin-top	Sets the amount of space that extends beyond an element's top border and that is not taken into account when calculating the height of the element.
overflow	This is used to define how an element will react to content within it that is larger than the element itself. For instance, what happens if you set the width and height of a `<div>` to 10 pixels by 10 pixels, and then try to display the full text of *Moby Dick* in it? This attribute provides the answer. When the value is `auto`, the browser can determine what to do. When the value is `hidden`, then the element will always be 10 pixels by 10 pixels, and anything that is larger than that will not be displayed. When the value is `scroll`, the element should provide scroll bars to be able to see the full content. Note that not all elements will observe this setting. A `<div>` will, however. If the value is `visible`, then the element will expand so that its contents are fully visible.
padding	Padding is the space that extends around an element up to, but not counting, the border, if the element has one. This attribute is a shortcut that allows you to set the padding on all four sides of an element. There are versions that can set just a single side (`padding-bottom`, `padding-top`, `padding-left`, and `padding-right`).
position	This defines whether an element is positionable, that is, you can manipulate its `left` and `top` properties, and if so, what kind of positioning to use. The value `absolute` means you specify coordinates relative to the browser window itself, so coordinates 0, 0 is the top-left corner of the browser window (the area when a page appears that is). `relative` is the other common value, and it indicates the position is relative to where the element would have naturally fallen in the document when rendered.
top	This sets the location of the top edge of a positionable element. This will either be measured relative to the browser window if the `position` attribute is set to `absolute`, or relative to the location the element would normally appear in the document when set to `relative`.
visibility	For positioned elements, this attribute tells whether the element is rendered on the screen. The difference between this and the `display` attribute is that when the value of `visibility` is `hidden`, the space where the element would appear is still reserved for the element.
width	Sets the width of an element. For this attribute to be settable, the `position` attribute must be set to `absolute`.
z-index	Sets where a positioned element appears in the stack order. Think of the elements on a page as a deck of playing cards. If you started with the bottommost card and assigned it a numeric value, and that numeric value increased as you went up through the desk, that would be a stacking order because those values would tell you where any given card is relative to another, either above it in the stack or below it. In terms of a web page, if you have two `<div>` elements with their `position` attributes sets to `absolute`, and their `left` attributes set to 10, and their `top` attributes set to 10, they would be overlapping. The value of the `z-index` attribute determines which is on top, and therefore visible, and which one is underneath, and therefore hidden. The one with the higher value will be on top.

Again, Table 2-4 does not contain all the attributes available in CSS, but these are the ones you will encounter in this book most frequently. If by chance you see one used that is not listed here and is not mentioned in the text, I recommend the website W3C Schools as a good reference (`www.w3schools.com/css/css_reference.asp`).

Summary

In this chapter, we examined the basic technologies and techniques that will be used in the remainder of the book to develop our Ajax applications. We described JavaScript in some detail, including somewhat more advanced topics and ways of making it more "professional" in nature. You learned about XML, including how to parse it on the client. We also touched on the topics of dynamic HTML and DOM manipulation as well as Cascading Stylesheets.

Although it is my hope that this chapter has served as an introduction for those of you who may not have had much exposure to the topics discussed, if you do fall in that category I highly recommend finding any of the very good books that go into these topics in even more detail. Although I believe this chapter has put you on a level playing field that will enable you to explore the applications to come, there is no way I could have covered all the finer points of all these things. You will only help yourself by exploring them further and in more exhaustive detail.

CHAPTER 3

The Server Side of the Equation

As with Chapters 1 and 2, you may well be able to skip this chapter if you are already knowledgeable in Java. If you can install a Java Development Kit (JDK), have worked with Tomcat, have written some simple Java programs, have written some servlets and JavaServer Pages (JSPs), can parse XML in Java, and can deploy and start a Web Application Archive (WAR) in Tomcat, then this chapter will have little to offer you. If any of that is new to you, though, or you would like to refresh your memory, read on! This chapter will discuss how to prepare your development environment for working with the example apps that represent the remainder of this book, and will give you a baseline of knowledge about Java development, and Java-based web development in particular. This chapter will also explain how to deploy and play with the sample apps that follow.

The Project Development Environment

In the course of this chapter, and indeed this entire book, an underlying assumption is being made. That assumption is that you are already fairly knowledgeable in the Java realm, and are really more interested in what may be somewhat new to you: Ajax and client-side development. It is assumed that you are more interested in seeing how Ajax fits in with the server-side Java code you already know how to write to a large extent (I hope you will learn a few things on the server side along the way, but by and large that is not the goal). Because of this assumption, this chapter will be different from Chapter 2 in that I will not be going over the basics of Java as I did with JavaScript and the like. I will, however, cover a few things that may not be part of your everyday repertoire, including Ant and Tomcat, and I'll include a brief section on servlets and JSPs. I will also form symmetry with the last chapter in that I will discuss ways of parsing XML on the server.

This first section is just a simple check to make sure your development environment is suitable for working with the projects in this book, which means ensuring you have a proper JDK installed on your system. All of the examples in this book were developed under JDK 1.4.2, but they should work just fine under 1.5. To ensure consistency and functionality of the projects, however, for the purposes of this book, if you do not have JDK 1.4.2 installed, download it from `http://java.sun.com` and install it. Do not worry about what subversion you get (i.e., 1.4.2_10 or something like that); any 1.4.2 version should be just fine. You should be able to install this JDK alongside an existing JDK without any trouble (check Sun's documentation to be sure you do not jeopardize any current JDK you may have). If by chance you have never installed a JDK before, simply download the installer appropriate for your operating system and execute it. You will be walked through the simple install process and should be all set in a matter of minutes.

You will also likely want to add the `xxxx/bin` directory to your path, where `xxxx` is the root of the JDK. Incidentally, I have gotten into the habit of always installing the JDK into `c:\jdk` under Windows, or `/home/jdk` on *nix systems. This allows me to upgrade my JDK without having to worry about anything else. As long as the directory structure is the same, which it has been for some time, the JDK is upgraded, and anything pointing to it still works unaltered. No environment variables to update, no scripts or such to change; it all just continues to work with the newer version. This is a matter of choice, of course; I have no compelling *technical* reason to do this, but I have found it saves me time and effort, so I offer the suggestion to you as well.

■ **Note** You *do not* need to download J2EE for the projects in this book. The only J2EE API used in this book is the servlet API, which is included with the applications.

Beyond the JDK, you are free to use whatever development environment you like. I personally believe that tools are great, but knowledge is better, and my development environment of choice is a fantastic text editor for Windows called UltraEdit (`www.ultraedit.com`). While UltraEdit is not free, I personally feel it is unparalleled. Another great text editor to consider is jEdit (`www.jedit.org/`). This editor is free and has the benefit of being cross-platform, and it is specifically geared for programmers with things like plug-ins. Either of these is a fine choice.

On the subject of IDEs, I have yet to meet an IDE that does not seem to get in my way more than it actually makes me more productive, so I have become extremely efficient working without one. Many people disagree with this approach, some very strongly so, and that is perfectly fine. Whatever your preferences are, whatever you feel makes you most efficient is great! If you feel you want or need an IDE, Eclipse (`www.eclipse.org/`) is a very popular choice, and it happens to be free. Another IDE worth mentioning, and the only one I have ever used that I could see someday using on a regular basis, is IntelliJ IDEA (`www.jetbrains.com/idea/`). While it is not free, there are a great many developers, and a growing number at that, who are absolutely in love with this product, so it may be worth a look if you are not yet familiar with it.

All of the examples in this book use Ant to build them, which means you can easily work with them from the command line, or from within any IDE, or from most good text editors. The choice is yours entirely; you will not be forced down either path by this book.

Speaking of Ant, let's get right to that!

Ant: Building Java Applications the Open Source Way

If you are not currently using Ant in your everyday development, this section may very well make this entire book worth its cost!

Ant is a product of the Apache Software Foundation, and you can find its home page at `http://ant.apache.org`. As is stated on the front page of the Ant website, "Apache Ant is a Java-based build tool. In theory, it is kind of like Make, but without Make's wrinkles."

If you are unfamiliar with Make, let me briefly describe it. Make is typically used in the C/C++ world (but not limited to C/C++) to translate source code into object code. It is not itself a compiler, but a utility that makes use of compilers, as well as sometimes other tools, to build a program. Make uses makefiles, which control the build process from start to finish. It is really a script for a build process.

Some of the "wrinkles" with Make that Ant seeks to address include the fact that Make is not cross-platform. Although there are implementations for most platforms, subtle differences sometimes creep in that have to be dealt with. Primarily because of this, Make tends to be more brittle and builds tend to break easier. Also, Ant has a great number of extensions that provide a lot of power. While Make can use most external tools, it tends to be not nearly as seamless or easy.

If you do not currently have Ant installed on your system, do so now. Installation amounts to the following simple steps:

1. Download the appropriate archive from the Ant website.
2. Decompress it where you would like Ant to be "installed." (There are no registry keys to create, no required environment variables, nothing of that sort… you could in fact copy the Ant directory from one PC to another and Ant would work, so it is not really installed per se—the only setup that is generally required is an environment variable pointing to the Ant binary so that you can execute it from anywhere, but strictly speaking, even that is in fact optional.)
3. Set an environment variable named `ANT_HOME` that points to the directory you decompressed Ant to (this is actually an optional step—Ant can usually guess the correct value—but I suggest you set it explicitly to avoid any possible problems).
4. Add the `ANT_HOME/bin` directory to your path.
5. Set an environment variable named `JAVA_HOME` that points to your JDK.

Once that is done, Ant should be all set for you to use.

Ant is different from other build tools such as Make in that it is not merely a wrapper around a command-line environment. Instead, it is a declarative tool, which is extensible via Java classes. Ant works by referencing a build file written in fairly straightforward XML, which is interpreted by Ant and executed as specified. For instance, Listing 3-1 shows a very simple Ant build file.

Listing 3-1. *A Simple Ant Build Script*

```
<project name="ASimpleBuildScript" default="compile" basedir=".">

  <description>
    This is an example of a simple Ant build script.
  </description>

  <property name="src" location="src" />
  <property name="temp" location="temp" />
  <property name="jar_dest" location="jardest" />
```

```
  <target name="init">
    <echo message="Build starting..." />
    <delete dir="${temp}" />
    <delete dir="${jar_dest}" />
    <mkdir dir="${temp}" />
    <mkdir dir="${jar_dest}" />
  </target>

  <target name="compile" depends="init" description="Compile app">
    <javac srcdir="${src}" destdir="${temp}" />
  </target>

  <target name="make_jar" depends="compile" description="Makes JAR file">
    <jar jarfile="${jar_dest}/app.jar" basedir="${temp}" />
  </target>

  <target name="clean" description="Clean up">
    <delete dir="${temp}" />
    <delete dir="${jar_dest}" />
  </target>

</project>
```

At this point you should go ahead and save that script to a file named `build.xml` in a directory of your choosing. Then, go to that directory via the command shell, enter **ant**, and press Enter. You should be greeted with something that looks like Figure 3-1.

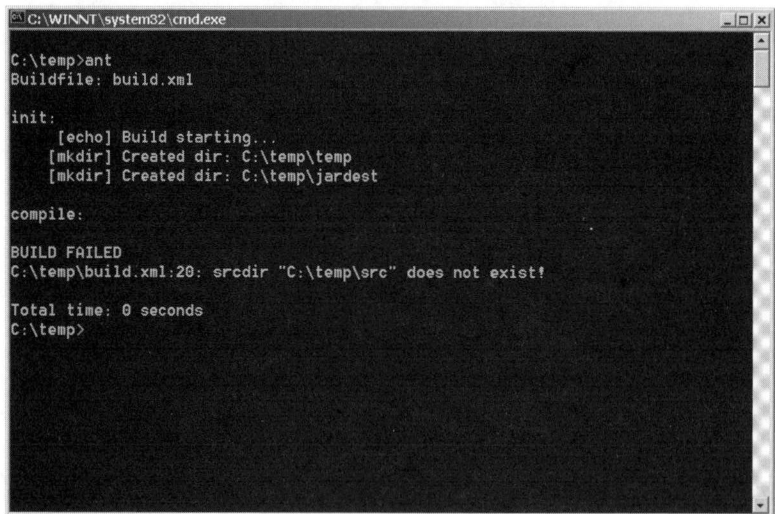

Figure 3-1. *Output of executing the Ant script shown in Listing 3-1*

Although that may look incorrect because of the BUILD FAILED message at the end, it really is not, and it should be obvious why in a moment. Let's now look at the specifics of this build file. The first things we see are

```
<project name="ASimpleBuildScript" default="compile" basedir=".">

  <description>
    This is an example of a simple Ant build script.
  </description>
```

The first line is the root element of the XML document, and it contains some basic information about the project this script builds, including its name and the base directory all script paths will be calculated from. (The value you see, a single period, denotes the current directory, and tends to be the most common value, but you can have your build script completely separate from the project and can specify the appropriate directory here.) The `default` attribute defines what target will be executed when none is specified. I will explain what a target is very soon.

The next section is simply a description of the script. This is useful because one of the things you can do is execute `ant -p` on the command line, and you will be presented with some information about the script, including this description. This is helpful if you are working with a new project and do not yet know its build script well.

After this we come to some properties:

```
  <property name="src" location="src" />
  <property name="temp" location="temp" />
  <property name="jar_dest" location="jardest" />
```

Properties are pretty much what you would expect: you can insert their values anywhere you like in the script; they act as replacement tokens. To use the value of the `src` property somewhere in the script for instance, you can insert `${src}` in the script, and the value "src" will be inserted before the script is interpreted. Here we are defining three properties: `src` is where the source files for the project can be found, `temp` is a temporary directory where our compiled classes will wind up, and `jar_dest` is where our JAR file will be created.

After this come four targets. A target in an Ant build script can be thought of much like a method in Java or a function in JavaScript. It is essentially a piece of the script that you can execute. So, for instance, you could do `ant clean` from the command line, and this would execute the target with the name `clean`.

The first target we encounter is the `init` target:

```
  <target name="init">
    <echo message="Build starting..." />
    <delete dir="${temp}" />
    <delete dir="${jar_dest}" />
    <mkdir dir="${temp}" />
    <mkdir dir="${jar_dest}" />
  </target>
```

The name attribute of the <target> tag is self-explanatory. The purpose of this target is to do some initial tasks to get the build ready to go. First, we display a message to the user saying the build is starting using the <echo> tag (since this is XML, everything you do will be in the context of markup tags like this). These tags are referred to as tasks in Ant parlance. Next, we delete our temp directory and our JAR destination directories using the <delete> task. Note the use of the properties we previously defined to reference the directories. This is a smart way to create a build script because all you need to do is change the property values to alter your script—no search-and-replace or manually editing the entire script. In fact, you can actually reference an external file that contains all your properties. This allows you to essentially separate the potentially variable parts of your scripts, the property values, from the "logic" of the build, the script itself.

Lastly, those same two directories are created anew so that they are present for the rest of the build. The <mkdir> task accomplishes this for us.

The next target we find is the compile target:

```
<target name="compile" depends="init" description="Compile app">
  <javac srcdir="${src}" destdir="${temp}" />
</target>
```

Here, we encounter two new attributes to the target tag: depends and description. description is easy to describe (pun intended): it tells us, we hope, what the target does and what it is for. If you go back and execute ant -p on the command line, you will see something like Figure 3-2.

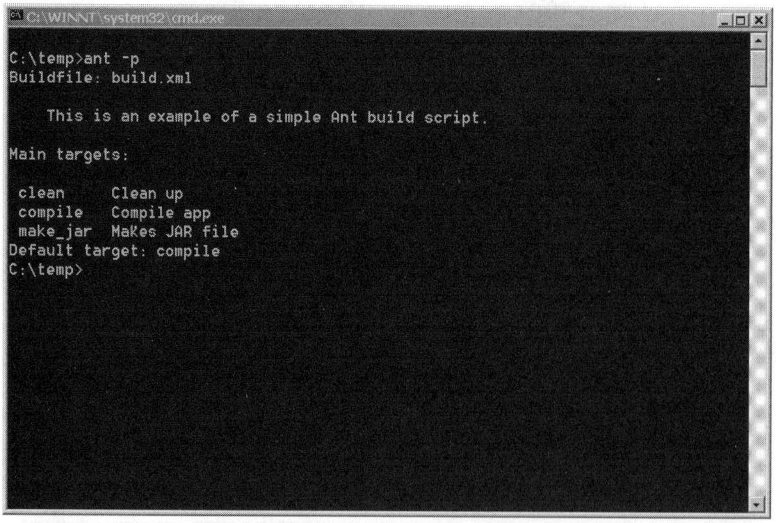

```
C:\WINNT\system32\cmd.exe

C:\temp>ant -p
Buildfile: build.xml

    This is an example of a simple Ant build script.

Main targets:

 clean      Clean up
 compile    Compile app
 make_jar   Makes JAR file
Default target: compile
C:\temp>
```

Figure 3-2. *Output of executing ant –p on the example script*

As you can see, the description attribute plays an important role: it gives us information on what the available targets are and what they do. Therefore, it is always a good idea to put meaningful descriptions on all your targets.

The depends attribute allows us to define a dependency chain among the targets. In other words, you can see from the ant -p output that the default target is compile. This means that if you execute just ant on the command line, the compile target will execute. Looking at the compile target, we see that it depends on the init target. So, Ant will execute that target before executing the compile target. Likewise, if the init target had a depends attribute defined, then the referenced target would be executed before init was, and so on, forming a chain. This is the typical approach to writing an Ant file. You will see an alternate approach shortly, one I prefer and will use in the build scripts throughout this book. Because the use of depends is typical, though, you should understand how it works.

Within the compile target we see the use of the <javac> task. This task has numerous options, but for this example we have used only two: srcdir, which defines where our Java source files can be found, and destdir, where our compiled classes should go. Note again the use of the properties in defining these paths. The <javac> task is very powerful and can compile an entire tree of source code, resolving dependencies (i.e., one class depends on another, which itself depends on the first) and will produce a proper package structure in the destdir.

After the compile target is the make_jar target:

```
<target name="make_jar" depends="compile" description="Makes JAR file">
  <jar jarfile="${jar_dest}/app.jar" basedir="${temp}" />
</target>
```

Notice that this target depends on the compile target. No sense making a JAR if we have not compiled first, and no sense making the developer have to manually execute compile before manually executing make_jar, and a dependency addresses both concerns. In this target we are using the <jar> task, which as its name implies, creates a JAR file named according to the value of the jarfile attribute, using the path pointed to by the basedir attribute as the source to build the JAR from.

Lastly is the clean target:

```
<target name="clean" description="Clean up">
  <delete dir="${temp}" />
  <delete dir="${jar_dest}" />
</target>
```

This is virtually identical to the init target except that it does not create the directories after deleting them. A target like this is typically used to clean up build artifacts before checking a project into source control. It generally is a stand-alone target, meaning it will not usually depend on other targets, and other targets will generally not depend on it.

At this point, I highly recommend spending some time with the Ant manual, available on the Ant website, and becoming familiar with the numerous tasks available. Once you get through the build-in standard tasks, you can start looking at the hundreds of additional add-on tasks available all over the Internet. Everything from FTP capabilities to SSH capabilities to source beautification functions to static code analyses are out there waiting for you!

I want to introduce you to just a few more specific tasks that Ant can perform, tasks that you will see in the build scripts for the projects in this book.

First, recall that I said I prefer not using the depends attribute. Although this is the canonical approach, to me, this makes a build script harder to follow and potentially more difficult to maintain because breaking the chain becomes a concern. It also makes your script coarser in terms of being able to perform smaller units of work; in other words, it is not as granular as I would like. It all feels more flimsy to me. It is also less programmatic and deterministic in my mind, which is something I value in a build script. I do not want the build tool making decisions about what to do—I want to explicitly tell it. To alleviate these things, I tend to use the `<antcall>` task. For instance:

```
<target name="build">
   <antcall target="compile" />
   <antcall target="make_javadocs" />
   <antcall target="make_jars" />
   <antcall target="checkstyle" />
   <antcall target="cleanup" />
</target>
```

All `antcall` does is allow you to call other targets from the current target. In other words, the targets become much more like functions. I will usually have properties defined that each target looks for. If the property associated with a given target is not present, then the target will not fire. In other words, I may have

```
<property name="do_compile" value="yes" />
```

Then, on the compile target I will add the `if` attribute:

```
<target name="compile" if="do_compile">
```

This says that if the `do_compile` property is defined, the target executes; if it is not defined, the target does not execute. In that way, I can alter what my build does simply by commenting out the appropriate properties. Since I have these properties in an external properties file, I never have to touch the actual build script itself. In addition, this has the benefit of not having to worry about command-line options. I always simply execute `ant` and let the default target (which `antcall`'s all the others) execute.

It is not my intention to convince you that this is the right or even the best way to write your scripts. I believe it is a matter of choice, and you should by all means make up your own mind. As I said earlier, this is not the canonical approach. However, it works very well, better than dependencies in my experience, and all the scripts in this book are written this way, so it certainly is worth understanding. If nothing else, you now know about the `antcall` task as well as the `if` attribute of the `<target>` tag!

The other concept that I want to introduce you to is `<macrodef>` task. In short, this allows you essentially to create your own tasks within the build script. The build scripts in this book use an Ant add-on called ant-dependencies. This add-on allows the script to download artifacts that the projects require from the Maven iBiblio repository. Maven (`http://maven.apache.org/`) is another build tool like Ant, but with some very different ways of doing things. One of the things it does is allow you to reference artifacts, for instance, Jakarta Commons JARs, and download them at compile time. This means you have to package less with your source code; the rest will be dynamically retrieved. iBiblio (`www.ibiblio.org/`) is a website dedicated to archiving virtual everything! One of the things they archive is various Java components. So, the ant-dependencies add-on allows you to download these components as part of the build process.

Here is an example of macrodef in action:

```
<macrodef name="get_dependencies">
  <sequential>
    <echo message="Retrieving compile-time dependencies..." />
    <setproxy proxyhost="${proxy_host}" proxyport="${proxy_port}" />
    <typedef classpath="ant-dependencies.jar"
     resource="dependencies.properties" />
      <dependencies pathId="compiletime_classpath" verbose="true">
        <!-- Servlet/JSP dependencies -->
            <dependency group="servletapi" version="2.3" />
            <!-- Checkstyle dependencies -->
            <dependency group="checkstyle" version="3.4" />
            <dependency group="antlr" version="2.7.5" />
            <dependency group="regexp" version="1.3" />
            <dependency group="commons-beanutils" version="1.7.0" />
            <!-- PMD dependencies -->
            <dependency group="pmd" version="3.2" />
            <dependency group="jaxen" version="1.0-FCS-full" />
            <dependency group="saxpath" version="1.0-FCS" />
      </dependencies>
    <echo message="Done" />
  </sequential>
</macrodef>
```

That is certainly a bit more complex than what we have seen thus far! In short, we are creating a task called get_dependencies so that you can later in the script do this:

```
<get_dependencies />
```

This will execute the code that is defined within the macrodef. Normally I would do this in the init task. <setproxy> is another standard Ant task, which defines a network proxy to be used. This may or may not be required on your network. The <typedef> target is used to work with Ant add-ons, as ant-dependencies does. It references the location where the classes are found for this extension, and any resource files it requires. Within it are definitions specific to the extension. In this case, we are creating a new property called compiletime_classpath, which is a special type of property in Ant that describes a classpath. All this means is that all the dependencies listed after this will be added to this classpath, and later targets can reference this classpath to do their work. This is a way of dynamically adding classes to the classpath during the build execution, a very handy thing to be able to do. After this is a series of <dependency> tags, which define the actual artifacts we want to pull down from the repository. Each defines the group they belong to, which is usually just the name of the component we want, plus the version of it we want.

It may have looked like a lot in the beginning, but I think you will agree in the end it makes quite a bit of sense.

Two other Ant tasks I would like to mention, since you will see them in the build scripts for the applications in this book, are <zip> and <jar> (and tangentially, <war>). The <zip> task creates a zip compressed file. Here's an example of its usage:

```
<zip destfile="MyProject.zip" basedir="./project">
  <include name="*.txt" />
</zip>
```

This task will create a zip file named MyProject.zip in the current directory consisting of all the files in the /project directory (relative to the current directory) that includes all files with a .txt extension.

The <jar> task is very similar:

```
<jar destfile="MyProject.jar" basedir="../" />
```

This will create a JAR file named MyProject.jar in the current directory, which includes all the files in all subdirectories starting with the directory that is the parent of the current directory.

Lastly, the <war> task is again very similar. The Ant manual gives a much better example than I could for this task, and here is that example:

Assume the following structure in the project's base directory:

```
thirdparty/libs/jdbc1.jar

thirdparty/libs/jdbc2.jar

build/main/com/myco/myapp/Servlet.class

src/metadata/myapp.xml

src/html/myapp/index.html

src/jsp/myapp/front.jsp

src/graphics/images/gifs/small/logo.gif

src/graphics/images/gifs/large/logo.gif
```

Now assume the WAR file myapp.war is created with

```
<war destfile="myapp.war" webxml="src/metadata/myapp.xml">
 <fileset dir="src/html/myapp"/>
 <fileset dir="src/jsp/myapp"/>
 <lib dir="thirdparty/libs">
  <exclude name="jdbc1.jar"/>
 </lib>
 <classes dir="build/main"/>
 <zipfileset dir="src/graphics/images/gifs" prefix="images"/>
</war>
```

The WAR will therefore consist of

```
WEB-INF/web.xml

WEB-INF/lib/jdbc2.jar

WEB-INF/classes/com/myco/myapp/Servlet.class

META-INF/MANIFEST.MF

index.html
```

```
front.jsp

images/small/logo.gif

images/large/logo.gif
```

Note that a JAR file is in fact a zip file; the same compression algorithm is used. A JAR file usually contains a manifest file, which gives extra information about the archive, but you can open a JAR file in a tool like WinZip, just the same as any zip file.

The `<war>` task is different than `<jar>` because it has an awareness of the structure of a webapp. This comes in handy if you have a source structure that is not itself a webapp. However, if your source is already structured as a webapp, you will get essentially the same result using `<jar>` as using `<war>`. That is why all the build scripts in this book use `<jar>` rather than `<war>`. In this instance, there isn't much difference.

And that is Ant in a very small nutshell. I have only just barely scratched the surface of what Ant can do, but I hope you will agree that it is definitely a very valuable tool to have in your tool chest.

Apache Tomcat: Something for Nothing!

Tomcat is one of those true gems of the open source world that is just so incredibly good and useful that it is amazing that anyone would be giving it away for free.

Tomcat is a servlet container, and in fact is *the* servlet container in the sense that it is the reference implementation of Sun's servlet and JSP APIs. It is another free product from the Apache Software Foundation (`http://tomcat.apache.org`), and if you take a moment to visit that page, you may be struck by how very little is there. You will not find a page bragging about all that Tomcat can do. To be sure, the available features are described on the site, but it is not promoting itself on the front page. If ever a product was deserving of a little self-promotion, Tomcat is it.

One of the key points about Tomcat is that it is very simple and lightweight. If you have never used it before, the steps to getting it up and running are as follows:

1. Download the appropriate distribution package. For most users, there are two relevant choices: the base distro package or the Windows installer package. The difference is that the base distro package you simply decompress to the directory where you would like Tomcat to live (which will be referred to as `TOMCAT_HOME` from here on out), while the installer package automates this process. I generally suggest grabbing the base distro package and doing the install steps manually. There are not many! This will be your only choice if setting Tomcat up on *nix.

2. If you use the Windows installer, there is nothing else to do. If you use the base distro package, however, you will have to set up an environment variable named `JAVA_HOME`, which you probably already have done when installing Ant, which points to your JDK installation (the root directory of the JDK).

3. Whichever package you got, at this point you can go into `TOMCAT_HOME`, and look in the bin directory there for the appropriate start-up script file, which is `startup.bat` for Windows systems, or `startup.sh` for *nix systems. Once you execute that, Tomcat should be running!

See, not a big deal! Once you have Tomcat running, you can try it out by navigating to `http://localhost:8080` in your web browser. The port 8080 is the default port for a fresh Tomcat install, but you may come across an install that is different at some point. If 8080 does not work, try 8181, which is another very common Tomcat port. The port is configurable (see the Tomcat documentation for a discussion of this as it is a bit out of the scope of this book). You should be greeted with the Tomcat home page, as shown in Figure 3-3. Note that it might look slightly different depending on what version of Tomcat you get.

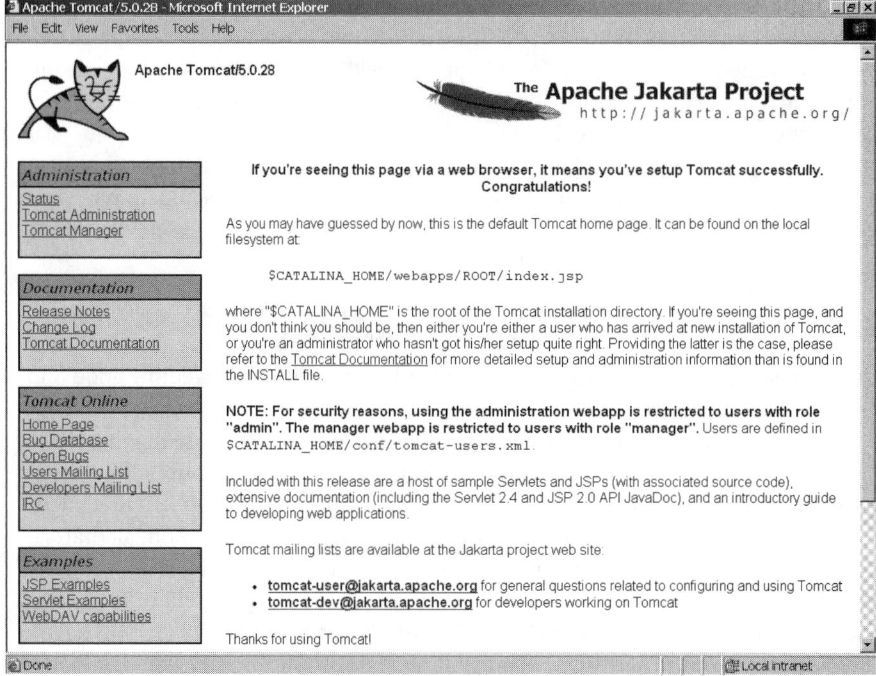

Figure 3-3. *The Tomcat home page*

Speaking of versions, the different branches of Tomcat implement different servlet and JSP spec versions. For the projects in this book you can choose any version of Tomcat in the 4.*x* or 5.*x* branch. One caveat is that the 5.*x* branch has in a sense been split further into the 5.0.*x* branch and the 5.5.*x* branch. The difference, the one that probably matters most here at least, is that the 5.5.*x* branch by default *requires* JDK 1.5. In order to use it with JDK 1.4, you will need to download an additional compatibility package. For this reason, I suggest, for the purposes of this book, not choosing a version from the 5.5.*x* branch. At the time of this writing, 5.0.28 was the latest stable 5.0.*x* branch version, and 4.1.31 is the latest 4.*x* branch version. I developed the projects in this book under 5.0.28, but if you would prefer to get 5.0.28, that will work fine, and so should any 5.5.*x* version as well if you decide you would rather have the latest and greatest, with the compatibility caveat taken into account.

Table 3-1 summarizes the servlet and JSP specs implemented by the various Tomcat versions.

Table 3-1. *Spec Versions Implemented by Various Tomcat Versions*

Servlet/JSP Spec	Tomcat Version
2.4/2.0	5.0.*x*
2.3/1.2	4.1.*x*
2.2/1.1	3.3.*x*

Once you have Tomcat up and running, there are just a few things to be aware of for the purposes of this book.

First, Tomcat ships with a number of webapps set up by default. I suggest removing them to make it easier to see what is going on. Especially under Windows, where Tomcat opens a console window that you can watch as your application runs to see log messages, it is helpful to have it start up as cleanly as possible. In addition, this will boost performance slightly, but perhaps most important, it will limit the messages written to the log to just those things that will be of interest to you, namely Tomcat messages about itself and messages from the app you are playing with.

To do this, you need to do two things. First, under `TOMCAT_HOME`, go into the `conf` directory. In there you should see a file named `server.xml` and another named `server-minimal.xml`. `server.xml` is the configuration file that describes, as I'm sure you have guessed, the Tomcat server instance as a whole, including information for various webapps. Make a backup copy of `server.xml` and then rename `server-minimal.xml` to `server.xml`. Next, go into the `webapps` directory under `TOMCAT_HOME` and move all the directories you see there *except* the `balancer` directory (if you do not see this directory, don't worry; it is not present in older versions of Tomcat). You can place them anywhere you like, in case you need them later. These are most of the webapps that are set up initially. Balancer is a special webapp that allows for load balancing. While you actually can remove it as well, there is some additional configuration that would be required elsewhere, so I find it easier to just leave it in place. Now, start Tomcat up again and you should notice a lot less happening at start-up in your console window. In addition, you will find that the default Tomcat page is no longer present. You now have an almost entirely clean Tomcat installation to play with that has as little as possible running on it by default.

The easiest way to deploy a webapp is to simply drop it in the `webapps` directory. If it is a WAR file, it should be automatically deployed (stop and restart Tomcat if it does not auto-deploy in a few seconds). If it is in exploded format, simply copy the directory into `webapps`. In either case, you can then access the webapp using the URL `http://localhost:8080/`*`xxxx`* where *`xxxx`* is the context. The context will simply be the name of the directory you copied into webapps if it was in exploded format. If you deployed a WAR file, chances are it is the name of the WAR file itself, but this is not necessarily true.

There is much more to Tomcat than this, but for what we'll be doing in this book, it is sufficient. Just to whet your appetite a bit and encourage you to explore Tomcat further, here are just some of the things Tomcat offers out-of-the-box:

- Container-managed JDBC connectivity, including connection pooling
- Load balancing
- A Java Naming and Directory Interface (JNDI) implementation

- Clustering support
- Java Management Extensions (JMX)
- Built-in web server functionality, with the ability to be fronted by "real" web servers like Apache, IIS, and Netscape

It is to a large degree a matter of semantics, but Tomcat is not technically an "app server," even though many people, including myself, refer to it as such. An app server, as defined by Sun, needs to include implementations of all J2EE APIs, but Tomcat does not. For instance, Tomcat does not support Enterprise JavaBeans, or EJBs (although there are other projects that integrate with Tomcat to provide this, including OpenEJB at `www.openejb.org`).

If any of the above is not familiar to you, the next section should help fill the gaps in your knowledge. Not to worry, it is ultimately pretty simple stuff!

Webapps, Servlets, JSPs, and Parsing XML on the Server

Web development with Java technologies can sometimes be a complex, overwhelming subject, especially for newcomers. There is quite a bit to learn, and lots of ways to do the same thing. However, at the end of the day, it generally boils down to just a few relatively simple concepts, namely webapps, servlets, and JSPs.

Webapps

In simplest terms, a webapp is simply a collection of resources—things like servlets, JSPs, images, stylesheets, and so on—which are packaged in a prescribed way and which can run within a servlet container. As you know, a Java application runs as an independent entity. If you write the class shown in Listing 3-2, you can compile it and execute it from the command line with nothing but a JDK installed (you can in fact execute it with just a Java Runtime Environment, or JRE, which a JDK includes).

Listing 3-2. *The Anti-"Hello World!" Java Application*

```
public class Test {
  public static void main(String[] args) {
    System.out.println("Goodbye cruel world!");
  }
}
```

Figure 3-4 shows what, I hope, is the obvious output of this application.

A webapp, on the other hand, will not work like this. A webapp requires resources that are provided by a container, which is essentially a Java application that acts as the parent of the webapp, providing it with various resources as required. This is usually referred to as a "servlet container." Tomcat is one such container. Jetty is another (`http://mortbay.org/jetty/index.html`).

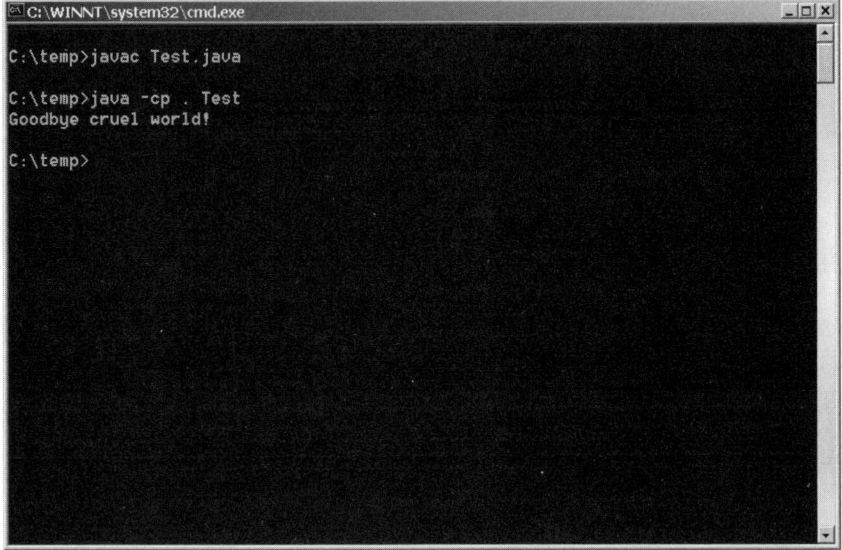

Figure 3-4. *That's one depressed Java application!*

There is also a larger class of container, a full-blown application server. These include IBM's WebSphere (www-306.ibm.com/software/websphere), BEA's WebLogic (http://e-docs.bea.com), Macromedia's JRun (www.macromedia.com/software/jrun), Apache's Geronimo (http://geronimo.apache.org), and Caucho's Resin (www.caucho.com). An application server, which does include a servlet container as part of it, also provides many more services such as things like JNDI directories, EJB containers, Web Services engines, and so forth.

In order for a collection of various resources to become a webapp, it has to be packaged a certain way. This means, to start, conforming to a certain directory structure. The structure looks like what you see in Figure 3-5.

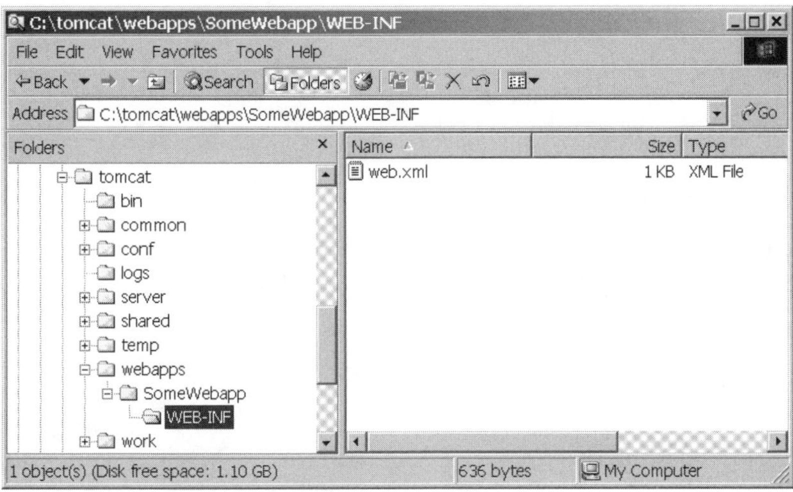

Figure 3-5. *The required directory structure of a webapp*

Not really much to it, is there? The SomeWebapp directory is where the webapp itself begins, but the key to making it a webapp and not just a collection of directories is the WEB-INF directory and its contents. This is the only real requirement in terms of required directories for it to be a webapp. Typically, however, you will see two directories underneath WEB-INF, classes and lib. The classes directory is where you would generally place any of the classes that make up your webapp. You would form a normal Java package hierarchy directory structure here and place your classes in it. You can also place here whatever resources you wish, things like properties files. The classes directory gets added to the classpath available to your webapp at runtime. The lib directory is where you would usually place any JAR files your webapp needs. Some people prefer to package their webapp classes in a JAR and place it here, in which case the classes directory can be left out. This is entirely a matter of preference. The JAR files in the lib directory are also added to the classpath at runtime.

One thing to keep in mind is that many servlet containers have complex class loaders that load JAR files from multiple locations. You wind up with a complex hierarchy of classes, some duplicates, at different levels. It is not at all uncommon to run into pathing issues where conflicts arise between classes in JARs in your webapp's lib directory and those elsewhere in the containers' classpath. The safest bet is generally to include any JARs that your webapp requires in the lib directory, and then deal with any conflicts that arise. Because most containers are smart enough to use the classes found in the lib directory first, many conflicts tend to be avoided this way (but not all unfortunately). The other benefit is that your app will not depend on classes being present in the container itself, so moving from one container to another becomes much easier because all the dependencies move along with the webapp.

Inside WEB-INF is where you will find the file web.xml, which is required to complete the transformation from collection of resources to webapp. This file is called a deployment descriptor, which is a complex way of saying that it is an XML description of your webapp that the container will use to activate it. web.xml can be very simple or very complex, depending on the needs of your app, what resources you use, and other factors. A relatively simple and fairly typical web.xml file might look like Listing 3-3.

Listing 3-3. *A Relatively Simple and Fairly Typical web.xml File*

```
<?xml version="1.0" encoding="ISO-8859-1"?>

<!DOCTYPE web-app PUBLIC  "-//Sun Microsystems, Inc.//DTD Web Application 2.3//EN"
"http://java.sun.com/dtd/web-app_2_3.dtd">

<web-app>

  <display-name>My Webapp</display-name>
  <description>This is just a simple deployment descriptor</description>

  <context-param>
    <param-name>someParameter</param-name>
    <param-value>someValue</param-value>
  </context-param>
```

```
  <filter>
    <filter-name>myFilter</filter-name>
    <filter-class>com.company.app.MyFilter</filter-class>
  </filter>
  <filter-mapping>
    <filter-name> myFilter </filter-name>
    <url-pattern>/*</url-pattern>
  </filter-mapping>

  <listener>
    <listener-class>com.company.app.MyContextListener</listener-class>
  </listener>

  <servlet>
    <servlet-name>myServlet</servlet-name>
    <servlet-class>com.company.app.MyServlet</servlet-class>
    <init-param>
      <param-name>initParam1</param-name>
      <param-value>value1</param-value>
    </init-param>
  </servlet>
  <servlet-mapping>
    <servlet-name>myServlet</servlet-name>
    <url-pattern>*.app</url-pattern>
  </servlet-mapping>

  <session-config>
    <session-timeout>20</session-timeout>
  </session-config>

  <welcome-file-list>
    <welcome-file>index.jsp</welcome-file>
  </welcome-file-list>

</web-app>
```

The interesting thing to note is that *everything* you see above inside the `<web-app>` root element is optional. Technically even the doctype is optional, although some containers will complain if it is not present, so it is probably fair to describe it as pseudo-required. Everything else is completely optional. Let's quickly run through this to get an idea what `web.xml` does for us. Note that this is only a subset of what can be present in `web.xml`.

The first thing we encounter is

```
  <display-name>My Webapp</display-name>
  <description>This is just a simple deployment descriptor</description>
```

Some visual editing tools use these two items. If you are not using such a tool, they really serve little purpose, although arguably just seeing them in the file itself is useful when you need to manually edit it. After that we see

```
<context-param>
  <param-name>someParameter</param-name>
  <param-value>someValue</param-value>
</context-param>
```

Context parameters are values that are available throughout your webapp. This is a good place to stash configuration values that your webapp needs, or things like data tables and so on. Context parameters, and indeed any of the parameter elements you will encounter in `web.xml`, form a map in memory, so you can retrieve a given parameter's value by referencing its name, as defined by the `<param-value>` and `<param-name>` elements correspondingly.

Next up we come to

```
<filter>
  <filter-name>myFilter</filter-name>
  <filter-class>com.company.app.MyFilter</filter-class>
</filter>
<filter-mapping>
  <filter-name> myFilter </filter-name>
  <url-pattern>/*</url-pattern>
</filter-mapping>
```

Filters, or servlet filters as they are sometimes called, are special Java classes, which are executed for each request that matches the value of their `<url-pattern>`. In other words, in this example, the filter named `myFilter`, as implemented by the `MyFilter` class in the `com.company.app` package, would be executed for every request made to this webapp, because it is mapped to the URL pattern `/*`. You can map it to any URL pattern you wish, such as `/admin/*` to only execute it for URLs in the admin path. You can also map it to a specific servlet and it will then only be executed when the request is going to that particular servlet. Note that you can define as many filters as you wish, and they will fire in the order they appear in `web.xml`. This collection of filters firing in a defined order is referred to as the filter chain.

After the filter definition we see

```
<listener>
  <listener-class>com.company.app.MyContextListener</listener-class>
</listener>
```

Listeners, like filters, are special Java classes (special in the sense that they implement a specified interface) that are fired in response to certain events within the container. Two types of listeners are `ContextListener` and `SessionListener`. The `ContextListener` fires when the webapp (the context in other words) starts up or is shut down, and the `SessionListener` can be fired when a user session is created or destroyed. There are some other events and even perhaps types of listeners, but those are by far the two most common. You can again define as many listeners as you like and they will be executed for each event in the order they appear in `web.xml`.

Next up is the servlet definition:

```
<servlet>
  <servlet-name>myServlet</servlet-name>
  <servlet-class>com.company.app.MyServlet</servlet-class>
  <init-param>
    <param-name>initParam1</param-name>
    <param-value>value1</param-value>
  </init-param>
</servlet>
<servlet-mapping>
  <servlet-name>myServlet</servlet-name>
  <url-pattern>*.app</url-pattern>
</servlet-mapping>
```

There are really two parts here: the <servlet> element and the <servlet-mapping> element, although they go hand in hand. The <servlet> element defines the servlet itself, and the <servlet-mapping>, like the <filter-mapping> we saw previously, determines what URLs will be handled by the servlet. In this example we are defining a servlet named mySerVlet, as implemented by the class MyServlet in the com.company.app package. We are also defining an initialization parameter for the servlet names initParam1 with the value value1. These initialization parameters are very much like the context parameters we used before, except that they generally apply only to the servlet, not the webapp as a whole. The <servlet-mapping> here is saying that any URL ending with .app will be handled by the servlet. You can map a servlet by path, as we saw with the filter, or you can make it by extension, as seen here. If you have ever used Struts, you will recognize that most developers tend to map the Struts Action servlet to the extension .do. There is no requirement with Struts, or with servlets in general—you are free to map both as you see fit—but .do is the typical Struts mapping, and many tend to use that with straight servlets as well.

After the servlet definition is a session configuration section:

```
<session-config>
  <session-timeout>20</session-timeout>
</session-config>
```

This section says that a user's session should time out after 20 minutes of inactivity.

Lastly, we have this section:

```
<welcome-file-list>
  <welcome-file>index.jsp</welcome-file>
</welcome-file-list>
```

The welcome file is the JSP that will be served if no resource is specified in the URL. In other words, if a user tries to access http://www.company.com/myapp, the welcome file will be returned because no resource was specified in this URL (remember that a resource ends with an extension). The welcome file listed here can also be a servlet; you simply replace the value of <welcome-file> with a URL that maps to the servlet. So, in this case, it could be hello.app, for example.

And that completes our rapid introduction to webapps.

■Note If anything in this section is new to you, I highly recommend at this point putting this book down, making sure you have Tomcat working, creating a simple webapp, and accessing it. To do so, create a file named `hello.htm` and put it in the root of the webapp (put whatever content in it you wish). Then, using the above `web.xml` as a template, delete everything from it except the `<web-app>` element and the doctype and `<welcome-file-list>` section and replace `index.jsp` with `hello.htm`. Then start Tomcat and access the webapp without specifying a resource and you should see your `hello.htm` page. Yes, a webapp does not actually have to have any servlets, JSPs, or indeed any Java at all in it!

Servlets

Servlets are nothing more than Java classes that extend a specific superclass, most usually `HttpServlet`. Within this class are a few (as few as one!) specific methods that represent the various lifecycle events a servlet can encounter. There is an `init()` method for when the servlet is first instantiated (which might be in response to the first request to it, or when the context started up). There is a `doPost()` method for when a POST HTTP request is received. There is a `doGet()` method for when a GET HTTP request is received. There are others, but generally those are the three you will be most interested in.

As they are Java classes, you can do virtually anything you want within them. In fact, there probably is nothing you *cannot* do, but there are some things you *should not* do (it is correct to say you are not "allowed" to do them, but that would be a slight misnomer because in fact the container will not stop you from doing them, but in terms of what the servlet spec says you "can" and "cannot" do, you cannot do them!).

For instance, spawning threads in a servlet is generally considered a bad idea. The reason is that once the request is handled, the thread can continue to exist but will not be under the control of the container. Therefore, the container cannot shut the thread down gracefully when the container goes down.

Also, because a servlet can handle multiple requests simultaneously, each being its own thread, and because there is in general only one instance of any given servlet, a servlet needs to be thread-safe, which means no instance fields, unless you want to synchronize them or are 100 percent certain they will be read-only after `init()` presumably sets them. Synchronizing anything in a servlet will lead to performance bottlenecks, though, so this is something to avoid whenever possible.

So, what does a simple servlet look like? Not much! Listing 3-4 shows an example of one.

Listing 3-4. *The Bart Simpson of Simple Servlet Examples*

```
import java.io.PrintWriter;
import java.io.IOException;
import javax.servlet.ServletException;
import javax.servlet.http.HttpServlet;
import javax.servlet.http.HttpServletRequest;
import javax.servlet.http.HttpServletResponse;
```

```
public class GraffitiServlet extends HttpServlet {

  public static String msg;

  public void init() throws ServletException {
    GraffitiServlet.msg = "Bart was here!";
  }

  public void doGet(HttpServletRequest request, HttpServletResponse response)
    throws ServletException, IOException {

    response.setContentType("text/html");
    PrintWriter out = response.getWriter();

    out.println("<html>\n<head>\n<title>SimpleServlet</title>\n</head>\n" +
       "<body bgcolor=\"#ffeaea\">\n");
    out.println("<h1>" + msg + "</h1>\n");
    out.println("</body>\n</html>");

    out.close();

  }
```

This servlet will result in the screen shown in Figure 3-6.

This servlet has only two methods: `init()` and `doGet()`. In `init()`, we set the `msg` member to our graffiti string. Then in `doGet()`, we get a `PrintWriter` from the `response` object. This then allows us to write out some HTML to the response, which will be returned to the client. Note that if you tried to submit a form to this URL using the POST method, this servlet would not respond. The default `doPost()` method in the `HttpServlet` class would execute, which does nothing. A typical thing to do in a servlet is have `doGet()` call `doPost()`, so that you can transparently handle both kinds of requests and not have duplicate code in two different methods.

■ **Note** If you want to try out this servlet, you will first need to compile it. Doing so requires that you have the servlet API in your classpath. There is a copy of this API in `TOMCAT_HOME` in the `common/lib` directory. There you should find a `servlet-api.jar` file. Add this to your classpath, save the code in Listing 3-4, and try to compile it. Once you have a class file, create a simple webapp as described in the previous section and name it `graffiti`, and copy the class file into `WEB-INF/classes`. Alter `web.xml` accordingly to point to this class file, and then start up Tomcat and try to access `http://localhost:8181/graffiti/doit.app`. You should see the same result as shown in Figure 3-6. For bonus points, try to write an Ant script to do the build for you.

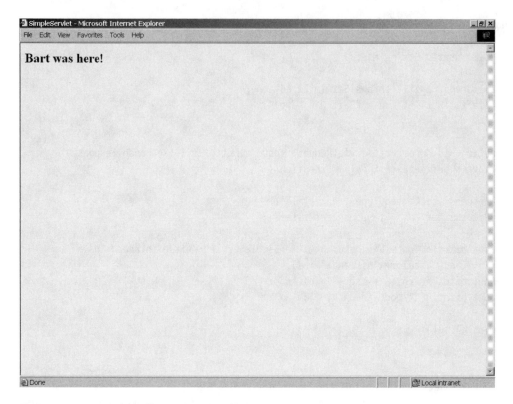

Figure 3-6. *Output of GraffitiServlet. Skinner is gonna go nuts!*

JSP

JSPs are, in short, a technology that allows you to insert Java code into an HTML page. When a JSP is requested, the container will convert it into a servlet, compile the servlet, and then execute it. This dynamic conversion and compiling is done automatically and can be done whenever the JSP changes, which makes JSPs a relatively easy way to develop webapps.

JSPs and servlets can work together very well, as things like the Struts framework shows. You can have a servlet execute that performs complex functions, and then forward the request along to a JSP to render the response. This provides some degree of separation between presentation and the logic of an application.

It is not, however, a perfect separation because it is very easy, and often too tempting to overcome, to just put Java code directly in the JSP. And why not? Especially if it can be dynamically converted to a servlet and compiled, then there is no application build process, no deployment, no stopping and restarting the container, and so forth. All of this is beneficial, especially during development, but even in production when those inevitable minor changes come up.

This, however, is a practice to be avoided whenever possible! Experience over the past few years has taught me, and anyone who has done Java-based web development, that the less code in your view layer, namely the JSPs, the better. Custom taglibs are available as an option, which is a way to create your own HTML tags that, when encountered on a page, fire Java code in a separate class. This is a step in the right direction, but even that is not perfect. Ideally, your

JSPs should be little more than a template for what the user will see, with little more than insertion of data into it.

Enough of the architectural lecturing. In this book you will see me break this rule about as often as I adhere to it; the difference is in the extent of the rule breaking. I will try to point out where I break the rule and why I did it, and I hope you will begin to form your own opinion on where the line is and when, if ever, you believe it is appropriate to cross it.

JSPs, being essentially HTML documents with bits of Java in it as described in the opening paragraph, are pretty simple. For instance, the JSP in Listing 3-5 shows a simple JSP page that will display all the request attributes, parameter, headers, and session attributes associated with the request. A session attribute is set from within the JSP itself.

Listing 3-5. *A Simple JSP That Shows All Request Attributes and Headers*

```
<%@ page language="java" import="java.util.Enumeration" %>

<%
  request.getSession().setAttribute("mySessionAttribute", "Hello again!");
%>

<html>
<head>
<title>SimpleJSP</title>
</head>

<body>

Request Parameters:<br>
<%
  for (Enumeration en = request.getParameterNames(); en.hasMoreElements();) {
    String next = (String)en.nextElement();
    out.println(next + " = " + request.getParameter(next) + "<br>");
  }
%>
<br><br>
Request Attributes:<br>
<%
  for (Enumeration en = request.getAttributeNames(); en.hasMoreElements();) {
    String next = (String)en.nextElement();
    out.println(next + " = " + request.getAttribute(next) + "<br>");
  }
%>
<br><br>
Request Headers:<br>
<%
  for (Enumeration en = request.getHeaderNames(); en.hasMoreElements();) {
    String next = (String)en.nextElement();
    out.println(next + " = " + request.getHeader(next) + "<br>");
  }
%>
```

```
<br><br>
Session Attributes:<br>
<%
  for (Enumeration en = request.getSession().getAttributeNames();
    en.hasMoreElements ();) {
    String next = (String)en.nextElement();
    out.println(next + " = " + request.getSession().getAttribute(next) + "<br>");
  }
%>

</body>
</html>
```

If you save the code from Listing 3-5, drop the file into the webapp that you previously created, and then access it, you should see something like Figure 3-7 (some variation is to be expected).

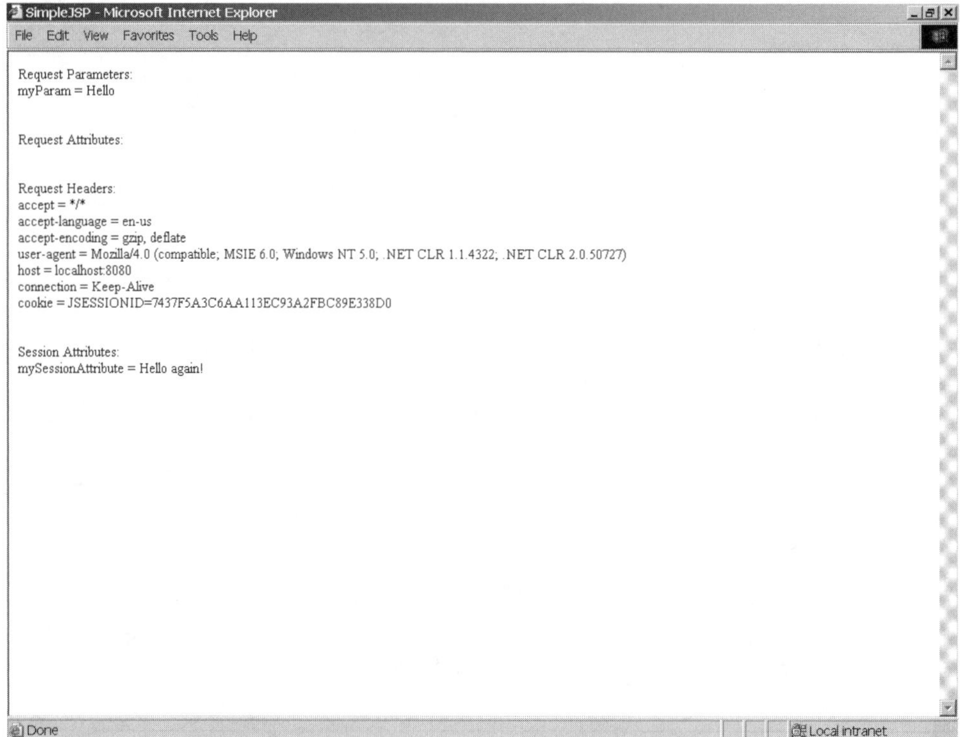

Figure 3-7. *Output of the simple JSP*

Parsing XML on the Server

Being able to parse XML has almost become a core skill in programming in general. It used to be something you did once in a blue moon, but nowadays it is almost at the vanguard of the things you will be doing on a seemingly everyday basis. Because of this, it makes sense to discuss it at least briefly here.

There are numerous ways to parse XML in Java, even more than there are in JavaScript. However, I find that the vast majority of the time, one tool will suffice: Commons Digester, or just plain Digester.

Digester (`http://jakarta.apache.org/commons/digester/`) is singularly one of the most useful components offered from the Apache Jakarta project. Reading from the Digester home page gives a good description for what Digester is and can do:

> *Basically, the Digester package lets you configure an XML -> Java object mapping module, which triggers certain actions called rules whenever a particular pattern of nested XML elements is recognized. A rich set of predefined rules is available for your use, or you can also create your own. Advanced features of Digester include:*
>
> - *Ability to plug in your own pattern matching engine, if the standard one is not sufficient for your requirements.*
> - *Optional namespace-aware processing, so that you can define rules that are relevant only to a particular XML namespace.*
> - *Encapsulation of Rules into RuleSets that can be easily and conveniently reused in more than one application that requires the same type of processing.*

The basic idea behind Digester is that an XML document is parsed. As certain elements in the document are encountered—elements that match a predefined rule—objects are created for these elements, or properties of a given object are set, or methods of a given object are called, and what you wind up with when the XML document is all parsed in an object graph containing new objects represents various elements in the XML document. Digester is one of those things that can seem a bit overwhelming at first, but once you get the hang of it you will not want to use anything else. Let's look at a simple example now.

Imagine we are writing a simple shopping cart web application, as seen on virtually any e-commerce website like Amazon.com. Imagine that in our application we have the following two classes, which represent the shopping cart and any items in the shopping cart:

```
package myApp;
public class ShoppingCart {
    public void addItem(Item item);
    public item getItem(int id);
    public Iterator getItems();
    public String getShopperName();
    public void setShopperName(String shopperName);
  }
```

```
package myApp;
public class Item {
  public int getId();
  public void setId(int id);
  public String getDescription();
  public void setDescription(String description);
}
```

Now let's assume that we have previously had a user who started shopping, maybe buying Christmas presents for his family (and himself!), dropped some items in their cart, and then left. Let's further assume that we wanted them to have a good shopping experience, so we saved the state of the shopping cart for later. Lastly, let's assume that we saved that state in the form of the following XML document:

```
<ShoppingCart shopperName="Rick Wakeman">
  <Item id="10" description="Child's bike (boys)" />
  <Item id="11" description="Red Blouse" />
  <Item id="12" description="Reciprocating Saw" />
</ShoppingCart>
```

Now, when the user comes back to our site, we want to read in this XML document and create a ShoppingCart object that contains three Item objects, all with their properties set appropriately to match the data in the XML document. We could do so with the following code:

```
Digester digester = new Digester();
digester.setValidating(false);
digester.addObjectCreate("ShoppingCart", "myApp.ShoppingCart");
digester.addSetProperties("ShoppingCart");
digester.addObjectCreate("ShoppingCart/Item", "myApp.Item");
digester.addSetProperties("ShoppingCart/Item");
digester.addSetNext("ShoppingCart/Item", "addItem", "myApp.Item");
ShoppingCart shoppingCart = (ShoppingCart)digester.parse();
```

If you have ever written XML parsing code in Java, you will recognize just how little there is to this, and how straightforward it looks. If you have never done so, trust me, this is fantastically quick and easy!

To break this down, let's look at the first two lines of code. The first line, obviously, instantiates a Digester object. You can reuse this object as required, providing any previous parse activities have been completed and provided you do not try to use the same instance from two different threads. The second line of code tells Digester that we do not want the XML document validated against a DTD.

After that comes a series of addXXX method calls, which each adds a particular rule to Digester. A number of built-in rules are available, and you can write your own as required.

All of the rules share the first method call parameter in common: the path to the element the rule will fire for. Recall that an XML document is a hierarchical tree structure, so to get to any particular element in the document you form a "path" to it that starts at the document root and proceeds through all the ancestors of the element. In other words, looking at the <Item> elements, the parent of all of the <Item> elements is the <ShoppingCart> element.

Therefore, the full path to any of the `<Item>` elements is `ShoppingCart/Item`. Likewise, if the `<Item>` element had an element nested beneath it, say `<Price>`, then the path to that element would be `ShoppingCart/Item/Price`. A Digester rule is "attached" to a given path and will fire any time an element with that path is encountered. You can have multiple rules attached to a given path, and multiple rules can fire for any given path.

In this example, our first rule, an `ObjectCreate` rule, is defined to fire for the path `ShoppingCart`. This means that when the `<ShoppingCart>` element is encountered, an instance of the class `myApp.ShoppingCart` will be created.

Digester uses a stack implementation to deal with the objects it creates. For instance, when the `ObjectCreate` rule fires and instantiates that `ShoppingCart` object, it is pushed onto the stack. All subsequent rules—until the object is popped off the stack either explicitly, as a result of another rule, or because parsing is completed—will work against that object. So, when the next rule, the `SetProperties` rule fires, it will set all the properties of the object on the top of the stack, in this case our `ShoppingCart` object, using the attributes of the `<ShoppingCart>` element in the document.

Next we see another `ObjectCreate` rule set up for the `<Item>` elements, and also another `SetProperties` rule for that same element. So, when the first `<Item>` element is encountered, the object is created and pushed onto the stack, meaning it is now on top of the `ShoppingCart` object.

Lastly, we see a `SetNext` rule. What this does is call a given method, `addItem()` in this case, on the *next* object on the stack, which would be the `ShoppingCart` object, passing it the object on the top of the stack, the `Item` object. At the end of this, the `Item` object on the top of the stack is popped off, revealing the `ShoppingCart` object, which is again the top object on the stack. This process repeats three times for each `<Item>` element.

At the end, the object on the top of the stack, which would be our `ShoppingCart` object at that point, is popped, and returned by Digester. We catch that return into the `shoppingCart` variable, and we now have a reconstituted shopping cart in the same state the user left it in!

Interestingly, Digester uses SAX (Simple API for XML) under the covers. SAX is an event-driven method of parsing XML, like Digester is (which stands to reason!), but functions at a lower level and tends to be quite a bit more work than Digester. Code like that shown in Listing 3-6 is typical.

Listing 3-6. *A Simple Example of Using SAX*

```
import java.io.*;
import org.xml.sax.*;
import org.xml.sax.helpers.DefaultHandler;
import javax.xml.parsers.SAXParserFactory;
import javax.xml.parsers.ParserConfigurationException;
import javax.xml.parsers.SAXParser;

public class ListElements extends DefaultHandler {

  public static void main(String argv[]) {
    if (argv.length != 1) {
      System.err.println("Usage: java xml_file");
      System.exit(1);
    }
```

```
    DefaultHandler handler = new ListElements();
    SAXParserFactory factory = SAXParserFactory.newInstance();
    try {
      SAXParser saxParser = factory.newSAXParser();
      saxParser.parse(new File(argv [0]), handler);
    } catch (Exception e) {
      e.printStackTrace();
    }
  }

  public void startElement(String inNamespaceURI, String inLName,
    String inQName, Attributes attributes) throws SAXException {
    String elementName = inLName;
    if (elementName.equals("")) {
      elementName = inQName;
    }
    if (elementName.equalsIgnoreCase("Band")) {
      System.out.print("***** ");
    }
    System.out.print("<" + elementName + "> found");
    if (!elementName.equalsIgnoreCase("BestBandsInTheWorld")) {
      String name = attributes.getValue("name");
      System.out.print(", name=" + name);
    }
    System.out.println("");
  }

}
```

You can try running this by saving the XML shown in Listing 3-7 to a file named `example.xml` and executing the application, passing `example.xml` to it on the command line.

Listing 3-7. *Example XML to Feed to the ListElements Application*

```
<BestBandsInTheWorld>
  <Band name="Shadow Gallery">
    <Bassists name="Carl Cadden-James" />
    <Guitarist name="Brendt Allman" />
    <Keyboardist name="Chris Ingles" />
    <Guitarist name="Gary Wehrkamp" />
    <Drummer name="Joe Nevolo" />
    <Singer name="Mike Baker" />
  </Band>
  <Band name="Dream Theater">
    <Drummer name="Mike Portnoy" />
    <Singer name="James LaBrie" />
    <Guitarist name="John Petrucci" />
    <Bassist name="John Myung" />
```

```
    <Keyboardist name="Jordan Rudess" />
  </Band>
</BestBandsInTheWorld>
```

You should see the result shown in Figure 3-8.

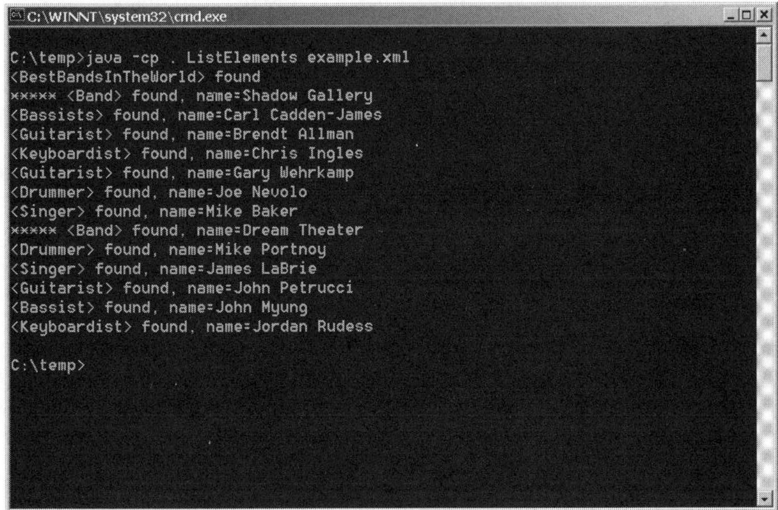

Figure 3-8. *Output of the simple SAX example using the example XML*

While I think you will agree this is not exactly rocket science, I hope you will also agree that Digester does make things easier, and certainly there is less code involved. Aside from being easier and perhaps more obvious, imagine if you wanted to write the code to implement some of the functionality that the Digester rules provide in pure SAX code. Does that sound like an especially pleasant experience? Not to me either! Still, SAX has its place at times, such as when you need to process an XML document straight through without creating object graphs, so I wanted to make you aware of it.

Although there are other ways to parse XML in Java as well, I believe Digester and sometimes SAX are all you need, and certainly all that will come up in the projects in this book. I will therefore leave it as an exercise for you the reader to discover those other methods on your own if you so choose. As you can tell by now, I am a big Digester booster, and I truly believe you will be too when you see what the alternatives are!

Installing and Playing with the Applications

All of the projects in this book are downloadable from the Apress website. You will be able to download them in two different forms: WAR file and exploded webapp form. The WAR file can simply be placed in the `TOMCAT_HOME/webapps` directory and Tomcat will deploy the application upon start-up (Tomcat may in fact be configured by default to deploy WARs as soon as it sees them present in the `webapps` directory). The exploded webapp can simply be copied to `TOMCAT_HOME/webapps` as well, and it will be active when Tomcat is restarted (it most likely will not become active until restart).

If you wish to use another app server, you should be able to do so without any problem. There is nothing in any of the projects that is specific to Tomcat, and nothing that is specific to any one operating system, so if you prefer to use WebSphere on Red Hat, you should be able to do so, although the deployment method could differ somewhat. However, most app servers have a directory where the exploded webapp winds up one way or another, so if you know that location then you should be able to copy the exploded form there and be good to go.

None of these applications requires a back-end database, even though in many cases that would have made sense. I did not, however, want to add additional setup for you to play with them. I wanted them to essentially be drop-and-play in nature, so even where a database would have made sense I chose to not use one. Likewise, each application is packaged with all the dependencies it requires so that you do not need to do much with classpaths and server setups. JNDI is not used anywhere, nor are any container-managed resources. I am certain you will spot instances where an application could have been made better if these things were used, but again, that would have run contrary to the drop-and-play goal. I hope you will view these as opportunities for you to expand the projects to gain experience rather than shortcomings. View these things as an opportunity to learn by doing!

I highly encourage you to play with all the projects even before you look at the chapters for them. Most of them, save perhaps Karnak, are useful and fun on their own (and Karnak is useful too, with some modifications). In fact, I myself have put together my own personal website that acts like something of a shell around some of these applications, so for instance I can send e-mails, read RSS feeds, and organize my schedule essentially from one place. This would be an excellent project for you to do yourself once you have explored these projects. I am sure you will have some great ideas by the end of this book for how to put them all together!

Summary

In this chapter we have briefly touched on the server-based technologies and techniques that will be used by the projects to come, including basic webapp structure, servlets, JSPs, Tomcat, and projects built with Ant. We also took a look at XML, specifically parsing XML with Commons Digester as well as the old standby, SAX. If any of this was new to you, and definitely if it was all new to you, I highly recommend taking some time to explore these topics in further detail, especially the last section dealing with webapps, servlets, and JSPs. The projects, which we'll begin to look at in the next chapter, will delve into these areas in much greater detail, but in a practical way. There will not be a great deal of discussion about the basic theory behind servlets, for example; we'll simply be using them. Therefore, if you do not already know the theory, you may not get as much out of the projects as you otherwise could.

PART 2

The Projects

Any sufficiently advanced technology is indistinguishable from magic.

—Arthur C. Clarke

For a successful technology, reality must take precedence over public relations, for Nature cannot be fooled.

—Richard Feynman

Everything should be made as simple as possible, but not one bit simpler.

—Albert Einstein

Knowledge is of two kinds. We know a subject ourselves, or we know where we can find information on it.

—Samuel Johnson

Knowledge is of two kinds. We know a subject ourselves, or we know how to type Google.

—Frank W. Zammetti

Always be wary of the Software Engineer who carries a screwdriver.

—Robert Paul

CHAPTER 4

Karnak: Type-Ahead Suggestions

In this chapter we will create an application that anticipates and suggests what we might type in a text box and provides options from which we can choose. To accomplish this, we will meet the first library we will use in this book: AjaxTags from the Java Web Parts project.

Requirements and Goals

The late, great Johnny Carson used to perform one of the best bits in late-night television, along with his ever-present sidekick Ed McMahon. In this bit, Johnny played the part of the Egyptian mystic The Amazing Karnak. Just in case you have never seen the bit, it went something like this…

Johnny, dressed in an utterly over-the-top headdress, would "divine" an answer to an as yet unasked question. He would do this while holding an envelope, which purportedly held the question, up to his forehead. As an example, he might say "Splsh. Bwah. Pouf." Ed would at this point repeat the answer for comic effect. Johnny would then, with flair, open the envelope and reveal the question: "What is the sound an exploding sheep makes?" Naturally, seeing it performed is about a billion times more entertaining than reading about it (unless you happen to be a sheep, in which case neither is likely to be terribly entertaining).

How is this relevant to Ajax programming, you may ask? In what might be considered the stretch of the year, we are about to build an application that will, in effect, give you answers (potentially) before you ask a question. Just like Google Suggest (`www.google.com/webhp?complete=1&hl=en`), we will build Karnak, the type-ahead suggestions application!

Let's start with some simple bullet points that will describe our main goals for this project:

- Since this is our first foray into Ajax in a real sense, we want to have as easy a time putting it together as possible, which means we will use our first Ajax library: AjaxTags in Java Web Parts.

- We are not going to try and out-Google Google, so our data set from which to suggest answers will be very limited and completely static.

- Very simply, as we type, we should get a list that appears below the text box we are typing in that contains a list of possible answers based on what we have typed thus far. We should then be able to select one of the answers and have the text box be populated with it.

- A selection will be made by using the up and down arrows to highlight suggestions, then clicking return to populate the text box. We are not going to do anything beyond that, i.e., no submitting the value to the server, as that isn't really relevant here and now.
- As we type more letters, the list of possible answers should shrink, further refining the matches.
- We will only try to match things that begin with a letter A–Z.
- The server side will be a single, simple servlet. This will suffice for our needs pretty well.

How We Will Pull It Off

Let's begin by getting familiar with the library we are going to use to build this application: AjaxTags, which is a subcomponent of the Java Web Parts project (`http://javawebparts.sourceforge.net`).

Java Web Parts was begun in May 2005 with the goal of being a repository for small, largely independent parts of general interest to Java web developers. It attempts to be completely framework-agnostic and covers a wide spectrum of needs. In Java Web Parts (JWP), you can find things like filters for doing compression, limiting concurrent session, and injecting dependencies into a request (think Spring or JSF's managed bean facility, but for any framework). You can also find various servlets for various functions, for instance, rendering a graphic text image from a supplied string. There is also an extremely powerful Chain of Responsibility (CoR) implementation, a helper class to calculate the size of a session or context object, classes to encode various types of response streams, taglibs for advanced GUI widgets and inserting general-purpose utility JavaScript functions into a page, a class that makes configuring your webapps via XML configuration files exceedingly simple, and much more. If you are doing web development with Java technologies, and that seems likely given you are reading this book, I suggest having a look at JWP at some point. Like the Jakarta Commons libraries, there is a wealth of timesaving things there that will make your life a lot easier.

However, perhaps the most popular feature of JWP is AjaxTags, a taglib that makes adding Ajax to JSPs child's play. AjaxTags was originally an extended version of the Struts HTML taglib, but was later spun off into a generic taglib that is not tied to Struts in any way. It can still be used in Struts-based applications, but it can be used in WebWork applications, JSF applications, or any other frameworks (or with just straight servlets). AjaxTags contains just four tags, two of which are used on a regular basis, the other two less frequently. AjaxTags works all its magic via XML configuration file; everything is done in a declarative way. What this means is that you will not have to write one bit of JavaScript yourself for most common Ajax functions. However, AjaxTags also offers a ton of flexibility beyond that, at the expense of having to write a little bit of script yourself. To reiterate, though, this is entirely optional, and you will find that you can do a great many things without any script writing, which is the goal of AJaxTags. AjaxTags is extensible, powerful out-of-the-box and, best of all, about as simple as Ajax can get!

Let's take a look at a quick example of using AjaxTags. I suggest throwing together a quick-and-dirty blank webapp and following along with these steps to really get a feel for AjaxTags. I also suggest opening up the AjaxTags API documentation in your browser to refer to along the way. You can find that documentation online at `http://javawebparts.sourceforge.net/javadocs/index.html`.

The first step is always to add two JAR files to your webapp in `WEB-INF/lib`: `javawebparts_taglib.jar` and `javawebparts_core.jar`. The latter is required for all JWP components. You will also need to add the Commons Logging JAR to your webapp as JWP depends on that. The next thing that needs to be done is to add two elements to your `web.xml` file, as shown in Listing 4-1.

Listing 4-1. *AjaxTags Required web.xml Entries*

```
<context-param>
  <param-name>ajaxTagsConfig</param-name>
  <param-value>/WEB-INF/ajax_config.xml</param-value>
</context-param>
<listener>
  <listener-class>javawebparts.taglib.ajaxtags.AjaxInit</listener-class>
</listener>
```

The `ajaxTagsConfig` context parameter tells AjaxTags where its configuration file is found. This is a context-relative path. You can place the file wherever you like in the context and can name it whatever you like. The context listener is responsible for initializing AjaxTags based on the content of the configuration file.

With those steps complete, you are now ready to add Ajax functionality to your application.

AjaxTags follows, mostly anyway, an event-driven model, so you will be thinking in terms of adding an Ajax event to a given element on a page. You can "Ajax-enable" any element on a page by "attaching" an Ajax event to it. For instance, create the simple JSP shown in Listing 4-2.

Listing 4-2. *Simple JSP*

```
<html>
  <head></head>
  <body>
    <input type="button" value="Click for AJAX">
    <br>
    <div id="results"></div>
  </body>
</html>
```

As the value of the button implies, we want to fire an Ajax event when the button is clicked. We want to have the server generate some response, and we then want to insert it into the `<div>` named `results`. To do this, we need to add three things to this page: first, as with all taglibs, the taglib declaration at the top of the page, and then two AjaxTags tags within it. Listing 4-3 shows our JSP with the three additions made.

Listing 4-3. *Simple JSP, with the Three AjaxTags Additions Made*

```
<%@ taglib prefix="ajax" uri="javawebparts/taglib/ajaxtags" %>
<html>
  <head></head>
  <body>
```

```
    <input type="button"
      value="Click for AJAX"><ajax:event ajaxRef="test/btnClick"/>
    <br>
    <div id="results"></div>
  </body>
</html>
<ajax:enable />
```

Note that the Tag Library Descriptor (TLD) for AjaxTags is included in the `javawebparts_taglib.jar`, so the taglib declaration is local. Skipping ahead to the `<ajax:enable />` tag at the end, this is always required and must always follow all other AjaxTags tags. It is usually best and simplest to just put it at the very end of the document, but this is not a requirement. There are no attributes for this tag as of the version of AjaxTags used in this project (a subsequent beta version adds a `debug` attribute), and its purpose is to render JavaScript required by all the other AjaxTags tags that appear previously in the document.

Next we come to the `<ajax:event>` tag, which follows the `<input>` element. This defines, as its name implies, an Ajax event. This tag must immediately follow the element you want to attach the event to, and I do mean very literally *immediately* after it! No spaces or anything else can be present between the close of the element you are attaching an Ajax event to and the `<ajax:event>` tag itself. This is because some JavaScript will be rendered in place of this tag that does some fairly interesting DOM magic to find the element preceding it and attach an event handler to it.

The `<ajax:event>` tag has a single attribute: `ajaxRef`. This is a link into the configuration file, which will define everything about this Ajax event. We will get to that configuration file in a moment. For now, just note that the `ajaxRef` is always in the form "xxxx/yyyy".

You can fire an Ajax event on any type of event you normally could for a given element, so in this case, a button has an `onClick` event, an `onFocus` event, an `onMouseDown` event, and so on, so you could fire an Ajax event in response to any of those.

Now let's look at the configuration file that accompanies this. If you are following along, create the `file ajax_config.xml` in the `WEB-INF` folder as shown in Listing 4-4.

Listing 4-4. *AjaxTags ajax_config.xml Configuration File*

```
<ajaxConfig>
  <form ajaxRef="test" isPage="true">
    <element ajaxRef="btnClick">
      <event type="onclick">
        <requestHandler type="std:SimpleRequest" method="get">
          <target>response.htm</target>
          <parameter />
        </requestHandler>
        <responseHandler type="std:InnerHTML">
          <parameter>results</parameter>
        </responseHandler>
      </event>
    </element>
  </form>
</ajaxConfig>
```

Let's now break this configuration file down piece by piece. First, we open with the `<ajaxConfig>` element, which is always the root of an AjaxTags configuration file. Next we come to a `<form>` element. Historically, when AjaxTags was a Struts extension, you could only Ajax-enable elements within an HTML form. This is no longer true, but the nomenclature remains. In fact, as we can see in this example, we do not have an HTML form on our page at all. The `<form>` element in the configuration file therefore represents what is termed a "virtual" form, meaning it really is not anything other than a grouping of Ajax-enabled events. When such a virtual form is defined, the `isPage` attribute must be set to true. In general, you should have no more than one virtual form per JSP page, although there is no technical reason you have to (it tends to be simpler if that rule is followed, though). A `<form>` element is given an `ajaxRef`, which can be anything you wish, but must be unique among `<form>` elements.

Within a `<form>` element are one or more `<element>` elements. These map to the elements you are attaching an Ajax event to. They too have an `ajaxRef` attribute, and can again be whatever you wish. The `ajaxRef` of `<element>` elements must be unique within the `<form>`, but they can be duplicated by other `<elements>` elements of other `<form>` elements.

Take a moment to look at the `ajaxRef` of the `<form>` and the `<element>`. Put them together, separated by a slash, and you will see that it matches the `ajaxRef` we used in the `<ajax:event>` tag on the page. This is how AjaxTags determine what configuration information a given Ajax event on the page will reference. Therefore, as mentioned earlier, the `ajaxRef` used in the `<ajax:event>` tag is always in the form "xxxx/yyyy", where xxxx is the `ajaxRef` of the `<form>` in the configuration file and yyyy is the `ajaxRef` of the `<element>` in the configuration file.

Each `<element>` can contain one or many `<event>` elements. These define the various events that will fire Ajax calls. In this case we are defining a single one: an `onClick` event handler. It should be noted that as AjaxTags does its thing, it will overwrite any event handler code attached to the element originally (this is no longer true in a subsequent beta version—the AjaxTags code will be appended to any existing handler code), so for instance if we had an `onClick` event attached to the button in the JSP, that handler would be overwritten by the AjaxTags handler. This is not usually a problem, but you should keep it in mind.

AjaxTags works by defining a request handler and a response handler for each event. A request handler is a JavaScript function that forms the request that will be made to the server. A response handler is a JavaScript function that will be executed when the response comes back from the server successfully. A number of request and response handlers are bundled with AjaxTags, and you will be able to perform all the most common Ajax tricks out of the box. However, AjaxTags also offers the flexibility for you to write your own.

In this case, we have a `<requestHandler>` element defined for this `<event>`. A `<requestHandler>` element has two attributes, *type* and *method*. *Type* names the request handler that will be used. Any of the built-in handlers begin with the prefix `std:`. For instance, here we are using the `std:SimpleRequest` handler, which simply accesses the referenced URL (we are playing the "HTML page as a server" trick here again). The `method` attribute is either `get` or `post`, whichever is appropriate for your application.

The `<requestHandler>` element contains the child `<target>` element, which is simply the URL the request goes to. Lastly we encounter the `<parameter>` child element. The meaning of this element will differ from handler to handler, but in the case of the `std:SimpleRequest` handler, nothing is passed to the server; the URL is simply accessed and the response grabbed.

The `<responseHandler>` defines the other side of the equation, namely what happens when the server's response is received. In this case we are using probably the most common built-in handler, the `std:InnertHTML` handler. For this handler, the `<parameter>` element does mean something, namely, it is the DOM ID of an element on the page whose innerHTML property will be updated with the response from the server.

An important consideration here is that many of the standard handlers, which we will discuss in a moment, need a reference to an actual HTML form to work. If a given element that you attach an Ajax event to is part of an HTML form, this will happen automatically by getting the parent of the element, which is the form, at runtime. However, in the case of "virtual" forms, this obviously would cause some of the handlers to break. To deal with this, the <event> element has an optional form attribute, which should contain the name of a real HTML form to reference. This can also be used if you want to configure an event within a real HTML form to use values from another HTML form. Although this is possible, it tends to be rather confusing and so I suggest you not do it.

So, let's follow this flow through. The user clicks the button. The event handler written out by the <ajax:event> tag fires and calls the configured request handlers. The handler does whatever it is supposed to, be it constructing an XML document, a query string, or whatever else, and then the URL referenced in the configuration file is accessed. The server process is executed and presumably constructs some sort of response. The response from the server comes back and is inserted into the <div> with the ID results in this case, or whatever else the configured response handler does. That's pretty simple, isn't it?

There is one more piece to the AjaxTags puzzle that we will need to become familiar with for this project: custom handlers. Recall that when you specify a handler type for an event, any that begin with std: means one of the built-in "standard" handlers is being referenced. What if the ones that exist do not quite meet your needs, as will be the case in this application? Well, AjaxTags offers you the ability to create your own, and it can be as simple or complex as you need.

All AjaxTags request handlers have a common function signature as follows:

```
StdQueryString (form, target, param, resHandler, resHandlerParam, method, mungedRef,
  timerObj, ajaxRef)
```

The definition of each of the parameters is as follows:

- StdQueryString is the JavaScript function name.
- form is a reference to the HTML form that is the parent of the element that fired the event, or the value of the form attribute of the <event> element as defined in the configuration file. This will be an object reference to the form at runtime.
- target is the URL the request is to be submitted to as defined in the configuration file. This can optionally include query string parameters in the configuration file.
- param is the value of the <parameter> element for the request handler as defined in the configuration file.
- resHandler is a reference to the JavaScript function that will server as the Ajax event callback function as defined in the configuration file.
- resHandlerParam is the value of the <parameter> element for the response handler as defined in the configuration file.
- method is the HTTP method of the handler as defined in the configuration file.

- `mungedRef` is the full ID of the element that fired the event. This will always be in the form `jwpatp_xxxx`, where `xxxx` is the `ajaxRef` of the element with the slash replaced by an underscore character.
- `timerObj` is a reference to the timer object that fired this handler, if this is used in conjunction with the `<ajax:timer>`, or `null` otherwise.
- `ajaxRef` is, as I'm sure you can guess, the `ajaxRef` of the element that fired the event. This is implicitly sent as a query string parameter with every request so the server side of things can make branch decisions based on this information if required.

As I mentioned earlier, this handler function can do whatever you need it to do. At the end, though, it is expected that you will make an Ajax request to a server (although even this is not required, but it would not be AjaxTags without it!). You are free to write your own code to do this, or you can even use another library if you wish. However, all the standard handlers use a common JavaScript function called `ajaxRequestSender()` that is automatically placed on the page by virtue of the `<ajax:enable>` tag. This function takes care of all the details of actually making the call. It does a number of important things for you, so it is suggested that custom handlers use it.

First, it makes sure that the URL the request goes to is always unique. This is important because certain browsers, Internet Explorer primarily, are a little too aggressive in caching of server responses, even those made via Ajax. You can easily run into a situation where your client-side Ajax code seems to be working flawlessly, yet your server logs show no activity. This is because a previous request was made, which the browser cached, and then the browser did not submit a new request subsequently and instead served the cached copy. This is only an issue with GET requests because POST requests are never cached. However, the `ajaxRequestSender()` function deals with this problem by appending a request parameter to the end of the URL as a query string named `ensureUnique`. You can effectively ignore this parameter, but it will ensure the URL is always unique and therefore caching issues will not bother even GET requests.

Second, `ajaxRequestSender()` deals with simultaneous Ajax requests for you. As we saw in the example in the first chapter, each Ajax request typically gets its own `XMLHttpRequest` object, and a reference to that object is stored somewhere for the callback handler to use. If one request is in progress, and another is fired, the first will effectively be lost in favor of the second. This is sometimes not a problem at all, and even desirable in some cases, but in most cases it is not what you want to happen. AjaxTags at present always ensures that the first request is not lost, and the second will proceed as expected as well.

Third, `ajaxRequestSender()` adds the `ajaxRef` query string parameter so the server process can always tell what element fired the event. This can be very important if you want to have a single class handle a number of different events.

And, believe it or not, we have just learned everything about AjaxTags that we need to make Karnak a reality! Now we can get down to it and do some work!

Visualizing the Finish Line

In building Karnak, let's first look at what the final product will be. Figures 4-1 and 4-2 show Karnak in action. Admittedly, there is not a whole lot to actually see in this case—it is, after all, a simple application—but even still, I have tried to spice it up just a bit.

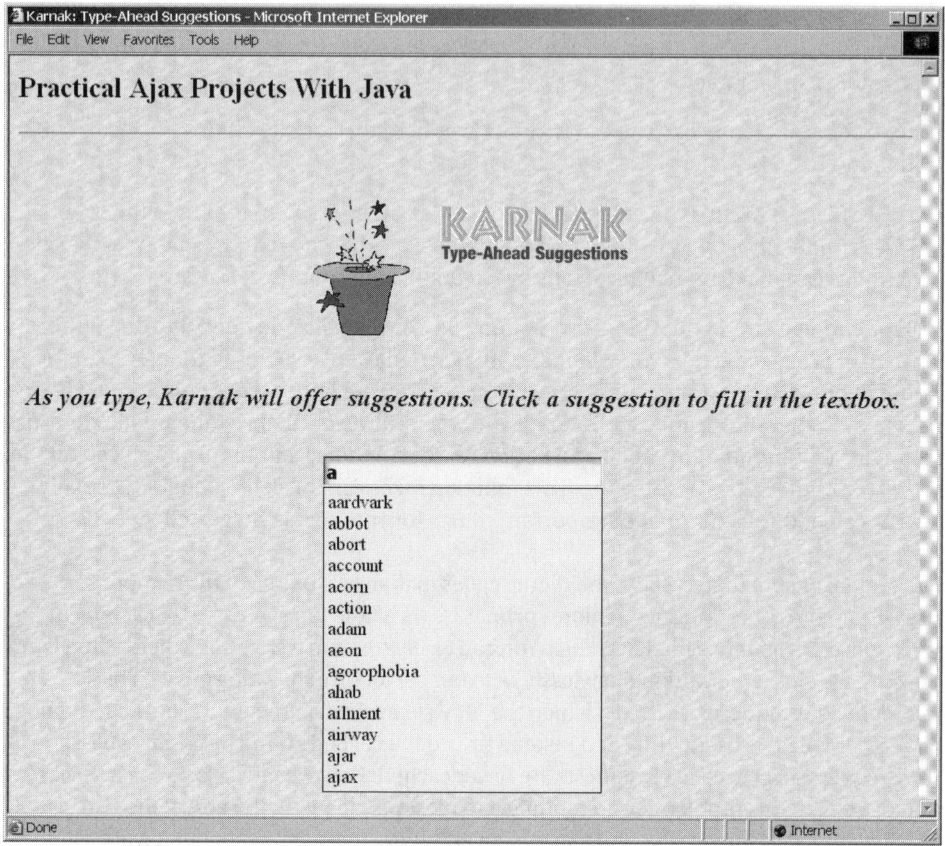

Figure 4-1. *Karnak in action!*

Figure 4-1 shows Karnak when a single letter is entered. A dropdown appears with matching items retrieved from the server.

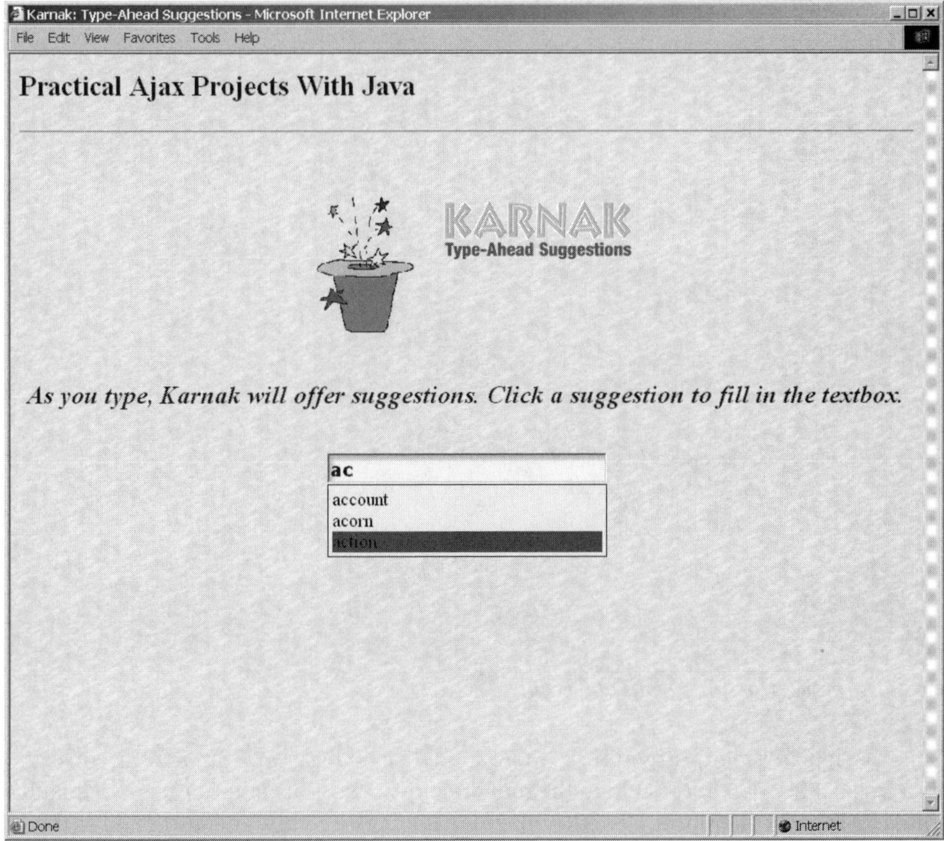

Figure 4-2. *Even more Karnak magic!*

In Figure 4-2 we see the selection further narrowed down by entering two letters. We can also see that one item has been highlighted and will presumably be the user's selection.

Now it is time to dive in and see how to put this thing together.

Dissecting the Solution

Let's begin by getting a feel for the file layout of this application. Figure 4-3 shows the structure.

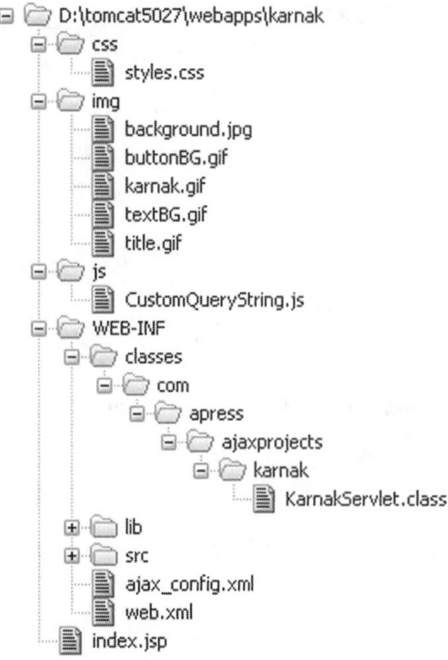

Figure 4-3. *Directory structure layout of Karnak*

This is a regular webapp structure, so there should be no real surprises. Karnak consists of only a single JSP, `index.jsp`, found in the root directory. This is also the configured default document. `index.jsp` references all of the images in the `img` directory, and also imports the stylesheet `styles.css` found in the `css` directory. We have a single JavaScript file, `CustomQueryString.js`, in the `js` folder. Note that this is *not* directly imported into `index.jsp` but is inserted by AjaxTags dynamically. The `WEB-INF/classes` directory is where the beginning of our server-side Java classes are located. Well, in reality, there is only a single class, `KarnakServlet.class`. The `src` directory is where all the source code for Karnak lives, plus the Ant build script. Again, only a single `KarnetServlet.java` file is there. The `lib` folder contains all the libraries Karnak depends on, and they are listed in Table 4-1.

Table 4-1. *The JARs Karnak Depends On, Found in WEB-INF.lib*

JAR	Description
`commons-logging-1.0.4.jar`	Jakarta Commons Logging is an abstraction layer that sits on top of a true logging implementation (like Log4J), which allows you to switch the underlying logging implementation without affecting your application code. It also provides a simple logger that outputs to `System.out`, which is what this application uses.
`javawebparts_core_v1.0_beta3.jar`	The Java Web Parts (JWP) core package, required by all other JWP packages.
`javawebparts_taglib_v1.0_beta4.jar`	The Java Web Parts (JWP) taglib package. This includes AjaxTags, which is used for this application.

With that out of the way, we can now begin to look at Karnak itself. First, let's look at the client side of the equation.

The Client-Side Code

We are going to have a single JSP, as shown in Listing 4-5.

Listing 4-5. *The Karnak JSP Page*

```
<%@ taglib prefix="ajax" uri="javawebparts/taglib/ajaxtags" %>

<html>
  <head>
    <title>Karnak: Type-Ahead Suggestions</title>
    <link rel="StyleSheet" href="css/styles.css" type="text/css" media="screen">
  </head>

  <body background="img/background.jpg">
    <h2>Practical Ajax Projects With Java</h2>
    <hr width="100%">
    <br><br>
    <center>
      <h2>
        <img src="img/karnak.gif" align="center" hspace="10"
          width="123" height="160">
        <img src="img/title.gif">
      </h2>
      <br>
      <div style="font-size:16pt;font-weight:bold;font-style:italic;">
        As you type, Karnak will offer suggestions.  Click a suggestion to
        fill in the textbox.
      </div>
      <br><br>
      <form name="TypeAheadSuggestionsForm" onSubmit="return false;">
        <input type="text" name="enteredTextbox" class="cssUserInput"
        style="width:300px;"><ajax:event
        ajaxRef="TypeAheadSuggestionsForm/enteredTextChange"/>
        <br>
        <div id="suggestions" class="cssSuggestionsDiv"></div>
      </form>
    </center>
  </body>

</html>
<ajax:enable />
```

This is a pretty typical JSP page, with the addition of the AjaxTags elements we have already seen, namely the taglib declaration at the top, the `<ajax:enable>` tag at the end, and a single

<ajax:event> tag "attached" to a text box input element. Note the use of the cssUserInput selector, which will be shown in a moment. This gives the nice inset look to the text box by setting its background to an image designed to give this effect. Also note the use of inline styling on the text above the text box. I did it this way simply to contrast the use of inline styles with using selectors throughout the rest of the page. Lastly, notice how the input text box uses both a style selector as well as an inline style, demonstrating that they can in fact exist together.

styles.css

Notice that we link in an external stylesheet here. That stylesheet is as you see in Listing 4-6.

Listing 4-6. *The Karnak Stylesheet*

```
/* This style will be applied to our suggestions div. */
.cssSuggestionsDiv {
  border           : 1px solid #000000;
  background-color : #f0f0f0;
  width            : 300px;
  text-align       : left;
  padding          : 4px;
  visibility       : hidden;
}

/* This style will be applied to the user input textbox. */
.cssUserInput {
  font-family      : verdana;
  font-size        : 12pt;
  font-weight      : bold;
  width            : 92%;
  background       : url(../img/textBG.gif);
}
```

There is not very much there. The first style class defined will be applied to the <div> where our suggestions will appear below the text box. The second class is applied to the text box where the user enters their text.

CustomQueryString.js

Next we come to where the majority of the heavy lifting is done, the external JavaScript file. Listing 4-7 shows that code in its entirety.

Listing 4-7. *The JavaScript Karnak Needs to Function*

```
// The following are constants for various keys that we check for throughout
// the following code.
KEY_RETURN = 13;
KEY_UP = 38;
KEY_DOWN = 40;
KEY_LEFT = 37;
```

```
KEY_RIGHT = 39;
KEY_SHIFT = 16;
KEY_CONTROL = 17;
KEY_ALT = 18;
KEY_ESC = 27;
KEY_INSERT = 45;
KEY_HOME = 36;
KEY_END = 35;
KEY_PAGEUP = 33;
KEY_PAGEDOWN = 34;
KEY_SCROLLLOCK = 145;
KEY_PAUSE = 19;
KEY_DELETE = 46;
KEY_PRINTSCREEN = 118;
KEY_NUMLOCK = 144;
KEY_CAPSLOCK = 20;
KEY_LEFT_WINDOWS = 91;
KEY_RIGHT_WINDOWS = 92;
KEY_CONTEXT = 93;
// The keycode that was pressed.
keyCodePressed = null;
// Attach a keyDown event handler to the document.  Note the slight difference
// between IE (which only needs the part outside the if block) and other
// browsers (which also need the captureEvents portion).
document.onkeydown = keyDown;
if ((document.layers) ? true : false) {
  document.captureEvents(Event.KEYDOWN);
}
// The number of the suggestion that was highlighted before the latest
// arrow key was pressed.
previousSuggestion = 0;
// The suggestion that is currently hightlighted.
currentSuggestion = 0;
// The number of suggestions currently displayed.
numSuggestions = 0;

// This is a custom AjaxTags request handler.  It constructs a query string
// and also deals with hiding and showing the suggestions div as appropriate.
function CustomQueryString(form, target, param, resHandler,
  resHandlerParam, method, mungedRef, timerObj) {
  // Get a reference to our input textbox.  The param names the
  // element that is the user entry textbox, but it does it directly, i.e.,
  // not as a DOM ID, so we need to eval() it to get a reference to it.
  textbox = eval(param);
  // Get a reference to our suggestions div.
  suggestionsDiv = document.getElementById("suggestions");
```

```
// If the value in the textbox is blank, just hide the suggestions div.
if (textbox.value == "") {
  previousSuggestion = 0;
  currentSuggestion = 0;
  keyCodePressed = null;
  document.getElementById("suggestions").style.visibility = "hidden";
  return;
}
// There must be some actual text...
// If return is pressed, populate the textbox, hide the suggestions div
// and we're done.
if (keyCodePressed == KEY_RETURN) {
  if (suggestionsDiv.style.visibility == "hidden") {
    alert(textbox.value);
    return;
  } else {
    if (currentSuggestion > 0) {
      textbox.value = document.getElementById("suggestion" +
        currentSuggestion).innerHTML;
      suggestionsDiv.style.visibility = "hidden";
      return false;
    }
  }
}
// If the up (KEY_UP=38) or down (KEY_DOWN=40) arrows are pressed...
if (keyCodePressed == KEY_UP || keyCodePressed == KEY_DOWN) {
  // Reset the previous selection, if any, to the unhighlighted state.
  if (previousSuggestion > 0) {
    document.getElementById("suggestion" +
      previousSuggestion).style.backgroundColor = "#f0f0f0";
  }
  // Up arrow...
  if (keyCodePressed == KEY_UP) {
    currentSuggestion--;
    if (currentSuggestion < 1) {
      currentSuggestion = 1;
    }
  }
  // Down arrow...
  if (keyCodePressed == KEY_DOWN) {
    currentSuggestion++;
    if (currentSuggestion > numSuggestions) {
      currentSuggestion = numSuggestions;
    }
  }
  // Record this as the previousSuggestion so we can reset it next time.
  previousSuggestion = currentSuggestion;
```

```
    // Highlight the new suggestion.
    document.getElementById("suggestion" +
      currentSuggestion).style.backgroundColor = "#ff0000";
    return false;;
  }
    // If we're here, it means none of our special keys (return, up and down
    // arrows) were pressed, so here we are going to fire an AJAX request.
    // Before we do that though, we need to reject a few other keys that would
    // cause an unnecessary AJAX call, and there's just no need for that!
    if (keyCodePressed != KEY_SHIFT && keyCodePressed != KEY_CONTROL &&
      keyCodePressed != KEY_ALT && keyCodePressed != KEY_ESC &&
      keyCodePressed != KEY_INSERT && keyCodePressed != KEY_HOME &&
      keyCodePressed != KEY_END && keyCodePressed != KEY_PAGEUP &&
      keyCodePressed != KEY_PAGEDOWN && keyCodePressed != KEY_SCROLLLOCK &&
      keyCodePressed != KEY_PAUSE && keyCodePressed != KEY_DELETE &&
      keyCodePressed != KEY_PRINTSCREEN && keyCodePressed != KEY_NUMLOCK &&
      keyCodePressed != KEY_CAPSLOCK && keyCodePressed != KEY_LEFT_WINDOWS &&
      keyCodePressed != KEY_LEFT && keyCodePressed != KEY_RIGHT &&
      keyCodePressed != KEY_RIGHT_WINDOWS && keyCodePressed != KEY_CONTEXT) {
      queryString = "?enteredText=" + escape(textbox.value);
      ajaxRequestSender(form, target, queryString, null, resHandler,
        resHandlerParam, method, true, mungedRef, timerObj);
    }
}

// This is the keyDown handler for the document.  It records the keycode that
// was pressed, which will be used in the AjaxTags request handler
// onKeyDown events to deal with highlighting suggestions.
function keyDown(e) {
  ev = (e) ? e : (window.event) ? window.event : null;
  if (ev) {
    keyCodePressed = (ev.charCode) ? ev.charCode:
      ((ev.keyCode) ? ev.keyCode : ((ev.which) ? ev.which : null));
  }
}
```

OK, that looks like quite a bit of code! In reality, though, a lot of it is comments anyway, but more important, you will see that it is not anything too complex. Let's tear it apart, shall we?

First, we have some code outside of any function. This sets up some page-scoped variables and executes some minor, but essential, code. Let's talk about the global variables first.

- `keyCodePressed`: On `keyDown` events anywhere on the page, we need to capture the key code that was pressed, which will then be used in the custom AjaxTags handler. The reason for this will be explained shortly.
- `previousSuggestion`: When the user presses the up and down arrow keys, we need to highlight the suggestions, if there are any currently displayed. This variable is used in that process.

- currentSuggestion: This is used in conjunction with the previousSuggestion variable.
- numSuggestions: This is the total number of suggestions currently visible. This too is used when highlighting suggestions.

Then there is the minor code that executes when the page loads (remember that JavaScript code outside functions will be executed as it is encountered as the page loads into the browser). This code attaches a function as an event handler to the document's onKeyDown event. Note that Netscape-based browsers, including Firefox, need to have some extra code executed to attach the event handler, namely the call to captureEvents(). That is the reason for the conditional logic there. By checking that document.layers is present, we can easily determine whether or not we are in Internet Explorer and call captureEvents() as appropriate.

Next we come to the custom AjaxTags request handler. Before we get into that, though, let's quickly look at the keyDown event handler function we have attached to the document, the function keyDown():

```
// This is the keyDown handler for the document.  It records the keycode that
// was pressed, which will be used in the AjaxTags request handler
// onKeyDown events to deal with highlighting suggestions.
function keyDown(e) {
  ev = (e) ? e : (window.event) ? window.event : null;
  if (ev) {
    keyCodePressed = (ev.charCode) ? ev.charCode:
      ((ev.keyCode) ? ev.keyCode : ((ev.which) ? ev.which : null));
  }
}
```

All this function does in essence is record the key code that was pressed. The first line contains some logic that is needed because Netscape-based browsers receive the event object, which contains all the relevant information about a given event, via a parameter to the event handler function, whereas Internet Explorer receives that object in the window object via the event property. The end result is that the variable ev contains the relevant event object.

The line inside the if block is a bit complex-looking (and I usually frown on trinary logic statements like this, especially strung together as this is, but it was actually cleaner to write it this way than a series of nested if statements), but it boils down to the fact that depending on what browser the page is in determines which property of the event object you need to go after to get the key code. In some it is charCode, in others is it keyCode, and in still others it is which. The key code is recorded in the page-scoped keyCode variable, and the function is done.

Now we come to the custom AjaxTags request handler named CustomQueryString(). If you look through the AjaxTags documentation, you will notice that there is a QueryString request handler included that does essentially what the custom handler does. Why do we need the custom handler then? The reason is because we need to be able to do different things when various keys are pressed, and also perform some other logic at the same time. If you recall, when you Ajax-enable an element with AjaxTags, it effectively overrides any event handler that was previously attached. There is no way with AjaxTags to fire two functions from the same event (this is addressed in subsequent versions with the ability to append the AjaxTags handler code to existing handler code, but it would still not be possible with a standard handler because it would always fire). Therefore, we could not use the standard QueryString request handler, and still be able to do all the other logic we need to do at the same time. The solution is therefore to write a custom handler that will in essence do the same thing that the standard QueryString handler does, plus all the extra logic we need to do.

So, the first thing our custom handler does is get some references to some elements on the page, as seen here:

```
// Get a reference to our input textbox.  The param names the
// element that is the user entry textbox, but it does it directly, i.e.,
// not as a DOM ID, so we need to eval() it to get a reference to it.
textbox = eval(param);
// Get a reference to our suggestions div.
suggestionsDiv = document.getElementById("suggestions");
```

We first get a reference to the text box where the user has presumably entered some text. This is done by calling eval() on the parameter defined in ajax_config.xml. The parameter value is not a DOM ID; it is a reference in the form document.form.element. The actual value is document.TypeAheadSuggestionsForm.enteredTextbox. So, in order to get a reference to it, we eval() that value, and the JavaScript interpreter hands us back the object we want. We also get a reference to the <div> where the suggestions are displayed, if any.

Next is a trivial rejection: if there is nothing entered in the text box, hide the suggestions <div> and exit. Some variables are also reset to ensure a consistent state. This is all mostly for the case where the user just deleted the last character in the text box. In that case there is no further work to do; we just need to be sure no suggestions are showing. The code that accomplishes all this follows:

```
// If the value in the textbox is blank, just hide the suggestions div.
if (textbox.value == "") {
  previousSuggestion = 0;
  currentSuggestion = 0;
  keyCodePressed = null;
  document.getElementById("suggestions").style.visibility = "hidden";
  return;
```

After that is code that deals with three "special" keys: Return or Enter (it's the same key code for either), up arrow, and down arrow. They are special in the sense that they are what we wrote a custom handler for. We need to do some "special" processing when they are pressed. When Return (or Enter—again, same thing) is clicked, the text box should be populated with whatever suggestion is currently highlighted, if any. That code is

```
// If return is pressed, populate the textbox, hide the suggestions div
// and we're done.
if (keyCodePressed == KEY_RETURN) {
  if (suggestionsDiv.style.visibility == "hidden") {
    alert(textbox.value);
    return;
  } else {
    if (currentSuggestion > 0) {
      textbox.value = document.getElementById("suggestion" +
        currentSuggestion).innerHTML;
      suggestionsDiv.style.visibility = "hidden";
```

```
        return false;
      }
    }
  }
```

Notice the way we get a reference to the currently highlighted suggestion. When the suggestion <div> is populated, each suggestion is given a DOM ID consisting of the word "suggestion" followed by a number, beginning with 1. As its name implies, the currentSuggestion variable stores the number of the currently highlighted suggestion. We also need to do something slightly different depending on whether suggestions are currently displayed. If they are, we just need to populate the text box with the selected suggestion. If they are not showing currently, this means the user selected a suggestion because the code could not reach this point unless some text had been entered (because of that earlier trivial rejection). In this case we will pop up an alert box showing what the contents of the text box currently are. You would in all likelihood make a submission to the server at this point to do something (like the actual search in the case of Google Suggest), but here a simple alert will suffice for our purposes.

Next, we come to the code that deals specifically with our other "special" keys, that is, the up and down arrows. Here is the relevant bit of code:

```
// If the up (KEY_UP=38) or down (KEY_DOWN=40) arrows are pressed...
if (keyCodePressed == KEY_UP || keyCodePressed == KEY_DOWN) {
  // Reset the previous selection, if any, to the unhighlighted state.
  if (previousSuggestion > 0) {
    document.getElementById("suggestion" +
      previousSuggestion).style.backgroundColor = "#f0f0f0";
  }
  // Up arrow...
  if (keyCodePressed == KEY_UP) {
    currentSuggestion--;
    if (currentSuggestion < 1) {
      currentSuggestion = 1;
    }
  }
  // Down arrow...
  if (keyCodePressed == KEY_DOWN) {
    currentSuggestion++;
    if (currentSuggestion > numSuggestions) {
      currentSuggestion = numSuggestions;
    }
  }
  // Record this as the previousSuggestion so we can reset it next time.
  previousSuggestion = currentSuggestion;
  // Highlight the new suggestion.
  document.getElementById("suggestion" +
    currentSuggestion).style.backgroundColor = "#ff0000";
  return false;
}
```

It is first important to remember that the flow of this code could only have reached this point if some text was actually entered, based on the logic that preceded it. This is significant because this is the only condition under which suggestions could be showing, which is the only situation where the up and down arrows actually have any meaning. The key codes 38 and 40 correspond to the up and down arrows, so we check for those, using our constants for code readability. If we find either has been pressed, we reset the state of the previously selected suggestion (the one that was last highlighted, if any) to the normal state (where the background color has the value `#F0F0F0`). Once that is done, we are ready to highlight a new suggestion.

I would like to point out that the better way to do this would be to have a highlighted and unhighlighted style class and change the suggestion's `className` attribute appropriately instead of altering the `backgroundColor` style attribute directly. This would further insulate the style information from the code. I did it this way simply to demonstrate that you in fact can.

The code then determines which specific key was pressed and increments or decrements the `currentSuggestion` variable appropriately, taking into account the bounds of the suggestion list. This means that when the up arrow is pressed, and the first suggestion is already highlighted, no change will in effect occur because 1 is the lower bounds of the list. Likewise, if we are on the last suggestion and the down arrow is pressed, nothing will in effect change because the variable `numSuggestions` holds the upper bounds of the list.

Once the new suggestion is made current, we record it also as the `previousSuggestion`. This is so that the next time an arrow key is pressed we know which suggestion to restore to the normal state. Lastly, the code updates the background color of the newly highlighted suggestion. Again, having a separate style class for this would have been better, but this simply shows it is not the only way.

The next thing that occurs is one last rejection to stop spurious Ajax events. Some keys that do not generally result in anything happening on the screen, or that do not result in any content change in the text box, still cause an Ajax event to fire. While the code functions when this happens, it is just a lot of unnecessary network traffic. Keys like Shift, Ctrl, Alt, Esc, Insert, and so forth are the ones I am referring to here. So, we do a quick check to see if the key that was pressed was any of them:

```
if (keyCodePressed != KEY_SHIFT && keyCodePressed != KEY_CONTROL &&
  keyCodePressed != KEY_ALT && keyCodePressed != KEY_ESC &&
  keyCodePressed != KEY_INSERT && keyCodePressed != KEY_HOME &&
  keyCodePressed != KEY_END && keyCodePressed != KEY_PAGEUP &&
  keyCodePressed != KEY_PAGEDOWN && keyCodePressed != KEY_SCROLLLOCK &&
  keyCodePressed != KEY_PAUSE && keyCodePressed != KEY_DELETE &&
  keyCodePressed != KEY_PRINTSCREEN && keyCodePressed != KEY_NUMLOCK &&
  keyCodePressed != KEY_CAPSLOCK && keyCodePressed != KEY_LEFT_WINDOWS &&
  keyCodePressed != KEY_LEFT && keyCodePressed != KEY_RIGHT &&
  keyCodePressed != KEY_RIGHT_WINDOWS && keyCodePressed != KEY_CONTEXT) {
```

If the key does not match any of the keys listed in this check, the Ajax event can fire. The next thing that occurs is the construction of the query string with this line:

```
queryString = "?enteredText=" + escape(textbox.value);
```

There is only a single parameter to pass, and because it is a user entry, we need to escape it to avoid any characters that would otherwise break the resultant URL. Then, last but certainly not least, the actual Ajax call is done with this line:

```
ajaxRequestSender(form, target, queryString, null, resHandler,
  resHandlerParam, method, true, mungedRef, timerObj);
```

As we discussed in our earlier look at AjaxTags, a few common usage functions are rendered by AjaxTags, one of which is `ajaxRequestSender()`. This function is what literally makes the call to the server. You do not have to use it—you can use your own code, or another library even, to make the actual call—but AjaxTags provides this as a convenience. All of the standard handlers use it, so there is some logic in using it yourself in your custom handlers.

The Server-Side Code

At this point we have literally examined the entire client side of this application! We now need to see what is happening on the server side of things, and how AjaxTags is tying it all together.

web.xml

The first thing to look at is `web.xml`, which is shown in Listing 4-8.

Listing 4-8. *Web.xml for the Karnak Application*

```
<?xml version="1.0" encoding="ISO-8859-1"?>

<!DOCTYPE web-app PUBLIC  "-//Sun Microsystems, Inc.//DTD Web Application 2.3//EN"
"http://java.sun.com/dtd/web-app_2_3.dtd">

<web-app>

  <!-- This parameter is needed to initialize AjaxTags.  It points to the -->
  <!-- context-relative configuration file. -->
  <context-param>
    <param-name>ajaxTagsConfig</param-name>
    <param-value>/WEB-INF/ajax_config.xml</param-value>
  </context-param>

  <!-- This listener is needed to initialize AjaxTags.  It uses the -->
  <!-- above parameter. -->
  <listener>
    <listener-class>javawebparts.taglib.ajaxtags.AjaxInit</listener-class>
  </listener>

  <!-- This is a simple servlet for this example that returns the HTML for -->
  <!-- the second select element.  It might be nice to have a special -->
  <!-- handler for populating an existing select, since it comes up so -->
  <!-- often, but for now you can do it this way out-of-the-box. -->
```

```
  <servlet>
    <servlet-name>KarnakServlet</servlet-name>
    <servlet-class>com.apress.ajaxprojects.karnak.KarnakServlet</servlet-class>
  </servlet>
  <servlet-mapping>
    <servlet-name>KarnakServlet</servlet-name>
    <url-pattern>/askKarnak</url-pattern>
  </servlet-mapping>

  <welcome-file-list>
    <welcome-file>index.jsp</welcome-file>
  </welcome-file-list>

</web-app>
```

If you have seen a web.xml file before, this will be no big deal for you. If this happens to be your first time, our previous discussions about XML being self-describing should be largely apparent here as you can probably discern the meaning of most of it without much trouble.

As we discussed when we looked at how AjaxTags works earlier, the first thing we see here is the context parameter ajaxTagsConfig, which points to our AjaxTags configuration file. The next thing we see is the AjaxTags listener, which is responsible for initializing AjaxTags when the context (the application) starts up. After that is a typical servlet definition, in this case pointing to the class KarnakServlet. This servlet is what will literally do the matching of what the user enters against our "database" of possible suggestions. We map this to the path /askKarnak. After that is a typical welcome page definition so that index.jsp is shown when no JSP is referenced in the URL.

ajax_config.xml

Now we get to the glue that really ties this all together: the AjaxTags configuration file, shown in Listing 4-9.

Listing 4-9. *AjaxTags Configuration File for Karnak*

```
<ajaxConfig>
  <!-- Define a custom request handler.  We could have used the -->
  <!-- std:QueryString handler, but we wouldn't be able to have as much -->
  <!-- control over keypress events that we need for this, so a custom -->
  <!-- handler it is! -->
  <handler name="CustomQueryString" type="request">
    <function>CustomQueryString</function>
    <location>js/CustomQueryString.js</location>
  </handler>
  <!-- Define a single form. -->
  <form ajaxRef="TypeAheadSuggestionsForm">
    <!-- Only the textbox is Ajax-enabled. -->
    <element ajaxRef="enteredTextChange">
```

```
      <!-- Any time a key is pressed (released actually), fire an event. -->
      <event type="onkeyup">
        <!-- We'll be using our custom request handler defined above. -->
        <requestHandler type="CustomQueryString" method="get">
          <target>askKarnak</target>
          <parameter>document.TypeAheadSuggestionsForm.enteredTextbox</parameter>
        </requestHandler>
        <!-- When we get back, just insert the returned results into the -->
        <!-- div named suggestions on the page, which contains the -->
        <!-- matching suggestions. -->
        <responseHandler type="std:InnerHTML">
          <parameter>suggestions</parameter>
        </responseHandler>
      </event>
    </element>
  </form>
</ajaxConfig>
```

Let's break this apart and examine it one piece at a time. The first thing we see is the configuration of a custom handler:

```
   <!-- Define a custom request handler.  We could have used the -->
  <!-- std:QueryString handler, but we wouldn't be able to have as much -->
  <!-- control over keypress events that we need for this, so a custom -->
  <!-- handler it is! -->
  <handler name="CustomQueryString" type="request">
    <function>CustomQueryString</function>
    <location>js/CustomQueryString.js</location>
  </handler>
```

As you can see from this listing, we are defining a custom handler named CustomQueryString. This is the name we will reference later on to use this handler. We also define it as a request handler (remember that AjaxTags has two types of handlers, request and response, which deal with communication from the client to the server in the case of the request handler, and then what happens with the response received from the server in the case of the response handler). We are also informing AjaxTags that the JavaScript function to call for this handler is CustomQueryString, which if you look back on Listing 4-7 you will see there, by virtue of the <function> element. Lastly, we are telling AjaxTags that this function can be found in an external JavaScript file in the <location> element. AjaxTags will insert the appropriate script import statement for us using this location.

Moving on, we come to the definition of the only Ajax event on this page:

```
<!-- Define a single form. -->
<form ajaxRef="TypeAheadSuggestionsForm">
  <!-- Only the textbox is Ajax-enabled. -->
  <element ajaxRef="enteredTextChange">
    <!-- Any time a key is pressed (released actually), fire an event. -->
    <event type="onkeyup">
      <!-- We'll be using our custom request handler defined above. -->
```

```
      <requestHandler type="CustomQueryString" method="get">
        <target>/askKarnak</target>
        <parameter>document.TypeAheadSuggestionsForm.enteredTextbox</parameter>
      </requestHandler>
      <!-- When we get back, just insert the returned results into the -->
      <!-- div named suggestions on the page, which contains the -->
      <!-- matching suggestions. -->
      <responseHandler type="std:InnerHTML">
        <parameter>suggestions</parameter>
      </responseHandler>
    </event>
  </element>
</form>
```

This is where everything is cobbled together to make this application work. First, recall that every element you wish to attach an Ajax event to in AjaxTags must be contained within a form, be it a real HTML form on the page or a "virtual" form, in which case it serves strictly as a container for other elements. In this case, we are referencing a real form, so the `ajaxRef` of the `<form>` element we see in Listing 4-9 should match the name of the form on the page, which it in fact does here. Within the form we are defining a single `<element>`, the text box the user types in. Note that the `ajaxRef` of the `<element>` does not have to match the name or DOM ID of the text box. In this case it does not match (but it can if you wish).

Within the `<element>` we are defining a single `<event>`, which we want to fire any time a key is pressed, or more precisely, when it is released by setting the type attribute to `onkeyup`. When this event fires we want to use our `CustomQueryString` as denoted in the `<requestHandler>` element. We also specify that we want our Ajax request to be made with the HTTP GET method. We configure the request handler to submit to the URL `/askKarnak`, which you will recall is the mapping we gave to our servlet. This handler also makes use of the `<parameter>` element to name the text box where users make their entries, as previously discussed.

Each Ajax event that AjaxTags handles has two sides to it: the request and the response. Having configured the request side of the equation, we now need to configure the response side. We do this within the `<responseHandler>` element. Here we are using the standard `InnerHTML` handler, which will take whatever the server returns and insert it into the named element using the `innerHTML` property, in this case the `<div>` with the ID `suggestions`.

That's all there is to it. As I mentioned at the start, AjaxTags really does make it quite easy!

KarnakServlet.java

There is one last piece of the puzzle to examine, and that is the servlet. Listing 4-10 shows the servlet in its entirety.

Listing 4-10. *The Complete Karnak Servlet*

```
package com.apress.ajaxprojects.karnak;

import java.io.IOException;
import java.io.PrintWriter;
import javax.servlet.http.HttpServlet;
```

```
import javax.servlet.http.HttpServletRequest;
import javax.servlet.http.HttpServletResponse;
import javax.servlet.ServletException;

/**
 * Simple servlet that returns the HTML to render the list of matching
 * suggestions based on the entered text passed in.
*/
public class KarnakServlet extends HttpServlet {

  private static String[][] words = {
    { "aardvark", "abbot", "abort", "account", "acorn", "action", "adam",
      "aeon", "agorophobia", "ahab", "ailment", "airway",  "ajar", "ajax", },
    { "bad", "bald", "band", "barrel", "beard", "bed", "beltway", "biff",
      "big", "bird", "bladder", "bones", "buddy", "burp", "butt", "buzz" },
    { "calm", "card", "cargo", "chase", "chasm", "chemical", "christmas",
      "congo", "congress", "consider", "cork", "crash", "creep", "crisp" },
    { "damn", "dastardly", "dean", "dell", "descent", "develop", "diet", "dig",
      "dilbert", "directory", "dog", "douglas", "drug", "druthers" },
    { "ear", "earlier", "ebert", "effort", "egg", "emergency", "enemy",
      "energy", "enterprise", "evening", "every", "exempt", "exhaust", "eye" },
    { "fan", "fantasy", "farm", "fender", "fish", "flew", "fling", "flung",
      "fly", "fog", "foghorn", "frank", "frenzy", "friend", "frog", "fumble" },
    { "gang", "gap", "gas","girl", "gleam", "going", "gone", "gong", "grand",
      "grasp", "great", "guinea", "gulf", "gulp", "gurgle", "guy" },
    { "halo", "ham", "hammer", "hang", "hearing", "heart", "hello", "help",
      "hermit", "hero", "hog", "howdy", "hubert", "hung", "hurry", "hurt" },
    { "ice", "implicate", "imply", "indecent", "indigo", "industry", "inside",
      "internet", "intimate", "intimidate", "into", "irrevocable" },
    { "jack", "jakarta", "jake", "jam", "jargon", "java", "JavaScript", "jerk",
      "jest", "john", "joke", "josh", "jug", "july", "june", "jury" },
    { "kangaroo", "karl", "kettledrum", "kill", "killer", "kilowatt", "kimbo",
      "kmew", "kmow", "knighthood", "knock", "kong", "konquer" },
    { "lamb", "lance", "learning", "lesson", "let", "liberace", "liberate",
      "lifelike", "like", "likes", "long", "lunch", "lunge", "lurch" },
    { "magic", "mammogram", "march", "may", "mercenary", "mercy", "merge",
      "microsoft", "mom", "mommy", "monday", "money", "munch", "munchies" },
    { "nag", "nanny", "narc", "narcotic", "natural", "nature", "nerd", "never",
      "nobody", "nonsense", "noon", "not", "nurture", "nut", "nuts" },
    { "offense", "offensive", "old", "operate", "operation", "operational",
      "opium", "orca", "organ", "orlando", "orphan", "ort", "overture" },
    { "pal", "pearch", "peas", "penny", "people", "perfume", "personal",
      "pod", "power", "prescott", "pretty", "programmer", "properties" },
    { "quadratic", "quadrinomial", "quadruple", "query", "question", "quibble",
      "quick", "quickest", "quickly", "quinn", "qwerty" },
```

```
  { "rambus", "rap", "rat", "really", "rear", "rebate", "refine",
    "regurgitate", "reject", "rejoice", "rock", "roger", "roll", "roster" },
  { "sack", "sad", "sam", "saturday", "say", "seattle", "september", "squash",
    "star", "still", "street", "stuck", "sucks", "sunday", "swish" },
  { "tag", "ted", "the", "thomas", "thursday", "tom", "tomcat","tone",
    "trace", "transformation", "travel", "troll", "tuck", "tuesday", "turd" },
  { "ugly", "unclean", "undercurrent", "underneath", "underverse",
    "unfettered", "universal", "unpleasent", "upside", "useless","utter" },
  { "valium", "vast", "vegas", "vegetable", "vehement", "veign","venue",
    "venus","verify","veterinarian", "virtue", "vogue" },
  { "wack", "wafer", "wag", "war", "water", "whimsical", "wicked", "wild",
    "wise", "wish", "wobble", "wonderful", "world", "wow", "wully" },
  { "xanadu", "xavier", "xenobiologist", "xenogeologist", "xenomorph",
    "xenophobia", "xigua", "xml", "xslt", "xteq", "xylophone" },
  { "yack", "yam", "year", "yell", "yellow", "yes", "yesterday", "yesteryear",
    "yoda", "yodel", "yogurt", "you", "yours", "yummy" },
  { "zammetti", "zap", "zapped", "zen", "zenith", "zero", "zest", "zinc",
    "zitto", "zone", "zoned", "zucchini", "zuckerman", "zygot" }
};

/**
 * doGet.
 *
 * @param  request          HTTPServletRequest.
 * @param  response         HTTPServletResponse.
 * @throws ServletException ServletException.
 * @throws IOException      IOException.
 */
public void doGet(HttpServletRequest request, HttpServletResponse response)
  throws ServletException, IOException {

  // Get the text the user entered and report it.
  String enteredText = (String)request.getParameter("enteredText");
  System.out.println(enteredText);

  // If anything was entered, find any matches, case-insensitive.
  StringBuffer sb = new StringBuffer(1024);
  int numSuggestions = 0;
  if (enteredText != null && !enteredText.equalsIgnoreCase("")) {
    enteredText = enteredText.toLowerCase();
    int i = ((int)enteredText.charAt(0)) - 97;
    if (i >= 0 && i <= 25) {
      for (int j = 0; j < words[i].length; j++) {
        if (words[i][j].startsWith(enteredText)) {
          // We found a match, construct the HTML for it.
          numSuggestions++;
          sb.append("<div id=\"suggestion" + numSuggestions + "\" ");
```

```
            sb.append(words[i][j]);
            sb.append("</div>\n");
          }
        }
      }
    }
    sb.append("<script>");
    sb.append("keyCodePressed=null;");
    sb.append("numSuggestions=" + numSuggestions + ";");
    sb.append("previousSuggestion=0;");
    sb.append("currentSuggestion=0;");
    sb.append("suggestionsDiv.style.visibility=\"visible\";");
    sb.append("</script>");
    PrintWriter out = response.getWriter();
    out.println(sb.toString());

  } // End goGet().


} // End class.
```

The first thing we notice is the huge array named `words`. As I mentioned earlier, we are not going to try to compete with Google, so this represents our "database." This is a two-dimensional array, where the first dimension is a letter of the alphabet and the second dimension is a list of words for that letter.

After that is the `doGet()` method, where all the work is actually done. The first thing we do is get what the user entered from the request object and display it:

```
    // Get the text the user entered and report it.
    String enteredText = (String)request.getParameter("enteredText");
    System.out.println(enteredText);
```

After that comes the code that literally does the matching:

```
// If anything was entered, find any matches, case-insensitive.
StringBuffer sb = new StringBuffer(1024);
Int numSuggestions = 0;
if (enteredText != null && !enteredText.equalsIgnoreCase("")) {
  enteredText = enteredText.toLowerCase();
  int i = ((int)enteredText.charAt(0)) - 97;
  if (i >= 0 && i <= 25) {
    for (int j = 0; j < words[i].length; j++) {
      if (words[i][j].startsWith(enteredText)) {
        // We found a match, construct the HTML for it.
        numSuggestions++;
```

Here, we first ensure that we actually got something from the user, which, if you look back on the request handler code, could never actually happen. But it is considered a best practice to always validate on the server what you may have already validated on the client, and that is precisely what this code is doing. Next, we convert the entered text to lowercase so that we are doing a case-insensitive search. Then we come to this line:

```
int i = ((int)enteredText.charAt(0)) - 97;
```

The purpose of this code is to determine which index into the first dimension of our array we should look into to get matching suggestions. We take the first character of the user's entry, get its character code (which for all intents and purposes in this case is its ASCII code), and subtract 97 from it. In ASCII 97 is a lowercase "a." So, if the user enters "acr", the character code of the first letter is 97, so subtracting 97 from it we get 0, which is the index into the `words` array where the words beginning with "a" are. If the user entered "z", we would get the value 122, minus 97 is 25, which is the index into the array where the words beginning with "z" are.

Once that is done, this code executes:

```
    if (i >= 0 && i <= 25) {
      for (int j = 0; j < words[i].length; j++) {
        if (words[i][j].startsWith(enteredText)) {
          // We found a match, construct the HTML for it.
          numSuggestions++;
```

Here, now that we have the first array dimension index, we cycle through the words in the second dimension and find any that start with what the user has entered. Those are our matching suggestions. For each item in the list, we increment our `numSuggestions` counter variable so that we can report back to the client how many suggestions there are (since that value is needed to make the highlighting of suggestions work), and we render the HTML that will be displayed in our `<div>` back on the page, as shown here:

```
          sb.append("<div id=\"suggestion" + numSuggestions + "\" ");
          sb.append(words[i][j]);
          sb.append("</div>\n");
        }
      }
    }
  }
  sb.append("<script>");
  sb.append("keyCodePressed=null;");
  sb.append("numSuggestions=" + numSuggestions + ";");
  sb.append("previousSuggestion=0;");
  sb.append("currentSuggestion=0;");
  sb.append("suggestionsDiv.style.visibility=\"visible\";");
  sb.append("</script>");
  PrintWriter out = response.getWriter();
  out.println(sb.toString());
```

The first thing that is rendered is the opening of the `<div>` tag. Then we render the DOM ID of the element, which is the word "suggestion" followed by a number (starting with 1). This results in each suggestion being a unique node in the DOM for us to manipulate for highlighting later. This is yet again an instance where the "proper" way probably would be to do this all through changing style classes. However, it is nice to see that it can be done in other ways, as we see here.

A `<script>` block is then rendered. This block resets some variables. Each time the server is consulted and the suggestions are updated, we want to make sure we have no spurious keyboard events fire, which is what setting `keyCodePressed` to `null` does. We also need to record the number of suggestions so that we can be sure not to highlight nonexistent items; that's what setting `numSuggestions` does. Setting `previousSuggestion` and `currentSuggestion` to 0 makes sure that the first suggestion that will be highlighted when the user uses the cursor keys will be the first one. Finally, we ensure that the suggestions `<div>` is visible, if it was not before.

Once we have built all the HTML, the `StringBuffer` is written out to the response, and the servlet has finished its task. Back on the client, the `std:InnerHTML` response handler inserts the content into the suggestions `<div>`'s `innerHTML` property, and the cycle is complete!

Suggested Exercises

With each project in this book, I will make suggestions for expanding the project that will serve as exercises for you to get your hands dirty a bit and (I hope) more fully absorb the information espoused in the chapter. For Karnak, I suggest the following:

- Add speed throttling. You may have realized that making an Ajax call on every keypress is a sure way to kill a server in a hurry. If you were to examine the code for Google Suggest, you would find that they do a pretty neat trick: they have some JavaScript that times how fast you are typing and will actually send fewer requests the faster you type. Adding this capability might be a bit of a challenge, but it would be well worth it.

- Expand the servlet to perform soundex matching as well as literal matching. The Jakarta Commons Codec package has a `Soundex` class that should make this fairly easy. (Incidentally, if you are not regularly using the Commons packages and thinking of them before you begin coding utility-type functions, you are doing yourself a disservice and missing out on some great work!) Perhaps present the suggestions with a divider between the literal matches and the soundex matches.

Summary

In this chapter we built our first, real Ajax application! We duplicated—to some degree at least—what the finest minds in Google have done and learned to do something that can be very useful in many web applications. You learned about AjaxTags from Java Web Parts and saw the ease with which you can build Ajax applications using that library. As Obi-Wan Kenobi said to Luke Skywalker when he was finally able to deflect the remote's lasers with the blast shield down, "You've taken your first step into a larger world."

CHAPTER 5

InstaMail: An Ajax-Based Webmail Client

This chapter will introduce an application called InstaMail, which is an Ajax-based webmail application. We'll use a new library (DWR) to build this application, and we'll also use some client-side DOM scripting and CSS to make this a little more "pretty" application than something like Karnak. In the end, we'll have a web application that you can run on a server and that will give you remote access to your POP3 account from anywhere. Although it will not be as full-featured as Microsoft Outlook, it will be more than capable of performing the basics.

Requirements and Goals

A while back, access to e-mail accounts was always through some bulky fat-client application. AOL was and still is perhaps the most famous; you may recall others like CompuServe and Delphi. Later on, and still to this day, we have applications like Microsoft Outlook and Outlook Express, Thunderbird, and Eudora, just to name a few.

More recently, though, over the past 2 to 3 years perhaps, people have started to realize that it would be nice to have e-mail available to them anywhere, not just on a PC or laptop with the client installed. That realization, along with the advent of the Internet and always-on access for many people, heralded the birth of the webmail client!

A webmail client is nothing more than a web application that runs on a server and acts essentially as a proxy between you and your POP3/IMAP account. POP3 is the most popular e-mail protocol out there for mail retrieval, and Simple Mail Transfer Protocol (SMTP) is the most common for mail transmission. It usually contains some basic functions, and increasingly even more advanced functions. Clearly it has to be able to send and receive messages from a POP3/SMTP account, and usually it will have some form of address book as well. Those are pretty much the basics that everyone expects to find. Things like multiple folder support, grouping of e-mail "conversations," rich e-mail editing, file attachments, and alerts are some of the more "advanced" features that can be found in many webmail applications today.

Here, we'll build ourselves a webmail client that covers those basics. Because the advanced features generally require knowing a little more about the server the application runs on than I can safely assume in the context of this book, we won't delve into many, if any, of those advanced features. However, as I am sure you can guess, they make for a very nice, easy list of suggested enhancements for you at the end!

Let's now codify the features this webmail application will support, and the general design goals:

- We want the user interface (UI) to be somewhat "pretty." Karnak was obviously a very simple interface, but here we'll try to take it just a little further.
- We should of course be able to view our POP3 Inbox and read messages in it, as well as delete messages.
- Sending a message as well is an obvious goal. We should be able to compose a new e-mail, either to a contact in our address book or to someone else, and we should also be able to reply to a received message, complete with quoting of the original message.
- To make things simple and stay focused on what we should be focused on, InstaMail will support a single e-mail client for a single user, and there will be no security per se, i.e., no username and password will be required to access InstaMail (they will still of course be required, usually to access the POP3/SMTP servers).
- We'll provide an address book from which a new message can be started. We'll store just some basic information for each contact, namely first name, last name, e-mail address, and comment. Comment can be any note you want to make about the contact.
- In addition to access to the Inbox, we'll maintain all sent messages locally.
- We'll be able to delete the message currently being read, or select a batch to delete from the Inbox view.
- In addition to the UI being a bit "pretty," we want to exercise some DHTML (Dynamic HTML) and CSS skills and incorporate some slightly "fancy" features, things like some button mouse-over effects and a Please Wait float-over. We won't go completely crazy—just enough to have fun!

That list should give us more than enough to do. It should also be a bit of a fun project to dissect, so without delay, let's get to it!

How We Will Pull It Off

We have seen AjaxTags from Java Web Parts now, and I hope you have come to appreciate what it can do for you. AjaxTags is far from the only option out there, though, and this time around we are going to play with something called Direct Web Remoting (DWR).

DWR (`http://getahead.ltd.uk/dwr`) is a free, open source product from a small IT consulting group called Getahead, whose members are Joe Walker and Mark Goodwin. DWR is an interesting approach to Ajax in that it allows you to treat Java classes running on the server as if they were local, that is, running within the web browser.

First we need to set up DWR. Unlike most of the other libraries described in this book, DWR consists of a server-side component as well as a client-side component. As such, it does require a bit of setup on the server, whereas most of the other libraries do not require any setup beyond importing the correct JavaScript code into your pages.

Setting up DWR basically boils down to adding a single JAR file to your webapp, adding a servlet definition to `web.xml`, and creating a single XML configuration file.

The first step is to copy the `dwr.lib` JAR into `WEB-INF/lib` of your webapp. Once that is done, you can move on to step two, which is defining the DWR servlet in `web.xml`, like so:

```
<servlet>
  <servlet-name>dwr-invoker</servlet-name>
  <display-name>DWR Servlet</display-name>
  <servlet-class>uk.ltd.getahead.dwr.DWRServlet</servlet-class>
  <init-param>
     <param-name>debug</param-name>
     <param-value>true</param-value>
  </init-param>
</servlet>

<servlet-mapping>
  <servlet-name>dwr-invoker</servlet-name>
  <url-pattern>/dwr/*</url-pattern>
</servlet-mapping>
```

This is just a typical servlet definition with a mapping to the `/dwr/*` path so that any request beginning with `/dwr` will be processed by the DWR servlet. This servlet is essentially the "traffic cop" that dispatches your requests to the appropriate class.

To make it all work, DWR requires that you write a single XML configuration file named `dwr.xml` and place it in `WEB-INF`, which is the third step. This file, among other things, determines what classes DWR can remote, and also provides information about the various classes it might have to deal with. A simple example of this configuration file might look like this:

```
<!DOCTYPE dwr PUBLIC "-//GetAhead Limited//DTD Direct Web Remoting 1.0//EN"
"http://www.getahead.ltd.uk/dwr/dwr10.dtd">

<dwr>
  <allow>
    <convert converter="bean"
      match="com.apress.ajaxprojects.instamail.MessageDTO" />
    <create creator="new" JavaScript="OptionsManager">
      <param name="class"
        value="com.apress.ajaxprojects.instamail.OptionsManager" />
    </create>
  </allow>
</dwr>
```

In this example, we are informing DWR that it has permission to convert any object of type `MessageDTO` into a corresponding JavaScript object. We are also informing DWR that calls to the class `OptionsManager` can be made. Any other class will not be allowed. Note that most of the basic Java types have converters enabled by default. More specifically, the following are automatically converted:

- All primitive types, boolean, int, double, etc.
- The class-based versions of these: Boolean, Integer, etc.
- java.lang.String
- java.util.Date and the three SQL derivatives
- Arrays of the above
- Collections (Lists, Sets, Maps, Iterators, etc.) of the above
- DOM objects (like Element and Document) from DOM, XOM, JDOM, and DOM4J

You generally will only have to inform DWR of your own custom classes. This means you have to give it permission to marshal the class to and from the client. This is done with the <convert> tag. As long as your class only contains the above-mentioned types, it should automatically work. If it contains other types, however, you will have to write your own converter for it. That topic is out of the scope of this book, so I refer you to the DWR website and documentation for details.

To make this all come together in your mind, we'll look at an example usage. First, we'll need our configuration file with the following contents:

```
<!DOCTYPE dwr PUBLIC "-//GetAhead Limited//DTD Direct Web Remoting 1.0//EN"
"http://www.getahead.ltd.uk/dwr/dwr10.dtd">

<dwr>
  <allow>
    <create creator="new" JavaScript="MyClass">
      <param name="class" value="com.company.app.MyClass" />
    </create>
  </allow>
</dwr>
```

This is saying that DWR is allowed to instantiate and call methods on the class MyClass in the com.company.app package. Further, it says that we'll interact with this object via the MyClass object on the client. Let's say the class looks like this:

```
package com.company.app;
public class MyClass {
  String sayHello(String name) {
    return "Hello, " + name;
  }
}
```

With DWR, you could have some JavaScript on a page to execute that method as follows:

```
MyClass.sayHello("Frank", sayHelloHandler);
var sayHelloHandler = function(data) {
  alert(data);
}
```

Notice how that first line looks exactly like a Java call to that class? The differences are that it looks like `sayHello()` is a static method, which it is not, and also the addition of the second parameter. The second parameter is telling DWR what JavaScript function should handle the return from the method call, and the fact that it looks static is simply a by-product of the DWR syntax.

The `sayHelloHandler` is akin to the regular Ajax callback you have seen before, but the details of it are hidden behind this simplified method call. The single parameter `data` represents the return from the method call, and this can actually be a simple Java type, a Java class (think collections, for example), or your own custom class. In this case it is just a standard `String`, so throwing it to an `alert()` call simply displays the result, "Hello, Frank" in this case.

As far as using DWR in your pages, all that is required is a few JavaScript file imports. You will always import `engine.js`, and usually `util.js`. In addition, for each class you will remote, you will import a JavaScript source file that contains essentially what can be thought of as the remote interface of the classes you will be calling methods on. Interestingly, all these JavaScript files are actually provided by the DWR servlet itself. In other words, there are no JavaScript files you have to remember to copy into your webapp. As long as `dwr.jar` is present, so are the JavaScript files! Even more interesting is the fact that the interface files are actually generated dynamically using reflection. From a technical standpoint, DWR is a very neat piece of engineering. The fact that it is so useful and makes Ajax so easy is all the more impressive.

Once you declare the servlet and create a config file, you can go to the following address: `http://localhost:8080/[YOUR-WEBAPP]/dwr/`.

Assuming your app server is listening on port 8080, replace `[YOUR-WEBAPP]` with the name (context) of the webapp, and you will be returned a page that details all the classes you have declared in the config file, as well as all the methods they expose. It will also give you details on what files to import into your pages, and provide test links to try the various methods. This is a very handy debugging tool, since if it works here then you know everything is working as far as DWR goes. It also is a great "getting started" tool because it gives you all the information you need to make use of the classes you have exposed.

DWR also supports integration with many of the most popular libraries of today, including Struts, Spring, Hibernate, and Beehive. For instance, you can have DWR call on Spring to create any configured Spring beans before making calls to its methods. If you are using any of these libraries, this integration will likely prove a boon to your work.

Lastly, DWR provides a handful of useful utility functions to do things like populate a table from a returned collection, set values in various form fields, and display returned objects in a useful way. We'll see many of these things as we explore the InstaMail application. We won't touch on everything DWR provides, of course, as it is a very rich library.

To explore DWR in more depth, as I highly recommend doing, visit `http://getahead.ltd.uk/dwr/` and have a look around.

Visualizing the Finish Line

InstaMail is a fairly good-looking application if I do say so myself! It is always worth noting that engineers often don't have the artistic eye that our web designer brethren possess. Even still, the engineers among us should always strive to do the best with the assets we have, and that is precisely what I have attempted to do here.

We should also not be ashamed to use the tools available to us! The basic page layout and graphics for InstaMail were generated with a program called Xara Webstyle, which is a godsend for those of us who are not artists at heart. Taking the basics that Webstyle provides, and after tweaking and extending it, we arrive at a look and feel that I am fairly happy with, and I hope you will be too! So, let's have a look at InstaMail!

The first view you will encounter when you access InstaMail is the Intro view (Figure 5-1). As it is shown here, InstaMail has not been used before, and therefore all you can do is go to the Options view to set up your e-mail account. If you had already done that, then you would see the row of buttons along the top and on the side that you will see in later views and the Getting Started verbiage would not be present at all. Note the link at the bottom. You can click on it at any time to get help on the current view.

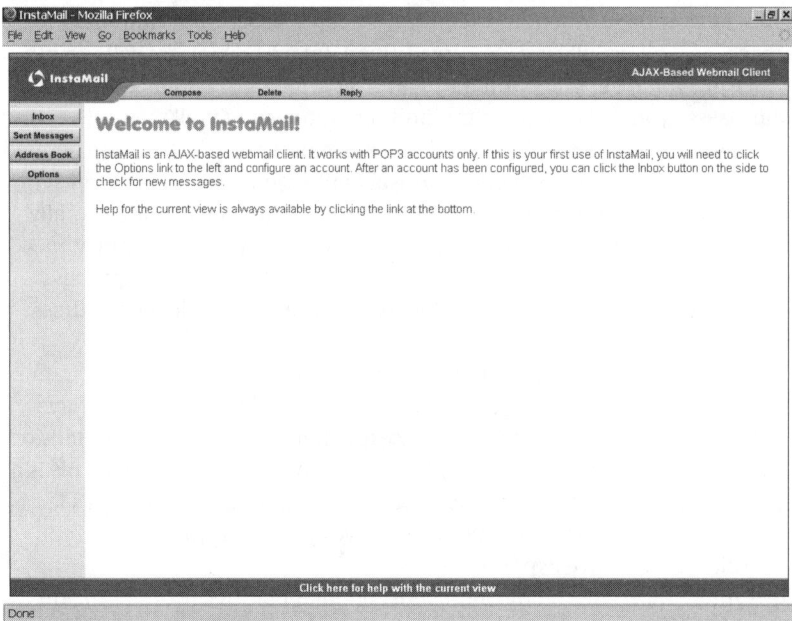

Figure 5-1. *The InstaMail Intro view*

Next up is the Inbox (Figure 5-2), which displays your incoming messages. You can check off a number of e-mails and delete them from here, and you can delete individual messages while you are viewing them.

The Sent Messages view (Figure 5-3) looks essentially just like the Inbox view, with some different fields showing. As with the Inbox, you can check off a batch of e-mails and delete them.

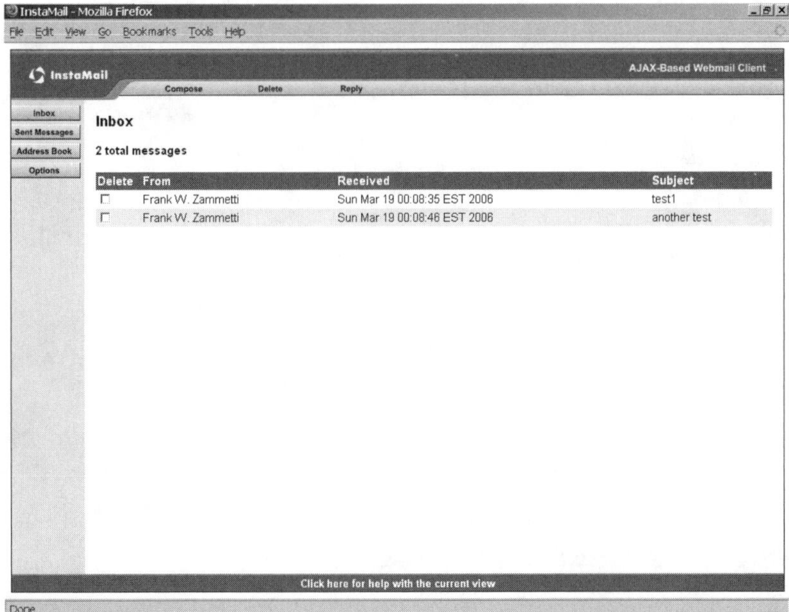

Figure 5-2. *The Inbox*

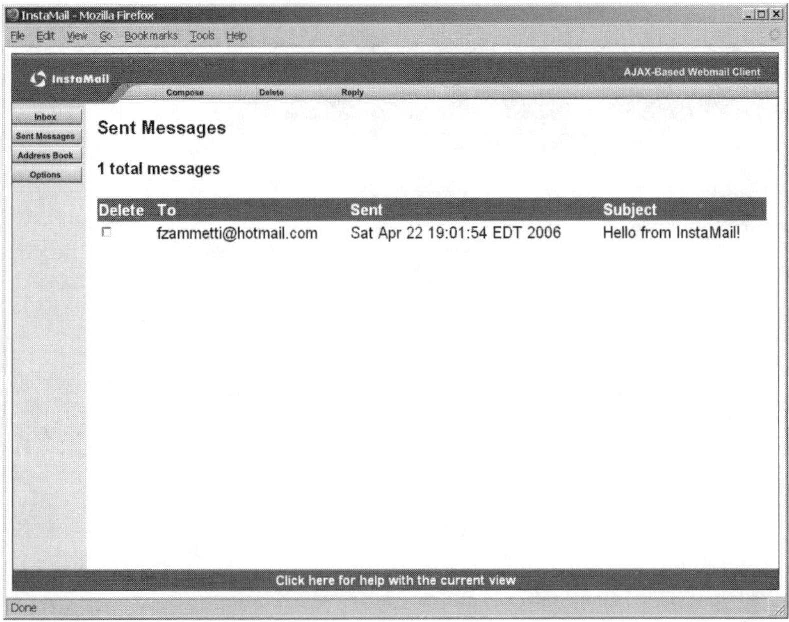

Figure 5-3. *The Sent Messages view*

Figure 5-4 shows how you'd compose a new message.

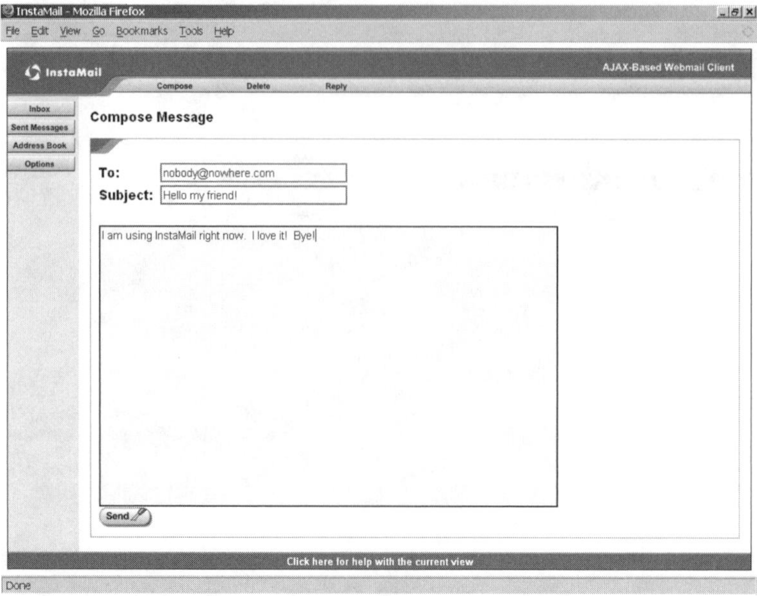

Figure 5-4. *Composing a new message*

Figure 5-5 shows the view you will see when you click on a message from either the Inbox or Sent Messages view.

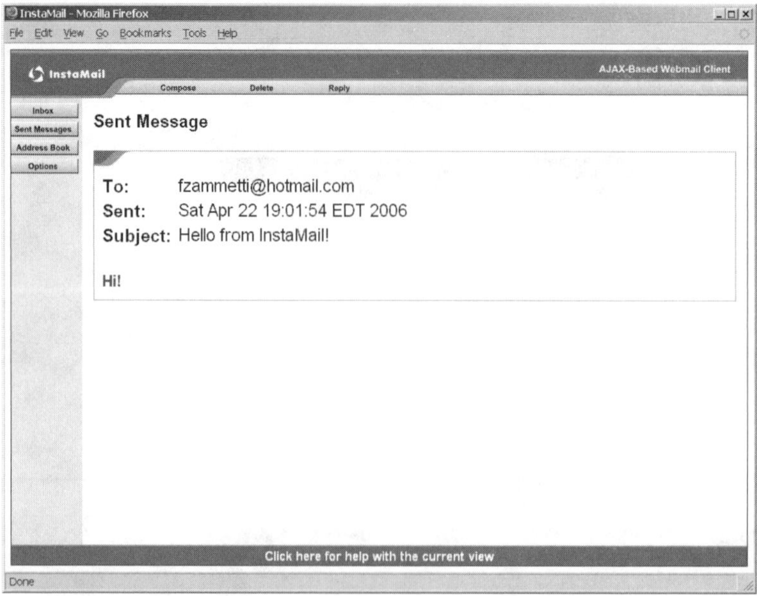

Figure 5-5. *Reading an existing message*

The address book (Figure 5-6) allows you to store contacts that you frequently correspond with. You can click on an existing contact, at which point you can edit their e-mail address and note, or delete them. This screen naturally allows you to add new contacts and delete existing contacts as well.

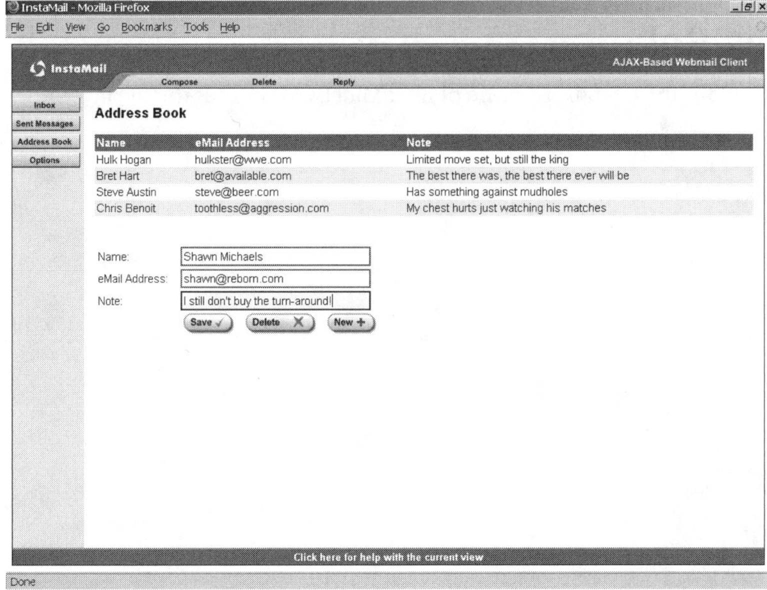

Figure 5-6. *The address book*

The Options view (Figure 5-7) is where users can set up their e-mail account; POP3 and SMTP can be used.

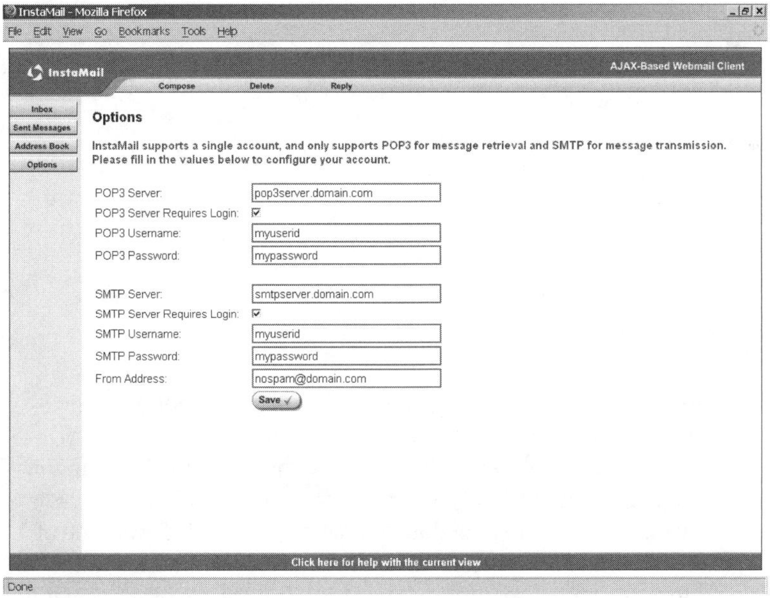

Figure 5-7. *The Options view*

And that is a quick tour of InstaMail. Now is the moment you've been waiting for: time to dive into the code!

Dissecting the Solution

Let's begin by getting a feel for the overall structure of InstaMail by looking at the file layout, shown in Figure 5-8.

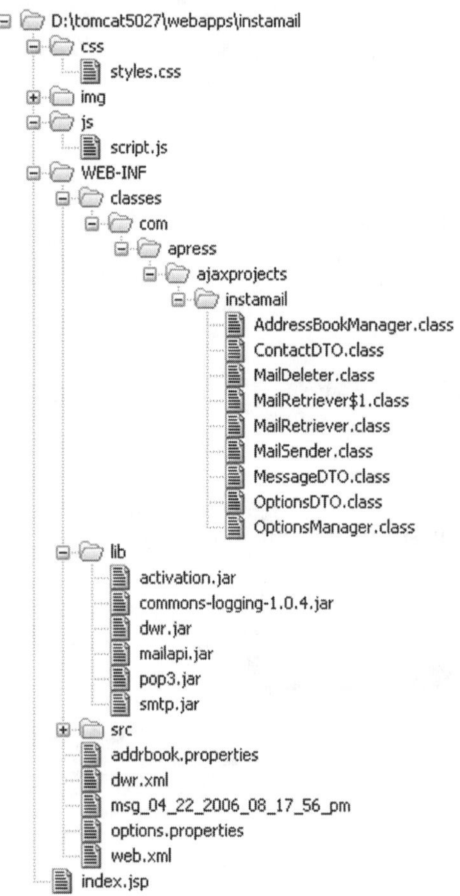

Figure 5-8. *Directory structure of InstaMail*

InstaMail consists of a single JSP page, `index.jsp`. All the markup for the entire application is in that one file. This file imports the stylesheet file `styles.css` in the `/css` directory. It also makes use of all the images in the `/img` directory, which I have not expanded here in the interest of keeping this layout image small (there are a rather large number of images involved, and listing them all would have more than doubled the height of this figure). All of the JavaScript for InstaMail, save a single `init()` function in `index.jsp`, is contained in the `script.js` file in the `/js` directory, which is also imported by `index.jsp`. We can also see here nine classes that make up the server side of the application in the `WEB-INF/classes` directory, in a typical package directory structure. Lastly, we can see the libraries that InstaMail makes use of in the WEB-INF/lib directory, and they are described in Table 5-1.

Table 5-1. *The JARs InstaMail Depends on, Found in WEB-INF/lib*

JAR	Description
activation.jar	JavaBeans Activation Framework, needed by the JavaMail API.
commons-logging-1.0.4.jar	Jakarta Commons Logging is an abstraction layer that sits on top of a true logging implementation (like Log4J), which allows you to switch the underlying logging implementation without affecting your application code. It also provides a simple logger that outputs to System.out, which is what this application uses.
dwr.jar	The JAR containing all the DWR classes.
mailapi.jar	The JavaMail API, the Sun-standard library for performing mail functions.
pop3.jar	JavaMail extensions for dealing with POP3 mail servers.
smtp.jar	JavaMail extensions for dealing with SMTP mail servers.

The WEB-INF/src directory contains all the source code for this project, including Ant build script.

The Client-Side Code

The first thing we'll look at with InstaMail is the config files, starting with web.xml, shown in Listing 5-1.

Listing 5-1. *InstaMail's web.xml Config File*

```
<?xml version="1.0" encoding="ISO-8859-1"?>

<!DOCTYPE web-app PUBLIC "-//Sun Microsystems, Inc.//DTD Web Application 2.3//EN"
"http://java.sun.com/dtd/web-app_2_3.dtd">

<web-app>

  <display-name>InstaMail</display-name>

  <servlet>
    <servlet-name>dwr-invoker</servlet-name>
    <servlet-class>uk.ltd.getahead.dwr.DWRServlet</servlet-class>
    <init-param>
      <param-name>debug</param-name>
      <param-value>true</param-value>
   </init-param>
  </servlet>
  <servlet-mapping>
    <servlet-name>dwr-invoker</servlet-name>
    <url-pattern>/dwr/*</url-pattern>
```

```
  </servlet-mapping>

  <!-- Session timeout config. -->
  <session-config>
    <session-timeout>30</session-timeout>
  </session-config>

  <!-- Welcome file config. -->
  <welcome-file-list>
    <welcome-file>index.jsp</welcome-file>
  </welcome-file-list>

</web-app>
```

Well, there certainly is not much to it, is there? The most important item is the DWR servlet definition. Here we are mapping it to the path /dwr/* and telling it we want to see debug information. Beyond that we are simply setting a session timeout of 30 minutes and setting index.jsp as our welcome page. Very concise indeed!

dwr.xml

Next up is dwr.xml, which is the DWR configuration file that was described earlier, shown in Listing 5-2.

Listing 5-2. *dwr.xml for InstaMail*

```
<!DOCTYPE dwr PUBLIC "-//GetAhead Limited//DTD Direct Web Remoting 1.0//EN"
"http://www.getahead.ltd.uk/dwr/dwr10.dtd">

<dwr>
  <allow>
    <convert converter="bean"
      match="com.apress.ajaxprojects.instamail.MessageDTO" />
    <convert converter="bean"
      match="com.apress.ajaxprojects.instamail.OptionsDTO" />
    <convert converter="bean"
      match="com.apress.ajaxprojects.instamail.ContactDTO" />
    <create creator="new" JavaScript="OptionsManager">
      <param name="class"
      value="com.apress.ajaxprojects.instamail.OptionsManager" />
    </create>
    <create creator="new" JavaScript="MailRetriever">
      <param name="class" value="com.apress.ajaxprojects.instamail.MailRetriever" />
    </create>
```

```
    <create creator="new" JavaScript="MailSender">
      <param name="class" value="com.apress.ajaxprojects.instamail.MailSender" />
    </create>
    <create creator="new" JavaScript="MailDeleter">
      <param name="class" value="com.apress.ajaxprojects.instamail.MailDeleter" />
    </create>
    <create creator="new" JavaScript="AddressBookManager">
      <param name="class"
        value="com.apress.ajaxprojects.instamail.AddressBookManager" />
    </create>
  </allow>
</dwr>
```

Like web.xml, this is not exactly a *War and Peace*-sized piece of code! To remind you, dwr.xml basically tells DWR, among other things, what classes it is allowed to create and access, and also what objects it can convert to and from JavaScript and Java. In this case we are listing the Data Transfer Objects (DTOs) that InstaMail uses as convertible, and we are listing the five main classes that contain the server-side functionality of the application. We'll of course be looking at them in detail soon, but their names alone should give you a very clear idea of what they do. Note that as shown here, there is no limitation on what methods or properties of the classes can be accessed. The only limitation is on those classes not listed, which cannot be remotely called at all.

DWR does offer some other capabilities by way of this config file that InstaMail does not require. For instance, you can tell DWR to use certain classes to create the classes you want to remote. Think of something like Spring, for example, which would create and initialize a bean for you before DWR passes through any calls to it. There is also some configuration you can do with regard to the method signatures of a class. DWR does its magic with a heavy dose of reflection, but sometimes it is not sufficient. You can give DWR "hints" about the data types and such that the signatures contain, to fill in the gaps.

styles.css

The next thing we are going to look at is the stylesheet that InstaMail uses. Because it is fairly long, I will not list it in its entirety here. However, it contains some interesting bits that I will call your attention to. First, here are some selectors that are used for the hover effect of the help link at the bottom:

```
.footer {
  font-size         : 10pt;
  font-weight       : bold;
  font-family       : Arial;
  color             : #ffffff;
  background-color  : #2661dd;
  border-top-color  : #ff7f00;
  border-top-width  : 2px;
  border-top-style  : solid;
  padding-top       : 2px;
  padding-bottom    : 2px;
}
```

```
.footerHover {
  font-size           : 10pt;
  font-weight         : bold;
  font-family         : Arial;
  color               : #000000;
  cursor              : pointer;
  background-color    : #ff7f00;
  border-top-color    : #ff7f00;
  border-top-width    : 2px;
  border-top-style    : solid;
  padding-top         : 2px;
  padding-bottom      : 2px;
}
```

Notice how the border is set on the top only? That is how the effect of having a divider line above it is achieved. The hover state alters the cursor, showing a pointer (or hand, depending on browser and OS) as well as altering the background color. This is a nice, simple, active feedback response for the user. This same effect is used within the message lists:

```
.msgListRow1 {
  font-size           : 12pt;
  font-weight         : normal;
  font-family         : Arial;
  color               : #000000;
  background-color    : #ffffff;
  cursor              : default;
}

.msgListRow2 {
  font-size           : 12pt;
  font-weight         : normal;
  font-family         : Arial;
  color               : #000000;
  background-color    : #efeff7;
  cursor              : default;
}

.rowHover {
  font-size           : 12pt;
  font-weight         : normal;
  font-family         : Arial;
  cursor              : pointer;
  background-color    : #ff7f00;
}
```

Why two selectors for the non-hover state, you ask? This is because of the row striping it. The rows of the result list alternate between shaded and nonshaded. This is a nice thing to do for users because it lets them track information across the screen easily, allowing them to keep the data that goes together straight in their minds. One way to accomplish this is to alternate what selector is used on a given row. Here, the rows alternate between using `msgListRow1` and `msgListRow2`.

One last selector I'd like to draw your attention to is the one used for the Please Wait float-over. A float-over, or simply a "floating layer," is a layer that floats over others—that is, has a higher `z-index`. Note that this differs from the `float` CSS attribute, which describes where one element is placed in relation to another vertically or horizontally. In this instance, float-over refers to the layer's position *on top* of other layers—that is, it "floats" over them.

Even though when you perform an operation in InstaMail that results in the Please Wait box being shown the layer behind it is hidden, it is still hovering over the layer, and this selector accomplishes that.

```
.cssPleaseWait {
  font-size           : 16pt;
  font-weight         : bold;
  font-family         : Arial;
  color               : #ffffff;
  position            : absolute;
  left                : 1px;
  top                 : 1px;
  width               : 330px;
  height              : 66px;
  background-color    : #ff7f00;
  display             : none;
  z-index             : 1000;
  border-top-width    : 4px;
  border-right-width  : 4px;
  border-left-width   : 4px;
  border-bottom-width : 4px;
  border-right-style  : solid;
  border-bottom-style : solid;
  border-top-style    : solid;
  border-left-style   : solid;
  border-right-color  : #2161de;
  border-bottom-color : #2161de;
  border-top-color    : #2161de;
  border-left-color   : #2161de;
}
```

The part that really makes it float over everything else is the `z-index`. This CSS attribute sets the depth of a given layer. For instance, if you have three `<div>`s on a page, all absolutely positioned at the same location, which one would you see? If you visualize the structure of those layers, it is a stack, three layers on top of each other. Which one is on the top of the stack? The answer is that it will always be the one with the highest `z-index` value. In this case, we give the Please Wait layer a `z-index` of 1000 so that it will definitely be on top of everything else.

index.jsp

The next piece to look at is index.jsp, which is the only document in InstaMail! Once again, because of its length, I will not list the entire source here but just call out details. The first detail we should look at is found in the <head> of the document, and is a collection of JavaScript imports:

```
<!-- DWR interfaces. -->
<script type="text/JavaScript" src="js/script.js"></script>
<script type="text/javascript" src="dwr/interface/OptionsManager.js"></script>
<script type="text/javascript" src="dwr/interface/AddressBookManager.js">
</script>
<script type="text/javascript" src="dwr/interface/MailRetriever.js"></script>
<script type="text/javascript" src="dwr/interface/MailSender.js"></script>
<script type="text/javascript" src="dwr/interface/MailDeleter.js"></script>
<script type="text/javascript" src="dwr/engine.js"></script>
<script type="text/javascript" src="dwr/util.js"></script>
```

Notice that the path for each of these contains the /dwr/ portion. That means that these will be served by the DWR servlet. Pause and think about that for a moment, because it is really pretty neat… DWR is serving JavaScript! You see, DWR, using the information provided in dwr.xml, generates some JavaScript code on the fly by using reflection to examine the classes we want to remote. Notice that the name of the requested JavaScript file in each line matches the name of one of the classes in dwr.xml. This is quite deliberate. The code that the servlet serves, and which we import into our page, is what allows us to call on methods of an object on the server as if it was on the client. Very cool!

I also want to mention that all the DWR documentation seems to show these imports with the context in the src URL, /instamail/dwr/interface/OptionsManager.js, for instance. This is not necessary, and it is in fact better I think to leave them relative, as shown here, so that changing the context name will not cause the application to break.

Immediately following those imports is a <script> block that contains a single function, init(), as shown here:

```
<script>

  // Initialize the application.  This has to be here as opposed to
  // script.js because there is some JSP scriptlet here that has to execute,
  // and that wouldn't have happened if it was in an external JS file.
  function init() {
    // There was a strange problem with Firefox... in some cases, no matter
    // what I did, the textboxes would still have values when I reloaded
    // the app. I never did figure out why this was, so all the textboxes
    // in the app are cleared here, which deals with the issue.  Same thing
    // for enabling text fields.  If anyone figures out why this happens,
    // I'd love to hear it!  Until then, I chalk it up as a Firefox quirk.
    setValue("contactNameEntry", "");
    setValue("contactAddressEntry", "");
    setValue("contactNoteEntry", "");
```

```
setValue("pop3ServerEntry", "");
setChecked("pop3ServerRequiresLoginEntry", null);
setValue("pop3UsernameEntry", "");
setValue("pop3PasswordEntry", "");
setValue("smtpServerEntry", "");
setChecked("smtpServerRequiresLoginEntry", null);
setValue("smtpUsernameEntry", "");
setValue("smtpPasswordEntry", "");
setValue("fromAddressEntry", "");
setValue("composeToEntry", "");
setValue("composeSubjectEntry", "");
setValue("composeTextEntry", "");
setDisabled("contactNameEntry", false);
setDisabled("contactAddressEntry", false);
setDisabled("contactNoteEntry", false);
setDisabled("pop3ServerEntry", false);
setDisabled("pop3ServerRequiresLoginEntry", false);
setDisabled("pop3UsernameEntry", false);
setDisabled("pop3PasswordEntry", false);
setDisabled("smtpServerEntry", false);
setDisabled("smtpServerRequiresLoginEntry", false);
setDisabled("smtpUsernameEntry", false);
setDisabled("smtpPasswordEntry", false);
setDisabled("fromAddressEntry", false);
setDisabled("composeToEntry", false);
setDisabled("composeSubjectEntry", false);
setDisabled("composeTextEntry", false);
// Start out on the Intro view.
currentView = "divIntro";
showView(currentView);
<%
  OptionsDTO options = new OptionsManager().retrieveOptions(
    pageContext.getServletContext());
    // The application has not yet been configured, so we want to
    if (options.isConfigured()) {
%>
      // The buttons start out not showing, to avoid JavaScript errors
      // if you hover over them before the page fully loads, but now
      // we can show them.
      setClassName("topButtons", "divShowing");
      setClassName("sideButtons", "divShowing");
      appConfigured = true;
<%
    } else {
%>
```

```
            // The application has not yet been configured.  In this case,
            // the buttons ARE NOT shown, and instead we show the normally
            // hidden "Getting Started" div.
            setClassName("divGettingStarted", "divShowing");
            appConfigured = false;
      <%
          }
      %>
    }

  </script>
```

As its name and comments imply, this function is called when the page loads to initialize InstaMail. In a bit we'll look at `script.js`, which contains the balance of the client-side code for InstaMail. I mention that because you may wonder why this script is in `index.jsp` as opposed to `script.js` with everything else. The reason is the scriptlet section at the end. If this was in the `.js` file, the server would not interpret the scriptlet, and thus the functions it performs would not work. It has to be in the JSP so that the container interprets it while rendering the HTML from the JSP.

The calls to `setValue()`, `setChecked()`, and `setDisabled()`, functions we'll examine shortly, are present to get around an issue I was seeing in Firefox. Even when reloading the page, for some reason, Firefox would continue to maintain any entries in text boxes. To this day I do not know why this was happening, although it did not occur in IE. To get around the problem I simply clear out all the text boxes and checkboxes and such when the page loads. In some ways this is better anyway, and more typical: most applications tend to have an initialization routine at the start anyway, so this is adhering to that pattern anyway.

The current view is set to the Intro view after the fields have been cleared. Lastly, the scriptlet section is encountered. The purpose of this section is simply to see if the app has been configured yet—that is, if an e-mail account has been set up. If it has not been configured yet, then all the buttons are hidden and the `divGettingStarted` `<div>` is shown, which is just some verbiage telling you that you need to set up an account, and a link to the Options view, since that is the only thing the user should be able to do in this state. Once the application is configured, all the buttons are shown as normal and `divGettingStarted` is hidden. Because we determine if the app has been configured by getting an `OptionsDTO` object, which has a field `configured` that will be set to true or false accordingly, we need this to execute on the server. It actually could have been another Ajax call to the server, but I felt this was a much simpler and cleaner way to do it. The trend in recent years has been to move away from scriptlets in JSPs, and I generally agree with that trend. However, I do not take it to the extreme of suggesting it should never be done, and in a case like this I felt it was acceptable, and probably even more desirable because the alternative is something like a custom tag, which seems like overkill, or else an extra Ajax call as I mentioned. With the extra call, you have to make sure the UI is not accessible to the user for the duration of the call; otherwise they could be performing functions that really should be disabled, and which would be disabled as a result of the Ajax call. The KISS principle (Keep It Simple, Stupid!) is something I adhere to, and this seems like a good example of following that principle.

After that comes the markup for InstaMail in its entirety. Notice as you use the application that there are a number of "views," a.k.a. screens, that you can flip between. Notice too that as you do so, you are never retrieving the page from the server. From the start, all the various views of the application are in your browser. Each view is its own `<div>` on the page, and the appropriate `<div>` is shown at the appropriate time. There is the Intro `<div>`, the Inbox `<div>`, the Sent Messages `<div>`, the Message `<div>`, the Address Book `<div>`, the Options `<div>`, and the Compose `<div>`. Looking through the contents of `index.jsp`, you will literally see those `<div>`s. This seemingly simple structure yields a great deal of power and makes for a very well-performing application. Think about it: the server only returns data to us; all the markup is already in the client. This is very bandwidth efficient, and yields fewer delays in switching views for the user. Something like clicking the Compose button is instantaneous. Even a small delay here, as would be present in a typical webapp where the server would be called upon to serve that page, would be perceived by the user in a negative way. This approach completely avoids that problem.

One thing I would like you to notice as you look through the markup is how few times you see the `style` attribute used on elements. Except for a few exceptions, only `class` is used. This is by design. The presentation has been abstracted out into the stylesheet almost entirely (and truthfully it could have been abstracted out entirely). Doing this cleanly separates what your application looks like from its structure, as we have discussed before. Even this application, however, does not go as far as is possible in this regard, but it does go further than some of the other applications in this book do.

Aside from these few points, the markup is actually rather unremarkable. I therefore leave it to you to examine in your own time. I believe you will find that there is really very little going on. What you will see, though, is a lot of calls to JavaScript functions that exist in `script.js`, and that is therefore our next destination.

script.js

The first thing you will see is a batch of image preloads, all looking like this:

```
img_send = new Image();
img_send.src = "img/send.gif";
img_send_over = new Image();
img_send_over.src = "img/send_over.gif";
```

An image preload is nothing but some JavaScript that loads an image from the server into the browser's memory. This is usually done for image rollovers, that is, when an image changes when you move your mouse over it. The preload stops the browser from having to go out to the server when your mouse moves over the image to get the alternate version. If it did this, the user would perceive a delay, which is unpleasant. This example shows preloading the two versions of the Send button: how the button looks when you are not hovering over it, and how it looks when you are. There are around 11 such preloads in `script.js`.

Following that are three global variables, described in Table 5-2.

Table 5-2. *Global Variables in script.js*

Global Variable	Description
currentView	This stores the name of the current view, that is, the name of the <div> that is currently visible.
checkboxNumber	Later on in the code, we'll be dynamically populating a table, and next to each item in the table will be a checkbox. Each checkbox needs to have a unique ID associated with it, and to do this we simply attach a number onto the end of its name. This variable is used during that process. With the way the table creation is done using DWR, making this variable global seems to be the only way to persist its value across function calls, which is what we need to do to make this work.
appConfigured	This is set during initialization, and it is used later on when a determination about the app being configured or not is required in the JavaScript.

Next up we see two functions that handle our mouse events for our buttons on the top and side:

```
// onMouseOver handler for buttons.
function btnMouseOver(obj) {
  id = obj.id;
  obj.src = eval("img_" + id + "_over").src;
  obj.style.cursor = "pointer";
}


// onMouseOut handler for buttons.
function btnMouseOut(obj) {
  id = obj.id;
  obj.src = eval("img_" + id).src;
  obj.style.cursor = "";
}
```

This is pretty typical mouse rollover code. We get the ID of the object that called the method, one of the buttons, and then use the `eval()` function to get a reference to the appropriate preloaded image. We then set the `src` of the button to the `src` of the preloaded image, completing the rollover (or rollout, as it were). In addition, the `cursor` style attribute is changed so that we get a pointer when we hover over a button.

After that are two similar functions for dealing with rows in either the Inbox or Sent Messages tables:

```
// onMouseOver handler for rows in Inbox or Sent Messages.
function rowMouseOver() {
  this.parentNode.className = "rowHover";
}
```

```
// onMouseOut handler for rows in Inbox or Sent Messages.
function rowMouseOut() {
  this.parentNode.className = this.parentNode.rowClass;
}
```

You may be wondering about that `rowClass` attribute. There is no such attribute in HTML! It is in fact a custom attribute that is used to store the class of the row that a cell uses. In DOM scripting, you can add attributes at will to nodes, or to HTML tags, which of course are themselves DOM nodes. This comes in very handy when you need to store bits of metadata about a node, as is the case here.

Contrast the two, and you will see they are obviously a bit different. Part of that is that it *had* to be, and part of it is that I *wanted* it to be for the sake of seeing two approaches. First, why it had to be… as we'll see shortly, the Inbox and Sent Messages view contain a table listing messages that you can click on to view the message. The contents of these tables are generated dynamically. Part of that generation is attaching event handlers to the cells in the table. As a preview, look at this snippet:

```
td1 = document.createElement("td");
td1.onmouseover = rowmouseover;
```

The first line should be obvious: it is asking the document object to create a new `<td>` element for us. Note that this element does not immediately become part of the DOM. Instead, it is simply created and returned to the caller. The second line attaches an event handler to the `onMouseOver` event. Recall from our earlier discussions of JavaScript in Chapter 2 that a function is an object. What we are in effect doing here is setting the `onMouseOver` property of the new `<td>` element to the `rowMouseOver` object, which just so happened to be a function. Note the syntax, though: there is no parameter list given when doing this. The fact is that it is not possible to pass parameters to a handler when you set it on an object like this. Therefore, unlike the button handlers, we could not pass the `this` reference to it.

Fortunately for us, the `this` reference is intrinsic when you attach an object to another in this manner! Recall how prototyping works in JavaScript and this should make sense. The `onMouseOver` property is now an object reference, which for all intents and purposes becomes a part of the object it is attached to, the `<td>` in this case. So, within this function, this has meaning.

So that is why it had to be different. As for why I wanted it to be different, I wanted to show you that you do not have to change style attributes directly, as we did for the `cursor` attribute of the buttons. Instead, you can just change the class appropriately. If you look at the `rowHover` style selector, you will see that the `cursor` attribute is set to `pointer`, the same as was done manually for the buttons. This is another example of abstracting out the display properties of your views. With this approach, you do not have to touch the code but just the stylesheet. This is generally better because it is less error prone and requires less (or at least different) expertise. Theoretically, nonprogrammers can alter the stylesheets themselves, for instance. Think of graphic designers, the people who have the expertise to make it look good rather than make it function.

Next in `script.js` is a batch of setXXXX and getXXXX functions. The purpose of these functions is to provide us a shortcut to setting and getting various properties of elements on the page. Consider this line:

```
document.getElementById("myDiv").style.display = "block";
```

We have seen this sort of thing before, and it is certainly not anything scary at this point. However, consider the analogy that is possible because of these functions:

```
setDisplay("myDiv", "block");
```

If nothing else, that is about half the amount of typing! More important, though, it is less error prone and makes the code look quite a bit cleaner and perhaps easier to comprehend. Simply stated, that is the reason for the series of getters and setters you see in the utility functions section.

Following this are a few more utility functions. Most of them simply make calls to the set methods described earlier. For instance, `hideAllLayers()` is called to, well, hide all the `<div>`s for all the views. This is done when a new one is being shown. Instead of needing to hide the currently showing `<div>`, they are all hidden and then the new one shown. Kind of a lazy approach to it, but it is a bit more foolproof.

After that is `showPleaseWait()`, which is responsible for showing our float-over. This is called pretty much whenever the view changes, or when any operation is undertaken that might take a moment (like saving options or creating a new contact, for example). It begins by calling `hideAllLayers()`, then calling `enableButtons(false);`, which hides all the buttons on the top and bottom. It would cause problems if the user clicked one of the buttons while an Ajax request was being processed, and the easiest way to avoid that is simply to hide the buttons. Again, this is perhaps a bit of a lazy approach, but is at the same time more foolproof. Once those things are done, `divPleaseWait` is centered on the page, taking into account the current size of the window. The code that accomplishes that is interesting:

```
// First we center the layer.
pleaseWaitDIV = getElement("divPleaseWait");
if (window.innerWidth) {
  lca = window.innerWidth;
} else {
  lca = document.body.clientWidth;
}
lcb = pleaseWaitDIV.offsetWidth;
lcx = (Math.round(lca / 2)) - (Math.round(lcb / 2));
iebody = (document.compatMode &&
  document.compatMode != "BackCompat") ?
  document.documentElement : document.body;
dsocleft = document.all ? iebody.scrollLeft : window.pageXOffset;
pleaseWaitDIV.style.left = (lcx + dsocleft - 120) + "px";
if (window.innerHeight) {
  lca = window.innerHeight;
} else {
  lca = document.body.clientHeight;
}
lcb = pleaseWaitDIV.offsetHeight;
lcy = (Math.round(lca / 2)) - (Math.round(lcb / 2));
iebody = (document.compatMode &&
  document.compatMode != "BackCompat") ?
  document.documentElement : document.body;
```

```
  dsoctop = document.all ? iebody.scrollTop : window.pageYOffset;
  pleaseWaitDIV.style.top = (lcy + dsoctop - 40) + "px";
  // Now actually show it.
  pleaseWaitDIV.style.display = "block";
```

The thing that makes this a bit tricky is that the values we need to do the calculations involved differ between browsers. Specifically, `innerWidth` is used in IE, while `clientWidth` is used in other browsers, and likewise for `innerHeight` and `clientHeight`. There is also some complication within IE itself in getting a reference to the document body element. There is a difference in the way you gain access to it when you're in strict CSS mode and when you're not. The trinary logic line you see getting a reference to `iebody` is where that logic comes in. At the end of the day, though, this all boils down to a relatively simple formula: take the width of the `divPleaseWait` `<div>`, subtract it from the width of the window, and divide by 2. Do the same for the height, and the results are your new X and Y coordinates. There is also a need to use some "magic numbers" in the calculations because of various elements of chrome on the browser windows that sometimes are not taken into account. You can consider them a fudge factor, a necessary evil!

The `hidePleaseWait()` function is called when an operation completes, that is, when an Ajax request returns. It does as it says: it hides the `divPleaseWait` `<div>` and displays the buttons again.

The `showView()` function accepts the name of one of the view `<div>`s and shows it. Lastly, the `enableButtons()` function accepts a boolean value. When true, all the buttons on the top and bottom are shown. When false, they are hidden.

Next up, going linearly through `script.js`, are all the functions that perform our Ajax. I would like to skip them for now and finish off the non-Ajax functions that follow them. I believe this will help you understand what is going on in the Ajax code a little easier.

The first non-Ajax function after that section is the `editContact()` function, called when the user clicks one of the existing contacts in the address book to edit it:

```
// Called to edit/delete an existing contact.
function editContact() {
  setValue("contactNameEntry", this.parentNode.cells[0].innerHTML);
  setValue("contactAddressEntry", this.parentNode.cells[1].innerHTML);
  setValue("contactNoteEntry", this.parentNode.cells[2].innerHTML);
  setDisabled("contactNameEntry", true);
  setDisabled("contactAddressEntry", false);
  setDisabled("contactNoteEntry", false);
}
```

Here, and elsewhere, you may have noticed the `this.parentNode` call. This is included due to the structure of the table that is constructed to list messages for either the Inbox or the Sent Messages view. Recall that both views have a checkbox as the first item on the row. Originally, I had all the `mouseOvers` and `onClick` events on the row, because that is where the information on the message is stored. Besides that, we really are interested in the row, not the individual cells. The problem I encountered, however, is that if you click one of the checkboxes in that setup, it fires the `onClick` event of the row! This is certainly not what we want. The way I chose to avoid this is to put the `mouseOvers` and `onClicks` on the individual cells, except for the one containing the checkbox. That is why if you hover over a row, notice that when you hover over the checkbox, the row does not highlight. This is perfectly OK and gets around this problem.

However, now when a cell is clicked, the information for the message is needed, and that exists on the row level, not the cell level. Therefore, we take the `this` reference, which is to the cell, and get a reference to its parent node, which is the row. We can then go ahead and access the information we need. In this function, we are setting the values of the edit boxes to the values for the contact the user clicks (the Address Book view has the same sort of table display, a master-detail view, as it is typically called). Again, we face the same problem. The element that generates the `onClick` event is a cell, but we need data on the row; hence we again need to go after the parent node of the cell. In this case, we then need to get the `innerHTML` values of the three cells in the row, which we do by way of an array reference to the array of cells that the parent `<tr>` element has.

Notice too that the contact name is not editable, and we therefore need to disable it. The contact name is, in a sense, the unique key, if this were a database table. Therefore, we do not want the user to be able to change that key, and hence the field is not editable.

Next up is `gotoComposeMessage()`. The only complication here is that if we are on the Address Book view, we assume that the user has selected a contact and wants to compose a message to them. In that case, we grab the e-mail address and populate the address field on the Compose view. Note that the showing and hiding of the Please Wait `<div>` is pretty much superfluous since the view switch is basically instantaneous. I only do it for the sake of consistency, since anywhere else the view changes, the Please Wait `<div>` is shown.

`gotoComposeReply()` comes next, and it is very much the same as `gotoComposeMessage()`. However, since the reply button only has meaning on the Message view, we need to check for that and abort if the user is seeing another view. Beyond that, like `gotoComposeMessage()`, we are prefilling the fields on the Compose view, namely the address of the sender of the message, the subject with "RE:" appended to the front, and the message itself is quoted below a divider line demarcating it from our reply.

The next function we see is `newContact()`. It is almost the same as `editContact()`, except that we are setting the entry fields to blanks, and of course making sure all three edit boxes are now enabled. Otherwise, it is much the same thing.

The last non-Ajax function we encounter is `gotoHelp()`. This is what gets called when the user clicks the help link on the bottom of the page. It is about as simple a help system as one could imagine: based on the current view, it pops a JavaScript `alert()` box with some text describing the current view. Perhaps not the fanciest way to provide online help, but it certainly gets the job done!

Now we'll start to look at the Ajax functions using DWR, which is where all the truly interesting stuff happens. First up is `gotoInbox()`, and its companion function, `replyGetInboxContents()`. You will see this function/companion function dichotomy repeat itself a number of times going forward. You will quickly understand why. Listing 5-3 shows this code in its entirety.

Listing 5-3. *The gotoInbox() Function and Its Companion, replyGetInboxContents()*

```
// Called when the Inbox link is clicked, shows divInbox.
function gotoInbox() {
  showPleaseWait();
  MailRetriever.getInboxContents(replyGetInboxContents);
}
// Our callback.
var replyGetInboxContents = function(data) {
```

```
  DWRUtil.removeAllRows("inboxTBody");
  checkboxNumber = 0;
  var  altRow = true;
  var getFrom = function(data) { return data.from; };
  var getReceived = function(data) { return data.received; };
  var getSubject = function(data) { return data.subject; };
  var getCheckbox = function(data) {
    var cb = document.createElement("input");
    cb.type = "checkbox";
    cb.id = "cb_received_" + checkboxNumber;
    cb.msgID = data.msgID;
    checkboxNumber++;
    return cb;
  };
  var count = 0;
  DWRUtil.addRows("inboxTBody", data,
    [ getCheckbox, getFrom, getReceived, getSubject ], {
    rowCreator:function(options) {
      count++;
      var row = document.createElement("tr");
      if (altRow) {
        row.rowClass = "msgListRow1";
        row.className = "msgListRow1";
         altRow = false;
      } else {
        row.rowClass = "msgListRow2";
        row.className = "msgListRow2";
         altRow = true;
      }
      row.msgType = data[options.rowIndex].msgType;
      row.msgID = data[options.rowIndex].msgID;
      return row;
    },
    cellCreator:function(options) {
      var cell = document.createElement("td");
      if (options.cellNum != 0) {
        cell.onclick = gotoViewMessage;
        cell.onmouseover = rowMouseOver;
        cell.onmouseout = rowMouseOut;
      }
      return cell;
    }
  });
  setInnerHTML("inboxCount", count + " total messages");
  currentView = "divInbox";
  showView(currentView);
  hidePleaseWait();
}
```

This function is called, as you might expect, when the Inbox button is clicked. From this point on you will notice that all of the Ajax functions have a similar pattern, that is, there is one function that is called in response to some event (usually user-initiated), and then an associated function. The associated function is akin to the Ajax callback function you attach to an `XMLHttpRequest` object. DWR hides all the details of Ajax from you, but it still is the same underlying principle.

In this case, we simply show the Please Wait float-over, and then this statement is executed:

```
MailRetriever.getInboxContents(replyGetInboxContents);
```

As previously discussed, DWR generates a JavaScript file for each object you want to remote. This JavaScript contains essentially "stub" objects that you call on, and DWR behind the scenes makes the remote call to the server-side object. This gives you the illusion of directly calling remote objects. That is precisely what this line is doing. It is calling the `getInboxContents()` method of the `MailRetriever` object, or more precisely, of a new `MailRetriever` object because a new object is created as a result of each call, so there is not just one object to call. The only parameter we pass in this case is the JavaScript callback function that will handle the return from the method call. This parameter is always present in all our Ajax code, and is always the last parameter.

When the call returns, the `replyGetInboxContents()` function is called. Notice the somewhat unusual way the function is defined: it is assigned to a variable! This gives us an easy way to refer to the function. You can in fact have the callback function inline in the method call, that is, something along the lines of

```
MailRetriever.getInboxContents(function replyGetInboxContents(str){alert(str);});
```

Most people, myself included, think that is just simply harder to read, and thus I try and avoid that where possible. The other problem is that should you want to share the callback with another Ajax call, you will not be able to do it if inlined because it is essentially an anonymous function.

Once we get into the callback function, the first thing we see is

```
DWRUtil.removeAllRows("inboxTBody");
```

`DWRUtil` is an object that DWR provides that is completely optional; it is not required for DWR to work. However, it provides some very handy functions, one of which is this `removeAllRows()` function. Its purpose is to remove all the rows from a given table (`<tbody>` more precisely). This is what we need to do here. When the Inbox is refreshed, we need to start with an empty table, and then create a row for each e-mail in the Inbox. This single line accomplishes that first part, clearing the table.

After that comes the following chunk of code:

```
checkboxNumber = 0;
var  altRow = true;
var getFrom = function(data) { return data.from; };
var getReceived = function(data) { return data.received; };
var getSubject = function(data) { return data.subject; };
```

```
var getCheckbox = function(data) {
  var cb = document.createElement("input");
  cb.type = "checkbox";
  cb.id = "cb_received_" + checkboxNumber;
  cb.msgID = data.msgID;
  checkboxNumber++;
  return cb;
};
var count = 0;
```

Recall our discussion of the checkboxNumber variable previously. This is used to append a number to the ID of each delete checkbox we'll create, so that they all have a unique ID. Numbering starts at 0, hence this line. The variable altRow is a simple boolean toggle flag that we'll use to set the appropriate class for each row in the table so that we get the alternating-band effect we want.

The next four functions are functions that are required by DWR, as we'll see shortly. Each one is analogous to an accessor (or getter) method on a JavaBean. In this case, DWR will call these functions and pass it an object referenced by the parameter data. The functions will access some property of that data, just like it was a JavaBean, and return it. Each of these functions corresponds to a cell in the table. This will become clear in a moment! The last function, the getCheckbox() function, will be called by DWR to create the delete checkbox for each row. Notice the use of the checkboxNumber variable. Also notice that the only parameter to this function is the data variable, which is created by DWR. It should now make sense why checkboxNumber has to be global: there is no other way to get it to this function! Since its value has to persist between invocations of this function, the variable has to exist outside the function.

After this comes a call to another very useful function from the DWRUtil object:

```
DWRUtil.addRows("inboxTBody", data,
  [ getCheckbox, getFrom, getReceived, getSubject ], {
  rowCreator:function(options) {
    count++;
    var row = document.createElement("tr");
    if (altRow) {
      row.rowClass = "msgListRow1";
      row.className = "msgListRow1";
      altRow = false;
    } else {
      row.rowClass = "msgListRow2";
      row.className = "msgListRow2";
      altRow = true;
    }
    row.msgType = data[options.rowIndex].msgType;
    row.msgID = data[options.rowIndex].msgID;
    return row;
  },
```

```
    cellCreator:function(options) {
      var cell = document.createElement("td");
      if (options.cellNum != 0) {
        cell.onclick = gotoViewMessage;
        cell.onmouseover = rowMouseOver;
        cell.onmouseout = rowMouseOut;
      }
      return cell;
    }
  });
```

addRows() is another table modification function, this one focused on creating rows. Its first argument is the ID of a <tbody> element to populate. The second argument is the data object passed to the callback, which is the return from the method call on the server-side object. In this case, as is logical for a table, it is a collection, where each element corresponds to a row. After that comes an array of function calls, and they should look very familiar to you! As I mentioned, each one corresponds to a cell in the table. So, here's what DWR is going to do:

1. Iterate over the data collection. For each element, create a <tr>.
2. Iterate over the collection of functions named. For each, create a <td>, call the function, and populate the <td> with the return from the function.
3. Add the <td> to the <tr>.
4. Add the <tr> to the table.
5. Continue this process until the data collection is exhausted.

The other parameter to the addRows() function is optional and is an array of functions that DWR will use to create each <tr> and <td>. The default implementations simply create a plain <tr> and <td> and return it, but the designers of DWR wisely recognized that many times you will need to do more than that, so they allow you to provide custom functions for creating these elements. In this case, I broke my own rule and made them anonymous inline functions. I did this more to demonstrate what that looks like, but since they are not going to be shared it is not such a bad thing. Still, I think you will agree that the syntax is a little funky perhaps?

Be that as it may, the first inline function deals with creating a row. We have a couple of considerations to take into account. First, we need to count how many rows there are, which remember, correspond to e-mails, so that we can display how many e-mails are in the Inbox for the user. So, with each invocation we increment the variable count. Second, we need to set the appropriate class for the row to get the banding effect we want. This is done by looking at whether altRow is true or false, and setting a different class accordingly, and of course flipping the value of altRow. Third, we need to attach some custom attributes to the <tr> that will allow us to identify the e-mail. In this case that means setting msgType to the msgType the server returns (which will always be "received" in the Inbox) and the msgID returned by the server (which is just the number of the message in the Inbox). Notice the array notation used to get that information. DWR passes us an options object, which includes the data object originally passed in to the callback. There does not seem to be a way to directly access the current row, that is, there does not appear to be something like options.currentRow available. However, we do have access to the index into the data array that is currently being rendered. In other words, we can tell what row we are working on. So, with that, we can use array notation against the data variable to get the information we need.

The second inline function deals with creating a cell. Recall previously I described the problem with putting event handlers on the row when the user clicks the delete checkbox. I mentioned that the handlers instead had to be attached to the cells. This is where that is done. The function first checks if this is the first cell being added, and if it is, then it is the cell with the checkbox, so no event handlers are attached. If it is any other cell, the `onClick`, `onMouseOver`, and `onMouseOut` events are hooked. That is all this function does.

Lastly, in our `gotoInbox()` function we find

```
setInnerHTML("inboxCount", count + " total messages");
currentView = "divInbox";
showView(currentView);
hidePleaseWait();
```

The first line uses one of our convenience functions to display for the user how many e-mails are in the Inbox, again using that `count` variable we saw before. The second line sets the view to the Inbox, which it may or may not have been already. The third line actually shows the view, and finally we hide the Please Wait float-over, and the function is done.

DWR, in addition to making Ajax and RPC very easy, also makes table manipulation very easy! Since this is a very common thing to do with Ajax, it is a very nice feature indeed.

Next up is the `gotoSentMessage()` function. This is called when the Sent Messages button is clicked. I am going to refrain from going over it because it is virtually identical to the `gotoInbox()` function we just looked at. The only real difference is that sent messages are identified by their filename as opposed to their `msgIDs`, as messages in the Inbox are. Aside from that, it is almost identical code. Do review it, though, to convince yourself of that, and to reinforce how DWR is used.

After that comes this function:

```
// Called when a message is clicked while divInbox or divSentMessages is
// showing, shows divMessage.
function gotoViewMessage() {
  var _msgID = null;
  var _msgType = null;
  var _filename = null;
  showPleaseWait();
  if (currentView == "divInbox") {
    _msgID = this.parentNode.msgID;
    _filename = null;
  }
  if (currentView == "divSentMessages") {
    _filename  = this.parentNode.filename;
    _msgID = null;
  }
  _msgType = this.parentNode.msgType;
  MailRetriever.retrieveMessage(_msgType, _filename, _msgID, replyRetrieveMessage);
}
```

```
// Our callback.
var replyRetrieveMessage = function(data) {
  setInnerHTML("msgSubject", data.subject);
  setInnerHTML("msgText", data.msgText);
  setInnerHTML("msgType", data.msgType);
  if (data.msgType == "received") {
    setInnerHTML("msgID", data.msgID);
    setInnerHTML("msgFromToLabel", "From: ");
    setInnerHTML("msgFromTo", data.from);
    setInnerHTML("viewTitle", "Received Message");
    setInnerHTML("msgSentReceivedLabel", "Received: ");
    setInnerHTML("msgSentReceived", data.received);
  }
  if (data.msgType == "sent") {
    setInnerHTML("msgFilename", data.filename);
    setInnerHTML("msgFromToLabel", "To: ");
    setInnerHTML("msgFromTo", data.to);
    setInnerHTML("viewTitle", "Sent Message");
    setInnerHTML("msgSentReceivedLabel", "Sent: ");
    setInnerHTML("msgSentReceived", data.sent);
  }
  currentView = "divMessage";
  showView(currentView);
  hidePleaseWait();
}
```

Review either the `gotoInbox()` or `gotoSentMessages()` function and you will see that the `gotoViewMessage()` function is in fact the `onClick` handler set for each cell. This function has a relatively simple job: get the details we need to identify an e-mail, which means the message type ("sent" or "received") and either the `msgID` or `filename`, whichever is appropriate. We have discussed why the cells have to be the trigger of the event, and we also discussed the use of the `parentNode` property to get at the information we need, and that is all that is going on here. Once the information is retrieved, a call is made to the `retrieveMethod()` method of the `MailRetriever` object on the server.

The callback takes the information retrieved from the server about the message and populates various fields on the screen, then shows the message view. Based on whether this is a sent message or a received message (remember, this function services both the Inbox view and the Sent Messages view), not only does the information have to be displayed but we need to update various labels on the screen as well. This callback is really quite straightforward.

The `doDelete()` function is next, called when the Delete button is clicked. The first thing it does is check the value of the `currentView` variable, and if it is not the message view, the Inbox view or the Sent Messages view, it tells the user it doesn't apply.

When the view is the message view, it is a fairly straightforward operation. All `doDelete()` has to do is grab the `msgType`, `filename`, and `msgID` values from the `<div>`s that data is in. Only the `filename` or the `msgID` is important, not both (i.e., when viewing the Inbox, the `msgID` applies; when viewing Sent Messages then `filename` applies), but it does no harm to send both since the server-side code looks at `msgType` and only cares about one or the other based on that. Once that is done, `deleteMessages()` of the `MailDeleter` object is called. The response handler simply looks at the current view and refreshes it. That means calling gotoInbox() if viewing the Inbox, which results in a new Ajax request, or gotoSentMessage() if viewing the Sent Messages (again resulting in another Ajax request). If the current view was the message view, it examines the value of the title on the page to determine if a received messages or a sent message was being viewed, and then calls gotoInbox() or gotoSentMessages() as appropriate.

Oops, I got ahead of things a bit there! What happens if the current view is the Inbox? In that case, we are dealing with the possibility of the user having checked off a number of e-mails to delete. The deleteMessages() method of the MailDeleter class actually accepts a comma-separated list of values, either filenames or msgIDs, depending on the view. When the view was the individual message view, there was just a single value. This is still a valid comma-separated list, of course; it just happens to have only a single value. For the other two views, though, we have to construct a list of all the checked items. To do so, we use this code:

```
var i = 0;
var obj = null;
var i = 0;
// Construct a CSV of MsgIDs for Inbox messages.
if (currentView == "divInbox") {
  msgType = "received";
  filenames = null;
  obj = getElement("cb_received_" + i);
  while (obj != null) {
    if (obj.checked) {
      if (msgIDs != "") {
        msgIDs += ",";
      }
      msgIDs += obj.msgID;
    }
    i++;
    obj = getElement("cb_received_" + i);
  }
}
```

Recall when we populated the table, we gave each checkbox a unique ID that ended with a number. Now you can see why: it facilitates us easily cycling through all the checkboxes looking for those that are checked. Of course, we do not know how many messages there are, and thus how many checkboxes there are (true, we could examine the value of the <div> where the message count is displayed, but that seems like a bit of a hack to me). So, we get an object reference to the first checkbox. Assuming we do not get null back, indicating the checkbox doesn't exist (there are no messages in this view), then we see if it is checked and add it to our CSV if so. We then try and get the next checkbox, and so on, building up our CSV string. Once we are done, the same process as for a single message occurs in terms of sending the request and refreshing the correct view when the call returns.

We now come to the sendMessage() function. This is relatively simple. First, we perform a check to be sure the user entered an e-mail address to send to, a subject and some text, and if not we tell the user we cannot yet send the message. Assuming they have entered all three, the sendMessage() method of the MailSender class is called. Notice the call in this case contains parameters:

```
  MailSender.sendMessage(composeTo, composeSubject, composeText,
    replySendMessage);
```

The last argument is still the callback function, but anything preceding that is taken by DWR to be arguments to the target method.

The response handler clears out the entry boxes and shows the Send Messages view. Sending a message could not be easier!

After that is the gotoAddressBook() function. This, like gotoSentMessages(), is very similar to gotoInbox() that we have examined, so please have a look; it will be very familiar! The only real difference is that because we do not have delete checkboxes in this view, there is no check when creating a cell to see which cell number we are creating. In fact, because there are no checkboxes I could have put the event handlers on the row this time. I did not do so just for the sake of consistency with the other functions.

saveContact() comes next, and there really is not much to it:

```
// Called to save a contact.
function saveContact() {
  contactName = getValue("contactNameEntry");
  contactAddress = getValue("contactAddressEntry");
  contactNote = getValue("contactNoteEntry");
  if (contactName == "" || contactAddress == "") {
    alert("Please enter both a name and address");
    hidePleaseWait();
    return false;
  }
  showPleaseWait();
  AddressBookManager.saveContact(contactName, contactAddress, contactNote,
    replySaveContact);
}
// Our callback.
var replySaveContact = function(data) {
  newContact();
  alert(data);
  hidePleaseWait();
  gotoAddressBook();
}
```

We once again have the typical two cooperative functions. A quick check to be sure the user entered all the required information, and then it is just a matter of an Ajax call to the AddressBookManager's saveContact() method, passing the appropriate arguments along. The server will respond with a success or failure message, so all the response handler has to do is display what was returned. This is akin to doing a System.out.println on the return from a method on the server, since saveContact() returns a plain old string. One problem I encountered is that there is sometimes a slight delay before the address book file is actually written to disk. Because of this, the returned message informs the user that they may have to click the Address Book link to see the new contact.

To go along with saveContact() is deleteContact():

```
// Called to delete a contact.
function deleteContact() {
  contactName = getValue("contactNameEntry");
  if (contactName == "") {
    alert("Please select a contact to delete");
    hidePleaseWait();
    return false;
  }
  showPleaseWait();
  AddressBookManager.deleteContact(contactName, replyDeleteContact);
}
// Our callback.
var replyDeleteContact = function(data) {
  newContact();
  alert(data);
  hidePleaseWait();
  gotoAddressBook();
}
```

Very much like saveContact(), deleteContact() checks for the required information, then makes an Ajax call to perform the delete. The response handler again simply displays the returned string and shows the address book again.

We are almost done exploring the client-side code—just two functions left (well, really four, but I have been counting the pairs as one in essence). Next we have gotoOptions(), called when the Options button is clicked:

```
// Called when the Options link is clicked, shows divOptions.
function gotoOptions() {
  showPleaseWait();
  OptionsManager.retrieveOptions(replyRetrieveOptions);
}
// Our callback.
var replyRetrieveOptions = function(data) {
  setValue("pop3ServerEntry", data.pop3Server);
  if (data.pop3ServerRequiresLogin == "true") {
    setChecked("pop3ServerRequiresLoginEntry", "true");
  } else {
    setChecked("pop3ServerRequiresLoginEntry", null);
  }
  setValue("pop3UsernameEntry", data.pop3Username);
  setValue("pop3PasswordEntry", data.pop3Password);
  setValue("smtpServerEntry", data.smtpServer);
  if (data.smtpServerRequiresLogin == "true") {
    setChecked("smtpServerRequiresLoginEntry", "true");
  } else {
    setChecked("smtpServerRequiresLoginEntry", null);
  }
```

```
  setValue("smtpUsernameEntry", data.smtpUsername);
  setValue("smtpPasswordEntry", data.smtpPassword);
  setValue("fromAddressEntry", data.fromAddress);
  currentView = "divOptions";
  showView(currentView);
  hidePleaseWait();
}
```

There really is not much to this. A call is made to the server, which returns the options, and the response handler then populates the fields of the Options view with the data.

One thing I would like to bring to your attention is that the call to `retrieveOptions()` returns an `OptionsDTO`, as we'll see when we look at the server-side code. Recall the `dwr.xml` configuration file, in which we allowed DWR to convert the `OptionsDTO`. DWR is able to essentially take that bean and convert it to a JavaScript object. Well, in fairness, I have not examined the DWR code in any great detail so I do not know if it is literally doing this. My suspicion is that DWR is reflectively grabbing all the field values from the `OptionsDTO` and adding it to the object that the data variable references. What is important, however, is that DWR is giving us the *illusion* of having that `OptionsDTO` on the client and allowing us to access its fields via the `data` variable. This is pretty cool! The cleanliness of the previous code in terms of actually accessing the options definitely is.

And now finally, we reach the final client-side code, and I am sure you can guess what it is: yep, it is `saveOptions()`!

```
// Called when the Save button is clicked when divOptions is showing.
function saveOptions() {
  pop3Server = getValue("pop3ServerEntry");
  pop3ServerRequiresLogin = getChecked("pop3ServerRequiresLoginEntry");
  pop3Username = getValue("pop3UsernameEntry");
  pop3Password = getValue("pop3PasswordEntry");
  smtpServer = getValue("smtpServerEntry");
  smtpServerRequiresLogin = getChecked("smtpServerRequiresLoginEntry");
  smtpUsername = getValue("smtpUsernameEntry");
  smtpPassword = getValue("smtpPasswordEntry");
  fromAddress = getValue("fromAddressEntry");
  if (pop3Server == "") {
    alert("You must enter a POP3 server address");
    hidePleaseWait();
    return false;
  }
  if (pop3ServerRequiresLogin == true &&
    (pop3Username == "" || pop3Password == "")) {
    alert("If the POP3 server requires login, then you must enter " +
      "both a POP3 username and password");
    hidePleaseWait();
    return false;
  }
```

```
  if (smtpServer == "") {
    alert("You must enter an SMTP server address");
    hidePleaseWait();
    return false;
  }
  if (smtpServerRequiresLogin == true &&
    (smtpUsername == "" || smtpPassword == "")) {
    alert("If the SMTP server requires login, then you must enter " +
      "both an SMTP username and password");
    hidePleaseWait();
    return false;
  }
  if (fromAddress == "") {
    alert("You must enter a from address");
    hidePleaseWait();
    return false;
  }
  showPleaseWait();
  OptionsManager.saveOptions(pop3Server, pop3ServerRequiresLogin,
    pop3Username, pop3Password, smtpServer, smtpServerRequiresLogin,
    smtpUsername, smtpPassword, fromAddress, replySaveOptions);
}
// Our callback.
var replySaveOptions = function(data) {
  alert(data);
  appConfigured = true;
  setClassName("divGettingStarted", "divHidden");
  showView(currentView);
  hidePleaseWait();
}
```

First, the options that the user entered are grabbed. Next, a series of validations are performed to be sure they entered all required information. Once that is done, the Ajax call is made to `saveOptions()` on the `OptionsManager` class, and all the options that were entered are passed along. The callback has only to display the result, again a simple string, and reshow the Options view.

The Server-Side Code

We are now ready to move on to the server-side code, which is encapsulated in a total of eight classes. Three of them are simple DTOs, nothing but data fields and their getter and setter methods. I will leave them to you to examine, but there is virtually no code to look at, save for the overridden `toString()` method.

OptionsManager.java

The first class to look at is the `OptionsManager` class, shown in Listing 5-4.

Listing 5-4. *The OptionsManager Class*

```
package com.apress.ajaxprojects.instamail;


import java.io.File;
import java.io.FileOutputStream;
import java.io.InputStream;
import java.io.IOException;
import java.util.Properties;
import javax.servlet.ServletContext;
import org.apache.commons.logging.Log;
import org.apache.commons.logging.LogFactory;


/**
 * This class deals with maintaining options, including the e-mail account.
 *
 * @author <a href="mailto:fzammetti@omnytex.com">Frank W. Zammetti</a>.
 */
public class OptionsManager {


  /**
   * Log instance.
   */
  private static Log log = LogFactory.getLog(OptionsManager.class);


  /**
   * Filename of the options file.
   */
  private static final String optionsFilename = "options.properties";


  /**
   * This method retrieves the options and returns them.  If no
   * optionsFilename file is found, a 'blank' DTO is returned.
   *
   * @param  sc ServletContext associates with the request.
   * @return    An OptionsDTO containing all the stored options.
   */
  public OptionsDTO retrieveOptions(ServletContext sc) {

    // Instantiate an OptionsDTO, and by default assume it will be configured.
    // This means the application has already been configured for use.  This
    // affects what the user can do when the app is accessed initially.
```

```
OptionsDTO options = new OptionsDTO();
options.setConfigured(true);

// Read in the options.
InputStream isFeedFile =
  sc.getResourceAsStream("/WEB-INF/" + optionsFilename);
Properties props = new Properties();
try {
  if (isFeedFile == null) {
    throw new IOException(optionsFilename + " not found");
  }
  props.load(isFeedFile);
  isFeedFile.close();
} catch (IOException e) {
  log.info("No " + optionsFilename + " file, a blank DTO will " +
    "be returned.");
  // Make sure the OptionsDTO is set as unconfigured so that when the
  // index.jsp page is loaded, all the user will be allowed to do is go to
  // the Options views.
  options.setConfigured(false);
  props.setProperty("pop3Server", "");
  props.setProperty("pop3ServerRequiresLogin", "false");
  props.setProperty("pop3Username", "");
  props.setProperty("pop3Password", "");
  props.setProperty("smtpServer", "");
  props.setProperty("smtpServerRequiresLogin", "false");
  props.setProperty("smtpUsername", "");
  props.setProperty("smtpPassword", "");
  props.setProperty("fromAddress", "");
}

// Populate OptionsDTO from options Properties.
options.setPop3Server(props.getProperty("pop3Server"));
options.setPop3ServerRequiresLogin(
  props.getProperty("pop3ServerRequiresLogin"));
options.setPop3Username(props.getProperty("pop3Username"));
options.setPop3Password(props.getProperty("pop3Password"));
options.setSmtpServer(props.getProperty("smtpServer"));
options.setSmtpServerRequiresLogin(
  props.getProperty("smtpServerRequiresLogin"));
options.setSmtpUsername(props.getProperty("smtpUsername"));
options.setSmtpPassword(props.getProperty("smtpPassword"));
options.setFromAddress(props.getProperty("fromAddress"));

return options;
```

```
} // End retrieveOptions().


/**
 * This method saves the options.
 *
 * @param  pop3Server               The POP3 server address.
 * @param  pop3ServerRequiresLogin Does the POP3 server require login?
 * @param  pop3Username             The POP3 username.
 * @param  pop3Password             The POP3 password.
 * @param  smtpServer               The SMTP server address.
 * @param  smtpServerRequiresLogin Does the SMTP server require login?
 * @param  smtpUsername             The SMTP username.
 * @param  smtpPassword             The SMTP password.
 * @param  fromAddress              From address for outgoing messages.
 * @param  sc                       ServletContext associated with the request.
 * @return                          A message saying the save was OK.
 */
public String saveOptions(String pop3Server, String pop3ServerRequiresLogin,
  String pop3Username, String pop3Password, String smtpServer,
  String smtpServerRequiresLogin, String smtpUsername,
  String smtpPassword, String fromAddress, ServletContext sc) {

    // Log what we received.
    log.info("\nSaving options:\n" +
    "pop3Server = " + pop3Server + "\n" +
      "pop3ServerRequiresLogin = " + pop3ServerRequiresLogin + "\n" +
      "pop3Username = " + pop3Username + "\n" +
      "pop3Password = " + pop3Password + "\n" +
      "smtpServer = " + smtpServer + "\n" +
      "smtpServerRequiresLogin = " + smtpServerRequiresLogin + "\n" +
      "smtpUsername = " + smtpUsername + "\n" +
      "smtpPassword = " + smtpPassword + "\n" +
      "fromAddress = " + fromAddress + "\n");

    String result = "";

    // Populate Properties structure.
    Properties props = new Properties();
    props.setProperty("pop3Server", pop3Server);
    props.setProperty("pop3ServerRequiresLogin",
      pop3ServerRequiresLogin);
    props.setProperty("pop3Username", pop3Username);
    props.setProperty("pop3Password", pop3Password);
    props.setProperty("smtpServer", smtpServer);
    props.setProperty("smtpServerRequiresLogin",
      smtpServerRequiresLogin);
```

```
      props.setProperty("smtpUsername", smtpUsername);
      props.setProperty("smtpPassword", smtpPassword);
      props.setProperty("fromAddress",  fromAddress);

      // Lastly, delete any existing optionsFilename file in WEB-INF and
      // write out a new version from the Properties object we just populated.
      // Return a message saying the operation was complete, or if any problems
      // occur, a message saying what went wrong.
      FileOutputStream fos = null;
      try {
        new File(sc.getRealPath("WEB-INF") + "/" + optionsFilename).delete();
        fos = new FileOutputStream(sc.getRealPath("WEB-INF") +
          "/" + optionsFilename);
        props.store(fos, null);
        fos.flush();
        result = "Options have been saved.";
      } catch (IOException e) {
        log.error("Error saving contact:");
        e.printStackTrace();
        result = "Options could not be saved.  " +
          "Please review logs for details.";
      } finally {
        try {
          if (fos != null) {
            fos.close();
          }
        } catch (IOException e) {
          log.error("Error closing fos: " + e);
        }
      }

      return result;

  } // End saveOptions().


} // End class.
```

This class has two static members, a Commons Logging `Log` instance, and a `String` that stores the name of the file where options will be saved.

The first method we find is `retrieveOptions()`, which, as its name implies, reads the options file and returns an `OptionsDTO` instance populated with the options. If the options file is not found—which most likely means this is the first time the user has used InstaMail—we throw an `IOException`, which is immediately caught, and the `OptionsDTO` is blanked out and returned. You may ask why the exception is thrown and immediately caught. Simply put, it allows the code to blank out the DTO to be in one place and handle not only the known situation of the file not being present (which is not a trigger of an exception by itself) but also any unexpected exceptions that might occur. I usually do not like using exceptions for flow control, which is more or less what this is, because exceptions incur a relatively high amount of overhead within the JVM to instantiate and throw. In this case, though, I felt it was acceptable because this is not a situation that should arise more than once, and it makes for more concise code.

The options are stored in the form of a standard Java properties file, so we wind up with a populated `Properties` object if the file is actually present. The code then takes the values from that structure and transfers it to the `OptionsDTO` and returns it.

Going along with `retrieveOptions()` is `saveOptions()`. This is even easier! We simply grab the incoming request parameters, which are our options; populate a `Properties` object from it; and then write it out using pretty typical code for writing out a properties file. A string is returned that will be displayed to the user indicating success or failure. Not much to it.

AddressBookManager.java

Now we'll have a look at the `AddressBookManager` class, as seen in Listing 5-5.

Listing 5-5. *The AddressBookManager Class*

```
package com.apress.ajaxprojects.instamail;


import java.io.File;
import java.io.FileOutputStream;
import java.io.InputStream;
import java.io.IOException;
import java.util.ArrayList;
import java.util.Collection;
import java.util.Iterator;
import java.util.Properties;
import javax.servlet.ServletContext;
import org.apache.commons.logging.Log;
import org.apache.commons.logging.LogFactory;


/**
 * This class deals with maintaining the address book.
 *
 * @author <a href="mailto:fzammetti@omnytex.com">Frank W. Zammetti</a>.
 */
public class AddressBookManager {


  /**
   * Log instance.
   */
  private static Log log = LogFactory.getLog(AddressBookManager.class);
```

```
/**
 * Filename of the address book.
 */
private static final String addrBookFilename = "addrbook.properties";


/**
 * This method retrieves the contents of the Address Book.
 *
 * @param  sc ServletContext associates with the request.
 * @return    A collection of ContactDTOs.
 */
public Collection retrieveContacts(ServletContext sc) {

  // Read in the address book.
  InputStream isFeedFile =
    sc.getResourceAsStream("/WEB-INF/" + addrBookFilename);
  Properties props       = new Properties();
  int        numContacts = 0;
  try {
    if (isFeedFile == null) {
      throw new IOException(addrBookFilename + " not found");
    }
    props.load(isFeedFile);
    isFeedFile.close();
    // Now we need to determine how many contacts there are.  To do this, we
    // divide the total number of properties read in by 3, since each
    // contact always has 3 items stored about them.
    if (props.size() != 0) {
      numContacts = props.size() / 3;
    }
  } catch (IOException e) {
    log.info("No " + addrBookFilename + " file, an empty address book will " +
      "be returned.");
  }

  // Now we cycle through the properties the number of times we calculated
  // there are contacts.  For each we construct a ContactDTO and add it to
  // the collection to be returned.
  log.info("numContacts = " + numContacts);
  Collection contacts = new ArrayList();
  for (int i = 1; i < numContacts + 1; i++) {
    ContactDTO contact = new ContactDTO();
    contact.setName(props.getProperty("name" + i));
    contact.setAddress(props.getProperty("address" + i));
    contact.setNote(props.getProperty("note" + i));
    contacts.add(contact);
  }
```

```
    return contacts;

  } // End retrieveContacts().


  /**
   * This method adds a contact to the Address Book.
   *
   * @param  inName    The name of the contact.
   * @param  inAddress The e-mail address for the contact.
   * @param  inNote    Any arbitrary note about the contact.
   * @param  sc        ServletContext associates with the request.
   * @return           A message saying the save was OK.
   */
  public String saveContact(String inName, String inAddress,
    String inNote, ServletContext sc) {

      // Log what we received.
      log.info("\nAdding contact:\n" +
        "inName = " + inName + "\n" +
        "inAddress = " + inAddress + "\n" +
        "inNote = " + inNote + "\n");

      String result = "";

      // In order to save a contact, we essentially need to write out the
      // entire address book, so the first step is to read it in.
      Collection contacts = retrieveContacts(sc);

      // Now we iterate over it, adding each to a Properties object.  Remember
      // that for each contact we are writing out three properties, the name,
      // the address and the note.  To name each uniquely, we append a number
      // onto it.
      Properties props = new Properties();
      int i = 1;
      for (Iterator it = contacts.iterator(); it.hasNext();) {
        ContactDTO contact = (ContactDTO)it.next();
        props.setProperty("name"    + i, contact.getName());
        props.setProperty("address" + i, contact.getAddress());
        props.setProperty("note"    + i, contact.getNote());
        i++;
      }

      // Now we add the new contact
      props.setProperty("name"    + i, inName);
      props.setProperty("address" + i, inAddress);
      props.setProperty("note"    + i, inNote);
```

```
    // Lastly, delete any existing addrBookFilename file in WEB-INF and
    // write out a new version from the Properties object we just populated.
    // Return a message saying the operation was complete, or if any problems
    // occur, a message saying what went wrong.
    FileOutputStream fos = null;
    try {
      new File(sc.getRealPath("WEB-INF") + "/" + addrBookFilename).delete();
      fos = new FileOutputStream(sc.getRealPath("WEB-INF") +
        "/" + addrBookFilename);
      props.store(fos, null);
      fos.flush();
      fos.close();
      result = "Contact has been added.\n\nPlease note that if the contact " +
        "does not show up immediately, you may have to click the " +
        "Address Book link once or twice.";
    } catch (IOException e) {
      log.error("Error saving contact:");
      e.printStackTrace();
      result = "Contact could not be added.  Please review logs for details.";
    } finally {
      try {
        if (fos != null) {
          fos.close();
        }
      } catch (IOException e) {
        log.error("Error closing fos: " + e);
      }
    }

    return result;

} // End saveContact().


/**
 * This method deletes a contact from the Address Book.
 *
 * @param  inName The name of the contact to delete.
 * @param  sc     ServletContext associates with the request.
 * @return        A message saying the delete was OK.
 */
public String deleteContact(String inName, ServletContext sc) {

    log.info("\nDeleting contact:\n" + inName + "\n");

    String result = "";
```

```
// To delete a contact, we need to read in the address book and
// re-write it out MINUS the contact to be deleted.  So, first thing,
// let's read it in.
ArrayList contacts = (ArrayList)retrieveContacts(sc);

// Now, let's go through and find the one to delete and do it.
for (int i = 0; i < contacts.size(); i++) {
  ContactDTO contact = (ContactDTO)contacts.get(i);
  if (contact.getName().equalsIgnoreCase(inName)) {
    contacts.remove(i);
    break;
  }
}

// Lastly, we construct a Properties object containing what is left of
// the address book, and write it out.
Properties props = new Properties();
int i = 1;
for (Iterator it = contacts.iterator(); it.hasNext();) {
  ContactDTO contact = (ContactDTO)it.next();
  props.setProperty("name"    + i, contact.getName());
  props.setProperty("address" + i, contact.getAddress());
  props.setProperty("note"    + i, contact.getNote());
  i++;
}
FileOutputStream fos = null;
try {
  new File(sc.getRealPath("WEB-INF") + "/" + addrBookFilename).delete();
  fos = new FileOutputStream(sc.getRealPath("WEB-INF") +
    "/" + addrBookFilename);
  props.store(fos, null);
  fos.flush();
  result = "Contact has been deleted.\n\nPlease note that if the " +
    "contact does not go away immediately, you may have to click the " +
    "Address Book link once or twice.";
} catch (IOException e) {
  log.error("Error deleting contact:");
  e.printStackTrace();
  result = "Contact could not be deleted.  Please review logs for " +
    "details.";
} finally {
  try {
    if (fos != null) {
      fos.close();
    }
  } catch (IOException e) {
    log.error("Error closing fos: " + e);
```

```
      }
    }

    return result;

  } // End deleteContact().


} // End class.
```

This is all pretty typical Java code, so I will not be going over it in detail here. There are two things I would like to point out, however. First, look at the method signatures. Do you see the `ServletContext` as an argument? In fact, look at any of the server-side class methods, except for the DTOs, and you will see this. The `ServletContext` is needed for various reasons throughout, usually to get reference to a file system location like the options file or address book file. However, look back at the client code that calls these methods... you won't see `ServletContext` mentioned!

This is another really neat DWR feature. In fact, I will quote directly from the DWR manual here:

> *It is possible to get access to the HTTP servlet objects without writing code that depends on DWR—just have the needed parameter (i.e. HttpServletRequest, HttpServletResponse, HttpSession, ServletContext or ServletConfig) declared on your method. DWR will not include it on the generated stub and upon a call of the method it will fill it in automagically.*

Basically, all that means is that if your server-side method signature includes one of these objects that DWR knows about, it will go ahead and pass it in without you doing a thing. This is actually fantastic when you think about it, because if you examine all the server-side code for InstaMail, except for the `ServletContext`, these classes are in no way web related; they are simple Plain Old Java Objects (POJOs). DWR is in effect performing a basic form of dependency injection[1] for you. Very handy indeed! While what DWR is doing may not be dependency inject in the truest sense, it has the same effect, which I think matters more.

The second thing I want to explain is the division by 3 you will see in the `retrieveContact()` method. Recall that for each contact we are saving three pieces of information: name, address, and a note. Therefore, when we read in the address book, we'll have three elements in our `Properties` object for each contact. To get the total number of contacts then, we need to divide by 3.

---

1. As defined in Wikipedia (`http://en.wikipedia.org/wiki/Dependency_injection`): "Dependency injection (DI) is a programming design pattern and architectural model, sometimes also referred to as Inversion of Control or IoC, although technically speaking, dependency injection specifically refers to an implementation of a particular form of IoC. The pattern seeks to establish a level of abstraction via a public interface, and to remove dependency on components by (for example) supplying a plug-in architecture. The architecture unites the components rather than the components linking themselves or being linked together. Dependency injection is a pattern in which responsibility for object creation and object linking is removed from the objects themselves and transferred to a factory. Dependency injection therefore is obviously inverting the control for object creation and linking, and can be seen to be a form of IoC."

MailSender.java

Now we come to the home stretch: the last three classes we need to look at: `MailSender`, `MailRetriever`, and `MailDeleter`. Clearly these are the classes that will do the majority of the work in InstaMail. After all, it is a mail client, and these classes clearly are working with mail messages, so let's jump right in to `MailSender`, as seen in Listing 5-6.

Listing 5-6. *The MailSender Class*

```
package com.apress.ajaxprojects.instamail;


import org.apache.commons.logging.Log;
import org.apache.commons.logging.LogFactory;
import javax.mail.Session;
import javax.mail.Message;
import java.util.Date;
import java.text.SimpleDateFormat;
import javax.mail.internet.MimeMessage;
import java.io.FileOutputStream;
import java.io.ObjectOutputStream;
import javax.mail.Transport;
import javax.mail.internet.InternetAddress;
import java.util.Properties;
import javax.servlet.ServletContext;


/**
 * This class is responsible for sending e-mails.
 *
 * @author <a href="mailto:fzammetti@omnytex.com">Frank W. Zammetti</a>.
 */
public class MailSender {


  /**
   * Log instance.
   */
  private static Log log = LogFactory.getLog(MailSender.class);


  /**
   * This method sends a message.
   *
   * @param  inTo      The recipient of the message.
   * @param  inSubject The subject of the message.
   * @param  inText    The text of the message.
   * @return           A string indicating success or failure.
   */
```

```
public String sendMessage(String inTo, String inSubject, String inText,
  ServletContext sc) {

  Transport          transport = null;
  FileOutputStream   fos = null;
  ObjectOutputStream oos = null;
  String             result = "";

  try {

    // Get the options, and also get the current date/time.  We do it once
    // here so just in case we cross a second boundary while processing,
    // we know the filename and the sent time will jive.
    OptionsDTO options = new OptionsManager().retrieveOptions(sc);
    Date       d       = new Date();
    log.info("options = " + options + "\n\n");
    // Construct Properties JavaMail needs.
    Properties props = new Properties();
    props.setProperty("mail.transport.protocol", "smtp");
    props.setProperty("mail.host",               options.getSmtpServer());
    if (options.getSmtpServerRequiresLogin().equalsIgnoreCase("true")) {
      props.setProperty("mail.user",     options.getSmtpUsername());
      props.setProperty("mail.password", options.getSmtpPassword());
    }
    log.info("props = " + props + "\n\n");
    // Create a JavaMail message.
    Session session = Session.getDefaultInstance(props, null);
    log.info("session = " + session + "\n\n");
    transport = session.getTransport();
    log.info("transport = " + transport + "\n\n");
    MimeMessage message = new MimeMessage(session);
    // Populate the data for the message.
    message.addRecipient(Message.RecipientType.TO, new InternetAddress(inTo));
    message.setFrom(new InternetAddress(options.getFromAddress()));
    message.setSubject(inSubject);
    message.setContent(inText, "text/plain");
    // Send it!
    transport.connect();
    transport.sendMessage(message,
      message.getRecipients(Message.RecipientType.TO));

    // We also need to save the message.  It will be saved in WEB-INF,
    // and the filename will be the current date and time, formatted nicely,
    // with "msg_" appended to the front.  That way we can easily list them
    // all later.  Note that all we are going to do is simply create a
    // MessageDTO, and serialize it.
    MessageDTO mDTO = new MessageDTO();
    mDTO.setFrom(options.getFromAddress());
```

```
        mDTO.setTo(inTo);
        mDTO.setSent(d.toString());
        mDTO.setReceived(null);
        mDTO.setSubject(inSubject);
        mDTO.setMsgText(inText);
        mDTO.setMsgType("sent");
        String filename = new SimpleDateFormat("MM_dd_yyyy_hh_mm_ss_a").format(d);
        filename = "msg_" + filename.toLowerCase();
        mDTO.setFilename(filename);
        fos = new FileOutputStream(sc.getRealPath("/WEB-INF") + "/" + filename);
        oos = new ObjectOutputStream(fos);
        oos.writeObject(mDTO);
        oos.flush();
        fos.flush();

        result = "Message has been sent";

      } catch (Exception e) {
        e.printStackTrace();
        log.error("Error sending message");
        result = "Error sending message: " + e;
      } finally {
        try {
          if (transport != null) {
            transport.close();
          }
          if (oos != null) {
            oos.close();
          }
          if (fos != null) {
            fos.close();
          }
        } catch (Exception e) {
          log.error("Exception closing transport, oos or fos: " + e);
        }
      }

      return result;

    } // End sendMessage().


} // End class.
```

MailSender has only a single purpose in life: to send a message via SMTP. As such, it has only a single method, sendMessage() (clearly I was not in a creative mode when it came to naming these three classes!). When a message is sent, MailSender also has to write it to disk since we want to retain all sent messages locally.

First we need to populate a `Properties` object for use with JavaMail, the standard Java API for working with e-mail. This object contains details like the SMTP server address, the username and password to use, and so forth. All of this is mandated by the JavaMail API. Once that object is ready, we open a session with the server and construct a `MimeMessage` object. This contains the text of the message, the recipient address, and the subject, among other things. Finally, the server is asked to send the message.

Once that is complete, we still have to save the local copy. To do this we populate a `MessageDTO` object. The filename we'll be saving is constructed as a string beginning with "msg_" and then containing the current date and time, down to the second. This should ensure, barring someone with a *very* quick finger or the computer having an incorrect date and time set, that each e-mail sent has a unique filename. Because all the messages begin with a known string "msg_", we can easily list them later, as you'll see in a moment. Finally, we use plain old Java serialization to save the message. Note that error handling is pretty minimal. If an error occurs, there likely is not a whole lot we can do about it, so we simply make sure that it gets reported to the user and that the details are logged. We also ensure that the connection to the server gets closed no matter what via `finally`, since otherwise no other mail client would be able to access the mailbox. (I found this out the hard way when, during testing, I locked my primary e-mail account! It was not until I realized I needed to shut down my Tomcat instance to close the connection that I was able to access it again.)

MailRetriever.java

Now that we have seen how messages are sent, let's see how they are received. Listing 5-7 shows the `MailRetriever` class, which is where this happens.

Listing 5-7. *The MailRetriever Class*

```
package com.apress.ajaxprojects.instamail;


import java.util.Properties;
import java.util.ArrayList;
import java.util.Collection;
import java.util.Date;
import java.io.File;
import java.io.FileInputStream;
import java.io.ObjectInputStream;
import java.io.FileFilter;
import javax.servlet.ServletContext;
import org.apache.commons.logging.Log;
import org.apache.commons.logging.LogFactory;
import javax.mail.Store;
import javax.mail.Session;
import javax.mail.Folder;
import javax.mail.Message;
```

```
/**
 * This class is responsible for getting lists of messages and individual
 * messages.
 *
 * @author <a href="mailto:fzammetti@omnytex.com">Frank W. Zammetti</a>.
 */
public class MailRetriever {


  /**
   * Log instance.
   */
  private static Log log = LogFactory.getLog(MailRetriever.class);


  /**
   * This method retrieves the contents of the Inbox.
   *
   * @param  sc  ServletContext of the incoming request.
   * @return     A collection of MessageDTOs.
   */
  public Collection getInboxContents(ServletContext sc) {

    Collection messages = new ArrayList();
    Folder     folder   = null;
    Store      store    = null;

    try {

      // Get the fromAddress from Options.
      OptionsDTO options = new OptionsManager().retrieveOptions(sc);
      log.info("options = " + options);
      String fromAddress = options.getFromAddress();

      Properties props = new Properties();
      props.setProperty("mail.transport.protocol", "pop3");
      props.setProperty("mail.host", options.getPop3Server());
      if (options.getPop3ServerRequiresLogin().equalsIgnoreCase("true")) {
        props.setProperty("mail.user",     options.getPop3Username());
        props.setProperty("mail.password", options.getPop3Password());
      }
      log.info("props = " + props);

      Session session = Session.getDefaultInstance(new Properties());
      log.info("session = " + session);
      store = session.getStore("pop3");
      store.connect(options.getPop3Server(), options.getPop3Username(),
        options.getPop3Password());
```

```
      log.info("store = " + store);
      folder = store.getFolder("INBOX");
      folder.open(Folder.READ_ONLY);
      log.info("folder = " + folder);
      int count = folder.getMessageCount();
      for(int i = 1; i <= count; i++) {
        Message message = folder.getMessage(i);
        MessageDTO mDTO = new MessageDTO();
        // Get from address.  Note that it will have quotes around it, so
        // we'll need to remove them.
        String from = message.getFrom()[0].toString();
        from = from.replaceAll("\"", "");
        mDTO.setFrom(from);
        mDTO.setTo(fromAddress);
        mDTO.setReceived(message.getSentDate().toString());
        mDTO.setSubject(message.getSubject());
        mDTO.setSent(null);
        mDTO.setMsgID(new Integer(i).toString());
        mDTO.setMsgType("received");
        mDTO.setFilename(null);
        messages.add(mDTO);
      }

    } catch (Exception e) {
      e.printStackTrace();
      log.error("Could not retrieve Inbox contents: " + e);
    } finally {
      try {
        if (folder != null) {
          folder.close(false);
        }
        if (store != null) {
          store.close();
        }
      } catch (Exception e) {
        log.error("Error closing folder or store: " + e);
      }
    }

    return messages;

  } // End getInboxContents().


  /**
   * This method retrieves the contents of the Sent Messages folder.
   *
   * @param  sc  ServletContext of the incoming request.
```

```
   * @return     A collection of MessageDTOs.
   */
  public Collection getSentMessagesContents(ServletContext sc) {

    Collection messages = new ArrayList();

    try {

      // First, get a list of File objects for all the messages stored
      // in WEB-INF.
      String path = sc.getRealPath("WEB-INF");
      File   dir  = new File(path);
      FileFilter fileFilter = new FileFilter() {
        public boolean accept(File file) {
          if (file.isDirectory()) {
            return false;
          }
          if (!file.getName().startsWith("msg_")) {
            return false;
          }
          return true;
        }
      };
      File[] files = dir.listFiles(fileFilter);
      if (files == null) {
        log.info("Directory not found, or is empty");
      } else {
        // Now that we know there are messages and we have a list of them,
        // go through each and reconstitute the serialized MessageDTO
        // for each and add it to the collection.
        for (int i = 0; i < files.length; i++){
          log.info("Retrieving '" + files[i] + "'...");
          FileInputStream   fis = new FileInputStream(files[i]);
          ObjectInputStream oos = new ObjectInputStream(fis);
          MessageDTO message = (MessageDTO)oos.readObject();
          oos.close();
          fis.close();
          messages.add(message);
        }
      }

    } catch (Exception e) {
      e.printStackTrace();
      log.error("Error retrieving sent messages list: " + e);
    }
```

```
  return messages;

} // End getSentMessagesContents().


/**
 * This method retrieves a single message and all the pertinent details of it.
 *
 * @param  msgType  The type of message to retrieve, either "sent" or
 *                  "retrieved".
 * @param  filename The name of the file the message is stored on disk under
 *                  if retrieving a Sent Message, null otherwise.
 * @param  msgID    The ID of the message if retrieving a message in the
 *                  Inbox, null otherwise.
 * @param  sc       ServletContext of the incoming request.
 * @return          The message requested.
 */
public MessageDTO retrieveMessage(String msgType, String filename,
  String msgID, ServletContext sc) {

  MessageDTO message = null;

  try {
    log.info("msgType = " + msgType);
    log.info("filename = " + filename);
    log.info("msgID = " + msgID);
    if (msgType.equalsIgnoreCase("sent")) {
      // Message from Sent Messages.
      String path = sc.getRealPath("WEB-INF");
      filename = path + File.separatorChar + filename;
      log.info("Retrieving '" + filename + "'...");
      File   dir  = new File(filename);
      FileInputStream   fis = new FileInputStream(filename);
      ObjectInputStream oos = new ObjectInputStream(fis);
      message = (MessageDTO)oos.readObject();
      oos.close();
      fis.close();
    }
    if (msgType.equalsIgnoreCase("received")) {
      // Message from Inbox.
      OptionsDTO options = new OptionsManager().retrieveOptions(sc);
      log.info("options = " + options);
      String fromAddress = options.getFromAddress();
      Properties props = new Properties();
      props.setProperty("mail.transport.protocol", "pop3");
      props.setProperty("mail.host", options.getPop3Server());
```

```
        if (options.getPop3ServerRequiresLogin().equalsIgnoreCase("true")) {
          props.setProperty("mail.user",     options.getPop3Username());
          props.setProperty("mail.password", options.getPop3Password());
        }
        log.info("props = " + props);
        Session session = Session.getDefaultInstance(new Properties());
        log.info("session = " + session);
        Store store = session.getStore("pop3");
        store.connect(options.getPop3Server(), options.getPop3Username(),
          options.getPop3Password());
        log.info("store = " + store);
        Folder folder = store.getFolder("INBOX");
        folder.open(Folder.READ_ONLY);
        log.info("folder = " + folder);
        int count = folder.getMessageCount();
        int i = Integer.parseInt(msgID);
        Message msg = folder.getMessage(i);
        message = new MessageDTO();
        // Get from address.  Note that it will have quotes around it, so
        // we'll need to remove them.
        String from = msg.getFrom()[0].toString();
        from = from.replaceAll("\"", "");
        message.setFrom(from);
        message.setTo(fromAddress);
        message.setReceived(msg.getSentDate().toString());
        message.setSubject(msg.getSubject());
        message.setSent(null);
        message.setMsgID(new Integer(i).toString());
        message.setMsgType("received");
        message.setFilename(null);
        message.setMsgText(msg.getContent().toString());
        folder.close(false);
        store.close();
      }
    } catch (Exception e) {
      e.printStackTrace();
      log.error("Error retrieving message: " + e);
    }

    return message;

  } // End retrieveMessage().


} // End class.
```

The first method we encounter is `getInboxContents()`. Similar to the `sendMessage()` method, we begin by populating a `Properties` object. Using that object, we then get a connection to the POP3 server and ask for the contents of the "INBOX" folder. This is one of the standard folder names that all POP3 servers understand. The JavaMail API gives us access to the number of messages in the folder we are working with, which is precisely what we need. Each e-mail in a POP3 folder has a number, starting with 1, so all we need to do is loop as many times as there are messages. For each, we retrieve it, and construct a `MessageDTO` object from the pertinent details (from, subject, receive time, etc.). These objects are added to a `List`, which is returned to the caller. DWR understands `Lists` intrinsically, so there is no extra work to do here.

The next method we see is `getSentMessagesContents()`. This is again pretty standard Java code. We first retrieve a list of all the files in the `WEB-INF` directory beginning with "msg_". Then for each we use the standard Java serialization mechanism to reconstitute our `MessageDTO` object. Each is again added to a `List` that is returned, and that's it! Certainly there are better ways to persist messages than object serialization, but without getting into a true persistence framework, I dare say the code is not likely to be any more concise and simple than this.

Finally, we have the `retrieveMessage()` function. This services requests to view an individual message for both the Inbox and Sent Messages views, so as expected, there is some branching logic. I thought about breaking these out into separate methods, but this way keeps the client code simpler, which to me is a more important consideration than the server-side code. And it is not as if a simple `if` branch is anything complicated.

In any case, the first branch takes us into retrieving a sent message. This is virtually identical to what we saw in the previous method, except that we are looking for a specific filename, which we are passed by the client-side code. So, we load it, reconstitute the object, and return it.

The other branch takes us into retrieving a message from the Inbox. Once again, this code is very much like that in the `getInboxContents()` method. Naturally there is no need to loop through the messages; we simply ask for the one we are interested in based on the `msgID` number passed in (which is just the index number of the message in the Inbox). Once we have it, we populate a `MessageDTO` object from it and return it to the caller.

MailDeleter.java

Only one thing is left to look at: the `MailDeleter` class, as seen in Listing 5-8.

Listing 5-8. *The MailDeleter Class*

```
package com.apress.ajaxprojects.instamail;


import org.apache.commons.logging.Log;
import org.apache.commons.logging.LogFactory;
import javax.mail.Session;
import javax.mail.Flags;
import javax.mail.Message;
import java.util.Date;
import java.text.SimpleDateFormat;
import java.util.StringTokenizer;
import javax.mail.internet.MimeMessage;
import java.io.FileOutputStream;
import java.io.File;
import java.io.ObjectOutputStream;
```

```
import javax.mail.Transport;
import javax.mail.internet.InternetAddress;
import javax.mail.Store;
import javax.mail.Folder;
import java.util.Properties;
import javax.servlet.ServletContext;


/**
 * This class is responsible for deleting e-mails.
 *
 * @author <a href="mailto:fzammetti@omnytex.com">Frank W. Zammetti</a>.
 */
public class MailDeleter {


  /**
   * Log instance.
   */
  private static Log log = LogFactory.getLog(MailDeleter.class);


  /**
   * This method deletes a message.
   *
   * @param  msgType   The type of message to delete, either "sent" or
   *                   "retrieved".
   * @param  filenames The names of the files the messages are stored on disk
   *                   under if deleting Sent Messages, null otherwise.  This
   *                   can be a comma-separated list of filenames, or just
   *                   a single value.
   * @param  msgIDs    The IDs of the messages if deleting messages in the
   *                   Inbox, null otherwise.  This can be a comma-separated
   *                   list of IDs, or just a single value.
   * @param  sc        ServletContext of the incoming request.
   * @return           A string indicating success or failure.
   */
  public String deleteMessages(String msgType, String filenames, String msgIDs,
    ServletContext sc) {

    log.info("\nAbout to delete message:\n" +
      "msgType = " + msgType + "\n" +
      "filenames = " + filenames + "\n" +
      "msgIDs = " + msgIDs + "\n");
```

```
String result = "Message(s) deleted.";
Store  store  = null;
Folder folder = null;

try {
  if (msgType.equalsIgnoreCase("sent")) {
    // Deleting from Sent Messages.
    StringTokenizer st = new StringTokenizer(filenames, ",");
    String errs = "";
    String path = sc.getRealPath("WEB-INF");
    while (st.hasMoreTokens()) {
      String fn = st.nextToken();
      fn = path + File.separatorChar + fn;
      boolean success = (new File(fn)).delete();
      if (!success) {
        if (!errs.equalsIgnoreCase("")) {
          errs += ", ";
        }
        errs += "Unable to delete '" + fn + "'";
      }
    }
    if (!errs.equalsIgnoreCase("")) {
      result = errs;
    }
  }
  if (msgType.equalsIgnoreCase("received")) {
    // Deleting from Inbox.
    OptionsDTO options = new OptionsManager().retrieveOptions(sc);
    log.info("options = " + options);
    StringTokenizer st = new StringTokenizer(msgIDs, ",");
    Properties props = new Properties();
    props.setProperty("mail.transport.protocol", "pop3");
    props.setProperty("mail.host", options.getPop3Server());
    if (options.getPop3ServerRequiresLogin().equalsIgnoreCase("true")) {
      props.setProperty("mail.user",     options.getPop3Username());
      props.setProperty("mail.password", options.getPop3Password());
    }
    log.info("props = " + props);
    Session session = Session.getDefaultInstance(new Properties());
    log.info("session = " + session);
    store = session.getStore("pop3");
    store.connect(options.getPop3Server(), options.getPop3Username(),
      options.getPop3Password());
    log.info("store = " + store);
    folder = store.getFolder("INBOX");
    folder.open(Folder.READ_WRITE);
    log.info("folder = " + folder);
```

```
        while (st.hasMoreTokens()) {
          String msgID = st.nextToken();
          int i = Integer.parseInt(msgID);
          Message message = folder.getMessage(i);
          message.setFlag(Flags.Flag.DELETED, true);
        }
      }
    } catch (Exception e) {
      log.error("Exception deleting POP3 message(s): " + e);
      e.printStackTrace();
      result = "An error occurred deleting message(s).  Please refer to " +
        "the logs for details.";
    } finally {
      try {
        if (folder != null) {
          folder.close(true);
        }
        if (store != null) {
          store.close();
        }
      } catch (Exception e) {
        log.error("Error closing folder or store: " + e);
      }
    }

    return result;

  } // End deleteMessages().


} // End class.
```

Just like the MailSender class, there is only a single method here to look at: deleteMessages(). Recall from our earlier look at the client-side code that this method expects to receive a comma-separated list of items to delete, either filenames when dealing with sent messages, or message IDs when dealing with received messages. So, after we branch based on whether we are deleting sent messages or received messages, as you might expect, the first thing we need to do is tokenize the string. When that is done, we enter a look until we have exhausted all the tokens. For each, in the case of sent messages, we get a reference to the file and delete it using the standard File.delete() method. If any errors are encountered, we record them in a string to be returned to the caller for display, but we keep going until no tokens are left.

For received messages, it is only slightly more difficult. One last time we see the Properties object being populated. We also see a session established with the POP3 server. We then loop, and for each token we retrieve the message from the server. (Remember that the token is the message number.) The way you delete a message with the JavaMail API is to retrieve it, and then set a flag marking it for deletion. The message will still not actually be deleted until you close the folder, and then only if you pass true to the close() method.

The same kind of minimalist error handling that we have seen before is again used. The outcome of the operation is returned to the caller for display.

And that wraps it up! We have just explored every part of InstaMail, and I hope you will agree that DWR really made it very nice, neat, and compact in terms of code size.

Suggested Exercises

I have purposely left open a number of items that I encourage you to pursue to make InstaMail even better. I believe these items will give you a good experience in using DWR. None of them should prove especially difficult, either.

- Allow for multiple e-mail accounts. Tangential to this is the ability for multiple users to log in and use a specific account.
- Allow for file attachments. I highly suggest looking at the Commons FileUpload component (`http://jakarta.apache.org/commons/fileupload/`) for this. It will save you a great deal of time and effort and make this enhancement almost child's play!
- Allow for "rich" e-mail content. Spend some time Googling for rich edit components to integrate. A number of them are available, and many of them are Ajax-enabled already.
- Allow for custom folders. It would be nice if you could create a Storage folder, for example, and move any e-mail you wanted into it.
- Use a database to store everything instead of the file system. I opted to use the file system in all applications in this book because I did not want you to incur the extra burden of having to set up and configure a database. That being said, many of the applications very much fit in the database mold, and InstaMail is a prime example. This would clearly make the application more scalable and robust and would allow for further functionality, including
    - Add search capabilities. It should be quick and easy to find any message.
    - Allow for paging of folder views. Notice how the Inbox and Sent Message views always show all their contents? Paging through them, say 25 messages at a time, would be very helpful when viewing large numbers of messages.

All of these should be pretty fun enhancements to make, and I do hope you will undertake them.

Summary

In this chapter we built a webmail client application utilizing Ajax techniques courtesy of the DWR library. We discovered how DWR allows us to essentially treat Java classes on the server as client-side components, calling methods on them, accessing properties, and so on. We saw how what is truly a small amount of code, with the right libraries, can yield a rather useful application. In addition, we explored just a few more advanced client-side presentation techniques using DOM scripting and CSS.

CHAPTER 6

AjaxReader: Because Every Ajax Book Has to Have One!

In this chapter we'll construct an RSS application that uses Ajax to do its thing. This has pretty quickly become something of the de facto standard in Ajax examples, and it seems no Ajax book is complete without it! This particular implementation will demonstrate the use of Ajax-Tags from Java Web Parts (JWP), which I believe you'll find is a fantastic and easy way to implement Ajax. In addition, I think you'll find it to be a particularly easy-to-follow implementation, which will make understanding how all the pieces fit together very easy.

Requirements and Goals

RSS (Really Simple Syndication) is a standard, lightweight XML format, which is used to distribute information in the form of news headlines and linked-to article contents. A website will publish an RSS "feed," a URL at which resides an XML document that, when parsed, produces a list of headlines, along with some other useful information—most important a link to another URL where the contents that apply to that headline can be found.

An RSS reader is nothing but an application that fetches these RSS feeds and displays their contents, and then allows the user to see the content for a given headline. Numerous readers are available, some built into web browsers, others stand-alone. Some have fancy features, like the ability to aggregate feeds into one display, or group feeds and open whole groups at a time, among other things. At the end of the day, though, any reader will parse a feed and display it, and that more or less sums up an RSS reader.

Because it is so relatively simple, an RSS reader is a good candidate for a web-based application, and is an excellent chance to demonstrate the use of Ajax, since an RSS reader is a classic summary/detail application. The feeds themselves represent summaries, and the headlines represent details, and the content under the headlines represent even further details that can be drilled down to. As such, not refreshing the summary just to display the details is a much desired attribute, and one for which Ajax is ideally suited.

So, in building our RSS reader, we have a few fairly simple requirements:

- As with most of the projects in this book, we want to do as little work as possible. Especially for such a relatively simple application, complexity is hard to justify!
- We should be able to see a list of feeds that we can click on to reveal headlines. We should then be able to click a headline to see the underlying content. All the while, we should still see our feed list, in case we want to jump to another feed.

- We should of course be able to add and delete feeds at will.
- We'll do one semi-fancy trick: we want to be able to hide the feed list (and the area where feeds are edited) to display more of the headlines and/or underlying contents. We'll still want to see a small area where we can click a button to go back to the headlines, as well as expand the feed list again.
- We want to be able to print articles, as well as browse them separately from the reader if we wish. To accomplish this, we'll provide the ability to open an article in a new window.
- All of this should be accomplished with as little server-side code as possible.

Choosing the right tools, these goals are fairly easily accomplished, and yet we'll wind up with a rather useful little application that can be run in virtually any servlet container with no difficulty.

How We Will Pull It Off

The first thing to decide is what to use to do the Ajax work. Many choices present themselves, as is always the case with Ajax projects. In this case, I have chosen to go with AjaxTags in Java Web Parts once more. This project presents the opportunity to look at a few more capabilities that AjaxTags has to offer, so why not? It will also result in a small amount of client-side code, which is always a good thing when you can achieve it.

On the server side of things, we'll go with straight servlets this time around. Because the Java code involved is really very simplistic, there is no need for a full framework to bog us down, and in this case that is most likely what would happen. You don't use dynamite to remove a few dead branches from a tree, and likewise you don't use a full-blown application framework to build what can be built with basic tools.

The only real complication involved is the parsing of the RSS feeds themselves. While RSS is not especially difficult—and thus I could have written parsing code to do it without much trouble—the bottom line is that reinventing the wheel is something you should strive to avoid when possible, especially if the wheel is something very generic and common, as parsing an RSS feed is. After all, RSS is meant to be simple and generic, not specific to any given application, so why should you want to write custom code to deal with it?

There are a few RSS parser libraries available, but perhaps the most popular is called ROME, which stands for Rss and atOM utilitiEs (`https://rome.dev.java.net/`). It is actually more than just RSS parsing utilities. It can parse other feed formats such as Atom. It can also generate feeds, saving you the trouble of having to create proper XML.

Using ROME is about as easy as it gets. For example:

```
String feedURL = "http://www.domain.com/someFeed";
URL feedURL = new URL(feedURL);
SyndFeedInput input   = new SyndFeedInput();
SyndFeed feed = input.build(new XmlReader(feedUrl));
```

This will retrieve the feed at the URL stored in `feedURL` and parse it. Once that is done, we can access various bits of information about it through the `feed` variable, like so:

```
// Get the list of headlines parsed from the feed.
List headlines = feed.getEntries();
```

We can iterate over that list and do something with each headline:

```
for (Iterator it = headlines.iterator(); it.hasNext();) {
  SyndEntryImpl entry = (SyndEntryImpl)it.next();
  String uri = entry.getUri(); // Get the URI the headlines' contents is at.
  String title = entry.getTitle(); // Get the headline title.
  // Get the headlines' description.
  String desc = entry.getDescription().getValue();
}
```

See, far from rocket science! But that is precisely what you should wind up saying about a good library: it should be quick and easy to use and not require an advanced degree in quantum chromodynamics. ROME succeeds in spades here.

We were already introduced to AjaxTags in the Karnak project, but we'll be pulling a few new tools out of the toolbox this time around, so let's discuss the new items now.

Aside from the `<ajax:event>` and `<ajax:enable>` tags that we learned about while exploring the Karnak project, AjaxTags contains two other tags: `<ajax:manual>` and `<ajax:timer>`. Let's talk about the timer tag first.

The timer tag allows us to set up a repeating Ajax event that fires continuously at a given interval. You configure it in `ajax_config.xml` just like any other event, using any of the same handlers, and so on. In your JSP, though, you do the following:

```
<ajax:timer ajaxRef="page/listFeeds" startOnLoad="true" frequency="1000" />
```

This sets up a timer that will fire every second (frequency is measured in milliseconds). The `startOnLoad` attribute tells AjaxTags to start the timer immediately when the page loads. If this is set to false, then you take responsibility for setting up a timer and starting it. This can be useful if you only wish to start the event based on some user event, say to continually update a table of data only after the user has submitted some display criteria.

That's really about all there is to the timer tag. Amazingly, the manual tag is even simpler! The manual tag basically renders the appropriate JavaScript function to execute an Ajax event. As with the timer tag, you configure the event the same way as any other AjaxTags event. For instance, imagine you saw the following on a page:

```
<ajax:manual ajaxRef="page/showHeadlines" manualFunction="doRefreshHeadlines" />
```

This would result in the following being rendered:

```
<script>function
doRefreshHeadlines(){StdSimpleXML(document.forms["feedForm"],
"/listHeadlines","feed,feedTitle=feedTitle",StdIFrameDisplay,
"ifContent", "POST","doRefreshHeadlines",null,"page/showHeadlines");}</script>
```

Notice that this is not attached to any page element. You have complete control over when and how you call `doRefreshHeadlines()`, or whether or not you ever call it. The code inside that function is equivalent to the code that would be generated by

```
<ajax:event ajaxRef="page/showHeadlines" />
```

The only difference is that the `<ajax:event>` tag would attach that code to the specified event handler of the preceding element. In `ajax_config.xml`, to use a manual event you simply specify the event type as `manual`. Likewise, for the timer tag, you specify `timer`. This tells AjaxTags that we are not attaching the code to a page element; it is instead stand-alone code for the developers' use.

You may wonder why the manual tag was invented. There were really two reasons. First, many times you'll want to return some markup as the result of an Ajax event that itself uses AjaxTags. This turns out to be problematic at present for a number of reasons. However, at the end of the day, what you are really interested in is the call to the specified request handler. Thus, the manual tag essentially bypasses the parts that can be problematic and gives you the same functionality under your complete control. The second reason is so that you have this control while still being able to work in an essentially declarative fashion (although obviously less so since you now have to write some minimal JavaScript yourself).

This tag makes AjaxReader possible, as we'll soon see!

Visualizing the Finish Line

Let's now get a picture, figuratively and literally, of AjaxReader by looking at some screenshots.

Figure 6-1 shows the first thing you will see when you start up AjaxReader. In this case, two RSS feeds have already been added, one for MSNBC (`www.msnbc.com`) and one for the venerable Slashdot (`www.slashdot.org`).

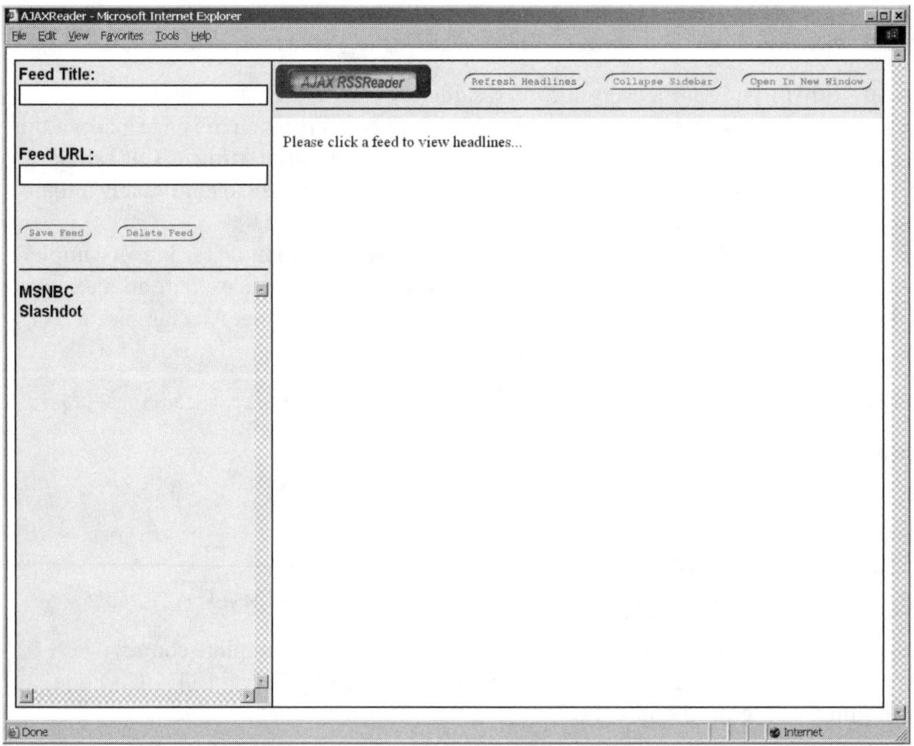

Figure 6-1. *The AjaxReader display when you first access it*

Figure 6-2 shows what it looks like when you are viewing headlines from a feed. You can also see how the text fields are highlighted when they get focus to add or make changes to a feed, and you can also see the hand pointer when you hover over a feed.

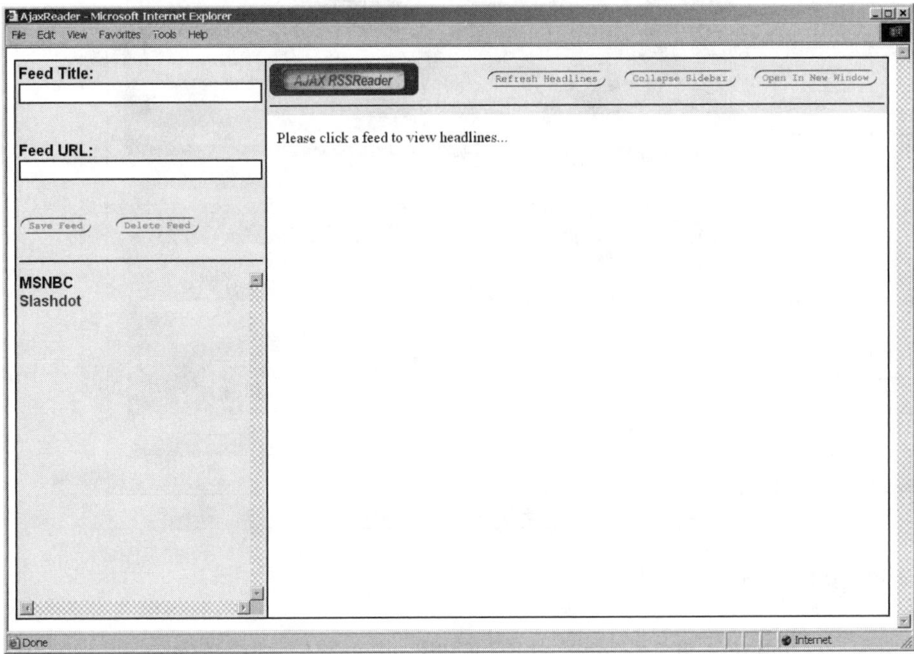

Figure 6-2. *Displaying the headlines for a selected feed*

Figure 6-3 is what AjaxReader looks like when you select a headline.

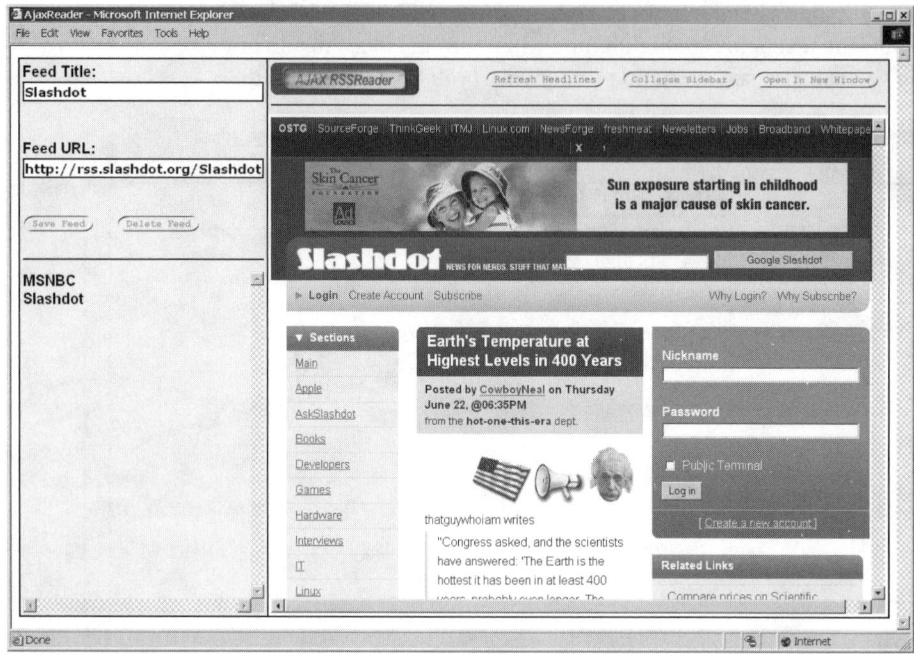

Figure 6-3. *Viewing a selected headline*

Figure 6-4 is again viewing a headline, but this time after the Collapse Sidebar button has been clicked. This gives a fuller view of the article to the reader.

Lastly, Figure 6-5 is a new window that is spawned by clicking the Open In New Window button. This is especially useful for printing an article, since doing so within the main window is difficult at best due to browser security restrictions (I will talk about this problem later on).

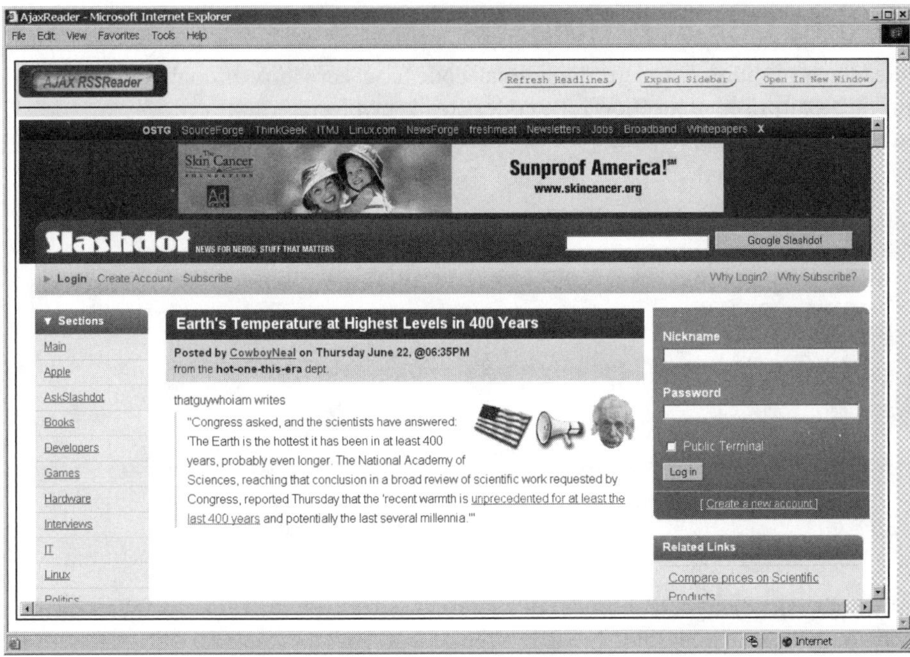

Figure 6-4. *The view with the sidebar collapsed for more reading room*

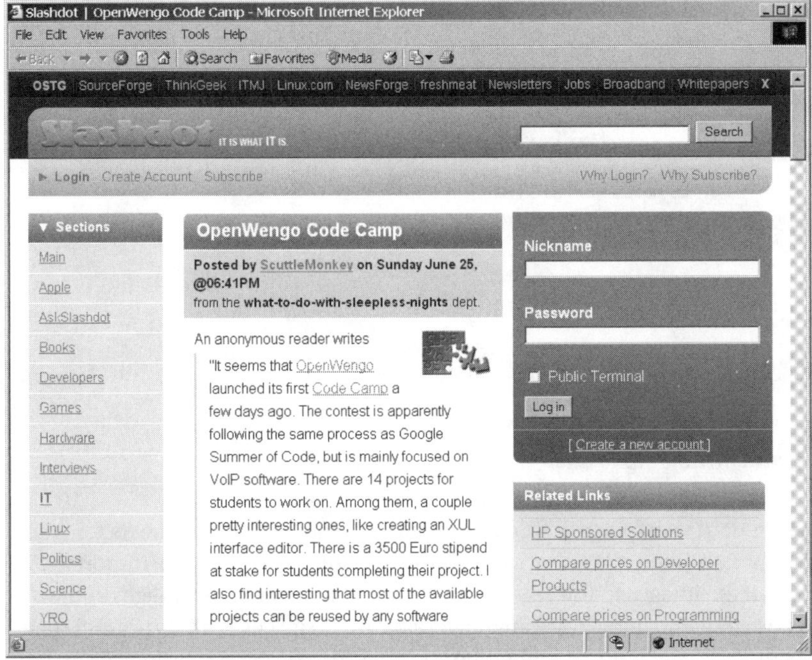

Figure 6-5. *A headline opened in a new window*

Dissecting the Solution

The AjaxReader application is an amazingly small code base. Let's look through it now, and I think you will be surprised at just how little code is really involved!

First, the bird's eye view, starting with the directory structure, shown in Figure 6-6.

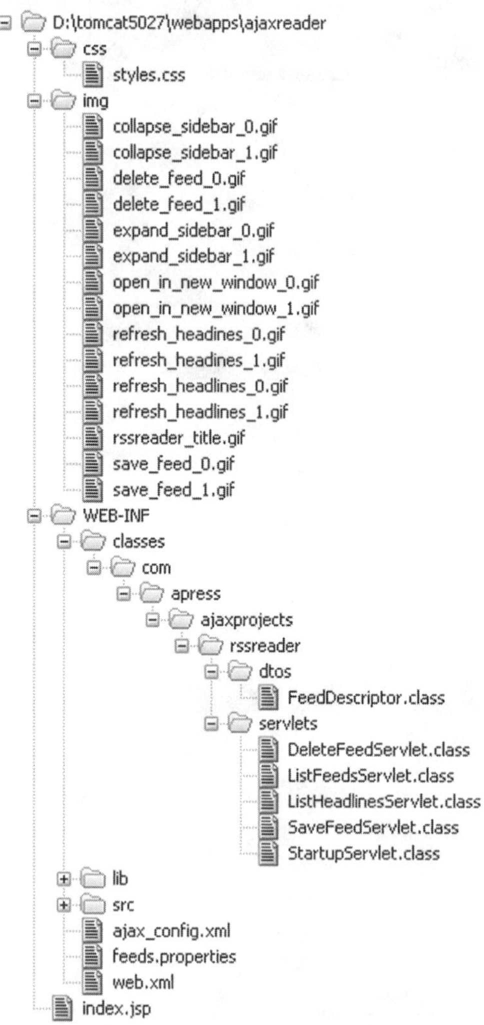

Figure 6-6. *Directory structure of AjaxReader*

It is of course a standard webapp structure with typical directories for stylesheets (`css`) and images (`img`). All our markup (`index.jsp`, that's it!) is in the root directory. This JSP imports `styles.css` and loads all the images in the `img` directory. Note that most of the images end with either `_0` or `_1`. The ones that end with `_0` are an image, a button in all cases, in its normal state. The ones that end with `_1` are the buttons in their hover states, that is, what they look like when the mouse hovers over them. We can see all our Java classes in the `WEB-INF/classes` directory, as expected. The `dtos` directory holds our single `FeedDescriptor` DTO, and the `servlets` directory holds all the servlets that make up AjaxReader. We also see two files in WEB-INF in addition to the usual web.xml: ajax_config.xml is the configuration file for AjaxTags, and feeds.properties is the file where feeds the user creates are stored. The lib folder is where all the JARs AjaxReader depends on are found. These are shown in Table 6-1.

Table 6-1. *The JARs AjaxReader Depends on, Found in WEB-INF.lib*

JAR	Description
commons-beanutils-1.7.0.jar	The Jakarta Commons BeanUtils library, needed by Digester.
commons-digester-1.7.0.jar	Jakarta Commons Digester is a library for parsing XML and generating objects from it. This is used to parse some messages passed to the server by the client code.
commons-lang-2.1.jar	Jakarta Commons Lang are utility functions that enhance the Java language. Needed by Digester.
commons-logging-1.0.4.jar	Jakarta Commons Logging is an abstraction layer that sits on top of a true logging implementation (like Log4J), which allows you to switch the underlying logging implementation without affecting your application code. It also provides a simple logger that outputs to System.out, which is what this application uses.
javawebparts_core_v1.0_beta4.jar	The JWP core package, required by all other JWP packages.
javawebparts_request_v1.0_beta4.jar	The JWP request package; includes some useful utility classes for dealing with HTTP requests.
javawebparts_taglib_v1.0_beta4.jar	The JWP taglib package. This includes AjaxTags, which is used for this application.
jdom-1.0.jar	An XML parsing tool, needed by ROME.
rome-0.7.jar	ROME is an RSS feed parser that this application uses to retrieve and work with RSS feeds.

The WEB-INF/src directory contains all the source code for this project, including the Ant build script.

The Client-Side Code

Let's first look at web.xml, shown in Listing 6-1.

Listing 6-1. *web.xml for AjaxReader*

```
<?xml version="1.0" encoding="ISO-8859-1"?>

<!DOCTYPE web-app PUBLIC  "-//Sun Microsystems, Inc.//DTD Web Application 2.3//EN"
"http://java.sun.com/dtd/web-app_2_3.dtd">

<web-app>

  <display-name>AjaxReader</display-name>
```

```
<!-- If you require a proxy on your network, set the following -->
<!-- as appropriate for your network.  If not needed, leave -->
<!-- them blank. -->
<context-param>
  <param-name>proxyHost</param-name>
  <param-value>someproxy.mynetwork.com</param-value>
</context-param>
<context-param>
  <param-name>proxyPort</param-name>
  <param-value>8080</param-value>
</context-param>

<!-- This parameter is needed to initialize AjaxTags.  It points to the -->
<!-- context-relative configuration file. -->
<context-param>
  <param-name>ajaxTagsConfig</param-name>
  <param-value>/WEB-INF/ajax_config.xml</param-value>
</context-param>

<!-- This listener is needed to initialize AjaxTags.  It uses the -->
<!-- above parameter. -->
<listener>
  <listener-class>javawebparts.taglib.ajaxtags.AjaxInit</listener-class>
</listener>

<!-- Servlet to do application setup. -->
<servlet>
  <servlet-name>StartupServlet</servlet-name>
  <servlet-class>
    com.apress.ajaxprojects.rssreader.servlets.StartupServlet
  </servlet-class>
  <load-on-startup>1</load-on-startup>
</servlet>
<!-- Servlet to list feeds. -->
<servlet>
  <servlet-name>ListFeedsServlet</servlet-name>
  <servlet-class>
    com.apress.ajaxprojects.rssreader.servlets.ListFeedsServlet
  </servlet-class>
</servlet>
<!-- Servlet to list headlines for a selected feed. -->
<servlet>
  <servlet-name>ListHeadlinesServlet</servlet-name>
  <servlet-class>
    com.apress.ajaxprojects.rssreader.servlets.ListHeadlinesServlet
  </servlet-class>
</servlet>
```

```
  <!-- Servlet to save a feed. -->
  <servlet>
    <servlet-name>SaveFeedServlet</servlet-name>
    <servlet-class>
      com.apress.ajaxprojects.rssreader.servlets.SaveFeedServlet
    </servlet-class>
  </servlet>
  <!-- Servlet to delete a feed. -->
  <servlet>
    <servlet-name>DeleteFeedServlet</servlet-name>
    <servlet-class>
      com.apress.ajaxprojects.rssreader.servlets.DeleteFeedServlet
    </servlet-class>
  </servlet>

  <!-- Servlet mappings. -->
  <servlet-mapping>
    <servlet-name>ListFeedsServlet</servlet-name>
    <url-pattern>/listFeeds</url-pattern>
  </servlet-mapping>
  <servlet-mapping>
    <servlet-name>ListHeadlinesServlet</servlet-name>
    <url-pattern>/listHeadlines</url-pattern>
  </servlet-mapping>
  <servlet-mapping>
    <servlet-name>SaveFeedServlet</servlet-name>
    <url-pattern>/saveFeed</url-pattern>
  </servlet-mapping>
  <servlet-mapping>
    <servlet-name>DeleteFeedServlet</servlet-name>
    <url-pattern>/deleteFeed</url-pattern>
  </servlet-mapping>

  <!-- Session timeout config. -->
  <session-config>
    <session-timeout>15</session-timeout>
  </session-config>

  <!-- Welcome file config. -->
  <welcome-file-list>
    <welcome-file>index.jsp</welcome-file>
  </welcome-file-list>

</web-app>
```

AjaxReader has a servlet (which we'll look at shortly) that goes out and grabs an RSS feed. This is a simple HTTP transaction. However, because some networks require a proxy to access the Internet, we see that we have two context parameters named `proxyHost` and `proxyPort`.

Set them as appropriate for your network, or leave them blank if you do not have to go through a proxy.

After that we see the usual `ajaxTagsConfig` context parameter that points to our `ajax_config.xml` file. Then we see the listener that is used to read in that config file and otherwise get AjaxTags ready to go.

Following that is a series of servlet declarations and mappings. Notice that the `StartupServlet` is the only one with a `<load-on-startup>` element. The job of this servlet is to initialize the application, which in this case means reading in the `feeds.properties` file and storing it in application scope. We'll look at each of these servlets in detail shortly, but for now just familiarize yourself with their mappings.

After that comes a typical session timeout setting, 15 minutes in this case, and finally a welcome file list. AjaxReader only has a single JSP in it, so naturally this is the welcome page!

ajax_config.xml

Next up in Listing 6-2 is `ajax_config.xml`.

Listing 6-2. *AjaxTags Configuration File for AjaxReader*

```
<ajaxConfig>

  <!-- Events within the feedForm. -->
  <form ajaxRef="feedForm" isPage="false">

    <!-- onClick event for the Add Feed button. -->
    <element ajaxRef="saveFeed">
      <event type="onclick">
        <requestHandler type="std:SimpleXML" method="post">
          <target>/saveFeed</target>
          <parameter>feed,feedTitle=feedTitleEdit,feedURL=feedURLEdit</parameter>
        </requestHandler>
        <responseHandler type="std:CodeExecuter">
          <parameter />
        </responseHandler>
      </event>
    </element>
    <!-- onClick event for the Delete Feed button. -->
    <element ajaxRef="deleteFeed">
      <event type="onclick">
        <requestHandler type="std:SimpleXML" method="post">
          <target>/deleteFeed</target>
          <parameter>feed,feedTitle=feedTitle</parameter>
        </requestHandler>
        <responseHandler type="std:CodeExecuter">
          <parameter />
        </responseHandler>
      </event>
    </element>
```

```
  </form>

  <!-- Events outside any real HTML form. -->
  <form ajaxRef="page" isPage="true">

    <!-- This configuration is used to set up a manual Ajax function -->
    <!-- that will be used when a feed in the feed list is clicked -->
    <!-- as well as when the Refresh Headlines button is clicked. -->
    <element ajaxRef="showHeadlines">
      <event type="manual" form="feedForm">
        <requestHandler type="std:SimpleXML" method="post">
          <target>/listHeadlines</target>
          <parameter>feed,feedTitle=feedTitle</parameter>
        </requestHandler>
        <responseHandler type="std:IFrameDisplay">
          <parameter>ifContent</parameter>
        </responseHandler>
      </event>
    </element>
    <!-- Timer event for the feeds list update. -->
    <element ajaxRef="listFeeds">
      <event type="timer" form="not_applicable">
        <requestHandler type="std:SimpleRequest" method="get">
          <target>/listFeeds</target>
          <parameter />
        </requestHandler>
        <responseHandler type="std:InnerHTML">
          <parameter>divFeedList</parameter>
        </responseHandler>
      </event>
    </element>

  </form>

</ajaxConfig>
```

There are essentially four different Ajax requests that the AjaxReader application can make of the server. The first is triggered when the user clicks the Save Feed button. This simply passes along some XML in the form

```
<feed>
  <feedTitle>xxx</feedTitle>
  <feedURL>yyy</feedURL>
</feed>
```

The `std:SimpleXML` request handler is used to do that. Upon return we use the `std:CodeExecutor` response handler. This is the first time we are seeing this handler. Its purpose in life is to assume that what the server returns is a chunk of JavaScript, so it executes it for us. This is great because we can return the following content from a servlet for example:

```
alert("hello!");
```

When std:CodeExecutor gets ahold of that, it executes it on the client, resulting in an alert pop-up greeting us. Executing returned JavaScript is actually a very common trick with Ajax. Google itself uses this technique to do its Google Suggests.

The next thing we see configured is the event attached to the Delete Feed button. It is almost identical to the Save Feed event, except that the XML only includes the feed title. Note that both of these are part of a real HTML form. This is required since the std:SimpleXML request handlers assumes the elements named are part of the parent for the element the event is attached to.

On the other hand, the next two elements that are configured are part of a "virtual" form, that is, they are not going to be attached to any element on the page. Instead, we have a manual event and a timer event. The manual event is used when the user clicks one of the feeds in the feed list. We again see the std:SimpleXML request handler in action, and just like the Delete Feed event, only the feed title is actually required. The response handler we use is the std:IFrameDisplay, which can be thought of as exactly like the std:InnerHTML handler, except that it writes to an iFrame instead. The last configured event is the timer event. Here, we are just sending a simple request, that is, no parameters or XML or anything else is required, and when the result comes back it is to be put into the divFeedList <div>. This is used to periodically refresh the feed list so that any updates the user makes will be reflected in the list very soon after. Note that the form attribute, as of this writing, is a required element when you are setting up a "virtual" form. The reason is that since the <form> element that is the parent is not a real HTML form, AjaxTags will use the value of this attribute for any handler that requires a reference to a real form. Even if you use a handler that does not require that, AjaxTags still expects to find a value there. However, if you are in fact using handlers that do not reference a form, as we are doing here with std:SimpleRequest, the value will not actually be used, so it can be anything you want, any string at all. The value not_applicable is reasonable in this case since it indicates to anyone reviewing the configuration file that the handler used does not require a reference to a form.

And that's it for configuration files! There is also a feeds.properties file that you will find in the WEB-INF directory. This file is written dynamically when you add, change, or delete feeds, so there is no need to look at it here. It is a plain old Java properties file and nothing more. The property name is the feed name, and the property value is the feed URL.

index.jsp

Now we can begin to look at actual application code. Listing 6-3 shows the first of this, the index.jsp file, the only JSP in AjaxReader!

Listing 6-3. *index.jsp, the AjaxReader Presentation Layer in Its Entirety*

```
<%@ taglib prefix="ajax" uri="javawebparts/taglib/ajaxtags" %>

<html>

  <head>
```

```
<link rel="stylesheet" href="css/styles.css" type="text/css">
<title>AjaxReader</title>

<script>


  // This variable deternmines what state our view is in.  Possible values:
  // 0 = Initial, when the page first loads
  // 1 = Headlines showing
  // 2 = Article showing
  var viewState = 0;


  // This variable stores the last link that was clicked when viewing
  // headlines for a feed.  This is used to open the article in a
  // new window.
  var lastClickedLink = null;


  // Image preloads.
  var open_in_new_window_0 = new Image();
  open_in_new_window_0.src = "img/open_in_new_window_0.gif";
  var open_in_new_window_1 = new Image();
  open_in_new_window_1.src = "img/open_in_new_window_1.gif";
  var refresh_headlines_0 = new Image();
  refresh_headlines_0.src = "img/refresh_headlines_0.gif";
  var refresh_headlines_1 = new Image();
  refresh_headlines_1.src = "img/refresh_headlines_1.gif";
  var collapse_sidebar_0 = new Image();
  collapse_sidebar_0.src = "img/collapse_sidebar_0.gif";
  var collapse_sidebar_1 = new Image();
  collapse_sidebar_1.src = "img/collapse_sidebar_1.gif";
  var expand_sidebar_0 = new Image();
  expand_sidebar_0.src = "img/expand_sidebar_0.gif";
  var expand_sidebar_1 = new Image();
  expand_sidebar_1.src = "img/expand_sidebar_1.gif";
  var save_feed_0 = new Image();
  save_feed_0.src = "img/save_feed_0.gif";
  var save_feed_1 = new Image();
  save_feed_1.src = "img/save_feed_1.gif";
  var delete_feed_0 = new Image();
  delete_feed_0.src = "img/delete_feed_0.gif";
  var delete_feed_1 = new Image();
  delete_feed_1.src = "img/delete_feed_1.gif";
```

```
// This function is called onLoad to initialize things.
function init() {
  // Size the divIFrame div so it takes up the whole window.  There is
  // a browser bug that causes setting the height to 100%, as we'd want
  // to do, to not work.  So, we need to do it via scripting.  And
  // of course, there is a difference between IE and FF in how it counts
  // the size of the document, so some branching logic is in order.  We
  // will use the typical check for the XMLHttpRequest object to
  // determine which browser we're running in.
  var dh = document.body.offsetHeight;
  if (window.XMLHttpRequest) {
    dh = dh - 84;
  } else {
    dh = dh - 120;
  }
  document.getElementById("divIFrame").style.height = dh + "px";
  window.frames["ifContent"].document.open();
  window.frames["ifContent"].document.write(
    "Please click a feed to view headlines...");
  window.frames["ifContent"].document.close();
  document.forms[0].feedTitle.value = "";
  document.forms[0].feedURL.value = "";
  document.forms[0].feedTitleEdit.value = "";
  document.forms[0].feedURLEdit.value = "";
  viewState = 0;

} // End init().


// Called when a feed is clicked in the feed list to show headlines.
// This is also called when the Refresh Headlines button is clicked,
// hence the need for the event to be passed in.
function showFeedHeadlines(inEvent, inFeedTitle, inFeedURL) {

  lastClickedLink = null;

  // When the page is first shown and user clicks Refresh button, that
  // isn't a valid condition, so quickly reject that with a message.
  if (viewState == 0 && inEvent == "refresh") {
    alert("Please select a feed first");
    return;
  }
  // When an article is showing...
  if (viewState == 2) {
    // We need to recreate the iFrame within the divIFrame div.  This
    // gets around browser security restrictions since we can't touch
    // the iFrame in most ways once an external article is showing.
```

```
      // Unfortunately, there doesn't appear to be a cross-browser way to
      // do this, so we have to branch based on browser type.  We'll use
      // the same check of XMLHttpRequest, even though we are not actually
      // using that object, since that is a pretty good way to determine
      // whether we're using IE vs. some other browser.
      if (window.XMLHttpRequest){
        var newIF = document.createElement("iframe");
        newIF.setAttribute("name", "ifContent");
        newIF.setAttribute("width", "100%");
        newIF.setAttribute("height", "100%");
        newIF.setAttribute("frameborder", "no");
        var dif = document.getElementById("divIFrame");
        dif.appendChild(newIF);
      } else {
        document.getElementById("divIFrame").innerHTML =
          "<iframe name=\"ifContent\" width=\"100" + "%" + "\" " +
          "height=\"100" + "%" + "\" frameborder=\"no\"></iframe>"
      }
    }
    // When refresh is clicked and a feed is shown...
    if (inEvent == "refresh") {
      inFeedTitle = feedForm.feedTitle.value;
      inFeedURL = feedForm.feedURL.value;
    }
    // Set values in form.
    feedForm.feedTitle.value = inFeedTitle;
    feedForm.feedURL.value = inFeedURL;
    feedForm.feedTitleEdit.value = inFeedTitle;
    feedForm.feedURLEdit.value = inFeedURL;
    // Write out contents to iFrame.
    window.frames["ifContent"].document.open();
    window.frames["ifContent"].document.write(
      "Please wait, retrieving headlines...");
    window.frames["ifContent"].document.close();
    // Call our manual Ajax function (which AjaxTags wrote for us) to do
    // the actual headlines refresh, and also udpate the view state
    // appropriately.
    doRefreshHeadlines();
    viewState = 1;
  } // End showFeedHeadlines().


  // Called to collapse or expand the sidebar so more of the feed
  // headlines or an article can be seen.
  function collapseExpandSidebar() {
```

```
      var tds = document.getElementById("tdSidebar");
      var o = document.getElementById("btnExpandCollapseSidebar");
      if (o.getAttribute("whichButton") == "collapse") {
        tds.style.display = "none";
        o.setAttribute("whichButton", "expand");
        o.src = "img/expand_sidebar_0.gif";
      } else {
        tds.style.display = "block";
        o.setAttribute("whichButton", "collapse");
        o.src = "img/collapse_sidebar_0.gif";
      }

    } // End collapseExpandSidebar().


    // Called when a link in the iFrame is clicked.
    function linkClicked(inLinkUri) {

      lastClickedLink = inLinkUri;
      viewState = 2;

    } // End linkClicked().


    // Called to open article in a new window.
    function openInNewWindow() {
      if (lastClickedLink != null) {
        var winOpts = "menubar,resizable,scrollbars,titlebar,status," +
          "toolbar,width=640px,height=480px,top=0px,left=0px";
        window.open(lastClickedLink, "Print", winOpts);
      }
    }


  </script>


</head>

<body onLoad="init();" class="cssMain">

  <!-- Ajax event to continually update our feed list. -->
  <ajax:timer ajaxRef="page/listFeeds" startOnLoad="true" frequency="1000" />
```

```
<!-- Function to be called when a feed is clicked. -->
<ajax:manual ajaxRef="page/showHeadlines"
  manualFunction="doRefreshHeadlines" />

<table border="1" cellpadding="0" cellspacing="0" bordercolor="#000000"
  width="100%" height="100%" class="cssMain" id="outerTable">
  <tr>
    <!-- Sidebar. -->
    <td width="250" id="tdSidebar" class="cssSidebar">
      <table border="0" cellpadding="4" cellspacing="0" width="100%"
        height="100%" class="cssMain">
        <tr>
          <!-- Feed Maintenance. -->
          <td height="200" valign="top">
            <form name="feedForm" onSubmit="return false;">
              <input type="hidden" name="feedTitle">
              <input type="hidden" name="feedURL">
              Feed Title:<br>
              <input type="text" name="feedTitleEdit" size="30"
                maxlength="50" class="cssTextbox"
                onFocus="this.className='cssTextboxActive';"
                onBlur="this.className='cssTextbox';">
              <br><br>
              Feed URL:<br>
              <input type="text" name="feedURLEdit" size="30"
                maxlength="100" class="cssTextbox"
                onFocus="this.className='cssTextboxActive';"
                onBlur="this.className='cssTextbox';">
              <br><br>
              <input type="image" src="img/save_feed_0.gif"
                hspace="2" valign="absmiddle" border="0"
                onMouseOver="this.src=save_feed_1.src;"
                onMouseOut="this.src=save_feed_0.src;">
              <ajax:event ajaxRef="feedForm/saveFeed" />
                 
              <input type="image" src="img/delete_feed_0.gif"
                hspace="2" valign="absmiddle" border="0"
                onMouseOver="this.src=delete_feed_1.src;"
                onMouseOut="this.src=delete_feed_0.src;">
              <ajax:event ajaxRef="feedForm/deleteFeed" />
            </form>
            <hr width="100%" color="#000000">
          </td>
        </tr>
        <tr>
```

```
        <!-- Feed List. -->
        <td valign="top">
          <div class="cssFeedList" id="divFeedList">
            Please wait,<br>retrieving feed list...
          </div>
        </td>
      </tr>
    </table>
  </td>
  <!-- Main content. -->
  <td>
    <table border="0" cellpadding="4" cellspacing="0" width="100%"
      height="100%" class="cssMain">
      <tr height="60" id="topBar">
        <!-- Control and title. -->
        <td width="100%" valign="middle" class="cssControlTitle">
          <table border="0" cellpadding="0" cellspacing="0" width="100%"
            height="100%" class="cssMain">
            <tr>
              <td width="220">
                <img src="img/rssreader_title.gif" valign="absmiddle">
              </td>
              <td align="right">
                <input type="image" src="img/refresh_headlines_0.gif"
                  hspace="10" valign="absmiddle" border="0"
                  onMouseOver="this.src=refresh_headlines_1.src;"
                  onMouseOut="this.src=refresh_headlines_0.src;"
                  onClick="showFeedHeadlines('refresh', '', '');">
                <input type="image" src="img/collapse_sidebar_0.gif"
                  id="btnExpandCollapseSidebar" hspace="10"
                  valign="absmiddle" border="0"
                  onMouseOver="this.src=eval(this.getAttribute('whichButton')+
                  '_sidebar_1').src;"
                  onMouseOut="this.src=eval(this.getAttribute('whichButton')+
                  '_sidebar_0').src;"
                  onClick="collapseExpandSidebar();"
                  whichButton="collapse">
                <input type="image" src="img/open_in_new_window_0.gif"
                  hspace="10" valign="absmiddle" border="0"
                  onMouseOver="this.src=open_in_new_window_1.src;"
                  onMouseOut="this.src=open_in_new_window_0.src;"
                  onClick="openInNewWindow();">
              </td>
            </tr>
```

```
                <!-- Divider line. -->
                <tr height="10">
                  <td class="cssDividerRow" valign="top" colspan="2">
                    <hr width="100%" color="#000000">
                  </td>
                </tr>
              </table>
            </td>
          </tr>
          <!-- Content. -->
          <tr>
            <td valign="top">
              <div id="divIFrame"><iframe name="ifContent" width="100%"
                height="100%" frameborder="no"></iframe></div>
            </td>
          </tr>
        </table>
      </td>
    </tr>
  </table>


</body>

<ajax:enable debug="false" />
</html>
```

Let's start with the markup first. The first thing we see is that when the page loads, in response to the onLoad event, a JavaScript function, init(), is called. This, as the name implies, initializes the application. We'll look at this function shortly. After that come two AjaxTags:

```
<!-- Ajax event to continually update our feed list. -->
<ajax:timer ajaxRef="page/listFeeds" startOnLoad="true" frequency="1000" />

<!-- Function to be called when a feed is clicked. -->
<ajax:manual ajaxRef="page/showHeadlines"
  manualFunction="doRefreshHeadlines" />
```

As previously discussed, the first tag, <ajax:timer>, sets up a periodic Ajax event that refreshes the list of feeds the user sees. The second, the <ajax:manual> tag, renders the appropriate JavaScript for us to make a manual Ajax call whenever we please. This will be called when one of the feeds in the feed list is clicked.

After that comes a fairly typical table-based layout. It consists of essentially three sections: a sidebar, a top bar, and a main content area. The sidebar is further subdivided into an area where feeds can be maintained, and then the list of feeds itself. The feed maintenance section consists of an HTML form named feedForm. Four fields are present in the form, two each for the feed title and feed URL. One of each is hidden and the remainder are editable by the user. The reason there seems to be duplication is that when a user clicks on a feed, we want to populate the edit boxes so that they can modify the feed. However, if we were to use the values of those fields when we retrieved headlines, we might run into problems because the user might have changed them on us. So, we use the hidden field values when retrieving headlines, but the editable fields when saving the feed.

We also have two graphical buttons on the form, one for saving the feed currently in the edit boxes, and one for deleting the feed. We use a typical JavaScript rollover effect to make them come alive. In case you have never seen that before, it is simply swapping the image that is displayed when the mouse hovers over the button, and swapping back the original image when the mouse leaves the button. This is done by setting the `src` attribute of the image (using the `this` keyword) to point to the `src` of an image that was previously loaded (you will see this when we look at the script on the page). Notice that they are *not* form submission buttons in the sense that we do not want them to actually submit the form. The form itself is not meant to be submitted; it is merely a container for the elements of the form so that we can use AjaxTags to work with it. This actually presents a subtle problem in some browsers because submitting the form happens concurrently with the Ajax event firing, which results in subtle, intermittent errors. The way to avoid this is to make sure the form does not get submitted, and that is the purpose of the `onSubmit` handler attached to the form. It simply returns false, which stops the form submission.

Each of the buttons has an Ajax event attached to it:

```
<input type="image" src="img/save_feed_0.gif"
  hspace="2" valign="absmiddle" border="0"
  onMouseOver="this.src=save_feed_1.src;"
  onMouseOut="this.src=save_feed_0.src;">
<ajax:event ajaxRef="feedForm/saveFeed" />
   
<input type="image" src="img/delete_feed_0.gif"
  hspace="2" valign="absmiddle" border="0"
  onMouseOver="this.src=delete_feed_1.src;"
  onMouseOut="this.src=delete_feed_0.src;">
<ajax:event ajaxRef="feedForm/deleteFeed" />
```

AjaxTags takes care of rendering the appropriate script for us onto these buttons.

Below the form is a `<div>` named `divFeedList`. I take the simple approach with the feed list and simply rewrite the entire contents of the `<div>` whenever the list is refreshed.

The main content area comes next, and this is divided into a top bar and the area where the headlines and articles are displayed. In the top bar we find three buttons:

```
<input type="image" src="img/refresh_headlines_0.gif"
  hspace="10" valign="absmiddle" border="0"
  onMouseOver="this.src=refresh_headlines_1.src;"
  onMouseOut="this.src=refresh_headlines_0.src;"
  onClick="showFeedHeadlines('refresh', '', '');">
<input type="image" src="img/collapse_sidebar_0.gif"
  id="btnExpandCollapseSidebar" hspace="10"
  valign="absmiddle" border="0"
  onMouseOver="this.src=eval(this.getAttribute('whichButton')+
  '_sidebar_1').src;"
  onMouseOut="this.src=eval(this.getAttribute('whichButton')+
  '_sidebar_0').src;"
```

```
    onClick="collapseExpandSidebar();"
    whichButton="collapse">
  <input type="image" src="img/open_in_new_window_0.gif"
    hspace="10" valign="absmiddle" border="0"
    onMouseOver="this.src=open_in_new_window_1.src;"
    onMouseOut="this.src=open_in_new_window_0.src;"
    onClick="openInNewWindow();">
```

Here again we see the image rollover effect being used to make the buttons reactive to the user. This is always a good thing since it both engages the user and gives them feedback that their actions actually result in something happening. We have all had applications freeze on us, or seemingly so, and we sit there wondering whether or not it is still working. Simple visual feedback cues like this help alleviate that problem.

You will see that each of these buttons has an `onClick` event handler attached. The first button, which refreshes headlines, calls the `showFeedHeadlines()` JavaScript function, which we'll see briefly. The second button calls `collapseExpandSidebar()` to show or hide the sidebar, thereby allowing the user to switch to a larger view if they wish. The third button calls the `openInNewWindow()` function and is meant to be used when you want to print an article, or just have a separate browser window to view it in.

Note the `whichButton` attribute on the Collapse Sidebar button. If you look up the `<input>` tag, you will not find that attribute. With HTML, you can attach arbitrary attributes to any tag you wish, and modern browsers will essentially add them to the DOM for that element. This is handy when you have a piece of information about the state of a specific tag you wish to store, for example, as is the case here. When the sidebar is showing, the button should say "Collapse Sidebar", but when the sidebar is hidden, the button should say "Expand Sidebar". While we could store this information in a JavaScript variable, it is more elegant to store it on the tag itself as a custom attribute, and that is precisely what `whichButton` is. With the value of this attribute, we can construct a complete variable name as appropriate for the current state of the button using the JavaScript `eval()` function. This function takes a string and evaluates it. In this case, the string it is evaluating is the name of one of the images constructed on the fly using the value of the `whichButton` attribute as part of it. Therefore, what `eval()` returns to us winds up being an object reference to one of the preloaded images. We then set the `src` attribute of the button to the `src` attribute of that image, and the image changes on the screen.

This attribute is also used in the `collapseExpandSidebar()` function, which we'll look at shortly.

The third button, the Open In New Window button, is necessary to allow for printing. The problem that arises is that the articles are displayed in an iFrame. Unfortunately, once you direct an iFrame to a URL outside the domain that served the original page (i.e., where AjaxReader was served from), you can no longer do most things with it. This is to avoid cross-domain scripting exploits. One big no-no is calling the `print()` method on the iFrame's window, which is how you might expect to be able to print. While some browsers seem to allow this by default, and while the ones that do not could probably be coerced into doing so by playing with security settings, we would not want to require a user to do this in order to print. So, what we do instead is open the article in a new window, from which the user can browse it at will, or print it—no problem. To do this, we need to record the URL that is clicked when viewing feed headlines. Then, when this button is clicked, we open the new window with that URL. We'll see how the URL is stored later when we begin to examine the script for AjaxReader. For now, just keep in mind that when you click a headline, the URL is recorded in a JavaScript variable, and that variable is used when you click the Open In New Window button.

The last bit of markup to discuss is the main content section. The important part is here:

```
<div id="divIFrame"><iframe name="ifContent" width="100%"
  height="100%" frameborder="no"></iframe></div>
```

You may be wondering why the iFrame is wrapped in a <div>. Why not just have the iFrame itself present? The reason relates to what happens when you click on one of the headlines and are viewing an article. Imagine clicking the Refresh Headlines button. If we did that, we would have to rewrite the contents of the iFrame again. But what domain was currently showing in the iFrame? Not the domain of AjaxReader in all likelihood! Therefore, we would bump up against the browser's security model, not allowing us to do it. By wrapping the iFrame in a <div>, we can rewrite the contents of the <div>, which means re-creating the iFrame entirely. Since the <div> will always be in the originating domain, no such security issues arise.

That covers the markup, now we can look at the script in the <head> of the page. The first thing we encounter there is a page-scoped variable named `viewState`. This stores a value that determines what our view currently looks like. Three values are possible: 0 indicates we are in our "initial" state, which is when the page first loads; 1 indicates the headlines of a feed are showing; and 2 indicates an article is being displayed. This information becomes important when various buttons are clicked. We also find a variable `lastClickedLink`. This stores the most recent link clicked when viewing headlines. This is needed when the Open In New Window button is clicked. Ideally, we could have just referenced the iFrame's `src` attribute to determine the URL to open in the new window, but unfortunately this runs afoul of browser security restrictions in most cases. To avoid that, we have an `onClick` event on the headlines that updates the value of this variable so we have it to open in a new window.

After that comes a section of image preloads. This is used for the image rollover effects. We instruct the browser to create `Image` objects for us, which causes it to go fetch the images specified and store them in memory. Note that this image retrieval happens immediately when the `src` attribute is assigned, which is precisely what we want because we want to have the image in memory (or in the local disk-based cache, at the browser's discretion) before we ever use them. This is important because imagine what would happen if you put your mouse over a button and the browser at that point went out to get the appropriate image, and then when your mouse left the button it went out again to get the next appropriate image. This would be a lot of network traffic for a trivial thing, and there would be delays just in the button changing appearance. Preloading the images avoids this problem.

Immediately following that is our `init()` function:

```
// This function is called onLoad to initialize things.
function init() {
  // Size the divIFrame div so it takes up the whole window.  There is
  // a browser bug that causes setting the height to 100%, as we'd want
  // to do, to not work.  So, we need to do it via scripting.  And
  // of course, there is a difference between IE and FF in how it counts
  // the size of the document, so some branching logic is in order.  We
  // will use the typical check for the XMLHttpRequest object to
  // determine which browser we're running in.
  var dh = document.body.offsetHeight;
```

```
  if (window.XMLHttpRequest) {
    dh = dh - 84;
  } else {
    dh = dh - 120;
  }
  document.getElementById("divIFrame").style.height = dh + "px";
  window.frames["ifContent"].document.open();
  window.frames["ifContent"].document.write(
    "Please click a feed to view headlines...");
  window.frames["ifContent"].document.close();
  document.forms[0].feedTitle.value = "";
  document.forms[0].feedURL.value = "";
  document.forms[0].feedTitleEdit.value = "";
  document.forms[0].feedURLEdit.value = "";
  viewState = 0;

} // End init().
```

This function performs a couple of tasks. First, it sets the size of the iFrame so it takes up the whole window. It would have been desirable to be able to simply set a height of 100% on the iFrame, but unfortunately, a bug in some browsers causes this to not work. Therefore, this bit of script is necessary. We basically just get the `offsetHeight` of the document, which is in essence the amount of space the document takes up in the browser window, and subtract a bit from it to account for the buttons and logo at the top. Unfortunately, a single value for both browsers does not suffice because the `offsetHeight` is calculated differently in Firefox versus Internet Explorer. So, through some trial and error (believe it or not!), I settled on the values 84 for Firefox and 120 for Internet Explorer as yielding just about the same effect. Note the use of the typical `XMLHttpRequest` browser branch check to determine which value to use. Even though Ajax is not involved at this point, this check is quick and easy and works well.

Second, it writes out a message in the iFrame telling the user to click a feed to view headlines. Third, it sets the values of our `feedForm` to all blanks. Last, it sets the `viewState` to 0. All but the first task might seem redundant, since by default the `feedForm` fields are all blank and `viewState` is 0 already. However, this function serves a dual purpose and will be called at various times later as well to "reset" the view, and that is why these functions are done here anyway.

After the `init()` function comes the `showFeedHeadlines()` function. This function is called when the user clicks a feed in the feed list. It is also called when the Refresh Headlines button is clicked. Because it serves both these purposes, it accepts a parameter, `inEvent`, which tells it where the call came from and it can branch its logic based on that. This parameter will always have one of two values, either "feed", when a feed in the feed list is clicked, or "refresh", when the Refresh Headlines button is clicked. Used in conjunction with the `viewState` variable, this function can always react accordingly.

For example, the first check performed is

```
if (viewState == 0 && inEvent == "refresh") {
  alert("Please select a feed first");
  return;
}
```

This covers the case of the user clicking the Refresh Headlines before a feed has been selected. When the value is "refresh" in any other view state, we simply need to populate the hidden form fields and submit an Ajax request:

```
// When refresh is clicked and a feed is shown...
if (inEvent == "refresh") {
  inFeedTitle = feedForm.feedTitle.value;
  inFeedURL = feedForm.feedURL.value;
}
```

This snippet retrieves the title and URL of the feed currently being viewed and puts them into two variables that will be used a few lines later to populate the form that will be used by the call to `doRefreshHeadlines()` later on that fires the Ajax event (note the method name was specified in the manual tag). And finally, if the `viewState` is 2, meaning articles are showing, then regardless of the value of `inEvent`, we need to create an empty iFrame again, so we do this:

```
// When an article is showing...
if (viewState == 2) {
  // We need to recreate the iFrame within the divIFrame div.  This
  // gets around browser security restrictions since we can't touch
  // the iFrame in most ways once an external article is showing.
  // Unfortunately, there doesn't appear to be a cross-browser way to
  // do this, so we have to branch based on browser type.  We'll use
  // the same check of XMLHttpRequest, even though we are not actually
  // using that object, since that is a pretty good way to determine
  // whether we're using IE vs. some other browser.
  if (window.XMLHttpRequest){
    var newIF = document.createElement("iframe");
    newIF.setAttribute("name", "ifContent");
    newIF.setAttribute("width", "100%");
    newIF.setAttribute("height", "100%");
    newIF.setAttribute("frameborder", "no");
    var dif = document.getElementById("divIFrame");
    dif.appendChild(newIF);
  } else {
    document.getElementById("divIFrame").innerHTML =
      "<iframe name=\"ifContent\" width=\"100" + "%" + "\" " +
      "height=\"100" + "%" + "\" frameborder=\"no\"></iframe>"
  }
}
```

Note again a branch based on browser type. The problem is that in Firefox, simply replacing the `innerHTML` attribute of the `<div>` does not result in the iFrame being inserted into the DOM, and we need that for things later. In Internet Explorer, it does get inserted into the DOM. So, for Firefox, we create a new iFrame element, set the appropriate attributes on it, and then append it to the `divIFrame` element. For Internet Explorer, simply setting `innerHTML` is sufficient.

After that comes code that would apply in all cases, namely setting the four form field values to what was passed in (or, if the event was a refresh, the values that were pulled from the form fields), writing out the Please Wait message to the iFrame, setting our `viewState` appropriately, and of course firing the Ajax event.

Next is the `collapseExpandSidebar()` function. This actually has nothing at all to do with Ajax; it is a strictly client-side DOM manipulation function. Its job, as you can guess from the name, is to collapse or expand (hide or show) the sidebar. To do this, the `whichButton` attribute of the button is interrogated to determine whether to collapse or expand the sidebar based on its current state. Also note the use of the `getAttribute()` function. This is a DOM manipulation function that must be used in some browsers (other browsers allow you to directly reference the attribute) to access custom attributes. There is a corresponding `setAttribute()`, which you can see used here as well to update the value of the `whichButton` attribute. Once the determination is made as to whether we are expanding or collapsing the sidebar, the `display` style attribute of the sidebar is set appropriately, and the `whichButton` attribute of the button is switched as well, along with the image of the button so it reflects the correct option.

The next bit of code on this page is the `linkClicked()` function. This is called any time a headline is clicked. Its sole purpose in life is to set the `viewState` to 2, the appropriate state indicator, and to set the `lastClickedLink` variable to the URL that is passed in, which is the URL of the headline that was clicked. Note that the call to this function is made from code that is rendered by the `ListHeadlinesServlet`, which we'll see very soon. I only mention this because if you search `index.jsp` for the usage of `linkClicked()`, you would find that nothing ever calls it, and I did not want you wondering why!

styles.css

There is also an external stylesheet involved here, and it is shown in Listing 6-4.

Listing 6-4. *The AjaxReader Stylesheet*

```
.cssMain {
  font-family      : arial;
  font-size        : 12pt;
  font-weight      : bold;
}

.cssFeed {
  color            : #000000;
  cursor           : normal;
}

.cssFeedHover {
  color            : #ff0000;
  cursor           : pointer;
}

.cssSidebar {
  display          : block;
  background-color : #f0f0f0;
}
```

```
.cssFeedList {
  width            : 100%;
  height           : 100%;
  overflow         : scroll;
}

.cssControlTitle {
  background-color : #f0f0f0;
}

.cssDividerRow {
  background-color : #f0f0f0;
}

.cssTextbox {
  font-family      : verdana;
  font-size        : 10pt;
  font-weight      : bold;
  border           : solid 2px #000000;
  background-color : #ffffff;
}

.cssTextboxActive {
  font-family      : verdana;
  font-size        : 10pt;
  font-weight      : bold;
  border           : solid 2px #ffa0a0;
  background-color : #ffff00;
}
```

Probably the only interesting thing in the stylesheet is the setting of the `cursor` attribute for the feed list items in the `cssFeedHover` selector. This gives us a nice pointing hand, or pointer arrow depending on your operating system, when you hover over a feed in the list. The same style selector also changes the color to red when hovered over. Again, visual cues to the user are always a good idea. Also note the other visual cues on the `cssTextboxActive` selector. This sets the background of the text box to yellow, and the border to a light red when it is the active text box.

The Server-Side Code

Now that we have looked at the rather petite presentation layer of AjaxReader, let's see what is happening on the server side of things.

FeedDescriptorDTO.java

AjaxReader consists of a grand total of six Java classes: five servlets and one DTO. We'll look at the DTO first, shown in Listing 6-5.

Listing 6-5. *The FeedDescriptorDTO in All Its (Imagined) Grandeur*

```
package com.apress.ajaxprojects.rssreader.dtos;


import java.lang.reflect.Field;


/**
 * This is a bean that represents a feed.
 */
public class FeedDescriptor {


  /**
   *
   */
  private String feedTitle;


  /**
   *
   */
  private String feedURL;


  /**
   * feedTitle mutator.
   *
   * @param inFeedTitle New feedTitle value.
   */
  public void setFeedTitle(String inFeedTitle) {

    feedTitle = inFeedTitle;

  } // End setFeedTitle().


  /**
   * feedTitle accessor.
   *
   * @return feedTitle current value.
   */
  public String getFeedTitle() {
```

```
    return feedTitle;

  } // End getFeedTitle().


  /**
   * feedURL mutator.
   *
   * @param inFeedURL New feedURL value.
   */
  public void setFeedURL(String inFeedURL) {

    feedURL = inFeedURL;

  } // End setFeedURL().


  /**
   * feedURL accessor.
   *
   * @return feedURL current value.
   */
  public String getFeedURL() {

    return feedURL;

  } // End getFeedURL().


  /**
   * Overriden toString method.
   *
   * @return A reflexively built string representation of this bean.
   */
  public String toString() {

    String str = null;
    StringBuffer sb = new StringBuffer(1000);
    sb.append("[" + super.toString() + "]=\n{{{{");
    try {
      Field[] fields = this.getClass().getDeclaredFields();
      for (int i = 0; i < fields.length; i++) {
        sb.append("\n" + fields[i].getName() + "=" + fields[i].get(this));
      }
      sb.append("\n}}}}");
```

```
      str = sb.toString().trim();
    } catch (IllegalAccessException iae) {
      iae.printStackTrace();
    }
    return str;

  } // End toString().


} // End class.
```

The FeedDescriptor DTO is nothing but a simple bean that stores information about a feed, namely its title and URL. Move along, nothing to see here!

StartupServlet.java

Now we come to the servlets, where we'll find there are some things to look at. First up is StartupServlet, as shown in Listing 6-6.

Listing 6-6. *StartupServlet*

```
package com.apress.ajaxprojects.rssreader.servlets;


import com.apress.ajaxprojects.rssreader.dtos.FeedDescriptor;
import java.io.InputStream;
import java.util.ArrayList;
import java.util.Iterator;
import java.util.Properties;
import javax.servlet.http.HttpServlet;
import javax.servlet.ServletConfig;
import javax.servlet.ServletContext;
import javax.servlet.ServletException;
import org.apache.commons.logging.Log;
import org.apache.commons.logging.LogFactory;


/**
 * Servlet called at application startup to set things up.
 *
 * @author <a href="mailto:fzammetti@omnytex.com">Frank W. Zammetti</a>.
 */
public class StartupServlet extends HttpServlet {


  /**
   * Log instance.
   */
```

```
  private static Log log = LogFactory.getLog(StartupServlet.class);


  /**
   * init.
   *
   * @throws ServletException if anything goes wrong.
   */
  public void init() throws ServletException {

    try {
      log.info("AjaxReader StartupServlet Initializing...");
      ServletConfig  servletConfig  = getServletConfig();
      ServletContext servletContext = servletConfig.getServletContext();
      // Get a stream on the feeds.properties file and load it in.
      InputStream isFeedFile =
        servletContext.getResourceAsStream("WEB-INF/feeds.properties");
      Properties properties = new Properties();
      properties.load(isFeedFile);
      ArrayList feeds = new ArrayList();
      // Iterate over all the feeds, create a FeedDescriptor DTO for each and
      // store the collection in application scope.
      for (Iterator it = properties.keySet().iterator(); it.hasNext();) {
        String feedTitle = (String)it.next();
        String feedURL   = properties.getProperty(feedTitle);
        FeedDescriptor feedDescriptor = new FeedDescriptor();
        feedDescriptor.setFeedTitle(feedTitle);
        feedDescriptor.setFeedURL(feedURL);
        feeds.add(feedDescriptor);
      }
      servletContext.setAttribute("feeds", feeds);
      log.info("feeds = " + feeds);
      log.info("AjaxReader StartupServlet Done");
    } catch (Exception e) {
      e.printStackTrace();
    }

  } // End init().


} // End class.
```

As you will recall from `web.xml`, `StartupServlet` is the only servlet that starts when the context starts; all others are initialized upon first use. The job of this servlet is to read in the `feeds.properties` file, construct a `FeedDescriptorDTO` for each feed found, and add it to a collection, which is stored in application context. This saves us from having to read to the file all the time; we instead keep it in memory and then only worry about updates to the feed list.

If you have ever worked with properties files, the code will look familiar to you. We simply get a stream on the properties file and feed that stream to the `Properties` class's `load()` method. We then iterate over the collection of properties, and for each we instantiate a `FeedDescriptorDTO` and populate it. Each DTO is placed into an `ArrayList`, which is then set as a servlet context attribute. This is the same as application scope, or context scope. Although there is not much to `StartupServlet`, it is an essential part of the application.

ListFeedsServlet.java

After `StartupServlet` comes the `ListFeeds` servlet, shown in Listing 6-7.

Listing 6-7. *The Servlet That Lists Our Feeds for Us, the Aptly Named ListFeedsServlet*

```
package com.apress.ajaxprojects.rssreader.servlets;


import com.apress.ajaxprojects.rssreader.dtos.FeedDescriptor;
import java.io.IOException;
import java.io.PrintWriter;
import java.util.ArrayList;
import java.util.Iterator;
import javax.servlet.http.HttpServlet;
import javax.servlet.http.HttpServletRequest;
import javax.servlet.http.HttpServletResponse;
import javax.servlet.ServletException;
import org.apache.commons.logging.Log;
import org.apache.commons.logging.LogFactory;


/**
 * Servlet to list feeds.
 *
 * @author <a href="mailto:fzammetti@omnytex.com">Frank W. Zammetti</a>.
 */
public class ListFeedsServlet extends HttpServlet {


  /**
   * Log instance.
   */
  private static Log log = LogFactory.getLog(ListFeedsServlet.class);


  /**
   * doGet.  Calls doPost() to do real work.
   *
   * @param  request          HTTPServletRequest.
   * @param  response         HTTPServletResponse.
```

```
   * @throws ServletException ServletException.
   * @throws IOException      IOException.
   */
  public void doGet(HttpServletRequest request, HttpServletResponse response)
    throws ServletException, IOException {

    doPost(request, response);

  } // End doGet().


  /**
   * doPost.
   *
   * @param  request          HTTPServletRequest.
   * @param  response         HTTPServletResponse.
   * @throws ServletException ServletException.
   * @throws IOException      IOException.
   */
  public void doPost(HttpServletRequest request, HttpServletResponse response)
    throws ServletException, IOException {

    log.info("ListFeedsServlet.doPost()");
    response.setContentType("text/html");
    PrintWriter out = response.getWriter();
    ArrayList feeds = (ArrayList)getServletContext().getAttribute("feeds");
    // Iterate over the collection of feeds and for each write out some
    // markup that will allow it to be clicked to display its headlines.
    // We want to highlight it when hovered over too.
    for (Iterator it = feeds.iterator(); it.hasNext();) {
      FeedDescriptor feedDescriptor = (FeedDescriptor)it.next();
      out.println("<div class=\"cssFeed\" onClick=\"" +
        "showFeedHeadlines('feed','" + feedDescriptor.getFeedTitle() + "'," +
        "'" + feedDescriptor.getFeedURL() + "');\"" +
        " onMouseOver=\"this.className='cssFeedHover';\"" +
        " onMouseOut=\"this.className='cssFeed';\"" +
        ">" + feedDescriptor.getFeedTitle() + "</div>");
    }

  } // End doPost().


} // End class.
```

ListFeedsServlet generates the markup that is displayed in the feed list section of the screen. The code gets the ArrayList from application context and iterates over it. For each we construct the appropriate markup for the feed.

Part of the generated markup is the `onClick` event handler. Notice that it calls the `showFeedHeadlines()` JavaScript function that we examined earlier, this time passing in `feed` as the first parameter. Recall how this is used to branch the logic within that function. We also attach `onMouseOver` and `onMouseOut` handlers to change the style class that the element is displayed with. This is how the color and cursor get changed when you hover over an item.

ListHeadlinesServlet.java

Next up in our cavalcade of servlets comes `ListHeadlinesServlet`, shown in Listing 6-8.

Listing 6-8. *ListHeadlinesServlet*

```
package com.apress.ajaxprojects.rssreader.servlets;


import com.apress.ajaxprojects.rssreader.dtos.FeedDescriptor;
import com.sun.syndication.feed.synd.SyndEntryImpl;
import com.sun.syndication.feed.synd.SyndFeed;
import com.sun.syndication.io.SyndFeedInput;
import com.sun.syndication.io.XmlReader;
import java.io.ByteArrayInputStream;
import java.io.IOException;
import java.io.PrintWriter;
import java.net.URL;
import java.util.ArrayList;
import java.util.Iterator;
import java.util.List;
import javawebparts.request.RequestHelpers;
import javax.servlet.http.HttpServlet;
import javax.servlet.http.HttpServletRequest;
import javax.servlet.http.HttpServletResponse;
import javax.servlet.ServletException;
import org.apache.commons.digester.Digester;
import org.apache.commons.lang.StringEscapeUtils;
import org.apache.commons.logging.Log;
import org.apache.commons.logging.LogFactory;


/**
 * Servlet to list headlines for a given feed.
 *
 * @author <a href="mailto:fzammetti@omnytex.com">Frank W. Zammetti</a>.
 */
public class ListHeadlinesServlet extends HttpServlet {
```

```
/**
 * Log instance.
 */
private static Log log = LogFactory.getLog(ListHeadlinesServlet.class);


/**
 * doGet.  Calls doPost() to do real work.
 *
 * @param  request          HTTPServletRequest.
 * @param  response         HTTPServletResponse.
 * @throws ServletException ServletException.
 * @throws IOException      IOException.
 */
public void doGet(HttpServletRequest request, HttpServletResponse response)
  throws ServletException, IOException {

  doPost(request, response);

} // End doGet().


/**
 * doPost.
 *
 * @param  request          HTTPServletRequest.
 * @param  response         HTTPServletResponse.
 * @throws ServletException ServletException.
 * @throws IOException      IOException.
 */
public void doPost(HttpServletRequest request, HttpServletResponse response)
  throws ServletException, IOException {

  try {

    log.info("ListHeadlinesServlet.doPost()");

    // We are going to use Commons Digester to parse the XML that was
    // POSTed to this servlet to get headlines for the specified feed.
    Digester digester = new Digester();
    digester.setValidating(false);
    // The XML has the form:
    // <feed>
    //   <feedTitle />
    // </feed>
    // We create a FeedDescriptor instance when <feed> is hit, then populate
    // it from the three child elements.
```

```
digester.addObjectCreate("feed",
  "com.apress.ajaxprojects.rssreader.dtos.FeedDescriptor");
digester.addBeanPropertySetter("feed/feedTitle", "feedTitle");
String         newFeedXML     = RequestHelpers.getBodyContent(request);
FeedDescriptor feedDescriptor = null;
feedDescriptor = (FeedDescriptor)digester.parse(
  new ByteArrayInputStream(newFeedXML.getBytes()));

// Show the FeedDescriptor we just filled in.
log.info("Feed = " + feedDescriptor);

// Now we go through our collection of feeds in application context
// and find the one we need so we can get the URL.
String    feedURL = null;
ArrayList feeds   = (ArrayList)getServletContext().getAttribute("feeds");
for (Iterator it = feeds.iterator(); it.hasNext();) {
  FeedDescriptor fd = (FeedDescriptor)it.next();
  if (fd.getFeedTitle().equals(feedDescriptor.getFeedTitle())) {
    feedURL = fd.getFeedURL();
    break;
  }
}

// Set up proxy, if configured.
String proxyHost = getServletContext().getInitParameter("proxyHost");
String proxyPort = getServletContext().getInitParameter("proxyPort");
if (proxyHost != null && !proxyHost.equalsIgnoreCase("") &&
  proxyPort != null && !proxyPort.equalsIgnoreCase("")) {
    System.getProperties().put("proxySet", "true");
    System.getProperties().put("proxyHost", proxyHost);
    System.getProperties().put("proxyPort", proxyPort);
}

// Use ROME to get the clicked feed.
URL           feedUrl = new URL(feedURL);
SyndFeedInput input   = new SyndFeedInput();
SyndFeed      feed    = input.build(new XmlReader(feedUrl));

// Now iterate over the headlines and construct our HTML.
List headlines = feed.getEntries();
StringBuffer sb = new StringBuffer(4096);
sb.append("<html><head><title></title></head><body\n<ul>\n");
for (Iterator it = headlines.iterator(); it.hasNext();) {
  SyndEntryImpl entry = (SyndEntryImpl)it.next();
  sb.append("<li><a href=\"" + entry.getUri() + "\" " +
    "onClick=\"window.parent.lastClickedLink='" +
    entry.getUri() + "';\"" +
```

```
        ">" + entry.getTitle() + "</a><br>" +
        entry.getDescription().getValue() +
        "<br><br></li>\n");
    }
    sb.append("</ul></body></html>");

    // Write the HTML to the output.
    response.setContentType("text/html");
    PrintWriter out = response.getWriter();
    out.println(sb.toString());

  } catch (Exception e) {
    // If any exceptions occur, we'll generically return content that
    // says the feed could not be retrieved.  Before that though, we'll do
    // our typical "minimal" exception handling.  At the end, note that
    // unlike the other servlets, the exception IS NOT rethrown.  We want
    // this servlet to be like Las Vegas: whatever happens here, stays here!
    System.err.println("ListHeadlinesServlet.doPost(): Exception: " + e);
    e.printStackTrace();
    response.setContentType("text/html");
    PrintWriter out = response.getWriter();
    out.println("<html><head><title>Error</title></head><body>" +
      "<font color=\"#ff0000\"Unable to retrieve and parse feed.  Sorry!  " +
      "Please try again.</font><br><br>Some things to check:<br><br>" +
      "* Is the feed's URL correct?<br>" +
      "* Are proxyHost and proxyPort set appropriately?");
  }


} // End doPost().


} // End class.
```

This first thing I would like to call out is this section of code:

```
// We are going to use Commons Digester to parse the XML that was
// POSTed to this servlet to get headlines for the specified feed.
Digester digester = new Digester();
digester.setValidating(false);
// The XML has the form:
// <feed>
//   <feedTitle />
// </feed>
// We create a FeedDescriptor instance when <feed> is hit, then populate
// it from the three child elements.
digester.addObjectCreate("feed",
  "com.apress.ajaxprojects.rssreader.dtos.FeedDescriptor");
```

```
digester.addBeanPropertySetter("feed/feedTitle", "feedTitle");
String         newFeedXML     = RequestHelpers.getBodyContent(request);
FeedDescriptor feedDescriptor = null;
feedDescriptor = (FeedDescriptor)digester.parse(
  new ByteArrayInputStream(newFeedXML.getBytes()));
```

Here we are using Commons Digester again to parse some incoming XML. In this case, what comes out of that is a FeedDescriptorDTO with the feedTitle populated (no feedURL is passed in). Following that, the collection of FeedDescriptorDTOs from application context is iterated over to find the matching item. When we find the one with a matching title, we grab the URL. I choose to do it this way rather than passing the URL in as well because Digester, while being extremely handy, is somewhat heavyweight and requires a fair amount of overhead. Because Digester uses Commons Beanutils under the covers, and since Beanutils does all its work with a healthy (or unhealthy, depending on your viewpoint!) dose of reflection, and since reflection is still even today a somewhat expensive thing to use (although not nearly as bad as it used to be—modern JVMs have come a long way!), you probably will not want to use Digester for anything more than small messages like we see here. Also, you can make things more efficient by keeping an instance of Digester around, since much of the overhead is actually in parsing the rules and setting them up. As long as you do not change the rules once you have an instance, you can keep it as a static member of some class and reuse it, thereby eliminating a lot of the overhead. For small messages like this, though, which are not really time-dependent (i.e., a few hundred milliseconds either way will not make much difference), you can get away without tricks like that. Therefore, the less you have to parse, the better. Since the minimum information we need from the client is the feed title—we can already determine the URL from what we have in application context—I felt this was a more efficient approach, even if only slightly so. Arguably the benefit decreases with a larger number of feeds, and there is likely a point where Digester would have been faster than the iteration, so think of it as an opportunity for you to improve the code!

The next section of code deals with setting up the network proxy, if one is defined in web.xml. If both the proxyPort and proxyHost parameters are not blank, then we set system properties based on their values. All Java network operations after that will use those proxy settings.

After that, we see ROME being used to parse the feed:

```
// Use ROME to get the clicked feed.
URL           feedUrl = new URL(feedURL);
SyndFeedInput input   = new SyndFeedInput();
SyndFeed      feed    = input.build(new XmlReader(feedUrl));
```

That should look quite familiar after our earlier discussion of ROME. Once the SyndFeed instance is populated, we just need to generate the response and write it out:

```
// Now iterate over the headlines and construct our HTML.
List headlines = feed.getEntries();
StringBuffer sb = new StringBuffer(4096);
sb.append("<html><head><title></title></head><body\n<ul>\n");
for (Iterator it = headlines.iterator(); it.hasNext();) {
  SyndEntryImpl entry = (SyndEntryImpl)it.next();
  sb.append("<li><a href=\"" + entry.getUri() + "\" " +
```

```
        "onClick=\"window.parent.lastClickedLink='" +
        entry.getUri() + "';\"" +
        ">" + entry.getTitle() + "</a><br>" +
        entry.getDescription().getValue() +
        "<br><br></li>\n");
    }
    sb.append("</ul></body></html>");

    // Write the HTML to the output.
    response.setContentType("text/html");
    PrintWriter out = response.getWriter();
    out.println(sb.toString());
```

From the SyndFeed instance we get the collection of headlines and iterate over it. For each item we generate the markup. Note the call to `window.parent.linkClicked()`. Recall that `linkClicked()` is a JavaScript function in `index.jsp`. This page, in terms of the DOM hierarchy in the browser, is the parent page of the iFrame this markup will be displayed in; hence we have to traverse the hierarchy to get to that function. Fortunately, there is an easy shortcut. Every window object in the browser, of which an iFrame is one, has a parent attribute that, as you might expect, holds a reference to the parent document. So, we reference that and we can directly call our function. Other than that, this is just straight markup to display the headline in a clickable fashion with the description below it.

One important point I'd like to make here is that you always have the option to use a JSP to generate your response; you virtually never have to do it in code as shown here. Other projects in the book will use the JSP approach, but I wanted to show this approach here. You may realize that best practices these days are to not generate responses in code like this, and I wholeheartedly recommend the same thing. But remember, it is always a choice, and sometimes you may have a good reason to not go the JSP route. In fact, you do not have to use JSP either. You can use any presentation technology you wish (Velocity, FreeMarker, etc.). It has been my experience that many people doing Ajax work do not even realize that JSPs, or other render technologies, can be used. I therefore want to make sure you realize this! Also, all of the same reasons to use JSPs in the first place apply, including no need to recompile to make changes, better separation of concerns, and so on. I do not believe there is a right and wrong answer—just two different approaches to the same thing that you as the developer should be aware of so that you can make an appropriate decision when the time comes.

Lastly, we notice that everything was wrapped in a `try...catch` block. The code is designed to react in the same way when any exception occurs: it returns a message to be displayed saying the feed could not be retrieved, and even suggests the two most likely culprits to the failure. Yes, I could have examined the failure and determined a more specific course of action, but in reality, I cannot think of too many failure conditions that could be recovered from, so there likely would not be much else to do anyway. This makes the code simple and yet still about as user-friendly as it is likely to ever be.

SaveFeedsServlet.java

Now we'll examine the servlet responsible for saving feeds we enter. This servlet is shown in Listing 6-9.

Listing 6-9. *SaveFeedServlet, Without Which We Could Not, Well, SAVE FEEDS!*

```
package com.apress.ajaxprojects.rssreader.servlets;


import com.apress.ajaxprojects.rssreader.dtos.FeedDescriptor;
import java.io.ByteArrayInputStream;
import java.io.File;
import java.io.FileOutputStream;
import java.io.IOException;
import java.io.PrintWriter;
import java.util.ArrayList;
import java.util.Iterator;
import java.util.Properties;
import javawebparts.request.RequestHelpers;
import javax.servlet.http.HttpServlet;
import javax.servlet.http.HttpServletRequest;
import javax.servlet.http.HttpServletResponse;
import javax.servlet.ServletException;
import org.apache.commons.digester.Digester;
import org.apache.commons.logging.Log;
import org.apache.commons.logging.LogFactory;


/**
 * Servlet to save a feed.
 *
 * @author <a href="mailto:fzammetti@omnytex.com">Frank W. Zammetti</a>.
 */
public class SaveFeedServlet extends HttpServlet {


  /**
   * Log instance.
   */
  private static Log log = LogFactory.getLog(SaveFeedServlet.class);


  /**
   * doGet.  Calls doPost() to do real work.
   *
   * @param  request          HTTPServletRequest.
   * @param  response         HTTPServletResponse.
   * @throws ServletException ServletException.
   * @throws IOException      IOException.
   */
```

```
public void doGet(HttpServletRequest request, HttpServletResponse response)
  throws ServletException, IOException {

  doPost(request, response);

} // End doGet().


/**
 * doPost.
 *
 * @param  request          HTTPServletRequest.
 * @param  response         HTTPServletResponse.
 * @throws ServletException ServletException.
 * @throws IOException      IOException.
 */
public void doPost(HttpServletRequest request, HttpServletResponse response)
  throws ServletException, IOException {

  try {

    log.info("AddFeedServlet.doPost()");

    // We are going to use Commons Digester to parse the XML that was
    // POSTed to this servlet to add the feed.
    Digester digester = new Digester();
    digester.setValidating(false);
    // The XML has the form:
    // <feed>
    //   <feedTitle />
    //   <feedURL />
    // </feed>
    // We create a FeedDescriptor instance when <feed> is hit, then populate
    // it from the three child elements.
    digester.addObjectCreate("feed",
      "com.apress.ajaxprojects.rssreader.dtos.FeedDescriptor");
    digester.addBeanPropertySetter("feed/feedTitle", "feedTitle");
    digester.addBeanPropertySetter("feed/feedURL", "feedURL");
    String newFeedXML = RequestHelpers.getBodyContent(request);
    FeedDescriptor feedDescriptor = null;
    feedDescriptor = (FeedDescriptor)digester.parse(
      new ByteArrayInputStream(newFeedXML.getBytes()));

    // Show the FeedDescriptor we just filled in.
    log.info("Feed = " + feedDescriptor);
```

```
// See if they entered both a title and URL.  If not, error.
if (feedDescriptor.getFeedTitle() == null ||
  feedDescriptor.getFeedTitle().equalsIgnoreCase("") ||
  feedDescriptor.getFeedURL() == null ||
  feedDescriptor.getFeedURL().equalsIgnoreCase("")) {

  log.info("Title and/or URL missing, cannot add");
  // Message to the user saying feed NOT added.
  PrintWriter out = response.getWriter();
  out.print("alert(\"Feed was not saved because title and/or URL was" +
    " blank.\");");
  out.flush();
  out.close();

// Title and URL present, can go ahead and add (or update).
} else {

  log.info("Title and URL present, checking for existence...");

  // See if a feed with this name already exists.  If it does, update
  // the URL with what we just received.
  boolean isAdd = true;
  ArrayList feeds = (ArrayList)getServletContext().getAttribute("feeds");
  for (Iterator it1 = feeds.iterator(); it1.hasNext();) {
    FeedDescriptor feed = (FeedDescriptor)it1.next();
    if (feedDescriptor.getFeedTitle().equalsIgnoreCase(
      feed.getFeedTitle())) {
      log.info("Feed already exists, updating URL...");
      // Set isAdd to false so we know this is an update.
      isAdd = false;
      feed.setFeedURL(feedDescriptor.getFeedURL());
    }
  }

  // Go ahead and add the feed if it's new (isAdd=true);
  if (isAdd) {
    log.info("Adding new feed...");
    feeds.add(feedDescriptor);
    getServletContext().setAttribute("feeds", feeds);
  }

  // Now take all the feeds in our collection, which now includes the
  // new one, and put them into a Properties object.
  Properties properties = new Properties();
```

```
        for (Iterator it = feeds.iterator(); it.hasNext();) {
          FeedDescriptor feed = (FeedDescriptor)it.next();
          properties.setProperty(feed.getFeedTitle(),
            (String)feed.getFeedURL());
        }

        // Lastly, delete any existing feed.properties file in WEB-INF and
        // write out a new version from the Properties object we just
        // populated.  We have now in effect added the new feed.
        new File(getServletContext().getRealPath("WEB-INF") +
          "/feeds.properties").delete();
        FileOutputStream fos =
          new FileOutputStream(getServletContext().getRealPath("WEB-INF") +
          "/feeds.properties");
        properties.store(fos, null);
        fos.close();

        // Add confirm message to the user and reset display.
        log.info("Outputting response success response");
        PrintWriter out = response.getWriter();
        out.println("init();");
        out.println("alert(\"The feed '" + feedDescriptor.getFeedTitle() +
          "' has been saved.  Your feed list should update shortly.\");");
        out.flush();
        out.close();

      }

    } catch (Exception e) {
      // No real error handling, but we do want to be sure we see any
      // exception that occurs.
      System.err.println("AddFeedServlet.doPost(): Exception: " + e);
      e.printStackTrace();
      throw new ServletException(e.getMessage());
    }

  } // End doPost().


} // End class.
```

This servlet starts out, in `doPost()`, by parsing some incoming XML in the same fashion as `ListHeadlinesServlet`. The only difference is that in this servlet, the XML we receive includes both the feed title and URL. Once we have a `FeedDescriptorDTO` populated as a result of the parsing with Digester, some checks are performed to be sure both a title and URL were in fact entered. If they were not, a response is rendered that consists of a JavaScript alert. If you look at the `ajax-config.xml` for this event, you will see that the response handler is the std:CodeExecutor. So, the handler assumes that what is being returned is a chunk of JavaScript and will immediately execute it.

Once the FeedDescriptorDTO is validated, a check is performed against the feeds in application scope to see if a feed with this name already exists, like so:

```
// See if a feed with this name already exists.  If it does, update
// the URL with what we just received.
boolean isAdd = true;
ArrayList feeds = (ArrayList)getServletContext().getAttribute("feeds");
for (Iterator it1 = feeds.iterator(); it1.hasNext();) {
  FeedDescriptor feed = (FeedDescriptor)it1.next();
  if (feedDescriptor.getFeedTitle().equalsIgnoreCase(
    feed.getFeedTitle())) {
    log.info("Feed already exists, updating URL...");
    // Set isAdd to false so we know this is an update.
    isAdd = false;
    feed.setFeedURL(feedDescriptor.getFeedURL());
  }
}
```

If the feed is not found, then this is essentially a straight add operation, so we set the isAdd variable so we can act accordingly later. If the feed is found, however, all we are doing is updating the URL (we can never alter the name of an existing feed because the name is in essence like a unique key field in a database table) of the existing FeedDescriptor from the application-scoped collection.

Next, we check to see if isAdd is true. If it is, we need to do the add, and two things are required to add a feed. First, the DTO is added to the application-scope collection. Second, the feeds.properties file is written out (re-created essentially) from that collection, which then includes the new feed. Lastly, we render a response, again a chunk of JavaScript, which first calls the init() function, and then pops an alert saying the feed was saved. The call to init() essentially resets the page to its initial state, which assures us that we are in a valid state after the feed appears in the feed list with the next refresh.

DeleteFeedServlet.java

And finally, we come to a servlet that is the Hyde to SaveFeedServlet's Jekyll, the ying to its yang: DeleteFeedServlet, as shown in Listing 6-10.

Listing 6-10. *DeleteFeedServlet, Code Written Expressly to Be Destructive!*

```
package com.apress.ajaxprojects.rssreader.servlets;


import com.apress.ajaxprojects.rssreader.dtos.FeedDescriptor;
import java.io.ByteArrayInputStream;
import java.io.File;
import java.io.FileOutputStream;
import java.io.IOException;
```

```
import java.io.PrintWriter;
import java.util.ArrayList;
import java.util.Iterator;
import java.util.Properties;
import javawebparts.request.RequestHelpers;
import javax.servlet.http.HttpServlet;
import javax.servlet.http.HttpServletRequest;
import javax.servlet.http.HttpServletResponse;
import javax.servlet.ServletException;
import org.apache.commons.digester.Digester;
import org.apache.commons.logging.Log;
import org.apache.commons.logging.LogFactory;


/**
 * Servlet to delete a feed.
 *
 * @author <a href="mailto:fzammetti@omnytex.com">Frank W. Zammetti</a>.
 */
public class DeleteFeedServlet extends HttpServlet {


  /**
   * Log instance.
   */
  private static Log log = LogFactory.getLog(DeleteFeedServlet.class);


  /**
   * doGet.  Calls doPost() to do real work.
   *
   * @param  request          HTTPServletRequest.
   * @param  response         HTTPServletResponse.
   * @throws ServletException ServletException.
   * @throws IOException      IOException.
   */
  public void doGet(HttpServletRequest request, HttpServletResponse response)
    throws ServletException, IOException {

    doPost(request, response);

  } // End doGet().


  /**
   * doPost.
   *
```

```
   * @param  request          HTTPServletRequest.
   * @param  response         HTTPServletResponse.
   * @throws ServletException ServletException.
   * @throws IOException      IOException.
   */
  public void doPost(HttpServletRequest request, HttpServletResponse response)
    throws ServletException, IOException {


    try {

      log.info("DeleteFeedServlet.doPost()");

      // We are going to use Commons Digester to parse the XML that was
      // POSTed to this servlet to add the feed.
      Digester digester = new Digester();
      digester.setValidating(false);
      // The XML has the form:
      // <feed>
      //   <feedTitle />
      // </feed>
      // We create a FeedDescriptor instance when <feed> is hit, then populate
      // it from the three child elements.
      digester.addObjectCreate("feed",
        "com.apress.ajaxprojects.rssreader.dtos.FeedDescriptor");
      digester.addBeanPropertySetter("feed/feedTitle", "feedTitle");
      String newFeedXML = RequestHelpers.getBodyContent(request);
      FeedDescriptor feedDescriptor = null;
      feedDescriptor = (FeedDescriptor)digester.parse(
        new ByteArrayInputStream(newFeedXML.getBytes()));

      // Show the FeedDescriptor we just filled in.
      log.info("Feed = " + feedDescriptor);

      if (feedDescriptor.getFeedTitle() == null ||
        feedDescriptor.getFeedTitle().equalsIgnoreCase("")) {
        // Message to the user saying feed NOT deleted.
        PrintWriter out = response.getWriter();
        out.print("alert(\"No feed selected to delete.\");");
      } else {

        // Now we go through our collection of feeds in application context
        // and remove the matching feed.
        ArrayList feeds = (ArrayList)getServletContext().getAttribute("feeds");
        int indexToDelete = -1;
        int i             = 0;
        for (Iterator it = feeds.iterator(); it.hasNext();) {
```

```
          FeedDescriptor fd = (FeedDescriptor)it.next();
          if (fd.getFeedTitle().equals(feedDescriptor.getFeedTitle())) {
            indexToDelete = i;
            break;
          }
          i++;
        }
        if (indexToDelete != -1) {
          feeds.remove(indexToDelete);
        }
        getServletContext().setAttribute("feeds", feeds);

        // Now take all the feeds in our collection, which now does not include
        // the deleted one, and put them into a Properties object.
        Properties properties = new Properties();
        for (Iterator it = feeds.iterator(); it.hasNext();) {
          FeedDescriptor feed = (FeedDescriptor)it.next();
          properties.setProperty(feed.getFeedTitle(), feed.getFeedURL());
        }

        // Lastly, delete any existing feed.properties file in WEB-INF and write
        // out a new version from the Properties object we just populated.
        // We have now in effect deleted the feed.
        new File(getServletContext().getRealPath("WEB-INF") +
          "/feeds.properties").delete();
        FileOutputStream fos =
          new FileOutputStream(getServletContext().getRealPath("WEB-INF") +
          "/feeds.properties");
        properties.store(fos, null);
        fos.close();

        // Delete confirm message to the user and reset display.
        PrintWriter out = response.getWriter();
        out.println("init();");
        out.println("alert(\"The feed '" + feedDescriptor.getFeedTitle() +
          "' has been deleted.  Your feed list should update shortly.\");");

      }

    } catch (Exception e) {
      // No real error handling, but we do want to be sure we see any
      // exception that occurs.
      System.err.println("DeleteFeedServlet.doPost(): Exception: " + e);
      e.printStackTrace();
      throw new ServletException(e.getMessage());
    }
```

```
  } // End doPost().


} // End class.
```

This servlet is in many ways very similar to the SaveFeedServlet we just looked at. The differences are that first, the incoming XML only contains the feed title; the URL is not required. Second, the verification of the DTO is limited to ensuring that a feed title was present. If none was present, then a message is returned to the user, again using JavaScript that is returned and the std:CodeExcutor AjaxTags response handler, telling them that a feed was not selected. Third, obviously the feed is removed from the application-scoped collection before the properties file is written out. Otherwise, the basic structure and flow is similar. The JavaScript returned when the feed is removed again contains a call to the init() function as well.

As you have seen, an RSS reader is not exactly rocket science, not for the basics anyway. Doing it with Ajax is a trivial exercise really, especially with AjaxTags around to save us the heavy lifting.

Suggested Exercises

Let's face it: an RSS reader is a fairly simple thing, even in its most advanced form. Aside from eye candy, there really is not much to the job! That being said, there are still some things you might consider doing with this application to make it that much better.

- Allow for automatic updating of feed headlines. This can be accomplished with another AjaxTags timer without too much trouble.
- Fix the flicker that you see in Firefox when the feed list is updated. For this you will need to write a custom AjaxTags handler that does essentially what the std:InnerHTML handler does, but only updates the <div> when the contents have actually changed (see how this is done in the AjaxChat project).
- Allow for grouping of feeds for easier administration.

Summary

In this chapter we examined a fairly simple RSS feed reader. You saw how AjaxTags can save you a ton of work and how it allows you to write an RSS reader with a minimum of effort.

CHAPTER 7

■ ■ ■

PhotoShare: Share Your Visual Life with Your Friends

In this chapter we'll become acquainted with an application called PhotoShare, which is a way to share photographs with family and friends. This application will make use of the Dojo library for its Ajax functionality, as well as a few other things. This project will be a bit fancier than the others; it uses DOM scripting and CSS to provide some special effects and coolness. This project will also demonstrate how you can create a simple application framework on the server side instead of just using straight servlets or a full-blown application framework like Struts.

Requirements and Goals

If you have ever spent any time with Flickr (`www.flickr.com`), you already know that posting and sharing photographs with family, friends, or even total strangers is a popular thing to do these days on the Web. While Flickr is probably the most famous and popular of these services, it is most definitely not the only example. Fotki (`www.fotki.com`), PBase (`www.pbase.com`), and Webshots (`www.webshots.com`) are other examples. And these were just the first four that came up in Google searching for "photo sharing"—there were another 129 million hits that I did not have time to explore!

Clearly, this is something that many people are interested in doing. So, it was a fairly natural application to write, and as it turns out, Ajax can be a part of it to good effect. In addition, because photographs is one example of what people think of when they use the term "multimedia," and because that word often tends to go hand in hand with cool special effects and such, this might also be a good opportunity to experiment with DOM scripting and CSS to see what we can achieve.

So, what will this PhotoShare application of ours be able to do? Let's create a quick list:

- We should be able to create collections of photographs so that people can organize them in any manner they find appropriate. If you would like a collection of photos of your kids, no problem! What about a collection of photos about your trip to Florida last winter? Absolutely! We'll of course want to be able to delete collections, too, just in case we need to clean up.
- Don't forget the obvious: we need to be able to add photos as well! As with collections, being able to delete them is also important.

- For each photo we add, we want to be able to record who added it, and also record a description about it. After all, you may know that Aunt Erma's cat's name is Mr. Tinkles, but not everyone else will.
- We want to be able to download photos for posterity's sake.
- We want to be able to print the photos, just in case someone wants a wallet-sized version of your shot of the Statue of Liberty at dusk.
- Because many times you take a picture with the camera turned on its side (landscape versus portrait), we should be able to rotate a picture to view it properly. We'll allow for it to be rotated in 90-degree increments clockwise, to get the right view of the picture.
- We'll present the collection of photos in the form of a filmstrip, which we can scroll up and down. The user will be able to click on a photo, and it will "grow" to a default size of 640×480 pixels (VGA resolution) as it flies into place.
- We'll again use some graphical buttons so that we can have some nice rollover effects.
- No security is involved in this application because, after all, we want people to be able to *share*, so locking someone out would kind of go against that idea.

Well, it seems as though we may have some opportunity for some fun. Let's get started.

How We Will Pull It Off

We have seen a number of options for doing Ajax so far in this book. We have seen the AjaxTags component of Java Web Parts. We have seen DWR, and we have seen "naked" Ajax. For this project, we'll use a library that has been gaining a big following of late, a library with a martial arts background apparently: Dojo!

On its front page, Dojo (`http://dojotoolkit.org`) explains what it is, and I see no need to try and paraphrase them, so here is a direct quote:

> *Dojo is the Open Source JavaScript toolkit that helps you build serious applications in less time. It fills in the gaps where JavaScript and browsers don't go quite far enough, and gives you powerful, portable, lightweight, and tested tools for constructing dynamic interfaces. Dojo lets you prototype interactive widgets quickly, animate transitions, and build Ajax requests with the most powerful and easiest to use abstractions available. These capabilities are built on top of a lightweight packaging system, so you never have to figure out which order to request script files in again. Dojo's package system and optional build tools help you develop quickly and optimize transparently.*
>
> *Dojo also packs an easy to use widget system. From prototype to deployment, Dojo widgets are HTML and CSS all the way. Best of all, since Dojo is portable JavaScript to the core, your widgets can be portable between HTML, SVG, and whatever else comes down the pike. The web is changing, and Dojo can help you stay ahead.*
>
> *Dojo makes professional web development better, easier, and faster. In that order.*

Yes, that does about sum it up! As I mentioned, Dojo has been gaining a following of late, and has even been integrated into some popular frameworks, WebWork from OpenSymphony for example (`www.opensymphony.com/webwork`).

Dojo is a rather large library, containing a myriad of packages and features. Dojo is not just about Ajax; it provides some functions that extend JavaScript itself, as well as general utility code for JavaScript applications. However, there is a downside to Dojo: it is still really in its infancy. One look at the online documentation and you will realize that using Dojo means that, to a large degree, you will be fending for yourself. Many of the packages do not, as of the time of this writing, appear to have any documentation at all. Examples are a bit thin at this point, and the planned features are not fully baked just yet.

For our purposes in PhotoShare, however, we'll only be using two parts of Dojo, and they happen to be pretty well developed at this point: the Ajax functionality and the event system functionality.

To begin using Dojo, you have a couple of options. Dojo comes in a number of "editions." So, if you are interested only in the Ajax functionality, you can download just the IO edition. If you are interested only in graphical user interface (GUI) widgets, you can download the widget edition. There is also a so-called "kitchen sink" edition that contains everything Dojo offers. For our purposes, I used the "Event + I/O" edition.

Once you have downloaded the proper edition, all you need to do is a typical JavaScript import of the `dojo.js` file, like so:

```
<script src="js/dojo.js"></script>
```

After that, you're all set. Dojo also offers an "import" feature. So, for instance, if you have downloaded the IO edition and later decide you want to use the event system, you can do this:

```
<script type="text/javascript">
    dojo.require("dojo.event.*");
</script>
```

Dojo will then take care of loading all the dependencies for you, and you will be good to go. You can do this for any of the features you want and also at any time. In other words, you don't need to have a bunch of imports at the top of the page for each package you want to use; you can instead treat it just like Java imports and let Dojo handle all the details (although the main import of `dojo.js` *is* still required).

Dojo offers Ajax functionality in the form of the `dojo.io` package. By the way, when I say "package" here, what that really means is objects within Dojo. This has the effect of mimicking packaging namespaces, which avoids naming conflicts between Dojo and your own objects. Anyway, with the `dojo.io` package, we are specifically interested in the `dojo.io.bind()` function, which is how we make an Ajax request. Using this function is pretty simple:

```
// An asynchronous request to foo.php that returns a JavaScript literal
// which is displayed via alert()
var bindArgs = {
    url: "foo.php",
    mimetype: "text/plain",
    error: function(type, errObj){
        alert("An error occurred!");
    },
```

```
    load: function(type, data, evt){
        alert(data);
    }
};

// Dispatch the request
var requestObj = dojo.io.bind(bindArgs);
```

Here we are seeing something that we have not seen before: setting up a JavaScript associative array. The bindArgs variable points to an array of objects, each of various kinds (the first two are strings, the last two are functions) and each associated with a specific name (url, mimetype, error, and load). This means that we can access an element of the array, mimetype say, by doing bindargs["mimetype"]. This is a handy way to pass a batch of information to a function as a single object, and Dojo uses this paradigm quite a bit. You can also use a slightly different form of this, which is in fact the form I use throughout PhotoShare. That form does away with the need to define bindArgs and instead supplies the same information as bindArgs does inline with the function call. The syntax is slightly funky, but is a bit more compact. Here is what the previous example looks like in that form:

```
dojo.io.bind({
  url: "foo.php",
  error: function(type, errObj) { alert("An error occurred!"); },
  load: function(type, data, evt) {
    alert(data);
  },
  mimetype: "text/plain"
});
```

As far as the various arguments go, url is of course the URL the request will be made to. The error argument points to a function that will be executed when an error occurs. The load argument is the Ajax callback function that you have seen many times already. The mimetype argument is the Multipurpose Internet Mail Extensions (MIME) type that will be used when interpreting the response. This is *not* the MIME type of the outbound request! You will also see two other arguments used in PhotoShare: transport and content. The transport argument simply defines the mechanism that will be used to make the request. Dojo offers a few, but for our purposes, all we care about is XMLHTTPTransport. The content argument is how we can pass request parameters to the URL. This argument takes the form of another associative array, describing the parameter names and values.

To see how this all fits together, let's look at a real usage of Dojo from PhotoShare, the request used to delete a photo:

```
dojo.io.bind({
  url: "deletePhoto.action",
  content: {collection: collectionName, filename: photoFilename},
  error: function(type, errObj) { alert("AJAX error!"); },
  load: function(type, data, evt) {
    alert(data);
    hidePleaseWait();
```

```
    loadCollection();
  },
  mimetype: "text/plain",
  transport: "XMLHTTPTransport"
});
```

For the time being, ignore what is actually happening in the `load` function, but instead look at how the `content` argument is used to send the name of the collection and the filename of the photo to delete (`collectionName` is a previously defined variable, as is `photoFilename`). As I am sure you can see, there really is not much to it.

The other piece of Dojo that will be used in PhotoShare is the event system. Simply put, this is an easy way to attach event handlers to any element on a page. As we have seen many times, we can define a JavaScript snippet that will fire when the mouse is moved over a given element like so:

```
<div id="myDiv" onMouseOver="alert('over');">Hover over me!</div>
```

You can also attach that event separately from the markup, like so:

```
<div id="myDiv">Hover over me!</div>
<script>
  document.getElementById("myDiv").onmouseover = function() { alert("over"); };
</script>
```

Normally if you were going to do this, the script here would probably be called when the page is loaded, not immediately after the markup, but the result is exactly the same. Dojo makes this a bit easier by providing the `dojo.event.connect()` function:

```
dojo.event.connect(document.getElementById("myDiv"), "onclick", "handleOnClick");
```

The first argument is the node to attach an event to, the second is the event to capture, and the third is the name of the function that will handle the event. This may not seem a whole lot better until you know one important fact: events are handled differently in Internet Explorer than in Firefox. In Firefox, the function that is called as the result of an event firing is passed an event object that contains all the information about the event. This comes in handy when you need to know, for instance, what element fired the event. In Internet Explorer, however, there is a system known as "event bubbling," which means that when an event fires, an event object is created, and then "bubbles up" through a hierarchy of elements, until one handles it. First, the element that actually fired the event gets the chance to handle the event. Then the parent of that element. Then the parent of *that* element. Then the document. Then the window. You get the point! However, in all of this, that event object is *not* passed to any event handler function. Instead, you have to go grab it by calling `window.event`. The Dojo `connect()` function handles this transparently for us and passes the event object to the handler function, regardless of what browser we're in. That one simple fact alone makes the `dojo.connect()` function a worthwhile thing to use because it removes the cross-browser concerns from our event handlers. Sweet!

One other point on `dojo.connect()` that I want to mention, even though it is not used in PhotoShare, is the fact that it allows you to connect multiple handler functions to an event on a single element, and Dojo guarantees that they fire in the order they are attached. This means you can have `doOnClick1()` and `doOnClick2()` for a button, and if you call `dojo.connect()`

twice with them in that order, then you are always guaranteed to get `doOnClick1()` firing, and then `doOnClick2()` firing. This is something you would have to write a fair bit of code to implement on your own, but Dojo makes it just that easy.

As I mentioned earlier, Dojo is a rather large library with many more packages than these two. Table 7-1 shows some of the other things Dojo offers.

Table 7-1. *Some of the Other Packages Dojo Offers*

Dojo Package	Description
`dojo.lang`	Utility routines to make JavaScript easier to use. Contains a number of functions for manipulating JavaScript objects, testing data types, etc.
`dojo.string`	String manipulation functions like `trim()`, `trimStart()`, `escape()`, etc.
`dojo.logging`	JavaScript logging.
`dojo.profile`	JavaScript code profiling.
`dojo.validate`	Data validation functions like `isNumber()`, `isText()`, `isValidDate()`, etc.
`dojo.crypto`	Cryptographic routines.
`dojo.storage`	Code that implements a durable client-side cache using Flash's cookie mechanism. This effectively gives you a client-side analogy to the `HttpSession` object on the server.
`dojo.Collections`	Various data structures like `Dictionary`, `ArrayList`, `Set`, etc.

Dojo also provides a nice set of GUI widgets, many of which provide a high "wow factor." Unfortunately, I found very little documentation on any of them, and that is the reason I chose not to use them in PhotoShare. If you can find examples of their usage, I do believe they will impress you.

I do feel it necessary to repeat my earlier warning about the current state of Dojo. Some fantastic work is being done there, but it is not yet a fully mature library that has all the documentation, examples, and completeness it eventually will. If you choose to use Dojo, be prepared, at least for a while longer, to deal with these things. As of this writing, Dojo 0.2.2 is the current version, and certainly things could have changed by the time this book was released. A great many influential people are very high on Dojo, and if nothing else, that should convince you it is worth looking at in more detail.

Visualizing the Finish Line

As always, let's take some time to familiarize ourselves with the application we'll be exploring.

The first screen, shown in Figure 7-1, is what users will see when they first access PhotoShare. Note that PhotoShare opens in a new window, which means that if you have pop-up blocking enabled, you may have to make an exception for PhotoShare or turn off blocking altogether.

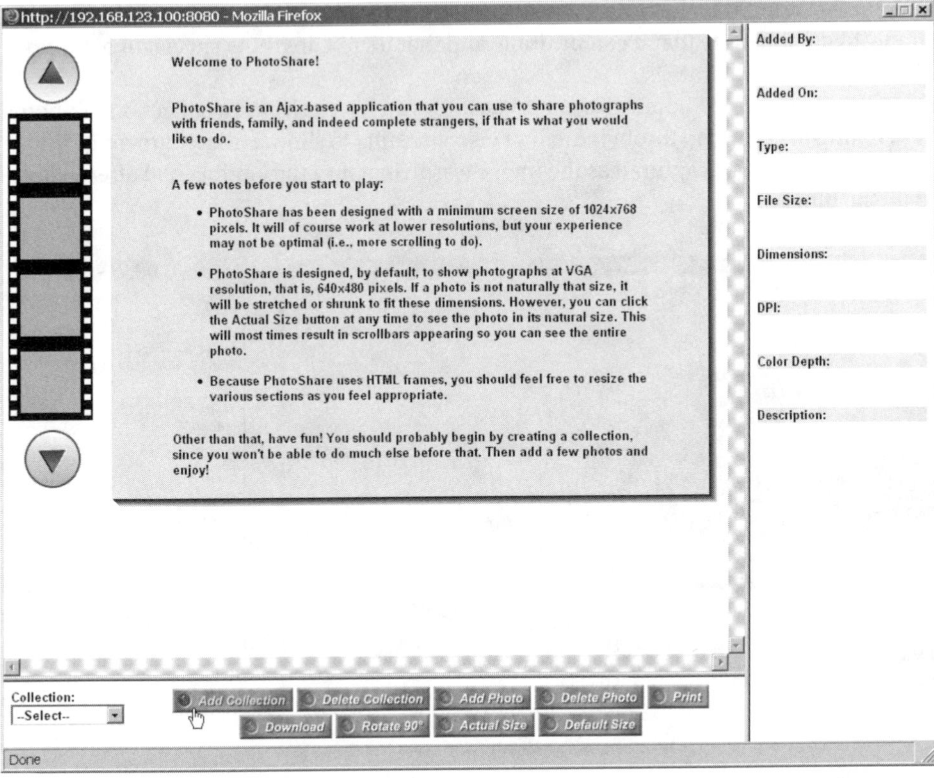

Figure 7-1. *The main PhotoShare screen as first seen*

Another interesting fact is that PhotoShare uses frames. Using frames is something I feel has gotten a bad rap over the years because many developers made quite a few mistakes early on, and because of that convinced themselves that frames were a problem. Some of those problems are quite legitimate, such as keeping the state of the frames in sync (imagine a menu frame and a main content area... if the menu should change according to what is in the main area, this is a synchronization issue). Another real problem is being able to bookmark a framed page. This is usually difficult, especially if you want to allow for bookmarking of pages within a framed site (more often than not, only the first frameset document gets bookmarked, unless you write some script to handle it).

However, in the world of Ajax, I believe that frames will begin to see more usage. The advantage of having a page split into essentially separate subpages is a very powerful paradigm, and because it is common in Ajax applications to not navigate from page to page as in a plain old website, many of the issues around frames cease to exist. Bookmarking is not usually a problem, for instance, because you never actually leave the URL you first accessed (remember, in an Ajax application, more times than not you will update subsections of a page, not navigate to a new one). Synchronization can still be an issue, but no more so than keeping `<div>`s synchronized in a single HTML document—so it is no worse than any other Ajax application without frames.

In any case, I wanted to do one application in this book with frames if for no other reason than simply to demonstrate that it can be done, and that it's not anything special or anymore difficult than one without frames.

Figure 7-2 shows what PhotoShare looks like after you have selected a collection of photos and are scrolling the filmstrip through them. It also attempts to show a photo "growing" into place. This screenshot was captured as the image was flying onto the landing pad after being clicked on the filmstrip.

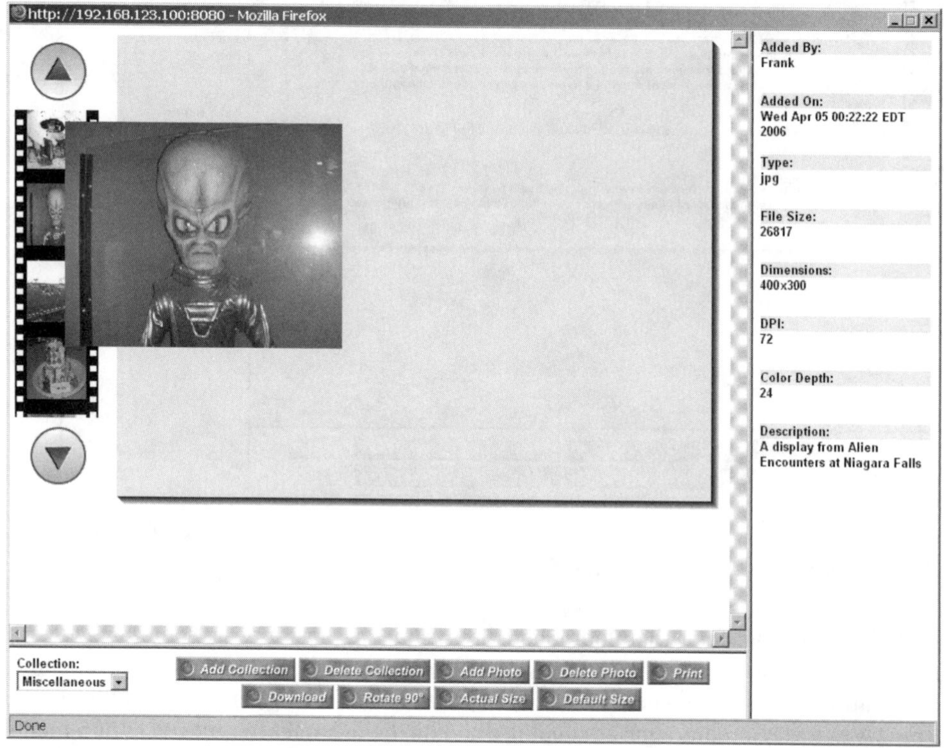

Figure 7-2. *A photo in the process of growing*

In Figure 7-3, you can see what the screen looks like after a photo has completely "grown" and is now at its default size. All the photos are initially shown at a size of 640×480 pixels, which is standard VGA size. This results in the photo appearing normal if it is actually 640×480 pixels in size, but if it is larger or smaller, it will be stretched or shrunk to fit that size. That is where the Actual Size button comes in, which we'll see in a moment. I did it this way because 640×480 pixels is a fairly typical size for photos; people tend to shrink larger ones down when they take them so they are not too big to e-mail, and most digital cameras do not shoot at a smaller size unless you specifically tell them to, which most people tend not to do.

Figure 7-4 shows the image after the rotate function has been used. Also, note that the image is smaller than in Figure 7-3. It is actually being viewed at its real, or "natural," size.

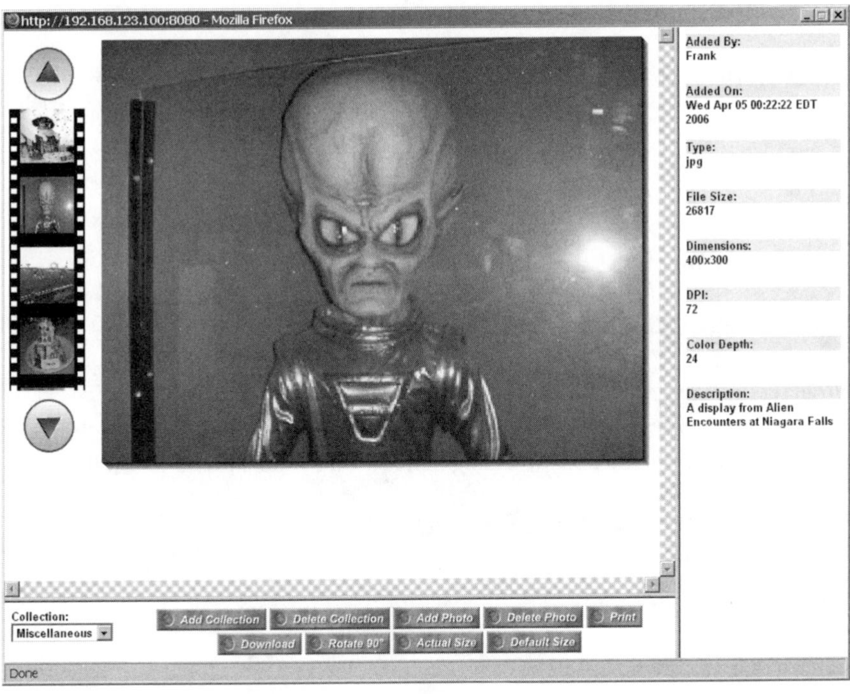

Figure 7-3. *Viewing a photo at its default size*

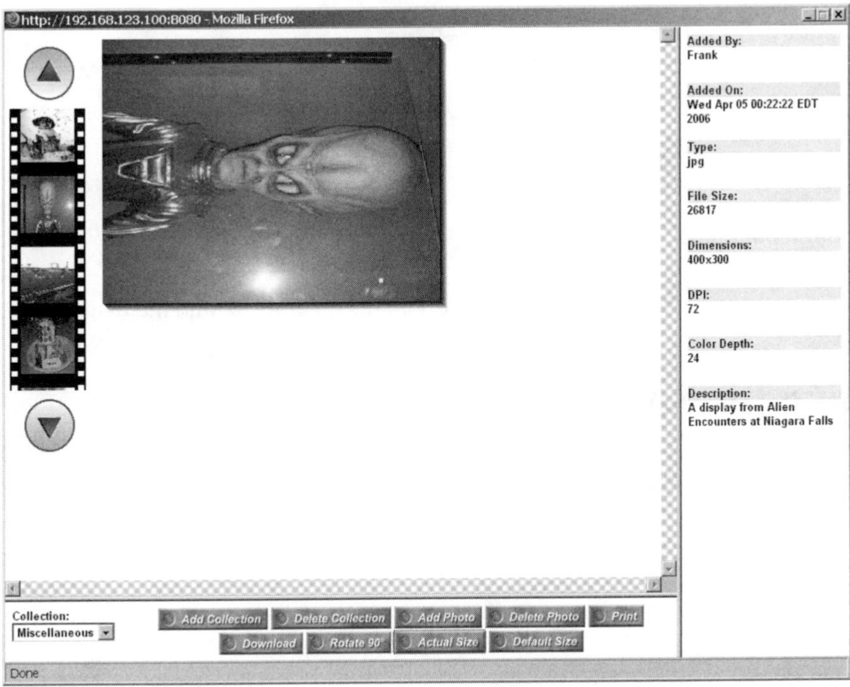

Figure 7-4. *Viewing a rotated image at its actual size*

Adding to a collection is done via a pop-up dialog, and Figure 7-5 shows this.

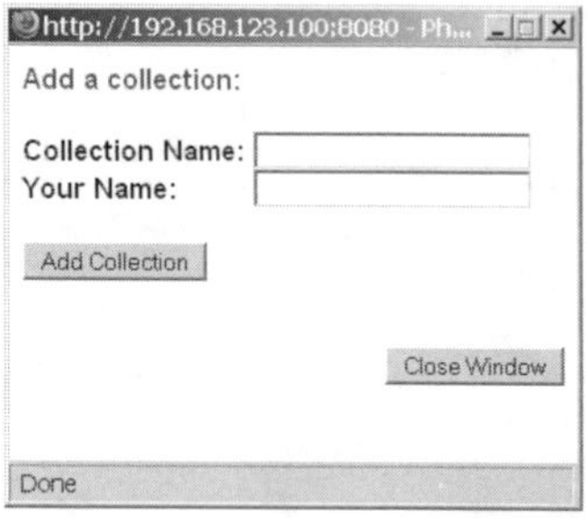

Figure 7-5. *Adding a collection*

Finally, in Figure 7-6, we see the pop-up dialog that is used to add a photo to a collection.

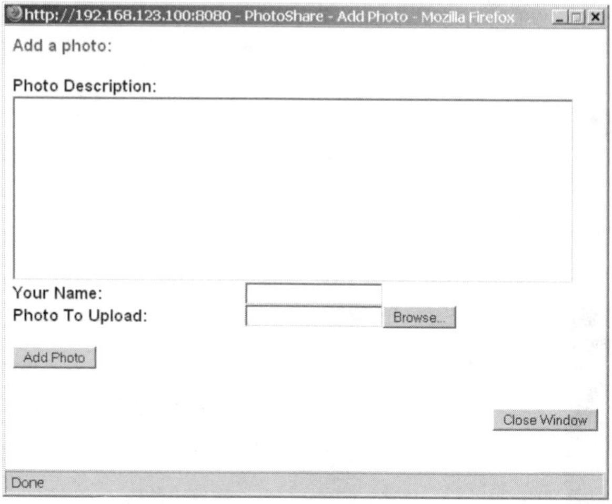

Figure 7-6. *Adding a photo*

Now that we know what the end result looks like, let's see the code behind the magic.

Dissecting the Solution

As has been the custom in this book, let's now look at the directory layout of PhotoShare (Figure 7-7) and familiarize ourselves with the important files involved.

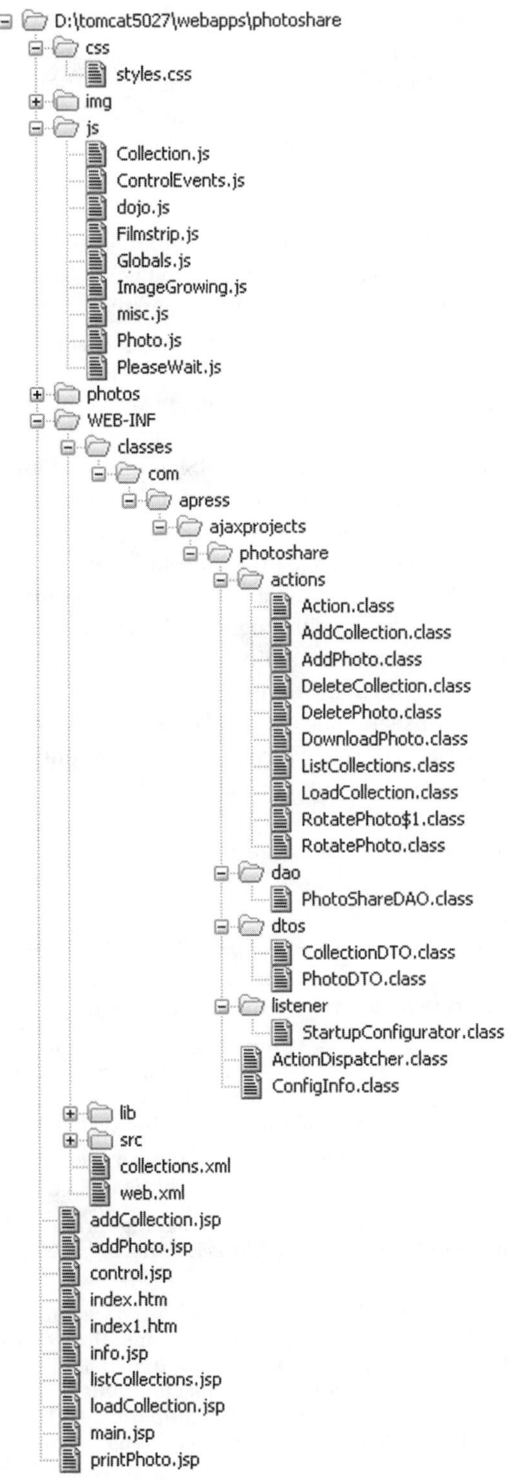

Figure 7-7. *Directory structure of PhotoShare*

We have here a usual webapp directory structure. The initial welcome page is `index.htm`. This is a simple page that opens a new window and loads `index1.htm` into it. `index1.htm` is a frameset document that defines the frame-based layout of the application. Into these frames the documents `main.jsp`, `info.jsp`, and `control.jsp` are loaded. `addCollection.jsp`, `addPhoto.jsp`, and `printPhoto.jsp` are pages that will be loaded into pop-up windows for the functions the user can perform (I'll bet you can guess which functions!). Lastly, `loadCollection.jsp` and `listCollections.jsp` are used to render the result of Ajax requests.

The `/css` directory contains a single `styles.css` file, which is imported into most of the previously mentioned pages. The `/img` directory, which I have not expanded in Figure 7-7 just to save space, contains a fair number of images that are used for the buttons and their rollover effect, as well as images to make the filmstrip. The `/photos` directory is where the photos that are added into PhotoShare by users will be stored.

The last directory is `/js`, and as you may have guessed, this is where all the JavaScript files are stored. These files are imported into the `main.jsp` page only. All the other frames will make use of any functions they may need by referencing them in the frame that JSP is rendered in. The `Collection.js` file contains the `Collection` object, which is a container for a number of photos. The `ControlEvents.js` file is where all the UI event handlers for the buttons and drop-down in the control frame are found. `dojo.js` is of course the Dojo library itself. `Filmstrip.js` contains the code that makes the filmstrip work, that is, scrolling, populating it, and so forth. `Globals.js` contains a bunch of global JavaScript variables used throughout PhotoShare. `ImageGrowing.js` is the code responsible for expanding a picture off the filmstrip and moving it onto the landing pad area when the user clicks on a photo in the filmstrip. `misc.js` contains some… wait for it… miscellaneous functions, things like initialization and other plumbing-type functions. `Photo.js` contains the code for the `Photo` object, which of course represents one of the photographs in a collection. Lastly, `PleaseWait.js` contains the code for the Please Wait overlay seen at various points while using PhotoShare.

The `WEB-INF/lib` folder is where you'll find all the JARs PhotoShare depends on (Table 7-2).

Table 7-2. *The JARs PhotoShare Depends On, Found in WEB-INF.lib*

JAR	Description
`commons-beanutils-1.7.0.jar`	The Jakarta Commons BeanUtils library, needed by Digester.
`commons-digester-1.7.0.jar`	Jakarta Commons Digester is a library for parsing XML and generating objects from it. This is used to parse some messages passed to the server by the client code.
`commons-fileupload.jar`	Jakarta Commons FileUpload is a library for accepting uploads and processing the resultant file via HTTP.
`commons-io.jar`	Jakarta Commons IO is a library containing various input/output (I/O) functions. This is required by FileUpload.
`commons-logging-1.0.4.jar`	Jakarta Commons Logging is an abstraction layer that sits on top of a true logging implementation (like Log4J), which allows you to switch the underlying logging implementation without affecting your application code. It also provides a simple logger that outputs to `System.out`, which is what this application uses.

JAR	Description
ImageTools.jar	This JAR contains a few classes for image manipulations used in PhotoShare, such as rotating images.
javawebparts_core_v1.0_beta3.jar	The Java Web Parts (JWP) core package, required by all other JWP packages.
javawebparts_taglib_v1.0_beta3.jar	The JWP taglib package. This includes AjaxTags, which is used for this application.
jstl.jar	The core JAR needed to support the JSP Standard Tag Library (JSTL).
standard.jar	The standard set of tags that JSTL provides.

The WEB-INF/src directory contains all the source code for this project, including the Ant build script.

The Client-Side Code

Now let's begin to look at the actual code behind PhotoShare. The first thing to look at is the single configuration file that PhotoShare depends on, and it is our standard web.xml, shown in Listing 7-1.

Listing 7-1. *PhotoShare's Lone Config File, web.xml*

```
<?xml version="1.0" encoding="ISO-8859-1"?>

<!DOCTYPE web-app PUBLIC  "-//Sun Microsystems, Inc.//DTD Web Application 2.3//EN"
"http://java.sun.com/dtd/web-app_2_3.dtd">

<web-app>

  <display-name>PhotoShare</display-name>

  <!-- Startup configuration of PhotoShare courtesy of the -->
  <!-- StartupConfigurator context listener. -->
  <listener>
    <listener-class>
      com.apress.ajaxprojects.photoshare.listener.StartupConfigurator
    </listener-class>
  </listener>

  <!-- Our main servlet that all requests go through.  This is akin to an -->
  <!-- MVC controller, like a very much trimmed down Struts ActionServlet -->
  <!-- (if you are familiar with Struts!) -->
  <servlet>
    <servlet-name>ActionDispatcher</servlet-name>
    <servlet-class>
      com.apress.ajaxprojects.photoshare.ActionDispatcher
    </servlet-class>
```

```
    <load-on-startup>1</load-on-startup>
  </servlet>
  <servlet-mapping>
    <servlet-name>ActionDispatcher</servlet-name>
    <url-pattern>*.action</url-pattern>
  </servlet-mapping>

  <!-- Session timeout config. -->
  <session-config>
    <session-timeout>30</session-timeout>
  </session-config>

  <!-- Welcome file config. -->
  <welcome-file-list>
    <welcome-file>index.htm</welcome-file>
  </welcome-file-list>

</web-app>
```

There is nothing unusual going on here. We see a single ContextListener, StartupConfigurator, which is responsible for initializing PhotoShare as far as the server side of the application goes. We'll see this class, or at least relevant bits of it, in a little while. We also have a single servlet mapped to *.action, so any URI ending with ".action" will be handled by this servlet. This servlet, which we'll look at in detail later, is responsible for instantiating a given Action class and executing it, and then acting on what that Action returns (which can be a forward, or a code indicating a page to go to, or null if the Action fully renders a response). After that is a typical session timeout value. In fact, PhotoShare does not use session at all, so for all intents and purposes the session timeout is irrelevant. I still like to have an explicit value set, just in case I decide to use session later. Lastly, we point the application to index.htm as our default page, which is coming up shortly. And that is literally all the configuration there is for PhotoShare!

index.htm

Let's now begin to examine the markup for PhotoShare. First up is the first page that is accessed, index.htm, as shown in Listing 7-2.

Listing 7-2. *The Starting Point, index.htm*

```
<html>
<head>
<title>PhotoShare</title>
<script>
  function openWindow() {
    // Open a window to display PhotoShare in.
    var winWidth = 1000;
    var winHeight = 750;
    var winLeft = (screen.width) ? (screen.width - winWidth) / 2 : 0;
```

```
    var winTop = (screen.height) ? (screen.height - winHeight) / 2 : 0;
    winOpts = "resizeable,width=" + winWidth + ",height=" + winHeight +
      ",top=" + winTop + ",left=" + winLeft;
    window.open("index1.htm", "PhotoShare", winOpts);
  }
</script>
</head>
<body onload="openWindow();">
The main PhotoShare window should have now appeared.  If it has not, please
ensure that you have scripting enabled in your browser, and that you do not
have a popup blocker that has blocked the window from opening.  You may need
to create an exception for PhotoShare, or disable any popup blocker entirely.
<br><br>
Please note that PhotoShare is designed for a screen resolution of 1024x768.
It will of course work at lower resolutions, but your experience will not
be optimal.
</body>
</html>
```

PhotoShare is opened in a new window with no *chrome*, meaning no toolbars or menus and such that are usually present on a browser window. I did this because I needed to maximize the amount of space available to PhotoShare, and in a typical browser setup, the chrome, just vertically (meaning the menus and toolbars and such), can take up approximately 170 pixels, perhaps more. That does not even count the status bar at the bottom. So, upon loading, this document calls `openWindow()`, which uses the `window.open()` method. This method accepts the HTML document to load, a title for the window, and a series of options (which are optional, hence the name!). In this case, the options we want to set are `resizable`, which indicates that the window is capable of being resized by the user; `width/height`, which set the size of the window (to 1000 pixels by 750 pixels correspondingly here, just small enough to fit on a 1024×768 resolution monitor) and `top/left`, which sets its position on the screen. `top` and `left` are calculated values that take the resolution of the screen into account via the `screen.height` and `screen.width` properties (`screen` is an intrinsic object made available by the browser to our script) and causes the opened window to be centered on the screen.

index1.htm

`index.htm` requests that `index1.htm` be opened in the new window, so let's examine `index1.htm`, shown in Listing 7-3.

Listing 7-3. *The Frameset Document, index1.htm*

```
<html>
  <frameset cols="*,200">
    <frameset rows="*,68">
      <frame name="fraMain" scrolling="yes" src="main.jsp">
      <frame name="fraControl" scrolling="no" src="control.jsp">
    </frameset>
```

```
      <frame name="fraInfo" scrolling="auto" src="info.jsp">
      <noframes>
        <body>
          Your browser doesn't support frames.
          Is it an abacus?!?
          Please upgrade!
        </body>
      </noframes>
    </frameset>
</html>
```

If you have ever worked with frames before, this will need no explanation at all. If frames are new to you, let me explain a bit. A frameset is nothing but a subdivision of a web page. In essence, each subdivision becomes a completely separate page. You can load a whole new HTML document in each, you can manipulate them individually, and so forth.

Each framed page begins with a frameset document that defines how the page is to be split into individual frames. That is what `index1.htm` is. In this case, we are saying that we have a frameset that is broken down into two columns. The second column will by default be 200 pixels wide (this is the photo info area), and the other column will fill the remainder of the width of the browser content area (this is where the filmstrip and photo viewing area is, as well as the control area). The first column is then further broken down into two rows. The second row is by default 68 pixels tall (this is the control area), and the other row will fill the remainder of the browser content area (again, the filmstrip and photo viewing area). In addition, a frameset document allows you to define a `<noframes>` section. This will be displayed in browsers that do not support frames. On a desktop PC, such a browser virtually does not exist any more, but some mobile browsers still do not support them. Even that is somewhat rare in my experience.

As you look at the PhotoShare application, try to visualize how the markup in Listing 7-3 relates to what you see on the screen in terms of how the frames are defined and translated visually.

info.jsp

Now that we have seen how the PhotoShare window is opened, and how the frameset itself is defined, we can now dive into the HTML documents that populate the frames, starting with the simplest document, shown in Listing 7-4: `info.jsp`.

Listing 7-4. *A Fairly Simple Page, info.jsp, Where Photo Info Is Displayed*

```
<html>
  <head>
    <title>PhotoShare - Info</title>
    <!-- Link in stylesheet. -->
    <link rel="stylesheet" href="css/styles.css" type="text/css">
  </head>
  <body class="cssMain">
    <table width="100%" border="0" cellpadding="0" cellspacing="0"
      class="cssMain">
```

```
      <tr class="cssInfoRowHeader"><td>Added By:</td></tr>
      <tr><td valign="top" height="24" id="addedBy"> </td></tr>
      <tr><td valign="top" height="10"> </td></tr>
      <tr class="cssInfoRowHeader"><td>Added On:</td></tr>
      <tr><td valign="top" height="24" id="addedOn"> </td></tr>
      <tr><td valign="top" height="10"> </td></tr>
      <tr class="cssInfoRowHeader"><td>Type:</td></tr>
      <tr><td valign="top" height="24" id="type"> </td></tr>
      <tr><td valign="top" height="10"> </td></tr>
      <tr class="cssInfoRowHeader"><td>File Size:</td></tr>
      <tr><td valign="top" height="24" id="fileSize"> </td></tr>
      <tr><td valign="top" height="10"> </td></tr>
      <tr class="cssInfoRowHeader"><td>Dimensions:</td></tr>
      <tr><td valign="top" height="24" id="dimensions"> </td></tr>
      <tr><td valign="top" height="10"> </td></tr>
      <tr class="cssInfoRowHeader"><td>DPI:</td></tr>
      <tr><td valign="top" height="24" id="dpi"> </td></tr>
      <tr><td valign="top" height="10"> </td></tr>
      <tr class="cssInfoRowHeader"><td>Color Depth:</td></tr>
      <tr><td valign="top" height="24" id="colorDepth"> </td></tr>
      <tr><td valign="top" height="10"> </td></tr>
      <tr class="cssInfoRowHeader"><td>Description:</td></tr>
      <tr><td valign="top" height="24" id="description"> </td></tr>
    </table>
  </body>
</html>
```

info.jsp is the markup for the photo info area on the right. As you can see, there is no JavaScript in this particular document; it is just straight markup. It is essentially nothing more than a table where we have a row that is a heading (i.e., the name of the piece of information about the photo), a row where the actual piece of information will appear, and a row with a nonbreaking space entity ( ), which just separates the data fields a little. The table itself has the cssMain style applied to it, which means by default all the text in the table will have that style applied to it. This is overridden on the rows where the headers are; those instead have the cssInfoRowHeader style applied to them.

control.jsp

Listing 7-5 shows the content of the control frame, control.jsp.

Listing 7-5. *Where All the Action Starts, control.jsp*

```
<html>
  <head>
    <title>PhotoShare - Control</title>
    <!-- Link in stylesheet. -->
    <link rel="stylesheet" href="css/styles.css" type="text/css">
    <script>
```

```
      // Preload all images for buttons in this frame.
      var add_collection_0 = new Image();
      add_collection_0.src = "img/add_collection_0.gif";
      var add_collection_1 = new Image();
      add_collection_1.src = "img/add_collection_1.gif";
      var delete_collection_0 = new Image();
      delete_collection_0.src = "img/delete_collection_0.gif";
      var delete_collection_1 = new Image();
      delete_collection_1.src = "img/delete_collection_1.gif";
      var add_photo_0 = new Image();
      add_photo_0.src = "img/add_photo_0.gif";
      var add_photo_1 = new Image();
      add_photo_1.src = "img/add_photo_1.gif";
      var delete_photo_0 = new Image();
      delete_photo_0.src = "img/delete_photo_0.gif";
      var delete_photo_1 = new Image();
      delete_photo_1.src = "img/delete_photo_1.gif";
      var print_0 = new Image();
      print_0.src = "img/print_0.gif";
      var print_1 = new Image();
      print_1.src = "img/print_1.gif";
      var download_0 = new Image();
      download_0.src = "img/download_0.gif";
      var download_1 = new Image();
      download_1.src = "img/download_1.gif";
      var rotate_0 = new Image();
      rotate_0.src = "img/rotate_0.gif";
      var rotate_1 = new Image();
      rotate_1.src = "img/rotate_1.gif";
      var actual_size_0 = new Image();
      actual_size_0.src = "img/actual_size_0.gif";
      var actual_size_1 = new Image();
      actual_size_1.src = "img/actual_size_1.gif";
      var default_size_0 = new Image();
      default_size_0.src = "img/default_size_0.gif";
      var default_size_1 = new Image();
      default_size_1.src = "img/default_size_1.gif";
    </script>
  </head>
  <body class="cssMain">
    <table width="100%" height="100%" cellpadding="0" cellspacing="0"
      border="0" class="cssMain"><tr>
      <td width="140" align="left" valign="top">
        Collection:<br>
        <span id="spnCollectionsList">
          <select id="collectionsList" class="cssMain"></select>
        </span>
      </td>
```

```
      <td align="center" valign="middle">
        <input type="image" src="img/add_collection_0.gif"
          id="btnAddCollection"
          onMouseOver="this.src=add_collection_1.src;this.style.cursor='pointer';"
          onMouseOut="this.src=add_collection_0.src;this.style.cursor='normal';">
        <input type="image" src="img/delete_collection_0.gif"
          id="btnDeleteCollection"
          onMouseOver=
          "this.src=delete_collection_1.src;this.style.cursor='pointer';"
          onMouseOut="this.src=delete_collection_0.src;this.style.cursor='normal';">
        <input type="image" src="img/add_photo_0.gif" id="btnAddPhoto"
          onMouseOver="this.src=add_photo_1.src;this.style.cursor='pointer';"
          onMouseOut="this.src=add_photo_0.src;this.style.cursor='normal';">
        <input type="image" src="img/delete_photo_0.gif" id="btnDeletePhoto"
          onMouseOver="this.src=delete_photo_1.src;this.style.cursor='pointer';"
          onMouseOut="this.src=delete_photo_0.src;this.style.cursor='normal';">
        <input type="image" src="img/print_0.gif" id="btnPrintPhoto"
          onMouseOver="this.src=print_1.src;this.style.cursor='pointer';"
          onMouseOut="this.src=print_0.src;this.style.cursor='normal';">
        <input type="image" src="img/download_0.gif" id="btnDownloadPhoto"
          onMouseOver="this.src=download_1.src;this.style.cursor='pointer';"
          onMouseOut="this.src=download_0.src;this.style.cursor='normal';">
        <input type="image" src="img/rotate_0.gif" id="btnRotatePhoto"
          onMouseOver="this.src=rotate_1.src;this.style.cursor='pointer';"
          onMouseOut="this.src=rotate_0.src;this.style.cursor='normal';">
        <input type="image" src="img/actual_size_0.gif" id="btnActualSize"
          onMouseOver="this.src=actual_size_1.src;this.style.cursor='pointer';"
          onMouseOut="this.src=actual_size_0.src;this.style.cursor='normal';">
        <input type="image" src="img/default_size_0.gif" id="btnDefaultSize"
          onMouseOver="this.src=default_size_1.src;this.style.cursor='pointer';"
          onMouseOut="this.src=default_size_0.src;this.style.cursor='normal';">
      </td>
    </tr></table>
  </body>
</html>
```

There is just a smidgeon of code in this document, starting with what appears in the <head>. This is a series of the usual image preloads that we have already seen a number of times in other projects in this book. The images are for the various buttons that appear on the bottom. In the markup itself, we lay everything out in a single table with a single row. The row has two columns. The first column is where the collections dropdown lives. Note that the <select> is wrapped in a <span>, and this is for very good reason, which we'll see later (think: how do I update that <select> when collections are added or deleted?). One thing to point out now is the difference between <div> and <span>. In short, the main difference is that you will get a line break after a <div>, but not with a <span>. In more detail, <div> is meant to define a logical division in a document, whereas <span> is meant simply to wrap a section of markup, typically to assign some style to it. In most cases, you will find that you can use them interchangeably. There may, however, be instances where that line break after a <div> (a paragraph break to be more accurate) will be a problem, as it was here because it would have been just enough vertical space to cause a scroll bar in the frame, and I did not want that to occur.

In the second column are all the buttons. We simply render them one right after another, and center the contents of the column, so in effect we have the same thing as a flow layout in an AWT/Swing application. Each button has `onMouseOver` and `onMouseOut` event handlers, which are responsible for flipping the image of the button to the hover state `onMouseOver`, and back to the normal nonhover state image when the mouse leaves the button. These handlers also flip the `cursor` style attribute so that we get a pointer (or hand, depending on browser and OS) when we hover over it. You may have noticed that there is no handler for `onClick`, so how can these buttons ever actually *do* anything? All will be revealed, my young Padawan learner! (Seriously, though, bad *Star Wars* jokes aside, it's kind of a neat thing that Dojo provides, and we'll see it in just a bit.)

main.jsp

`main.jsp` is up next, and it is in fact where most of the real action is. However, because of its size, I will only be calling out relevant parts here. You should review it completely on your own before continuing.

To begin with, wow, lots of imports! With all the JavaScript externalized, that is to be expected. We of course import Dojo, as well as all the code that makes up PhotoShare itself. When this document loads, the `init()` function is called, which, as you probably have guessed, is responsible for initializing PhotoShare, as far as the client side of the house goes. We'll see that soon.

We have our Please Wait float-over, initially hidden, which is identical to what was seen in InstaMail.

After that we see a table opened, essentially splitting this frame in two—the first half (well, less than half really) for the filmstrip, and the other half for the photo viewing area—and the "landing pad," which is where a photo winds up after it is finished growing.

The first markup we see is this:

```
<!-- Up button. -->
<img src="img/up_button_0.gif" id="up_button" class="cssUpButton"
  onMouseOver="buttonOver(this);this.style.cursor='pointer';"
  onMouseOut="buttonOut(this);this.style.cursor='normal';">

<!-- Hide area for top of filmstrip. -->
<img src="img/film_tile_hide.gif" class="cssFilmstripTopHide">
<br>

<!-- Filmstrip photo "holes". -->
<img src="img/film_tile.gif" id="filmTile0" class="cssFilmTile0">
<img src="img/film_tile.gif" id="filmTile1" class="cssFilmTile1">
<img src="img/film_tile.gif" id="filmTile2" class="cssFilmTile2">
<img src="img/film_tile.gif" id="filmTile3" class="cssFilmTile3">
<img src="img/film_tile.gif" id="filmTile4" class="cssFilmTile4">
```

```
<!-- Placeholders for images on filmstrip. -->
<img onClick="imgClick(0);" arrayIndex="" src="img/film_placeholder.gif"
  width="64" height="64" id="pic0"
  onMouseOver="this.style.cursor='pointer';"
  onMouseOut="this.style.cursor='normal';"
  style="position:absolute;top:16px;left:19px;z-index:200;">
<img onClick="imgClick(1);" arrayIndex="" src="img/film_placeholder.gif"
  width="64" height="64" id="pic1"
  onMouseOver="this.style.cursor='pointer';"
  onMouseOut="this.style.cursor='normal';"
  style="position:absolute;top:96px;left:19px;z-index:200;">
<img onClick="imgClick(2);" arrayIndex="" src="img/film_placeholder.gif"
  width="64" height="64" id="pic2"
  onMouseOver="this.style.cursor='pointer';"
  onMouseOut="this.style.cursor='normal';"
  style="position:absolute;top:176px;left:19px;z-index:200;">
<img onClick="imgClick(3);" arrayIndex="" src="img/film_placeholder.gif"
  width="64" height="64" id="pic3"
  onMouseOver="this.style.cursor='pointer';"
  onMouseOut="this.style.cursor='normal';"
  style="position:absolute;top:256px;left:19px;z-index:200;">
<img onClick="imgClick(4);" arrayIndex="" src="img/film_placeholder.gif"
  width="64" height="64" id="pic4"
  onMouseOver="this.style.cursor='pointer';"
  onMouseOut="this.style.cursor='normal';"
  style="position:absolute;top:336px;left:19px;z-index:200;">

<!-- Hide area for bottom of filmstrip. -->
<img src="img/film_tile_hide.gif"
  style="position:absolute;top:408px;left:6px;z-index:300;">

<!-- Down button. -->
<img src="img/down_button_0.gif" id="down_button"
  style="position:absolute;top:418px;left:23px;z-index:400;"
  onMouseOver="buttonOver(this);this.style.cursor='pointer';"
  onMouseOut="buttonOut(this);this.style.cursor='normal';">
```

Note that I removed a small section that defines the imgGrowing <div>. I wanted you to see only the markup that defines the filmstrip together, and that is what the previous snippet is. Let me explain the "theory," such as it is, behind how the filmstrip works. If you have ever implemented a scroller before, especially if you, like me, spent a lot of time writing demos on the Commodore 64 back in the '80s, this will be instantly familiar to you. If this is your first exposure to it, note that virtually all scrollers work in the same basic way, so you can apply this going forward whenever you need such a thing.

The filmstrip is set up as a series of "tiles," in this case what is shown in Figure 7-8.

Figure 7-8. *The tile image that makes up the filmstrip*

A series of five of these filmstrip tiles are laid out to form a vertical line, so what you see is basically a filmstrip with room for five "frames" (a frame means a photo here, but if this were a real filmstrip, it would be a frame). Above and below this line of filmstrip tiles are two square images that are pure white, matching the background of the page. These images are the same size as the filmstrip tile, 90×80 pixels. They are our "hider" tiles. One hider tile is overlaid on the first filmstrip tile on the top. The effect is that only four of the filmstrip tiles are now visible. The other hider tile is placed on the bottom of the filmstrip, right after the last filmstrip tile.

Assuming a collection is selected, an array is populated that contains the images for our photos. On top of the filmstrip tiles are placed the photos from the array. This is done by setting the `z-index` style attribute of the photo to something higher than that of the filmstrip tile, and ensuring that the photo lines up with the gray area on the tile (which is 64×64 pixels in size).

Now, the trick with the hider tiles is that they too have a higher `z-index` style attribute assigned to them than do the filmstrip tiles, and also higher than the photos on the tiles. In other words, imagine if a photo is occupying the gray space on a filmstrip tile. Any portion of both the photo and filmstrip tile that overlaps the hider tile will not be visible. So, what will happen if one of the tiles overlaps another? Simply put, part of the filmstrip tile, and photo, if the tile has a photo on it, will be obscured by the hider tile because it will be behind the hider tile. Are you beginning to see why it's called a hider tile? Simply put, it "hides" part of the filmstrip, and any photo that is on it.

So, let's imagine what happens if we shift all five of our filmstrip tiles 10 pixels down at the same time (the photos get shifted right along with them all the time). Part of the filmstrip tile that was obscured by the hider tile up top will now be visible, and the hider on the bottom will now hide 10 pixels of the tile on the bottom. That is exactly what happens when you hover over the up or down buttons: all the tiles are shifted one pixel at a time.

Clearly that is not the whole story. What happens when all the tiles are shifted from the starting positions 80 pixels in either direction by virtue of the user scrolling it up or down using the arrow buttons? Well, that is where the scrolling actually takes place. What we do is we rotate the array that contains the image in the appropriate direction. We then reset the positions of the tiles and photos so that either the tile on the top or bottom is behind the hider, depending on which way the scroll went. We then update the photos on the tiles, and voilà, a scroll is born!

I realize that explanation may seem a bit confusing; this is one of those things that is far easier to understand visually. Fortunately, there is an easy way to see exactly what is happening. Go into `main.jsp` and remove these two bits of code:

```
<!-- Hide area for top of filmstrip. -->
<img src="img/film_tile_hide.gif" class="cssFilmstripTopHide">
<br>
```

and

```
<!-- Hide area for bottom of filmstrip. -->
<img src="img/film_tile_hide.gif"
  style="position:absolute;top:408px;left:6px;z-index:300;">
```

This removes the hider images from the equation, and you can clearly see the images shifting "behind" them, and then flipping back when the filmstrip is scrolled 80 pixels up or down by you hovering over the scroll buttons. The rotating of the array should also be apparent at that point. Note that the images of the buttons are laid out over those hider tiles, so they are still present. Since they have a transparency to them, though, I believe it actually helps see what is happening.

After that we see this section:

```
<!-- Placeholders for images on filmstrip. -->
<img onClick="imgClick(0);" arrayIndex="" src="img/film_placeholder.gif"
  width="64" height="64" id="pic0"
  style="position:absolute;top:16px;left:19px;z-index:200;">
<img onClick="imgClick(1);" arrayIndex="" src="img/film_placeholder.gif"
  width="64" height="64" id="pic1"
  style="position:absolute;top:96px;left:19px;z-index:200;">
<img onClick="imgClick(2);" arrayIndex="" src="img/film_placeholder.gif"
  width="64" height="64" id="pic2"
  style="position:absolute;top:176px;left:19px;z-index:200;">
<img onClick="imgClick(3);" arrayIndex="" src="img/film_placeholder.gif"
  width="64" height="64" id="pic3"
  style="position:absolute;top:256px;left:19px;z-index:200;">
<img onClick="imgClick(4);" arrayIndex="" src="img/film_placeholder.gif"
  width="64" height="64" id="pic4"
  style="position:absolute;top:336px;left:19px;z-index:200;">
```

These are the images that will actually be our photos. Initially they start out as nothing but placeholders, using a 1×1 transparent pixel image as a placeholder. Note the custom `arrayIndex` property. This is how we determine what index into the `photos` array of the `Collection` object (which we'll see shortly) is used as the source of the image when a collection is being viewed.

After that comes the landing pad markup. This is nothing but a giant `<div>` that starts out with some introductory text in an internal `<div>` (`landingPadText`). This text will be hidden when a collection is selected. The landing pad is sized to 640×480 pixels, our default photo size.

Finally of interest in this document is the markup dealing with the shadow you see on the landing pad:

```
<!-- Shadow for landing pad. -->
<div id="shadow1" style="position:absolute;left:117px;top:11px;width:640px;
  height:480px;background-color:#000000;z-index:8;"></div>
<div id="shadow2" style="position:absolute;left:118px;top:12px;width:640px;
  height:480px;background-color:#202020;z-index:7;"></div>
<div id="shadow3" style="position:absolute;left:119px;top:13px;width:640px;
  height:480px;background-color:#404040;z-index:6;"></div>
```

```
<div id="shadow4" style="position:absolute;left:120px;top:14px;width:640px;
  height:480px;background-color:#606060;z-index:5;"></div>
<div id="shadow5" style="position:absolute;left:121px;top:15px;width:640px;
  height:480px;background-color:#808080;z-index:4;"></div>
<div id="shadow6" style="position:absolute;left:122px;top:16px;width:640px;
  height:480px;background-color:#a0a0a0;z-index:3;"></div>
<div id="shadow7" style="position:absolute;left:123px;top:17px;width:640px;
  height:480px;background-color:#c0c0c0;z-index:2;"></div>
<div id="shadow8" style="position:absolute;left:124px;top:18px;width:640px;
  height:480px;background-color:#e0e0e0;z-index:1;"></div>
<div id="shadow9" style="position:absolute;left:124px;top:18px;width:640px;
  height:480px;background-color:#fafafa;z-index:0;"></div>
```

Unfortunately, while Internet Explorer provides access to DirectX filters, including drop-down shadows, Firefox and most other browsers do not. (By the way, although they are not used in this book, if you should want further information on using those filters, you'll find a good reference here: `http://msdn.microsoft.com/library/default.asp?url=/workshop/author/filter/reference/reference.asp`.) There is no good way that I am aware of to achieve a drop shadow on arbitrary page elements that is cross-browser. Therefore, for the time being, you'll always have to do something special for each browser, or as I have done, find a way to "fake it." In any case, a drop shadow is simply a series of lines, most commonly to the right and bottom of an element, where the lines start out black close to the image and gradually get lighter and lighter until they match the background. To achieve that effect, I have a series of `<div>`s, each with a color lighter than the last, and each offset to the right and down from the starting position of the landing pad. This winds up giving the desired effect.

addCollection.jsp

With that out of the way, we now come to `addCollection.jsp`, which provides the content of the Add Collection dialog. This JSP is shown in Listing 7-6.

Listing 7-6. *The Content of the Add Collection Dialog, addCollection.jsp*

```
<%@ taglib prefix="c" uri="http://java.sun.com/jstl/core" %>
<html>
  <head>
    <title>PhotoShare - Add Collection</title>
    <!-- Link in stylesheet. -->
    <link rel="stylesheet" href="css/styles.css" type="text/css">
    <script>
      function init() {
        // If this document was loaded as a result of just successfully adding
        // a collection, we need to update the collection list dropdown.
        if ("<c:out value='${message}'/>".indexOf("added") != -1) {
          opener.window.top.fraMain.updateCollectionsList();
        }
      }
    </script>
  </head>
```

```
  <body onLoad="init();" class="cssMain">
  <div class="cssMessage"><c:out value="${message}"/><br><br></div>
  <form name="addCollectionForm" method="post" action="addCollection.action">
    <table border="0" cellpadding="0" cellspacing="0" class="cssMain">
      <tr>
        <td>Collection Name: </td>
        <td>
          <input type="text" size="24" name="name"
            value="<c:out value="${param.name}"/>">
        </td>
      </tr>
      <tr>
        <td>Your Name: </td>
        <td>
          <input type="text" size="24" name="creator"
            value="<c:out value="${param.creator}"/>">
        </td>
      </tr>
      <tr><td colspan="2"> </td></tr>
      <tr>
        <td colspan="2"><input type="submit" value="Add Collection"></td>
      </tr>
    </table>
  <form>
  <br>
  <p align="right">
    <input type="button" value="Close Window" onClick="window.close();">
  </p>
  </body>
</html>
```

This is mostly straightforward markup, so we probably do not need to look it over in too much detail. Note the use of JSTL to populate the values of the input fields. This is so that if an error occurs, we'll have our values back. JSTL is preferable to a simple scriptlet here (`<%=request.getParameter("creator")%>`, for example) because the first time the dialog is shown, those parameters are not present in the request, and the scriptlet would output `null`. We would have to add logic to handle that. JSTL does that for us, so we can keep our page code a bit cleaner.

JSTL is also used in the `init()` function. The purpose of this function, called on page load, is to update the list of collections when a collection is added. We look for the string "added" in the response message from the server, which indicates the add was successful, and if it is found we call `updateCollectionsList()` in `main.jsp`, which is the `opener` for this dialog and therefore the user of the `opener` in the line `opener.window.top.fraMain.updateCollectionsList();`. Because the `opener` is a frameset document, we need to navigate down the DOM tree, starting from the `top`, referencing the frame we want to call the function in (`fraMain`), and finally call the function itself.

addPhoto.jsp

In the same vein, Listing 7-7 shows addPhoto.jsp, the content of the Add Photo dialog.

Listing 7-7. *The Content of the Add Photo Dialog, addPhoto.jsp*

```
<%@ taglib prefix="c" uri="http://java.sun.com/jstl/core" %>
<html>
  <head>
    <title>PhotoShare - Add Photo</title>
    <!-- Link in stylesheet. -->
    <link rel="stylesheet" href="css/styles.css" type="text/css">
    <script>
      function init() {
        // Set the value of the hidden form field that contains the collection
        // name to that of the selected collection in the dropdown.
        document.getElementById("hiddenCollection").value =
          opener.window.top.fraControl.document.getElementById(
            "collectionsList").value;
        // If this document was loaded as a result of just successfully adding
        // a photo, we need to reload the collection.
        if ("<c:out value='${message}'/>".indexOf("added") != -1) {
          opener.window.top.fraMain.loadCollection();
        }
      }
    </script>
  </head>
  <body onLoad="init();"  class="cssMain">
  <div class="cssMessage"><c:out value="${message}"/><br><br></div>
  <form name="addPhotoForm" enctype="multipart/form-data" method="post"
    action="addPhoto.action">
    <input type="hidden" id="hiddenCollection" name="collection">
    <table border="0" cellpadding="0" cellspacing="0" width="100%"
      class="cssMain">
      <tr>
        <td colspan="2">Photo Description: </td>
      </td>
      <tr>
        <td colspan="2">
          <textarea name="description" cols="69" rows="10">
            <c:out value="${param.description}"/>
          </textarea>
        </td>
      </tr>
      <tr>
        <td>Your Name: </td>
```

```
        <td align="left">
          <input type="text" name="adder"
            value="<c:out value="${param.adder}"/>">
        </td>
      </tr>
      <tr>
        <td>Photo To Upload: </td>
        <td align="left"><input type="file" name="photo"></td>
      </tr>
      <tr><td colspan="2"> </td></tr>
      <tr>
        <td colspan="2"><input type="submit" value="Add Photo"></td>
      </tr>
    </table>
  <form>
  <br>
  <p align="right">
    <input type="button" value="Close Window" onClick="window.close();">
  </p>
  </body>
</html>
```

This is almost the same as the addCollection.jsp that we just looked at, so we won't delve into it too much. The only thing to note is that this particular function, on the server, requires the name of the collection the photo is being added to. So, the init() function gets the function from the dropdown in the fraControl frame (notice the DOM traversal here as before) and populates a hidden form field so it will be submitted with the rest of the form data. The only other difference is that when a photo is added to a collection, we obviously need to refresh the collection. To do that, we simply reload the collection, just like when the dropdown selection changes.

listCollections.jsp

The code shown in Listing 7-8, listCollections.jsp, is a bit of a different animal than the rest.

Listing 7-8. *A Page That Renders an Ajax Result, listCollections.jsp*

```
<% /*
      This JSP is responsible for rendering the markup for the collections
      select dropdown in the control frame.  It uses the collections request
      attribute set there by the ListCollections Action.
   */
%>
<%@ page language="java" import="java.util.*" %>
<select id="collectionsList" class="cssMain"
  onChange="parent.fraMain.loadCollection();">
  <option value="none">--Select--</option>
```

```
  <%
    HashMap collections = (HashMap)request.getAttribute("collections");
    for (Iterator it = collections.keySet().iterator(); it.hasNext();) {
      String name = (String)it.next();
  %>
      <option value="<%=name%>"><%=name%></option>
  <%
    }
  %>
</select>
```

Remember when we looked at control.jsp, I mentioned the fact that the <select> was wrapped in a <span>? Well, now we can see why. The updateCollections() function makes an Ajax request that eventually winds up in this JSP. The JSP renders the markup for the <select>. Upon returning to the client-side JavaScript, the innerHTML of that <div> will be replaced with what the JSP rendered.

You may be wondering if updating a <div> is the only way to update a <select>. The answer is no. You can also write script that manipulates the existing <select>, clears it of options, and then inserts them via DOM methods. This is perfectly valid as well. However, the difference in code is pretty substantial: essentially one line of code to update the <div> versus numerous lines to use the DOM. I would say that unless you have a reason to script the DOM, in situations like this I would go with the less code-intense approach.

loadCollection.jsp

Listing 7-9 shows loadCollection.jsp, which is very much along the same lines as listCollections.jsp, but a bit different at the same time.

Listing 7-9. *A JSP That Renders XML to Return to the Client, loadCollection.jsp*

```
<% /*
      This JSP is responsible for rendering the XML that describes a collection
      when one is selected by the user.  This XML is generated using the
      collection request attribute, which is a CollectionDTO.
    */
%>
<%@ page language="java"
     import="java.util.*,com.apress.ajaxprojects.photoshare.dtos.*" %>
<% CollectionDTO collection = (CollectionDTO)request.getAttribute("collection"); %>
<collection name="<%=collection.getName()%>"
  createdBy="<%=collection.getCreatedBy()%>"
createdOn="<%=collection.getCreatedOn()%>">
  <%
    ArrayList photos = collection.getPhotos();
    for (Iterator it = photos.iterator(); it.hasNext();) {
      PhotoDTO photo = (PhotoDTO)it.next();
  %>
```

```
      <photo addedBy="<%=photo.getAddedBy()%>"
        addedOn="<%=photo.getAddedOn()%>"
        type="<%=photo.getType()%>"
        fileSize="<%=photo.getFileSize()%>"
        dimensions="<%=photo.getDimensions()%>"
        dpi="<%=photo.getDpi()%>"
        filename="<%=photo.getFilename()%>"
        colorDepth="<%=photo.getColorDepth()%>">
      <%=photo.getDescription()%>
      </photo>
  <%
    }
  %>
</collection>
```

OK, so this should look a little bit familiar. It is similar to `listCollections.jsp`, with one big difference: this time we are not rendering markup to be inserted in a `<div>`; we are rendering XML. There is no difference as far as JSPs go between rendering markup and rendering XML. Further, you could render any old text you want in whatever custom form you create; a JSP does not care. I have found that people many times forget this, and especially when doing Ajax, they think that the response must be rendered in code in a servlet (or Struts `Action`, or what have you). This of course is not true, and forgetting it will nearly always lead to writing more code than you have to. Especially when you can use JSTL in a JSP, there is little reason not to use JSPs to render whatever the result of your Ajax call is. In this particular case I did not use JSTL because it was all just simple calls to getters in a bean anyway, so the benefit of using JSTL is not as apparent as in other cases. Also, it is always good to remember that as nice as JSTL and other taglibs can be, you can still always do the basics underneath it all, and seeing that on occasion is a good thing.

Collection.js

Now that all of the markup is out of the way, we can get to some actual code. The first bit we'll look at, shown in Listing 7-10, is `Collection.js`.

Listing 7-10. *JavaScript for the Collection Object as Defined in Collection.js*

```
// Collection object.
function Collection() {
  this.name = null;
  this.createdBy = null;
  this.createdOn = null;
  this.photos = new Array();
  this.currentArrayIndex = null;
}
Collection.prototype.setName = function(inName) {
  this.name = inName;
}
```

```
Collection.prototype.getName = function() {
  return this.name;
}
Collection.prototype.setCreatedBy = function(inCreatedBy) {
  this.createdBy = inCreatedBy;
}
Collection.prototype.getCreatedBy = function() {
  return this.createdBy;
}
Collection.prototype.setCreatedOn = function(inCreatedOn) {
  this.createdOn = inCreatedOn;
}
Collection.prototype.getCreatedOn = function() {
  return this.createdOn;
}
Collection.prototype.addPhoto = function(inPhoto) {
  this.photos.push(inPhoto);
}
Collection.prototype.getPhoto = function(inIndex) {
  return this.photos[inIndex];
}
// Function to load the images fom the server for each photo in the collection.
Collection.prototype.loadPhotoImages = function() {
  for (var i = 0; i < this.photos.length; i++) {
    this.photos[i].loadImage();
  }
}
// Method to rotate an array in the "down" direction on the filmstrip.
Collection.prototype.rotateArrayDown = function() {
  var l = this.photos.length - 1;
  var o1 = this.photos[0];
  for (var i = 0; i < l; i++) {
    this.photos[i] = this.photos[i + 1];
  }
  this.photos[l] = o1;
}
// Method to rotate an array in the "up" direction on the filmstrip.
Collection.prototype.rotateArrayUp = function() {
  var l = this.photos.length - 1;
  var o1 = this.photos[l];
  for (var i = l; i > 0; i--) {
    this.photos[i] = this.photos[i - 1];
  }
  this.photos[0] = o1;
}
```

```
Collection.prototype.toString = function() {
  return "Collection=[name=" + this.name +
    ",createdBy=" + this.createdBy +
    ",createdOn=" + this.createdOn + ",photos={" + this.photos + "}]";
}
```

The `Collection` class is the equivalent of a simple JavaBean in JavaScript. The only real "meat" is in the `loadPhotoImages()`, `rotateArrayDown()`, and `rotateArrayUp()` functions. We have an array named `photos`. This is a collection of `Photo` objects, which we'll see next. `LoadPhotoImages()` simply iterates over this array and calls the `loadImage()` function on the `Photo` objects, which results in a call to the server to load the image. `rotateArrayDown()` and `rotateArrayUp()` are called when the filmstrip has been scrolled 80 pixels in either direction to rotate the elements of the array in the appropriate direction. Recall the discussion of how the filmstrip works (and I hope you tried my suggestion to see it a bit more clearly). This code is responsible for moving the photos up and down the filmstrip. It *looks* like the photos themselves are moving up and down, but in fact just the data in the array is shifting, and the image sources are updated according to the new state of the array.

Photo.js

In Listing 7-11 we see `Photo.js`, which as you can guess is where the `Photo` object seen in describing the `Collection` object is.

Listing 7-11. *JavaScript for the Photo Object as Defined in Collection.js*

```
// Photo object.
function Photo() {
  this.type = null;
  this.addedBy = null;
  this.addedOn = null;
  this.fileSize = null;
  this.dimensions = null;
  this.width = null;
  this.height = null;
  this.dpi = null;
  this.filename = null;
  this.colorDepth = null;
  this.description = null;
  this.image = null;
}
Photo.prototype.setType = function(inType) {
  this.type = inType;
}
Photo.prototype.getType = function() {
  return this.type;
}
```

```
Photo.prototype.setAddedBy = function(inAddedBy) {
  this.addedBy = inAddedBy;
}
Photo.prototype.getAddedBy = function() {
  return this.addedBy;
}
Photo.prototype.setAddedOn = function(inAddedOn) {
  this.addedOn = inAddedOn;
}
Photo.prototype.getAddedOn = function() {
  return this.addedOn;
}
Photo.prototype.setFileSize = function(inFileSize) {
  this.fileSize = inFileSize;
}
Photo.prototype.getFileSize = function() {
  return this.fileSize;
}
// Set the dimensions of the photo.  Expects the argument to be in the form
// widthxheight.
Photo.prototype.setDimensions = function(inDimensions) {
  this.dimensions = inDimensions;
  var a = inDimensions.split("x");
  this.width = a[0];
  this.height = a[1];
}
Photo.prototype.getDimensions = function() {
  return this.dimensions;
}
Photo.prototype.getWidth = function() {
  return this.width;
}
Photo.prototype.getHeight = function() {
  return this.height;
}
Photo.prototype.setDpi = function(inDpi) {
  this.dpi = inDpi;
}
Photo.prototype.getDpi = function() {
  return this.dpi;
}
Photo.prototype.setFilename = function(inFilename) {
  this.filename = inFilename;
}
Photo.prototype.getFilename = function() {
  return this.filename;
}
```

```
Photo.prototype.setColorDepth = function(inColorDepth) {
  this.colorDepth = inColorDepth;
}
Photo.prototype.getColorDepth = function() {
  return this.colorDepth;
}
Photo.prototype.setDescription = function(inDescription) {
  this.description = inDescription;
}
Photo.prototype.getDescription = function() {
  return this.description;
}
// Loads the image from the server corresponding to this photo.
Photo.prototype.loadImage = function() {
  this.image = new Image();
  this.image.src = "photos/" + this.filename;
}
Photo.prototype.getImage = function() {
  return this.image;
}
Photo.prototype.toString = function() {
  return "Photo=[type=" + this.type + ",addedBy=" + this.addedBy +
    ",addedOn=" + this.addedOn + ",fileSize=" + this.fileSize +
    ",dimensions=" + this.dimensions + ",dpi=" + this.dpi +
    ",filename=" + this.filename + ",colorDepth=" + this.colorDepth +
    "]";
}
```

Again, for all intents and purposes `Photo` is really just a simple bean, a bunch of setters and getters and not too much more. You can see the `loadImage()` function mentioned previously, which when executed results in a call to the server (or a retrieval from the local browser cache if the photo is already present) to get the image itself. Note that the dimensions of the photo are sent by the server in width×height form, so the `setDimensions()` function splits that into its constituent parts so that we can have access to the height and width individually.

Globals.js

The `Globals.js` file contains some global variables that are used throughout the rest of the JavaScript, so it makes sense to look at that next. Listing 7-12 shows this file in its entirety. I think that the comments themselves tell the full story, so there is probably no need to repeat them here. I suggest you examine the listing to gain a feel for what the various variables are, as we'll be seeing them again in the rest of the JavaScript to come.

Listing 7-12. *JavaScript Containing All the Global Variables Used in PhotoShare*

```
// This flag will be set to true when the server is called upon to do
// some processing.  This will be used to lock out some functions during
// that period.
```

```
var processing = false;

// The left and top coordinates of the upper-left corner of
// the landing pad area.
var landingPadLeft = 116;
var landingPadTop = 10;

// This is a reference to the currently active Collection object.
var currentCollection = null;

// This is a reference to the currently displayed photo.
var currentPhoto = null;

// The index into the image array of the current image.
var currentArrayIndex = null;

// This is the amount the current photo is rotated in degrees.
var rotationAmount = null;

// ***** Variables used to grow an image. *****
var growTimer = null; // Timer used to grow an image.
var growIndex = null; // Index into growCoordinates when growing an image.
var growCoordinates = null; // The array of coordinates that represent a
                        // straight line path from the starting location
                        // of a thumbnail to the fully expanded version.
var growWidthStep = null; // How much a thumbnail grows horizontally along
                      // the path to full.
var growHeightStep = null; // How much a thumbnail grows vertically along the
                       //path to full.
var growWidth = null; // The current width of the growing image.
var growHeight = null; // The current height of the growing image.
var growWidthFinal = null; // The target width of the growing image.
var growWidthHeight = null; // The target height of the growing image.

// ***** Variable used to scroll the filmstrip. *****
var scrollTimer = null; // Timer used for scrolling the filmstrip.
var y_offset = null; // How far the filmstrip is scrolled up or down.

// "The Pixel of Destiny" (Google for it, you'll love it!)
var img_film_placeholder = new Image();
img_film_placeholder.src = "img/film_placeholder.gif";

// Images for up button rollover.
var img_up_button_0 = new Image();
img_up_button_0.src = "img/up_button_0.gif";
var img_up_button_1 = new Image();
img_up_button_1.src = "img/up_button_1.gif";
```

```
// Images for down button rollover.
var img_down_button_0 = new Image();
img_down_button_0.src = "img/down_button_0.gif";
var img_down_button_1 = new Image();
img_down_button_1.src = "img/down_button_1.gif";
```

misc.js

`misc.js` is the next file to look at; it's shown in Listing 7-13.

Listing 7-13. *JavaScript for Miscellaneous Code, misc.js*

```
// This function is called when PhotoShare first loads to perform various
// initializiation tasks.
function init() {
  // Use Dojo to attach events to our control buttons and dropdown.
  var evNode = null;
  evNode = parent.fraControl.document.getElementById("btnAddCollection");
  dojo.event.connect(evNode, "onclick", "addCollection");
  evNode =
    parent.fraControl.document.getElementById("btnDeleteCollection");
  dojo.event.connect(evNode, "onclick", "deleteCollection");
  evNode = parent.fraControl.document.getElementById("btnAddPhoto");
  dojo.event.connect(evNode, "onclick", "addPhoto");
  evNode = parent.fraControl.document.getElementById("btnDeletePhoto");
  dojo.event.connect(evNode, "onclick", "deletePhoto");
  evNode = parent.fraControl.document.getElementById("btnPrintPhoto");
  dojo.event.connect(evNode, "onclick", "printPhoto");
  evNode = parent.fraControl.document.getElementById("btnDownloadPhoto");
  dojo.event.connect(evNode, "onclick", "downloadPhoto");
  evNode = parent.fraControl.document.getElementById("btnRotatePhoto");
  dojo.event.connect(evNode, "onclick", "rotatePhoto");
  evNode = parent.fraControl.document.getElementById("btnActualSize");
  dojo.event.connect(evNode, "onclick", "setActualSize");
  evNode = parent.fraControl.document.getElementById("btnDefaultSize");
  dojo.event.connect(evNode, "onclick", "setDefaultSize");
  // Reset all globals to their initial states.
  resetVars();
  // Set the pictures on the filmstrip to their correct positions.
  setPicLocations();
  // Ask the server to get the list of collections and update the dropdown.
  updateCollectionsList();
}

// This is called to reset all variables to their initial states.  This
// happens at startup of course, and also when a collection is selected.
function resetVars() {
  // Kill grow timer, if running.
```

```
  if (growTimer != null) {
    window.clearTimeout(growTimer);
    growTimer = null;
  }
  // Kill scroll timer, if running.
  if (scrollTimer != null) {
    window.clearTimeout(scrollTimer);
    scrollTimer = null;
  }
  // Hide growing image, if showing.
  var o = document.getElementById("imgGrowing");
  o.style.display = "none";
  o.style.top = "0px";
  o.style.left = "0px";
  // Point the photos on the filmstrip away from the image array in the
  // collection and "blank" them out.
  document.getElementById("pic0").arrayIndex = null;
  document.getElementById("pic0").src = img_film_placeholder.src;
  document.getElementById("pic1").arrayIndex = null;
  document.getElementById("pic1").src = img_film_placeholder.src;
  document.getElementById("pic2").arrayIndex = null;
  document.getElementById("pic2").src = img_film_placeholder.src;
  document.getElementById("pic3").arrayIndex = null;
  document.getElementById("pic3").src = img_film_placeholder.src;
  document.getElementById("pic4").arrayIndex = null;
  document.getElementById("pic4").src = img_film_placeholder.src;
  // Reset all other variables appropriately.
  currentCollection = null;
  currentPhoto = null;
  growIndex = null;
  growCoordinates = null;
  growWidthStep = null;
  growHeightStep = null;
  growWidth = null;
  growHeight = null;
  growWidthFinal = null;
  growWidthHeight = null;
  y_offset = 0;
  rotationAmount = 0;
}

// This function is called to update the list of collections in the dropdown.
function updateCollectionsList() {
  // Don't do it if server is processing.
  if (processing) { return false; }
  // Snap photo to landing pad, if growing.
  snapImageToLandingPad();
```

```
  // Show Please Wait floatover.
  showPleaseWait()
  // Make AJAX call.
  dojo.io.bind({
    url: "listCollections.action",
    error: function(type, errObj) { alert("AJAX error!"); },
    load: function(type, data, evt) {
      parent.fraControl.document.getElementById(
        "spnCollectionsList").innerHTML = data;
      hidePleaseWait();
    },
    mimetype: "text/html",
    transport: "XMLHTTPTransport"
  });
}

// Resets the landing pad to its default size.
function resetLandingPad() {
  o = document.getElementById("landingPad")
  o.style.width = "640px";
  o.style.height = "480px";
}

// Resets the landing pad shadow layers to the proper size when showing a
// photo at actual size.
function setShadowActualSize() {
  for (var i = 1; i < 10; i++) {
    o = document.getElementById("shadow" + i)
    o.style.width = currentPhoto.getWidth();
    o.style.height = currentPhoto.getHeight();
  }
}

// Resets the landing pad shadow layers to the proper size when showing a
// photo at default size.
function setShadowDefaultSize() {
  for (var i = 1; i < 10; i++) {
    o = document.getElementById("shadow" + i)
    o.style.width = 640;
    o.style.height = 480;
  }
}
```

Recall when we looked at `control.jsp` that I mentioned that there were no `onClick` handlers for any of the buttons? Now we can see why! In the `init()` function, we use the Dojo event system, via the `dojo.event.connect()` function, to attach the appropriate `onClick` handlers to the buttons. The benefits to doing this were already enumerated in the "How We Will Pull It Off" section.

The resetVars() function does exactly as its name suggests: resets our global variables as appropriate. It also stops any timers that may currently be running. Obviously, there would not be any at startup, but this function also gets called at various times throughout the lifecycle of PhotoShare, such as when a collection is selected, and at that point there could be an active timer that we would want stopped.

Next we see the updateCollection() function. In most of the functions in PhotoShare, you will see this bit of code first:

```
// Don't do it if server is processing.
if (processing) { return false; }
// Snap photo to landing pad, if growing.
snapImageToLandingPad();
```

The first line is a quick rejection to see if the server is currently processing for us, in other words, if an Ajax request has been made and a request has not arrived yet. In nearly every case, when that is the state, we do not want a new function to fire, so we quickly check the value of the processing variable and immediately return if it is true. The second line immediately cancels a photo that might be growing and "snaps" it to the landing pad as if its growth cycle had completed. This will have no real effect if the photo is already on the landing pad.

listCollections() then makes an Ajax request to the server to get the list of collections. The response to this request is rendered by the listCollections.jsp that we saw earlier. Once the response comes back, we update the <div> that the <select> is in:

```
parent.fraControl.document.getElementById(
  "spnCollectionsList").innerHTML = data;
```

Once more we see the DOM traversal that needs to occur because we are accessing something in another frame. Lastly, we call hidePleaseWait();, which (I hope you guessed) hides the Please Wait float-over, which was shown via a call to showPleaseWait() before the request was made.

The resetLandingPad() function is next, and that simply resets the size of the landing pad to its default 640×480-pixel size.

The next function we find is setShadowActualSize(). This is called when the Actual Size button is clicked, to show the photo at its natural actual size, not our 640×480 default. Recall that the shadow <div>s are always sized to 640×480 by default and simply offset down and to the right from the landing pad to give the shadow effect. What happens if the photo is not 640×480 naturally, though? We can easily update the size of the landing pad based on the values we get back from calling getWidth() and getHeight() on the currentPhoto object, but what about the shadows? Well, we have to do essentially the same thing, but look through all 10 of them. That does the trick. Correspondingly, the setShadowDefaultSize() function that follows does the same thing, but this time we just set the width and height to 640 and 480 respectively; there's no need to look at the size of the currentPhoto.

PleaseWait.js

In Listing 7-14, we look at a quick hit, so to speak: the PleaseWait.js file.

Listing 7-14. *PleaseWait.js*

```
// Called to show the Please Wait layer when an operation begins.
function showPleaseWait() {
  processing = true;
  // First we center the layer.
  var pleaseWaitDIV = document.getElementById("divPleaseWait");
  var lca;
  if (window.innerWidth) {
    lca = window.innerWidth;
  } else {
    lca = document.body.clientWidth;
  }
  var lcb = pleaseWaitDIV.offsetWidth;
  var lcx = (Math.round(lca / 2)) - (Math.round(lcb / 2));
  var iebody = (document.compatMode &&
    document.compatMode != "BackCompat") ?
    document.documentElement : document.body;
  var dsocleft = document.all ? iebody.scrollLeft : window.pageXOffset;
  pleaseWaitDIV.style.left = (lcx + dsocleft - 120) + "px";
  if (window.innerHeight) {
    lca = window.innerHeight;
  } else {
    lca = document.body.clientHeight;
  }
  lcb = pleaseWaitDIV.offsetHeight;
  lcy = (Math.round(lca / 2)) - (Math.round(lcb / 2));
  iebody = (document.compatMode &&
    document.compatMode != "BackCompat") ?
    document.documentElement : document.body;
  var dsoctop = document.all ? iebody.scrollTop : window.pageYOffset;
  pleaseWaitDIV.style.top = (lcy + dsoctop - 40) + "px";
  // Now actually show it.
  pleaseWaitDIV.style.display = "block";
}

// Hides the Please Wait float-over.
function hidePleaseWait() {
  pleaseWaitDIV =
    document.getElementById("divPleaseWait").style.display = "none";
  processing = false;
}
```

Refer to Chapter 5, the InstaMail project, for an explanation of this code, as it was already broken down there.

ImageGrowing.js

Another relatively quick hit is the ImageGrowing.js file. I have again chosen to call out only the interesting portions of this code, so please check it out before reading further.

The first function, calcLine(), is a JavaScript implementation of the Bresenham line-drawing algorithm. This is perhaps the most common algorithm in all of graphics. Going into its theory is a bit beyond the scope of this book; if you would like to get into such details, Wikipedia is your friend: http://en.wikipedia.org/wiki/Bresenham%27s_line_algorithm. For our purposes, it should be enough to know that we are not trying to draw a line here. What we are trying to do is generate a list of coordinates from the position of a clicked photo on the filmstrip to the location of the landing pad in a straight line. We'll update the position of an image each time a timer fires and go through this list of coordinates. That will give us the effect of the photo "flying" into place.

The next function we see is growImage(). This is the function that will be called in response to a timer firing once a photo is clicked on the filmstrip. Its job is first to move the photo along the path calculated by calcLine(), and also expand the image from its thumbnail size of 64×64 pixels to the default size of 640×480 pixels, and it should accomplish this complete growth at the same time we reach the end of our path. This will give us the appearance that the photo is not only flying onto the landing pad, but is growing at the same time.

Let's take a look at this code in detail. The first bit we see is this:

```
var o = document.getElementById("imgGrowing");
// If the growing image has not reached its final location yet...
if (growIndex < growCoordinates.length) {
  // Set its location to the next coordinates in the path.
  o.style.left = growCoordinates[growIndex][0] + "px";
  o.style.top = growCoordinates[growIndex][1] + "px";
```

When a photo is clicked, one effect is that the imgGrowing image's src is set to that of the photo that was clicked. So from then on, we are manipulating the imgGrowing image. The first thing we do is we see if we have run through the array of coordinates calculated by calcLine() yet. If not, we still have growing and moving to do. So, we first update the location of imgGrowing with the next coordinates in the array. Remember that the left and top style attributes must have a numeric value followed by the units indicator, px in this case.

The next thing we need to do is make the image grow, and that is accomplished with this snippet of code:

```
  // Expand it a little more.
  o.width = growWidth;
  o.height = growHeight;
  growWidth += growWidthStep;
  growHeight += growHeightStep;
```

Here we are setting the value of the width and height style attributes of imgGrowing to the current calculated width and height. We then add the step variables to the current values accordingly. The growWidthStep and growHeightStep variables are calculated when the photo is first clicked. First we calculate the line coordinate array. Then we calculate the delta in the starting and ending size of the photo, which is always 640 – 64 for the width and 480 – 64 for the height, which is the default 640×480-pixel size minus the thumbnail size of 64×64 pixels.

Then, we take those two numbers, 576 and 416, and divide them by the number of elements in the array. Remember that the line calculation has taken into account what photo was clicked, how the filmstrip was scrolled at the time, and other factors because all of those things affect the starting position. Once we do that division, we have the number of pixels the image must grow width-wise and height-wise for each movement along the line so that when it reaches the landing pad, it is at full size (in reality it can wind up being a little smaller because of rounding errors, but it turns out to not be a big enough difference to matter, and the `snapImageToLandingPad()` function takes care of that situation for us).

Speaking of the `snapImageToLandingPad()` function... The first thing that function does is stops the timer used to grow the image, if it was running. Then it sets the coordinates of the `imgGrowing` image to match the landing pad, and also sets the size of the image to the default size. Lastly, it calls on the `setShadowDefaultSize()` function so that the landing pad shadow is sized correctly.

ControlEvents.js

I have saved the longest, and meatiest, bit for last: `ControlEvents.js`. This file contains all the JavaScript that handles the events fired from the control frame by clicking the buttons and making a change in the dropdown. Because it is so long, it will not be listed in its entirety here. Instead, I will just call out the important parts.

First, note that all the functions begin the same way:

```
// If an operation is in progress, usually involving the server, don't do it.
if (processing) { return false; }
```

As previously discussed, none of the buttons should do anything when we have an active Ajax request being processed, and this line ensures that.

After that, most of them perform some input validations before proceeding. For example, the `addPhoto()` function checks if the `currentCollection` variable is `null`, which would mean a collection has not yet been selected, in which case adding a photo clearly has no meaning.

Once the validations are done, we see

```
// If photo happens to be growing, cut it short.
snapImageToLandingPad();
```

This too we have seen before. We want the photo, if it happens to be growing and flying towards the landing pad, to immediately complete its journey before we perform the requested function. That is what `snapImageToLandingPad()`, which we have previously seen, does.

In `addCollection()` and `addPhoto()`, we are opening a new window that is a dialog used to, obviously, add a collection or photo. The line that actually opens the window is similar to what we saw in `index.htm`:

```
window.open("showAddCollection.action", "", "width=340,height=240");
```

Note that the document we are requesting ends in `.action`, which means our servlet is going to handle it. We'll see the code behind that in a moment, but in short, this will cause an `Action` to execute, which will do nothing but immediately return and indicate what JSP to return. It is considered a "best practice" to have all requests in a webapp go through whatever server-side framework you are using. I made an exception when populating the frameset in `index1.htm`, but that is a fairly minor exception. Even still, arguably, they should go through the servlet as well. This allows you to enforce added degrees of security, perform tasks common to all requests, and things of that nature.

deleteCollection(),deletePhoto, loadCollection(), and rotatePhoto() all result in Ajax calls using Dojo. They are all pretty similar, but I would like to call your attention to loadCollection(), since more is happening there than the others, and yet since they are all so similar, you will get the basic idea of all of them from this one. Here is the Ajax call using Dojo:

```
dojo.io.bind({
  url: "loadCollection.action",
  content: {collection: collectionName},
  error: function(type, errObj) { alert("AJAX error!"); },
  load: function(type, data, evt) {
    // Now that we have received back the XML describing the collection,
    // we'll use JSDigester to parse it.
    var jsDigester = new JSDigester();
    jsDigester.addObjectCreate("collection", "Collection");
    jsDigester.addSetProperties("collection");
    jsDigester.addObjectCreate("collection/photo", "Photo");
    jsDigester.addSetProperties("collection/photo");
    jsDigester.addBeanPropertySetter("collection/photo",
      "setDescription");
    jsDigester.addSetNext("collection/photo", "addPhoto");
    currentCollection = jsDigester.parse(data);
    // Now the XML has been parsed and we have a populated Collection
    // object to play with.  Now, we'll tell the collection object
    // to go load all the photos.
    currentCollection.loadPhotoImages();
    // And now, update the filmstrip.
    updatePics();
    hidePleaseWait();
  },
  mimetype: "text/plain",
  transport: "XMLHTTPTransport"
});
```

So, what is going on here? Well, first, recall that dojo.io.bind() is the function that Dojo provides to send Ajax requests to the server. This function uses a number of arguments, and these are passed in as an associative array. The first one is url, which is just the URL the request will be submitted to. Next is content, which is how we define query parameters. In this case, we are sending in a parameter named collection, and its value is that of the collectionName variable, which we got a few lines prior by getting the value of the dropdown in the fraControl frame. Next is error, which is the function that will handle any errors. All the Ajax requests are set to simply display an alert saying an error has occurred. These are all "work or fail" kinds of requests, meaning retrying automatically is probably not viable, so a simple message should suffice. Let's skip the load parameter for just a moment and come back to it. Following that is mimetype, which is the MIME type of the response from the server, not the type of the request being made. You may be wondering why we are using a MIME type of text/plain here instead of the more intuitive text/xml. The reason is that when the MIME type is text/xml, the

XMLHttpRequest object performs the extra step of parsing the returned response so that it is accessible via the responseXML property as a DOM object. However, since we are going to use JSDigester to parse the response instead, there is little reason to incur the extra overhead of that automatic parsing by XMLHttpRequest. Granted the overhead in this instance would be quite minor, but it is still a good practice to not incur it if you don't really have to. Lastly, transport defines how the call will be made, via XMLHttpRequest in this case.

Now, circling back around the load parameter, this is the function that will be executed when the response is received from the server. In this case, we are using JSDigester to parse the response. As previously mentioned, JSDigester is a client-side implementation of the Commons Digester component. It allows you to use a rules-based mechanism to parse XML using a stack-based approach. What that means is that you set up a series of rules for parsing the XML document, each of which fires when certain "events" occur, such as encountering a specific element, or that element being closed, and so forth. This is at a higher level than SAX, although SAX is actually used underneath JSDigester.

JSDigester, and its big brother Commons Digester, is used by adding rules to a Digester instance (JSDigester instance in the case of JSDigester). The first rule we see added here is an objectCreate rule. This rule says that when the XML element named "collection" is encountered, an instance of the Collection class should be created. This is the JavaScript object defined in Collection.js. The next rule, a setProperties rule, says that when the XML element named "collection" is encountered, we should take the attributes of that element and use them to set the properties of the object on the top of the stack, which is the last object created since it gets pushed onto the stack at creation time. So, our Collection object will now be populated from the attributes of the <collection> element. Next we have another objectCreate rule, which will create an instance of Photo from Photo.js whenever the XML document named "photo" is encountered that is a child of the "collection" element ("collection/photo"). Remember that the Photo object will now be pushed onto the stack and will be the top object. So, the next rule, another setProperties rule, will now work on the Photo object to populate its properties from the attributes of the <photo> tag. Next we add a beanPropertySetter rule, which sets a specific property of the object on the top of the stack with the text of an XML element. So, for instance, we have in the XML document <photo>Some description</photo>, and we want to set the description property of the Photo object on the top of the stack to the string "Some description". That is exactly what this rule does for us. Lastly, we have a setNext rule. This takes the object on the top of the stack, our Photo object, and adds it to the *next* object on the stack, our Collection object, using the addPhoto() function of the Collection object.

So, when all is said and done and this loadCollection() function ends, we'll have ourselves a Collection object that contains some number of Photo objects in its internal array. We set the currentCollection variable to this object, and call the updatePics() function so the changes become visible, and that's that!

The last bit of code that I would like to explain is in the rotatePhoto() function:

```
// Only allow updates in 90 degree increments clockwise.
rotationAmount += 90;
if (rotationAmount == 360) {
  rotationAmount = 0;
}
var photoFilename = currentPhoto.getFilename();
// Show the please wait floatover.
showPleaseWait();
```

```
// Make AJAX call.
dojo.io.bind({
  url: "rotatePhoto.action",
  content: {filename: photoFilename, degrees: rotationAmount},
  error: function(type, errObj) { alert("AJAX error!"); },
  load: function(type, data, evt) {
    document.getElementById("imgGrowing").src = null;
    document.getElementById("imgGrowing").src =
      "photos/" + data;
    hidePleaseWait();
  },
  mimetype: "text/plain",
  transport: "XMLHTTPTransport"
});
```

The first part is fairly obvious. Since we are only allowing for clockwise rotation in 90-degree increments, the only "complexity" is to reset the `rotationAmount` to 0 when we hit 360. After that, we get the filename of the photo currently being viewed and send that as a part of the query string in the Ajax request, along with the `rotationAmount`, of course. Note that the original photos are never actually modified; the rotation results in a temporary file being written out. The response from the server to this Ajax request is actually the name of that temporary file. So, all we need to do is update the `src` attribute of the image being viewed, which you'll recall is always `imgGrowing`, and the rotated version of the photo will be retrieved and displayed.

The Server-Side Code

With our exploration of the client side of PhotoShare complete, now we'll move on to the server side of things.

ConfigInfo.java

The first class to examine is `ConfigInfo`. This class is not listed here because it is a very simple JavaBean class. In fact, it is nothing more than a static `HashMap`, and a method to add an element to that `HashMap`, a method to get an element from that `HashMap`, and one to return the entire `HashMap`. This class is where we store our `Action` configurations, as created in the `StartupConfigurator` class.

StartupConfigurator.java

The `StartupConfigurator` class is also not listed in its entirety here because a fairly large portion of this class is simply repetitive code. I will instead just describe portions of it and point out where the repetition is. I suggest that you review the entire class at your leisure.

Execution begins in the `contextInitialized()` method. The first thing it does is calls `initConfigInfo()`. All of the operations that our application can perform—more specifically, the URLs that the server will respond to—are defined by populating a plain old `HashMap` with some specific members. Let's take a look at one such configuration:

```
hm = new HashMap();
hm.put("path",    "showAddCollection");
hm.put("class",
  "com.apress.ajaxprojects.photoshare.actions.AddCollection");
hm.put("method", "showScreen");
hm.put("ok",      "addCollection.jsp");
ConfigInfo.addConfig(hm);
```

This is simply saying that when the URL /showAddCollection.action is received, we want the class AddCollection to be instantiated. We then want the showScreen() method of that class called. This method is expected to return a String. If it returns the string "ok", then the request will be forwarded to the addCollection.jsp. If this looks similar to Struts, or indeed many other webapp frameworks, that is no accident! We are in fact creating a small, simple framework for our application. In the interest of keeping the amount of code down a bit, I decided not to read this information in from a configuration file. Besides that concern, this is not meant to be a general-purpose framework as Struts is. This is a specific application with specific needs, so hard-coding this configuration information is not a terrible sin in my estimation. Anyway, the class that is instantiated here is called an Action class.

There are a series of these HashMap populations, and this is the repetition I was referring to. They are all very much similar to the previous code snippet. You will notice that some do not define return codes that will be recognized when an Action returns them. This is by design. An Action can also, in our small framework world, return null, which means the response is fully formed and nothing else should be done. It can also return a string that starts with /, which indicates that we should forward to that URL directly. Both of these are needed by some Actions in PhotoShare, and we'll see that soon.

After initConfigInfo() completes, the code gets a stream to the collections file, which is always stored in WEB-INF. This stream is then passed to the init() method of our DAO, which we'll look at shortly.

ActionDispatcher.java

After that comes the ActionDispatcher class. Review this class before continuing as it is not listed in its entirety here.

ActionDispatcher is akin to the Struts ActionServlet, or the front servlet in most other web frameworks. It is where all requests that go to the server for PhotoShare are handled. It is actually a pretty simple bit of code. First, we have a couple of lines that get us just the document portion of the requested URL:

```
String path     = request.getServletPath();
String pathInfo = request.getPathInfo();
if (pathInfo != null) {
  path += pathInfo;
}
if (path.charAt(0) == '/') {
  path = path.substring(1);
}
int dotPos = path.lastIndexOf(".");
path = path.substring(0, dotPos);
```

We then see if that document name can be found in our ConfigInfo object. If not, we throw an exception. If so, we continue processing.

Using reflection, we instantiate an instance of the class specified in the HashMap we retrieved from ConfigInfo. A real general-purpose framework would check to ensure that the class is an instance of the base Action class, via inheritance, and handle it gracefully if it was not. However, we are not trying to out-Strut Struts here, so we can forgo that check. So, once we have that Action instance, we set the request, response, session, and servlet context that are associated with the request being services on the Action. This allows us to make Actions that are basically just POJOs, that is, we do not have to supply specific methods with specific signatures. As long as a given method returns String, that is the only requirement. The method named in the HashMap is then executed, and the return value is grabbed. The code then examines the string that was returned. If it is null, nothing else will happen; the request is considered completely services. If it is not null, the first character is examined. If it is a "/" character we assume it is a valid URL and forward to it. If it does not begin with a "/" character, then we look it up in the HashMap. If it is found, we get the value associated with the key (vis-à-vis, the return value from the Action) and forward to that.

And that is ActionDispatcher in a nutshell.

CollectionDTO.java and PhotoDTO.java

In the interest of space, I will be skipping the CollectionDTO and PhotoDTO classes, as they are pretty typical DTOs. However, I would like to draw your attention to the getAsXML() methods. First, here is the version from CollectionDTO:

```
/**
 * This method is called to get a string of XML representing this DTO.
 *
 * @return A string of XML representing this DTO.
 */
public String getAsXML() {

  StringBuffer sb = new StringBuffer(512);
  sb.append("<collection name=\"" + name + "\" ");
  sb.append("createdBy=\"" + createdBy + "\" ");
  sb.append("createdOn=\"" +
    new SimpleDateFormat("MM/dd/yyyy hh:mma").format(createdOn) +
    "\">\n");
  for (Iterator it = photos.iterator(); it.hasNext();) {
    PhotoDTO dto = (PhotoDTO)it.next();
    sb.append(dto.getAsXML());
  }
  sb.append("</collection>\n");
  return sb.toString();

} // End getAsXML().
```

And here is the version from PhotoDTO:

```
/**
 * This method is called to get a string of XML representing this DTO.
 *
 * @return A string of XML representing this DTO.
 */
public String getAsXML() {

  StringBuffer sb = new StringBuffer(1024);
  sb.append("<photo addedBy=\"" + addedBy + "\" ");
  sb.append("addedOn=\"" +
    new SimpleDateFormat("MM/dd/yyyy hh:mma").format(addedOn) +
    "\" ");
  sb.append("type=\"" + type + "\" ");
  sb.append("fileSize=\"" + fileSize + "\" ");
  sb.append("dimensions=\"" + dimensions + "\" ");
  sb.append("dpi=\"" + dpi + "\" ");
  sb.append("filename=\"" + filename + "\" ");
  sb.append("colorDepth=\"" + colorDepth + "\">\n");
  sb.append(description + "\n");
  sb.append("</photo>\n");

  return sb.toString();

} // End getAsXML().
```

These methods are pretty obvious, but I wanted to point out that they are used when writing out the collections file. Each object knows how to create its own XML, so we just have to ask each object to do so and then combine it all together.

PhotoShareDAO.java

We now come to the PhotoShareDAO. Since it is probably the longest listing in PhotoShare, I have again chosen to call out the especially interesting pieces and will not be listing the entire class here. Since we have seen other DAOs in this book already, and since this one is in many ways very similar, reviewing it in depth here is probably not necessary. Once again, though, reviewing it on your own is very much encouraged.

PhotoShareDAO is a singleton, so we have the typical getInstance() method referencing a private static PhotoShareDAO field and a private no-argument constructor.

If you recall from the discussion of StartupConfigurator, a stream is gotten to the collections file and then passed to the init() method of PhotoShareDAO. This method then uses Commons Digester to parse the XML and generate CollectionDTO objects, which themselves contain PhotoDTO objects. We have discussed JSDigester already, and I would like you to note the similarity between that code and the code in init() here. In fact, to cement your understanding of how Digester works in general, if Digester is new to you, I suggest examining this method and making sure it all makes sense in your mind. However, there are a few new things here, so let's have a look at them now:

```
// Configure BeanUtils to handle our date.
String pattern = "MM/dd/yyyy hh:mma";
Locale locale = Locale.getDefault();
DateLocaleConverter converter = new DateLocaleConverter(locale, pattern);
converter.setLenient(true);
ConvertUtils.register(converter, java.util.Date.class);
// Read in collections config and create beans, hand off to DAO.
Digester digester = new Digester();
digester.setValidating(false);
digester.push(this);
```

The first thing to note is that Digester uses another Commons library, BeanUtils, to populate fields in the objects it creates. BeanUtils handles conversions from strings, which is what Digester is reading in from an XML file, to various Java types. Most of them are built in and automatic for all intents and purposes. Some are slightly more problematic. Dates, for instance, tend to sometimes cause problems. For us, the important consideration is that we want the date to be in a certain format. So, we are creating a converter, which is simply a class that can convert from one type to another. In this case we are creating a `DateLocaleConverter`, which is a class that BeanUtils supplies. Here we set it to use the default locale on the server and also a particular date format that we specify. We then register that converter with `ConvertUtils`, a class in the BeanUtils library, and that will be used from then on when setting the value of a `Date` field in an object.

Something else we see for the first time here is a call to `setValidating()` on the Digester instance. This simply tells Digester that we do not want the XML being parsed to be validated against a DTD. Lastly, we push the instance of the `PhotoShareDAO` onto the stack. This means that when Digester begins its work, this will be the first object on the stack. This is done because the way the rules are set up, we'll be creating a `Collection` object. This will wind up being the top object on the stack. We'll be telling Digester to use a `setNext` rule when the `<collection>` element is encountered. This will call `addCollectionDigester()`, a method of `PhotoShareDAO`, to add the created collection, since `PhotoShareDAO` is where we'll be storing our collections data.

You will notice that there is an `addCollectionDigester()` method and an `addCollection()` method. The first is used when reading in the collections config file during initialization. Since at that point we just want to add the `Collection` object to the collections, that is all `addCollectionDigester()` does. `addCollection()` by contrast is called when a user adds a collection via the UI. In that situation, we also need to rewrite the collections file—hence the need for two different methods. It probably would have been possible to introduce branching logic to handle both situations from one method, but this approach seems a lot cleaner and simpler to me.

The `writeCollectionsFile()` method is a fairly typical file-writing method that is used to write out our collections config file. Note the use of the `getAsXML()` method on each `CollectionDTO` object. That method will in turn call the `getAsXML()` methods on each of the `PhotoDTO` objects it contains, so that the string it ultimately returns represents the entire collection, photos and all.

With `PhotoShareDAO` now out of the way, we have only one package of classes left to explore, and that is all the various `Actions` that PhotoShare is comprised of.

Action.java

Next up is the Action class, which is the base class for all our other Actions. Because it is a relatively simple class, it is not listed here, but again, please do examine it before continuing.

The Action class is nothing but a simple JavaBean that has getters and setters for request, response, session, and servlet context. Recall that any subclass does not need to provide any particular methods with any particular signatures, yet naturally they will need access to those objects. With this base class, that access is automatically provided. This class also provides a default implementation of the execute() method. This is handy if we wanted to simply forward to a JSP while still going through the framework. We could have an Action configuration that named this Action class as the class to instantiate, and then named the execute() method as the method to execute. The developer would not need to implement a subclass of the Action class, which saves some work. If you are familiar with Struts, this is equivalent to the ForwardAction metaphor, except that there us not even a special class that has to be used; the base class takes care of it just fine.

One last thing this base class provides is the setMessage() method. This simply sets a request attribute named "message" to the value passed to it. This is used on the client side to display response messages to the user, specifically when the Add Photo and Add Collection dialogs are used. Many frameworks provide fancier alternatives to this, but for the purposes of PhotoShare, this suffices.

AddCollection.java

The AddCollection Action class is the first true Action we'll examine (see Listing 7-15).

Listing 7-15. *AddCollection Action Class for Adding Collections*

```
package com.apress.ajaxprojects.photoshare.actions;

import com.apress.ajaxprojects.photoshare.dao.PhotoShareDAO;
import com.apress.ajaxprojects.photoshare.dtos.CollectionDTO;
import java.util.Date;
import org.apache.commons.logging.Log;
import org.apache.commons.logging.LogFactory;

/**
 * This class adds a collection.
 */
public class AddCollection extends Action {

  /**
   * Log instance.
   */
  private static Log log = LogFactory.getLog(AddCollection.class);

  /**
   * Called by ActionDispatched to show the Add Collection dialog.
   *
```

```
   * @return Result.
   */
  public String showScreen() {

    log.info("Entry...");
    setMessage("Add a collection: ");
    log.info("Exit");
    return "ok";

  } // End showScreen().

  /**
   * Called by ActionDispatched to add a collection.
   *
   * @return Result.
   */
  public String addCollection() {

    log.info("Entry...");

    // Display incoming parameters.
    String name    = (String)(getRequest().getParameter("name"));
    String creator = (String)(getRequest().getParameter("creator"));
    log.info("name = "    + name);
    log.info("creator = " + creator);

    // Create and populate CollectionDTO from input.
    CollectionDTO collection = new CollectionDTO();
    collection.setName(name);
    collection.setCreatedBy(creator);
    collection.setCreatedOn(new Date());

    // Call on DAO to add collection and write out the collections.xml file.
    PhotoShareDAO dao = PhotoShareDAO.getInstance();
    String result = dao.addCollection(getServletContext(), collection);
    setMessage(result);

    log.info("Exit");

    return "ok";

  } // End addCollection().

} // End class.
```

This is nothing more than instantiating a CollectionDTO, populating it from request parameters, and handing it to the PhotoShareDAO to deal with. Lastly, we call setMessage() with the result from the call to addCollection(), so the user can be told what happened.

AddPhoto.java

The next class to look at is AddPhoto. In the interest of space, we'll just look at segments of this class. AddPhoto is the Action that accepts an upload of a photo. Yet another Commons library is used here, FileUpload. This is a handy library that deals with the complexity of a multipart submission for us. The first bit of code is asking FileUpload to parse the incoming request for us:

```
// Create a factory for disk-based file items
FileItemFactory factory = new DiskFileItemFactory();
// Create a new file upload handler
ServletFileUpload upload = new ServletFileUpload(factory);

// Parse the request... thank you FileUpload!
List items = null;
try {
  items = upload.parseRequest(getRequest());
} catch (FileUploadException fue) {
  fue.printStackTrace();
  log.error("Error uploading file: " + fue);
  setMessage("An error occurred.  Details can be found in the logs.");
  return "ok";
}
```

This results in a List of FileItem objects. Each of these objects can be either a file that was uploaded or a form field. So, what we need to do is iterate over this List now, and for each, determine whether it is our uploaded file (and save a reference to it if so), or if it is one of the form fields, use the value to populate a PhotoDTO:

```
// Iterate over the parsed items.  It's either a form field or the photo
// itself, handle each accordingly: build up a PhotoDTO from the form
// fields, or grab the file for later processing.
PhotoDTO dto = new PhotoDTO();
Iterator it  = items.iterator();
FileItem theFile = null;
while (it.hasNext()) {
  FileItem item = (FileItem)it.next();
  if (item.isFormField()) {
    String name  = item.getFieldName();
    String value = item.getString();
    if (name.equalsIgnoreCase("collection")) {
      dto.setCollection(value);
    }
    if (name.equalsIgnoreCase("adder")) {
      dto.setAddedBy(value);
    }
```

```
        if (name.equalsIgnoreCase("description")) {
          dto.setDescription(value);
        }
      } else {
        theFile = item;
      }
    }
```

After that, the DTO continues to be populated. The type of the photo is parsed out of the filename (we simply grab the extension of the filename, and that becomes our type). The size of the file is gotten by calling the `getSize()` method of the `FileItem` that is the uploaded photo that we saved a reference to. We then construct a filename to save the photo under. This filename is constructed by taking the name of the collection, with spaces replaced with underscores, and appending to it the name of the person who uploaded it (again with spaces replaced by underscores), and then appending the current date and time, down to the second, and then using the extension of the uploaded file. This pretty well ensures uniqueness of the filename (not absolutely perhaps, but good enough).

Once all that is done, we ask FileUpload to write the file out for us, and it very politely obliges! Once that is done, we still have a few pieces of information that we need to capture about the photo. Since this information could not easily be retrieved before writing the file out, we can only now do it. To get the information we need—dimensions, color depth, and DPI—we use a class named `ImageInfo`, which is a public domain piece of code released some time ago. Because its operation is definitely out of the scope of this book, it is included as part of the `ImageTools.jar`. The full source for it is available on the Apress website. This class accepts a path to the file to examine. It can then be called on to provide the information we need, which we then set in our DTO. Once that is done, the last thing we do is call on `PhotoShareDAO` to add the photo to the collection. This results in the collections file being rewritten. The result is set using `setMessage()`, and the request is complete.

DeleteCollection.java

In Listing 7-16 we see the `DeleteCollection` Action.

Listing 7-16. *DeleteCollection Action Class for Deleting Collections*

```
package com.apress.ajaxprojects.photoshare.actions;

import com.apress.ajaxprojects.photoshare.dao.PhotoShareDAO;
import java.io.IOException;
import java.io.PrintWriter;
import org.apache.commons.logging.Log;
import org.apache.commons.logging.LogFactory;

/**
 * This class deletes a specified collection.
 */
public class DeleteCollection extends Action {
```

```
  /**
   * Log instance.
   */
  private static Log log = LogFactory.getLog(DeleteCollection.class);

  /**
   * This is called to delete a collection.
   *
   * @return Result.
   */
  public String execute() {

    log.info("Entry...");

    // Display incoming parameters.
    String name = (String)(getRequest().getParameter("name"));
    log.info("name = " + name);

    // Call on DAO to delete collection and write out the collections.xml file.
    PhotoShareDAO dao = PhotoShareDAO.getInstance();
    String result = dao.deleteCollection(getServletContext(), name);
    try {
      getResponse().setContentType("text/plain");
      PrintWriter out = getResponse().getWriter();
      out.println(result);
      out.flush();
    } catch (IOException ioe) {
      ioe.printStackTrace();
      log.error("Unable to write response.  See log for details.");
    }

    log.info("Exit");

    return null;

  } // End execute().

} // End class.
```

Like AddCollection, this is nothing but getting the name of the collection to delete from the request parameters, and passing it to the PhotoShareDAO's deleteCollection() method to do the actual deletion. The result is again captured. In this case, however, instead of setting the message request attribute, I instead opted to write the response manually. This was done basically just to demonstrate doing this as well.

DeletePhoto.java

Listing 7-17 shows the DeletePhoto Action.

Listing 7-17. *DeletePhoto Action Class for Deleting Photos*

```
package com.apress.ajaxprojects.photoshare.actions;

import com.apress.ajaxprojects.photoshare.dao.PhotoShareDAO;
import java.io.IOException;
import java.io.PrintWriter;
import org.apache.commons.logging.Log;
import org.apache.commons.logging.LogFactory;

/**
 * This class deletes a specified photo.
 */
public class DeletePhoto extends Action {

  /**
   * Log instance.
   */
  private static Log log = LogFactory.getLog(DeletePhoto.class);

  /**
   * Called by ActionDispatched to delete a photo.
   *
   * @return Result.
   */
  public String execute() {

    log.info("Entry...");

    // Display incoming parameters.
    String filename   = (String)(getRequest().getParameter("filename"));
    String collection = (String)(getRequest().getParameter("collection"));
    log.info("filename = " + filename);
    log.info("collection = " + collection);

    // Call on DAO to delete photo.
    PhotoShareDAO dao = PhotoShareDAO.getInstance();
    String result = dao.deletePhoto(getServletContext(), filename, collection);
    try {
      getResponse().setContentType("text/plain");
      PrintWriter out = getResponse().getWriter();
      out.println(result);
      out.flush();
    } catch (IOException ioe) {
```

```
      ioe.printStackTrace();
      log.error("Unable to write response.  See log for details.");
    }

    log.info("Exit");

    return null;

  } // End execute().

} // End class.
```

DeletePhoto is virtually identical to DeleteCollection, except that we need both the photo's filename and collection in order to delete it. The DAO again does the real work for us, and again the response is written out manually. Note that for both classes, the return from the method is null, indicating to ActionDispatcher that the response is fully formed, so no forward is required.

DownloadPhoto.java

Next up (in Listing 7-18) is the DownloadPhoto class.

Listing 7-18. *DownloadPhoto Action Class for Downloading a Photo*

```
package com.apress.ajaxprojects.photoshare.actions;

import org.apache.commons.logging.Log;
import org.apache.commons.logging.LogFactory;

/**
 * This class rotates a specified photo 90 degrees clockwise.  After this
 * executes, the RetrievePhoto Action will be executed to return the
 * rotated photo.
 */
public class DownloadPhoto extends Action {

  /**
   * Log instance.
   */
  private static Log log = LogFactory.getLog(RotatePhoto.class);

  /**
   * Called by ActionDispatched to download a photo.
   *
   * @return Result.
   */
  public String execute() {
```

```
    log.info("Entry...");

    // Display incoming parameters.
    String filename = (String)(getRequest().getParameter("filename"));
    log.info("filename = " + filename);

    // Just set the Content-Disposition to attachment, with a filename
    // matching that of the photo the user wants to download, and then
    // forward to the photo file itself.  Done!
    getResponse().setHeader("Content-Disposition", "attachment;" +
      "filename=\"" + filename + "\"");

    log.info("Exit...");

    return "/photos/" + filename;

  } // End execute().

} // End class.
```

To download a photo, all that is required is to set the `Content-Disposition` header to indicate an attachment. This causes the browser to display a Save As dialog, rather than trying to open the returned object with an appropriate handler helper (or application). Once that is done, we simply return the path to the image. `ActionDispatcher` will see the "`/`" at the beginning of the returned value and will immediately forward to it, treating it as a URL.

ListCollections.java

Now we come to Listing 7-19, which shows the `Action` class `ListCollections`.

Listing 7-19. *ListCollections Class*

```
package com.apress.ajaxprojects.photoshare.actions;

import com.apress.ajaxprojects.photoshare.dao.PhotoShareDAO;
import java.util.HashMap;
import org.apache.commons.logging.Log;
import org.apache.commons.logging.LogFactory;

/**
 * This class returns a list of all existing collections.
 */
public class ListCollections extends Action {

  /**
   * Log instance.
   */
  private static Log log = LogFactory.getLog(ListCollections.class);
```

```
  /**
   * Called by ActionDispatched to list all collections.
   *
   * @return Result.
   */
  public String execute() {

    log.info("Entry...");

    // Ask the DAO for a list of collections, and add it to request.
    PhotoShareDAO dao = PhotoShareDAO.getInstance();
    HashMap collections = dao.getCollectionList();
    log.info("collections = " + collections);
    getRequest().setAttribute("collections", collections);

    log.info("Exit...");

    return "ok";

  } // End execute().

} // End class.
```

ListCollections is another simple Action. All it needs to do is call on the PhotoShareDAO via the getCollectionList() method, and then set the result in request as an attribute named collections. The request will then be forwarded to the listCollections.jsp page. If you look back to that, it should be obvious how the attribute is accessed and the response generated. HTML markup is generated by this JSP for the collection dropdown. The <div> that <select> lives in is then updated with this generated markup, and the collections list has in effect been updated.

LoadCollection.java

The next Action to examine is the LoadCollection Action, which can be seen in Listing 7-20.

Listing 7-20. *LoadCollection Class*

```
package com.apress.ajaxprojects.photoshare.actions;

import com.apress.ajaxprojects.photoshare.dao.PhotoShareDAO;
import com.apress.ajaxprojects.photoshare.dtos.CollectionDTO;
import org.apache.commons.logging.Log;
import org.apache.commons.logging.LogFactory;


/**
 * This class is called when the user selects a collection.  It returns
 * XML that is converted on the client to a JavaScript array.
 */
```

```
public class LoadCollection extends Action {

  /**
   * Log instance.
   */
  private static Log log = LogFactory.getLog(LoadCollection.class);

  /**
   * Called by ActionDispatched to load a collection.
   *
   * @return Result.
   */
  public String execute() {

    log.info("Entry...");

    // Display incoming parameters.
    String collection = (String)(getRequest().getParameter("collection"));
    log.info("collection = " + collection);

    // Get the CollectionDTO.
    PhotoShareDAO dao = PhotoShareDAO.getInstance();
    CollectionDTO dto = dao.getCollection(collection);

    // Put the DTO in request so we can use it to render XML in the JSP.
    getRequest().setAttribute("collection", dto);

    log.info("Exit...");

    return "ok";

  } // End execute().

} // End class.
```

LoadCollection is yet another simple Action (are you seeing a pattern here?). It has only to grab the name of the collection to load from the request parameter, and then call on PhotoShareDAO to provide a fully populated CollectionDTO object by calling the getCollection() method. That object is then set in a request as an attribute named collection, and it's finished. This request will then wind up in loadCollection.jsp, XML is generated from this JSP, which is then returned to the client. The client code then parses the XML with JSDigester, and a client-side version of the CollectionDTO, in the form of a Collection object, is created. Variables are reset, and the collection is asked to load the images for all the photos. That is how a collection is loaded!

RotatePhoto.java

Finally, after a long journey, we come to the RotatePhoto class. Once again, in the interest of space, it is not shown here in its entirety.

RotatePhoto begins by getting the filename of the photo to rotate and the number of degrees to rotate from the request parameters. It then loads the image using standard AWT functions. Once the image is loaded, it needs to be converted to a BufferedImage, and in order to do that we use a class named ImageHelper. The toBufferedImage() method does the conversion for us. ImageHelper, like ImageInfo before it, is a class that is contained in the ImageTools.jar file, and is outside the scope of this book. The source again is available on the Apress website if you wish to examine it.

A call to the rotate() method of ImageHelper performs the actual rotation for us. Once that is done, we have only to save the file. Like the AddPhoto action, we again construct a filename, but slightly different this time. This time, we start with the string "tempPhoto_", and then append the current date and time to it with spaces and colons replaced with underscores. We then use the JDK ImageIO class to write out the file.

One thing I skipped there was the call to deleteTempFiles(), whose code looks like this:

```
/**
 * This method deletes all temp photo files.
 */
private void deleteTempFiles() {

  // First, get a list of File objects for all the temp files, if any,
  // stored in /photos.
  String path = getServletContext().getRealPath("photos");
  File   dir  = new File(path);
  FileFilter fileFilter = new FileFilter() {
    public boolean accept(File file) {
      if (file.isDirectory()) {
        return false;
      }
      if (!file.getName().startsWith("tempPhoto_")) {
        return false;
      }
      return true;
    }
  };
  File[] files = dir.listFiles(fileFilter);
  if (files != null) {
    // Now that we know there are temp files and we have a list of them,
    // delete each
    for (int i = 0; i < files.length; i++) {
      log.info("Deleting temp file '" + files[i] + "'...");
      files[i].delete();
    }
  }

} // End deleteTempFiles().
```

This method is responsible for deleting any files in the /photo directory that begin with the string "tempPhoto_". There should only ever be one anyway, but this ensures that is true.

Once the file is written out, we generate the response for the client, which is just the filename of the temp file we just wrote out. The client will then update the `src` of the `imgGrowing` image to point to this temp image; hence the user will see a rotated version of the image. Note that every time a new photo is selected, the `rotationAmount` JavaScript variable gets reset, so the next time users view a photo they had previously again, it will be in its unrotated, normal orientation again.

And with that, we have now examined PhotoShare in its entirety! I hope you have enjoyed your ride.

Suggested Exercises

As with all the other applications in this book, I have left open some avenues for enhancements for you to explore. Here are just a few suggestions:

- Implement a few more image-manipulation functions. Things like mirroring, flipping, and even a one-touch photo enhancement feature are all possible. This will not actually aid you in exploring Ajax, but it would certainly be a nice enhancement to provide.
- Allow for editing of existing photo descriptions. You can present a dialog to edit the current description, and then submit the change via Ajax.
- Add a function to e-mail a link to a specific photo to a friend. You will have to create a new `Action` that accepts a collection name and a photo identifier so that you can automatically load the collection as well as the requested photo.
- Make the edit fields on the dialogs highlight in some way when they get focus. This is always a nice thing to do in any UI so that the user knows which field is currently active, and I purposely did not do it in this application so you would have the opportunity to do so! Perhaps try to be a little fancy with it and do not just update the background color but also instead fade it through a few colors (i.e., start with a dark blue when it initially gets focus and quickly fade to a light blue background).
- Rewrite the application so that when a photo is uploaded, thumbnails are created, and use those on the filmstrip. To go along with this, only load the actual photo when the user clicks it. This will make the collection initially load a lot faster, but will introduce a delay when a photo is clicked before it begins to grow. So, you will have to modify the UI to handle this in such a way as to not annoy the user terribly. A float-over that explains that the image is being retrieved might do the trick.

Summary

In this chapter we have dissected the PhotoShare application and learned about the Dojo library. We have seen how a bit of scripting and CSS/DOM manipulation can yield a somewhat fancy application with some neat special effects. We have also seen how to construct our own simple application framework for the server components of the application. All in all, it has been a fun little project!

CHAPTER 8

The Organizer: Get Yourself Organized Now!

In this chapter, we'll build what is commonly called a PIM application, or Personal Information Manager. This application, which we'll call The Organizer, will include the ability to write notes to yourself, set up tasks to accomplish, store all your contacts, and make appointments. We'll learn about about another real web application framework, WebWork. We'll use a very popular Ajax library named Prototype for our Ajax functionality.

Requirements and Goals

The requirements for The Organizer are actually rather straightforward, since PIM applications are a fairly common thing. So, without further ado, our goals are as follows:

- First, we'll allow for multiple user accounts, so we'll need all the requisite account management functions, including creating, updating, and deleting accounts. Each user will maintain his or her own accounts, and we'll not have any administrative-type functionality on top of that (an obvious enhancement suggestion!).
- When a user logs in, they will start at a Day At A Glance screen, which will list those tasks and appointments for the current day.
- The Organizer will consist of four basic units of functionality: notes, tasks, contacts, and appointments.
- For notes, we should be able to record a subject and some text. That is really about it!
- For each task, we should be able to record a subject, a due date, a priority rating (high, normal, or low), a status (complete or incomplete), and some comments about the task.
- For contacts, we'll have a fair amount of data we can capture, including home phone, address, fax number, cell number, spouse, children, and so forth. We'll have much the same data for work information, with some extras like assistant, manager, title, company, and so forth. Lastly, we'll have essentially duplicates of most of these as *other*, so that for instance you can have a home address, a work address, and some other address, and likewise for most pieces of information.

- For appointments, we of course need to be able to create them, and record the subject of the appointment, what date it is, what time it starts and ends, and some comments about it.
- For appointments, we'll provide four different views: day view, week view, month view, and year view. We should be able to select a date to use as the basis for any of these views.
- We should be able to not only create notes, tasks, contacts, and appointments, but also modify and delete existing instances.
- We want to use a real framework for this application, not something we invent ourselves.

As you can see, these goals and requirements are not anything special as far as PIM applications go. But we have enough there to make life interesting, so let's figure out exactly how we are going to do it.

How We Will Pull It Off

One of the things I would like to touch upon in this project that I have not previously talked about is the methodology behind building this application. I want to describe how I went about putting it together, especially because it was done in an extremely short amount of time.

I approached this project with a service-oriented architecture (SOA) mentality. Basically, I identified all the individual functions that would be needed, and proceeded to code each as a separate, independent service. Especially when you are working with an Ajax application, this is a fairly natural way to look at things because you can visualize all the code that runs on the client as being the application itself, while the functions you call on the server are services that the application needs to do its work.

So, instead of thinking of pages, and a navigation flow through them, I thought about what functions are required for notes, for instance. Well, clearly we need to be able to list notes, so that is one service. We need to be able to create a note, so that is another service. It would be nice to be able to update an existing note, so there is another service. Finally, being able to delete a note makes sense, so that is yet another service.

Once I had done that bit of planning, I created a page to test each function. These were plain HTML pages with nothing fancy in them. For instance, the test page to create a note was

```
<html>
  <head>
    <title>The Organizer</title>
 </head>
  <body>
    Create Note
    <br><br>
    <form action="noteSave.action">
      subject: <input type="text" name="subject"><br>
      <textarea cols="40" rows="15" name="text"></textarea>
      <input type="submit" value="Create Note">
    </form>
  </body>
<html>
```

So, I wound up with 30 or so of these types of test pages, with little to no navigation between them (there had to be some for things like logon functionality, but by and large they were completely separate). I knew that the final application would not use these; in fact, it would probably not use anything remotely similar. At that point, I had not yet decided whether the server would return XML, HTML, or something else.

And that is precisely the important point! This application differs from all the others in this book in that every single response from the server to an Ajax request is rendered via JSP. We have seen this before, but this is the first application where that is the sole mechanism by which responses are created. The great thing about this is that you can decide how to return the response later; it becomes merely an implementation detail that can be deferred. This, coupled with the SOA approach, means that your application can change forms very easily, and you do not have to decide everything up front, which for me is the way I prefer to work (for me, early coding *is* design many times… I can quickly determine what will work and what will not that way).

Once I got to the point where all the individual pages worked with the server-side services, I then created the main JSP that would be the client-side code of the application. For each of the test JSPs, I ultimately decided to use them to return straight HTML, so I then coded them for real (which took only a few minutes per JSP, since the basic outline was already there). Once that was done, it was just a matter of the plumbing on the client side to glue all these discrete services and their responses together and turn it into a coherent whole.

I very much recommend this approach. Do not even think about Ajax initially; simply determine the discrete functions your application needs, the services the server must provide, and go to it. Once all the services are implemented, *then* you can begin to think about what the application looks like and how those services get cobbled together to form the larger whole. If you have JSPs (or some other flexible rendering technology like Velocity, for instance), then you do not even have to initially think about what the server returns for each service. I have found this approach works very well.

With that out of the way, we'll look at the four main tools we'll use to make this happen: Prototype, WebWork, HSQLDB, and Spring JDBC.

Prototype

Prototype is one of the most popular JavaScript libraries out there. Notice I did not call it an Ajax library; it is much more than just Ajax. It is the basis of many Ajax libraries and is integrated into many frameworks, so it is definitely worth taking a look at.

There is an often-stated criticism of Prototype—that it is dangerous because it extends basic JavaScript objects. This can have unintended side effects in other JavaScript code. There are examples on the Web of iterations of arrays not working because the `Array` object is extended, among other problems. Although this may be true, the simple fact is that Prototype is used by many other libraries with no bad side effects, so the case may be overstated. Then again, it may not! The point is that it is something you should be aware of. Some of the basic JavaScript objects, including `Object`, `Number`, `Function`, `String`, `Array`, and `Event`, are extended by Prototype and are therefore different than they usually are. While the intent is that these changes should not affect existing code, nor should it cause any problems for new code, there does seem to be instances where it can and does cause problems.

Prototype introduces a number of shortcuts to JavaScript. For instance:

```
$("newNote").style.display = "none";
```

What exactly is going on here? Simply put, `$()` is a function that is used in place of the ubiquitous `document.getElementById()`. There are a number of variations on this theme, including `$F()`, which gets a named form element, `$A()`, which converts its single argument to an array, `$H()`, which converts objects into enumerable `Hash` objects that resemble associative arrays, and `$R()`, which is simply shorthand for writing new `ObjectRange(lowerBound, upperBound, excludeBounds)` (the `ObjectRange` is an object that represents a range of values, with upper and lower bounds). You will see the `$()` function used often in this project; the others are not used.

The other important part of Prototype, for this project, is the `Ajax` object. This is where all the Ajax functionality lives. We'll use two functions of this object in this project: `Request()` and `Updater()`. The difference is that `Request()` just sends the request you set up, and then calls a function you specify to handle the response. `Updater()` is designed for perhaps the most common Ajax use case: updating an element on the page (a `<div>`, more often than not) with the server's response. Here is an example of the `Request()` function:

```
new Ajax.Request("myServer.action", {
  method : "post",
  postBody : Form.serialize($(myForm)),
  onSuccess : function(resp) {
   alert("Server returned to us");
  }
});
```

So, we call this function, passing it a number of arguments. The first argument is simply the URL to submit to, some resource named `myServer.action` in this case (assume we have this mapped to a servlet, for example). We specify we want a POST done, and then we populate the `postBody`. To do this, we use a very neat function of Prototype: `Form.serialize()`. This function accepts a reference to a form, gotten by using the `$()` operator we saw previously. It then takes that form and constructs a query string from all its elements. In this case the query string is added to the body of the request, as is typical when POSTing data elements. The last thing we do is specify the function to call when the request successfully completes, in this case an inline function. You can just as easily reference another stand-alone function, or function that is a member of some object—whatever you prefer. Prototype provides a number of callbacks like this, including `onComplete` and `onFailure`, so you can hook into the `XMLHttpRequest` lifecycle easily.

The `Ajax.Updater()` function is virtually identical; the only difference is that there is a parameter before the URL: the ID of an element on the page to update. The other difference is that typically you will not have `onSuccess` defined because `Ajax.Updater()` is essentially including its own version of that callback.

There is a fair bit more in Prototype than is used in this project, so I encourage you to explore it. One other frequent criticism of Prototype is that, unfortunately, documentation and support is sparse, and worse, the code is barely documented at all (although that is in line with the idea of keeping JavaScript as small as possible, so I for one am not sure it is such a bad thing). In fact, if you go to the main Prototype site (`http://prototype.conio.net`), I think you will be dismayed at how little is there. Fortunately, a gentleman named Sergio Pereira has put together a very good bit of documentation, which you can find here: `http://www.sergiopereira.com/articles/prototype.js.html#Enumerating`. It is well worth a few minutes to peruse this documentation. I think you will agree that, criticisms aside, Prototype has a fair bit to offer.

WebWork

In this book we have created a number of application frameworks to make the server component of the applications a little more flexible and consistent. We'll also be introduced to a "real" framework named Struts in the next chapter (although I would be willing to bet you already are familiar with Struts to some extent—most Java web developers are).

WebWork is a project under the OpenSymphony banner (`http://opensymphony.com`) that is somewhat similar to the Apache Foundation. WebWork, to quote directly from the WebWork site, is "a Java web-application development framework. It is built specifically with developer productivity and code simplicity in mind, providing robust support for building reusable UI templates, such as form controls, UI themes, internationalization, dynamic form parameter mapping to JavaBeans, robust client and server side validation, and much more."

WebWork is very similar to Struts in most respects. In fact, as of this writing, WebWork is undergoing incubation at Apache and will in fact become Struts 2.0 (which is now being called the Struts Action 2 framework). If you have any experience at all with Struts, even the little bit you would get from looking at AjaxChat in Chapter 9, then WebWork will be quite familiar to you. If you have never seen Struts before, don't worry; WebWork is really quite simple!

In WebWork, the basic unit of work is the `Action`. This is a class that will perform some function in response to some URL being called by a client. `Actions` in WebWork are also holders for incoming request parameters. As an example, look at this class:

```
package.apress.ajaxprojects.theorganizer.actions;
import webwork.action.*;
public class LogonAction {
  private String username;
  private String password;
  public void setUsername(String username) {
    this.username = username;
  }
  public void setPassword(String password) {
    this.password = password;
  }
  public String execute() {
    if (username.equals("bill") && password.equals("gates")) {
      return Action.SUCCESS;
   } else {
      return Action.ERROR;
    }
  }
}
```

This could be an `Action` in WebWork that responds to the user entering their credentials and clicking a Logon button on a page. So, how do we hook this up to a URL? By creating a file called `xwork.xml` and placing it in `WEB-INF/classes` of our webapp. The contents of this file might be something like this:

```
<!DOCTYPE xwork PUBLIC "-//OpenSymphony Group//XWork 1.0//EN"
"http://www.opensymphony.com/xwork/xwork-1.0.dtd">
  <xwork>
```

```
  <include file="webwork-default.xml"/>
  <package name="default" extends="webwork-default">
    <default-interceptor-ref name="completeStack"/>
     <action name="logon"
       class="com.apress.ajaxprojects.theorganizer.actions.LogonAction">
       <result name="success">main.jsp</result>
       <result name="error">logon.jsp</result>
     </action>
  </package>
</xwork>
```

WebWork by default maps itself to all requests ending in `.action`. So, when the user clicks the Logon button, it submits a form to `logon.action`. WebWork intercepts this, and looks up logon in `xwork.xml`. It finds it, and instantiates the class named, `LogonAction` in this case. By default, WebWork will call a method named `execute()`, which is expected to return a `String`. The return value should map to one of the result names configured for this `Action`. In this case, if the user is valid (obviously this is not NSA-level security!), it returns the value of the `SUCCESS` constant found in the `Action` class in WebWork. This causes `main.jsp` to be returned. If the entered credentials are not valid, then `ERROR` is returned, which causes `logon.jsp` to be returned, which is presumably where the user started, instead.

One interesting feature of WebWork is autopopulation of incoming request parameters. That is how we were able to examine the username and password without doing anything. Before WebWork calls `execute()`, it takes all the request parameters, and calls setter methods on the `Action`, if they exist. In this case, it calls `setUsername()` and `setPassword()`, so that when `execute()` is finally called, the parameters are all there for us already; there's no need to directly access the request object as is typically necessary without a framework like this.

WebWork allows you to also specify what method to execute in the `Action` by adding a `method` attribute to the `<action>` element. In this way, you can group common functionality together in a single `Action` and call different methods depending on which `Action` mapping is called.

One other feature of WebWork that is used in The Organizer that I would like to make you aware of is the `ActionContext`. `ActionContext` is an object that is populated with various pieces of information on a per-request basis. For instance, you can get to the request object through the `ActionContext`. `ActionContext` is implemented as a `ThreadLocal`, which means there is a separate copy of its variables for each thread. The thing that makes this neat is that there is no need to pass `ActionContext` to any method in an `Action`, and indeed, WebWork will not. You can always access `ActionContext` by doing the following:

```
ActionContext context = ActionContext.getContext();
```

You could now get to request by doing the following:

```
HttpServletRequest request =
  (HttpServletRequest)context.get(ServletActionContext.HTTP_REQUEST);
```

The key point to this is that you can do this from *anywhere*. In other words, if your `Action` calls on another class, which itself calls another class, you can still use the previous code to get to things, as long as it all is executing within the same thread. This can actually be abused fairly easily because it means you might be tempted to go directly to the request object from a business delegate class, for instance, which would not be good separation of concerns. As long as you can exercise discipline and not be tempted to do that, and in fact never use this capability outside of `Actions`, then what you get are very clean `Actions` that are Plain Old Java Objects (POJOs); there are no classes to extend, no interfaces to implement (an oft-stated failing of Struts is that you are forced to extend a base `Action` class, so you lose your one opportunity to extend). Note that the requirement to implement interfaces or extend classes isn't typically necessary in WebWork, although there *are* in fact interfaces to implement and classes to extend, all of which can provide additional capabilities and services automatically to your application, as we'll see in this code.

WebWork is a rather expansive framework covering far more than I can possibly describe here. WebWork in fact has some built-in Ajax functionality, including integration with DWR and Dojo out of the box. I encourage you to spend some time looking at the WebWork documentation to see what it offers. Especially if you have experience with Struts, since WebWork is the future of Struts, it would be a good idea to become familiar with it in my opinion. This project will give you a good basis to start with, because it does not delve too deeply into WebWork. In fact, aside from what we have seen here, the only other features used are some of the WebWork JSP tags, which we'll see later. As a gentle introduction to WebWork, though, The Organizer should serve you very well!

HSQLDB

HSQLDB, formerly called Hypersonic SQL, is a lightweight 100 percent pure Java SQL database engine. It supports a number of modes, including in-memory (for use with applets and such), embedded (which is how we'll be using it here), and client-server mode, which is basically a stand-alone database server. HSQLDB is the embedded database engine used in OpenOffice, and that is a pretty good pedigree if you ask me!

You can find HSQLDB's website here: `www.hsqldb.org`. One of the great things about HSQLDB is how drop-dead simple it is to use. First, one of its very convenient features is that if you attempt to access a database that does not exist, it will go ahead and create it for you. So, to get a database set up, this is all we have to do:

```
Class.forName(Globals.getDbDriver()).newInstance();
Connection conn = DriverManager.getConnection("jdbc:hsqldb:c:\temp\myDatabase",
  "sa", "");
conn.close();
```

This will create a new directory named `myDatabase` in `c:\temp`, and will create a basic database for us. At this point, we can go ahead and use standard JDBC and SQL to create tables, insert data, or whatever we want to do. There is no complex startup procedure and no setup code. There are not even any classes to import specific to HSQLDB!

HSQLDB is housed in a single JAR file with no outside dependencies. The JAR file is less than 1MB in size, so when they say "lightweight," they aren't kidding! Yet, it supports many features, such as views, temp tables and sequences, referential integrity, triggers, transaction support, Java stored procedures and functions, and even `Object` data types!

If you need to do database work in your application, and if you do not have or want a full-blown relational database management system (RDBMS), HSQLDB is a great solution. In fact, even if you *do* have a full-blown RDBMS like Oracle or SQL Server, you might want to think about HSQLDB anyway.

Spring JDBC

Unless you have been living under the proverbial rock for the past year or so, you have almost certainly heard of the Spring framework. You most likely heard about it first in the context of dependency injection, or IoC (Inversion of Control). This is probably what it is most well known for. However, Spring is much more than that.

Spring is what is termed a "full-stack" framework, meaning it pretty well covers all the bases a J2EE developer might need. It takes a layered approach, meaning that each "module" of functionality can be, more or less, used independently, and you can add only the functionality you need. Spring runs the gamut from dependency injection as mentioned, to web Model-View-Controller (MVC), to various general-purpose utility functions such as string manipulations and such, Object-Relational Mapping (ORM), and JDBC.

Speaking of JDBC, that is in fact the unit of functionality The Organizer directly uses (WebWork itself uses some other features, such as dependency injection, but the application code itself does not). The Spring JDBC package includes classes that make working with JDBC easier and, more important, less error-prone. One of the banes of JDBC programming is that developers are sometimes forgetful beasts, and neglect to do things like release database connections when they have finished with them. This leads to resource leaks, and eventually a crashed application, or worse yet, an entire server. With Spring JDBC, these types of mistakes are virtually impossible.

With Spring JDBC, database access basically boils down to two steps. First, get a data source to work with, and two, execute the pertinent SQL. For step one, the following code is used:

```
dataSource = new DriverManagerDataSource();
dataSource.setDriverClassName(Globals.dbDriver);
dataSource.setUrl(Globals.dbURL);
dataSource.setUsername(Globals.dbUsername);
dataSource.setPassword(Globals.dbPassword);
```

The `Globals` class contains a number of constants used in The Organizer, including the details of connecting to the database, such as the driver to use, the URL, the username, and the password. Once we have a data source, step two is accomplished like this:

```
JdbcTemplate jt = new JdbcTemplate(dataSource);
List notes = jt.queryForList(
  "SELECT * FROM myTable"
);
```

The `JdbcTemplate` class is our gateway into the world of Spring JDBC. As you can see, it provides a `queryForList()` method, which returns us a `List` representing the result set. No more messing around with `ResultSet` objects! Other methods are provided, such as `queryForMap()`, which is used to retrieve a single record from the database and get a `Map` in return, making it very simple to access the fields of the record.

Note that I am not showing any connection-handling code. That is because the data source and template handle all that for us. No worries about closing the connection or dealing with statements and that sort of typical JDBC work.

One last thing I'd like to mention about Spring JDBC is that it wraps `SQLExceptions` in custom exception classes so that your code can be abstracted away from the standard JDBC classes entirely. As an example, when creating a new account in The Organizer, you could select a username that is already in use. In that case, the `JdbcTemplate` class will throw a `DataIntegrityViolationException` object, which we catch and handle appropriately.

The JDBC package is just one small part of Spring. A great deal more information is available to help you develop your applications better and faster. Take some time to check out what Spring has to offer; I think you will love what you find: `www.springframework.org`.

Visualizing the Finish Line

If you are familiar with the Macintosh family of computers from Apple, and more specifically, the more recent user interfaces they offer, then The Organizer will look familiar because the overall style is based on the "aqua" look and feel. Buttons and tabs have a bubble-shaped styling with a gentle gradient luster to them. Of course, in black and white in a book you cannot get the full effect, so go play a bit before continuing!

Now, let's familiarize ourselves with the application just a bit.

Figure 8-1 shows the Day At A Glance view. This is the first thing a user sees after they log on. It presents the user with the tasks and appointments for the current day.

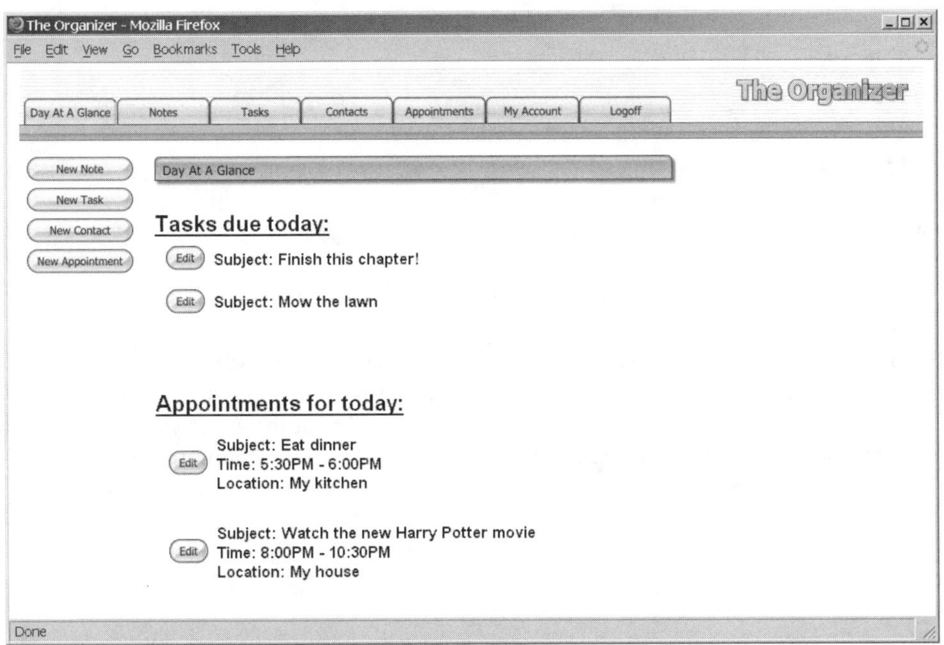

Figure 8-1. *The Organizer's Day At A Glance screen, the first thing seen by the user after logging on*

Along the top are tabs for the major areas of functionality: notes, tasks, appointments, contacts, and maintenance of your user account. You also have the ability to jump back to the Day At A Glance view at any time, as well as log off.

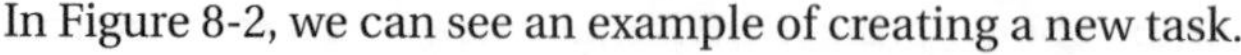

In Figure 8-2, we can see an example of creating a new task.

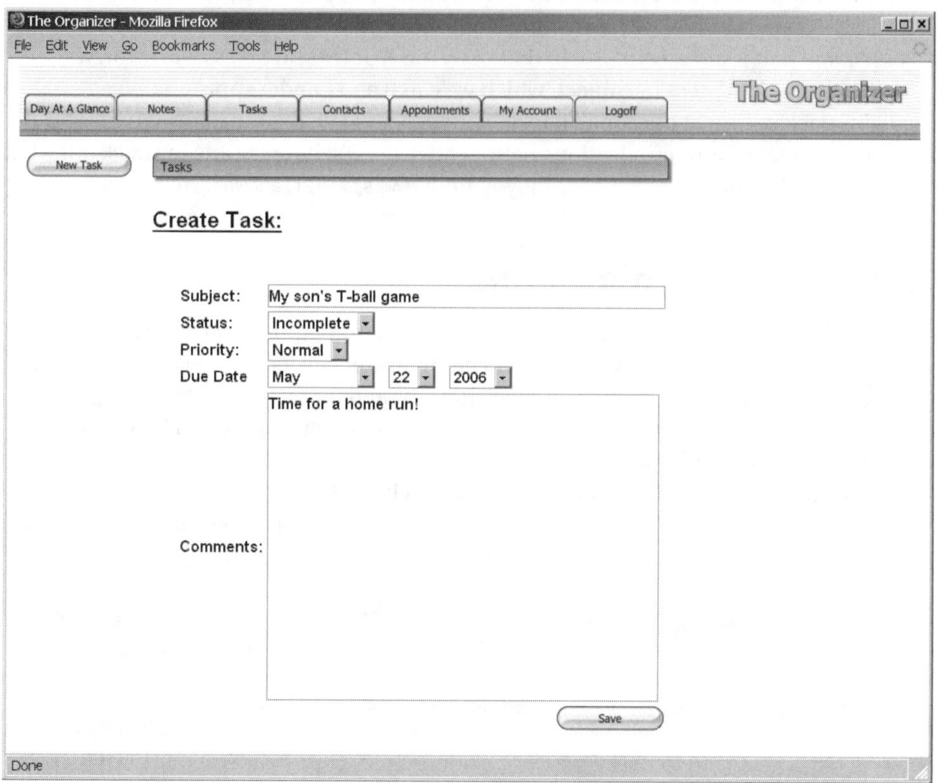

Figure 8-2. *Creating a new task*

Figure 8-3 shows editing an existing note. Creating a note looks virtually identical, except for different headings and so forth.

One last example is shown in Figure 8-4. This is the week view, showing all the appointments for the current week. All of the other views look the same; they just show different appointments, that is, appointments for the current month, day, or the entire year. You can select a date to use as the basis for this. So, if you wanted to see all the appointments for 2007, for instance, you can select any date in 2007, and the year view will show the appropriate appointments.

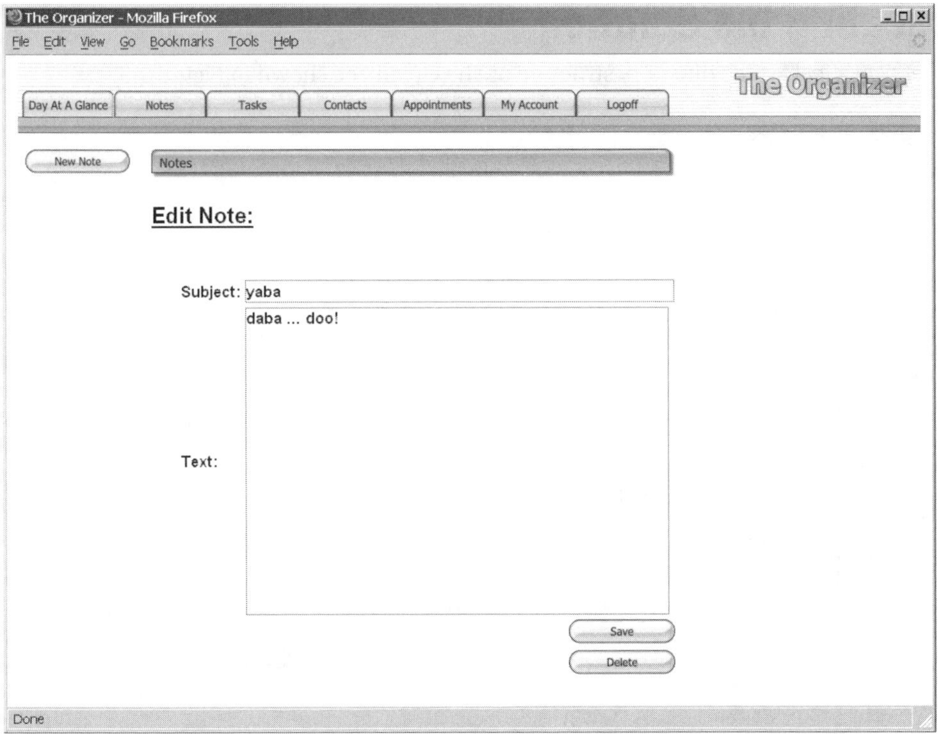

Figure 8-3. *Editing an existing note*

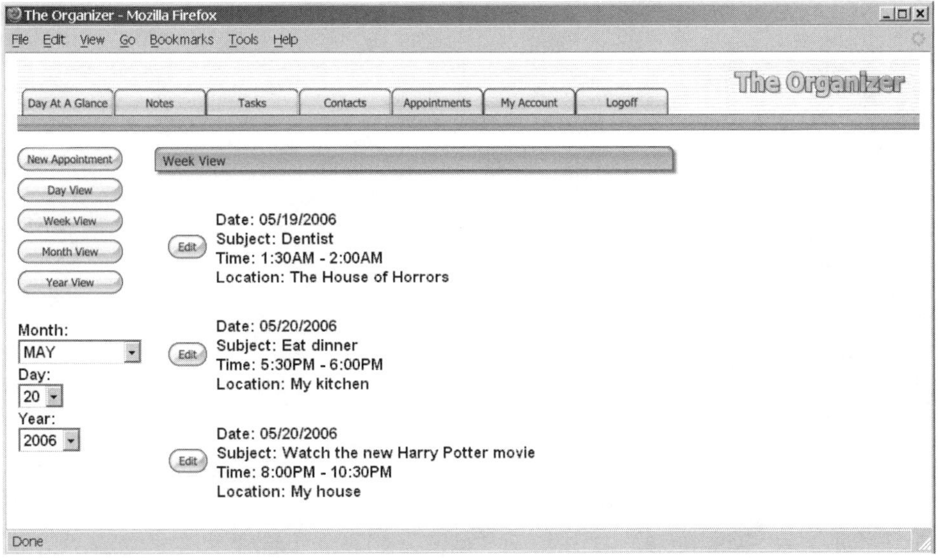

Figure 8-4. *Viewing appointments for the current week*

And now, without further ado: the code!

Dissecting the Solution

First, let's get a feel for the directory structure of The Organizer, shown in Figure 8-5.

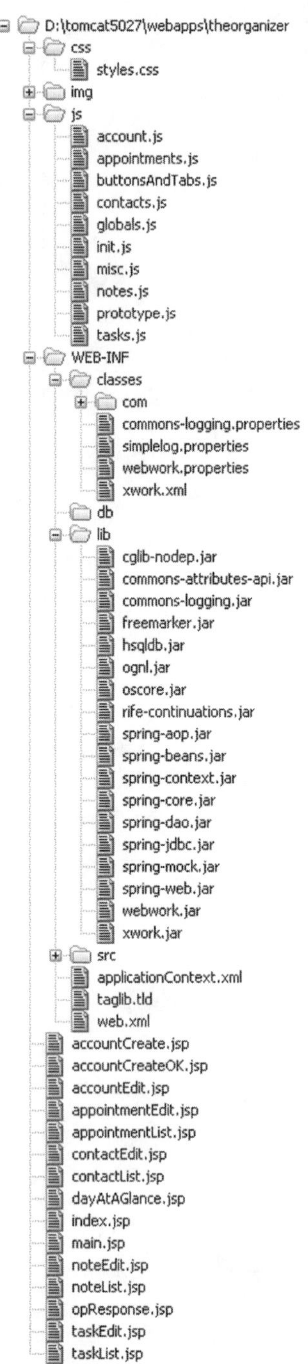

Figure 8-5. *Directory structure layout of The Organizer*

In the root directory we have a number of JSPs, which we'll be looking at shortly. In the `/css` directory is our stylesheet, `styles.css`. The `/img` directory, which is not expanded here to conserve space, contains all the image resources, including image rollovers, headers, and so forth. The `/js` directory contains all the JavaScript used in this application. In `/WEB-INF` we find the usual `web.xml`, plus `applicationContext.xml`, which is the Spring framework configuration file. We also find `taglib.tld`, the taglib descriptor for the WebWork tags. One new thing here that we haven't seen in any other projects in this book is the content of `/WEB-INF/classes`, most notably, `xwork.xml` and `webwork.properties`. Both of these are configuration files for WebWork. They need to be accessible via a class loader and so cannot be in `/WEB-INF` and must instead be in `/WEB-INF/classes` (or somewhere else accessible via a class loader, although this is the typical location). We also see two files, `commons-logging.properties` and `simplelog.properties`, which combine to configure logging for the application. Our source files, as usual, are found in `WEB-INF/src`, which is not shown here but is pretty much the same as every other source directory in this book.

Finally, the `/WEB-INF/lib` folder contains all the libraries that The Organizer depends on; they are listed in Table 8-1.

Table 8-1. *The JARs That the Organizer Depends On, Found in WEB-INF.lib*

JAR	Description
`cglib-nodep.jar`	Required by WebWork. CGLib is a powerful, high-performance, and high-quality code generation library. It is used to extend Java classes and implements interfaces at runtime.
`commons-attributes-api.jar`	Required by WebWork. Commons Attributes provides a runtime API to metadata attributes such as doclet tags, inspired by the Nanning and XRAI projects as well as JSR 175 and C# attributes.
`commons-logging.jar`	Required by WebWork. Jakarta Commons Logging is an abstraction layer that sits on top of a true logging implementation (like Log4J), which allows you to switch the underlying logging implementation without affecting your application code. It also provides a simple logger that outputs to `System.out`, which is what this application uses.
`freemarker.jar`	Required by WebWork. FreeMarker is a "template engine," a generic tool to generate text output (anything from HTML to autogenerated source code) based on templates. It's a Java package—a class library for Java programmers. It's not an application for end users in itself, but something that programmers can embed into their products.
`hsqldb.jar`	HSQLDB, our embedded SQL database engine.
`ognl.jar`	Required by WebWork. OGNL stands for Object-Graph Navigation Language. It is an expression language for getting and setting properties of Java objects. You use the same expression for both getting and setting the value of a property.
`oscore.jar`	Required by WebWork. OSCore is a set of utility classes that are common to the other components of OpenSymphony. Contains essential functionality for any J2EE application.

continued

Table 8-1. *Continued*

JAR	Description
rife-continuations.jar	Required by WebWork. RIFE/continuations is a subproject of RIFE that aims to make its support for continuations in pure Java available as a general-purpose library.
spring-aop.jar	Spring framework AOP (Aspect-Oriented Programming) package. Core Spring AOP interfaces, built on AOP Alliance AOP interoperability interfaces.
spring-beans.jar	Spring framework Spring beans package. This package contains interfaces and classes for manipulating JavaBeans.
spring-context.jar	Spring framework context package. This package builds on the beans package to add support for message sources and for the Observer design pattern, and the ability for application objects to obtain resources using a consistent API.
spring-core.jar	Spring framework core classes package. Provides basic classes for exception handling and version detection, and other core helpers that are not specific to any part of the framework.
spring-dao.jar	Spring DAO (Date Access Objects) package. Exception hierarchy enabling sophisticated error handling independent of the data access approach in use.
spring-jdbc.jar	Spring JDBC package. The classes in this package make JDBC easier to use and reduce the likelihood of common errors.
spring-mock.jar	Spring mock objects package.
spring-web.jar	Spring web package. Includes various web-related classes.
webwork.jar	The WebWork JAR, where most of WebWork lives.
xwork.jar	XWork is a command pattern framework that is used to power WebWork as well as other applications. XWork provides an Inversion of Control container, a powerful expression language, data type conversion, validation, and pluggable configuration.

The Client-Side Code

Let's begin by looking at the configuration files, beginning with web.xml. The four elements that are of importance are these:

```
<!-- WebWork filter. -->
<filter>
  <filter-name>webwork</filter-name>
  <filter-class>
    com.opensymphony.webwork.dispatcher.FilterDispatcher
  </filter-class>
</filter>
<filter-mapping>
  <filter-name>webwork</filter-name>
  <url-pattern>/*</url-pattern>
</filter-mapping>
```

```
<!-- Spring IoC. -->
<listener>
  <listener-class>
    org.springframework.web.context.ContextLoaderListener
  </listener-class>
</listener>

<!-- The Organizer initialization. -->
<listener>
  <listener-class>
    com.apress.ajaxprojects.theorganizer.listener.ContextListener
  </listener-class>
</listener>

<!-- WebWork taglib. -->
<taglib>
  <taglib-uri>webwork</taglib-uri>
  <taglib-location>/WEB-INF/taglib.tld</taglib-location>
</taglib>
```

The first filter mapping is what makes WebWork "go." Instead of using a servlet, as Struts and most other MVC frameworks do, WebWork uses a filter. One thing of note is that even though the filter is mapped to `/*`, which means all incoming requests are handled by the filter, in fact by default only requests ending with `.action` will be handled by WebWork. The "real" filtering is done within the filter itself.

The listener is for Spring functionality needed by WebWork to function. Likewise, the second listener is needed by The Organizer. Some onetime initialization is performed by this listener, as we'll see when we get to that class.

Lastly, we need a declaration of the WebWork taglib, which references the TLD in `WEB-INF`. This is nothing but your standard, everyday taglib definition file, so I will not be reviewing it here.

applicationContext.xml

The `applicationContext.xml` file that is also found in `WEB-INF` is the Spring configuration file. Because The Organizer does not use Spring's dependency injection capabilities, this file is essentially empty, but it is still required to be present.

webwork.properties

The other configuration files are located in `WEB-INF/classes`. First up is `webwork.properties`. This is a standard Java properties file where you can change various default settings of WebWork. The only one you will find in this particular file is `webwork.objectFactory = spring`, which tells WebWork to use Spring for creating objects.

commons-logging.properties, simplelog.properties

Two other files of interest are `commons-logging.properties` and `simplelog.properties`. Jakarta Commons Logging (JCL) is used by The Organizer for its logging functions, and further, the `SimpleLog` is used, which is a logger that JCL provides that simply writes its output to `STDOUT`.

These two files allow us to configure that. First, in commons-logging.properties, we find the single line

```
org.apache.commons.logging.Log=org.apache.commons.logging.impl.SimpleLog
```

This is what informs JCL to use SimpleLog. In simplelog.properties, we have some settings for this logger:

```
org.apache.commons.logging.simplelog.defaultlog=info
org.apache.commons.logging.simplelog.log.com.apress.ajaxprojects=info
```

This says that, by default, only messages of level info and higher will be logged by this logger. We then further say that any class that is in the package com.apress.ajaxprojects, or any child package of that package, will be logged if the message is of level info or higher. It is important to set both a default level and specific level for the classes in The Organizer because other classes in the application may also use JCL, and if they do, we want to be able to control their logging level separately. For instance, WebWork itself uses JCL, and if the default level is changed to debug, for instance, you will see a great deal more messages logged coming from WebWork. If you wish to see more messages from The Organizer, set the second line to a level of debug or trace. It is helpful to be able to set this level during development as much more will be caught and displayed.

xwork.xml

The last file you will find in this directory is perhaps the most important: xwork.xml. If you have any experience with Struts, this is analogous to struts-config.xml. If you have never used Struts, then simply put, xwork.xml is the file that maps incoming request URIs to specific Action classes. That is at least its most important purpose.

xwork.xml is a fairly lengthy file, so I will only show a small portion of it here:

```
<!-- Retrieve a list of all notes (initial notes view). -->
<action name="noteList"
  class="com.apress.ajaxprojects.theorganizer.actions.NoteAction"
  method="list">
  <result name="success">noteList.jsp</result>
</action>

<!-- Show the create note view. -->
<action name="noteCreateShow"
  class="com.apress.ajaxprojects.theorganizer.actions.ForwardAction">
  <result name="success">noteEdit.jsp</result>
</action>

<!-- Create (create) a new note. -->
<action name="noteCreate"
  class="com.apress.ajaxprojects.theorganizer.actions.NoteAction"
  method="create">
  <result name="success">opResponse.jsp</result>
  <result name="error">noteEdit.jsp</result>
</action>
```

These three blocks are referred to as Action mappings. The first mapping is used when we want to see a list of notes for the current user. This mapping is saying that when a request comes in for the resource noteList.action, the class NoteAction should be instantiated, and the list() method should be called. This method will be expected to return a String that matches one of the <result> elements. success is one of the typical return strings. Notice there are two different results for the noteCreate mapping. This is so that if any sort of error occurs when saving the note (which is when this mapping would be executed), then the noteEdit.jsp page would be returned, presumably with some sort of error message for display to the user.

With the configuration files out of the way, let's now turn our attention to the source files, starting with the client side of the house.

styles.css

This is of course the stylesheet for The Organizer, and there is not really much to it. We have a grand total of nine selectors. The first is cssTopNav, which styles the upper portion of the screen where the tabs appear. Note the use of a background image that is repeated horizontally across the <div> this will ultimately be applied to. cssSideNav is the area where the buttons appear on the left-hand side. cssMain is for the main content in the middle. Note the usage of the four padding attributes. This sets a few pixels of space around all four edges so that the buttons and the tab bar at the top do not bump into the main content. Next we find the cssDAAGItem selector, which styles the tasks and appointments seen on the Day At A Glance screen. Likewise, cssDAAGHeading is the tasks and appointments header that defines each section. cssScrollContent is also used to style the main content in order to give us a scrolling <div>. This is done with the goal of avoiding the entire page scrolling if the content is too large vertically (it still can depending on your screen resolution, but that is largely unavoidable without resorting to frames). cssError is used to show the errors that can occur when logging on. Finally, cssInput0 and cssInput1 are used to style all input elements in the application. The one ending with 0 is what the element will look like what it does not have focus, and the one ending with 1 is what it looks like when it has focus (a different background color).

index.jsp

This is the default welcome page as defined in web.xml and serves as our logon page. We start with a normal taglib declaration for the WebWork tags. After that is our stylesheet import, and an import of the JavaScript file buttonsAndTabs.js. We'll look at this in more detail later, but for now suffice it to say that the code required to do the rollovers of the buttons is in it. After that we have a <script> block containing two variables: tabsButtonsEnabled and rolloverImages. The former determines whether or not the buttons are enabled, and the latter will store the preloaded images for the buttons. Those images are loaded on page load by calls to the createRolloverImages() function. In short, this function accepts the name of a button and loads the images for it and stores them in the rolloverImages array.

After that we see the following block:

```
<ww:if test="message!=null">
  <div class="cssError"><ww:property value="message" /></div>
</ww:if>
<ww:else>
  <div class="cssError"> </div>
</ww:else>
```

This is our first encounter with the WebWork tags. The `<ww:if>` tag is used to perform a logic comparison. Recall that when a URI mapped to WebWork comes in, an `Action` is executed. This `Action` can contain fields that correspond to incoming request parameters, as well as any other fields we wish, which can be used in the JSP. For instance, in the `AccountAction`, which is the `Action` that will be called to create a new account, we find a field named `message`. This is used to communicate errors to the user when logging on—if the username is not found, for instance. This `<ww:if>` tag is simply checking whether or not that field is `null`. WebWork knows to go look for the field in the current instance of the `AccountAction` class; we do not have to be anymore specific than naming the field. If the field it not `null`, we use the `<ww:property>` tag to display the value. If it is `null`, we output a nonbreaking space HTML entity so that the space reserved for the message is still present (to avoid the input fields being pushed down when a message is displayed).

After this block we come across a `<ww:form>` tag. This is the WebWork version of the standard `<form>` tag. We specify the URL to submit the form to, as well as the style class to apply to the form. Within the form we find a `<ww:textfield>` tag, which renders an `<input type="text">` tag.

Note the value attribute of these tags. For example, on the tag for the username, we find `%{username}`. This is how you specify fields in the `Action` to populate the value attribute with.

We lastly have a `<ww:submit>` tag; this one is of type `image`.

If you are observant, you may be scratching your head here a bit... how exactly do all the fields line up so nicely on the screen when there is no hint of structure in the markup? The answer is that the WebWork tags render a table structure for the form for us! Note the `label` attribute on the fields—this is the first column of a table. The field itself is the second column. WebWork does all this for us by default. WebWork supports various "themes," which change what gets rendered by the tags. The default theme is `XHTML`, which is what is rendered here (take a look at the generated source!). The other theme you will see in this project is `simple`. This basically tells WebWork to not render the table and such for us, but to just render the form field tag. There is also an `Ajax` theme, which provides automatic Ajax functionality on the form.

accountCreate.jsp

This is the JSP that is shown when the user clicks the Create Account button on the logon screen. It is quite similar to `index.jsp`. In fact, if you compare the two, they are virtually identical, so I will forgo looking over it here.

accountCreateOK.jsp

This is the JSP that renders the server's response when an account has been successfully created. It is nothing more than a message saying the account has been created, and a button that, when clicked, leads the user to the Day At A Glance view. The same JavaScript used for the buttons on the `accountCreate.jsp` is used here for the button and rollover on it.

main.jsp

This JSP is loaded after a user has been validated during logon, or when they click the OK button after creating an account. It is the unchanging content of The Organizer, including the tabs at the top and the buttons along the side. It is responsible for loading all the JavaScript required by the application in one go.

In fact, after the importing of the stylesheet, we find a block of 10 JavaScript file imports, nine for The Organizer itself, and one for the Prototype library.

After that, the markup begins. The markup can be logically divided into three sections: the top navigation bar, the side navigation bar, and the main content area.

For each of the tabs along the top navigation bar, we find a very similar chunk of markup:

```
<td valign="bottom"><img src="img/notes0.gif" id="notes"
  onClick="showNotes();"
  onMouseOver="rollover(this);"
  onMouseOut="rollout(this);"></td>
```

We have ourselves a table cell with an image inside it. The image of the tab starts off in its nonhighlighted (0) state. We give it an ID to refer to later, and attach the appropriate `onClick` event handler. We also assign `onMouseOver` and `onMouseOut` handlers using the `rollover()` and `rollout()` JavaScript functions that we'll see shortly.

After that we find a section that looks almost identical to the tabs, but this time it is for the buttons along the side. The interesting thing to note is that all the buttons are always present from the start. The appropriate buttons for a given view are shown, while the rest are hidden. Also in this section you will find some `<select>` elements. These are used to select a date when looking at appointments. Note that unlike the buttons and tabs, they have `onFocus` and `onBlur` handlers as well. This allows us to have the background change colors when a given control gets focus. The `onChange` event is also hooked so that any change in these fields results in the current view being updated (if applicable).

Lastly, we have a table cell with two `<span>` tags within it, one with the ID `mainContent` and one with the ID `pleaseWait`. The `mainContent` `<span>` is where the result returned by the server for any of our Ajax calls will be placed. Only this section will be dynamically updated; everything else remains the same (I am not counting the buttons being shown and hidden according to the view—I am referring to the fact that the rendered content remains the same everywhere but in `mainContent`). The `pleaseWait` `<span>` is where the Please Wait message is. These two `<span>`s are alternately displayed and hidden as required. Note that `<span>` is used instead of `<div>` to avoid unwanted line breaks after each, important for making the layout work as expected.

dayAtAGlance.jsp

The Day At A Glance screen is the first thing a user sees when they log on to the application, and this is the JSP responsible for rendering it. More specifically, when `main.jsp` loads, it calls a JavaScript function `init()`, which makes an Ajax request for this view. This JSP renders the response, and it is displayed in the `mainContent` `<div>`. The Day At A Glance view shows tasks that are due today, as well as appointments for today.

Let's examine the code that renders the tasks due today:

```
<div class="cssDAAGHeading">Tasks due today:</div>
<ww:if test="%{!tasks.isEmpty()}">
  <ww:iterator value="tasks">
    <form>
      <input type="hidden" name="createdDT" value="<ww:property
        value="createdDT"/>">
```

```
          <table border="0" cellpadding="0" cellspacing="0" class="cssDAAGItem">
            <tr>
              <td width="1">
                <input type="image" src="img/edit0.gif" id="edit"
                  align="absmiddle" onmouseover="rollover(this);"
                  onmouseout="rollout(this);"
                  onclick="taskRetrieve(this.form);return false;">
              </td>
              <td width="10"> </td>
              <td>
                Subject: <ww:property value="subject" />
              </td>
            </tr>
          </table>
        </form>
      </ww:iterator>
    </ww:if>
    <ww:else>
      There are no tasks to display
    </ww:else>
```

Here we meet a new WebWork tag: `<ww:iterator>`. This tag iterates over a collection that is a field in the current `Action`, in this case, the collection of tasks for today. Before that iteration begins, though, we check to see if the collection is empty. If it is, the `<ww:else>` tag executes, and we render a message saying there are no tasks to display. If it is not empty, however, we iterate over the collection. For each element, we output some markup. Notice the use of the `<ww:property>` tag again, and also notice how we only have to name the field to reference. This name is always a field of the current object from the collection. There is no need to give the current object a name, as is typical with other taglibs. The WebWork tags are smart enough to know that the name specified by the `value` attribute of the `<ww:property>` tag is a member of the current object from the collection. Cool!

The code that renders the markup for the appointments is basically the same, except that of course there are different fields to display, such as start time, end time, and location.

accountEdit.jsp

This is a simple JSP that is rendered as the result of an Ajax request when the user clicks the My Account tab. It is just a simple form that gives the user the ability to change their password, since this is currently all that can be edited (the username is essentially the key of the table, so it cannot be changed).

opResponse.jsp

This JSP renders the response to many different Ajax events, including saving notes, setting (or deleting) tasks and appointments, or creating new items. It handles all of these by going through a batch of `if` blocks to tailor itself appropriately to the operation that was performed. For instance, one of the things that is different depending on what operation was performed is the graphical header that is displayed. WebWork is kind enough to put the requested URI in the request as an attribute, so we can interrogate that value to see what operation was performed. So, if we are doing something with an appointment, for instance, this block of code will execute:

```
if (requestURI.indexOf("appointment") != -1) {
  headerFile = "appointments"; whatItem = "Appointment";
  targetFunc = "showAppointments();";
}
```

The `headerFile` variable is the name of the header graphic, minus path and extension. `whatItem` is text that will be displayed, such as "Appointment has been created". `targetFunc` is the name of the JavaScript function that will be executed when the user clicks the OK button.

The other variable that has to be set is `whatOp`, which is what operation was just performed. The code that does this is as follows:

```
if (requestURI.indexOf("create") != -1) { whatOp = "created"; }
if (requestURI.indexOf("update") != -1) { whatOp = "updated"; }
if (requestURI.indexOf("delete") != -1) { whatOp = "deleted"; }
```

By inserting these four variables' values into the markup, we can generate an output appropriate for the operation that was just performed, and make the OK button go to the appropriate view afterward. It's very handy to have this all in one file rather than a separate JSP for each response… imagine, three JSPs for each unit of functionality: one JSP for updating, one for deleting and one for creating, and those three types for each of the note, task, contact, and appointment function groups. Twelve JSPs versus a single one with some branching logic—I know I prefer the one!

appointmentEdit.jsp, contactEdit.jsp, noteEdit.jsp, taskEdit.jsp

I am grouping these four together because, essentially, they are all the same. True, they have different input fields on them, but the basic structure and function is identical in all of them. These are the JSPs used to show the forms for editing or creating an appointment, contact, note, or task.

We start out with a block of code to put the appropriate heading on the page:

```
<div class="cssDAAGHeading">
<%
  String requestURI = (String)request.getAttribute("webwork.request_uri");
  requestURI = requestURI.toLowerCase();
  if (requestURI.indexOf("create") != -1) {
    out.println("Create Note:");
  } else {
    out.println("Edit Note:");
  }
%>
</div>
<br>
```

We again do this by interrogating the request URI that led to this JSP, and render the appropriate text, "Create Note" or "Edit Note".

After that is a typical WebWork-based input form. Since this page will function as both edit and create, we need to output the values found in the Action instance as the value of the various form fields so that when we are editing we start out with the current values. In the Action itself we find that we have a NoteObject that stores all the values for the note. This has a subject field. To set the value of the text field to that value, we use the %{note.subject} notation. Note the reference to the note field, and then the subject field in that object.

As I mentioned, all four of these JSPs are essentially the same; the only difference relates to the fields present in the rendered form. Have a look at all of them to see this for yourself.

I will, however, point out one section in the taskEdit.jsp that is of interest:

```
<tr>
  <td><label>Due Date</label></td>
  <td>
    <ww:select name="dueMonth" theme="simple"
      list="#{'':'', '01':'January', '02':'February', '03':'March',
      '04':'April', '05':'May', '06':'June', '07':'July', '08':'August',
      '09':'September', '10':'October', '11':'November',
      '12':'December'}"
      cssClass="cssInput0"
      onfocus="this.className='cssInput1';"
      onblur="this.className='cssInput0';" />
     
    <ww:select name="dueDay" theme="simple"
      list="#{'':'', '01':'01', '02':'02', '03':'03', '04':'04', '05':'05',
      '06':'06', '07':'07', '08':'08', '09':'09', '10':'10', '11':'11',
      '12':'12', '13':'13', '14':'14', '15':'15', '16':'16', '17':'17',
      '18':'18', '19':'19', '20':'20', '21':'21', '22':'22', '23':'23',
      '24':'24', '25':'25', '26':'26', '27':'27', '28':'28', '29':'29',
      '30':'30', '31':'31'}"
      cssClass="cssInput0"
      onfocus="this.className='cssInput1';"
      onblur="this.className='cssInput0';" />
     
    <ww:select name="dueYear" theme="simple"
      list="#{'':'', '2006':'2006', '2007':'2007', '2008':'2008',
      '2009':'2009', '2010':'2010', '2011':'2011', '2012':'2012',
      '2013':'2013', '2014':'2014', '2015':'2015', '2016':'2016',
      '2017':'2017', '2018':'2018', '2019':'2019', '2020':'2020'}"
      cssClass="cssInput0"
      onfocus="this.className='cssInput1';"
      onblur="this.className='cssInput0';" />
  </td>
</tr>
```

Recall earlier when discussing WebWork in general when I mentioned how the WebWork tags were nice enough to render a table structure for us so that our forms automatically take on a nice, clean appearance. This was a result of the default XHTML theme. However, in the case of the due date for a task, I wanted to have three <select> dropdowns in a row. This is not possible by default because after the first one, the WebWork tag would close the table row. Instead, I had to set the theme of the tags to simple, which makes WebWork just render the input element, not the table code. I take responsibility for that. In this way, I can have my three <select> dropdowns in a row, and it is still nice and clean code.

Also notice the use of the <ww:select> tag. This tag allows you to populate the options for the dropdown from a collection in the Action, or with a literal list, as is done here. I think this also makes the code cleaner, because the alternative is a batch of <option> tags, as in a typical <select>, which are usually put on a separate line each. So with the <ww:select> tag, we wind up with fewer lines of code, and fewer characters typed, which is always good for us lazy programmers! Being able to reference a collection in the Action is even cooler, but to me it only makes sense if you have a dynamic list, or something read from a database, for instance. For static, known lists such as these, I find it just as easy to put them in the JSP itself. Your mileage may vary!

This JSP actually provides the capability to create a new note or edit an existing note, but it also provides the necessary markup to delete a note. This is done by a simple check at the end to see whether or not the requested URI was created. If it wasn't, it means we are editing an existing item. In that case, the Delete button is rendered.

appointmentList.jsp, contactList.jsp, noteList.jsp, taskList.jsp

As with the edit pages, the list JSPs are all pretty much the same. If you've seen one, you've seen 'em all, as the saying goes! So, let's get the "if you've seen one" part out of the way:

```
<%@ taglib prefix="ww" uri="webwork" %>

<img src="img/head_notes.gif">
<br><br>

<div class="cssScrollContent">

  <ww:if test="%{!notes.isEmpty()}">
    <ww:iterator value="notes">
      <form>
        <input type="hidden" name="createdDT" value="<ww:property
          value="createdDT"/>">
        <input type="image" src="img/edit0.gif" id="edit" align="absmiddle"
          onmouseover="rollover(this);" onmouseout="rollout(this);"
          onclick="noteRetrieve(this.form);return false;">
         
        Subject: <ww:property value="subject" />
      </form>
    </ww:iterator>
  </ww:if>
  <ww:else>
    There are no notes to display
  </ww:else>

</div>
```

That's it, completely. It is nothing more than iteration over a `List` in the `Action`, and generating markup for each item (or generating text saying there are no notes to display). Everything here we have seen before; it should just about be second nature by this point!

One thing to note is the `return false;` at the end of the `onClick` event handler. You will see this throughout the code for this project. The reason for it is that Internet Explorer will do a double-submit when you click these buttons: the one manually done by virtue of the call to `noteRetrieve()`, or whatever the event handler calls, and one for the automatic form submission. Returning false indicates to the browser that the automatic submission should not occur. Interestingly, this is not necessary in Firefox.

globals.js

The `globals.js` file contains a small handful of global variables, four in fact. The first, `rolloverImages`, stores the preloaded images for all the button and tab rollovers used in the application. This is an associative array, so we can pull out the images for a given button, for instance, by referencing it by name. No need to worry about index numbers! The next variable, `tabsButtonsEnabled`, tells us whether the user can click buttons or tabs at the moment. This is used to disable buttons and tabs when an Ajax request is working. Next is the `currentView` variable, which as its name implies, tells us what view we are currently looking at: `taskView`, `noteView`, `accountView`, and so on. The variable `subView` is used for appointments to record whether we are looking at day view, week view, month view, or year view when viewing appointments.

init.js

This source file contains a single function, `init()`, amazingly enough! This function is called from the `onLoad` event handler of the `main.jsp` page. Its job is, unsurprisingly, to initialize the application on the client. It performs three basic functions.

First, it preloads all the images for buttons and tabs. To do this, it makes use of a function `createRolloverImages()`, found in `buttonsAndTabs.js`. It accepts the name of the button or tab to load. It then creates two `Image` objects for it and loads the appropriate GIF file into it. It then adds these images to the `rolloverImages` array, keyed by name. This saves us from a lot of repetitive image preload code.

Second, it sets the `<select>` dropdowns in the left-hand side of the screen to the current date. These dropdowns are used when dealing with appointments to set the current date, which is then used as the basis for all the appointment views. This code makes use of the function `locateDDValue()` found in `misc.js`, which locates and selects a specified value in a specified `<select>` element. Note that this code uses the Prototype `$()` function to reference the dropdowns, like so:

```
locateDDValue($("dsMonth"), month);
```

Third, `init()` throws up an alert dialog to welcome the user to the system, and then calls `showDayAtAGlance()`, which fires off an Ajax request to get the result of the Day At A Glance service.

misc.js

This file contains a handful of, well, miscellaneous functions, which did not fit elsewhere. First up is showPleaseWait(), which is called whenever an Ajax request is made. It inserts the Please Wait message into the mainContent area.

Second is showDayAtAGlance(). This fires off an Ajax request to get the contents of the Day At A Glance view. Let's look at this function:

```
function showDayAtAGlance() {

  if (tabsButtonsEnabled) {
    showPleaseWait();
    new Ajax.Updater("mainContent", "dayAtAGlance.action", {
      method : "post",
      onSuccess : function(resp) {
        currentView = "dayAtAGlance";
        setupSidebarButtons("newNote", "newTask", "newContact",
          "newAppointment");
        hidePleaseWait();
      },
      onFailure : ajaxError
    });
  }

} // End showDayAtAGlance().
```

You will find that all of the Ajax calls in The Organizer have the same basic form. First, we only fire the request if tabsButtonsEnabled is true. When it is false, it means an Ajax request is already processing. It is set to false by the call to showPleaseWait(), which hides the main content and shows the Please Wait message (the pleaseWait <span> we saw earlier in main.jsp). Next, we use the Ajax.Updater() function call. Updater() is a convenience method that performs what is probably the most common Ajax function: updating some element on the page, usually a <div>, with the response from the server. The first argument passed to this function is the ID of the element to update. The second argument is the URL to send the request to. After that comes a collection of arguments, including what method to use, POST in all cases in this application; the function to call when the response is successfully returned (usually an anonymous function listed inline, as is shown here); and a function to execute when a failure occurs, in this case a call to ajaxError(), which is also found in misc.js (it is just an alert message saying an error has occurred). Note the call to hidePleaseWait() in the success handler. This shows whatever the server returned, which is now in the mainContent <span> in main.jsp, and also reenables the buttons and tabs.

After that we find logoff(), which is called when the user clicks the logoff tab. This does nothing but set the location of the window to logoff.action, which calls an Action that terminates the session and forwards to index.jsp, where the user can log on again if they wish.

Lastly, locateDDValue() is used to find and locate a value in a given <select> element. This is just a simple iteration over the options in the <select>, and when the matching element is found (ignoring case), it is selected.

buttonsAndTabs.js

This file contains all the code that makes the tabs and buttons work. There are four functions in it. First up is `setupSidebarButtons()`. This is called any time the view changes, that is, when a response to an Ajax request comes back from the server. Its job is to enable the appropriate buttons. Passed into this function is a variable argument list. What this means is that you could call this function any of the following ways:

```
setupSidebarButtons();
setupSidebarButtons("newNote");
setupSidebarButtons("newNote", "newTask");
setupSidebarButtons("newNote", "newTask", "newContact");
setupSidebarButtons("newNote", "newTask", "newContact", "newAppointment");
```

Implicitly available to every JavaScript function is an object named `arguments`. You access it by doing `xxxx.arguments`, where `xxxx` is the name of the function. So, in this case we do `var args = setupSidebarButtons.arguments;`. This object is an array of the arguments passed to the function. In the case of the first call earlier, this would be an empty array; in the second call, an array with a single element; and so on. So, in this function, we iterate over the array, and for each, enable the named button, like so:

```
  for (i = 0; i < args.length; i++) {
    $(args[i]).style.display = "block";
  }
```

In this way, the code that calls this function can set up whichever buttons are appropriate without having to explicitly pass an array or have a set number of arguments that this function accepts, each corresponding to a specific button. Variable argument lists are a powerful feature of JavaScript, and one that is used frequently in various libraries you may encounter.

The next function we find is `createRolloverImages()`, which we have seen used previously. Now we can see what it actually does:

```
function createRolloverImages(inName) {

  var img = new Image();
  img.src = "img/" + inName + "0.gif";
  rolloverImages[inName + "0"] = img;
  img = new Image();
  img.src = "img/" + inName + "1.gif";
  rolloverImages[inName + "1"] = img;

} // End createRollover().
```

Recall that this function is passed the name of a button or tab to load images for. So, using that name, we instantiate two `Image` objects, and then proceed to load them with the images whose name we form by taking the name passed in and appending either 0 or 1 to the end, 0 for the normal nonhover version and 1 for the hover version. We then add these two `Image` objects to the `rolloverImages` array that we saw in `Globals.js`. Recall that this is an associative array, and we'll reference the images by name, including the 0 or 1 at the end.

Lastly in this source file are the two functions that actually make use of the `rolloverImages` array, `rollover()` and `rollout()`. These correspond to the `onMouseOver` and `onMouseOut` events of all buttons and tabs. They both work the same way: first, we check to see if buttons and tabs are enabled, and only continue if they are. That way, we can lock out the buttons and tabs from being clickable by the user when an Ajax request is processing. Next, we see if we were passed a DOM ID of the button or tab as the second argument to this function (the first being a reference to the button or tab object itself). This ID is actually the name of the image file, sans the 0 or 1 at the end, which is appended by the two functions to form the full filename. The reason the ID is passed manually here is because of a bug in WebWork at the time of this writing where the ID would not be rendered on these elements in the forms. So, any of the buttons that are part of a form—that is, those in the main content area—would not work with this function because all this function should need is the object reference, from which the ID can be retrieved. Since it is not being rendered, however, this will not work. So, in some cases the ID is manually passed in, and in other cases it is not (it is passed in manually on WebWork-generated buttons). If no ID was passed in, we grab it from the object.

Finally, using this ID, we get the appropriate image from the `rolloverImages` array, and update the button (or tab) with it.

account.js

This JavaScript file contains the code that deals with accounts. Three functions are present: `showMyAccount()`,`accountUpdate()`, and `accountDelete()`. All of them have the same basic form as the `showDayAtAGlance()` function that we saw previously. `showMyAccount()` is the function called when the user clicks the My Account tab, and it returns the markup for the form to edit the account. `accountUpdate()` is called to save the updated account (which is just the ability to change the password in actuality). Lastly, `accountDelete()` is called when the user clicks the Delete Account button.

appointments.js, contacts.js, notes.js, tasks.js

I have lumped all four of these together again because they are all basically the same, so just reviewing one is probably sufficient.

In each of these files you will find seven functions. Using `notes.js` as the example, we first find `showNotes()`, which is called when the user clicks the Notes tab. This makes an Ajax call via Prototype in the same manner as we saw in `showDayAtAGlance()` and uses the `Ajax.Updater()` function to display the returned result, which is a list of notes in this case. After that is `doNewNote()`, which is called when the user clicks the New Note button. This displays the form generated by `noteEdit.jsp`. Next is `noteCreate()`, which makes the call to save a new note as a result of the user clicking the Save button when they have previously clicked New Note. After that comes `noteRetrieve()`, which is called when the user clicks the Edit button next to a note they wish to edit. It again displays the result of the rendering of `noteEdit.jsp`. After that is `noteUpdate()`, which updates an existing note when the user clicks Save on the note editing screen. After that is `noteDelete()`, called when the user wants to delete a note. The result of both of the previous functions is that `opResponse.jsp` is rendered and returned, tailored to the function that was performed as previously described. Finally is the function `validateNote()`, which performs some validations before submitting a note, either a new one or one being edited.

As mentioned, the other three files are quite the same, but please do examine them anyway to see that for yourself. There are a few exceptions to this. First, in `appointments.js`, you will find that in the `appointmentRetrieve()` function, I use `Ajax.Request()` rather than `Ajax.Updater()`. This is because simply updating the `mainContent <div>` is not sufficient because there are <select> elements that must have a value selected. By using AjaxRequest() instead, we have complete control over what happens when the response is successful, and in this case that means using the previously described locateDDValue() function to select a value in those <select> fields. Also in appointments.js are a few additional functions, namely doWeekView(),doMonthView(), and doYearView(). These are the functions that are called when the applicable button is clicked to change the current view. This makes the same call as does showAppointments(), which could be thought of as showDayView() because that is what it is doing. We pass to the server the name of the view we want, and it obliges with the applicable data. Also, you will find a dsSelectorChange(), which is the function called by the onChange event of the date selector on the side. This simply calls showAppointments(), doDayView(), doMonthView(), or doYearView(), depending on what the current view is, so that the data can be updated using the selected date as the basis.

Also note that the functions listed, aside from the initial showNotes() function and the validateNote() function in our example, make up a typical CRUD (Create, Retrieve, Update, Delete) collection of functions that are the hallmark of many data entry applications, which is essentially what this is after all. This CRUD pattern is repeated on the server side, as we'll now see.

The Server-Side Code

With the client-side code out of the way, we can now begin to explore what makes The Organizer tick on the server side of the fence.

Globals.java

The Globals class is a simple holder of static values such as database driver name, database username and password, and so on. The only thing of real interest here is the dbURL field, which is the only nonfinal field. This is of course the URL string to use for the database. The issue is that this value has to be constructed dynamically because it is a file system path to the WEB-INF/db directory. This path is constructed in ContextListener.java and then set in Globals so it is available to the rest of the application.

ContextListener.java

This class is executed when the context starts up to do some basic application initialization. There are basically three important tasks it performs. First, it constructs that dbURL value mentioned in describing Globals.java using the following code:

```
String dbURL = "jdbc:hsqldb:" +
  inEvent.getServletContext().getRealPath("/WEB-INF") +
  "/db/theorganizer";
Globals.setDbURL(dbURL);
```

As mentioned before, this constructs a real file system path to the WEB-INF/db directory, and it also names the database, theorganizer specifically.

Next it creates the database, if it does not already exist. The following code accomplishes that:

```
Class.forName(Globals.getDbDriver()).newInstance();
Connection conn = DriverManager.getConnection(Globals.getDbURL(),
  Globals.getDbUsername(), Globals.getDbPassword());
conn.close();
```

HSQLDB does its thing here and creates the database if it does not already exist; otherwise it just initializes the database engine.

The last step is to create the database tables. This is accomplished with a series of calls to the createTable() method of the TableDAO class, which we'll see later. We pass to this method the name of the table to create, using the constant table names declared in Globals.java. As a prelude to looking at that DAO, the createTable() method will retrieve metadata about the database, and check to see if the named table exists. If it does, it returns right away, and if it does not exist, the method goes ahead and creates the table. All of the database setup is encapsulated and automatic in the code, no there are no SQL scripts or things like that to run.

AccountObject.java

The AccountObject class is the class that represents a user account. It is a simple JavaBean with two fields: username and password. As with all the other object classes, as well as all the Action classes, my typical toString() method is present so that we can easily display the contents of an instance of these classes. Otherwise, this is a rather boring class!

AppointmentObject.java, ContactObject.java, NoteObject.java, TaskObject.java

I once again have chosen to lump all these together because they are quite similar. I could have easily listed AccountObject here as well since they are all nothing but plain old JavaBeans. As such, they are not worth discussing very much except to say that they each map to a record in the corresponding database table: appointments, contacts, notes, or tasks. Speaking of database tables…

TableDAO.java

The TableDAO object is a data access object that has one purpose in life: to create the database tables The Organizer needs to function. It is used exactly once, at application startup, and is called from ContextListener.

In the constructor, a data source is created, as we saw when we discussed HSQLDB. This is typical of all the DAOs in this application. After that, we have a single method, createTable(), which accepts as an argument the name of the table to be created. It begins its work by getting metadata on the database, like so:

```
Connection       conn  = dataSource.getConnection();
DatabaseMetaData dbmd  = conn.getMetaData();
ResultSet        rs    = dbmd.getTables(null, null, "%", null);
boolean          found = false;
while (rs.next()) {
  String s = rs.getString(3);
  if (s.equalsIgnoreCase(inTableName)) {
    found = true;
  }
}
rs.close();
```

If the table requested to be created is found, we'll not do anything after this. If it is not found, though, we do some branching logic based on which table was requested, and the appropriate SQL is executed to create the table. For instance, to create the accounts table, we use the following code:

```
log.info("Creating " + inTableName + " table...");
JdbcTemplate jt = new JdbcTemplate(dataSource);
if (inTableName.equalsIgnoreCase(Globals.TABLE_ACCOUNTS)) {
  jt.execute(
    "CREATE TABLE accounts ( " +
    "username VARCHAR(20), " +
    "password VARCHAR(20) " +
    ");");
  jt.execute("CREATE UNIQUE INDEX username_index ON accounts (username)");
```

Here we see a standard `CREATE TABLE` query, and then a bit of SQL to create a unique index on the username field. This disallows creating an account that already exists.

There are a total of five tables: `accounts`, `notes`, `tasks`, `contacts`, and `appointments`. Figure 8-6 shows a basic schema diagram of the database.

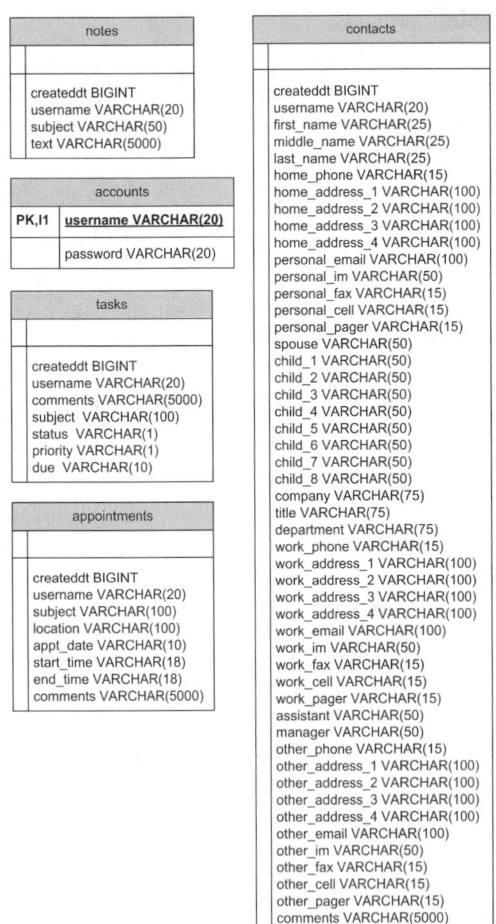

Figure 8-6. *Simple database schema diagram of The Organizer's database*

AccountDAO.java

The AccountDAO class deals with operations for user accounts. Specifically, we again see the CRUD pattern emerging: we have an accountCreate() method, an accountRetrieve() method, an accountUpdate() method, and an accountDelete() method. All but the accountRetrieve() method accepts a single argument, an AccountObject instance. The accountRetrieve() method accepts a username to look up. All but the accountRetrieve() method are simple SQL calls using the Spring JdbcTemplate class we have previously seen.

accountRetrieve() is not much more, but let's have a quick look at it:

```
public AccountObject accountRetrieve(final String inUsername) {

  log.debug("AccountDAO.accountRetrieve()...");

  log.debug("username to retrieve : " + inUsername);
  JdbcTemplate jt = new JdbcTemplate(dataSource);
  List rows = jt.queryForList(
    "SELECT * FROM accounts WHERE username='" + inUsername + "'"
  );
  AccountObject account = null;
  if (rows != null && !rows.isEmpty()) {
    account = new AccountObject();
    Map m = (Map)rows.get(0);
    account.setUsername((String)m.get("USERNAME"));
    account.setPassword((String)m.get("PASSWORD"));
  }
  log.info("Retrieved AccountObject : " + account);

  log.debug("AccountDAO.accountRetrieve() Done");
  return account;

} // End accountRetrieve().
```

This too uses JdbcTemplate to query for the record matching the requested username. We use the queryForList() method and then grab the first element of the List, which should contain only a single record. We create an AccountObject from it, populating the username and password from the Map in the List. queryForList() returns a List of Maps, where each Map represents a row in the result set, but since it is a Map, it is a bit easier to deal with. The created object is then returned, or null is returned if the matching record was not found.

AppointmentDAO.java, ContactDAO.java, NoteDAO.java, TaskDAO.java

Yet again, I have chosen to group four classes together because they are virtually identical in the end. These are the four DAO classes that deal with appointments, contacts, notes, and tasks, respectively. As in the AccountDAO class, you will find four methods in each class corresponding to the CRUD operations.

You will also find one additional method in each, an xxxList() method, where xxx is the object we are dealing with: appointment, contact, note, or task. Each of these methods performs a query to get a list of items for the user, and returns a list of the appropriate object type, either AppointmentObject, ContactObject, NoteObject, or TaskObject. Each of them accepts a username argument.

In addition, in the TaskDAO class, the listTasks() method also accepts a boolean that tells it to either return only those tasks due today or return all of them. When true is passed, only tasks due today are returned, and this is used when rendering the Day At A Glance view. When false is passed, all tasks are returned, which is used when rendering the view the user sees when they click the Tasks tab.

Likewise, the listAppointments() method is a bit different. In addition to username, it accepts a Date object, and a string telling it which view to return (day, week, month, or year). The Date object is used as the basis for the view. This method performs a number of steps to generate the appropriate list, so let's walk through those steps.

First, a list of all appointments for the user is obtained from the database:

```
log.debug("Servicing '" + inViewType + "' view...");
log.debug("username to retrieve appointments for : " + inUsername);
JdbcTemplate jt = new JdbcTemplate(dataSource);
List appointments = jt.queryForList(
  "SELECT createddt, subject, location, start_time, end_time, appt_date " +
  "FROM appointments WHERE username='" + inUsername + "' order by " +
  "appt_date, start_time"
);
```

Next, the day, month, year, and week of month are extracted from the date passed in:

```
GregorianCalendar gc = new GregorianCalendar();
gc.setTimeInMillis(inDate.getTime());
int day         = gc.get(Calendar.DATE);
int month       = gc.get(Calendar.MONTH) + 1;
int year        = gc.get(Calendar.YEAR);
int weekOfMonth = gc.get(Calendar.WEEK_OF_MONTH);
```

Note that the month value is incremented by 1. This is because the month returned from the gc.get(Calendar.MONTH) call is 0–11, but the month stored in the database is 1–12, so to be able to do comparisons later, we need the value to be in the range 1–12.

The code then begins to iterate over the result set List. For each, it extracts the appointment's date and extracts from that the same information as was extracted from the date passed in, as shown in the previous code. This is a bit different because the date is actually stored as a character string in the database, so we have to do some string parsing to get the same information:

```
String appointmentDate = (String)m.get("APPT_DATE");
int m_month = Integer.parseInt(appointmentDate.substring(0, 2));
int m_day = Integer.parseInt(appointmentDate.substring(3, 5));
int m_year = Integer.parseInt(appointmentDate.substring(6, 10));
int m_weekOfMonth = (new GregorianCalendar(
  m_year, m_month - 1, m_day)).get(Calendar.WEEK_OF_MONTH);
```

The variable m here is the Map of the current row in the result set. Now that we have the same information for both the date passed in and the date of the appointment we are currently examining, we can do some simple comparisons to determine if the appointment should be shown in the requested view, and if it should, we set the variable takeIt to true. For instance, if the day view was requested, the following logic is performed:

```
if (inViewType.equalsIgnoreCase("day")) {
  if (day == m_day && month == m_month && year == m_year) {
    takeIt = true;
  }
}
```

There is one such block of logic for each view type—a total of four if blocks. Then comes one last block, whose job it is to create a new AppointmentObject and populate it if the appointment is to be shown:

```
if (takeIt) {
  AppointmentObject appointment = new AppointmentObject();
  appointment.setCreatedDT(((Long)m.get("CREATEDDT")).longValue());
  appointment.setUsername(inUsername);
  appointment.setAppointmentDate((String)m.get("APPT_DATE"));
  appointment.setSubject((String)m.get("SUBJECT"));
  appointment.setLocation((String)m.get("LOCATION"));
  appointment.setStartTime((String)m.get("START_TIME"));
  appointment.setEndTime((String)m.get("END_TIME"));
  appointmentsOut.add(appointment);
}
```

The code is added to the appointmentsOut List, and is returned, and that is how the list of appointments for a given view is generated.

ForwardAction.java

In some cases in the application—for instance, when the user clicks the New Account button—we just want to return the outcome of a JSP rendering without actually doing any other work, essentially forwarding the request directly to a JSP. In this case, we still want the request to go through the WebWork framework as this is generally considered a best practice. The ForwardAction is a simple Action that is used in these situations. All it does is returns Action.SUCCESS, which causes the <forward> named success to be forwarded to. There is no actual work to be done, so this Action is in effect just a dummy Action so that we can still use the framework to make the request. Struts has a similar construct, also named ForwardAction.

LogonAction.java

The LogonAction class, not surprisingly, handles when the user is attempting to log on. It uses the default execute() method, which means that WebWork will execute this method without being told to. The real work of this Action is encapsulated in the following code snippet:

```
// Get the user.
AccountDAO    dao     = new AccountDAO();
AccountObject account = dao.accountRetrieve(username);
```

```
// See if they exist, and if their password is correct.
if (account == null) {
  log.info("User not found");
  message = "User not found";
  return Action.ERROR;
} else {
  if (!password.equalsIgnoreCase(account.getPassword())) {
    log.info("Password incorrect");
    message = "Password incorrect";
    return Action.ERROR;
  }
}
```

It calls on the AccountDAO to get the account for the username that came from the request parameters (remember, WebWork will have called setUsername() on this class before calling execute(), so the username field now has the parameter value). If it is not found, the appropriate message is set in the Action, and Action.ERROR is returned, which returns us to index.jsp, where the message field is used to display the error. If the account is found, and the password is incorrect, we return the appropriate message there (I realize this is not a security best practice, but we are not trying to build Fort Knox here!). If the account is found and the password is correct, Action.SUCCESS will be returned, and the AccountObject is also put in session, where it will be used later to get the username for SQL queries (so the username is never passed again as a request parameter).

LogoffAction.java

I will give you just one guess what this Action is for. Yes, it handles when the user wants to log off! The pertinent code is rather short and sweet here:

```
ActionContext      context = ActionContext.getContext();
HttpServletRequest request =
  (HttpServletRequest)context.get(ServletActionContext.HTTP_REQUEST);
HttpSession        session = request.getSession();
session.invalidate();
```

Recall in our earlier discussion of WebWork we talked about the ActionContext—how it is a ThreadLocal and how it is easy to get a reference to it, and through it, to the usual suspects: HttpServletRequest, HttpSession, and so on. That is precisely what we do here. The only job to be performed here is to invalidate the session, at which point the user is directed to index.jsp and is "logged off."

AccountAction.java

The AccountAction handles all operations required to work with user accounts. Just like in the DAOs, there are methods corresponding to the typical CRUD operations, and in the Actions (not just this one, but the AppointmentAction, ContactAction, NoteAction, and TaskAction classes as well) they are literally named create(), retrieve(), update(), and delete().

Each one looks suspiciously like the code you saw in the LogonAction. This is no accident. The fundamental structure is essentially the same for all these Actions and all these methods. One difference you will spot is in the create() method:

```
if (!password.equalsIgnoreCase(password_2)) {
  log.debug("Password not matched");
  message = "Password not matched";
  return Action.ERROR;
}
```

The typical "enter your password twice to verify" paradigm is used, and this is where that validation occurs.

Another difference is when we ask the AccountDAO to actually add the new account to the database. In this case, the possibility exists that the username is already in use, in which case an exception will be thrown. Remember that Spring will wrap the underlying SQLException into something more generic, so we have to catch that and handle it accordingly:

```
AccountDAO dao = new AccountDAO();
try {
  dao.accountCreate(account);
} catch (DataIntegrityViolationException dive) {
  // Username already exists.
  log.debug("Username already exists");
  message = "That username already exists.  Please try another.";
  return Action.ERROR;
}
```

DayAtAGlanceAction.java

This Action is called to show the contents of the Day At A Glance view. It boils down to simply calling two different DAOs to get the list of tasks due today as well as the list of appointments for today:

```
// First, get the list of tasks due today.
TaskDAO taskDAO = new TaskDAO();
tasks = taskDAO.taskList(username, true);

// Next, get the list of appointments for today.
AppointmentDAO appointmentDAO = new AppointmentDAO();
appointments = appointmentDAO.appointmentList(username, new Date(), "day");
```

Nothing to it!

AppointmentAction.java, ContactAction.java, NoteAction.java, TaskAction.java

Last but not least are the four Actions that deal with appointments, contacts, notes, and tasks. I have decided to group them together because of their extreme similarity to one another, as well as to the other Actions we have already looked at. As with the other Actions, you will again find the four CRUD methods, and they are essentially identical; just the SQL queries and objects they work with differ. Note that there are no validations performed in any of these. There is very little input validation to be performed at all outside of account creation, and those validations are handled in the client code (not the most robust design, I acknowledge, but sufficient for our purposes).

You will also find in each a `list()` method, which returns an appropriate list of the object corresponding to the item the Action is from. You will also find one more method in each, named `getXXXXObject()`, where `XXXX` is `Appointment`, `Contact`, `Note`, or `Task`. The purpose of this method is to save some redundant code. When creating or updating an item, we need to construct the appropriate object: `AppointmentObject`, `ContactObject`, `NoteObject`, or `TaskObject`. When we are creating a new appointment, we want to populate the object with the input from the user. When updating an existing appointment, the DAO will do this for us from the database. However, in both cases, some bits of information will be the same, such as username. So, to avoid having this code redundantly in both methods, I elected to break it out to a separate method. When editing an item, there is no harm in the object being populated from the input parameters; the fields in the `Action` will in fact be `nulls` and initial values, but they will be overwritten with what the DAO gets from the database, so there is no harm in it.

Just to be sure there are no surprises, let's look at an example of each of these methods from the `NoteAction` class. First, `create()`:

```
public String create() {

  log.info("\n\n--------------------------------------------------------------");

  log.debug("NoteAction.create()...");

  // Display incoming request parameters.
  log.info("NoteAction : " + this.toString());

  // Call on the NoteDAO to save the NoteObject instance we are about to
  // create and populate.
  NoteObject nte = getNoteObject();
  NoteDAO    dao = new NoteDAO();
  // Need to override the createdDT that was populated by getNoteObject().
  nte.setCreatedDT(new Date().getTime());
  dao.noteCreate(nte);

  log.debug("NoteAction.create() Done");

  return Action.SUCCESS;

} // End create().
```

Nope, nothing surprising there. We get a `NoteObject`, and then a `NoteDAO` instance. We set the `createdDT` field of the `NoteObject` to the current time, and call `noteCreate()` in the DAO, passing it the `NoteObject`. Simple!

How about the `retrieve()` method?

```
public String retrieve() {
```

```
    log.info("\n\n---------------------------------------------------------");

    log.debug("NoteAction.retrieve()...");

    // Display incoming request parameters.
    log.info("NoteAction : " + this.toString());

    // Retrieve the note for the specified user created on the specified date
    // at the specified time.
    AccountObject account  = (AccountObject)session.get("account");
    String        username = account.getUsername();
    NoteDAO       dao      = new NoteDAO();
    note = dao.noteRetrieve(username, createdDT);
    log.debug("NoteAction : " + this.toString());

    log.debug("NoteAction.retrieve() Done");

    return Action.SUCCESS;

  } // End retrieve().
```

Here we have just a little bit more going on. We get the username from the AccountObject in session, and we pass that along to the noteRetrieve() of the NoteDAO instance we create. note, which is a field of the Action of type NoteObject, is set to the object returned by the call. Again, very simple.

Any chance that update() has much more going on?

```
  public String update() {

    log.info("\n\n---------------------------------------------------------");

    log.debug("NoteAction.update()...");

    // Display incoming request parameters.
    log.info("NoteAction : " + this.toString());

    // Call on the NoteDAO to save the NoteObject instance we are about to
    // create and populate.
    NoteObject nte = getNoteObject();
    NoteDAO    dao  = new NoteDAO();
    dao.noteUpdate(nte);

    log.debug("NoteAction.update() Done");

    return Action.SUCCESS;

  } // End update().
```

Nope, wouldn't appear so! This is even a bit simpler: a call to getNoteObject() gets us a NoteObject with all the input parameters already populated, and then it is nothing more than passing that object along to the noteUpdate() method of the DAO. Piece of cake!

Next we look at the delete() method:

```
public String delete() {

  log.info("\n\n--------------------------------------------------------------");

  log.debug("NoteAction.delete()...");

  // Display incoming request parameters.
  log.info("NoteAction : " + this.toString());

  // Call on the NoteDAO to delete the NoteObject instance we are about to
  // create and populate.
  AccountObject account  = (AccountObject)session.get("account");
  String        username = account.getUsername();
  NoteDAO       dao      = new NoteDAO();
  NoteObject    nte      = new NoteObject();
  nte.setCreatedDT(createdDT);
  nte.setUsername(username);
  dao.noteDelete(nte);

  log.debug("NoteAction.delete() Done");

  return Action.SUCCESS;

} // End delete().
```

Once more we find that it is sweet and to the point. To delete any given item we have to supply the DAO with the username and the createdDT value, which as you recall serves as essentially the unique key for any item. More specifically, the username and createdDT serve as something of a composite key. To remind you, the createdDT is the date and time the item was created in milliseconds. So, for a given user, it is virtually impossible that two items of the same type could ever get the same createdDT value.

The list() method is also very simple:

```
public String list() {

  log.info("\n\n--------------------------------------------------------------");

  log.debug("NoteAction.list()...");

  AccountObject account  = (AccountObject)session.get("account");
  String        username = account.getUsername();
  NoteDAO       dao      = new NoteDAO();
  notes = dao.noteList(username);
  log.debug("NoteAction : " + this.toString());
```

```
    log.debug("NoteAction.list() Done");

    return Action.SUCCESS;

  } // End list().
```

Just get the username from the AccountObject in session and pass it along to the noteList() method in the DAO, and we are done!

Just for the sake of completeness at this point, let's take a look at the getNoteObject() method:

```
  private NoteObject getNoteObject() {

    AccountObject account  = (AccountObject)session.get("account");
    String        username = account.getUsername();
    NoteObject    nte      = new NoteObject();
    nte.setCreatedDT(createdDT);
    nte.setUsername(username);
    nte.setSubject(subject);
    nte.setText(text);
    return nte;

  } // End getNoteObject();
```

Hopefully that is pretty much exactly what you expected to see!

Again, all of these methods are very similar in all four of these Actions. The differences lie in what fields are present in the Action, and by extension, what fields these methods deal with, and of course what objects they work with, and what DAOs—all the things you would expect to be different. The basic, underlying structure and flow of the code is the same, though, with one exception: the list() method of the AppointmentAction.

```
  public String list() throws ParseException {

    log.info("\n\n--------------------------------------------------------");

    log.debug("AppointmentAction.list()...");

    AccountObject    account  = (AccountObject)session.get("account");
    String           username = account.getUsername();
    AppointmentDAO   dao      = new AppointmentDAO();
    Date             d        = null;
    SimpleDateFormat sdf      = new SimpleDateFormat();
    sdf.applyPattern("MM/dd/yyyy");
    d = sdf.parse(month + "/" + day + "/" + year);
    appointments = dao.appointmentList(username, d, view);
    log.debug("AppointmentAction : " + this.toString());
```

```
    log.debug("AppointmentAction.list() Done");

    return Action.SUCCESS;

  } // End list().
```

Here, some additional code is required to take the month, day, and year selected in the date selector on the left side of the screen and make a `Date` object out of it. Not exactly a big deal, but I wanted to point it out nonetheless.

Well, that about does it! We have now examined all the code that makes up The Organizer. I don't know about you, but I need a vacation!

Suggested Exercises

The Organizer is not meant to compete with the likes of Lotus Notes or Microsoft Outlook. Indeed, that level of functionality is far beyond what could be described in a book such as this. However, with just a few enhancements, The Organizer could offer a lot more to its users than the basics it offers now. Here are some suggestions for you to try that will challenge your newly gained knowledge of Prototype, HSQLDB, WebWork, and Spring:

- Integrate The Organizer and InstaMail. It would be nice if you could have one unified address book (the one in The Organizer is more robust and is the natural choice), and it would also be nice if you could send an e-mail at the click of a button while looking at the contact list in The Organizer.
- Graphical views for the appointments would allow you to see your appointments for a given time span.
- A busy search function would let you choose any user(s) in the database, and see whether they have appointments scheduled for a given time period.
- Allow for automated e-mail notifications when tasks are due and when appointments will soon begin. The code from InstaMail should be easy transportable to accomplish this. For bonus points, send e-mails to your cell phone's e-mail address so you can get your alerts on the go. Most cell providers offer this functionality nowadays; check with them for the details.

Summary

In this chapter we constructed something that is genuinely useful to anyone with a hectic lifestyle. If you were to host this application on an Internet-facing server, the ability to have access to your contacts, to-do lists, notes, and appointments from virtually anywhere would be a very handy thing. This chapter also discussed the Prototype library, which underpins a great many Ajax libraries. We also explored the WebWork application framework, which is set to become the next Struts. And last but not least, we explained how to use an embedded database named HSQLDB in our applications.

CHAPTER 9

■ ■ ■

AjaxChat: Chatting, the Ajax Way!

This chapter will be the first of two projects in this book that presents an Ajax project done with straight Ajax. That means this application will not be using any library or toolkit—it will just be you and JavaScript! In previous chapters, we explored a number of very fine libraries, and even more are available that we haven't mentioned. However, there is no requirement that you use any of them, and many times you may find it more appropriate or desirable to just use your JavaScript Fu and do it all yourself. Here we'll build ourselves a nice little multiuser, multiroom chat application, much like the Yahoo! chat rooms. Even better, we'll build this application using Struts on the server to make it that much more interesting!

Requirements and Goals

Chat rooms have been with us for a very long time now. In fact, it is chat rooms, those gathering places where you can talk in real time with your fellow computer users, that draw many people to the Internet in the first place (e-mail tends to be the biggest draw, but chat rooms are not too far behind for many people).

If you think about what a chat room application must require, it becomes clear that we'll need a server component. There has to be some broker in between all the chatter that deals with keeping track of the various chat rooms available, who is logged in and chatting in what room, and those types of system-level considerations. More important, though, is some arbiter of messages—a way for all the people currently chatting in a given room to see the various messages.

In a "real" chat application, such as those you might find on AOL, for instance, it is likely that the server actually pushes new messages out to the users in the room. That way, there is no delay between when someone says something and when everyone else in the room sees it.

If you were going to build a purely HTML-based chat application, as we are about to do, you'd have to consider all of these points. However, because the Web is based on a pull model of client-server interaction, ignoring things like applets and such, you clearly need to go about things a little differently. Could you have a meta refresh tag on a page that periodically asked the server for any new messages? Yes, but then you would be redrawing the entire screen each time, which would be rather inefficient, especially if you built it with something like JSP or another dynamic rendering technology where the server would be responsible for that redrawing.

There must be a better way, and of course there is: Ajax!

The AjaxChat application will have a number of requirements based on these, and a few others, as follows:

- The application must support multiple users and multiple rooms. We won't enumerate any specific scalability requirement except to say that a reasonably sized group of friends should be able to chat simultaneously, so something in the 10-user range should do fine.
- We have seen a number of solutions that use servlets on the back-end, so this time we'll do something a little more interesting and robust and build AjaxChat using Struts.
- We want to be able to adjust the font size of messages displayed in the room we are chatting in, to allow for people (like me!) with bad eyesight to have an easier time of it.
- Just for fun, we want the ability to show our messages in one color and other people's messages in another.
- The server will need to properly deal with things like duplicate users and users who do not properly log off. We won't, however, require a login per se—that is, user accounts will not be created and persisted.
- There should be an option to clear the "history" in a room so that a user can have a clean display at any time.

This should be a fun project! Let's now figure out how we are going to accomplish all that we have set out for ourselves.

How We Will Pull It Off

Because we are not using any Ajax library this time around, we do not have anything to introduce in that regard. What I will introduce is a whole server-side framework, as well as a tag library, namely Struts and JSTL (the Java Standard Template Library, a standardized tag library from Sun), respectively. If you are already familiar with these and do not feel that you need a refresher, you can safely skip this section.

In a nutshell, Struts is a Java framework for building web-based applications that implements the Model-View-Controller (MVC) design pattern. More precisely, it implements the Model 2 MVC architecture.

Basically, this means that there is a central entity, known as the controller, through which all requests are routed. This controller determines what action should be performed and delegates the request to a handler. Once the handler completes its task, the controller comes in again and determines where the request should go next.

In a Struts-based application, the controller is actually a loose conglomeration of a couple of things. First up is the `ActionServlet`. This is a typical servlet, the kind that performs some tasks common to all requests. Perhaps the most important task is delegating the request to a `RequestProcessor`, at least as far as Struts is concerned—this is where all the work in servicing a given request occurs. Ultimately, the `RequestProcessor` determines which `Action` to execute (an `Action` is the Struts term for the handler). This determination is made based on the URI requested and configuration stored in an XML file.

The `Action` then executes, and this is where your application really begins. The canonical approach is then to have the `Action` call upon some other class or classes to do the work of servicing the request. At the end of the Action, an object is returned that tells the RequestProcessor where to go next, which is typically a JSP.

The JSPs make up the view, the V in MVC, of a Struts application. The model, the M in MVC, is generally comprised of the classes your Actions call upon. The controller, the C in MVC, is the combination of ActionServlet, RequestProcessor, and Actions.

If you have never dealt with Struts, all of this is considerably easier than it might sound right now. To demonstrate that, let's look at a very simple Struts application. In this application, we'll ask the user to enter a first name and last name, and then we'll greet them nicely. To do this we need to create two JSPs, one class and one configuration file.

To begin, download and install the simple Struts example webapp for this chapter from the Apress website's Source Code section. Alternatively, you can create this webapp from scratch by first going to http://struts.apache.org and downloading the Struts 1.2.7 binary distribution. You should generally be able to use any newer version of Struts as well since the Struts team is usually quite good about ensuring backward compatibility. That being said, grab 1.2.7 if you can, just in case. This will give you the libraries and other files you need. A Struts webapp is no different from any other webapp except that there are a few required JARs to include. There's still a web.xml file and the same directory structure you are already familiar with.

First let's look at web.xml, shown in Listing 9-1.

Listing 9-1. *web.xml from Simple Struts Example*

```
<?xml version="1.0" encoding="ISO-8859-1"?>

<!DOCTYPE web-app PUBLIC "-//Sun Microsystems, Inc.//DTD Web Application 2.2//EN"
"http://java.sun.com/j2ee/dtds/web-app_2_2.dtd">

<web-app>

  <context-param>
    <param-name>javax.servlet.jsp.jstl.fmt.localizationContext</param-name>
    <param-value>MessageResources</param-value>
  </context-param>

  <servlet>
    <servlet-name>action</servlet-name>
    <servlet-class>org.apache.struts.action.ActionServlet</servlet-class>
    <init-param>
      <param-name>config</param-name>
      <param-value>/WEB-INF/struts-config.xml</param-value>
    </init-param>
    <init-param>
      <param-name>application</param-name>
      <param-value>MessageResources</param-value>
    </init-param>
    <load-on-startup>1</load-on-startup>
  </servlet>
```

```
  <servlet-mapping>
    <servlet-name>action</servlet-name>
    <url-pattern>*.do</url-pattern>
  </servlet-mapping>

  <welcome-file-list>
    <welcome-file>index.jsp</welcome-file>
  </welcome-file-list>

</web-app>
```

The context parameter javax.servlet.jsp.jstl.fmt.localizationContext tells JSTL that we want to internationalize our messages. This will be discussed later on, so for now let's move on.

Struts uses the FrontController pattern, which means all requests are routed through a single servlet, in this case the ActionServlet. This is a typical setup of that servlet. The config parameter defines where the Struts application configuration file will be found, and struts-config.xml in WEB-INF is the typical location and name for this file. The application parameter is used to define a properties file that will serve to provide messages throughout the application. The servlet is mapped to any URI ending with *.do, again, typical of Struts applications. Note the <load-on-startup> element. This is required because the first page, as we'll see, uses a forward defined in struts-config.xml, which will only be read when the servlet starts. If we did not start the servlet immediately, then the first request to index.jsp would fail with a NullPointerException because the config file has not yet been read.

The next file of interest is the message resources file, shown in Listing 9-2.

Listing 9-2. *Simple Struts Example Message Resource Bundle File*

```
title=Simple Struts Example
entryPrompt=Please enter your first and last name and click submit:
firstNamePrompt=First Name:
lastNamePrompt=Last Name:
returnToEntryPage=Return to entry page
nameNotEntered=I can't greet you if you don't enter your name!
hello=Hello,
```

This file is called a message resource bundle. It is nothing but a Java properties file that maps key names to message text. Note that the name of the file is MessageResources_en.properties. The MessageResources portion you will recognize from the ActionServlet configuration. The _en part is the locale. In other words, if you wanted to localize your application in German, create a file called MessageResources_de.properties and change the text accordingly (the keys remain the same, of course). Struts and JSTL (which we'll discuss shortly) can automatically switch between them based on the locale the browser passes in. This makes providing internationalization (i18n) support in your application child's play! Note that there are actually two resource bundles, one with no locale part in its name, and the one with _en in it. The one without _en is the default bundle, as this will be used when no locale-specific version is found.

The next file up for review is struts-config.xml, shown in Listing 9-3.

Listing 9-3. *struts-config.xml for Simple Struts Example App*

```
<?xml version="1.0" encoding="ISO-8859-1" ?>

<!DOCTYPE struts-config PUBLIC
"-//Apache Software Foundation//DTD Struts Configuration 1.2//EN"
"http://jakarta.apache.org/struts/dtds/struts-config_1_2.dtd">

<struts-config>

  <form-beans>
    <form-bean name="mainForm" type="org.apache.struts.action.DynaActionForm">
      <form-property name="firstName" type="java.lang.String" />
      <form-property name="lastName" type="java.lang.String" />
    </form-bean>
  </form-beans>

  <global-forwards>
    <forward name="showMainPage" path="/main.jsp" />
  </global-forwards>

  <action-mappings>
    <action path="/greetPerson"
      type="com.apress.ajaxprojects.simplestruts.GreetPersonAction"
      name="mainForm" scope="request" validate="false">
      <forward name="default" path="/greeting.jsp" />
    </action>
  </action-mappings>

  <message-resources parameter="MessageResources" />

</struts-config>
```

There is quite a bit more that can be present in `struts-config.xml`, but as a simple example, this is all we'll include. The first element, the `<form-beans>` element, defines `ActionForm` objects, known as form beans. In Struts, a form bean maps to an HTML form. When the HTML form is submitted, Struts populates the `ActionForm` from the request parameters. Likewise, when a page is displayed, Struts will populate the HTML form from the `ActionForm`. This means you do not have to deal with marshaling and unmarshaling data. Struts can also handle many types of conversions from Strings to native types because it uses Commons BeanUtils to populate the `ActionForm`. That being said, the original intent of an `ActionForm` was to be a Data Transfer Object (DTO) between the browser and the control layer of the application, and as such, only `Strings` should generally be present in an `ActionForm`. There is some controversy about this nowadays, but that is in line with the original intent.

In this particular case, we are using a `DynaActionForm`. A plain old `ActionForm` requires you to write a class that extends `ActionForm`. This class tends to be little else but private `String` members and a public getter and setter for each. As you can imagine, that code is fairly mundane and tedious to write and maintain. The `DynaActionForm` alleviates the needs to write such a class by defining the class via XML. In this case we are creating a form bean with two fields, firstName and lastName, and defining their types as String. We also give a name to this bean definition, mainForm. This will be used later in the configuration to reference the bean.

The next section is the <global-forwards> section. In Struts, after your code has executed in an Action class (coming soon!), you reference a given forward configured in struts-config.xml. This forward names the path to go to. Here we have declared a single forward named showMainPage, which points to the main.jsp page. This allows you to separate the actual JSP to go to from what the Actions do. For instance, if we have an Action that returns the showMainPage forward, and we later decide that instead of main.jsp being shown we want to show someOtherPage.jsp, all we need to do is change the path configured in the forward; the code in the Action remains the same.

The next section is where the majority of work is done in a struts-config.xml file, the action mappings. An action mapping corresponds to a URI that a client can request, and what happens when that URI is requested. In this case, we have defined something to happen when the URI greetPerson.do is requested (remember that the Struts ActionServlet will only react to a URI ending with the configured extension, .do in this case). When that URI is requested, Struts will do a number of things. First, it will find the matching <action> mapping, and see if it has a value for the name attribute. This references a form bean, mainForm in this case. Next, it looks for the scope attribute. If scope is "session", Struts will check if the form bean exists in session already. If not, Struts will create a new instance of it. If scope is "request", Struts will instantiate a new instance with every request. At that point, now that Struts has an instance of the form bean, whether a new one or a recycled one from session, it populates it from the request parameters. Next, it looks at the validate attribute. If this were true, the validate() method of the form bean would be called, where you could write code to ensure valid user input. If that code indicates validation has failed, Struts would look for an input attribute, which would name the page we were coming from, and it would return to that page.

However, in this example, no validation is being done, so the input attribute is not present. Next, Struts looks at the type attribute and instantiates an instance of the named class. Assuming it is a subclass of Action (if it was not then Struts would throw an exception), the execute() method of the action is called. This method returns an ActionForward, which corresponds to a forward in struts-config.xml. The forward can be either a global forward as previously discussed, or a <forward> element configured as a child of the <action> mapping. In this example, we have one such forward named default. Struts will then forward the request to the path named by the forward, greeting.jsp in this case.

The last element to discuss is the <message-resources> element. This is the same thing as the init parameter of the ActionServlet. This information is required by Struts in both places to function properly.

Now, let's examine the code in Listing 9-4, which is the source for our single Action in the example application.

Listing 9-4. *The GreetPersonAction Class*

```
package com.apress.ajaxprojects.simplestruts;


import javax.servlet.http.HttpServletRequest;
import javax.servlet.http.HttpServletResponse;
import org.apache.struts.action.Action;
import org.apache.struts.action.ActionForm;
```

```
import org.apache.struts.action.ActionForward;
import org.apache.struts.action.ActionMapping;
import org.apache.struts.action.DynaActionForm;

public class GreetPersonAction extends Action {

  public ActionForward execute(ActionMapping mapping, ActionForm form,
    HttpServletRequest request, HttpServletResponse response) throws Exception {

      // Get the two parameters from request.
      DynaActionForm f         = (DynaActionForm)form;
      String         firstName = (String)f.get("firstName");
      String         lastName  = (String)f.get("lastName");

      // See if they entered a first and last name.
      if (firstName == null || lastName == null ||
        firstName.equalsIgnoreCase("") || lastName.equalsIgnoreCase("") ) {
        // They didn't so mildly scold them.
        request.setAttribute("greeting",
          getResources(request).getMessage(getLocale(request),
          "nameNotEntered"));
      } else {
        // They did, so greet them.
        request.setAttribute("greeting",
          getResources(request).getMessage(getLocale(request),
          "hello") + " " + firstName + " " + lastName + "!");
      }

      // Return the ForwardConfig that tells us where to go next.
      return mapping.findForward("default");

    } // End execute().

} // End class.
```

As mentioned, all Actions ultimately extend, or inherit, from the base Action class, as we have done here. An Action should override the execute() method. This method receives as parameters the action mapping that corresponds to this request, the ActionForm instance (or null if there was none), and the request and response objects being serviced. Notice that all ActionForms, like Actions, extend from a common class, ActionForm in this case.

The first thing this class does is retrieve the firstName and lastName parameters from the request by way of the ActionForm. We need to cast the ActionForm to DynaActionForm first, then we simply call the get() method, requesting the appropriate parameter.

The next thing we do is check if firstName and lastName were entered. If they were not, we return a message saying that we cannot greet them. To do this, we call

```
getResources(request).getMessage(getLocale(request), "nameNotEntered")
```

This looks up the message nameNotEntered in our resource file, taking the locale into account. We then simply set this text into a request attribute named greeting. If the user did enter the parameters, though, we set a string under the same request attribute key that greets them by name, again using the resource bundle to keep it internationalized.

At the end, we return the forward named default. By calling mapping.findForward(), we are asking the action mapping to find that forward. If it did not find one under the mapping itself, as we have configured here, it would then look up a global forward under the same name.

When this returns, Struts forwards to the appropriate path, a JSP in this case, and the request completes.

The last thing to look at is the three JSPs that comprise our view, shown in Listings 9-5, 9-6, and 9-7.

Listing 9-5. *index.jsp*

```
<%@ taglib prefix="logic" uri="http://jakarta.apache.org/struts/tags-logic" %>
<logic:redirect forward="showMainPage" />
```

It is fairly typical to have a Struts app start with a page similar to that shown in Listing 9-5. This is also the default welcome page of the webapp as defined in web.xml. This page does nothing but immediately redirect to a forward named showMainPage. In essence, this allows us to “bootstrap” the application startup, and perhaps perform some extra initialization tasks. We are not doing any of that here, however.

This page makes use of one of the Struts taglibs, Logic. This taglib contains the redirect function that is used to launch things.

Listing 9-6. *main.jsp*

```
<%@ taglib prefix="html" uri="http://jakarta.apache.org/struts/tags-html" %>
<%@ taglib prefix="fmt" uri="http://java.sun.com/jstl/fmt" %>
<html:html>
  <head>
    <title><fmt:message key="title" /></title>
  </head>
  <style>
    .cssEntryPrompt {
      font-family          : sans-serif;
      font-size            : 14pt;
      font-style           : italic;
      font-weight          : bold;
    }
    .cssLabel {
      font-family          : sans-serif;
      font-size            : 12pt;
      background-color     : #f0f0f0;
    }
    .cssText {
      font-family          : sans-serif;
```

```
      font-size           : 12pt;
      background-color    : #ffff00;
    }
    .cssBtn{
      color               : #050;
      font-family         : sans-serif;
      font-size           : 84%;
      font-weight         : bold;
      background-color    : #fed;
      border              : 1px solid;
      border-top-color    : #696;
      border-left-color   : #696;
      border-right-color  : #363;
      border-bottom-color : #363;
    }
  </style>
  <body>
    <div class="cssEntryPrompt"><fmt:message key="entryPrompt" /></div>
    <br>
    <html:form action="/greetPerson.do">
      <table border="0" cellpadding="2" cellspacing="2">
        <tr>
          <td class="cssLabel"><fmt:message key="firstNamePrompt" /> </td>
          <td class="cssText"><html:text property="firstName" /></td>
        </tr>
        <tr>
          <td class="cssLabel"><fmt:message key="lastNamePrompt" /> </td>
          <td class="cssText"><html:text property="lastName" /></td>
        </tr>
        <tr>
          <td colspan="2" align="right"><html:submit styleClass="cssBtn"/></td>
        </tr>
      </table>
    </html:form>
  </body>
</html:html>
```

Listing 9-6 shows the first page the user actually sees. Here, we are simply prompting them for their first name and last name. This will be our first introduction to JSTL as well.

Before that, though, we see that we are using another Struts taglib, the HTML taglib. This is probably the one that is used most often. Virtually every HTML tag has a corresponding Struts HTML tag. Probably the most important of those is the `<html:form>` tag, and the tags that are children of it (`<html:text>` and `<html:submit>`, for instance).

The `<html:form>` element, at its simplest, takes just the `action` attribute, which corresponds to the action mapping defined in `struts-config.xml`. With this information, Struts can generate the appropriate `action` attribute for the form tag, taking URL structure into account. It can also determine the `ActionForm`, if any, to use to populate this form.

Under the <html:form> element we see the <html:text> elements. These map to properties of the ActionForm reference in the mapping. Struts can then pull the appropriate values from the bean and add value attributes to these elements. So, for instance, if the user entered a first name but not a last name, and we were doing validation on the bean, when control was returned to this page the first name the user entered could be populated automatically so they would not have to enter it again, which is good UI design.

Lastly we have an <html:submit> tag, which renders a typical form submit button.

Mixed in with all this Struts HTML taglib stuff is some JSTL in the form of the <fmt:message> tag. JSTL, which is an acronym for Java Standard Tag Library, is a set of custom tags created by Sun that performs common tasks in JSP development. In fact, the Struts taglibs existed for a long time before JSTL came out, but JSTL now can do almost everything the Struts taglibs can, except for the HTML taglib, so in general you will want to favor JSTL over Struts taglibs if for no other reason than they are more standardized. They also happen to be quite a bit simpler and much more logical to boot. There is no analogy for the Struts HTML taglib in JSTL, though, so you will still use that taglib.

The <fmt:message> tag simply inserts a message, in this case taken from our message resource bundle. We simply specify the key of the message to insert, and JSTL takes care of it, including using the proper locale (that was the purpose of that context parameter in web.xml by the way—to tell JSTL we want to enable internationalization support).

Listing 9-7. *greeting.jsp*

```
<%@ taglib prefix="html" uri="http://jakarta.apache.org/struts/tags-html" %>
<%@ taglib prefix="fmt" uri="http://java.sun.com/jstl/fmt" %>
<%@ taglib prefix="c" uri="http://java.sun.com/jstl/core" %>
<html>
  <head>
    <title><fmt:message key="title" /></title>
  </head>
  <style>
    .cssMessage {
      font-size   : 14pt;
      color       : #ff0000;
      font-style  : italic;
      font-weight : bold;
    }
  </style>
  <body>
    <div class="cssMessage"><c:out value="${requestScope.greeting}" /></div>
  </body>
  <br>
  <html:link forward="showMainPage">
    <fmt:message key="returnToEntryPage" />
  </html:link>
</html>
```

Listing 9-7 shows the greeting.jsp page, which is what the user sees when they click Submit on the form on the main.jsp page. Here we are using the code JSTL taglib, prefixed with the letter c. The <c:out> tag is used to display values from various places. In this case we want to display the request attribute named greeting. To do this, we use what is known as JSTL Expression Language, or EL. EL allows us to easily reference information from a number of various scopes, in this case requestScope.

It is worth noting that in the latest servlet spec, you do not even have to use the <c:out> tag; you can simply put ${requestScope.greeting}. This would also necessitate changing the <web-app> tag in web.xml to specify version 2.4 and also specify the correct namespaces. The full tag would then be

```
<web-app version="2.4" xmlns="http://java.sun.com/xml/ns/j2ee"
  xmlns:xsi="http://www.w3.org/2001/XMLSchema-instance"
  xsi:schemaLocation="http://java.sun.com/xml/ns/j2ee
  http://java.sun.com/xml/ns/j2ee/web-app_2_4.xsd">
```

I chose not to do this in this book to ensure a wider range of app servers and versions that the apps would run under. However, it is hard to argue that it is not a cleaner syntax, so if you know that your app server supports the 2.4 servlet spec, I encourage you to change a few of the <c:out> tags accordingly, just to see it in action.

The other new tag here is the <html:link> tag. This is the Struts wrapper around the HTML <a> tag. It again allows us to reference a given forward, and Struts deals with all the path construction issues for us.

So, how does this all work? First, what the user sees is shown sequentially in Figures 9-1, 9-2, and 9-3.

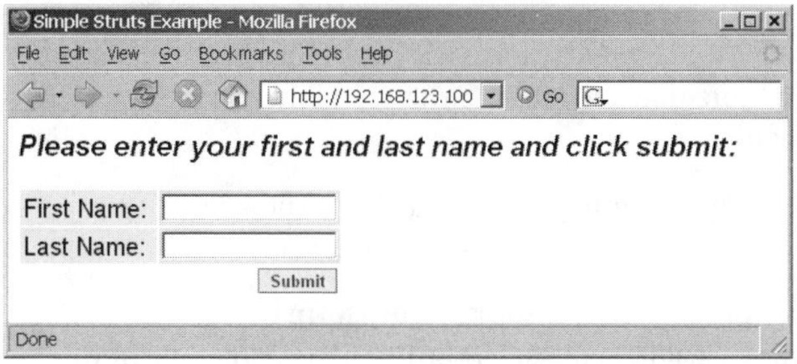

Figure 9-1. *The first page the user sees*

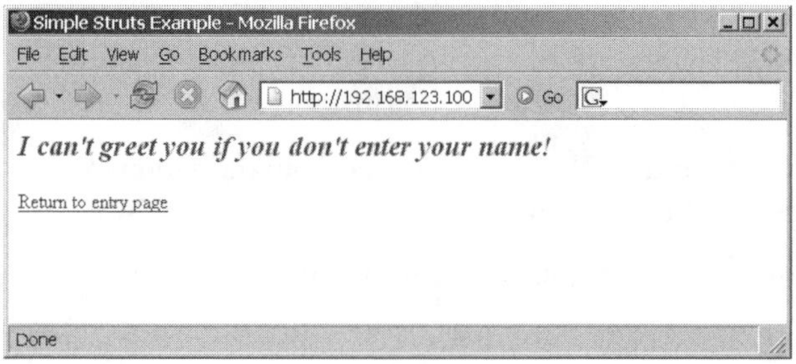

Figure 9-2. *The second page the user sees if they do not enter both a first and last name*

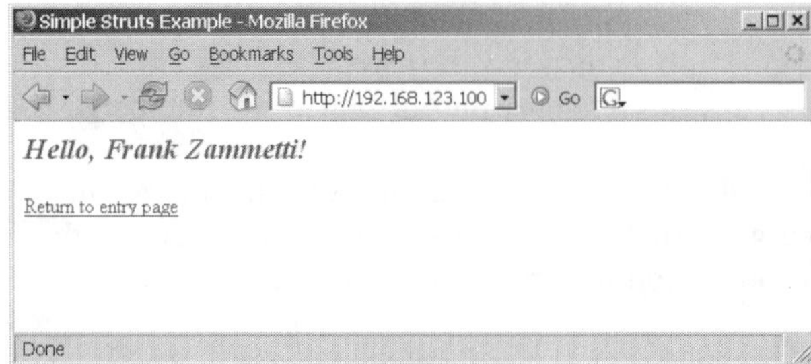

Figure 9-3. *The second page the user sees if they enter both a first and last name*

Not much to look at, but then, it does not need to look like much! Even still, just a few minor CSS usages—like the font settings on the entry page, with the instructions in italic; the background colors in the table; the Submit button being stylized; and finally the greeting in large, bold red text—all spruce things up just a little.

To make sure this is all clear with regard to Struts, let's walk through the exact sequence of events that occurs:

- The user accesses the application, for example, using the URL `http://localhost:8080/simplestruts` (your URL may vary depending on your configuration).
- The `index.jsp` page is rendered, which returns a redirect to the browser.
- The browser is redirected to `showMainPage.do`, which causes `main.jsp` to be rendered.
- The page is rendered, and the user sees the entry form with no values in it because no form bean has been created yet (note that `showMainPage.do` is a global forward, which does not reference any form bean).
- The user simply clicks Submit without entering any information. The URI `greetPerson.do` is requested, which hits the Struts `ActionServlet`.
- `ActionServlet` sees that this mapping references the `mainForm` form bean, so it checks what scope the bean is in. In this case it is "request", so Struts simply creates a new instance of the form bean and populates it from the request.
- `ActionServlet` then instantiates `GreetPersonAction`. In point of fact, Struts instantiates all `Actions` when it starts up, so in reality the `Action` is not instantiated with each request. This is not terribly important except for the fact that you need to avoid using class members in an `Action` because otherwise the `Action` will not be thread-safe. In any case, however, Struts then calls `execute()` on the `Action` instance.
- In `GreetPersonAction`, the `firstName` and `lastName` are retrieved from the action form Struts passed in. They are checked to be sure something was entered.
- If either or both were not entered, a message mildly scolding the user is placed in the request attribute greeting.
- If both were entered, a greeting message is placed in that same attribute.

- The forward named default is then looked up and returned. In this case it is a local forward defined for the mapping, which causes Struts to forward the request to `greeting.jsp`.
- The JSP `greeting.jsp` displays the request attribute set in the `Action` and displays a link to return to `main.jsp` where the entry form is.

And that, in an admittedly very brief nutshell, is Struts! Struts has a great deal more to offer, and if you have never used it before then you should definitely go have a look now. For this purposes of this project, however, you should now be ready to proceed.

Visualizing the Finish Line

So, getting back to the task at hand, creating AjaxChat, we first should know what we're building, so what follows is some screenshots and description of AjaxChat. The application essentially consists of three distinct screens: the "login" screen, the list of rooms (called the lobby), and the chat room itself.

Figure 9-4 shows the login screen. This screen is pretty simple, although we do have some eye candy in the form of a shadowed inset text box and a metallic-looking button. This screen is just a greeting and a place to enter a username. It is not a security login, mind you; it is simply a way for users to give themselves a name to chat under.

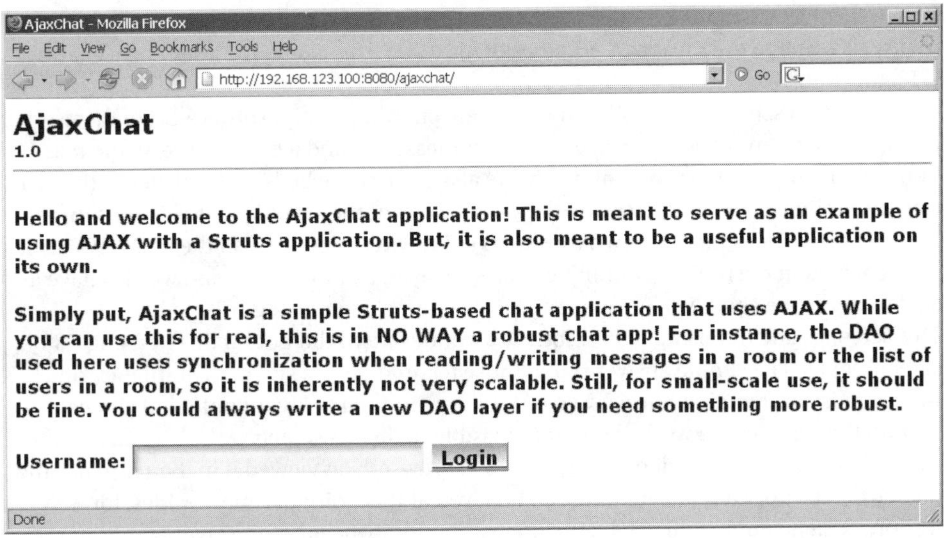

Figure 9-4. *The AjaxChat login page*

The next screen, the room list screen, is shown in Figure 9-5. This screen shows all the available chat rooms, and how many users are chatting in each. It also provides a logout button. This serves to clear out the user's session and ensures that they do not appear to still be chatting in any rooms.

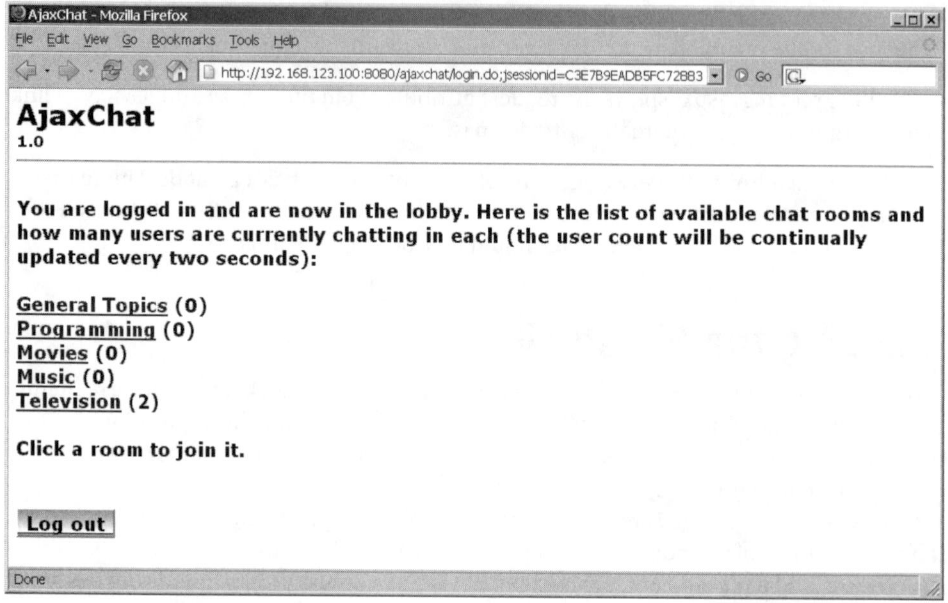

Figure 9-5. *The rooms list page*

Lastly, we come to the meat and potatoes of AjaxChat: the screen representing a chat room (Figure 9-6).

The chat room screen tells us what room we are chatting in, and shows a list of the users in the room with it. It provides a place to enter our messages, and a place to see all the messages posted to the room since we entered it. We also have some bells and whistles in the form of two icons for increasing or decreasing the size of the font the message scroll is seen in, as well as select boxes to change our own message's color and the color of all the messages of all the other chatters in the room. Naturally, we have a way to exit the room, and we also have a button that clears the chat history so we can have a nice, clean message display.

This screen is laid out using tables. You may wonder why I did not do this by using CSS layout techniques. The simple answer is that those techniques are still in their infancy, and cross-browser issues remain to be worked out. Tables are still my layout option of choice, and will be until those issues are worked out. It *is* possible to do this screen with CSS and no tables, but it would have been fragile depending on which browser you viewed it in. Better to use the technology that is more ubiquitous and well behaved at this point in time. Besides, for web applications, CSS layout is somewhat less interesting simply because the layout tends to not change as much. For websites, where content delivery is the primary concern, CSS layout has much more to offer.

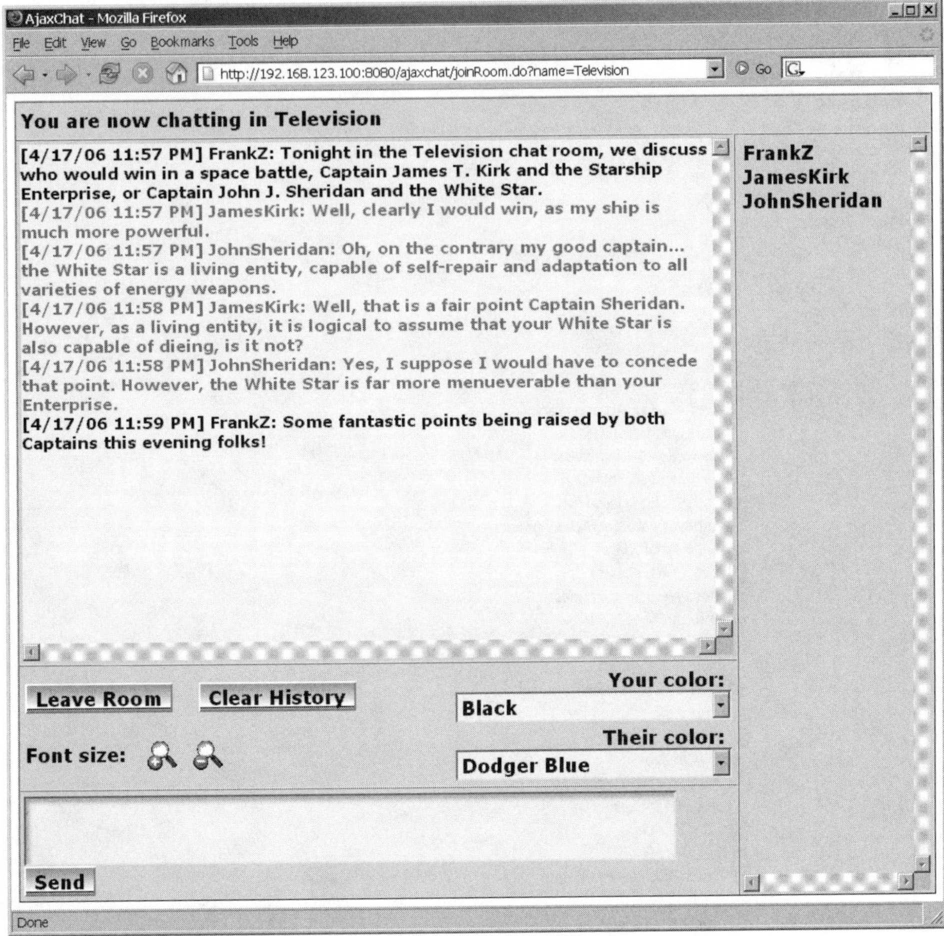

Figure 9-6. *Where it all happens: the chat room screen*

Enough of the tables versus CSS layout debate—let's get into some code!

Dissecting the Solution

As with other projects in this book, download the full source from the Apress website and follow along here. There is too much code to commit to print here, but I will call out bits and pieces where appropriate; otherwise, downloading and following along is very important.

To begin, let's look at the file layout of the project, as shown in Figure 9-7.

Figure 9-7. *Directory structure layout of AjaxChat*

Once more, we see our typical webapp structure. AjaxChat consists of three JSPs:

- `index.jsp`, which is our welcome page and where the user "logs in"
- `lobby.jsp`, which is where the chat room list is
- `room.jsp`, which of course is the JSP for inside a chat room

Interestingly, they go in exactly that order in terms of complexity!

All three of them reference the stylesheet `styles.css` in the `css` directory. All three also make use of the `buttonBG.gif` and `textBG.gif` images for stylizing buttons. The last two images, `zoomDown.gif` and `zoomUp.gif`, are used in the room to provide for text zooming capabilities.

In the `inc` directory we find a single file, `color_options.inc`. This file is included in the `room.jsp` file when rendered (a server-side include) and contains all the `<option>`s for the dropdowns where colors can be selected. Because there are so many of them, having it all in one place is definitely advisable.

The `WEB-INF` directory contains `web.xml`, as usual for a Java webapp, and also contains `struts-config.xml`, the Struts configuration file. In this directory you will also find `app-config.xml`, which is a custom configuration file where a few parameters for the application are stored. Lastly, you will find `rooms-config.xml`, which is the file where the chat rooms available to chatters are stored.

The `WEB-INF/classes` directory is where the beginning of our server-side Java classes are. We can see that there are quite a few, and we'll of course be going over them all in detail. In brief, however, the classes found in the `action` directory are our Struts `Actions`. The single class found in the `actionform` directory is our Struts `ActionForm` (only one is found here; two others are `DynaActionForms` defined in `struts-config.xml`). The single class in the `daemon` directory is a background thread that will be used to clean up users when they leave the application. The `dao` directory contains the single data access object AjaxChat uses. The `dto` directory contains three data transfer object classes used by AjaxChat to store information about rooms, users, and individual messages. In the `filter` directory you will find a single servlet filter used to check whether a request references a valid session as far as AjaxChat is concerned. The `listener` directory contains a single `ContextListener` that is used to initialize AjaxChat. Finally, the root `ajaxchat` directory contains a single class that is used to store some configuration information.

Finally, the `WEB-INF/lib` folder contains all the libraries that AjaxChat depends on, and they are listed in Table 9-1.

Table 9-1. *The JARs That AjaxChat Depends On, Found in WEB-INF.lib*

JAR	Description
`commons-logging-1.0.4.jar`	Jakarta Commons Logging is an abstraction layer that sits on top of a true logging implementation (like Log4J), which allows you to switch the underlying logging implementation without affecting your application code. It also provides a simple logger that outputs to `System.out`, which is what this application uses.
`commons-beanutils-1.7.0.jar`	The Jakarta Commons BeanUtils library, needed by Digester.
`commons-digester-1.7.jar`	Jakarta Commons Digester is a library for parsing XML and generating objects from it. It is used to parse some messages passed to the server by the client code.
`commons-lang-2.1.jar`	Jakarta Commons Lang are utility functions that enhance the Java language. Needed by Digester.
`commons-validator-1.0.2.jar`	The Commons Validator package, used to provide declarative validation in Struts applications.

continued

Table 9-1. *Continued*

JAR	Description
javawebparts_listener_v1.0_beta3.jar	The Java Web Parts (JWP) listener package, which contains, among other things, a listener for doing application configuration.
javawebparts_core_v1.0_beta3.jar	The JWP core package, required by all other JWP packages.
jstl.jar	The core JAR needed to support JSTL.
standard.jar	The standard set of tags that JSTL provides.
struts-1.2.7.jar	The Struts framework itself.

The Client-Side Code

We'll start our dissection by looking at the configuration files for this application. Let's begin by looking at web.xml.

web.xml

The first context parameter, javax.servlet.jsp.jstl.fmt.localizationContext, tells JSTL we want to internationalize our messages. It also serves to provide the base filename for the properties file.

Next we see the configFile context parameter. This will be used by our ContextListener to locate the configuration file for the application. In this case we are telling it to look for app-config.xml in the WEB-INF directory, relative to the context.

The last context parameter we see is configClass. This is the class that will be populated with our configuration information, com.apress.ajaxprojects.ajaxchat.AjaxChatConfig in this case.

After the context parameters comes a single filter configuration of the SessionChecker filter. We'll go into what that filter does later, but for now it is enough to know that it will fire for every request ending in *.do made to this context.

After the filter configuration comes a ContextListener configuration. Here we are using the AppConfigContextListener that can be found in Java Web Parts. This listener allows us to read in a configuration file and populate a config object in various ways. Here, we have a very simple configuration, so the default behavior is used: the named class will be instantiated, each element in the config file will be read in, and the corresponding setter in the instantiated object will be called. This listener can deal with more complex config files, as well as provide a default simple bean for storing the configuration information. Have a look; it is a pretty handy part!

The next section of web.xml declares our Struts Action servlet. This will look very much like we saw earlier in our brief foray into the world of Struts. Note the detail and debug parameters. This determines the level of logging Struts will do for us.

After that comes configuration of the session timeout. We set the value so that a session will expire after one minute. This is because a session is not established until after the user "logs in," and after that we have Ajax calls continually firing every few seconds. So, a session should never get close to a minute old. If it does, and the session expires, it likely means the user navigated away from the chat application, and we want to catch that situation as quickly as possible so we can clear them out of any room they were in. A minute is usually the smallest value you can set for a session timeout, although some containers may allow for a finer level of granularity. A minute should work for us, though.

Lastly, we configure the welcome page to `index.jsp`, so any request that comes in that does not reference a particular document (or end in `*.do`) will be routed to this JSP, which is our application's starting point.

struts-config.xml

The next configuration file we'll examine is `struts-config.xml`. Here we see a mixture of `DynaActionForms`, as we saw earlier, as well as "regular" `ActionForms`, that is, one for which you provide a class extending `ActionForm`. This is done simply to demonstrate that both work fine when doing Ajax in a Struts-based application. The `LobbyActionForm` and `LoginActionForm` correspond to the `lobby.jsp` page and the `index.jsp` page, respectively. The `ajaxPostMessageActionForm` is the bean that will be used when posting a message in a room. Many times you will see that an Ajax-based webapp goes directly to the request object to get incoming parameters, but I wanted to show that an Ajax request that is not XML-based would populate an `ActionForm` just the same as a non-Ajax request.

After that come the action mappings. They are broken down into those that deal with Ajax requests and those that do not. There is nothing different about them; I just organized them that way for clarity's sake. The mappings are described in Table 9-2.

Table 9-2. *The Action Mappings Used in AjaxChat*

Path	Description
`/login`	This mapping is called when the user clicks the Login button on the starting page (`index.jsp`).
`/logout`	This mapping is called when the user clicks the Logout button on the lobby screen (`lobby.jsp`).
`/lobby`	This mapping is called to show the lobby screen (`lobby.jsp`). This is essentially a "setup" `Action` for that screen.
`/joinRoom`	This mapping is called when the user clicks on one of the chat rooms to enter it on the lobby screen (`lobby.jsp`).
`/leaveRoom`	This mapping is called when the user clicks the Leave Room button on the chat room screen (`room.jsp`).
`/ajaxListUsersInRoom`	This mapping is called via an Ajax call to refresh the list of users in the room when chatting in a room (the right-hand pane on the side, `room.jsp`). Note that this is called periodically to keep the list of users fresh.
`/ajaxPostMessage`	This mapping is called via an Ajax call to post a message to the room the user is currently chatting in (`room.jsp`).
`/ajaxGetMessages`	This mapping is called periodically to get the list of messages posted to the room since the last one the client viewed (`room.jsp`).
`/ajaxLobbyUpdateStats`	This mapping is called periodically to refresh the number of chatters in each room when on the lobby screen (`lobby.jsp`).

Conceptually, as far as the Ajax-related mappings go, only the `ajaxPostMessage` mapping is really an "input" mapping, meaning it is the only one that uses an `ActionForm`. No validation is performed on it, as per the mapping configuration.

The last item in `struts-config.xml` is the message resource bundle declaration. This is the same as we saw before, so there's no need to go into it.

app-config.xml

You will find two other configuration files involved in this application: `app-config.xml` and `room-config.xml`. The former defines overall application settings, and the latter is a list of the available chat rooms. First is `app-config.xml`, shown in Listing 9-8.

Listing 9-8. *app-config.xml for AjaxChat*

```
<config>

  <!-- maxMessages is the maximum number of messages that will be stored in -->
  <!-- the messages collection of each room.  Any time a message is posted -->
  <!-- to a room, the number of messages in the collection is checked -->
  <!-- against this value.  If the count exceeds this value, the collection -->
  <!-- is cleared before the new messages is stored.  This is just a -->
  <!-- memory-saving measure, and probably makes things a bit more -->
  <!-- efficient too. -->
  <maxMessages>250</maxMessages>

  <!-- userInactivitySeconds is the maximum number of seconds that can -->
  <!-- elapse between Ajax requests before a user is considered inactive. -->
  <!-- When a user is considered inactive, they are forcibly removed -->
  <!-- from all rooms and from the application.  This is to deal with the -->
  <!-- case of a user closing the browser window without properly logging -->
  <!-- out, or possibly a JavaScript error that stops the Ajax request -->
  <!-- timers.  Note that this was originally done in a SessionListener, -->
  <!-- but because of problems seem in some containers, this had to be -->
  <!-- done instead. -->
  <userInactivitySeconds>15</userInactivitySeconds>

</config>
```

The comments pretty much tell the whole story. If they were paying me by the page I would be inclined to regurgitate the comments here, but they aren't, so I won't!

rooms-config.xml

Moving on, we come to `rooms-config.xml`, shown in Listing 9-9.

Listing 9-9. *rooms-config.xml for AjaxChat*

```
<rooms>
  <room name="General Topics" />
  <room name="Programming" />
  <room name="Movies" />
  <room name="Music" />
  <room name="Television" />
</rooms>
```

This is literally nothing more than a listing of the available chat rooms in XML format. The only information it conveys is the name of the room, so it really is as simple as it looks.

index.jsp

Now that we have the configuration files out of the way, let's move on the JSPs that make up AjaxChat. I am a big believer in simplicity and having as few source files as possible, and so there are a grand total of three JSPs to look at. First up is `index.jsp`.

Most of this we have seen already in our simple Struts example. Note the use of JSTL to display the page title and the two chunks of text at the top of the page. After that we see this section:

```
<logic:messagesPresent>
  <font color="#ff0000">
    <html:messages id="error">
      <bean:write name="error" />
    </html:messages>
  </font>
  <br/><br/>
</logic:messagesPresent>
```

Contained within Struts are functions for returning messages to the client. It does this by placing the messages under a known request attribute key. Rather than having to pull that attribute out yourself and see if there were any messages passed back, you can use the `<logic:messagesPresent>` tag, which will render the content it encloses only if there are messages present. `<html:messages>` will loop through the messages and display them. Here we tell it to display errors, which is a known value to Struts. The `<bean:write>` tag literally writes out the error message.

This page contains a single form where the user can enter their username. One neat trick is this part:

```
<html:submit styleClass="cssButton">
  <fmt:message key="labels.loginButton" />
</html:submit>
```

You cannot embed one custom tag within another, which means this won't work:

```
<html:submit styleClass="cssButton"
  value="<fmt:message key="labels.loginButton" />" />
```

This will not be interpreted and will result in an exception being thrown. The solution is to use the fact that a <submit> tag can wrap some text, which becomes the value, that is, the label, of the button. In this way, we can still use our internationalized message bundle.

lobby.jsp

Next is the JSP lobby.jsp. Let's talk about the markup first, since it is simpler. First, we display a heading at the top and the version of the application. We then show a message for the user. After this is the <div> with the id roomList:

```
<div id="roomList">
  <c:forEach var="roomName" items="${LobbyActionForm.rooms}">
    <a href="<c:url value="joinRoom.do">
      <c:param name="name" value="${roomName}" /></c:url>">
      <c:out value="${roomName}" />
    </a>
    <br/>
  </c:forEach>
</div>
<br/>
```

Here we are introduced to some new JSTL tags. First is the <c:forEach> tag. This tag accepts an EL expression in the items attribute that tells it to find a bean named LobbyActionForm in any scope (request scope in this case) and iterate over the rooms collection in it, which in this case is a simple Java String, and for each element present it to us under the name roomName. If we had instead had a collection of RoomDTO objects in the rooms collection, I might have set the var attribute to room, and then later I could reference individual properties of the object by modifying the EL expressions. Here, though, we have just a String. We are constructing a URL from this that the user can click to join the room, so we use the <c:url>, which constructs a URL for us. We need to append a parameter named name to the URL as a query string, and give it the value of the room name. Because the room names could have spaces or other problematic characters in a URL, using the <c:param> tag inside the <c:url> tag is good because it deals with encoding the parameter properly for us. After that we use the <c:out> tag, which writes out the value named. In this case we use an EL expression, which tells the tag to write out the roomName variable, which is our room name. Just to drive the point home (especially if JSTL is new to you), if we were dealing with a collection of RoomDTO objects instead of just Strings, and var had the value room instead, the EL expressions could be ${room.roomName} instead, to reference the roomName property of the current RoomDTO object referenced by the room variable.

The interesting thing to note is that this whole section is only important when the page is first shown. After that, we'll have a periodic Ajax event that overwrites the contents of the <div>. While it is true that what is written out is essentially the same, with the addition of the number of chatters in each room, the difference is that it will be written from with a Struts Action and will not use JSTL like this.

With the markup complete, we can now shift our attention to the JavaScript on the page. First, we encounter a few page-scoped variables, as summarized in Table 9-3.

Table 9-3. *Page-Scoped Variables on lobby.jsp*

Variable	Description
`assureUnique`	Internet Explorer is perhaps a little overaggressive in its caching scheme with regard to GET requests. If the URL is identical, IE will use a previously cached result, if any. Here this would mean that the stats would never be updated after the first time. To avoid this, we append a parameter to the requested URL that makes it unique with every request, thereby avoiding this problem.
`xhrLobbyUpdateStats`	This is a reference to the `XMLHttpRequest` object that will be used to fire the periodic Ajax stats update event.
`timerLobbyUpdateStats`	This is a reference to the timer that will fire to make our periodic stats update happen.
`lobbyUpdateStatsDelay`	This is the number of milliseconds between stats update requests. The default is 2 seconds (2,000 milliseconds).
`sendAjaxRequest`	When the user clicks the logout button, it is possible for an Ajax event to fire after the session has been invalidated, which leads to an exception being thrown. So, when the logout button is clicked, this variable gets set to false, which will cause no subsequent Ajax events to fire.

On page load, the `init()` function is called. Its sole purpose is to start up the timer that will fire our periodic Ajax stats update request. The function that the timer points to is `lobbyUpdateStats()`:

```
/**
 * This function is called as a result of the firing of the
 * timerLobbyUpdateStats timer to make an Ajax request to get counts of
 * users chatting in each room.  This happens continually as the user
 * sits in the lobby.
 */
function lobbyUpdateStats() {

  // Only fire a new event if a previous one has completed, or if the
  // XMLHttpRequest object is in an uninitialized state, or one has not
  // yet been instantiated.
  if (xhrLobbyUpdateStats == null || xhrLobbyUpdateStats.readyState == 0 ||
    xhrLobbyUpdateStats.readyState == 4) {
    // Create XMLHttpRequest object instance based on browser type.
    try {
      if (window.XMLHttpRequest){
        xhrLobbyUpdateStats = new XMLHttpRequest();
      } else {
        xhrLobbyUpdateStats = new ActiveXObject('Microsoft.XMLHTTP');
      }
      // Set the JavaScript function that will act as a callback for
      // any events the instance fires.
```

```
        xhrLobbyUpdateStats.onreadystatechange = lobbyUpdateStatsHandler;
        // Set the target URI for the request.  Note that we append a
        // value that will ensure that the URL is always unique.
        // This is to deal with caching issues in IE.
        target = "<html:rewrite action="ajaxLobbyUpdateStats" />" +
          "?assureUnique=" + assureUnique++;
        // One minor problem that
        if (sendAJAXRequest) {
          xhrLobbyUpdateStats.open("get", target, true);
          xhrLobbyUpdateStats.send(null);
        }
      } catch(e) {
        alert("Error in lobbyUpdateStats() - " + e.message);
      }
    }
    // Restart the timer no matter what happened above.
    timerLobbyUpdateStats = setTimeout("lobbyUpdateStats()",
      lobbyUpdateStatsDelay);

  } // End lobbyUpdateStats().
```

First we do a check of the status of the previous Ajax request, if any. If one had fired, `xhrLobbyUpdateStats` would not be `null`. In that case, we also want to make sure the request completed, or no request took place. Only then should a new event fire.

Once that determination is made, we instantiate a new `XMLHttpRequest` object, in the typical fashion that we have seen previously in this book. We point it to the `lobbyUpdateStatsHandler` callback function, and set the URL appropriately. Notice the use of the `<html:rewrite>` tag. This is a Struts tag from the HTML taglib that writes a proper URL based on a given action mapping. It takes into account the context, current location of the page, and so forth to render a URL that will work properly. Also, we append the `assureUnique` query string parameter to get around the previously mentioned IE caching concern. After that, we fire the request, but only if the `sendAjaxRequest` variable is true. Note that this is done as late in the process as possible so that the user clicking the logout button would register as close to the request being sent as possible in order to avoid micro-timing issues where the two events are close together, but not quite close enough, and the Ajax request fires after the button has been clicked. If that were to happen, it is possible for the session to have been invalidated before the Ajax request hits the server, in which case an exception occurs. While that scenario is technically still possible, checking the variable at this point rather than earlier in the function reduces the chances of it happening as much as possible. Lastly, we fire the timer again so that the next Ajax event will fire. Note that this happens regardless of whether the request gets sent, thereby setting up a continuous loop of requests (or at least potential requests).

Once the Ajax request returns, control winds up in the `lobbyUpdateStatsHandler()` function:

```
/**
 * This is the Ajax callback handler that updates the display.
 */
function lobbyUpdateStatsHandler() {
```

```
    if (xhrLobbyUpdateStats.readyState == 4) {
      if (xhrLobbyUpdateStats.status == 200) {
        // Get the returned XML and parse it, creating our HTML for display.
        newHTML = "";
        msgDOM  = xhrLobbyUpdateStats.responseXML;
        root    = msgDOM.getElementsByTagName("rooms")[0];
        rooms   = root.getElementsByTagName("room");
        for (i = 0; i < rooms.length; i++) {
          room = rooms[i];
          roomName = room.getAttribute("name");
          users = room.getAttribute("users");
          url = "<a href=\"<c:url value="joinRoom.do?name=" />";
          newHTML += url + escape(roomName) + "\">" + roomName + "</a>";
          newHTML += " (" + users + ")<br/>";
        }
        // Update the display.
        objRoomList = document.getElementById("roomList");
        objRoomList.innerHTML = newHTML;
      } else {
        alert("Error in lobbyUpdateStatsHandler() - " +
          xhrLobbyUpdateStats.status);
      }
    }

  } // End lobbyUpdateStatsHandler().
```

First, the result of the event is checked to make sure it completed successfully. Remember that this function will be called numerous times during the lifecycle of the request, but we really only care about when it completes successfully. Our response is a chunk of XML in the form

```
<rooms>
  <room name="xxx" users="yyy" />
</rooms>
```

This is relatively easy to parse. In fact, all we do is get a reference to the XML DOM through the `responseXML` property of `XMLHttpRequest`. We then get the root node (`rooms`), and then from that we get the collection of `<room>` elements. We then iterate over that collection, and for each we get the `name` and `users` attributes. From that we construct the appropriate markup.

Note the use of the `<c:url>` tag here, which we do so that if cookies are disabled, the URL will be rewritten to include the session ID. You should realize that this executes when the page is rendered, *not* on the client when the function is called.

In contrast to the `<c:url>` tag, note that here, we have to handle escaping the room name ourselves since we cannot execute custom tags on the client, and it is at that point that we would know the room name, not when the page is rendered. So, while this produces similar markup to what we saw earlier with JSTL and Struts tags (the only difference is the addition of the user counts here), we cannot use those tags now because their chance to execute has already passed. Instead we construct it using simple string manipulations, and using the JavaScript `escape()` function to URL encode the room name appropriately. `escape()` is a built-in function of JavaScript used to URL encode a string. There is a corresponding `unescape()` function as well to reverse the encoding process.

Once the string of markup is completely formed, we update the `roomList <div>`, and our chore is done! Note too that we'll get an error pop-up if anything but an OK response is received from the server. This is not especially robust error handling, but it gets the job done. Since chances are that a non-200 HTTP result is unrecoverable anyway, there is no point in trying to handle this anymore gracefully than we have.

room.jsp

Finally, we come to the page for the chat room itself, `room.jsp`. Let's again examine the markup first. I do not want to go over all of it because it is, by and large, just plain old HTML with some JSTL mixed in to insert content and you will likely have no trouble examining it yourself. Overall, though, we are looking at a table structure that contains four rows. The first row is the header that stretches across the entire window and displays the current room. The next row contains the chat history area and the user list area. Note that the user list spans across three rows to take up the remainder of the window after the header row. The third row is where the user controls are found, and the fourth row is where the user text input box is found.

One note of interest is in the header. You see the following line:

```
<c:out value="${roomName}" />
```

This is displaying the value of an object named `roomName`, which happens to be in session scope, and is set when the user enters a room. It is simply a `String`. Here we are using an EL expression to display it.

You may momentarily get a quizzical look on your face when you see this piece of code:

```
<input type="button"
  value="<fmt:message key="labels.leaveRoomButton" />"
  class="cssButton" onClick="leaveRoom();" />
```

You may be saying to yourself, "Wait a minute—a few pages back you said you could not nest one tag inside another, yet here you are doing exactly that!" The difference is that you cannot nest *custom* tags within each other. Here we are nesting a JSTL tag within a plain old HTML tag. That works just fine. Earlier I mentioned you could not set the value of the `value` attribute on a Struts `<html:submit>` tag with a JSTL tag, and that is correct. Those are two custom tags, two entities that the JSP interpreter has to interpret. Here it is just inserting a dynamic value into a static piece of text that just happens to be an HTML tag. Incidentally, I had that same quizzical look on my own face for a few seconds over this distinction too!

You will notice the mouse event handlers on the two magnifying glass icons. These set the cursor to a pointer hand (or an arrow on some operating systems and browsers) when you hover over them. This serves as a nice visual cue that it is an interactive element. It is always a good idea to provide such cues to your user whenever possible. This will lead to less confusion over what they can do at any given time, and also gives a more polished appearance to your webapps.

Lastly, notice that the values for the color dropdowns are included. Because both `<select>` boxes have the same values, it would make no sense to duplicate that in both places; hence an include avoids the redundant code.

Now it is time to look at the JavaScript that makes this all work. As I'm sure you can guess, this is where most of the action takes place. First up are again some page-scoped variables, as shown in Table 9-4.

Table 9-4. *Page-Scoped Variables on room.jsp*

Variable	Description
`AssureUniqueUsersInRoom`	This is analogous to the `assureUnique` variable we saw in the `lobby.jsp` page. This is used to ensure a unique request when updating the list of chatters in the room.
`assureUniqueGetMessages`	This is used to ensure a unique request when retrieving messages.
`scrollChatFontSize`	This is the font size the chat history pane is currently displayed in.
`oldUserListHTML`	When we retrieve an updated list of users in the room, we compare it to the HTML currently being displayed. If it is different than this value, and only if it is different, we update the display. This helps avoid a nasty flickering issue that plagues some versions of Firefox. The flicker, while actually still occurring, is barely perceptible because it happens only when people join and leave the room instead of with each request, and this happens infrequently, relative to the frequency of the regular requests at least.
`xhrListUsersInRoom`	The `XMLHttpRequest` object used to retrieve the updated list of users chatting in the room.
`XhrGetMessages`	The `XMLHttpRequest` object used to retrieve the messages posted to the room since the last update request was sent.
`timerListUsersInRoom`	This is the timer that fires periodically to update the user list.
`timerGetMessages`	This is the timer that fires periodically to update the chat history pane.
`listUsersInRoomDelay`	This is the delay between updates of the user list (defaults to 2 seconds).
`getMessagesDelay`	This is the delay between updates of the chat history pane (defaults to 1 second).

The room screen works by having two timers running at all times: one to update the list of messages posted to the room, and the other to update the list of users chatting in the room. Both are these timers are initially kicked off in the `init()` function, called in response to the `onLoad` event. That is all the `init()` function does.

The `listUsersInRoom()` is the function that the timer fires for updating the user list. If you compare this to the `lobbyUpdateStats()` function on the `lobby.jsp` page, you will see that they are virtually identical. For this reason, I'll refrain from going over it in detail. In fact, the same is true of the `getMessages()` function, which is the function fired in response to the other timer. Therefore I won't go over it either. Please do look at it, though, to convince yourself that it is not doing anything differently than you already saw on the `lobby.jsp` page.

The `listUsersInRoomHandler()` function is the callback that does the work when the Ajax call to update the user list returns. It looks like this:

```
/**
 * This function handles state changes for the listUsersInRoom Ajax request.
 */
function listUsersInRoomHandler() {

  if (xhrListUsersInRoom.readyState == 4) {
    if (xhrListUsersInRoom.status == 200) {
      // Get the returned XML and parse it, creating our HTML for display.
      newHTML = "";
      msgDOM  = xhrListUsersInRoom.responseXML;
      root    = msgDOM.getElementsByTagName("users")[0];
      users   = root.getElementsByTagName("user");
      for (i = 0; i < users.length; i++) {
        newHTML += users[i].getAttribute("name") + "<br/>";
      }
      // Update the display.
      if (oldUserListHTML != newHTML) {
        oldUserListHTML = newHTML;
        document.getElementById("userList").innerHTML = newHTML;
      }
    } else {
      alert("Error in listUsersInRoomHandler() - " +
        xhrListUsersInRoom.status);
    }
  }

} // End listUsersInRoomHandler().
```

We are again receiving a response in the form of XML, which looks like this:

```
<users>
  <user name="xxx" />
</users>
```

To parse this document, we start by getting the root element. As we saw previously, we do this by getting a collection of all `<users>` elements and then accessing the first element of the array. From there we get a collection of all the `<user>` elements. We then iterate over that collection and construct some HTML for each, which is in this case just the username with a line break after it. We now compare this constructed HTML to the HTML that was last inserted into the `userList` `<div>`. We do this by comparing what we just built to the value of the `oldUserListHTML` variable, which we stored the last time we updated the `<div>`. You may be wondering why this variable is needed rather than just retrieving the `innerHTML` property of the `<div>`. This is because what some browsers return for the value of that attribute does not precisely match what you inserted. The browser may make minor changes (which do not affect what actually is displayed) such as inserting or removing line breaks. If the browser does this, then our comparison would always yield a false result, and we would therefore be updating the `<div>` more often than we need to. If the value of `oldUserListHTML` is identical to what we just built, there is no reason to update the `<div>`. In Firefox at least, there is a flicker every time you update the `<div>` (this is a known issue, at least in some versions of Firefox). So, we do not want to update the `<div>` anymore than we need to so that the flickering is kept to a minimum. Once our HTML is formed and we have confirmed it is different than what is there now, we insert it into the userList <div> by setting its innerHTML property. And that is how we update a user list!

The next function we come across is the getMessagesHandler(), the callback for the Ajax call that updates the list of messages posted to the room. This is far and away the most complex bit of JavaScript in this application, but even still, it follows a very typical flow: get an XML document, get a collection of some set of tags, iterate over the collection constructing some HTML markup from it, and then insert that markup into a <div>. The XML we are getting back from the server this time looks like this:

```
<messages>
  <message>
    <postedBy>xxx</postedBy>
    <postedDateTime>yyyy</postedDateTime>
    <msgText>zzzz</msgText>
  </message>
</messages>
```

So, we begin with the usual: get the root element <messages>. Then, get a collection of all <message> elements and begin to iterate over it.

As we construct the HTML for each, we find ourselves using the getElementsByTagName() function, which is new. The syntax we wind up using, to get the postedBy value for instance, is

```
postedBy = message.getElementsByTagName("postedBy")[0].firstChild.nodeValue;
```

message is the reference to the <message> element we are currently processing. We request a collection of all the <postedBy> elements under this <message> element. This returns an array again, and since we know we have to deal with only one of them, we again go after the first element in the array. From there we ask for the first child node of that <postedBy> element by accessing the firstChild property. Finally, we grab the nodeValue property, which is what we ultimately were after. It may seem a little convoluted, but that's XML parsing in JavaScript without a library!

This is the way each of the elements under <message> is dealt with. However, recall that we can have separate colors for our messages and for others. The code that accomplishes that is

```
txtColor = "";
if (postedBy == "<c:out value="${user.username}" />") {
  txtColor = document.getElementById("yourColor").value;
} else {
  txtColor = document.getElementById("theirColor").value;
}
newHTML += "<font color=\"" + txtColor + "\">" +
  "[" + postedDateTime + "] " + postedBy + ": " + msgText +
  "</font><br/>";
```

You can see another JSTL tag used here that is doing nothing but outputting the username field of the user object found in session scope. Once again, as we saw with the <c:url> tag previously, this is evaluated when this page is rendered, which means this comparison is actually comparing postedBy to a static string. We match this against the username of the person who posted the message we are working on, and set the color appropriately based on the selections in the dropdowns.

There's one last piece of code to look at in this function:

```
// Update the display.  Note that the first time through we want to
// completely overwrite what's there (just  ), all other times
// we want to add on to what's there.  This is done to avoid the
// borders collapsing and there being a minor visual glitch.
objChatScroll = document.getElementById("chatScroll");
if (newHTML != "") {
  if (objChatScroll.innerHTML == " ") {
    objChatScroll.innerHTML = newHTML;
  } else {
    objChatScroll.innerHTML += newHTML;
  }
}
// Lastly, always scroll to the bottom.
objChatScroll.scrollTop = 1000000;
```

When the page is first displayed, the content of our chat history pane is just a nonbreaking space entity (` `), which needs to be overwritten the first time we update that pane. Any time after that, though, we need to append our markup to it so that we achieve an actual history display. So, we check the current value of the history pane and if it's ` ` then we overwrite; otherwise we append. Lastly, we update the `scrollTop` property of the history pane so that no matter what happens, we'll be at the bottom of the history so that we'll see the most recent messages immediately.

After this comes the `leaveRoom()` method, which is a one-liner that is called when you click the Leave Room button. It simply sets the `location` property of the window to bring the user back to the lobby screen. Notice the use of the Struts `<html:rewrite>` tag to get a URL appropriate for the task, using the `leaveRoom` action mapping. Nice to not have to write the URL yourself, is it not? More important, if you rearrange your pages and change your action mappings, Struts will take care of it for you; there's no need to update the JSP (so long as the mapping name doesn't change).

The `clearHistory()` function comes next, which is called in response to clicking the Clear History button, obviously enough! It simply sets the `innerHTML` of the chat history pane to the ` ` entity, which mimics its starting state.

After that is a utility function, `fullTrim()`. It accepts a string, trims all whitespace from both ends of it, and returns the result. This function is used when posting a message to make sure the user actually entered something, which we'll see shortly. In fact, we'll see that right now!

The `postMessage()` function is called when the user clicks the Send button. It spawns an instance of `XMLHttpRequest`, and sends the text the user entered as a query string parameter. It of course uses the `escape()` function to properly URL encode the string; otherwise things would break pretty quickly during a conversation! Once the message is sent, we also clear out the user entry text box and set focus to it, which is how most chat clients work, so users will probably expect it here as well. Notice that the new message is *not* manually put into the history on the client. Instead, it will only be shown in the history when the next update cycle completes. This saves us from dealing with some synchronization complexities, and also ensures that the message actually got posted to the room.

Following postMessage() are two final functions: increaseChatScrollFontSize() and its bizarre evil twin, decreaseChatScrollFontSize(). Both of these functions work by changing the value of the scrollChatFontSize variable by 2 in the appropriate direction. It then checks the value to be sure it is 8 or more and 48 or less, which are the lower and upper bounds allowed. Finally, it sets the fontSize property of the style object of the chattScroll <div> to the new value. Note that it appends the string "pt" to the end. Firefox requires this, while IE does not, although it works just fine in IE, so this is a nice cross-browser way to change the font size.

AjaxChat uses a stylesheet named styles.css in the /css subdirectory. It is a fairly straightforward stylesheet, so we won't examine it in detail here. One thing I do want to point out, however, is the use of the overflow attribute on the cssRoomUserList and cssRoomChatScroll classes. Setting these attributes to scroll causes the <div> to have scroll bars when the content is larger than its area. That is how we get vertical scroll bars on those sections. They may appear to be inline frames, but they aren't—they are simply layers.

Lastly, as far as presentation goes, we find a file named color_options.inc in the /inc subdirectory. This contains the markup for all the options contained in our color selection dropdowns, a small sample of which is seen here:

```
<option value="#f0f8ff" style="color:#f0f8ff;">Alice Blue</option>
<option value="#faebd7" style="color:#faebd7;">Antique White</option>
<option value="#00ffff" style="color:#00ffff;">Aqua</option>
<option value="#7fffd4" style="color:#7fffd4;">Aquamarine</option>
<option value="#f0ffff" style="color:#f0ffff;">Azure</option>
```

The Server-Side Code

Now that we have examined all the files that effectively make up the presentation of AjaxChat, we'll now begin to explore the server-side code, starting with a simple class, AjaxChatConfig.

AjaxChatConfig.java

AjaxChatConfig is a typical JavaBean with fields that correspond to the possible parameters in app-config.xml. It also contains what is my typical toString() method that I use in most beans:

```
/**
 * Overridden toString method.
 *
 * @return A reflexively built string representation of this bean.
 */
public String toString() {

  String str = null;
  StringBuffer sb = new StringBuffer(1000);
  sb.append("[" + super.toString() + "]={");
  boolean firstPropertyDisplayed = false;
  try {
    Field[] fields = this.getClass().getDeclaredFields();
```

```
      for (int i = 0; i < fields.length; i++) {
        if (firstPropertyDisplayed) {
          sb.append(", ");
        } else {
          firstPropertyDisplayed = true;
        }
        sb.append(fields[i].getName() + "=" + fields[i].get(this));
      }
      sb.append("}");
      str = sb.toString().trim();
    } catch (IllegalAccessException iae) {
      iae.printStackTrace();
    }
    return str;
  } // End toString().
```

This code uses reflection to display the beans' contents, which is very handy during debugging. Note that the fields and accessor methods are all static. This is an easy way to have a global settings cache in effect. You may notice that the mutator methods are not static. This is because Commons Digester is used to populate this object, and Digester requires that it be able to instantiate the object. Therefore, while there is probably no harm in making them static, there is no need either. It is therefore a little safer to make them nonstatic, so that if someone were inclined to improperly populate this object manually, they would have to instantiate it to do so.

LobbyActionForm.java (and all the ActionForms essentially)

Next up we'll look at the one `ActionForm` in AjaxChat, `LobbyActionForm`. As you will recall, a Struts `ActionForm` is really just a simple JavaBean that happens to extend from a specific class (`ActionForm`). It is, like our `AjaxChatConfig` object, just a collection of fields, accessors, and mutators. Also again we see the same `toString()` method as before.

MessageDTO.java

AjaxChat makes use of three DTOs to pass information around. The first of these is the `MessageDTO`.

Notice here that the `postedBy` member is actually of type `UserDTO`, which we'll see in a moment. This DTO contains all the pieces of information that together make up a message posted to a chat room, including who posted it, when the post was made, and of course the text of the message. Otherwise, it is once more just a simple, perfectly typical JavaBean.

RoomDTO.java

The next DTO is the `RoomDTO`. This DTO does a little more than other DTOs, as we'll see. The reason this DTO is slightly different than the rest is that when AjaxChat starts up, an instance of this class will be instantiated for each room configured, and that object will be stored in the `AjaxChatDAO` that we'll look at shortly. It is not simply a container for pieces of information, as most DTOs are. Instead, you could almost think of this DTO as more of a domain object than anything else because it contains some functional code as well. For instance, when a user is added to the room, the `addUser()` method is fired:

```
/**
 * Adds a user to the list of users chatting in the room.  The user WILL NOT
 * be added if they are already in the collection, which should deal with
 * the user clicking the Refresh button on their browser.
 *
 * @param inUser The user to add to the list of users chatting in the room.
 */
public void addUser(UserDTO inUser) {

  if (log.isDebugEnabled()) {
    log.debug("RoomDTO addUser()...");
  }
  boolean userAlreadyInRoom = false;
  for (Iterator it = users.iterator(); it.hasNext();) {
    UserDTO user = (UserDTO)it.next();
    if (user.getUsername().equalsIgnoreCase(inUser.getUsername())) {
      userAlreadyInRoom = true;
    }
  }
  if (!userAlreadyInRoom) {
    if (log.isDebugEnabled()) {
      log.info("Adding user to room: " + inUser);
    }
    users.add(inUser);
    Collections.sort(users);
  }

} // End addUser().
```

This method checks to see if the user is already in the room, and of course does not allow them to join the room if they are. This should generally not happen; the check is performed because it theoretically could under certain very unusual circumstances. This would require certain things happening with precise timing, so it is extremely unlikely. Still, the check is performed to ensure a user is not put in a room twice. This method also sorts the list of users once the user has been added to the collection of users chatting in the room so that when it is displayed it is in alphabetical order (better to do this sort only when someone joins the room to avoid the overhead of doing it with each user list update request).

Just in case you are new to Jakarta Commons Logging (JCL), let me mention that the following code is how logging is done in JCL:

```
if (log.isDebugEnabled()) {
  log.debug("RoomDTO addUser()...");
}
```

The `if` check you see first is called a "code guard." The reason for this is that logging statements, in some cases, should be avoided if not necessary. One of the criteria that determines that necessity is often whether the application is being run in "debug" mode. So, logging statements should generally be wrapped in a code guard to see if the application is running at some specific logging level.

When I said that logging should be avoided in some cases, interestingly, this is *not* one of those cases! When `log.debug()` is called, it will do the equivalent of `log.isDebugEnabled()`. So, you may think that is less efficient because the check will be performed twice here, and you would be right. However, imagine the following logging statement:

```
log.debug("User: " + UserDTO.getName() + ", Age: " + UserDTO.getAge());
```

If you were to execute that without a code guard, the check would only be performed once. However, the problem is that regardless of whether the message actually gets logged—that is, whether the check returns true or false—the string concatenation will always be performed first. Therefore, even if the application is not in debug mode, which means the message would not be logged, you still incur the overhead of the string construction, and that overhead far exceeds that of doing the check twice. So, wrapping such a line in a code guard means that if the message is not going to be logged, that will be determined before the message is constructed, making it considerably more efficient.

So, why is a code guard not necessary in this case? It should be obvious by now: there is no string construction, so there is no penalty for letting `log.debug()` do the check itself, and it would still only happen once. Is there any harm in doing this anyway? In absolute terms, yes, because you will always have a double comparison when the message is to be logged. However, it is a relatively small penalty to pay, and code guards *are* a good habit to have, especially if you ever need to add to the message later—it will be one less thing to think about.

Another place where there is more going on than in a typical DTO is in the `getMessages()` method:

```
/**
 * This method returns all messages after the given datetime.
 *
 * @param  inDateTime  The Datetime from which all subsequent messages
 *                     will be returned.
 * @return             List of messages.
 */
public Vector getMessages(Date inDateTime) {

  if (log.isDebugEnabled()) {
    log.debug("RoomDTO getMessages()...");
  }
  // Scan through the list of messages for the room and find any that were
  // posted after the given datetime, add those to a list to return.
  Vector al = new Vector();
  for (Iterator it = messages.iterator(); it.hasNext();) {
    MessageDTO message = (MessageDTO)it.next();
    if (message.getPostedDateTime().after(inDateTime)) {
```

```
      if (log.isDebugEnabled()) {
        log.debug("Returning message: " + message);
      }
      al.add(message);
    }
  }
  return al;

} // End getMessages().
```

When the client requests the chat history be updated, this method is called. It looks at the date and time that the last such request was made, and only returns messages posted subsequent to that.

One last item to point out is the postMessage() method:

```
/**
 * Posts a message to the room.
 *
 * @param inMessage A MessageDTO instance containing all the necessary
 *                  details for the message being posted.
 */
public void postMessage(MessageDTO inMessage) {

  if (messages.size() > AjaxChatConfig.getMaxMessages()) {
    messages.clear();
  }
  messages.add(inMessage);

} // End addMessage().
```

When a message is posted to the room, a check is made to see if the size of the collection of messages in the room has exceeded the limit configured in the app-config.xml file. If that threshold has been exceeded, the history is deleted. This is simply to conserve memory resources on the server. The messages collection in this DTO can really be thought of as a buffer. Remember that a client always gets only those messages posted subsequent to the last request they made for the list. Therefore, they will never be able to get the entire chat history this collection stores unless there happened to be more posts than the limit is configured for (250 by default). Remember that the update interval for the chat history is 1 second by default. What this all boils down to is that there would have to be over 250 messages posted to the room in a single second before any client appears to have "lost" messages (i.e., did not see a message posted to the room). In other words, there is a buffer of 250 messages per room. You would not want the collection to grow unbounded because after a while the memory utilization would become a problem. At the same time, you do not want the buffer to be so small that there is a chance of missing messages, and 250 seems like a reasonable value to attain both goals.

UserDTO.java

The last DTO in the queue to review is the UserDTO. Again, there is nothing especially unusual going on here. Note that the Comparable interface is implemented, which is why the compareTo() method is implemented. This allows us to sort the list of users as seen in the RoomDTO. This bean stores the username, as well as when the last Ajax request was received. This is how we determine which messages from the chat history to return with each update request.

GetMessagesAction.java

We now come to the action package, which contains all our Struts Actions. The first one we encounter is named GetMessagesAction.

The first thing done here is to get a reference to the current session. We then synchronize on the session. Why, you ask? Because some containers do not provide thread safety to the session object, which in fact is not mandated by the servlet spec, and therefore the application is responsible for ensuring noncorruption of data. Once that is done, we get from the session the UserDTO object. From it we pull the UserDTO object, and set its lastAjaxRequest field to the current date and time. This is used by the UserClearerDaemonThread to remove “stale” users from the room they were chatting in.

We also get the name of the room the user is chatting in, and we also look for an attribute named lastDateTime in session. This stores the date and time of the last message that was sent to the client. With these two pieces of information, we can call the getMessages() method of the AjaxChatDAO, which returns to us a Vector of messages.

The Action then iterates over that Vector and constructs the XML we previously saw from it and writes it to the response. Note that the postedDateTime is saved for each message, so that when the last message is processed, that value is stored in session under lastDateTime. Therefore, the next time this Action is executed, only messages posted after the last one sent during this cycle will be returned.

```
// Now iterate over the collection of messages we got and construct our
// XML.
StringBuffer xmlOut = new StringBuffer(4096);
xmlOut.append("<messages>");
for (Iterator it = messages.iterator(); it.hasNext();) {
  MessageDTO message = (MessageDTO)it.next();
  xmlOut.append("<message>");
  xmlOut.append("<postedBy>" +
    StringEscapeUtils.escapeXml(message.getPostedBy().getUsername()) +
    "</postedBy>");
  xmlOut.append("<postedDateTime>" +
    new SimpleDateFormat().format(message.getPostedDateTime()) +
    "</postedDateTime>");
  xmlOut.append("<msgText>" +
    StringEscapeUtils.escapeXml(message.getText()) + "</msgText>");
  xmlOut.append("</message>");
  lastDateTime = message.getPostedDateTime();
}
xmlOut.append("</messages>");
```

Note that null is returned, which indicates to Struts that the response is now fully formed and no forward or redirect should take place. This is typical in an Action that services an Ajax request.

JoinRoomAction.java

Next up in our barrage of Struts Actions is JoinRoomAction. This is a pretty simple one. We retrieve the name of the room the user wants to join from the LobbyActionForm. We then store that in session, and call the addUserToRoom() method of the AjaxChatDAO, which takes care of all the heavy lifting. From there we return the showroom forward, which sends the user the room.jsp page, and they are then in the room and ready to chat.

LeaveRoomAction.java

LeaveRoomAction is next, and is the antithesis of JoinRoomAction. This works essentially the same as JoinRoomAction, but the removeUserFromRoom() AjaxChatDAO method is used instead.

ListUsersInRoomAction.java

The ListUsersInRoomAction is used to, wait for it… list the users chatting in a room! This Action is called in response to an Ajax request, so we need to update the lastAjaxRequest field in the UserDTO object so that the UserClearedDaemonThread will not remove the user. After that, it is a simple matter of getting the name of the room the user is in from session, and passing that along to the getUserList() method of the AjaxChatDAO.

From that method we get back a Vector of UserDTO objects, which we iterate over and construct XML for, as described earlier. Here again we return null so Struts knows the response is done, and that is that.

LobbyAction.java

The LobbyAction is the code that executes when the lobby page is shown. Before explaining this class, I would like to note the usage of Commons Logging throughout the AjaxChat code base. Each class instantiates a static instance of Log, and this is used throughout for various messages, like so:

```
/**
 * Log instance.
 */
private static Log log = LogFactory.getLog(LobbyUpdateStatsAction.class);
```

Commons Logging, if you have never used it before, is nice because it sits between your code and the code of some logging package such as Log4J. It insulates your code from the underlying logging implementation, so that if you later decide to use J2EE logging instead of Log4J, your code will not need to be touched; only the configuration of the logging package does.

Moving on to the Action code itself, the first thing we see is again an update of the lastAjaxRequest field in the UserDTO because this Action services another Ajax request. After that, we call the getRoomsUserCounts() method of the AjaxChatDAO. This returns to us a LinkedHashMap. This collection was chosen because it allows us to have a known iteration order over the collection while still allowing for random access to the elements by key value. In fact, the next thing we do is indeed iterate over the collection.

We construct our XML during this iteration. Note the use of the `escapeXml()` method in `StringEscapeUtils`. This is a method in the Commons Lang package, which produces a `String` that is safe for insertion into XML—that is, certain characters are converted to entity strings. Since we cannot be sure what the developer has configured for the room names, this is a necessary safety. Once the XML is constructed and written to the response, we are done, so `null` is returned.

LoginAction.java

In Listing 9-10 we see the `LoginAction` class. This is worth looking at its entirety here.

Listing 9-10. *LoginAction Class*

```
package com.apress.ajaxprojects.ajaxchat.action;

import java.util.Date;
import javax.servlet.http.HttpServletRequest;
import javax.servlet.http.HttpServletResponse;
import javax.servlet.http.HttpSession;
import org.apache.commons.logging.Log;
import org.apache.commons.logging.LogFactory;
import org.apache.struts.action.Action;
import org.apache.struts.action.ActionForm;
import org.apache.struts.action.ActionForward;
import org.apache.struts.action.ActionMapping;
import org.apache.struts.action.ActionMessage;
import org.apache.struts.action.ActionMessages;
import com.apress.ajaxprojects.ajaxchat.dao.AjaxChatDAO;
import com.apress.ajaxprojects.ajaxchat.dto.UserDTO;
import com.apress.ajaxprojects.ajaxchat.filter.SessionCheckerFilter;

/**
 * This is a Struts Action that is called when the user clicks the Login button
 * on the welcome screen.
 *
 * @author <a href="mailto:fzammetti@omnytex.com">Frank W. Zammetti</a>.
 */
public class LoginAction extends Action {

  /**
   * Log instance.
   */
  private static Log log = LogFactory.getLog(LoginAction.class);
```

```
/**
 * Execute.
 *
 * @param  mapping   ActionMapping.
 * @param  inForm    ActionForm.
 * @param  request   HttpServletRequest.
 * @param  response  HttpServletResponse.
 * @return           ActionForward.
 * @throws Exception If anything goes wrong.
 */
public ActionForward execute(ActionMapping mapping, ActionForm inForm,
  HttpServletRequest request, HttpServletResponse response) throws Exception {

  if (log.isDebugEnabled()) {
    log.debug("execute()...");
  }

  HttpSession session = request.getSession();
  if (log.isDebugEnabled()) {
    log.debug("session = " + session);
  }
  synchronized (session) {

    // Get the username the user entered.
    String username = (String)request.getParameter("username");
    if (log.isDebugEnabled()) {
      log.debug("username = " + username);
    }

    ActionForward af = null;
    if (session != null &&
      session.getAttribute(SessionCheckerFilter.LOGGED_IN_FLAG) != null) {
      // User is already logged in, they probably hit refresh while in the
      // lobby, so go there now.
      if (log.isDebugEnabled()) {
        log.debug("User already logged in");
      }
      // There is still a minor potential problem... if by chance the user
      // was logged in and the app was restarted and sessions were persisted,
      // the user object in session can be null.  So, we'll check for that,
      // and re-create the user if applicable.
      if (session.getAttribute("user") == null) {
        if (log.isDebugEnabled()) {
          log.debug("User object null in session, so re-creating");
        }
```

```
        UserDTO user = new UserDTO(username);
        user.setLastAJAXRequest(new Date());
        session.setAttribute("user", user);
      }
      af = mapping.findForward("gotoLobby");
    } else {
      if (username == null || username.equalsIgnoreCase("")) {
        // Username was not entered, so they can't come in.
        if (log.isDebugEnabled()) {
          log.debug("Username not entered");
        }
        ActionMessages msgs = new ActionMessages();
        msgs.add(ActionMessages.GLOBAL_MESSAGE,
          new ActionMessage("messages.usernameBlank"));
        saveErrors(request, msgs);
        af = mapping.findForward("fail");
      } else {
        if (AjaxChatDAO.getInstance().isUsernameInUse(username)) {
          // The username is already in use, so they can't have it.
          if (log.isDebugEnabled()) {
            log.debug("Username already in use");
          }
          ActionMessages msgs = new ActionMessages();
          msgs.add(ActionMessages.GLOBAL_MESSAGE,
            new ActionMessage("messages.usernameInUse"));
          saveErrors(request, msgs);
          af = mapping.findForward("fail");
        } else {
          // Everything is OK, so create a new UserDTO and put it in session.
          if (log.isDebugEnabled()) {
            log.debug("Username being logged in");
          }
          UserDTO user = new UserDTO(username);
          user.setLastAJAXRequest(new Date());
          session.setAttribute("user", user);
          session.setAttribute(SessionCheckerFilter.LOGGED_IN_FLAG , "yes");
          // Lastly, add this user to the list of logged on users.
          AjaxChatDAO.getInstance().logUserIn(user);
          af = mapping.findForward("gotoLobby");
        }
      }
    }

    if (log.isDebugEnabled()) {
      log.debug("LoginAction complete, forwarding to " + af);
    }
```

```
      return af;

    }

  } // End execute().

} // End class.
```

LoginAction is a bit of a misnomer because a login per se is not occurring. Instead, we are simply determining that the username entered is unique and that the user is not already logged in. So, the first check that is done is to be sure the session does not contain the LOGGED_IN_FLAG value. If it is present, the user is already logged in and we send them right to the lobby. We also in this case check for the UserDTO in session. If it is not present, we re-create it. This is done because in some rare circumstances, where the app server is persisting sessions and it is restarted while the user is logged in, the session can be re-created but not all the data within it. This may be a bug in one particular app server I ran this app on (Resin), but in any case, adding this code solved the problem, and it does no harm if things are working as expected anyway.

Next, if the LOGGED_IN_FLAG is not found in session, then the username request parameter is examined. If none was entered, the user will be returned back to the login screen with a message indicating the error. Assuming they did enter a username, though, we call on the AjaxChatDAO to see if the username is already in use. If it is, the user is sent back to the login page with a message indicating they need to select a new username. Lastly, if all of these checks are passed, a new UserDTO is created and populated with the username and the current date and time to represent the last Ajax request. Although there has not been an Ajax request yet, we want to start with a date and time recorded so that the UserClearerDaemonThread will not immediately boot the user, should that fire before the first real Ajax request is made in the lobby. Lastly, we ask the AjaxChatDAO to add this user to the list of logged-in users, and send them to the lobby to begin.

LogoutAction.java

Of course, a LoginAction would be little good without a LogoutAction! As the comments indicate, there is not much to do here. We call on the AjaxChatDAO to remove the user from all rooms. This is really redundant, as they would have been removed when exiting a room, but because a client might use the back button or other manual navigation mechanisms that might avoid the leave room code, this avoids the problem of having users lingering in a room they are no longer chatting in. In addition, we return a nice message informing them they have logged out, invalidate the session, and finally forward back to index.jsp. The message is a standard Struts feature, and can be seen here:

```
// Display a nice message for the user informing them they are logged out.
ActionMessages msgs = new ActionMessages();
msgs.add(ActionMessages.GLOBAL_MESSAGE,
  new ActionMessage("messages.loggedOut"));
saveErrors(request, msgs);
```

We are pulling a message from our message bundle, and setting it under the GLOBAL_MESSAGE key, which the Struts tags we saw earlier on the index.jsp page can find.

SaveErrors() is a method of the Action base class that takes care of all the details of getting this back to the view (the JSP) for us.

PostMessageAction.java

Finally, as far as Actions go, we see the PostMessageAction, which, as you can guess, is called via Ajax to post a message to the room.

This Action makes use of the DynaActionForm declared in struts-config.xml to receive the text of the message to post. Using this, along with the username taken from the UserDTO object in session, a MessageDTO object can be constructed that is passed to the AjaxChatDAO for storage. The lastAjaxRequest field is also updated to avoid the user being booted for inactivity.

UserClearerDaemonThread.java

AjaxChat actually commits a Java webapp faux pas by spawning a background thread to do some periodic processing. The UserClearerDaemonThread class is the culprit.

Spawning threads in a webapp is generally frowned upon and should only be done with extreme caution. The reason is that the container is not in control of the resource, and cannot deal with its lifecycle correctly. In this case, it is a fairly noncritical function, and one that can be interrupted with no ill effect (i.e., you would not want to spawn a thread that updated a database because if the server shuts down in the middle of an update you will probably wind up with inconsistent data). With a few caveats in mind, background threads like this are relatively safe, although you still generally want to try to find another way of accomplishing your goals if possible. Also, it is virtually never good to spawn a thread to process a request, so if you find yourself thinking of doing that, I highly recommend you revisit your design first.

The purpose of this thread is to clear out any users who do not properly log out of the application. If they navigate to another page, or close their browser, the application needs to clear them out as soon as possible. The problem is, the obvious answer to this, a SessionListener, is not implemented precisely the same way in all containers. Some of them inform you when the session is about to be destroyed, others only *after* it has been destroyed. The problem is, we always need access to the UserDTO object in session so that we can get the username and clear them out of the collection of chatters in each room. Therefore, we cannot count on a SessionListener to do the trick. So, this background thread performs the function. It fires every few seconds, as configured in app-config.xml, and calls the removeInactiveUsers() method of the AjaxChatDAO, which we'll be looking at next. This fulfills our needs, and avoids any container differences.

It is also worth noting that this thread will be started as a daemon thread. This is necessary so that the container can shut down and not be held up by the thread, which will happen under some containers, Tomcat as an example. Making it a daemon thread avoids this problem.

AjaxChatDAO.java

AjaxChatDAO is the largest single class in AjaxChat, and it is truly where the majority of the server-side logic of the application resides. Listing 9-11 shows the entire code for this class.

Listing 9-11. *AjaxChatDAO Class*

```
package com.apress.ajaxprojects.ajaxchat.dao;

import java.io.InputStream;
import java.io.IOException;
import java.util.Date;
import java.util.Iterator;
import java.util.LinkedHashMap;
import java.util.Vector;
import org.apache.commons.digester.Digester;
import org.apache.commons.logging.Log;
import org.apache.commons.logging.LogFactory;
import com.apress.ajaxprojects.ajaxchat.AjaxChatConfig;
import com.apress.ajaxprojects.ajaxchat.dto.MessageDTO;
import com.apress.ajaxprojects.ajaxchat.dto.RoomDTO;
import com.apress.ajaxprojects.ajaxchat.dto.UserDTO;
import org.xml.sax.SAXException;

/**
 * This Data Access Object (DAO) is really the heart and soul of the app.  All
 * the real work is done here in terms of recording messages, dealing with
 * users and rooms and most everything else.  It's probably a bit more
 * than what a DAO is supposed to generally be, but in this case I don't think
 * it's a big deal.  Besides, the idea is that if you want to make this a more
 * robust application, with real message persistence and such, then all you
 * should probably have to mess with is this class.  That's the intent anyway.
 *
 * @author <a href="mailto:fzammetti@omnytex.com">Frank W. Zammetti</a>.
 */
public final class AjaxChatDAO {

  /**
   * Log instance.
   */
  private static Log log = LogFactory.getLog(AjaxChatDAO.class);

  /**
   * This class is a singleton, so here's the one and only instance.
   */
  private static AjaxChatDAO instance;

  /**
   * Collection of RoomDTO objects.
   */
  private LinkedHashMap rooms = new LinkedHashMap();
```

```
/**
 * Collection of UserDTO objects of currently logged in users.
 */
private Vector users = new Vector();

/**
 * Make sure instances of this class can't be created.
 */
private AjaxChatDAO() {
} // End constructor.

/**
 * Complete the singleton pattern.  This method is the only way to get an
 * instance of this class.
 *
 * @return The one and only instance of this class.
 */
public static AjaxChatDAO getInstance() {

  if (log.isDebugEnabled()) {
    log.debug("getInstance()...");
  }
  if (instance == null) {
    instance = new AjaxChatDAO();
    instance.init(null);
  }
  return instance;

} // End getInstance().

/**
 * Initialize.  Read in room-list.xml file and create RoomDTOs for each
 * and add it to the collection of rooms.  Note that the first time
 * getInstance() is called, we pass in null for the isConfigFile parameter,
 * and hence the config file is not read.  Before this DAO can really be
 * used, init() must be called, handing it an InputStream to the config
 * file.  This is done from ContextListener.
 *
 * @param isConfigFile InputStream to the config file.
 */
public synchronized void init(InputStream isConfigFile) {

  if (log.isDebugEnabled()) {
    log.debug("init()...");
  }
  if (isConfigFile != null) {
    // Read in rooms config and create beans, hand off to DAO.
```

```
    Digester digester = new Digester();
    digester.setValidating(false);
    digester.push(this);
    digester.addObjectCreate("rooms/room",
      "com.apress.ajaxprojects.ajaxchat.dto.RoomDTO");
    digester.addSetProperties("rooms/room");
    digester.addSetNext("rooms/room", "addRoom");
    try {
      digester.parse(isConfigFile);
      log.info("***** Rooms = " + rooms);
    } catch (IOException ioe) {
      ioe.printStackTrace();
    } catch (SAXException se) {
      se.printStackTrace();
    }
  }

} // End init().

/**
 * Adds a room to the collection of rooms.
 *
 * @param inRoom The room to add.
 */
public synchronized void addRoom(RoomDTO inRoom) {

  if (log.isDebugEnabled()) {
    log.debug("addRoom()...");
  }
  if (log.isDebugEnabled()) {
    log.debug("Adding room " + inRoom);
  }
  rooms.put(inRoom.getName(), inRoom);

} // End addRoom().

/**
 * Removes a room from the collection of rooms.
 *
 * @param inRoomName The namr of the room to remove.
 */
public synchronized void removeRoom(String inRoomName) {

  if (log.isDebugEnabled()) {
    log.debug("removeRoom()...");
  }
  RoomDTO room = (RoomDTO)rooms.get(inRoomName);
```

```
    if (room.getUserList().size() == 0) {
      rooms.remove(inRoomName);
      if (log.isDebugEnabled()) {
        log.debug("removeRoom() removed room " + inRoomName);
      }
    } else {
      if (log.isDebugEnabled()) {
        log.debug("removeRoom() Room not removed because " +
          "there are users in it");
      }
    }

  } // End removeRoom().

  /**
   * Add a message to the list of messages in the named room.
   *
   * @param inRoom    The name of the room to post the message to.
   * @param inMessage The message to post.
   */
  public synchronized void postMessage(String inRoom, MessageDTO inMessage) {

    if (log.isDebugEnabled()) {
      log.debug("postMessage(): inRoom = " + inRoom +
        " - inMessage = " + inMessage + "...");
    }
    RoomDTO room = (RoomDTO)rooms.get(inRoom);
    room.postMessage(inMessage);

  } // End postMessage().

  /**
   * Gets all messages in a named room newer than the specified datetime.
   *
   * @param  inRoom     The name of the room to get messages for.
   * @param  inDateTime The date/time to start retrieval from.  We'll actually
   *                    get any message subsequent to this datetime.
   * @return            List of messages for the named room.
   */
  public synchronized Vector getMessages(String inRoom, Date inDateTime) {

    if (log.isDebugEnabled()) {
      log.debug("getMessages(): inRoom = " + inRoom +
        " - inDateTime = " + inDateTime + "...");
    }
    RoomDTO room = (RoomDTO)rooms.get(inRoom);
    return room.getMessages(inDateTime);
```

```
} // End getMessages().

/**
 * Returns a list of all rooms.  Note that this returns the room name only,
 * it DOES NOT return a list of RoomDTOs.
 *
 * @return List of all rooms names.
 */
public synchronized Vector getRoomList() {

  if (log.isDebugEnabled()) {
    log.debug("getRoomList()...");
  }
  Vector roomList = new Vector();
  for (Iterator it = rooms.keySet().iterator(); it.hasNext();) {
    roomList.add((String)it.next());
  }
  if (log.isDebugEnabled()) {
    log.debug("roomList = " + roomList);
  }
  return roomList;

} // End getRoomList().

/**
 * Returns a Map of rooms, keyed by room name, with the number of users
 * chatting in each as the value.
 *
 * @return List of all rooms and user counts.
 */
public synchronized LinkedHashMap getRoomUserCounts() {

  if (log.isDebugEnabled()) {
    log.debug("getRoomUserCounts()...");
  }
  LinkedHashMap roomList = new LinkedHashMap();
  for (Iterator it = rooms.keySet().iterator(); it.hasNext();) {
    String roomName = (String)it.next();
    roomList.put(roomName,
      new Integer(((RoomDTO)rooms.get(roomName)).getUserList().size()));
  }
  if (log.isDebugEnabled()) {
    log.debug("roomList = " + roomList);
  }
  return roomList;

} // End getRoomUserCounts().
```

```
/**
 * Returns a list of all users currently chatting in a given room.  Note that
 * this returns the username only, it DOES NOT return a list of UserDTOs.
 *
 * @param  inRoom The name of the room to get the user list for.
 * @return        List of all usernames chatting in a named room.
 */
public synchronized Vector getUserList(String inRoom) {

  if (log.isDebugEnabled()) {
    log.debug("getUserList(): inRoom = " + inRoom + "...");
  }
  Vector userList = null;
  RoomDTO room = (RoomDTO)rooms.get(inRoom);
  userList = room.getUserList();
  if (log.isDebugEnabled()) {
    log.debug("userList = " + userList);
  }
  return userList;

} // End getUserList().

/**
 * Adds a user to the specified room.
 *
 * @param inRoom The room to add to.
 * @param inUser The user to add.
 */
public synchronized void addUserToRoom(String inRoom, UserDTO inUser) {

  if (log.isDebugEnabled()) {
    log.debug("addUserToRoom()...");
  }
  RoomDTO room = (RoomDTO)rooms.get(inRoom);
  room.addUser(inUser);

} // End addUserToRoom().

/**
 * Removes a user from the specified room.
 *
 * @param inRoom The room to add to.
 * @param inUser The user to remove.
 */
public synchronized void removeUserFromRoom(String inRoom, UserDTO inUser) {
```

```
  if (log.isDebugEnabled()) {
    log.debug("removeUserFromRoom()...");
  }
  RoomDTO room = (RoomDTO)rooms.get(inRoom);
  room.removeUser(inUser);

} // End removeUserFromRoom().

/**
 * Removes a user from all rooms.  This is kind of a safety net when a
 * user's session is destroyed.
 *
 * @param inUser The user to remove.
 */
public synchronized void removeUserFromAllRooms(UserDTO inUser) {

  if (log.isDebugEnabled()) {
    log.debug("removeUserFromAllRooms()...");
  }
  for (Iterator it = rooms.keySet().iterator(); it.hasNext();) {
    String  roomName = (String)it.next();
    RoomDTO room     = (RoomDTO)rooms.get(roomName);
    room.removeUser(inUser);
  }

} // End removeUserFromAllRooms().

/**
 * Adds a user to the list of logged on users.
 *
 * @param inUser The user to log in.
 */
public synchronized void logUserIn(UserDTO inUser) {

  if (log.isDebugEnabled()) {
    log.debug("logUserIn()...");
  }
  users.add(inUser);
  if (log.isDebugEnabled()) {
    log.debug(inUser.getUsername() + " logged in");
  }

} // End logUserIn().
```

```
/**
 * Removes a user from the list of logged on users.
 *
 * @param inUser The user to log out.
 */
public synchronized void logUserOut(UserDTO inUser) {

  if (log.isDebugEnabled()) {
    log.debug("logUserOut()...");
  }
  String  usernameToLogOut = inUser.getUsername();
  int     i                = 0;
  int     indexToRemove    = -1;
  for (Iterator it = users.iterator(); it.hasNext();) {
    UserDTO user = (UserDTO)it.next();
    if (usernameToLogOut.equalsIgnoreCase(user.getUsername())) {
      indexToRemove = i;
      break;
    }
    i++;
  }
  if (indexToRemove != -1) {
    users.remove(indexToRemove);
    if (log.isDebugEnabled()) {
      log.debug(usernameToLogOut + " logged out");
    }
  }

} // End logUserIn().

/**
 * Checks to see if a given username is in use in any room.
 *
 * @param  inUsername The name to check.
 * @return            True if the name is in use, false if not.
 */
public synchronized boolean isUsernameInUse(String inUsername) {

  if (log.isDebugEnabled()) {
    log.debug("isUsernameInUse()...");
  }
```

```
    boolean retVal = false;
    for (Iterator it = users.iterator(); it.hasNext();) {
      UserDTO user = (UserDTO)it.next();
      if (inUsername.equalsIgnoreCase(user.getUsername())) {
        retVal = true;
      }
    }
    if (log.isDebugEnabled()) {
      log.debug("Returning " + retVal);
    }
    return retVal;

  } // End isUsernameInUse().

  /**
   * This method goes through the collection of users and determines which, if
   * any, are inactive.  Any that are inactive are removed.  This is called
   * from the UserClearerDaemon thread.
   */
  public synchronized void removeInactiveUsers() {

    if (log.isDebugEnabled()) {
      log.debug("removeInactiveUsers()...");
    }
    Vector usersToRemove = new Vector();
    for (Iterator it = users.iterator(); it.hasNext();) {
      UserDTO user           = (UserDTO)it.next();
      long    now            = new Date().getTime();
      long    lastAJAXRequest = user.getLastAJAXRequest().getTime();
      if ((now - lastAJAXRequest) >=
        (AjaxChatConfig.getUserInactivitySeconds() * 1000)) {
        if (log.isDebugEnabled()) {
          log.debug("User " + user.getUsername() + " will be removed");
        }
        usersToRemove.add(user);
      }
    }
    for (Iterator it = usersToRemove.iterator(); it.hasNext();) {
      UserDTO user = (UserDTO)it.next();
      removeUserFromAllRooms(user);
      logUserOut(user);
    }

  } // End removeInactiveUsers().

} // End class.
```

The first important note is that this is a Singleton class. This is done so that we have one unique collection of rooms and users to deal with.

Recall that in the ContextListener, we get a stream to the rooms-list.xml config file and pass it to the init() method of the AjaxChatDAO. Now we can see here that Commons Digester is used to parse that file and create from it a collection of RoomDTO objects for each room. Note that to do this, the DAO itself is pushed onto the Digester stack so that the addRoom() method can be called for each <room> element encountered. AddRoom() is responsible for adding the RoomDTO to the rooms collection. Note that there is a corresponding removeRoom() method, although it is not used in this application. I wrote that so that I could create an admin screen later for maintaining the room list on the fly, but that does not exist today (feel free to add it!).

The postMessage() method is next, and it is just a pass-through to the postMessage() method of the RoomDTO that the message is bound for, and we have already examined that. The same is true of getMessages() as well as addUserToRoom() and removeUserFromRoom(). Therefore, I will not go into these methods since we have already touched on them in examining the DTOs.

The next method in the DAO is getRoomList(), which returns a Vector of strings where each string is the room name.

After that is getRoomUserCounts(). This simply iterates over the list of rooms and for each gets the list of users chatting in it and gets the size of that collection. It wraps this in an Integer and puts it into a LinkedHashMap where the key names are the room names. This is done so that the order of the rooms is maintained yet we can get the values for an individual room by name.

The getUserList() method that follows returns the list of users for a given room. Note that like the getRoomList() method, this just returns a Vector of strings where each element is the username. It does not return a collection of UserDTOs.

The removeUserFromAllRooms() method is called when the user logs out and is just a safety net to be sure the user gets cleared out of all rooms. This should always be a redundant thing to do, but better safe than sorry. To do this, the method simply iterates over the rooms collection and calls removeUser() from each.

After that is the logUserId() method, which simply adds the user to the users collection. That is all "logging in" means in this context. The corresponding logUserOut() method removes the user from the collection, but note that it has to do a little more work to accomplish this because trying to modify a collection that you are iterating over causes an exception. Since we have a Vector as the collection, we in fact do have to iterate over it to find the user to remove. So, we first locate the element in the Vector to remove, and after the iteration loop is done, only then do we remove the element.

The isUsernameInUse() method is used during login to ensure that the user entered a unique username. It simply iterates over the users collection and looks for a match (ignoring case). It returns true if the username is found, and returns false otherwise.

The last method in the DAO is removeInactiveUsers(). This method is called from the UserClearerDaemonThread. It iterates over the users collection and for each item it checks the lastAjaxRequest attribute. If the difference between the current time and the last request is greater than our inactivity threshold, the user is marked for removal. After the iteration loop completes, we then iterate over the collection of users to remove what was created during the first iteration, and for each user we call the removeUserFromAllRooms() method and then the logUserOut() method.

You may have noticed that every method in AjaxChatDAO is synchronized. The purpose is to maintain thread safety when modifying the rooms and users collections, as well as in effect the underlying RoomDTOs and UserDTOs. This approach limits scalability as all incoming requests are in effect serialized. However, without a more robust mechanism—a relational database perhaps—such synchronization is pretty well unavoidable. It may be possible to create a more robust memory-only DAO that avoids at least some of the synchronization, but the overhead of synchronization involved is no longer as drastic as it was in prior JVMs, and as such it is not quite as big a concern as it once was. That being said, there is no denying the scalability of AjaxChat is inherently limited using this DAO.

SessionCheckerFilter.java

AjaxChat makes use of a single servlet filter named SessionCheckerFilter. You can think of this as the "security" of AjaxChat. When fired, it first looks at the incoming request path. Because a session will not be established for a user until they log in, we must not process any paths that occur before that point. That means any requests for index.jsp, styles.css, any of the image files (assuming they are all GIFs), the login action mapping, and the logout action mapping will not be checked (in essence, the filter will ignore this request and just let it pass). Any other path will be checked, though. When one of these other paths is requested, we grab the session object, and then look for the attribute defined by the LOGGED_IN_FLAG constant. If it is present, the user has been logged in and the request can continue. If it is *not* present, then the user was not logged in, and the filter redirects to the index.jsp page. It also puts a Struts ActionMessage in the request, which will be displayed to the user.

ContextListener.java

The final class to examine in AjaxChat is the ContextListener class. This listener performs two important functions. First, it gets a stream on the rooms-config.xml file and passes it along to the AjaxChatDAO to be read. The DAO will read the file and create RoomDTO objects for each configured room. The other important task of this listener is to kick off our UserClearerDaemonThread. Note, as previously mentioned, that it is started as a daemon thread to allow for proper container shutdown. Also note that the priority of the thread is bumped down as low as possible. This thread, while important, is not time-critical, so the lower priority is acceptable.

```
// Lastly, start a background daemon thread that will periodically clear
// out inactive users from rooms.  This was originally done via
// SessionListener, but because of some problems seem in some container
// implementations (Resin, I'm looking at you!), this had to be done
// instead.
Thread userClearerDaemonThread = new UserClearerDaemonThread();
userClearerDaemonThread.setPriority(Thread.MIN_PRIORITY);
userClearerDaemonThread.setDaemon(true);
userClearerDaemonThread.start();
```

Whew, what a ride! That was quite a bit of code to go through, but I hope you will agree that it was not anything incredibly complex. More important, I hope it demonstrates how Ajax makes this app possible and better than could be done without it (and without applets, ActiveX, or similar technologies… it is still straight HTML and JavaScript after all!).

Suggested Exercises

A number of enhancements readily present themselves with this project. Here are just a few of the ideas you may wish to explore on your own:

- Provide the ability to send a private message to a selected user. In fact, start by creating a context menu option for the user list to present options. This could take the form of opening a new window that, in essence, duplicates the chat room, but with only you and the selected user in it.
- Another context option for the user list that would be a good enhancement is the ability to ignore selected users. We know how obnoxious some people can get in chat rooms, so the ability to filter out the garbage would be very useful!
- Create a more robust DAO layer. Since the current DAO uses synchronization all over the place, scalability will obviously be limited (exactly how far this application can scale would be a fun exercise itself). There are more clever ways to implement the DAO that can avoid most or all synchronization.
- Provide the ability to capture a transcript of the chat session and copy it to the users clipboard.
- Use a JSP to write out the room names and statistics in the lobby. Instead of writing out the new `<div>` contents in the `Action`, forward to a JSP to do it. For bonus points, include this JSP into the `lobby.jsp` so that the code that initially populates the `<div>` (as seen in `lobby.jsp` now) is the same code that updates it later, perhaps putting a question mark in the number of chatters initially.
- Add graphical smileys. Everyone loves his or her emoticons!

Summary

In this chapter we examined the AjaxChat application, an Ajax-ified version of the venerable Internet chat application. We saw how, instead of resorting to a library, we can use straight Ajax code without it becoming a nightmare of tangled spaghetti.

CHAPTER 10

■ ■ ■

AJAX Warrior: Back to the Future in a Fun Way!

Well, the road has been long! We've explored six other applications together, learned a great deal about using Ajax in various ways, and produced some really useful stuff from it all. Now we stand on the verge of a great journey. You are about to embark on a quest of understanding, and of entertainment. We will control the vertical. We will control the horizontal. We will venture forth into a land of strange creatures, magic, powerful enemies, and heroic deeds. As your guide, I'll take you into our final Ajax project, and what a dandy it is: a game! In this chapter you'll see more ways of using "naked" Ajax. You'll learn about something called JSON, a data interchange format that is all the rage in these Web 2.0 days, and you'll see a good amount of CSS and DOM scripting techniques. You'll be introduced to even more JavaScript tricks and even produce another kind of server-side application framework. At the end of it all, you get to slack off a bit and play a game that I hope you'll find entertaining as well as educational. Let the adventure begin!

Requirements and Goals

AJAX Warrior tells the story of the mythical land of Xandor. The evil Lord Mallizant has stolen the five sacred artifacts of Xandor: the Crystal Skull, the Scroll of Life, the Medallion of the Sun, the Staff of Tiuwahha, and the Ankh. He has banished the good king Chimley from his home in Castle Faldon and hidden the artifacts throughout the lands, protected in stone and guarded by evil magic. However, before Chimley was banished, he managed to steal the five keys needed to open the magical doors, and he has scattered three of them throughout the communities of Xandor and given two of them to custodians.

Your job, as the AJAX Warrior, is to first retrieve the five keys, and then retrieve the five artifacts. Once all five artifacts are in your possession, they will be reunited, and Mallizant will instantly die (he is now tied to their fate, much like Sauron in *Lord of the Rings*). Along the way you'll have to do battle with Mallizant's minions, a variety of beasts with varying degrees of fighting abilities. You'll need to speak to the inhabitants of Xandor because remember, two of them will have keys you need, and some will give you clues on where to find the other keys and even the artifacts themselves. Oh, and be sure not to kill one of the key masters; needless to say, your quest will be unceremoniously cut short if you do that!

OK, back here in the real world...

What exactly are we going to accomplish with this game? What are some of the specifics we're going to implement? Let's now enumerate at least a few of them:

- We'll have maps that are 100×100 tiles in size, where each tile is 32×32 pixels in size. This should give us a decent-sized world to inhabit.
- There will be four communities in Xandor: Castle Faldon, an unnamed village, and two towns named Rallador and Triyut. Each of them is also represented by a 100×100 map.
- The player will be able to cast a number of different spells, including a healing spell, a Fire Rain spell (for combat), and a Freeze Time spell (to stop the passage of time for every being but the player).
- The player will be able to possess a number of weapons, including a dagger, staff, and mace.
- We should be able to save a game in progress, and continue that game at will. Of course, that save should be done on the server.
- We'll be able to talk to some characters in the game. Some characters will be belligerent, though, and will not talk to us, but will instead attack us all the time.
- When talking to a character, we'll use a script system that allows for some variability depending on what the player says. As we reply to the character, their "karma" will increase or decrease depending on our responses. If their karma reaches zero, they will run away. If we're talking to a key master, we have to get their karma to 15, at which point they'll give us the key. So, it is important for the player to talk "properly" to each character.
- The player will be able to view their inventory of spells and weapons, will be able to call up help at any time, and will be able to cast spells at any time. They'll also be able to toggle between Attack mode, which means they'll attack any character they encounter, and Talk mode, which means they'll enter into conversation with any nonbelligerent character they encounter (provided they speak the language of the character!).
- Lastly, we want to have the vast majority of the true game logic on the server, *not* the client. The client should, for the most part, just be responsible for showing outcomes. We'll also do all our Ajax functions "nakedly," that is, without using any Ajax library, and we'll also use a new communication technique: JSON.

Whew, that sure is a lot of work! And just to remind you, these are only *some* of the goals. We'll discover other things that I've implemented as we dissect the solution, but these are probably the most important goals.

So, without further ado, here we go!

How We Will Pull It Off

In creating AJAX Warrior, I decided to go with "naked" Ajax, which means not using any library or toolkit at all. Developing games is usually a complex endeavor. I have written a number of games over the years, and I can say that they tend to be more complex than any of the enterprise-class development I do for a living. Because of this, I wanted to have the maximum degree of control over how things happened, and the best way to do that in my estimation is not to rely on any library.

Multipurpose Functions and Centralized Ajax

In exploring this application, you'll see a new technique to use when coding your own Ajax. This technique is a way to have a JavaScript function serve a dual purpose: to fire off an Ajax request, and to be its own callback. Let's jump directly into some code to see how this might work (Listing 10-1).

Listing 10-1. *An Example Ajax Function*

```
/**
 * Picks up an item the player is currently on.
 */
function pickUpItem() {

  if (xhr.request == null) {

    sendAJAX(pickUpItem, "pickUpItem.command", "", null);

  } else {

    if (xhr.json.iu == "true") {
      updatePlayerInfo(xhr.json.pn, xhr.json.ht, xhr.json.hp, xhr.json.gp);
    }
    // Always display the message.
    updateActivityScroll(xhr.json.mg);
    return true;

  } // End xhr.request == null if.

} // End pickUpItem().
```

Listing 10.1 shows one of the functions from the game code; specifically, the function is called when the player wants to pick up an item such as gold, spell scrolls, or health packs. We'll hold off on getting into the details of what is actually happening until later, but you need to recognize that here some branching is being done.

When the player wants to pick up an item, this function is called. It first checks to see if there is currently an Ajax request being processed by seeing whether or not `xhr.request` is `null` (again, do not get hung up on the details!). This would only be `null` if no Ajax request is currently in progress. In that case, it continues on and calls the `sendAJAX()` function, whose purpose I'm willing to bet you can guess! Note the first parameter passed to this function: it is a reference to the `pickUpItem()` function! This will be recorded as the desired callback function for the Ajax request.

Note that I said it will be recorded—it will not actually be registered with the `XMLHttpRequest` object associated with the request, as you might expect. Instead, `sendAJAX()` itself is the callback. To understand this, let's look at `sendAJAX()`, shown in Listing 10-2. However, I'm only going to show a trimmed version as the actual function is rather long and gets into details that we'll examine later. Listing 10.2 will give you the basic outline of its operation.

Listing 10-2. *The sendAJAX() Function (Trimmed Down)*

```
function sendAJAX(inCallback, inURL, inQueryString, inPostData) {

  if (xhr.request == null) {

    // Instantiate new XMLHttpRequest object.
    if (window.XMLHttpRequest) {
      xhr.request = new XMLHttpRequest();
    } else if (window.ActiveXObject) {
      xhr.request = new ActiveXObject("Microsoft.XMLHTTP");
    }

    // Make AJAX call.
    xhr.callback = inCallback;
    xhr.request.onreadystatechange = sendAJAX;

    // POST if inPostData is not null, GET otherwise.
    if (inPostData == null) {
      xhr.request.open("get", inURL + inQueryString, true);
    } else {
      xhr.request.open("post", inURL + inQueryString, true);
    }
    xhr.request.send(inPostData);

  } else {

    if (xhr.request.readyState == 4 && xhr.request.status == 200) {

      // Now call the callback function we recorded when initiating the
      // request.
      var clearVars = xhr.callback();

      // Finally, clear our variables associated with AJAX requests, if the
      // callback instructed us to (it wouldn't if it made another AJAX call).
      if (clearVars) {
        xhr.clearXHRVars();
      }

    } // End result status check.

  } // End XMLHttpRequest null check.

} // End sendAJAX().
```

So, let's follow the bouncing ball:

1. The player wants to pick up an item, so they press the Pick Up Item key, which calls `pickUpItem()`.
2. Assuming no other Ajax request is currently in progress, `sendAJAX()` is called.
3. `sendAJAX()` records the callback that `pickUpItems()` sent it, which is actually `pickUpItems()`, but it registers *itself* as the callback with the new `XMLHttpRequest` instance.
4. The request returns to `sendAJAX()`, and when a good response is received, that is, `readyState == 4` and `status == 200`, it calls the "real" callback, `pickUpItems()`.
5. `pickUpItems()` does its thing, and returns true.
6. Execution winds up back in `sendAJAX()`, where, seeing the result of calling the "real" callback was true, it nulls the variable holding the reference to the `XMLHttpRequest` object (`xhr.request`).

You may be asking yourself, "Isn't that a bit more complicated than it needs to be?" I do not believe so. There are two main benefits to this technique.

First, all of the actual Ajax code is centralized in `sendAJAX()`; it does not need to be duplicated anywhere else. Not only is this good in terms of code structure, it is also efficient because certain common things can be dealt with here instead of everywhere else—for instance, reacting to when the player dies. Instead of having to worry about all the various situations in which this could occur, we instead check for it in `sendAJAX()`. Since it can only occur as a result of some request to the server, it will be handled globally.

Second, this effectively eliminates concurrent Ajax requests, which could very well be a bad thing! Since all Ajax calls go through one function, and since this one function will only fire if another request is not already in progress, that problem is eliminated.

If both `pickUpItem()` and `sendAJAX()` checking to see if `xhr.request` is `null` seems redundant to you, just remember that both are Ajax callback functions. What would happen if we removed the check from `pickUpItems()`? We would not be able to differentiate between when we need to make the Ajax request—that is, when `xhr.request` is `null`—or when we need to handle the response—that is, when `xhr.request` is not `null`. What about if we remove it from `sendAJAX()`? In that case, we could again not determine if we can make an Ajax request, or whether we are being called as a result of a response returning from the server. It is not really about serializing Ajax requests, as you might initially expect, but that is a side effect, and fortunately, one we need anyway!

I hope you agree that this is a fairly elegant way to write Ajax code. I do not know if there is an actual name for this approach, but if not, feel free to refer to it as the Zammetti Approach!

JSON

At this point in this book, we've seen a number of ways to return data from the server from an Ajax request. We've seen XML. We've seen delimited strings. We've seen JavaScript being returned. We've even seen objects being returned (well, not really, but effectively that is what it looks like with DWR). For this project, we'll become familiar with another way to return data that is quickly becoming a big favorite of web developers: JSON.

JSON stands for JavaScript Object Notation. I feel this is a bit of a misnomer because while it *can* represent an object, it often does not. But that is just a name thing; the basic idea is that it is a way to structure data that is returned to a caller.

JSON is billed as being a lightweight, system-independent data interchange format that is easy for humans to read, easy for computers to parse, and easy for computers to generate. It uses a syntax that will be immediately familiar to most programmers who have any experience with a C-family language (including Java and JavaScript). It is built on two basic concepts that are pretty much universal in programming: a collection of name/value pairs, such as `Maps`, keyed lists, associative arrays, and so forth, and an order list of values, such as `Lists` or arrays.

Well, enough CompSci gobbly-gook! Let's see what JSON looks like:

```
{"firstName":"Frank","lastName":"Zammetti","age":"33"}
```

Really? Is that all there is to it? I wish I could try to impress you with my advanced knowledge, but no, that actually is all there is to it! As you can see, it looks similar to an array in Java, but not quite because two elements are defined between each delimiter. The item to the left of the colon is the key and the value to the right is the value. Each pair is separated by a comma, and the whole thing is wrapped in curly braces. Simple!

Where it gets really pretty cool is when you want to handle a JSON response in JavaScript. All you have to do is this:

```
eval("json = (" + xhr.responseText + ")");
```

The result, assuming `xhr` was the `XMLHttpRequest` that handled the response, is that a new variable, `json`, will be available to your script. From then on, if you want to get the first name in the response, you simply do this:

```
alert(json.firstName);
```

Really, that's it! The `eval()` call created the `json` variable, giving it the value of the response. The `json` variable is an associative array in JavaScript, so you can access the members just as you would any other associative array. Neat, huh?

You can send JSON to the server as well (although this project doesn't do that). If you go to `www.json.org/java/index.html`, you'll find some Java classes that help you generate and parse JSON. In this project, the only concern is generating JSON, and because again I wanted to have maximum control over the process, I wrote the code to do it myself. Of course, we're only talking about generating a string here; it certainly is not rocket science, as you'll see when we get to that code later.

I should mention that JSON is a general-purpose messaging format, and as such you can use it quite effectively outside Ajax work. Many people have taken to it much more than XML because it is less verbose but tends to be similarly human-readable. I'm sure we've all seen "bad" XML that is difficult to comprehend. Likewise, you can make JSON difficult to understand if you try.

Interestingly, to a certain extent, this project does just that that! For example, here's a real JSON response in AJAX Warrior:

```
{"dm":"false","pn":"Aragorn The Weak","ht":"100","hp":"1","gp":"10","iu":"true",
"vu":"true","di":"false","wn":"false","ec":"false","mo":"o","es":"false","md":"g
ggggggssss[[ggggggggggggggggggg([[[[[[[[[[gggggggg[ggggggggGgg[[[[gggggggggg[[[[
[(gggggg[[[[[[[[[[[[[[[[[[[[g^gggggg[[[[ggggggggg[[gggggggggggfggggggggggggfgggg
gggggggg"}
```


That does not look terribly readable to me! The names of the elements are obviously not meant for human consumption. Although you can probably guess quite a few of them, some you may not. The reason this is the case is that for a game, you want things to happen as quickly as possible in general. Therefore, I chose to make the JSON messages essentially unreadable to a human, who would likely never have to read them except perhaps for debugging purposes. So I made them as small and efficient as possible so as to (a) not take too long to generate or parse and (b) not take too long to transmit across the wire.

Most applications tend not to be quite as time-sensitive as a game, though, so I suggest always making your JSON (or XML for that matter!) as human-readable as possible. Saying `displayMessage` instead of `dm` and `playerName` instead of `pn`, for example, is what I recommend in such a case.

To learn more about JSON, check out the official JSON website, `www.json.org`. You'll find some reference materials and even code to help you work with JSON in a variety of languages, so if nothing else that might be worth it to you.

At this point, you are ready to use JSON, believe it or not! Go forth and be fruitful with your new knowledge!

With that out of the way, let's get into AJAX Warrior!

Visualizing the Finish Line

I suggest you spend some time playing AJAX Warrior before going forward. I hope you find it fun! It certainly is not something that would likely take more than an hour to finish, or even that long. There are a great many images I could show here, but because we have a lot of code to examine, I'm only going to show a handful of screens that are representative of the game. You'll see two pretty cool screens if you die or win the game, and they are not shown here. That should give you some incentive to play for a while!

The first screen I want to show you is the title screen, shown in Figure 10-1.

We have a nice little title banner up at the top, and an area for scrolling text. The player can switch this area between the story of the game, instructions, and some important notes (and they *are* important, so if you have not done so already, read them!). After that we have an entry box for the user to enter their name, as well as two buttons: one to start a new game, and one to continue an existing game.

Next up (Figure 10-2) is a shot that resembles what you'll see when AJAX Warrior begins. I say *resembles* because some of the setup of the game is random, so you may see something slightly different each time you start the game.

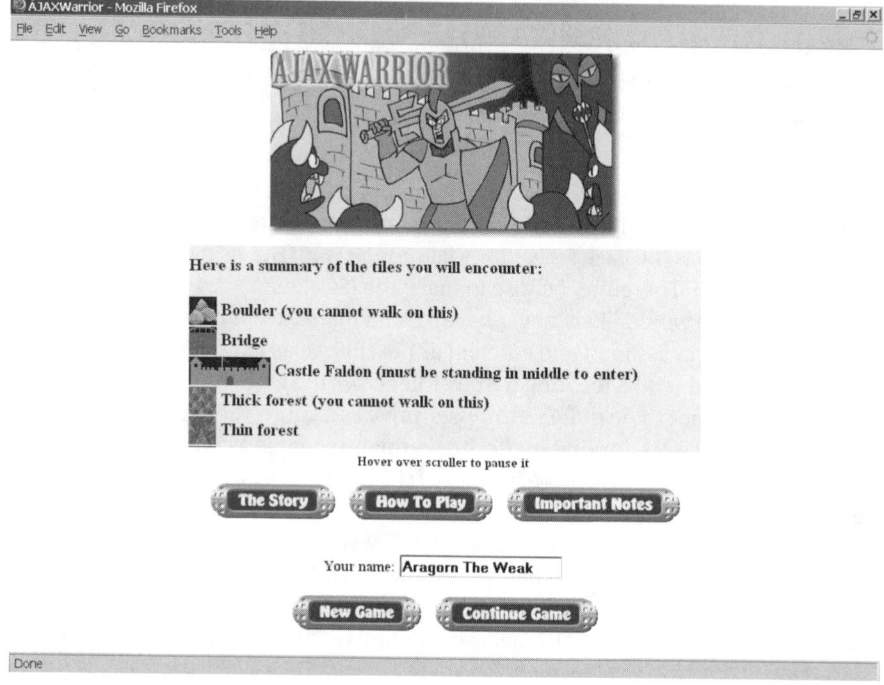

Figure 10-1. *The AJAX Warrior title screen*

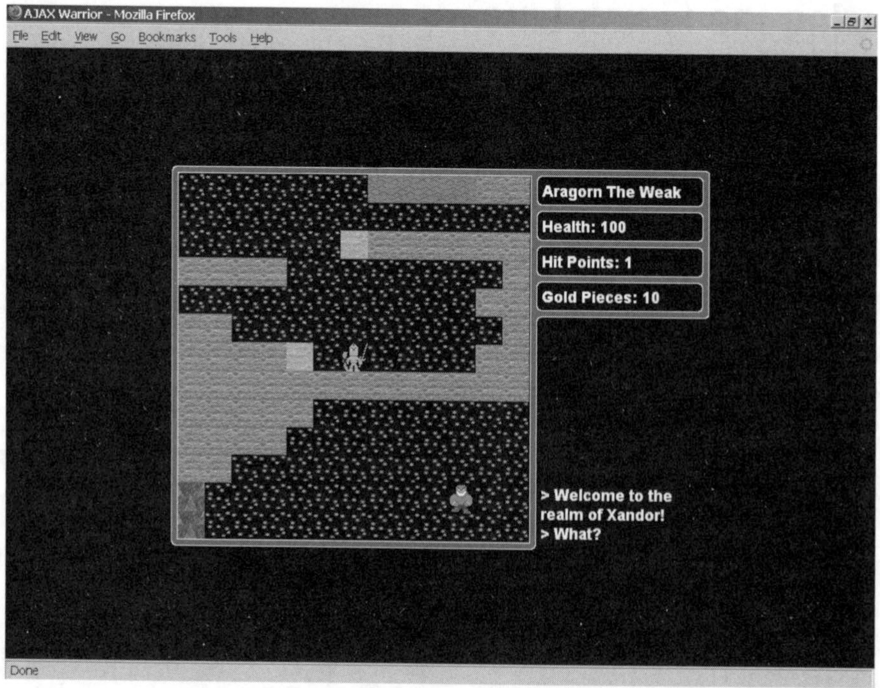

Figure 10-2. *The player's first look at AJAX Warrior*

What does it look like when you are doing battle with a character in the game? Figure 10-3 provides the answer.

Figure 10-3. *Oh no, time to fight!*

One of the other activities you can engage in while playing is talking to characters, and in fact, this is a must because some will give you clues you'll need, and more important, some will provide you with items that are essential to winning the game. Figure 10-4 shows a conversation with a character.

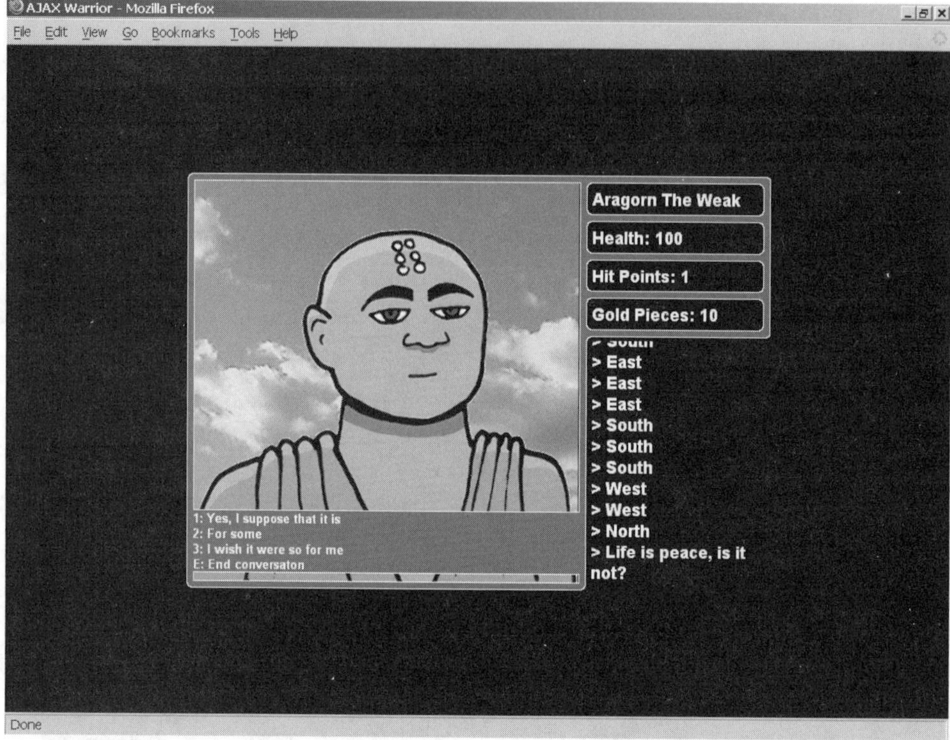

Figure 10-4. *Hopefully he won't just want to talk about the weather!*

Lastly, although it is a somewhat pedestrian screen as compared to the others, Figure 10-5 shows what viewing your inventory looks like.

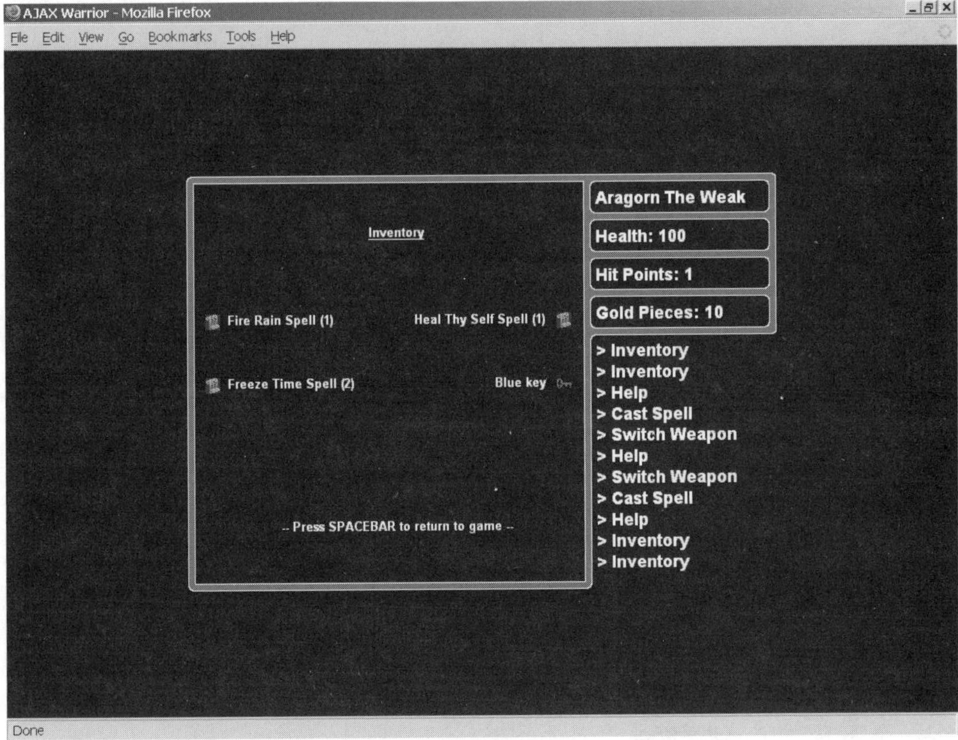

Figure 10-5. *Whaddaya got?*

Now that we know what AJAX Warrior looks like, we have only one small, minor, itsy-bitsy task to accomplish: tearing it apart and seeing what makes it tick!

Dissecting the Solution

First, please be sure to download the entire source for this project form the Apress website. Unlike many of the other projects in this book, I cannot list much of the source because this chapter is already rather long without it. It will therefore be important for you to have the source to look at as we go through the project.

Let's get a feel for the directory structure of AJAX Warrior. Unlike most of the other applications in the book, there is quite a lot to see here. Although it is still a typical webapp structure, there is more on top of that, and Figure 10-6 shows it. In this case, to conserve space, I have not expanded most of the branches to show the contents, so this is truly showing only the directory structure.

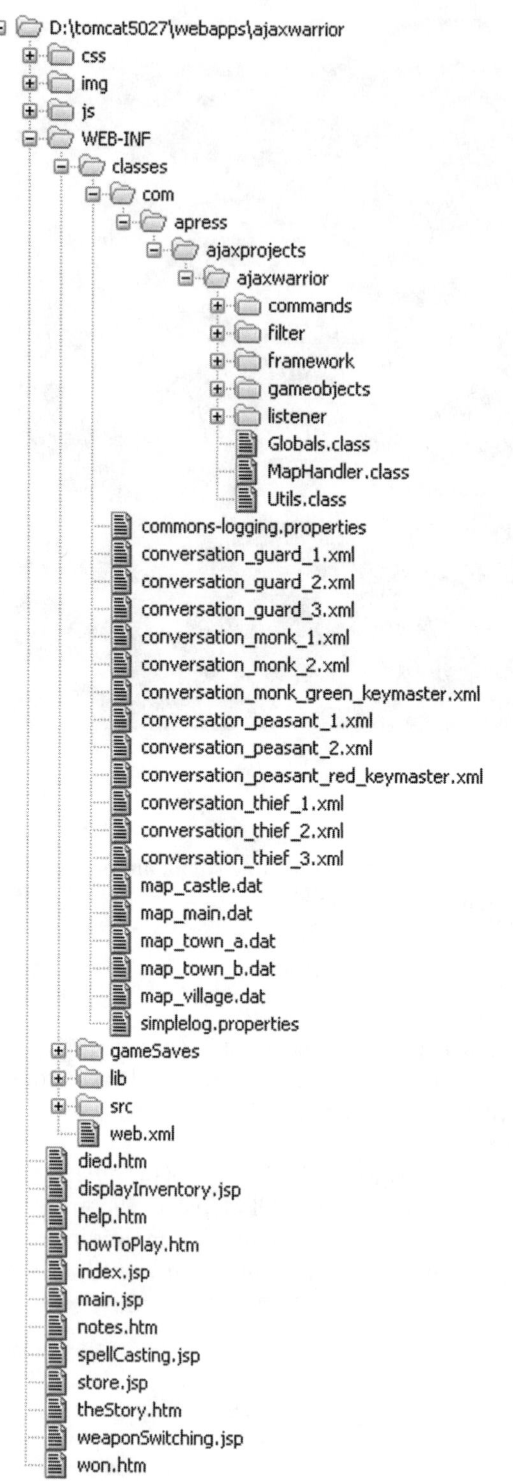

Figure 10-6. *Directory structure layout of AJAX Warrior*

At this point, the directory structure should be very familiar to you. In the root directory you'll find a number of HTML and JSP files, 13 of them. `index.jsp` is our welcome page. `main.jsp` is the actual game markup. All of the others are returned either as the result of an Ajax request (`died.htm`, `displayInventory.jsp`, `help.htm`, `spellCasting.jsp`, `store.jsp`, `weaponSwitching.jsp`, and `won.htm`). In the `/css` directory we find our typical single stylesheet, `styles.css`. In the `/img` directory are all the images for the application. The `/js` directory contains all the JavaScript for the game. We'll go over each one in some detail, and the same goes for the HTML and JSP files. However, Table 10-1 offers a breakdown of what the various JavaScript files contain.

Table 10-1. *Breakdown of the Numerous JavaScript Source Files in AJAX Warrior*

JavaScript File	Description
`ActivityScroll.js`	Contains code for working with the activity scroll (the area to the right below the player's information where messages are shown)
`BattleFuncs.js`	Contains code used when the player is fighting a character
`CastSpell.js`	Contains code used when the player is casting a spell
`Conversation.js`	Contains code used when the player is talking to a character
`GameFuncs.js`	Contains core game code—updating the map on the screen, for instance
`GameStateObject.js`	Contains a class that stores all the data defining the state of the game as far as the client side goes
`GlobalsObject.jsp`	Contains a class that houses constants and preloaded images
`Init.js`	Contains code that initializes the game
`KeyHandler.js`	Contains code that handles all keystrokes in the game
`SendAJAX.js`	Contains code that performs all Ajax requests throughout the game
`StoreFuncs.js`	Contains code used when the player is in a store
`SwitchWeapon.js`	Contains code used when the player wants to switch what weapon they are currently using
`UtilsObject.js`	Contains a handful of utility-type functions
`Vars.js`	Contains the few global (page-scoped) variables used in AJAX Warrior
`ViewChangeFuncs.js`	Contains code for switching between the various views in the game
`XHRObject.js`	Contains variables needed when making Ajax requests

After that we see the standard `WEB-INF` directory. There's nothing unusual, except you see a new directory: `/gameSaves`. As the name implies, this is where saved game data will be stored so that a player can continue a game later on.

Finally, the `WEB-INF/lib` folder contains all the libraries that AJAX Warrior depends on; they are listed in Table 10-2.

Table 10-2. *The JARs That AJAX Warrior Depends on, Found in WEB-INF.lib*

JAR	Description
`commons-logging-1.0.4.jar`	Jakarta Commons Logging is an abstraction layer that sits on top of a true logging implementation (like Log4J), which allows you to switch the underlying logging implementation without affecting your application code. It also provides a simple logger that outputs to `System.out`, which is what this application uses.
`commons-beanutils-1.7.0.jar`	The Jakarta Commons BeanUtils library, needed by Digester.
`commons-digester-1.7.jar`	Jakarta Commons Digester is a library for parsing XML and generating objects from it. This is used to parse some messages passed to the server by the client code.
`commons-lang-2.1.jar`	Jakarta Commons Lang are utility functions that enhance the Java language. Needed by Digester.
`javawebparts_request_v1.0_beta4.jar`	The Java Web Parts (JWP) request package; includes some useful utility classes for dealing with HTTP requests.
`javawebparts_core_v1.0_beta4.jar`	The JWP core package; required by all other JWP packages.

Before we start looking at the code, let me begin by saying that in this chapter I will rarely, if ever, list entire files, as I've tried to do throughout the rest of the book. One of my goals while writing this book was to make it so that you could be reading it without a computer in front of you and be able to understand what was going on. Therefore, I felt it was important to show complete listings as much as possible. I could not always do this; my editor had something to say about it! In this chapter, however, the decision was very easy: there's simply too much code, too many source files, for me to list them all. And once a few of them were not going to be listed, it was easy to decide to not list any of them in their entirety. Therefore, for this project, it is especially important that you download the source from the Apress website and follow along as you read.

Enough prefacing—let's get to it!

Of Maps and Conversations

The first topic I'd like to look at is not really code, but it is very important: maps and conversations. First, maps.

All of the maps used in AJAX Warrior are 100×100 elements. Each element is a character, and each character maps to a specific tile graphic (i.e., "m" is thin mountains, "w" is shallow water, and so on). The map files are stored in `WEB-INF/classes`, and so are accessible, as they are in the classpath. Printing a map here would be quite a waste of space, and would not look like anything but gibberish. However, I encourage you to look at one or two of them, and also look at the `Global.java` file to see what the various characters are.

Second, conversations. When the player talks to a character, it is not purely random, nor is it purely scripted. It is a web of conversation "nodes." Each node defines what the character says, and three replies the player can give. For each reply, the change in the character's karma is stored, as well as the next node to jump to. The character's karma is important because as the player talks to the character, the character's karma goes up and down (or stays the same). If it reaches zero, the character is spooked and runs away. If it reaches 15, *and* the character is one of the two key masters, then they'll give the player the key (if they are not key masters, it doesn't really matter).

For each type of character that the player can talk to—guards, thieves, monks, and peasants—there are three unique conversation webs. One peasant and one monk is a key master. The conversations are stored as XML files, also in `WEB-INF/classes`. That XML looks like this:

```
<conversation id="thief_1">
  <node id="3" response="What do you want?">
    <reply id="1" karma="0" target="5">Nothing, I was just saying hello</reply>
    <reply id="2" karma="-2" target="10">I want to kill all thieves</reply>
    <reply id="3" karma="1" target="9">Umm, interesting conversation starter</reply>
  </node>
  <node id="4" response="That is none of my concern">
    <reply id="1" karma="-1" target="8">
      What I say should be of great concern
    </reply>
    <reply id="2" karma="0" target="14">I understand</reply>
    <reply id="3" karma="1" target="6">
      Well, let's talk about something else
    </reply>
  </node>
</conversation>
```

As you may have guessed, writing these XML files by hand is a bit tedious. So, in the source directory you'll find a Microsoft Excel spreadsheet. If you have Excel, load it up and play a bit. You'll find that each conversation is mapped out in a separate tab, and macros are mapped to buttons to validate the scripts and write out the XML. A script has to pass a number of validations, including making sure that there are no unreachable nodes; that no reply references its node; that there is a positive, negative, and neutral karma adjustment reply for each node; and that the character response and replies do not exceed a maximum length.

Make no mistake; it still can be a bit tedious to write a script, even with this spreadsheet. But it is considerably easier than doing it manually, and the validations ensure that the scripts will make some kind of sense!

The Client-Side Code

Although it is not strictly speaking client-side code, let's begin by looking at `web.xml`, just to be sure there is nothing fishy going on there—and as it turns out, there's not! We have our typical welcome page defined as `index.jsp`, and a session timeout value set to 60 minutes. We also see a single servlet defined:

```
<servlet>
  <servlet-name>FrontServlet</servlet-name>
  <servlet-class>
    com.apress.ajaxprojects.ajaxwarrior.framework.FrontServlet
```

```
    </servlet-class>
    <load-on-startup>1</load-on-startup>
  </servlet>
  <servlet-mapping>
    <servlet-name>FrontServlet</servlet-name>
    <url-pattern>*.command</url-pattern>
  </servlet-mapping>
```

All of the requests made during our game—all our Ajax requests—will go through this servlet, allowing us to have a centralized place to handle some common functions, as we'll see later.

We then see a single filter defined:

```
  <filter>
    <filter-name>sessionCheckerFilter</filter-name>
    <filter-class>
      com.apress.ajaxprojects.ajaxwarrior.filter.SessionCheckerFilter
    </filter-class>
  </filter>
  <filter-mapping>
    <filter-name>sessionCheckerFilter</filter-name>
    <url-pattern>*.command</url-pattern>
  </filter-mapping>
```

Although we'll see it later, the purpose of this filter is to be sure that a game has been correctly started for any request that passes through our servlet. If a game has not been properly started, the request is directed back to `index.jsp`. All our requests will end with `.command`, which is what we map the servlet to.

Lastly, we have a single context listener:

```
  <listener>
      <listener-class>
        com.apress.ajaxprojects.ajaxwarrior.listener.ContextListener
      </listener-class>
  </listener>
```

This listener will handle any server-side application initialization that should occur at startup. Again, we'll see this in detail later.

index.jsp

The next thing to examine is `index.jsp`. This is the initial page the player sees, the one with the AJAX Warrior title banner and the scrolling area. The first thing found in the code is some image preloads for the buttons you see on the screen. There are two images for each button: a normal version and the version seen when you hover over the button with the mouse. After that is a batch of variables beginning with `vs_`, which are used for the vertical scroller in the middle of the page.

The first executable code we see is the `init()` function, which is called in response to the page's `onLoad` event:

```
function init() {

  vs_contain = document.getElementById("vs_container");
  vs_content = document.getElementById("vs_contents");
  layerCenterH(vs_contain);
  layerCenterH(document.getElementById("controls"));
  <% if (request.getAttribute("Error") != null) { %>
  alert("<%=request.getAttribute("Error")%>");
  <% } %>
  switchContents("theStory");

} // End init().
```

First, references are grabbed to two `<span>` elements: `vs_container` and `vs_contents`. Note that `<span>` is used instead of `<div>` to avoid the line break that `<div>` puts after itself. The `vs_` portion stands for (v)ertical (s)croll, and `vs_container` is the `<span>` with the gray background and is the area the scroller takes up. The `vs_contents` `<span>` is where the actual contents that will be scrolled go. Note that these two reference variables are page-scoped and are used throughout the rest of the page.

After that, we use the `layerCenterH()` function that we have previously seen in a number of chapters to center the vertical scroller. The same is done for the controls `<div>`, which contains all our buttons and a text box for entering a name.

After that we have a JSP scriptlet that renders an alert if an attribute named `Error` is found in the request. This will be present if the name the player enters is already in use, or if they tried to continue a game that does not exist.

Finally, `switchContents()` is called, passing in the ID of a `<div>` that contains text we want to scroll:

```
function switchContents(inWhichText) {
  stopScroller();
  vs_content.innerHTML = document.getElementById(inWhichText).innerHTML;
  resetScroller();
  startScroller();
} // End switchScrollText();
```

As you can see, the scroll is first stopped by calling `stopScroller()`, and the contents of the `<span>` that `vs_content` points to are updated with the contents of the `<div>` passed in. Then the scroller is reset by calling `resetScroller()` (so that if it was previously scrolling it will start from the beginning of the new content), and it is then started again by calling `startScroller()`. `switchContents()` is called when the user clicks The Story, How To Play, or Important Notes button.

Speaking of `resetScroller()`, let's see what it looks like:

```
function resetScroller() {
  // Determine milliseconds
  vs_milliseconds = 1000 / vs_scroll_speed;
  // Get height of container
  vs_container_height = vs_contain.style.height.substr(0,
    vs_contain.style.height.length - 2);
```

```
    // Get height of contents
    vs_contents_height = vs_content.scrollHeight;
    // Start off bottom
    vs_contents_top = (1 * vs_container_height) + 20;
    vs_content.style.top = vs_contents_top;
    // Make contents visibile
    vs_content.style.visibility = "visible";
  } // End resetScroller().
```

The variable vs_milliseconds specifies how many times per second the timer that causes the contents to scroll will be fired. vs_scroll_speed specifies how many lines the contents should scroll up per second, so dividing 1,000 by this number gives us the number of milliseconds required between each move (since there are 1,000 milliseconds in a second). vs_container_height is the height of the container <span>, and likewise, vs_contents_height is the height of the actual contents to be scrolled, both of which are needed to determine when scrolling has completed and the contents should recycle and scroll again. Note that the value returned by getting the value style.height is in the form 99px, where 99 is the actual height. So, we need to strip the px portion since we just want the number, hence the use of the substr() function. vs_contents_top is a variable that controls the value of the top style attribute. The way the scroll works is quite simple: the vs_contents <span> is set up to clip the contents, which means that scroll bars will not be present if the contents of the <span> are larger than the span itself, and the <span> will not resize to accommodate the contents. So, if we set the value of the top style attribute of the contents to something larger than the height of the container <span>, the contents won't be visible. If we then slowly subtract from that top value, the contents will slowly scroll up from the bottom of the container <span>. If we keep doing this until the contents have completely scrolled up (which means the top style attribute will be a negative value at that point, which is perfectly valid), we have ourselves a vertical scroller!

The startScroller() function is literally only this line:

```
vs_interval_id = setInterval('doScroller()', vs_milliseconds);
```

This simply sets up a timeout that fires after the amount of milliseconds determined in resetScroller(). As you can probably guess, stopScroller() is nothing but clearing this timeout, and also hiding the contents of the scroller.

The last scroller-related function is the target of the timeout, doScroller(), and I think you'll be surprised at how simplistic it is:

```
function doScroller() {
  // Only do this if we're not paused
  if (!vs_pause) {
    // Move up one pixel
    vs_contents_top--;
    // If we've scrolled off the top, reset to off the bottom
    if (vs_contents_top < -vs_contents_height) {
      vs_contents_top = (1 * vs_container_height) + 20;
    }
    // Reposition contents layer
    vs_content.style.top = vs_contents_top;
  }
} // End doScroller().
```

Yes, that is indeed it! We first check the value of the vs_pause variable, which is set to true when the player hovers over the scroller. This allows the player to pause the scroller to read it. If that variable is false, though, we simply subtract 1 from the vs_contents_top variable. We then check to see if we've scrolled all the way, which is done by comparing the value of vs_contents_top with the height of the contents stored in the variable vs_contents_height. When the former is less than negative the height, the scroll is complete. To make that a bit clearer, let's say the height of the contents is 200 pixels. When the top style attribute of the contents is less than –200, the scroll has completed. Remember, the contents of the container <span> will clip, so that if the contents are –200 pixels above the top of the container, it is no longer visible. At that point, the top attribute is reset to essentially push the contents down below the container, and finally, the top style attribute of the contents <span> is updated with the new value of the vs_contents_top variable.

The markup on the page is quite simple as well. We have a <div> with the ID pleaseWait. This is displayed when the user clicks New Game or Continue Game. This is done to avoid some JavaScript errors that can occur because of the image rollovers on the buttons. In essence, the page will be overwritten in memory with the actual game, but the screen will not immediately be updated. This means that if you roll over a button, the JavaScript that handled the rollover will have been overwritten, and an error occurs. The error is actually "invisible" to the user, but I did not like seeing it showing up even just in the debugger in Firefox, and this gets around it.

Following that is the AJAX Warrior title banner. Immediately after that are the two <span> elements for the vertical scroller. Note the onMouseOver() handler on the container; this handler is used to pause the scroller.

After that is our control <div>. This contains the buttons, as well as the text box for entering the player's name. The latter is part of a form that is submitted to startGame.command. Note the hidden whatFunction field. This will be populated either with the value "newGame" or "continueGame", depending on which button the player clicks. When the form is submitted, the checkName() function is called. This verifies that something was entered, and that it does not contain any invalid characters (since this will be a filename, only numbers, letters, dashes, underscores, and spaces are allowed).

Following that are three JSP includes: one for the contents of The Story, one for the contents of How To Play, and one for the contents of Important Notes. The files included are, unimaginatively, theStory.htm, howToPlay.htm, and notes.htm. Each is nothing but plain text wrapped in a <div>. Have a peek if you don't believe me!

main.jsp

Once the form is submitted and the server determines the correct outcome, either index.jsp will be shown again (if an error occurred, such as the game the player wants to continue cannot be found) or main.jsp will be shown. Let's now jump right into main.jsp. Refer to the listing for this JSP that you've downloaded from the Apress website.

There really is not any actual code here, just a whole batch of JavaScript imports... a JSP scriptlet wrapped in a JavaScript <script> block (I'll explain this in just a moment)... and finally, a whole bunch of <div> elements.

Let's jump back to that scriptlet for a moment. We'll learn shortly that there is a GameState object that stores, well, information about the current state of the game. In fact, there are *two* such objects, one server side and one client side. They both store different sets of information, but to properly save and restore a game, we need to save and restore both objects.

When main.jsp loads, recall that it could be as a result of a new game being started or an existing game being continued. In the latter case, we'll find that a serialized version of the client-side GameState object will have been put in request as an attribute under the name clientSideGameState. To continue the game, we need to reconstitute this serialized version into a real GameState object. The details of that reconstitution will be explored when we get to the JavaScript source, but in short, the string is put into a page-scoped variable named clientSideGameState. This variable is then passed to the init() function as a result of the onLoad event handler.

As for the <div> elements, divGame is the entire game area. Everything else is contained with this element. divBorder is the container of the border image. divMap is the actual gameplay area. imgCharacter, which is an <img> tag and not a <div>, is where the close-up of a character the player is talking to appears. divTalkingReplies is the blue box superimposed over the character listing the replies the player can give during conversation. divInventory, divSpellCasting, divWeaponSwitching, divStore, divHelp, and divGameEnd are areas that will have dynamic content placed (except divHelp, divGameEnd, and divStore, which are static) and will obscure the gameplay area. divName, divHealth, divHitPoints, and divGoldPieces are areas that will display the player's current information on the right. Finally, divActivityScroll is the area to the right below the player's information where messages are displayed.

styles.css

Note that all of these have a specific style class applied, and those classes are found in styles.css. They define font styles and colors and such, but also define positioning for the elements. All of the attributes used should by now be quite familiar to you; nothing fancy is going on. The one aspect that deserves some discussion is positioning.

It's important to remember that all of these are children of the divGame element. So, when we position another element within that one using the absolute value for the position attribute, it is an absolute value that is relative to the containing element. That may be a bit confusing, but you have to think like Einstein in terms of relativity. Usually, when absolute positioning is used, it is absolute relative to the page itself, which makes it seem really absolute, but in fact it is still relative.

The positioning may be easier to comprehend if you see it graphically. Figure 10-7 shows an exploded view of where the various layers get positioned. I use the border as the reference because in reality, all of the positioning is based on fitting into specific areas of the border. Recall, however, that the border is not the outer element; it is a container within a <div>. But the border is absolutely positioned within that container and is sized to fill the entire container; therefore, for all intents and purposes, you can think of all the other <div> elements as positioned relative to the border, as the diagram shows.

If you are uncertain about all this, an easy way to see is to add display:none; to the cssBorder class in styles.css and then start the game. With the border not visible, note that all the other elements are still where they should be. Again, because they are positioned absolutely within the divGame container, not with regard to the border, they appear to be positioned relative to the border.

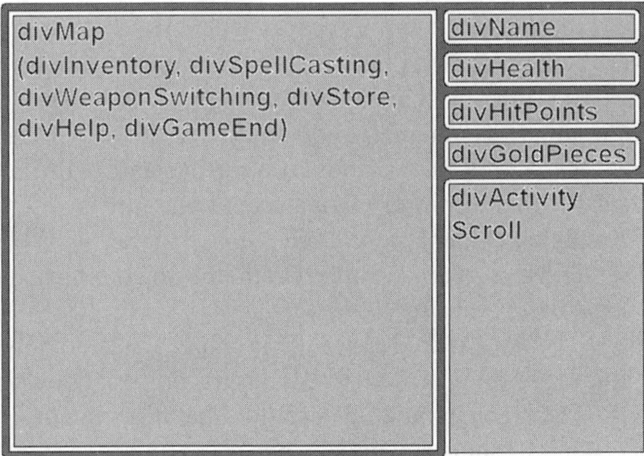

Figure 10-7. *How the various <div> elements relate to one another positionally*

died.jsp

Well, now, that is quite a dreary heading! This HTML document is displayed when the player dies (or when they kill a key master, since the game cannot be won at that point). Listing 10-3 contains the entire contents of this file.

Listing 10-3. *died.htm, in its Entirety*

```
<img src="img/game_lost.gif">
<div style="position:absolute;top:130px;left:2px;width:416px;height:100px;">
  <center>
    Thou art dead!
    <br>
    Please do try again!
    <br><br>
    Press any key to go to start screen.
  </center>
</div>
```

What happens is that with each of our JSON responses from the server, two elements are present: `di` and `wn`. `di` will be true if the player died; `wn` will be true if the player won the game (regardless of what the request was, since at least dying can happen in multiple ways). When the JavaScript function that sends Ajax requests (which we'll explore in a moment) sees that `di` is true in the response, it immediately sends another Ajax request targeting `died.htm`. The contents of this file are used to populate the `divGameEnd <div>` in `main.jsp`, and those contents are then displayed. This process is identical for when the player wins the game, and the markup is essentially identical to that shown in Listing 10-3, with a different image and different text, of course.

displayInventory.jsp

This file is a bit meatier. Here we're constructing markup to display the player's inventory. The markup is constructed by first getting the GameState object instance from request, and then getting the inventory collection from it. For now, it is enough to understand that the GameState object is an object on the server that stores all the information about the current state of the game. Things like the player's name and health, their inventory, what weapon they are currently using, and so on are found there. Recall that earlier I mentioned that there is a GameState object on both the client and server. The server-side object contains much more information, but both objects serve the same basic purpose.

Once we have the inventory collection, it is first checked to see if it is empty. If it is, some simple markup telling the user they are holding nothing is rendered. If it is not empty, though, the code begins to iterate over the collection. For each item, we determine what it is and output the appropriate markup. For instance, if it is the blue key, we see this:

```
case Globals.ITEM_KEY_BLUE:
  out.print("<img src=\"img/item_key_blue.gif\" " +
    "align=\"absmiddle\" width=\"16\" height=\"16\">");
break;
```

Globals is a class that contains a large number of constants used throughout the code. One of them is the code representing the blue key.

Note that the rendered markup is forming a table with two columns. So, we need to keep track of whether the item we're adding is in the first or second column so that we can end the row properly when the time comes. The firstColumn variable is used to keep track of that.

For each item in the inventory, we make a call to Utils.getDescFromCode(). Utils is a class that contains a handful of utility functions, getDescFromCode() among them. This function returns a descriptive string for the item code passed in; for instance, if we pass it A, which is the code for the blue key, it will return Blue key.

help.htm

This is the help screen the player sees when they press the H key during play. It is a pretty pedestrian piece of code and is just plain old HTML. I therefore leave this in your capable hands to check out.

spellCasting.jsp

This is the page that we display when the player wants to cast a spell. It is conceptually (and even structurally) very similar to displayInventory.jsp. Like that JSP, we get the inventory of the player from GameState, and check to see if it's empty. If it is, we render the markup to tell that to the player. If it isn't, we begin to iterate over it.

This time around, we know that there are only three possible spells, and we want to have specific keys the user can press for each to cast them. So, we switch on the inventory code and display the appropriate text for the spells only. We must also keep track of which spells the player has. Think of it this way: there is some JavaScript floating around somewhere that we'll see shortly that handles key presses. When the spell casting display is showing, the player can press F, H, or T, corresponding to the spells they can cast. However, how does that JavaScript know which of those is valid, because remember, the player may not have any spells, or may not have them all? It would be nice to not have to go to the server just to find out the player doesn't have a spell they requested casting. So, we construct a list of the spells the player has as we render this markup. This is a space-separated list of the codes for the spells. So, in other words, if the player had all the spells, we would get the string "` ; . dummy"; each of those is the code for a given spell (the codes will become a bit clearer later—just go with the flow for now!). At the end of string we also put "dummy", so that when the string is tokenized, there is always a value at the end and not a delimiter, which would cause a problem.

This is where it gets a bit interesting: at the very end of `spellCasting.jsp`, we see this line:

```
<script>gameState.spellsPlayerHas = "<%=spellsPlayerHas%>";</script>
```

Recall that this page will be rendered and returned as the result of an Ajax call. The JavaScript making that call looks for a script block in the response, and if found, `eval()`'s it. So, in this case, the result is that the `spellsPlayerHas` field of the client-side `gameState` object will be populated with the string that was constructed listing what spells the player has. So, that field can then be used when the player presses a key, say T, to see if they have that spell. If not, the keystroke is ignored.

store.jsp

The player can enter a store in the two towns and purchase various items. This JSP is the markup that is displayed when the player is in the store. It is nothing but a `<table>` listing all the items and how much they cost. The costs are taken from the `Globals` object. Aside from that, there's not much to see here, so have a quick peek and let's move along.

weaponSwitching.jsp

This is the file that renders the markup seen when the player wants to switch weapons. It is once again very much along the same lines as `spellCasting.jsp` and `displayInventory.jsp`. The only real difference is that because "Bare hands" is always an available option, there is never the possibility of inventory being empty or the player not having any spells to cast, as in the other two JSPs. So, there is no branch checking for emptiness here. Aside from that, it is very similar. Again, we have a string of weapons the player has built up, and again, a `<script>` block at the end is rendered and will be `eval()`'d to get the value into the `gameState` object to use when keystrokes are handled.

And with that, we have seen all of the markup for AJAX Warrior, and we've examined the stylesheet used. Now let's move on to the JavaScript, where most of the action is.

Globals.js

The first JavaScript file I'd like to discuss is `GlobalsObject.js`. This file contains the definition of a single JavaScript class, `GlobalsObject`. This is similar to the `Globals` class on the server in that it stores some constants used throughout the code. The vast majority of what is in this object are preloaded images. Note that the extension of this file is `.jsp` and not `.js` as the rest are. The reason is that we need to reference the values in the `Globals` class on the server, and we could not do that unless this was a JSP. The container will kindly evaluate the JSP for us, even when a `<script>` tag on a page includes it.

Let's look at a snippet of the beginning of this code:

```
function GlobalsObject() {

  // Viewport Sizes.
  this.TILE_WIDTH = <%=Globals.TILE_WIDTH%>;
  this.TILE_HEIGHT = <%=Globals.TILE_HEIGHT%>;
  this.VIEWPORT_WIDTH = <%=Globals.VIEWPORT_WIDTH%>;
  this.VIEWPORT_HEIGHT = <%=Globals.VIEWPORT_HEIGHT%>;
  this.VIEWPORT_HALF_WIDTH = <%=Globals.VIEWPORT_HALF_WIDTH%>;
  this.VIEWPORT_HALF_HEIGHT = <%=Globals.VIEWPORT_HALF_HEIGHT%>;
```

As you are well aware by now, we create a class in JavaScript by creating a function. Inside it we can define fields by using the `this` keyword. So here we are adding some fields: `TILE_WIDTH`, `TILE_HEIGHT`, `VIEWPORT_WIDTH`, `VIEWPORT_HEIGHT`, `VIEWPORT_HALF_WIDTH`, and `VIEWPORT_HALF_HEIGHT`. The values for these fields are all taken from the server-side `Globals` class (they are static finals). Since there is no such thing as final in JavaScript, we cannot get the true constants effect here; these fields are still alterable. We just have to hope the programmer is smart enough to not do so.

There are constants here mimicking almost all of the values in the server-side `Globals` class. As I mentioned earlier, most of the contents are image preloads. For instance:

```
  this.imgITEM_GOLD = new Image(<%=Globals.TILE_WIDTH%>, <%=Globals.TILE_HEIGHT%>);
  this.imgITEM_GOLD.src = "img/item_gold.gif";
```

This is the preloaded image for the chest of gold the player can pick up. We also see some constants defined for key handling, like so:

```
  this.KEY_SPACEBAR = 32;
  this.KEY_LEFT_ARROW = 37;
  this.KEY_RIGHT_ARROW = 39;
  this.KEY_UP_ARROW = 38;
  this.KEY_DOWN_ARROW = 40;
```

The numbers are the key codes that will be received in our keystroke event handlers when the player presses a key. Better to reference these constants throughout the code than the numeric values themselves!

Init.js

The `init()` function, contained in `init.js`, is called `onLoad` of `main.jsp`. It is responsible for initialization tasks for the game. These include

- Instantiating a number of objects such as `GameStateObject` and `GlobalsObject`
- Clearing out the activity scroll (the area to the right where messages appear)
- Reconstituting the `GameStateObject` instance if a game is being continued (in fact, the object referenced by the `gameState` variable itself does this, but `init()` makes the decision whether to ask the object to do it)
- Centering the game in the window
- Creating the 169 images that are the tiles our map display is built from

- Hooking the keyUp event handler so we can process key presses
- Hiding the various secondary displays (inventory, spell casting, help, weapon switching, and the store) since they are not hidden initially
- Making the initial Ajax request to display the map

I think that for the most part this code is pretty self-explanatory, but one part is worth a second look—the code that creates those map tile images:

```
var x;
var y;
for (y = 0; y < Globals.VIEWPORT_HEIGHT; y++) {
  for (x = 0; x < Globals.VIEWPORT_WIDTH; x++) {
    var newImg = document.createElement("img");
    newImg.style.position = "absolute";
    newImg.style.left = (x * Globals.TILE_WIDTH) + "px";
    newImg.style.top = (y * Globals.TILE_HEIGHT) + "px";
    newImg.width = Globals.TILE_WIDTH;
    newImg.height = Globals.TILE_HEIGHT;
    newImg.id = "tile-" + y + "-" + x;
    var map = document.getElementById("divMap");
    map.appendChild(newImg);
    document.getElementById("tile-" + y + "-" + x).src =
      Globals.imgTILE_BLANK.src;
  }
}
```

When you're playing the game and you see the map, you're seeing a viewport on a larger world. The map for the entire world of Xandor, for instance, is 100 tiles wide by 100 tiles high. However, you only see 13×13 of that at a time. The viewport is a grid of 13×13 images (169 in total). So, to display a viewport on the map, we get a chunk of the map that is 13 lines tall and 13 characters wide, where each character is a code representing a specific tile type (i.e., mountains, water, a town). So, the bottom line here is we need 169 images on the page whose src attribute we can update to reflect the tile that should currently be shown in it to form the viewport on the map.

However, it would be unwieldy to actually have 169 <img> tags on the page. Instead, we use some DOM functions to create them. We begin with a loop, which iterates the number of times there are lines in the viewport (13). Another loop inside that iterates for each character in the row (13). For each, we create a new <img> object. We set its position style attribute to absolute, and set its width and height to the width and height defined in Globals for a tile (32×32 pixels). We then set its left and top positions, using the value of the loops to form a grid. We then give it an ID formed by taking the string "tile-" and appending the y loop value and x loop value, separated by a dash. Finally, we get a reference to the divMap <div>, and append the new image object as a child of it. Finally, we get a reference to the <img> we just added and set its src to our blank tile. And that's how we get a grid of images to create our map viewport.

GameState.js

I have mentioned this GameState object thing a few times, and now it is time to check it out.

The GameStateObject is, by and large, just a JavaBean, or what would be the equivalent of a JavaBean in JavaScript. We have some fields here: activityScroll, which is an array that contains the messages seen in the activity scroll to the right; currentView, which is a reference to the <div> we are currently seeing (divMap, divInventory, etc.); and previousView, which is used when we view inventory, help, spell casting, or weapons switching, so we know whether we should show the map again, or whether we were in the middle of battle and should show the battle view again. spellCast and weaponSwitched are two simple true/false flags used to determine when a spell was just cast or when a weapon was just switched. weaponsPlayerHas and spellsPlayerHas are the strings generated by weaponSwitching.jsp or spellCasting.jsp to tell us which weapons or spells the player currently has. talkAttackMode determines whether the player is currently in Talk mode (blue border) or Attack mode (red border, which means the player will attack any character they come in contact with). currentWeapon specifies which weapon the player is currently using. fireProjectile, similar to spellCast and weaponSwitched, tells when a projectile weapon (slingshot or crossbow) has been fired. All of the variables prefixed with "projectile" are used when an arrow is flying either from the player or from a character. battleEnemyTurn is another flag that is set to true when in battle it is the character's turn to move.

Next we have the serialize() function. This is used when the player requests that the game be saved. This function constructs some XML representing the current gameState object. However, as it turns out, it's not important to save *all* the data contained in this object, so we ignore the unimportant fields and only serialize what we absolutely have to in order to persist the state of the game. This is equivalent to marking a field transient in Java, but since there is no notion of transient fields in JavaScript (mostly because there is no inherent notion of serialization), we simply ignore what we do not need to save.

To go along with serialize() is reconstitute(), which is called when a game is loaded (as a result of a call from that branching logic in Init.js we saw earlier). Recall that what the server returns to us is the same data that serialize() constructed, but as a delimited string (delimited by ~~~). So, we split this string, and set the fields of the gameState object based on its values. No big deal.

Utils.js

Utils.js contains a single class, UtilsObject, which itself contains two functions that we have previously seen: layerCenterH() and layerCenterV(). Although this is the first time we've seen them as two functions like this, we have in fact seen and examined the code they contain: in InstaMail in Chapter 5 and PhotoShare in Chapter 7. In those chapters, we combined the code and used it to center the Please Wait layers. Here, I've broken them out into two separate callable functions for more flexibility. Both functions accept a reference to some element on a page, and they then center that element, horizontal or vertically as applicable. Since we reviewed those functions in previous chapters, I will not go into detail here.

Vars.js

One of the things I wanted to demonstrate with this application is the concept of not polluting global namespace, or not using a lot of global variables. When you're trying to write more robust, professional-quality JavaScript, it is a good idea, as it is in Java (although you do not have a choice in Java as you do in JavaScript) to deal in objects as much as possible. So, instead of having the functions in `Utils.js` in page scope, for instance, I created a `UtilsObject` to house them. The benefit to this is that it avoids naming conflicts. If you wanted to have `layerCenterH()` at page scope, you could; the two would not conflict.

However, it is virtually impossible for an application of this complexity to not have *some* global variables, and indeed we have a few. But very few indeed:

```
var Globals = null;
var Utils = null;
var gameState = null;
var xhr = null;
```

That is the entire contents of `Vars.js`, minus the comments. `Globals` is a reference to the instance of the `GlobalsObject` class. `Utils` is a reference to the `UtilsObject` class. `gameState` is a reference to the `GameStateObject` class, and `xhr` is a reference to the `XHRObject` class.

XHRObject.js

Speaking of the `XHRObject`, we now come to `XHRObject.js`, which defines that class. Listing 10-4 shows the entire contents of this file. (Sorry, I said I wouldn't do this too often!)

Listing 10-4. *Against My Own Rule, the Entire XHRObject.js File*

```
/**
* This object contains three variables used to make Ajax requests.  The member
 * variable request is actually the XMLHttpRequest instance.  The callback
 * member is the function that is the callback for the current Ajax request.
 * The json member is the parsed JSON response.
 */
function XHRObject() {

  this.request = null;
  this.callback = null;
  this.json = null;

  /**
   * Function to null our XMLHttpRequest-related vars.
   */
  this.clearXHRVars = function() {
    this.callback = null;
    this.json = null;
    this.request = null;
  } // End clearXHRVars().

} // End XHRObject.
```

As the comments say, this object contains some fields used during Ajax request sending. `request` is literally the current `XMLHttpRequest` instance, `callback` is a reference to the function that is the callback for the request, and `json` is the parsed JSON response from the server.

SendAJAX.js

Having seen the `XHRObject` class, let's now see what makes use of it: the `sendAJAX()` function contained in `SendAJAX.js`. This function is used by all the other game code to make Ajax requests.

`sendAJAX()` accepts a number of parameters. First, it accepts a reference to the function that will be the callback. This will nearly always be the function that called `sendAJAX()`. It also accepts, as you would expect, the URL to submit the request to. It accepts both a query string (fully formed) and POST data. It technically will accept and use both; however, the call method (GET or POST) is determined by the presence of post, so if you send POST data to `sendAJAX()`, the method will be POST, regardless of whether or not there is a query string (but the query string *will* be used even if POSTing).

As we discussed in the "How We Will Pull It Off" section earlier, this function sets itself up as the callback in the newly instantiated `XMLHttpRequest`. So, first it checks whether there is already an `XMLHttpRequest` object reference in `gameState` (the `xhr` field). If so, then `sendAJAX()` proceeds (via an `if` branch) to check the status of the request. When that request completes, the results sent back by the server will be processed.

If there is no existing request in progress, the function instantiates a new `XMLHttpRequest` object, and attaches a parameter to the query string that has a value of the current date/time in milliseconds. This ensures that the browser will not cache the response and thereby cause it to appear as if the server is not responding (which it isn't because the request would never have reached the server). It then sets the method based on whether or not `inPostData` is `null`, and fires off the request.

When the response is received, the `else` part of the branch logic is fired, continually of course, until the response is good. When it is, the response is first `eval()`'d into `xhr.json`, which we'll reference from then on.

A number of various checks are then performed. If the `ex` member is present in `xhr.json`, then an exception occurred on the server and an alert box is displayed to let the player know. If the `di` member is set to true in `xhr.json`, then the player died, and the player's information is updated (so that their health can be shown as 0). Also, the activity scroll is updated so that the final message from the server is seen, and the game end screen is shown via the line

```
showGameEnd("died");
```

`showGameEnd()` accepts the values "died" and "won", and loads the appropriate content (`died.htm` or `won.htm`).

If the `ct` member is present in `xhr.json`, that means we are beginning to talk to a character, so the `startTalking()` function is called to do that (we'll see that in a bit).

If the `mo` member in `xhr.json` indicates we are now in Battle mode, and the current view is *not* Battle mode, that means we need to switch to Battle mode now. We do this by setting the current view to `battle`, and calling `updateMap()`, which will redraw the screen in Battle mode.

Lastly, if the mo member in xhr.json indicates we are not in normal (i.e., walking around the map) mode, and the current mode on the client is Battle, then we are coming out of battle, which again requires setting the current view and calling updateMap().

Note that each of these checks results in returning from the function. Before that, however, a call to xhr.clearXHRVars(); is made, which nulls out the xhr.request, xhr.json, and xhr.callback fields. It is only at this point that another Ajax request could occur (recall that the check to see if xhr.request is null is the first thing this function does).

Now, if none of these conditions applied, then sendAJAX() needs to call on the original callback that was passed into it. It does so, and captures the result. If the result is true, then xhr.clearXHRVars() is called. If false, it does not make that call. That way, if the callback function itself wants to make an Ajax request, it can do so. Think about what would happen if xhr.clearXHRVars() was called in that case—it would step on that new Ajax request and the request would not go through. Fortunately, this situation only comes up a few times, a majority of the time the callback will return true.

ActivityScroll.js

This source file contains a single function, updateActivityScroll(), which is called any time a new message should be displayed to the user in the activity scroll on the right side.

The activity scroll itself, as you might recall from our discussion of GameStateObject, is just an array. It always has 11 elements, which is how many can fit in the area allotted on the screen for messages. The messages are displayed top to bottom. In other words, each time the activity scroll is updated, it is redisplayed in full, and item index 0 is always the text shown at the top of the screen area, and so on down. So, in order for this to be a "scroll," we need to shift the contents of the array "up," that is, toward the 0 index. The 0 index element will fall into the "bit bucket." Fortunately, JavaScript arrays have some neat utility functions, among them shift(), which does precisely what we need. Also quite convenient is the push() method, which adds an element to the end of the array. This is nice because we don't have to worry about replacing a certain index or anything like that; shift() reduces the array's size to 10 elements, and push() then brings it back up to 11, and the net result is precisely what we want. Once that is done, we generate some simple markup from the contents of the array, and update the divActivityScroll <div>. The last piece of the puzzle is to scroll the contents of the <div> far enough so that the last element is always shown entirely. The problem here is that some messages returned by the server will actually take up two lines. So, if we didn't do this final scroll, we'd find that some messages get cut off on either the top or bottom, and sometimes the activity scroll text would extend downward a bit; both results are undesirable. Scrolling the whole <div> to an arbitrarily large value effectively pushes all the text down as far as it will go so that nothing is cut off, and in doing so, the <div> does not need to scroll.

StoreFuncs.js

I want to jump around just a bit here and look at the two functions in this file that relate to when the player is in a store and can purchase items. These two functions are perhaps the simplest examples that show the structure that most of the remaining functions will take. Listing 10-5 shows this code.

Listing 10-5. *The Entire Contents of StoreFuncs.js*

```
/**
 * This function is called when the player steps on a store trigger tile.
 */
function showStore() {
  if (xhr.request == null) {
    sendAJAX(showStore, "store.jsp", "", null);
  } else {
    showSecondaryView(xhr.request.responseText, Globals.VIEW_STORE);
    return true;
  } // End xhr.request == null if.
} // End showStore().


/**
 * This function is called when the player purchases an item in a store.
 */
function purchaseItem(inWhichItem) {
  if (xhr.request == null) {
    sendAJAX(purchaseItem, "purchaseItem.command", "?whichItem=" +
      inWhichItem, null);
  } else {
    updateActivityScroll(xhr.json.mg);
    return true;
  } // End xhr.request == null if.
} // End purchaseItem().
```

Both of these functions are called to fire off an Ajax request. `showStore()` is called when the user steps onto a tile right in front of a store, thereby entering the store. `purchaseItem()`, as one would expect, is called when the player decides on an item to purchase. Note the overall structure of both: a simple `if` checks to see whether `xhr.request` is `null`, and an `else` block. If it is `null`, a call to `sendAJAX()` is made. If it is not `null`, the `else` block kicks in, and the store view is shown (in the case of `showStore()`) or the activity scroll is updated (in the case of `purchaseItem()`). Most of the other functions we'll look at have this same basic structure, so it is important to understand the flow through them. To help with that understanding, Figure 10-8 shows a flow diagram of a call to one of them, and how `sendAJAX()` is involved.

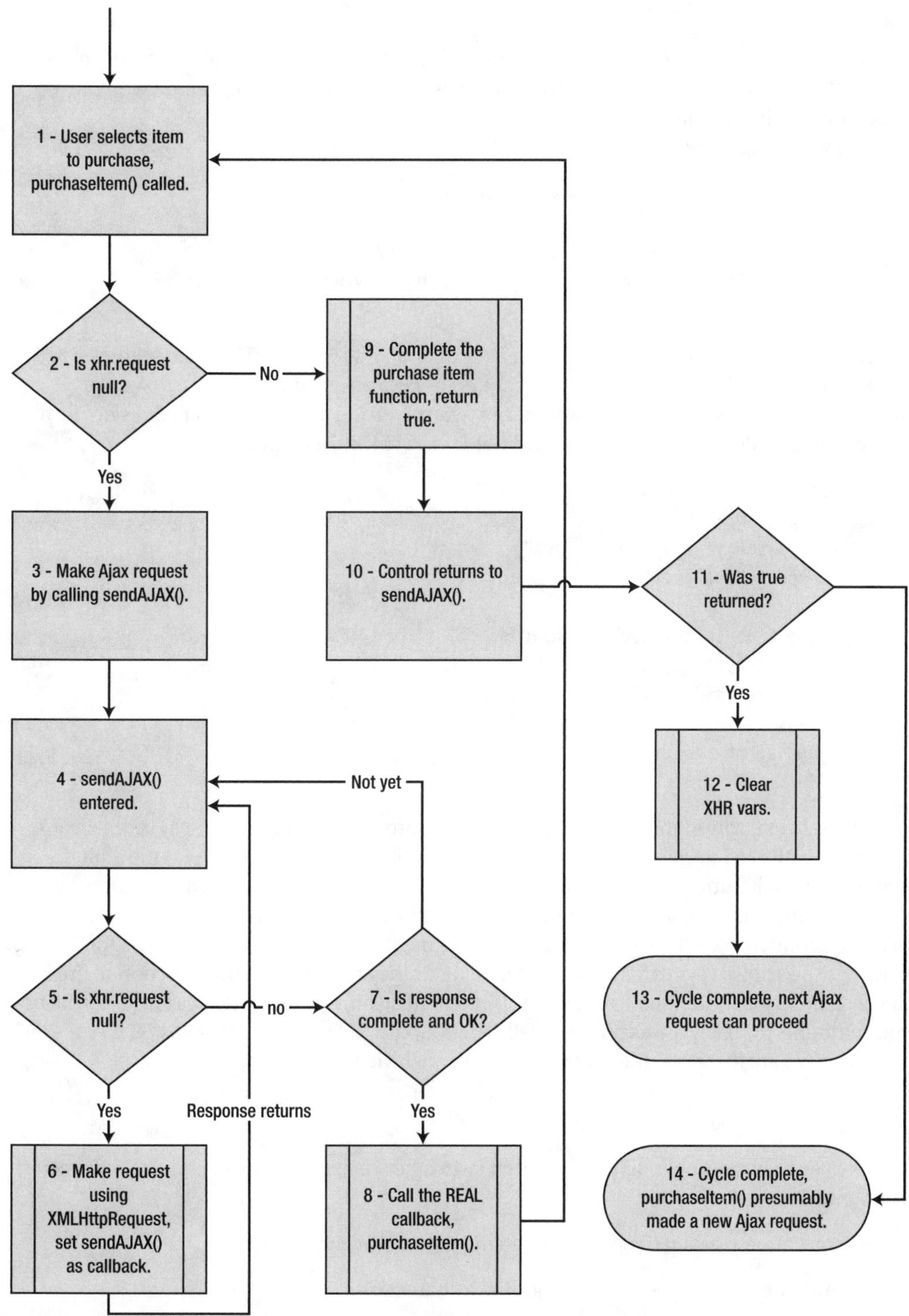

Figure 10-8. *Flow diagram of a typical Ajax request in AJAX Warrior*

KeyHandler.js

The next important piece of code to examine is the key handler code as defined by the function keyUp(). This function handles all the key presses in the game (as registered with the browser in the init() function).

The first thing we see is our code to get the key code pressed in a cross-browser fashion:

```
var ev = (e) ? e : (window.event) ? window.event : null;
if (ev) {
  keyCodePressed = (ev.charCode) ? ev.charCode:
    ((ev.keyCode) ? ev.keyCode : ((ev.which) ? ev.which : null));
}
```

After that comes an if statement with a number of else ifs in it. The logic branches depending on which view is current, since different keys are valid in different views. For instance, the E key, which enters a community when walking around the map, does not have any meaning while in battle. Within each if block is a switch, like the following:

```
switch (keyCodePressed) {
  case Globals.KEY_LEFT_ARROW:
    updateActivityScroll("West");
    updateMap("left");
  break;
  case Globals.KEY_RIGHT_ARROW:
    updateActivityScroll("East");
    updateMap("right");
  break;
 … and so on …
}
```

The vast majority of the cases simply call the appropriate function, such as updateMap() shown here (the call to updateActivityScroll() as well is common). There is some added complexity when buttons are pressed when the spell casting view or weapon switching views are shown; they can be called from either normal or battle view, so the code has to switch back to the appropriate view. Likewise, the cases for Battle mode are a bit more complex; for instance, the arrows keys can indicate movement, or they can indicate the direction of fire if the player previously pressed F for Fire Projectile. But again, by and large, this entire chunk of code amounts to "If key X was pressed, call function X()… if key Y was pressed, call function Y," and so on (where there is a different set of ifs for each view).

ViewChangeFuncs.js

This file contains a number of functions that switch between the various views in the game. The views are

- Normal view (when the player is walking around the map)
- Battle view (when the player is fighting a character)

- Inventory view (when the player is viewing their item inventory)
- Spell casting view (when the player wants to cast a spell)
- Weapon switching view (when the player wants to switch what weapon they are currently using)
- Help view (when the player is viewing the game help)
- Talking view (when the player is talking to a character)
- Store view (when the player is looking at the items they can purchase in a store)
- Game end view (when the player has either died or won the game)

`showHelp()` is called to show game help. `showMapView()` is called to show the normal map view. `showGameEnd()` is called to show the game end view (passing it the value "won" or "died" to indicate which view to show). `displayInventory()` is called to show the player's inventory.

All of these views make use of the `showSecondaryView()` function. This function accepts two parameters: the first is the markup to display, and the second is which view to display. Using these parameters, it populates the appropriate `<div>` and shows it, and also sets the `currentView` member of `gameState` appropriately.

You might be wondering why there is no `showSpellCasting()` or `showWeaponSwitching()` function, or others that change the view. The reason is that the ones that have functions here are essentially information-only views; no functionality is hidden within them. When you view inventory, you cannot select an item to use, for instance. However, spell casting requires two things: showing the spell casting view, and handling the casting of a spell. Because of this, you'll find a `castSpell()` function elsewhere that does what any of these would do—that is, show the spell casting view—but it also handles when the user picks a spell to cast. We'll see how that works soon.

CastSpell.js

Well, since I went and just brought it up, let's take a quick look at `castSpell()` right now! You can refer to the source file downloaded from the Apress website.

As before, you can see the overall structure repeated in terms of the branching logic based on whether or not `xhr.request` is `null`. When this function is called (which means the user pressed the C key), we need to simply show the spell casting view. In this case, the parameter `inWhichSpell` would not be passed, so the `else` block of the `if (inWhichSpell)` check is executed. This sets `gameState.spellCast` to false, and fires off an Ajax request to retrieve the markup for the spell casting view. When `sendAJAX()` receives the response, it calls back to `castSpell()`. At this point, the `else` block of the `if(xhr.request == null)` check executes. Within it, the `else` block of the `if (gameState.spellCast)` executes. This switches to the spell casting view and also evaluates that `<script>` block we spoke of earlier that lists what spells the player can cast. Now, at this point, you'll recall that the `keyUp()` function will be using a different set of `if` checks. So, when the user now presses a button corresponding to a spell they want to cast, it calls `castSpell()` again, but this time it passes in the code for the spell the player wants to cast. So, the `if (inWhichSpell)` check winds up executing the `if` portion, which makes an Ajax request to cast the spell. When sendAJAX() gets the response back, it again calls back to castSpell(). Again, the else block of the if (xhr.request == null) check executes, but time, because gameState.spellCast is true, the if portion of the if (spellCast) check executes. This updates the player's information and outputs whatever message the server returned to the activity scroll. That is a complete spell casting cycle from start to finish. That is also how a single function, castSpell(), can handle all the various flows through it.

Also in this JavaScript file is a function doesPlayerHaveSpell(). This is called when a key is pressed in Spell Casting mode to determine if the spell requested is one the player has to cast. It checks against the string eval()'d previously to get the value of gameState.spellsPlayerHas. This is nothing but a simple array scan to see if the requested code is present.

SwitchWeapon.js

If you just read the section on CastSpell.js, then you already more or less know all about SwitchWeapon.js! It is virtually identical. Please do have a look, and compare the two so as to be sure I am not pulling your leg.

Conversation.js

This source file contains four functions related to talking to a character: startTalking(), showNodeReplies(), stopTalking(), and talkReply().

startTalking() is, quite logically, what is called when the player comes in contact with a character they'll talk to. It is fairly straightforward: it shows the appropriate character image, switches to the talking view, shows the initial thing the character says (the character always talks first; pretend the player said "Hello!" automatically), and finally it shows the initial set of replies the player can make.

showNodeReplies() is the function that literally shows those replies, grabbing them from the xhr.json field.

stopTalking() does precisely what it says: it stops talking by setting the view back to normal (map) view.

Finally, talkReply() send an Ajax request when the player selects their reply. Let's have a quick look at this code:

```
function talkReply(inWhichReply) {

  if (xhr.request == null) {

    sendAJAX(talkReply, "talkReply.command", "?reply=" + inWhichReply, null);

  } else {

    if (xhr.json.mo == Globals.MODE_NORMAL) {
      updateMap();
      document.getElementById("imgCharacter").src =
        Globals.imgTransparent.src;
      showMapView();
```

```
    } else {
      showNodeReplies();
    }
    return true;

  } // End xhr.request == null if.

} // End talkReply().
```

OK, so, as usual, we have the typical branching we've seen a number of times now. What is interesting is the `else` block, when the response comes back. If the `mo` member of the `xhr.json` reply indicates we are now in normal mode, that means either the character got spooked by us and ran away, or they gave us a key. In either case, we're going to switch back to normal map view, and call `updateMap()` to get the correct view again. If the response did not indicate a switch back to normal mode, then the conversation is continuing, in which case the server will have returned a new set of replies the player can make. So, we call on `showNodeReplies()` once more to display them.

And that's how we talk to a nonexistent monk, thief, peasant, or guard!

GameFuncs.js

`GameFuncs.js` contains what would be considered the "core" client-side code of AJAX Warrior.

The first function we encounter is `updatePlayerInfo()`:

```
function updatePlayerInfo(inName, inHealth, inGoldPieces, inHitPoints) {

  document.getElementById("divName").innerHTML = inName;
  document.getElementById("divHealth").innerHTML = "Health: " + inHealth;
  document.getElementById("divHitPoints").innerHTML =
    "Hit Points: " + inGoldPieces;
  document.getElementById("divGoldPieces").innerHTML =
    "Gold Pieces: " + inHitPoints;

} // End updatePlayerInfo().
```

Pretty simple: pass if the player's name, health, gold pieces, and hit points, and the appropriate `<div>` elements will be updated.

Next up is `toggleTalkAttack()`:

```
function toggleTalkAttack(inWhichState) {

  if (xhr.request == null) {

    sendAJAX(toggleTalkAttack, "toggleTalkAttack.command", "", null);

  } else {
```

```
    updateActivityScroll(xhr.json.mg);
    // Change the border state.
    if (gameState.talkAttackMode == Globals.PLAYER_TALK_MODE) {
      document.getElementById("imgBorder").src = Globals.imgATTACKING.src;
      gameState.talkAttackMode = Globals.PLAYER_ATTACK_MODE;
    } else {
      document.getElementById("imgBorder").src = Globals.imgTALKING.src
      gameState.talkAttackMode = Globals.PLAYER_TALK_MODE;
    }
    return true;

  }

} // End toggleTalkAttack().
```

Once more, our typical function structure. When the reply returns from the server, we display the message we got back telling us what mode we are now in, and we then toggle the mode as recorded in `gameState`. Finally, we update the border image as appropriate: red for Attack mode, blue for Talk mode.

After that comes `enterCommunity()`. This is a simple call to the server that switches what map we are using from the main Xandor map to one of the community maps (unless the player wasn't standing on a community, in which case the message returned will indicate that). A call is then made to `updateMap()`, passing it `null`, which means it will return the chunk of the map corresponding to where the player begins inside a community.

`pickUpItem()` is next, and it is yet another simple Ajax call to the server. When the response returns, the player's information is updated (because if they picked up gold or a health pack, their info might have changed), and the function also displays whatever message the server returned.

`SaveGame()` is up next:

```
function saveGame() {

  if (xhr.request == null) {

    // Serialize the gameState object.
    var serializedGameState = gameState.serialize();
    sendAJAX(saveGame, "saveGame.command", "", serializedGameState);

  } else {

    updateActivityScroll(xhr.json.mg);
    return true;

  } // End xhr.request == null if.

} // End saveGame().
```

Here, we see a call to gameState.serialize(), which returns to us a string of XML representing the pertinent details of the gameState instance. An Ajax call is then made, passing this string as POST data (because it is passed as the last parameter; note the third parameter is an empty string—that is the query string). Upon return, we simply display the messages as returned by the server.

Last, we find updateMap(). This is quite a large function, but it's also quite simple. First, if xhr.request is null, we see

```
var queryString = "";

// Null means the player isn't moving.  Happens when the page is first
// shown, and in various other limited situations.
if (inMoveDir != null) {
  queryString = "?moveDirection=" + inMoveDir;
}

sendAJAX(updateMap, "updateMap.command", queryString, null);
```

If a move direction was passed in, we build a query string with that information. This will in essence allow the server to scroll the map, moving our viewport into the map. If it is null, that indicates it is the initial request for map data; in that case, the server will return the viewport for the player's starting location on the map.

Once the response comes back, we have

```
// Update the activity scroll, if applicable.
if (xhr.json.dm == "true") {
  updateActivityScroll(xhr.json.mg);
}
```

This code checks whether the dm element is xhr.json is true, which indicates that there is a message that needs to be displayed. In that case, we pass it to updateActivityScroll() to take care of that for us.

Then comes a big segment of code, part of which looks like this:

```
// Update the viewport, if applicable.
if (xhr.json.vu == "true") {
  var i = 0;
  var x;
  var y;
  for (y = 0; y < Globals.VIEWPORT_HEIGHT; y++) {

    for (x = 0; x < Globals.VIEWPORT_WIDTH; x++) {

      var tile = document.getElementById("tile-" + y + "-" + x);

      switch (xhr.json.md.charAt(i)) {
```

```
case Globals.TILE_BLANK:
  tile.src = Globals.imgTILE_BLANK.src;
break;
case Globals.TILE_BRIDGE:
  tile.src = Globals.imgTILE_BRIDGE.src;
break;
case Globals.TILE_FOREST_THIN:
  tile.src = Globals.imgTILE_FOREST_THIN.src;
break;
          ... and so on...

        }

      }

    }
```

We're going to loop through all the images in the grid (remember all those images we created in `init()`?). For each, we'll examine the corresponding element in the `xhr.json` reply to determine what kind of image should be shown; should it be a mountain, water, a town? Note that this all will happen only if the `vu` member of `xhr.json` is found to be true, which indicates the view has been updated. There's no sense doing all this work if the player has not moved anywhere!

Following this giant `switch` is one more chunk of code:

```
  // Finally, always place the player in the center if not in battle.
  // If in battle, place it where specified.
  if (gameState.currentView == Globals.VIEW_BATTLE) {
    var tile = document.getElementById("tile-" +
      xhr.json.cy + "-" + xhr.json.cx);
      if (gameState.battleEnemyTurn) {
        tile.src = Globals.imgCHARACTER_PLAYER.src;
      } else {
        tile.src = Globals.imgCHARACTER_PLAYER_BATTLE.src;
      }
  } else {
    var tile = document.getElementById("tile-" +
      (Globals.VIEWPORT_HALF_HEIGHT) + "-" +
      (Globals.VIEWPORT_HALF_WIDTH));
    tile.src = Globals.imgCHARACTER_PLAYER.src;
  }

} // End viewUpdated check.

// Update the player info, if applicable.
if (xhr.json.iu == "true") {
  updatePlayerInfo(xhr.json.pn, xhr.json.ht, xhr.json.hp, xhr.json.gp);
}
```

```
// If the last character move resulted in us entering a store, fire
// off the Ajax request to get the markup.  Note the return false... we
// will be starting a new Ajax request, so we don't want to null out the
// applicable variables.  However, before we can start that request, we
// have to null out the variables manually.
if (xhr.json.es == "true") {
  xhr.clearXHRVars();
  showStore();
  return false;
}

// Default return.
return true;
```

First, we need to place the player on the map. Wouldn't be much good without 'em! This will be different depending on whether we are in Battle mode. In this mode, the player can move around the entire viewport, whereas in normal mode they are always simply placed in the middle. Also, in Battle mode, when it is the player's turn, a flashing border appears around the player, and likewise when it is the character's turn. To do this, we need to use a different image depending on whose turn it is since the flashing border is done with nothing but an animated GIF.

After that, we update the player's information, if the `vu` member of `xhr.json` is true.

Finally, if the `es` member of `xhr.json` is true, it means the player is entering a store. In that case, we need to fire off a new Ajax request. So, we call `clearXHRVars()`; otherwise we wouldn't be able to make the new call because `sendAJAX()` would block it (or more precisely, act like it was being called back by `XMLHttpRequest`, which would cause an infinite loop). We then call `showStore()` to make the new call.

BattleFuncs.js

`BattleFuncs.js` contains the functions used during battle with a character. There are three functions: `battleMove()`, `battleEnemyMove()`, and `showProjectile()`.

`battleMove()` is called when the player moves when it is their turn. It is passed the direction the player moved, and an Ajax call is made. When the response is received, the `ph` element of `xhr.json` is checked for. If found, it means that the player fired a projectile weapon (slingshot or crossbow). Note that `ph` indicates whether or not the player hit the character, but here we are only checking whether it is present; whether it hit or not is irrelevant at this point (it will be present either way). If it is found, then a number of fields in `gameState` are updated, including what coordinates the projectile starts at (the player's location), where it stops (either the character or the edge of the viewport), what direction it's traveling in, whether or not it hit the character, and so on. At the end, a timer is started that fires `showProjectile()` every 100 milliseconds.

`ShowProjectile()` is responsible for actually showing an arrow flying (whether fired from the player or a character). It works by updating the coordinates of the arrow with every iteration and overwriting the appropriate tile. It restores the previous tile to what it was before the arrow was on it. When the end is reached, it stops the timer and branches, depending on whose turn it was. If it was the player's turn, it fires off a new Ajax request to allow the character a turn. If it was the character's turn, the player's information is updated. Recall that `sendAJAX()` determines when the player dies, so there is no need to do that check here. Likewise, if we have killed the character, `sendAJAX()` will take care of returning us to normal view as well.

Finally, battleEnemyMove() is quite similar to battleMove(). The primary difference is that when it completes, it doesn't do anything (like battleMove() has to call battleEnemyMove()) because it is the player's turn again. Therefore, the code just needs to wait for the player's input.

Note the following:

```
gameState.projectileX = parseInt(xhr.json.p1);
gameState.projectileY = parseInt(xhr.json.p2);
gameState.projectileEndX = parseInt(xhr.json.p3);
gameState.projectileEndY = parseInt(xhr.json.p4);
```

JSON is pretty ignorant when it comes to data types. That is to say, everything is a string! Here, had we simply set the fields to xhr.json.p1, for instance, when we tried to increment their values later on, we would have gotten string concatenations instead of math (I know this because I made this mistake; I included comments to prove it!). So, by using parseInt(), we get true numeric values instead. Review the discussion in Chapter 2 about data typing in JavaScript if you are unclear about this.

And with that, we have completely looked at the client side of things. Whew, quite a ride! Now we're ready to plunge into the server side of things, and there's at least as much code to look at there, so let's jump right in!

The Server-Side Code

While the server-side code of AJAX Warrior is not all that complex for the most part, there is a fair amount of it. It helps to understand the overall package structure first.

There are a number of packages, all of them under com.apress.ajaxprojects.ajaxwarrior. The first is commands. AJAX Warrior uses its own simple framework consisting of a front servlet and a number of commands, each corresponding to some specific call the client can make. Those commands are found in the commands package.

The filter package contains a single servlet filter that performs a check to ensure that a game has been properly started before the request can continue.

The framework package contains the classes that make up the application framework, including the front servlet.

The gameobjects package contains classes that make up the game itself. These are, for the most part, DTO-type objects.

The listener package contains a single context listener used to initialize the game at startup.

There are a few classes in the ajaxwarrior package itself, and it is in those classes that we'll begin our exploration.

Globals.java

The Globals class is nothing but a holder for a whole bunch of constants used throughout the game code. It includes fields for the tiles that appear in the maps, such as TILE_BRIDGE and TILE_WATER_SHALLOW. It includes fields for items such as ITEM_GOLD and ITEM_HEALTH. It contains fields as well for characters, artifacts, and so on. It also includes a number of strings, such as PLAYER_NO_WALK_TILES, which contains the codes for the tiles that the player cannot walk on. It includes fields like TILE_WIDTH and TILE_HEIGHT, which define how big a tile is (32×32 pixels). It also includes fields like PLAYER_START_HEALTH and PLAYER_MAX_HEALTH, which define characteristics of the player at startup and as the game progresses. There is no executable code in this class to speak of; it is simply a value holder.

Utils.java

You know all those JSON messages we've been talking about? Well, in the `Utils` class you'll find the `writeJSON()` method that creates these messages. Let's have a look at that method now. Please refer to its source as downloaded from the Apress website.

As you can see, it boils down to basically building up the contents of a `StringBuffer` and then outputting that to the response object passed in. The first check performed is to see if we are writing JSON as the result of an exception. If so, the response is simply the `ex` member and the message, which the client will display for us.

After that, a number of checks are performed on the input parameters, for instance to deal with a `null` map chunk, which is the data the client will use to render the current view of the map. Since the view will not always be updated, `null` can be passed here, in which case we need to avoid `NullPointerExceptions`. Likewise, if the view *is* being updated, then the incoming map chunk, which is an `ArrayList`, has to be converted to a `String`, and that is done too.

The JSON message varies depending on what is happening in the game. For instance, when we are in Battle mode, the elements `cx` and `cy` are present; otherwise they are not. Likewise, if a projectile weapon has been fired, then the `p1`, `p2`, `p3`, `p4`, `ph`, and `pd` elements will be present; otherwise they are not. This all keeps the messages as small and efficient as possible by generally not passing superfluous data.

The other method found in this class is `getDescFromCode()`, which is used to get a descriptive string for a given item code. This is used when displaying inventory, for instance. Note that for spells, this method also displays the number of that spell the player has in parentheses after the spell description.

MapHandler.java

The `MapHandler` class is far and away the largest class in all of AJAX Warrior, but it has to be; it has quite a lot of responsibility! In fact, if any class were to be called the heart and soul of this application, `MapHandler` probably stands the best chance of winning that title. Let's jump right in, shall we?

I'll begin by giving you a rundown of the data fields in this class:

- `static Log`: Log instance
- `ArrayList mainItems`: The collection of items placed on the main map
- `ArrayList townAItems`: The collection of items placed on the townA map
- `ArrayList townBItems`: The collection of items placed on the townB map
- `ArrayList villageItems`: The collection of items placed on the village map
- `ArrayList castleItems`: The collection of items placed on the castle map
- `ArrayList mainCharacters`: The collection of characters placed on the main map
- `ArrayList townACharacters`: The collection of characters placed on the townA map
- `ArrayList townBCharacters`: The collection of characters placed on the townB map
- `ArrayList villageCharacters`: The collection of characters placed on the village map
- `ArrayList castleCharacters`: The collection of characters placed on the castle map

- String currentMapString: String name of the current map
- ArrayList currentMap: Pointer to the map that is currently in use
- ArrayList previousMap: Pointer to the previous map that was used before the battle began
- ArrayList currentItems: Pointer to the items collection that is currently in use
- ArrayList currentCharacters: Pointer to the characters collection that is currently in use
- ArrayList battleMap: The battle map currently in use
- Random generator: Random number generator

Now we'll start exploring the methods by looking at the constructor. The constructor is a series of calls to placeItems(), which is responsible for randomly creating and placing items on the map (such as gold, health packs, and spell scrolls). There is also code specifically to add all the keys and artifacts. This is done for all five maps (four communities and the main map). After that come similar calls to placeCharacter(), which randomly places various characters on each map. The key masters are added explicitly in the constructor as well.

Next up we find the ubiquitous getChunk() method. This method is called frequently from various commands at various times. Its job is to return an ArrayList that represents the viewport of the map. In other words, the collection will contain 13 rows (because that is the height of the viewport as defined in Globals) where each row has 13 characters (because that is also the width of the viewport as defined in Globals) and each character is one tile on the map that the player sees. This ArrayList will be returned as one giant string to the client, which will then use it to render the current view. getChunk() begins by calling getBaseMapChunk(), which is where the actual map data is retrieved. It then superimposes over that map data the items that are currently on the map with this code:

```
for (Iterator it = currentItems.iterator(); it.hasNext();) {
  GameItem item = (GameItem)it.next();
  x = item.getXLocation();
  y = item.getYLocation();
  // If the next item in the collection is within the viewport, replace
  // the appropriate tile with the appropriate character tile.
  if (x >= inCurrentLocationX &&
    x <= (inCurrentLocationX + (Globals.VIEWPORT_WIDTH - 1)) &&
    y >= inCurrentLocationY &&
    y <= (inCurrentLocationY + (Globals.VIEWPORT_HEIGHT - 1))) {
    int row = y - inCurrentLocationY;
    int col = x - inCurrentLocationX;
    StringBuffer targetRow =
      new StringBuffer((String)chunk.get(row));
    targetRow.replace(col, col + 1, Character.toString(item.getType()));
    chunk.set(row, targetRow.toString());
  }
}
```

As you can see, it is nothing more than iterating over the collection of items, and for each, determining whether it is actually in the player's view. If it is, the appropriate character in the appropriate ArrayList element is replaced with the tile code for the item.

The characters are then superimposed onto the map data with code that is virtually identical to that which we have just seen. The end result is that the ArrayList that getChunk() returns is an accurate view of the map, items, and characters within view of where the player is standing on the map.

The next method we find is getBaseMapChunk(), which, as mentioned earlier, returns the chunk of the map for the viewport. It is nothing but a loop that iterates the number of times the viewport is high (13 currently) and retrieves the appropriate ArrayList elements and returns them.

After that comes getCenterTile(), which is another commonly used function. Its purpose is to retrieve the code of the tile where the player is standing, which is always the center tile in the viewport. This is used many times to determine when the player is standing on items, characters, tiles they cannot actually walk on, and so forth.

Next up we run into switchMap(). This method is called, for instance, when entering a community. All of the methods in this class work against the currentMap variable, which points to the appropriate ArrayList for the map the player is currently on (i.e., Xandor, a town, etc.). When the player enters a community, we need to point to a different ArrayList, and switchMap() does this. We pass it the name of the map we want to switch to, and it handles all the heavy lifting with code like this:

```
currentMap        = GameMaps.castleMap;
currentItems      = castleItems;
currentCharacters = castleCharacters;
currentMapString  = inWhichMap;
```

An if…else check determines which block to execute, and there are five blocks similar to this. currentMap is pointed at the appropriate ArrayList in the GameMaps class, and the items and characters are also updated. We also record the string that was passed into this method for logging purposes.

There is also one special value that can be passed in: "previous". This value is used primarily when battle ends in order to get us back onto the previous map without us knowing what it was. In other words, because the player can enter into battle while walking around Xandor, or while in any of the communities, the code cannot be written to return to any specific map; it can only determine what map to return to at runtime, and it does this based on this "previous" value.

The placeItems() method comes next. Passed into this method is the name of the map we're placing items on. Based on that value, a few lines of code execute, such as the following if the value was "main":

```
mainItems         = new ArrayList();
targetCollection  = mainItems;
mapBeingPopulated = GameMaps.mainMap;
numberOfItems     = Globals.NUM_ITEMS_ON_MAIN_MAP;
```

Here, we're first creating a whole new collection of items for this map. We're then pointing the `targetCollection` variable to that collection. This again allows the remainder of the code to be generic and we don't have to know what map we are dealing with. We also need a reference to the map itself that we're adding items to; we'll need to check on it later when we want to determine if the target tile is a valid one for an item to be placed on. Lastly, we get the number of items that should be on this map from `Globals`.

At this point, we begin a loop that iterates the number of times now specified by the `numberOfItems` variable. For each iteration of the loop, we randomly decide what kind of item we're going to place—health, spell scroll, or gold chest—and instantiate a `GameItem` object for it. At this point, we also randomly decide the quantity of each and set it on the object. Next, we randomly pick a tile to place the item on. We call on the `isItemSafeTile()` method, which returns true if it's OK to place an item on the tile, and returns false if not. If we get back false, we choose another location, and keep doing so until we find a safe location. Finally, when we have a location, we add the item to the `targetCollection`, and we are done.

The next method we stumble upon is `placeCharacters()`. This method starts off exactly the same as `placeItems()` in terms of pointing to the correct collection to add to (and first clearing it), pointing to the correct map data, and so forth. It then enters the same kind of loop. However, this method doesn't do any of the actual work! Instead, it makes a call to `createCharacter()`, which returns a `GameCharacter` object. Note that each character is given an ID based on the index of the loop. This is important because this ID is used later when removing a character from the collection, such as when the player kills the character in battle. It then calls `charPickLocation()`, passing it the `GameCharacter` object. These are broken out because they are needed at other times, such as when the player kills a character, so that we can create a new one. Once this is done, the character is added to the collection, and that is that.

The `removeCharacter()` method comes next, and as we mentioned earlier, the ID of the character to remove is passed in. The collection to remove from is determined by examining the `currentMapString` variable, which, as you'll recall, is set by calling `switchMap()`. After that, it is a simple loop to find and remove the character:

```
int i = -1;
for (Iterator it = targetCollection.iterator(); it.hasNext();) {
  i++;
  GameCharacter gc = (GameCharacter)it.next();
  if (inID.equalsIgnoreCase(gc.getId())) {
    // i is now the index of the character to delete.
    break;
  }
}
targetCollection.remove(i);
```

`createCharacter()` is the next method we find. As you'll recall, this is the first one called by `placeCharacters()`. Its job it to randomly determine the characteristics of the new character. First, it instantiates a `GameCharacter` object. Next, it randomly decides what direction the character is going to be moving in. Then, it randomly decides what type of character it is, and sets the applicable characteristics. There is a big `switch` statement in which each case is a specific character type. They are all quite similar, so I'll show just the one for a guard as an example:

```
// Guard.
case 1:
  // 0_thru_2 + 1 = 1_thru_3
  b = generator.nextInt(3) + 1;
  character.setTalkConversation(
    GameConversations.getConversation("guard_" + b));
  character.setImmobile(false);
  character.setType(Globals.CHARACTER_GUARD);
  // Guards will be belligerent about 20% of the time.  0_thru_100
  b = generator.nextInt(101);
  if (b < 20) {
    character.setBelligerent(true);
  }
  character.setGreenKeymaster(false);
  character.setRedKeymaster(false);
  character.setHitPoints(generator.nextInt(26) + 15);
  character.setHealth(generator.nextInt(21) + 80);
  // 0_thru_4
  w = generator.nextInt(5);
  switch (w) {
    case 0:
      character.setWeapon(Globals.WEAPON_DAGGER);
      break;
    case 1:
      character.setWeapon(Globals.WEAPON_STAFF);
      break;
    case 2:
      character.setWeapon(Globals.WEAPON_MACE);
      break;
    case 3:
      character.setWeapon(Globals.WEAPON_SLINGSHOT);
      break;
    case 4:
      character.setWeapon(Globals.WEAPON_CROSSBOW);
      break;
    default:
      log.error("** THIS SHOULD NEVER HAPPEN!");
      break;
  }
  break;
```

The first thing decided is which of the three guard conversations this character will use. Next, we call `setImmobile(false)` to indicate that this character moves around (some do not). Next, we determine whether or not the guard is belligerent (i.e., will always attack the player). We do this by picking a number between 0 and 100. If the value is < 20, then the guard is belligerent. This in effect means that about 20 percent of the time, guards will be belligerent. Well, that would be true if the random number distribution were truly random! It is close enough for our purposes, though; we aren't creating NSA code hashes here after all!

Next, since a guard is not a key master, we pass false to both `setRedKeymaster()` and `setGreenKeymaster()`. After that, we randomly decide on the guard's hit points. Since a guard is likely a pretty strong character, their hit points will always be between 15 and 35. Next we set their health, and again, because guards are quite strong, that value will always be between 20 and 100.

Finally, we randomly decide what kind of weapon the guard has. Guards can use all the weapon types (some characters cannot), so we have a lot of options to randomly choose from.

As I mentioned, this code is similar for all the character types. The ranges of the random values for things like health and hit points are of course different, and some characters, such as serpents, always use a specific weapon (a crossbow in that case), and some characters are always belligerent or never belligerent, so that decision is not present for some. But overall, the basic code structure is the same.

`charPickLocation()` is the next method. Its job is to choose a random location on the map for a character. This code is very similar to that seen in `placeItems()`, and it performs the same check to be sure the tile is valid for a character. Of course, this function uses a different string from `Globals`, since the tiles a character can be on are somewhat different from the tiles an item can be on.

The next method up for bid on The Code Is Right (sorry, couldn't resist!) is `getItem()`:

```
public GameItem getItem(final  int inCurrentLocationX,
  final int inCurrentLocationY) {

  // Calculate the X and Y coordinates the player is standing on.
  int x = inCurrentLocationX + Globals.VIEWPORT_HALF_WIDTH;
  int y = inCurrentLocationY + Globals.VIEWPORT_HALF_HEIGHT;
  // Now iterate over the collection of items for the current map and when
  // we find the item with those X/Y coordinates, return item to caller.
  int i = 0;
  GameItem gi = null;
  for (Iterator it = currentItems.iterator(); it.hasNext();) {
    gi = (GameItem)it.next();
    if (x == gi.getXLocation() && y == gi.getYLocation()) {
      break;
    }
    i++;
  }
  return gi;

} // End getItem().
```

As the name makes clear, it is used to retrieve a `GameItem` object for a specified tile on the map. Specifically, this is used in `PickUpItemCommand` when the player tries to pick up an item. Since we know the player is always in the middle of the viewport, we need to calculate the exact X/Y coordinate for the item because the `inCurrentLocationX` and `inCurrentLocationY` will actually be the upper-left corner of the viewport because that's always what "current location" of the player means outside of battle. So, we simply figure out that X/Y coordinate, then iterate over the collection for the `currentItems` and find the one with those coordinates and return it, or return `null` if it is not found (i.e., the player was not on an item when they pressed P).

`removeItem()` is the next method in line, and it works very similarly to `getItem()` in terms of calculating the X/Y coordinates and iterating over the collection until the item is found. The difference is that when it is found, the loop is exited and the index of the item found is removed.

The next four methods are `isNoWalkTile()`, `isCharacterNoWalkTile()`, `isItemTile()`, and `isItemSafeTile()`. I am grouping them because they are all pretty much the same: they return true or false to indicate whether the specified tile

- Is one that a player cannot walk on
- Is one that a character other than the player cannot walk on
- Currently has an item on it
- Is one we can place an item on

They all work by referencing some constant string in `Globals` (`PLAYER_NO_WALK_TILES`, `CHARACTER_NO_WALK_TILES`, `ITEM_TILES` and `ITEM_SAFE_TILES`, respectively) and seeing if the tile code passed in is found in the string. If so, true is returned; otherwise false is returned. These methods are used in various situations such as placing an item on the map, determining if the player's desired move should be allowed, and so on.

The next method is a pretty big one, `moveCharacters()`. This is called after the player makes a move to move all the characters on the map. First, it begins to iterate over the collection of characters on the map. It gets a reference to the next character in line and checks to see if it is immobile. If it is, then this iteration of the loop is ended with a `continue` keyword.

Next, we get the pertinent details about the character, such as its current location, move direction, and so forth. We now perform a check to determine how far away from the player the character is. If the character is belligerent, and if they are within view of the player, then the character will move toward the player. This is a very basic pursuit algorithm common in many games. One extra thing we do here is we check to see if the character is exactly one space away from the character diagonally. If so, we *do not* move them. This avoids a situation where the character appears to "jump" right on top of the player rather than actually pursue them. This is caused by the fact that if this check was not present, the X *and* Y coordinates would get updated by the subsequent code, which would result in the character now occupying the same tile as the player, causing combat to begin. This would not allow the player the possibility of running away from a character with the character in pursuit, and I felt that was an important thing to allow for.

Once the character's location is updated, we check to see if they wound up on a tile they cannot walk on. If so, we revert to the previous location. This too allows for the player to escape, for instance by walking over a bridge, which characters cannot walk on.

If the character *is not* belligerent or is out of view of the player, we just move it according to its current direction of movement. We first, however, check to see if we have moved a required number of tiles in that direction as defined in `Globals`. If we have, a new direction of travel is chosen.

If the character is still moving, though, we randomly determine whether to move them or not. Thirty percent of the time, a character will not move for this iteration.

A final check is performed to ensure that the character does not walk off the edges of the map. If they get within two tiles of the edge, they revert to their previous location. Note that eventually they'll walk away from the edge; they won't just get stuck there.

When all is said and done, the location of the player is updated (which may not be changed from what it was when this method started), and we update their direction of movement, since that could have changed too.

And that is character movement in a (rather large) nutshell.

The next method seen in this class is `isTileAlreadyOccupied()`. This method returns true if a character already occupies the specified tile. This method is used, for instance, to determine if a character can be placed on a tile when generating the characters for the map.

The next method, `touchingCharacter()`, is used to determine when battle should begin because the player and a character are "touching," that is, occupying the same tile. Here's its code:

```
public GameCharacter touchingCharacter(final int inCurrentLocationX,
  final int inCurrentLocationY, final ArrayList inChunk) {

  GameCharacter gc = null;
  char playerTile = getPlayerTile(inChunk);
  // Calculate the true X/Y coordinate of the player.
  int x = inCurrentLocationX + Globals.VIEWPORT_HALF_WIDTH;
  int y = inCurrentLocationY + Globals.VIEWPORT_HALF_HEIGHT;
  // See if the tile the player is on is a character tile.
  for (int i = 0; i < Globals.CHARACTER_TILES.length(); i++) {
    if (playerTile == Globals.CHARACTER_TILES.charAt(i)) {
      // OK, the tile the player is on is a character.  Now we need to find
      // the character.
      for (Iterator it = currentCharacters.iterator(); it.hasNext();) {
        GameCharacter g = (GameCharacter)it.next();
        if (x == g.getXLocation() && y == g.getYLocation()) {
          gc = g;
        }
      }
      break;
    }
  }
  return gc;

} // End touchingCharacter.
```

As you can see, the applicable `GameCharacter` instance is returned, or `null` is returned if the player is not in contact with a character.

We are almost done! The next method (other than the getter and setter for the `currentMapString` field and the `toString()` method) is `createBattleMap()`. When the player enters into battle, the map they see is constructed by filling the viewport with whatever tile they player is standing on—such as grass or mountains. Here's the code that accomplishes that:

```
public ArrayList createBattleMap(final int inCurrX, final int inCurrY,
  final GameCharacter inCharacter) {
```

```
    ArrayList chunk = getBaseMapChunk(inCurrX, inCurrY);
    char playerTile = getPlayerTile(chunk);
    // Now generate our battle map, which is the size of our viewport, filling
    // it with nothing but the tile the player was standing on (which should
    // always be a ground tile, i.e., dirt, etc.)
    battleMap = new ArrayList();
    for (int y = 0; y < Globals.VIEWPORT_HEIGHT; y++) {
      battleMap.add(StringUtils.repeat(
        Character.toString(playerTile), Globals.VIEWPORT_WIDTH));
    }
    // Now get the battle map, with the character superimposed into it.
    ArrayList bm = getBattleMap(inCharacter);
    previousMap = currentMap;
    currentMap  = battleMap;

    // Return the battle map.
    return bm;

  } // End createBattleMap().
```

As you can see, we get the chunk of the map for the viewport, and then get the tile the player is on. We then construct a chunk to fill the viewport using that tile. We use the handy `repeat()` method of the `StringUtils` class from Commons Lang. This returns to us a string filled with the specified character of length `Globals.VIEWPORT_WIDTH`. We do this `Globals.VIEWPORT_HEIGHT` times, filling an `ArrayList` with each iteration, and return it. That is our battle map!

Finally, we come to the last method in this big class: `getBattleMap()`. This simply returns the battle map that was created by `createBattleMap()`, with one difference: the character is superimposed onto it in its current location, like so:

```
  public ArrayList getBattleMap(final GameCharacter inCharacter) {

    int col = inCharacter.getXLocation();
    int row = inCharacter.getYLocation();
    ArrayList bm = new ArrayList(battleMap);
    StringBuffer targetRow =
      new StringBuffer((String)bm.get(row));
    targetRow.replace(col, col + 1, Character.toString(inCharacter.getType()));
    bm.set(row, targetRow.toString());
    return bm;

  } // End getBattleMap().
```

ClientSideGameState.java

The ClientSideGameState object is a simple JavaBean, which is used to store a representation of the client-side GameStateObject that we saw earlier. Internally, it has an ArrayList for the activity scroll, and two String fields, one for currentWeapon and another for talkAttackMode (and the applicable getters and setters). It also has a String activityScrollEntry, but this is used only to populate the instance using Digester when the game is saved, which we'll see later when we discuss the SaveGameCommand class.

Aside from the usual JavaBean methods, there is also a getAsString() method:

```
public String getAsClientString() {

  // Construct a delimited string where ~~~ is the delimiter sequence.
  StringBuffer sb = new StringBuffer(1024);
  sb.append(StringEscapeUtils.escapeJavaScript(talkAttackMode) + "~~~");
  sb.append(StringEscapeUtils.escapeJavaScript(currentWeapon) + "~~~");
  for (Iterator it = activityScroll.iterator(); it.hasNext();) {
    sb.append(StringEscapeUtils.escapeJavaScript((String)it.next()) + "~~~");
  }
  return sb.toString();

} // End getAsClientString
```

This method is used when a game is being continued. It constructs a delimited string, delimited by three tildes in a row (~~~) because that should be a safe delimiter in terms of it never naturally occurring in any of the data. Recall that the reconstitute() function of the client-side GameStateObject knows how to parse this string and use it to populate the GameStateObject instance. Now you know how it gets the string in the first place!

GameCharacter.java

The GameCharacter class is a simple JavaBean. It represents a character in the game that the player can interact with. It contains these fields:

- String id: The ID of this character.
- char type: The type of the character.
- int xLocation: The horizontal location of this character.
- int yLocation: The vertical location of this character.
- boolean belligerent: True if this character is belligerent toward the player, false if not.
- int health: The health of this character.
- int hitPoints: How many hit points this character has.
- char weapon: What weapon this character is holding.
- boolean greenKeymaster: True if this character can tell where the green key is, false if not.
- boolean redKeymaster: True if this character can tell where the red key is, false if not.

- `int moveCount`: A counter for how many tiles the character has moved in a given direction so far.
- `char moveDir`: The direction the character is currently moving in (`n`, `s`, `e`, `w`).
- `boolean immobile`: This flag is set to true when the character doesn't move.
- `GameConversation talkConversation`: The `GameConversation` this character will use.

There is no executable code other than the getters and setters (well, aside from the usual `toString()` method that I tend to use in DTO-type classes such as this).

GameConversation.java

`GameConversation` is another simple JavaBean, or DTO-type class. This one represents and stores a conversation as read in from one of the conversation XML files we looked at earlier. Internally it contains a `String id` field that the conversation is known by, and a `HashMap` containing all the nodes from the XML file, keyed by node ID. Like `GameCharacter`, there is no executable code in this class beyond getters, setters, and `toString()`.

GameConversations.java

`GameConversations` is a class that contains the collection of `GameConversation` objects in an internal `HashMap`.

When AJAX Warrior starts up, the `loadConversation()` method of this class is called repeatedly, one for each conversation script to be loaded (this call is made from the `ContextListener` class, which is coming up). This method uses Commons Digester to parse the conversation XML file, populate a `GameConversation` object, and add it to the collection. Have a look at the Digester rules in the class; I believe that the comments pretty well spell out how it works.

There is finally a `getConversation()` method, which accepts an ID and returns the appropriate `GameConversation` object.

GameItem.java

`GameItem` is yet another simple JavaBean that represents an item in the game such as a health pack, spell scroll, key, or artifact. The members of this class are

- `char type`: The type of the item
- `int xLocation`: The horizontal location of this item
- `int yLocation`: The vertical location of this item
- `int value`: The value of this item, either the number of scrolls if it's a spell scroll, the amount of health if it's a health pack, or the amount of gold pieces if it's a treasure chest
- `char spellType`: What type of spell this is, if it is a spell scroll

Once again, you'll find no meat here: just getters, setters, and `toString()` as far as actual code goes. (I am not counting a field definition as executable code—obviously it *is*, but I think you know what I mean!)

GameMaps.java

The GameMaps class is very much similar to the GameConversations class. It is a container of map data, although unlike GameConversation, there is no GameMap class because each map is nothing but a string of characters. However, internally, each map is stored as an ArrayList, where each 100 characters make up an element in the list. The reason I did it this way was so that it would be quick and easy to access a given row—no offset math to perform to get the proper substring or anything like that. It also makes expanding the maps very easy (hint, hint!).

Each of the five maps has its own ArrayList: mainMap, townAMap, townBMap, villageMap, and castleMap. The method loadMap() is called for each of these maps from the ContextListener class at startup, and the name of the map to load is passed in. The following code is then used to read the file and populate the appropriate ArrayList:

```
try {
  loader = Thread.currentThread().getContextClassLoader();
  stream = loader.getResourceAsStream(
    "map_" + inWhichMap + ".dat");
  isr    = new InputStreamReader(stream);
  br     = new BufferedReader(isr);
  String line = null;
  mapToLoad.clear();
  int lineCount = 0;
  int charCount = 0;
  while ((line = br.readLine()) != null) {
    lineCount++;
    charCount += line.length();
    mapToLoad.add(line);
  }
  log.info("Map loaded (lines: " + lineCount + ", chars:" +
    charCount + ")");
  if (log.isDebugEnabled()) {
    log.debug("GameMaps." + mapVarName + "=\n" + mapToLoad);
  }
} catch (Exception e) {
  e.printStackTrace();
} finally {
  try {
    br.close();
    isr.close();
    stream.close();
  } catch (Exception e) {
    log.debug("Exception closing: " + e);
  }
}
```

Prior to this, the variable mapToLoad is pointed to the appropriate ArrayList field, so this code works for any of the maps. Note that way the thread's class loader is used to gain access to the files—which explains why they have to be in WEB-INF/classes: they have to be in the classpath for the class loader in order for them to be found.

GameState.java

GameState is the class that stores the current state of the game: information such as what map is in use, what inventory the player has, what character they are talking to, and so on. This class is largely just a simple JavaBean with a bunch of fields and the appropriate getters and setters. There is, however, some actual code in it. First, let's see what fields are present:

- int currentLocationX: Player's current X location on the current map.
- int currentLocationY: Player's current Y location on the current map.
- boolean inCommunity: Flag to tell us whether we are in a community.
- int mainLocationX: Player's X location on the main map, saved when entering a community.
- int mainLocationY: Player's Y location on the main map, saved when entering a community.
- int mapLocationX: Player's X location on the current map, saved when entering battle.
- int mapLocationY: Player's Y location on the current map, saved when entering battle.
- String name: Player's name.
- int health: Player's health.
- int hitPoints: Player's hit points.
- int goldPieces: Player's gold pieces.
- boolean attackMode: Flag that tells us whether the player is currently in Attack mode.
- MapHandler mapHandle: The MapHandler object associated with this game.
- LinkedHashMap inventory: A Map of all the items the player is currently holding.
- char currentMode: The current mode the game is in.
- boolean playerWon: A flag that gets set when the player has won.
- boolean playerDied: A flag that gets set when the player has died.
- GameCharacter talkCharacter: The GameCharacter object the player is currently talking to, if any.
- String talkNode: What node in the conversation is current, if player is talking to a character.
- int karma: The current karma value of the character the player is talking to.
- GameCharacter battleCharacter: The character the playing is doing battle with.
- char currentWeapon: The weapon the player is currently using. If a blank space, then the player is using their bare hands.
- boolean freezeTime: A flag that indicates whether the Freeze Time spell has been cast.

- int freezeTimeCounter: A counter specifying how many moves are left for the Freeze Time spell.
- int winsToHPIncrease: The number of battle wins the player must get before the next hit point increase.
- int numBattleWins: A counter of how many wins the player has had since the last hit point increase.
- ClientSideGameState clientSideGameState: The client-side GameState object representation.

Aside from the pedestrian getters and setters, we have addToInventory():

```
public void addToInventory(final char inItem, final Object inValue) {

  // If the item being added is a spell, we want to increase the
  // count for that spell by 1, if there are any in inventory already, or just
  // add if fresh if it is not there already.
  if (inItem == Globals.SPELL_FIRE_RAIN ||
    inItem == Globals.SPELL_HEAL_THY_SELF ||
    inItem == Globals.SPELL_FREEZE_TIME) {
    Integer iSpellCount = (Integer)inventory.get(Character.toString(inItem));
    if (iSpellCount == null) {
      iSpellCount = new Integer(0);
    }
    int spellCount = iSpellCount.intValue();
    spellCount += ((Integer)inValue).intValue();
    inventory.put(Character.toString(inItem), new Integer(spellCount));
  } else {
    // The item is NOT a spell, just add it outright.
    inventory.put(Character.toString(inItem), inValue);
  }

} // End addToInventory.
```

For spells, there is an added complication: we need to add some number of spells to the count for that spell if the player already has that spell, or we need to add the spell fresh if they do not have it already. If it is not a spell, it is a straightforward add. Note that in all cases except spells, we have nothing to add—there is no Integer value to add; it is just a placeholder. So, in those cases, the caller of this method would have passed a new Object, just to have something to add.

There is, as you've probably guessed, a corresponding removeFromInventory() method. It works very similarly to this, except in reverse. Again for spells, the count is retrieved and reduced by 1. If that leaves 0, then the spell is removed from the inventory entirely.

Lastly, we have a checkGameWon() method. This method simply checks the inventory to see whether the player has all five artifacts. If they do, the method returns true, and the player will be shown the game end screen with the game won graphic.

This object is serialized when a game is saved, so by extension, anything it is composed of must likewise be `serializable`. Most of the classes in this package in fact are, for just this reason.

Lastly, note the `clientSideState` field. This is the string (XML) representation of the `GameStateObject` on the client, sent in when the game is saved. So, by serializing this object, we in effect save the client-side state as well, with no extra effort required.

GameTalkNode.java

Once more, we have a simple JavaBean. This class represents one of the nodes in a conversation (i.e., one row in the Excel spreadsheet). <sarcasm>It contains an overwhelming number of fields: 3!</sarcasm>

- `String id`: The ID of this node
- `String response`: The character's response for this node
- `LinkedHashMap replies = new LinkedHashMap()`: The collection of possible player replies

There is no executable code, other than the getters and setters, in this class.

GameTalkReply.java

The final class in the `gameobjects` package is `GameTalkReply`. It contains the individual pieces of information for a reply that a player can make for a given node. The `replies` member of the `GameTalkNode` is a collection of three `GameTalkReply` objects. That is also why a `LinkedHashMap` is used: I wanted the iteration order to be known, and `LinkedHashMap` provides that (but still gives you the benefit of a `Map`). This class contains these fields:

- `String id`: The ID of this reply; always `1`, `2`, or `3`
- `int karma`: The change in karma this reply will elicit
- `String target`: The node this reply will jump to
- `String replyText`: The text of this reply

There is no executable code, other than the getters and setters, in this class.

■ Note One general note about the classes in the `gameobjects` package: All of them, except for `GameMaps` and `GameConversations`, implement `Serializable` because they are saved as part of `GameState` when the player saves their game. These two exceptions do not need to be saved as they are read in when the application starts and are not altered after that. They also contain a rather large amount of data potentially, so we wouldn't want to store them in session, nor would we want to write them to persistent storage. The session object can be rather large by virtue of the fact that a single `GameConversation` object may be stored in it when the player is talking to a character. There is no sense is exacerbating the situation by storing *all* of them and then *all* of the maps!

SessionCheckerFilter.java

This filter is responsible for checking any request that comes into the front servlet and determining whether a game has been properly started. If not, the request is redirected back to the starting page (index.jsp). The doFilter() method starts by getting the path that was requested. It then checks to see if the /startGame command was requested. This is the very first request that would go through the front servlet in the normal flow, and at that point the game wouldn't have been properly started. So, if this exception wasn't present, the game could never be started because this filter would always redirect the request.

If the request was not to the /startGame command, we check for the presence of the Globals.GAME_PROPERLY_STARTED attribute in session. Only if it is present do we allow the request to continue; otherwise we redirect to index.jsp.

The idea is simply to not allow requests to the game that are not within the context of a properly started game.

ContextListener.java

The ContextListener class executes when the context starts up and is responsible for performing some basic initialization required before any game can actually start: reading in the maps and the conversation XML files. In fact, contextInitialized() is simply a series of calls to GameMaps.loadMap()—five in total, and for each call we pass the name of the map to load. After that is a series of calls to GameConversations.loadConversation—12 in total, and for each call we pass the name of the conversation to load.

So, all of the *actual* work is done by the GameMaps and GameConversations classes, which we'll see in a bit. We simply pass them the name of the map or conversation to load, and they take care of the details.

FrontServlet.java

The FrontServlet class is the single servlet that makes up, along with the CommandResult class in the com.apress.ajaxprojects.ajaxwarrior.framework package, the framework AJAX Warrior is built on. It is not quite Struts or JSF, but it does the trick!

FrontServlet's doGet() method calls on doPost(), where the work is done. This work consists of the following:

1. For the requested URL, everything is stripped off except the command. For example, the form in index.jsp submits to /startGame.command, so everything is stripped off until we just have startGame, which is the requested command.
2. For the requested command, the appropriate Command class is instantiated, passing the HttpServletRequest, HttpServletResponse, and ServletContext objects to its constructor.
3. The exec() method of the Command class is then called, and the result, which is a CommandResult object, is captured.
4. The finish() method of the Command class is called.
5. The CommandResult is examined. If it is null, the response is assumed to be finished and that is the end of processing. If it is not null, doRedirect() is called. If it returns true, a redirect to the URI set in the CommandResult is sent to the client. If it returns false, a forward is done to the URI.

If an exception occurs at any point in this process, Utils.writeJSON() is called so that the exception can be returned to the client for display via an alert pop-up.

As you can see, this is not a full-featured framework. And since all of the commands are hard-coded in it, it is not terribly flexible. However, it *is* more than adequate for our purposes, and allows us a centralized location to do the common tasks required of most tasks, which keeps redundant code to a minimum. If this were a game I was intent on selling on its own, I would certainly begin by externalizing the command mappings, and extending the framework from there. But this will suffice for the purposes of this book.

CommandResult.java

As mentioned earlier, a CommandResult object is returned by any Command. Again, because this isn't a full-fledged framework, the resource to return to the client is defined by each Command, rather than by any centralized location (i.e., declared forwards in Struts, for instance). The CommandResult has two members: path and redirect. The path is the URI to forward or redirect to (a forward is a transfer to another resource on the server that doesn't involve the client; a redirect is a response to the client telling it to make a new request for a resource and providing the address for the client to request). redirect is true when we want to do a redirect, and false otherwise (which means do a forward). There is a getter and a setter method for both fields, and that's all there is to the class.

As noted in the discussion of FrontServlet, a Command can return null instead of a CommandResult instance. In fact, this is what the majority of them do because they'll have called Utils.writeJSON(), at which point the response is fully formed.

Command.java

Jumping over to the com.apress.ajaxprojects.ajaxwarrior.commands package, we first find the Command class. This is a base class that all other Commands inherit from. It has a number of protected fields: HttpServletRequest request, HttpServletResponse response, HttpSession session, ServletContext ServletContext, GameState gameState, and MapHandler mapHandler. This means that any class inheriting from Command will automatically have access to these members, which makes for very clean code.

Here's the constructor responsible for populating these members:

```
public Command(final HttpServletRequest inRequest,
  final HttpServletResponse inResponse,
  final ServletContext inServletContext) {

  request        = inRequest;
  response       = inResponse;
  session        = request.getSession(true);
  servletContext = inServletContext;
  gameState      = (GameState)session.getAttribute("gameState");
  // When the StartGameCommand is called before a game has started, gameState
  // will be null, so we have to check for that lest we throw an NPE.
  if (gameState != null) {
    mapHandler = gameState.getMapHandler();
  }

} // End constructor().
```

The Command class has two other methods: exec() and finish(). The exec() method implements the behavior of the Command. finish() is called by FrontServlet after exec() has been called. Let's look at finish() now:

```
public void finish() {

  if (gameState != null) {
    gameState.setMapHandler(mapHandler);
    session.setAttribute("gameState", gameState);
  }
  log.debug("Command done");

} // End finish().
```

Obviously there isn't much to it, but this method's role is vital. Many of the Commands will alter various elements in GameState. This object is stored in session, and must be updated when each Command completes. finish() does this, and also updates mapHandler in gameState. The MapHandler instance is also updated by most Commands, and so must be updated in gameState as well.

BattleMoveCommand.java

We have seen a couple of relatively small and simple commands, but now it is time to look at a larger and more complex one. This is the command that is called when the player makes a move during battle.

First we get a reference to the GameCharacter object that the player is battling from gameState. Next, we record the player's current location, as well as the location of the character. Then, we get the direction in which the player moved from the request. If that direction begins with the string "projectile_", it means that the player has fired a slingshot or crossbow. In that case, we begin to populate a HashMap that will contain all the details of the projectile firing we'll need, beginning with the location where the projectile starts, which is the same as the player's location. Both locations are put into the HashMap under the keys p1 and p2, respectively.

Next, we find a giant switch statement with eight cases. The first four are quite simple: whichever direction the player moved in, assuming they did not fire a projectile, we update the player's location as appropriate.

If the player fired a projectile, however, we determine whether or not the character is hit. This amounts to checking that either the X or Y coordinate matches that of the player, depending on which direction the player fired in. For instance, to determine if the player hit the character while firing up, we do this:

```
if (currentLocationX == gcXLocation && currentLocationY > gcYLocation) {
  log.info("Projectile hit (up)");
  projectileHitEnemy = true;
  projectileInfo.put("ph", "true");
  projectileInfo.put("p3", Integer.toString(gcXLocation));
  projectileInfo.put("p4", Integer.toString(gcYLocation));
} else {
  message = "You missed!";
```

```
    projectileInfo.put("p3", Integer.toString(currentLocationX));
    projectileInfo.put("p4", Integer.toString(0));
  }
```

Obviously, in this case, the X coordinates must be the same, and the Y location of the player must be greater than the character's Y location. If both conditions are true, we put an element in the HashMap named ph set to true, and we set the ending coordinates of the projectile's travel to the coordinates of the character. If the projectile misses, we set an appropriate message to display to the user, and set the ending coordinates of the projectile's travel to the edge of the viewport.

After doing all that, we check to see if the projectile hit the character by checking the flag variable projectileHitEnemy. If it's true, we call the calculateDamage() function to determine how much hurt we put on our enemy.

The underlying calculation performed takes the DAMAGE_BASIS value (which is some value less than 1) and multiplies that by the amount of damage defined for the current weapon in use, or bare hands. Next, the code divides the hit points of the player by the HIT_POINT_DIVIDER value, and multiplies that outcome by the current value of damage. Finally, the code checks to make sure at least 1 unit of damage is done, and also that the amount of damage is not greater than the value of COMBAT_MAX_DAMAGE. Finally, this final damage value is returned.

Next, the code performs a check to see whether the player ran away from battle by moving off an edge of the viewport. If so, the mode is switched back to normal and the player is called an unworthy coward (I never said it was a kind game!).

Next, the code sees if the player and the character now occupy the same space. If so, the first thing done is to move the player back to where they were before this move. Next, the calculateDamage() method is again used because now the player has attacked the character. The code then checks to see if the enemy was vanquished. If so, one last check is performed: was this one of the key masters, and if so, does the player have their key already? If it was a key master and the player does not already have their key, tell the foolish human the quest is over because there is no longer any way to win the game! Finally, if the player did not kill the character, the code reports back to the player how much damage they did.

After this block of code, we have a bit more work to do. First, we set the player's coordinates to the updated values. These values may or may not be different from before. They'll be different unless the player attacked the character.

This block of code is last:

```
// See if the player defeated the enemy.
if (battleEnds) {
  HashMap vals = endBattle(gameState, mapHandler, gc, ranAway);
  // Update the message to return as long as we didn't run away.
  if (!ranAway) {
    message = (String)vals.get("message");
  }
  mapData = (ArrayList)vals.get("chunk");
} else {
  // Get the map data we'll return, still showing battle mode.
  mapData = mapHandler.getBattleMap(gc);
}
```

Regardless of how the battle ended, if it did end, we call the endBattle() method. This method performs a number of common functions always needed when battle ends. First, it restores the previous map and the player's location on it. Second, if the player did not run away, which would mean they won, then we calculate randomly how much gold they got, and we also figure out if it is time to "level up"—that is, increase their hit points. Initially, it takes five battle victories to increase your hit points. After that, it takes 10 victories, then 15, then 20, and so on. Third, the removeCharacter() method of MapHandler is called to get rid of the character. Fourth, createCharacter() and charPickLocation() of the MapHandler class are called, in that order, to generate and place a new character randomly. Lastly, the appropriate map chunk is retrieved and returned.

Note that this endBattle() method, as well as calculateDamage(), are broken out as separate methods because they are used from the BattleEnemyMoveCommand that we'll look at next.

Finally, once endBattle() completes, we generate our JSON response as usual and this command is finished.

BattleEnemyMoveCommand.java

If you read the description of BattleMoveCommand, then you essentially already know all about BattleEnemyMoveCommand. This command, as the name implies, is called after the player moves when it is the character's turn.

One difference is a block of code you'll see almost immediately in exec():

```
// If time is frozen, get outta Dodge quickly.
if (gameState.isTimeFrozen()) {
  log.debug("Freeze Time spell in effect");
  int ftc = gameState.getFreezeTimeCounter();
  ftc--;
  if (ftc <= 0) {
    log.debug("Freeze Time spell ended");
    gameState.setFreezeTime(false);
  } else {
    gameState.setFreezeTimeCounter(ftc);
  }
  Utils.writeJSON(false, null, null, false, gameState, false, response,
    false, false, null);
  return null;
}
```

If the player previously cast a Freeze Time spell, then the enemy cannot move now, and this code takes care of that. The spell is in effect for 15 moves, meaning the player can move 15 times before the character can move again.

After that, the code is effectively the same as in BattleMoveCommand, except obviously checks are performed to see whether the *character* fired a projectile weapon, whether or not the *player* was hit, whether or not the *player* died, and so on. Characters cannot cast spells, so it is a little simpler by comparison.

As noted, this command makes use of the calculateDamage() and endBattle() methods in BattleMoveCommand, so some redundancy is cut out there.

CastSpellCommand.java

This command is called when the player wants to cast a spell, whether it is during battle or just walking around.

The first step it performs is to get the code of the spell the player selected to cast from the request. Next, a simple rejection is performed:

```
// First, do any simple rejections based on mode.
if (gameState.getCurrentMode() == Globals.MODE_NORMAL) {
  if (whichSpell == Globals.SPELL_FIRE_RAIN) {
    message = "You can only cast that spell in battle";
    canCastSpell = false;
  }
}
```

This code handles the case of the player trying to cast a Fire Rain spell while not in battle, which cannot be done.

Next, assuming `canCastSpell` is true (as it would be unless the rejection fired) is to switch on the type of spell. For Heal Thy Self, we simply set the player's health to 100, and subtract 1 from the inventory count for that spell. For Freeze Time, we call `gameState.setFreezeTime(true)`, which will indicate to other commands that time is frozen. Of course, we again remove it from inventory.

If the spell is Fire Rain, we call `gameState.getBattleCharacter()` to get the `GameCharacter` we are doing battle with. We then calculate how much damage the spell does by multiplying the player's hit points by 2, and then limiting it to 20 points, and subtracting that amount from the character's health. Next, we determine whether or not the player killed the character like so:

```
if (gcHealth <= 0) {
  HashMap vals = BattleMoveCommand.endBattle(gameState, mapHandler,
    gc, false);
  mapData = (ArrayList)vals.get("chunk");
  message = (String)vals.get("message");
  viewUpdated = true;
} else {
  gc.setHealth(gcHealth);
  message = "You cast Fire Rain.  You did " + damage +
    " points damage (" + gcHealth + " remaining)";
}
```

If the player did kill the character, we call the `BattleMoveCommand.endBattle()` method, which returns to us the map chunk the player should now see (which would be from the map they were on when they entered into battle), as well as the message (which tells them how much gold they won, and whether they increased their hit points). If the character still survives, we send back a message stating how much damage was done and how much health the character has left, and set the new health value for the character.

DisplayInventoryCommand.java

This is a very simple command that does two things. First, it puts the current `gameState` instance in the request as an attribute under the key `gameState` (I was not feeling particularly creative that day!) and then forwards to displayInventory.jsp. The response is rendered and returned to the client, which displays the new view with the returned markup.

EndConversationCommand.java

As the name implies, this command is called when the player presses E during conversation to end talking right away. Its exec() method is pretty straightforward:

```
public CommandResult exec() throws Exception {

  log.debug("EndConversationCommand.exec()...");

  // Put us back in normal mode.  Be sure the character moves off the
  // player.
  gameState.setCurrentMode(Globals.MODE_NORMAL);
  GameCharacter gc = gameState.getTalkCharacter();
  mapHandler.charPickLocation(mapHandler.getCurrentMapString(), gc);
  gameState.setTalkNode(null);
  gameState.setTalkCharacter(null);

  // Get the chunk of the map data corresponding to the player's new
  // viewport on the map.
  ArrayList chunk = mapHandler.getChunk(gameState.getCurrentLocationX(),
    gameState.getCurrentLocationY());

  // Create our JSON string with the pertinent information and write it out
  // to the response.
  Utils.writeJSON(false, "You abruptly end the conversation.  Shame on thee!",
    chunk, true, gameState, false, response, false, false, null);

  log.debug("EndConversationCommand.exec() done");

  return null;

} // End exec().
```

There isn't too much going on. The mode is reset in gameState to indicate the player is no longer talking. Then, the character the player was talking to is randomly placed somewhere on the map. This is done so that the character is not right next to the player when the map is shown again, and a conversation cannot be immediately struck up. Finally, the current talk node and character are cleared in gameState, since there is no point in them hanging around. Lastly, our JSON response is written telling the player they quit the conversation; the response also includes the map chunk that will be displayed. All done!

EnterCommunityCommand.java

When the player steps onto a town, castle, or village on the map, they can enter that community, and this command is called on to perform that function.

First, the player's current coordinates on the map are saved in gameState. This is done so that upon exiting the community, we can put them right back where they were. Next, the map chunk representing the current viewport is gotten from mapHandler, and then getPlayerTile() is used to get the code of the tile the player is standing on.

At that point, it comes down to a big switch statement where each case is a specific community. As an example, here's what happens when the player is standing on the village:

```
message = "You have entered the unnamed village";
viewUpdated = true;
gameState.setInCommunity(true);
currentLocationX = Globals.COMMUNITY_STARTING_X;
currentLocationY = Globals.COMMUNITY_STARTING_Y;
gameState.setCurrentLocationX(currentLocationX);
gameState.setCurrentLocationY(currentLocationY);
mapHandler.switchMap("village");
chunk = mapHandler.getChunk(currentLocationX, currentLocationY);
```

We first set the message that the player will see in the activity scroll, and we set the flag in gameState that indicates the player is in a community by calling setInCommunity() on GameState. Next, we change the player's coordinates on the map to the starting coordinates as defined in Globals. Next, we call mapHandler.switchMap(), passing it the value "village". This switches the current map that mapHandler will work with to the map for the village. Finally, we get the initial chunk of the map for the community by calling mapHandler.getChunk().

After that, we simply call Utils.writeJSON(), and we're done. Of course, if the code found that the player was not standing on a community at all, a suitable message is returned informing them that there is nothing to enter.

PickUpItemCommand.java

When a player tries to pick up an item, this command is called.

The first thing it does is retrieve the chunk of the map that is the current viewport. It then retrieves the tile the player is standing on by using this line of code:

```
char centerTile = mapHandler.getPlayerTile(chunk);
```

This is a simple method that always returns the center tile of the viewport, which is always the tile the player is standing on (when not in battle, which is the only time a player can pick up an item). A call to mapHandler.isItemTile() is then made to determine whether or not the tile the player is standing on is an item they can pick up. If not, a message saying there is nothing to pick up is returned.

At this point, if it *was* an item they can pick up, the following line of code is hit:

```
GameItem item = mapHandler.getItem(currentLocationX, currentLocationY);
```

This line gets the appropriate GameItem object for the item being picked up, which is then added to the player's inventory. If the item is gold, a check is done to see whether the player is at maximum gold capacity, and an appropriate message is returned. If it is a health pack, a check is done to see whether the player is at maximum health, and an appropriate message is returned. If the item is a spell, the appropriate number of that type of spell is added to inventory. Keys and artifacts are simply added to inventory.

Assuming the item was picked up, the flag variable removeItemFromMap is set to true. Next, this check is performed:

```
if (removeItemFromMap) {
  mapHandler.removeItem(gameState.getCurrentLocationX(),
    gameState.getCurrentLocationY());
}
```

As the name says, the removeItem() method of mapHandler removes the item from the collection of items for the current map. However, it also adds a new item randomly to the map (not necessarily the same type of item that was just picked up).

Lastly, a call to gameState.checkGameWon() is made. If the player now has all five artifacts, the response indicates that the player has won, and the appropriate game end screen is shown.

PurchaseItemCommand.java

This command is executed when the player chooses an item in a store to purchase. First, the code of the item they wish to purchase is grabbed from the request. Then, the cost of that item is retrieved from the Globals class. Next, if the player has enough gold to purchase the item, a message is constructed saying what item they purchased, and the item is added to their inventory. If they do not have enough gold, then a message is returned indicating that.

Finally, in either case, we call Utils.writeJSON() with the message, and we are done.

SaveGameCommand.java

This command is executed when the player requests that their game be saved. It is a fairly simple piece of code.

First, the serialized version of the client-side GameStateObject is retrieved from the request using the RequestHelpers.getBodyContent() method from Java Web Parts (remember, the XML was POST'd to this command). Then, we use Commons Digester to parse the XML. The result is that we get a ClientSideGameState object populated with the activity scroll history and both talkAttackMode and currentWeapon populated. This object is then added to GameState.

As this point, we use an ObjectOutputStream's writeObject() method to write out the serialized GameState object. Finally, we write a simple JSON response saying the game was saved. Nothing to it! (You really have to love Java's support for serialization!)

ShowCastSpellCommand.java

This command is virtually identical to DisplayInventoryCommand, except that it forwards to weaponSwitching.jsp instead. 'Nuf said!

ShowSwitchWeaponCommand.java

This command, like ShowCastSpellCommand, is the same as DisplayInventoryCommand, except that the forward is to weaponSwitching.jsp this time around.

StartGameCommand.java

This command is called when the user clicks either the New Game or Continue Game button on the title screen. There are basically two logical flows through this. The first is for starting a new game.

First, the command captures the name that the player entered and uses it:

```
fis = new FileInputStream(servletContext.getRealPath("/WEB-INF") +
  "/gameSaves/" + fileName + ".sav");
request.setAttribute("Error", "A game with the name you " +
  "entered already exists.\\n\\nPlease select a new name and " +
  "try again.  Sorry!");
result = new CommandResult("index.jsp");
```

The expectation here is that the file will *not* be found, meaning that a game with this name has not already been started. The name the player enters is lowercased, and spaces are converted to underscores; that becomes the save filename. If a file with that name is found in `WEB-INF/gameSaves`, then we send the player back to `index.jsp`.

However, if a file with that name is *not* found, then a `FileNotFoundException` is thrown. In that case, the following code executes:

```
gameState  = new GameState();
mapHandler = new MapHandler();
gameState.setCurrentMode(Globals.MODE_NORMAL);
gameState.setCurrentLocationX(Globals.PLAYER_START_X);
gameState.setCurrentLocationY(Globals.PLAYER_START_Y);
gameState.setName(playerName);
gameState.setHealth(Globals.PLAYER_START_HEALTH);
gameState.setHitPoints(Globals.PLAYER_START_HIT_POINTS);
gameState.setGoldPieces(Globals.PLAYER_START_GOLD_PIECES);
gameState.setInventory(new LinkedHashMap());
gameState.setMapHandler(mapHandler);
gameState.setCurrentWeapon(Globals.WEAPON_NONE);
gameState.setWinsToHPIncrease(Globals.HIT_POINT_INCREASE_INCREMENT);
log.debug("StartGame.exec() done (NEW game starting)");
session.setAttribute(Globals.GAME_PROPERLY_STARTED, "true");
result = new CommandResult("main.jsp");
```

This is the sum total of what is required to begin a new game. Not really very much!

After this block of code you'll find the code that executes when a game is being continued. The same kind of file existence check is again performed. If the file is found, we use the `readObject()` method of the `ObjectInputStream` class to get our serialized `GameState` object back as a real object. A flag is also set to indicate that the file was found and the object restored.

Shortly thereafter, that flag is checked. If true, the `GAME_PROPERLY_STARTED` session attribute is set, and the request is forwarded to `main.jsp`, where the game starts up. If the flag was false, we return a message to the user indicating that the file was not found. This is done by sticking the message in a request as an attribute under the key `Error`. `index.jsp` looks for this attribute and renders the appropriate JavaScript `alert()` code to display it to the user.

SwitchWeaponCommand.java

This command is called when the user wants to switch weapons. It is the command called to switch weapons, not just to show the weapon switching view. Its exec() method is

```
public CommandResult exec() throws Exception {

  log.debug("SwitchWeaponCommand.exec()...");

  // Retreive which weapon the player is switching to.
  String paramWhichWeapon = request.getParameter("whichWeapon");
  char whichWeapon = paramWhichWeapon.charAt(0);
  // Set it as current.
  gameState.setCurrentWeapon(whichWeapon);

  // Report back to the user.
  String message = "You are now using your " +
    Utils.getDescFromCode(gameState.getCurrentWeapon(), gameState);

  // Create our JSON string with the pertinent information and write it out
  // to the response.
  Utils.writeJSON(false, message, null, false, gameState, false, response,
    false, false, null);

  log.debug("SwitchWeaponCommand.exec() done");

  return null;

} // End exec().
```

We get the code of the weapon the player wants to switch to, and set the new weapon in gameState. Finally, we write out a JSON response indicating what weapon they are now using.

TalkReplyCommand.java

This command handles the situation where the user is talking to a character and selects one of the three possible replies. The first thing this command does is get a reference to the appropriate GameReply object that corresponds with what the user selected.

Next, it adjusts the karma of the character according to the value of the reply. Then, it checks the karma to see if it is equal to or less than zero. If it is, the following code executes:

```
// Yep, karma at or below 0, run away, run away!!
gameState.setCurrentMode(Globals.MODE_NORMAL);
// Move character so we aren't standing on them.
mapHandler.charPickLocation(mapHandler.getCurrentMapString(), gc);
gameState.setTalkNode(null);
gameState.setTalkCharacter(null);
charResponse = "Argh!  Get away now!";
```

```
// Get the chunk of the map data corresponding to the player's new
// viewport on the map.
chunk = mapHandler.getChunk(gameState.getCurrentLocationX(),
  gameState.getCurrentLocationY());
viewUpdated = true;
```

Here we see that the game state is changed back to normal, which will cause the client side of things to exit Talk mode. Next, we randomly relocate the character so they are not near the player when the view is switched back to the map. We also clear out the current node and character in `gameState`. Next, we send a message to the client saying the character ran away, and finally, we get the viewport map chunk that will be rendered on the client. When all is said and done, this will be used in rendering the JSON response.

Another possible outcome of the karma adjustment is that the character's karma is now equal to or greater than 15. In that case, *if* the character is one of the key masters, the player is given the key. The code for that looks like this:

```
// The character is the green key master and their karma is high enough, so
// now they'll give the player the key.
gameState.setCurrentMode(Globals.MODE_NORMAL);
charResponse = "I place my hope in thee, here is the Green key!";
gameState.addToInventory(Globals.ITEM_KEY_GREEN, new Object());
// Make them no longer a key master, so they don't give us the key again.
gc.setGreenKeymaster(false);
// Move character so we aren't standing on them.
mapHandler.charPickLocation(mapHandler.getCurrentMapString(), gc);
gameState.setTalkNode(null);
gameState.setTalkCharacter(null);
// Get the chunk of the map data corresponding to the player's new
// viewport on the map.
chunk = mapHandler.getChunk(gameState.getCurrentLocationX(),
  gameState.getCurrentLocationY());
viewUpdated = true;
```

The code that deals with the red key master is identical to this, except we replace `green` with `red`. We again set the mode to normal, and then add the appropriate key to the player's inventory. We then change the character so that is no longer a key master; that way, if the player happens to talk to that character again, the player won't be given the key again. Again, the character is relocated, and the applicable variables in `gameState` are nulled. The map chunk is retrieved and is ready for inclusion in the JSON response.

There's another possible outcome of this command: if this is simply another node in the conversation—that is, the character does not run away, and no key is given. In that case, we simply get the target of the reply, and set its ID in `gameState` as the current talk node. Finally, we get the character's response from the target node and return that as the message in the JSON response.

In a nutshell, that's how talking to characters works, as far as the server side of the house goes.

ToggleTalkAttackCommand.java

This command is called to toggle the user between Talk and Attack mode. The code in exec() is

```
public CommandResult exec() throws Exception {

  log.debug("ToggleTalkAttackCommand.exec()...");

  // Simply flip the field and return a message stating the new mode.
  gameState.setAttackMode(!gameState.getAttackMode());
  String message = null;
  if (gameState.getAttackMode()) {
    message = "Attack Mode";
  } else {
    message = "Talk Mode";
  }

  // Create our JSON string with the pertinent information and write it out
  // to the response.
  Utils.writeJSON(false, message, null, false, gameState, false, response,
    false, false, null);

  log.debug("ToggleTalkAttackCommand.exec() done");

  return null;

} // End exec().
```

Nothing special is going on here. We call setAttackMode() on gameState, passing it the negation of its current value. Then we write out the JSON response indicating the mode the player is now in. Short and sweet!

UpdateMapCommand.java

Now, here, near the end, we come to the single biggest command in AJAX Warrior. The UpdateMapCommand is responsible for handling the redrawing of the current map display when the player moves. However, it does quite a bit more than that. Let's walk through it, shall we?

First we determine in which direction the player moved by retrieving the moveDirection request parameter. If this parameter is not present, it means it is an initial view of the map—that is, when the game first starts, or when we enter a community. (Yes, this command handles walking around Xandor as well as walking around any community. It is all the same as far as the code goes; we just use a different map data set.) Also, if moveDirection is null, we want to be sure to set the flag in the JSON response to indicate the player information should be updated so that when the game is first started, that information is displayed.

Next, based on the direction of movement requested, we update the player's map coordinates. Immediately after that, we do some bounds checking to be sure they do not scroll off an edge of the map.

Note that the coordinates of the player are a little misleading. The currentLocationX and currentLocationY members of GameState, which convey this information, really are the coordinates of the upper-left corner of the viewport. So, when the coordinates are 0 and 0, then the player will see the upper-left corner of the map, and won't be able to move up or left any further.

The next check only applies if the player is currently inside a community. If they are, and if they are now on one of the exit tiles—either the tile they started out on or the tile directly above or below it—then the community will be exited. To accomplish this, the following code executes:

```
gameState.setInCommunity(false);
gameState.restoreMainLocation();
mapHandler.switchMap("main");
// Get the chunk of the main map after the location is restored.
ArrayList chunk = mapHandler.getChunk(gameState.getCurrentLocationX(),
  gameState.getCurrentLocationY());
Utils.writeJSON(false, "Exited community", chunk, true, gameState,
  false, response, true, false, null);
log.debug("UpdateMap.exec() (exited community) done");
return null;
```

I suspect this code is quite self-explanatory at this point!

Now, after this code, we again get the chunk of the map representing the viewport. We do this because at this point, the player's coordinates could have changed, and the remainder of the checks we need to do have to be on the *new* coordinates.

The next check performed is this one:

```
char centerTile =  mapHandler.getPlayerTile(chunk);
if (mapHandler.isNoWalkTile(centerTile)) {
  log.debug("Is no walk tile, restoring previous");
  message = "Can't move there!";
  currentLocationX = previousLocationX;
  currentLocationY = previousLocationY;
}
```

If the new tile the player would be standing on is one they cannot stand on, like water for instance, then we need to restore their previous location and return a message saying they cannot walk there.

The next set of checks reveals whether the player is walking on one of the special "hidden" door tiles—the tile that must be passed through in order to get to one of the artifacts and that requires a specific key to get through. If the player does not have the appropriate key, the previous location is restored, and the player is hurt a bit. Five of these checks are performed, one for each hidden door. Here's what one of them looks like:

```
if (centerTile == Globals.TILE_WALL_HIDDEN_RED &&
  gameState.getInventory().get(
    Character.toString(Globals.ITEM_KEY_RED)) == null) {
  gameState.setHealth(gameState.getHealth() - 10);
```

```
      message = "You do not have the Red key!  Evil magic attacks you!";
      currentLocationX = previousLocationX;
      currentLocationY = previousLocationY;
      playerInfoUpdated = true;
      if (gameState.getHealth() <= 0) {
        gameState.setPlayerDied(true);
      }
    }
```

Note that we have to check to see whether the player died, and set the flag in gameState if so, in order for the appropriate game end view to be shown.

At this point we once again get the map chunk because the coordinates could be different now. Once we do that, we check to see whether the player is now standing on a swamp tile. If so, we reduce their health by 1 and again restore the previous coordinates.

After that, we store whatever the current coordinate values are in gameState. These final values take into account all the previous possible changes and resets to the previous coordinates.

Almost done now! If the player did in fact move, and if the Freeze Time spell is not in effect, then we call on the moveCharacters() method of mapHandler to move all the characters on this map.

Finally, if the Freeze Time spell is in effect, we count down how many moves remain before the spell runs out, and reset things if it does run out.

That is the end of the conditional portions of this command. What remains is what will always happen, beginning with a final get of the map chunk.

Next, we check to see whether the player is touching a character by calling the touchingCharacter() method of mapHandler. If this method returns true, we determine whether the character is belligerent, and if the player is in Attack mode or Talk mode. If the character is belligerent, or if the player is in Attack mode, then battle begins. If the character is nonbelligerent and the player is in Talk mode, then a conversation begins.

Only one more possibility to deal with! If we stepped on a store tile, and as long as we did not enter into battle (which could happen if a character happened to be standing on a store trigger tile), then we switch to the Store mode.

And of course, at the end, our JSON response is constructed and returned.

Whew! Take a breath! We have now completely explored AJAX Warrior!

Suggested Exercises

Ah yes, suggestions for a game… the best thing about game programming is there are absolutely no limits! You can carry things just as far as your imagination will allow. There are no stuffy corporate rules about how things have to be done, no predefined conceptions of what reality is. Oh, to be sure, the big game houses approach their development efforts about as seriously and professionally as any Fortune 500 business does theirs. But games have always held a special place in programming. Smaller companies, some run out of people's garages early on, can produce something that a great many people will love, and can do so based on nothing but their imagination and their own desire to produce something fun.

So, what kinds of exercises might be worthwhile for you to do with AJAX Warrior? Here is just a small list of suggestions:

- More spells! If you have ever played Dungeons and Dragons, you know that there are more spells that a player can cast than you can shake a magic staff at. Have fun adding as many as you can think of. Because some may require more than simply updating statistics, for instance, you might actually want to show a spell or two being cast and its effect; this would most definitely put your skills to the test.
- Expand the world of Xandor. I purposely tried to design everything to be expandable, which explains why I used the `Globals` class so often. Make the maps bigger, and add some other communities. You could also add more diverse tiles, more characters, more items to retrieve, and so forth.
- Enhance the gameplay with puzzles. Perhaps in addition to getting the appropriate key, the player can solve some sort of puzzle to get through the hidden doors.
- Include a tunnel system. This is something I would have loved to put in this game but simply did not have enough time to do so. The ability to go into tunnels from the mountains, and showing it with a very simple 3-D engine, is doable and would be very interesting.
- Include a boss battle. A final battle with Mallizant would be great. I thought it was a bit of a cop-out to not do it myself, but there are certain time pressures in writing a book! Also, think of how *Lord of the Rings* ended: Sauron is tied to the ring, so once it was destroyed in Mount Doom, he died immediately. I figure Mallizant is the same way: he's tied to the five artifacts he stole. At least, that's my story, and I'm sticking to it!

Summary

Now *that* was one big chapter! I hope you feel, as I do though, that it was well worth the effort. In this chapter we touched on a number of things: JSON, associative arrays, a new way to structure Ajax functions, a new server-side framework, and even a bit of basic game theory. We saw a fair bit of CSS and DOM scripting techniques, and picked up some new JavaScript tricks as well. Most important, we have seen just how fun game programming can be!

APPENDIX A

The XMLHttpRequest Object

More often than not, chances are you will use some sort of library to do your Ajax work. Some of the libraries out there—only a handful of which we talked about in this book—really do make it far easier to work the "Ajax way." That being said, there are times when you will want to go "bare metal," so to speak, and use the `XMLHttpRequest` object yourself. In those instances, this appendix will be an invaluable aid to you.

What Is the XMLHttpRequest Object?

`XMLHttpRequest` is an object (an ActiveX object in Microsoft Internet Explorer, a native component in most other browsers) that allows a web page to make a request to a server and get a response back without reloading the entire page. The user remains on the same page, and more important, they will not actually see the processing occur—that is, they will not see a new page loading, not by default at least. Using the `XMLHttpRequest` object makes it possible for a developer to alter a page previously loaded in the browser with data from the server without having to request the entire page from the server again.

What Browsers Support the XMLHttpRequest Object?

`XMLHttpRequest` is present in Internet Explorer 5.0 and higher, Apple's Safari 1.2 and higher, Mozilla's Firefox 1.0 and higher, Opera 7.6 and higher, and Netscape 7 and higher. Other browsers may or may not support it, so you should check for the capability before attempting to use it if you intend to support alternative browsers.

Also of note is a little JavaScript library by Andrew Gregory that allows for cross-browser Ajax support without dealing with the details of what browsers support the object and how. There are some limitations, but it is of interest nonetheless. You can find information on it here: `www.scss.com.au/family/andrew/webdesign/xmlhttprequest`.

Is the XMLHttpRequest Object a W3C Standard? (Or Any Other Kind of Standard for That Matter!)

No, the `XMLHttpRequest` object is not a W3C standard, or a standard of any other standards body. The W3C DOM Level 3 specification's "Load and Save" capabilities would provide similar functionality, but currently no browsers implement the Level 3 specification. Therefore, until that specification is widely adopted, if you need to send an HTTP request from a browser and get a response from a server, aside from the normal page navigation mechanism, the `XMLHttpRequest` object is the only viable option, along with some of the lesser-used (nowadays) alternatives like Java applets and ActiveX controls.

How Do I Use the XMLHttpRequest Object?

In Mozilla, Firefox, Safari, and Netscape, you create an instance of the `XMLHttpRequest` object by doing the following:

```
<script>var xhr = new XMLHttpRequest();</script>
```

For Internet Explorer:

```
<script> var xhr = new ActiveXObject("Microsoft.XMLHTTP");</script>
```

Here is an example of using the `XMLHttpRequest` object:

```
<script>

  var xhr = null;
  if (window.XMLHttpRequest){
    xhr = new XMLHttpRequest();
  } else {
    xhr = new ActiveXObject("Microsoft.XMLHTTP");
  }
  if (xhr) {
    var url = "/someURI";
    xhr.onreadystatechange = xhrCallback;
    xhr.open("get", url, true)
    xhr.send()
  }

  function xhrCallback() {
    if (xhr.readyState == 4) {
      if (xhr.status == 200) {
        alert("Ok");
```

```
      } else {
        alert("Problem retrieving Ajax response");
      }
    }
  }

  </script>
```

XMLHttpRequest Object Method and Properties Reference

Tables A-1 and A-2 outline the methods and properties available on the `XMLHttpRequest` object, representing the full API interface to that object through which you will interact with it.

Table A-1. *XMLHttpRequest Object Methods*

Method	Description
`abort()`	Stops the request that the object is currently processing. Note that like clicking the Stop button in your browser, the server will not be notified and will continue to process the request.
`getAllResponseHeaders`	This method returns all of the headers, both keys and values, as a string.
`getResponseHeader("key")`	This method returns the specified header value as a string.
`open("method", "url" [,asyncFlag [,"username" [,"password"]]]`	Contrary to its name, this does not appear to literally open anything. Instead, it just sets the parameters for the pending request. The value of `method` may be any valid HTTP method, `get` and `post` being the most common. `asyncFlag` is either true or false. Setting this to false will cause all JavaScript on the page to halt until the request returns. This is generally not desirable because if the server is unavailable, or the operation simply takes a long time, the user interface will seem to freeze to the user. Use with caution! `username` and `password` are used to make requests to URLs protected with Basic Auth security. Note that these two parameters, as well as `asyncFlag`, are optional, while `method` and `url` are required.
`send(content)`	This method transmits the pending request, and optionally sends a POST body or serialized DOM object (i.e., XML document). If POSTing simple parameters, content should be a string in the form "name1=value1&name2=value2"—in other words, a query string minus the initial question mark.
`setRequestHeader("key", "value")`	Sets an HTTP header that will be set on the outgoing response.

Table A-2. *XMLHttpRequest Object Properties*

Property	Description
`onReadyStateChange`	This is a pointer to the function that will serve as the event handler for the request this object instance is processing. Note that this function will be called multiple times during the lifecycle of the request.
`readyState`	This is an integer representing the status of the request. Possible values are 0 (uninitialized), 1 (loading), 2 (loaded), 3 (interactive), and 4 (complete).
`responseText`	This is a textual string version of the response from the server. Even if the response was XML, you will still find the actual text of the response here.
`responseXML`	If the response from the server was XML, the object will do the extra work of parsing it and generating a real DOM-compatible object that you can manipulate with DOM methods.
`status`	This is the numeric HTTP result code returned by the server, such as 404 if the resource is not found, or 200 if the result was OK.
`statusText`	This is a textual message string describing the status code.

XMLHttpRequest Object Status Codes

Table A-3 lists the status codes that can show up in the `readystate` field of the `XMLHttpRequest` object during the lifecycle of a request as your callback function is repeatedly called.

Table A-3. *XMLHttpRequest Object readystate Status Codes*

Numeric Code	Description
0	Uninitialized. This is the value the `readystate` field will have initially before any operation is begun.
1	Loading. This means the `open()` method has been successfully called, but `send()` has not yet been called.
2	Loaded. This means `send()` has been called, and the object has completed the request, but no data has been received yet. Headers and status, however, *are* available at this point.
3	Receiving (or Interactive). This means the response is being chunked back to the client. `responseText` at this point will hold the response as received thus far.
4	Loaded (or Completed). The request has completed and the full response has been received.

APPENDIX B

Libraries, Websites, and Books, Oh My!

Throughout this book, we've referenced a number of libraries, websites, and books for you to get further information or see examples. Here is a concise list of all those references for your convenience, even for those libraries that are used as part of an application but not specifically described (but, uh, please do still read this book, OK?).

Libraries/Toolkits/Products

- Adobe (formerly Macromedia) Flash (`www.adobe.com/products/flash/flashpro`): Flash is not just a vector animation tool; it is truly a full-fledged development environment allowing you to create multimedia-rich websites that will run identically across most modern platforms (if a supported Flash player is available, which is mostly the case these days).
- Adobe (formerly Macromedia) Flex (`www.adobe.com/flex`): A rich client development framework that can greatly simplify creation of dynamic web applications.
- Apache Ant (`ant.apache.org`): The de facto standard in Java build tools.
- Apache Geronimo (`geronimo.apache.org`): An Apache application server.
- Apache Jakarta Commons (`jakarta.apache.org/commons`): Under the Commons banner you will find a number of very useful libraries, including Commons Logging, BeanUtils, FileUpload, Commons Chain, and much more. In short, if you aren't using Commons today, you should be tomorrow!
- BEA WebLogic (`www.bea.com`): Another of the big players in the application server market; provides much the same capabilities as WebSphere (although both vendors have their advantages and disadvantages).
- Caucho's Resin (`www.caucho.com`): Another application server, fairly popular with web hosts.
- Dojo (`dojotoolkit.org`): A popular Ajax toolkit that, in addition to its Ajax functionality, provides a lot of nifty client-side functions such as collections and client-side session storage, as well as a number of excellent GUI widgets.

- DWR, or Direct Web Remoting (`getahead.ltd.uk/dwr`): A very popular Ajax library that provides a syntax in JavaScript to call objects on the server, making them appear to be running locally (in terms of the JavaScript you write).
- Eclipse (`www.eclipse.org`): Probably the most popular Java IDE out there, and free to boot!
- FreeMarker (`freemarker.sourceforge.net`): A Java-based template engine, used by default by WebWork.
- HSQLDB (`www.hsqldb.org`): Free, lightweight (but not in terms of functionality!), pure-Java database engine.
- IBM WebSphere (`www-306.ibm.com/software/websphere`): A full-blown Java application server providing many services, including servlets, JSP, JNDI, EJB, and so on.
- IntelliJ IDEA (`www.jetbrains.com/idea`): If you want an IDE and don't mind paying for it, this is probably the best available.
- Java Web Parts (`javawebparts.sourceforge.net`): A collection of handy classes and utilities such as servlets, filters, taglibs, a Chain of Responsibility (CoR) implementation, and much more, to help web developers working in Java.
- jEdit (`www.jedit.org`): A fantastic text editor, this one is free and open source, and more important, features a large number of plug-ins that perform a great deal of tasks, bringing it closer to a full-blown IDE than just a text editor.
- Jetty (`http://mortbay.org/jetty/index.html`): Jetty is a 100 percent Java HTTP server and servlet container. This means that you do not need to configure and run a separate web server (like Apache) in order to use Java, servlets, and JSPs to generate dynamic content.
- JSLib (`http://jslib.mozdev.org`): A JavaScript library from the Mozilla Foundation that includes such features as an SAX XML parser.
- JSTL (`java.sun.com/products/jsp/jstl`): JavaServer Pages Standard Tag Library, a set of simple, common tags to be used in JSPs to make your life easier and your pages cleaner.
- Macromedia JRun (`www.macromedia.com/software/jrun`): Another entry in the server market.
- Maven (`maven.apache.org`): An increasingly popular build tool, Maven is designed to do most things for you without you having to write build scripts as you do with Ant.
- OpenEJB (`http://sourceforge.net/projects/openejb`): An open source, modular, configurable, and extendable Enterprise JavaBeans (EJB) container system and EJB server.
- Prototype (`prototype.conio.net`): JavaScript library for doing Ajax, as well as some other handy things.
- ROME (`https://rome.dev.java.net`): A Java library for working with RSS feeds.
- Sarissa (`http://sourceforge.net/projects/sarissa`): Billed as a general-purpose XML processing tool for JavaScript, it includes XSLT processing and much more.

- Spring Framework (www.springframework.org): A massive framework that covers a great many of the bases J2EE developers need, including an Inversion of Control (IoC) container, Aspect-Oriented Programming (AOP) support, and JDBC utility classes.
- Struts Action Framework (struts.apache.org): Perhaps the most popular web framework out there utilizing the Model-View-Controller (MVC) pattern.
- Tomcat (tomcat.apache.org): The reference implementation of the servlet and JSP specs, Tomcat is a fast, simple, standards-compliant, and powerful servlet container favored by many developers and hosting environments alike.
- UltraEdit (www.ultraedit.com): In my opinion, the best text editor available for Windows.
- Velocity (jakarta.apache.org/velocity): A Java-based template engine; an alternative to JSPs.
- WebWork (www.opensymphony.org/webwork): A popular MVC framework, which is, as of this writing, the future of Struts.
- Xara Webstyle (www.xara.com/products/webstyle/): For those of us who can do some graphics work but are *far* from artists ourselves, Webstyle is a fantastic tool to create graphics for the Web that make us *look* like we know what we're doing!
- XML4Script (http://xmljs.sourceforge.net/website/documentation-w3cdom.html): Another JavaScript library for parsing XML.

Websites

- Adaptive Path (www.adaptivepath.com): The company that Jesse James Garrett works for.
- "Ajax: A New Approach to Web Applications," by Jesse James Garrett (www.adaptivepath.com/publications/essays/archives/000385.php): The article where Ajax got its name.
- BackBase (www.backbase.com): Providers of excellent Ajax applications and toolkits.
- CSS Zen Garden (www.csszengarden.com): If you want to see what is possible with CSS layout, look no further than this site.
- Excite (www.excite.com): A great example of a portal site.
- Flickr (www.flickr.com): Ajax-enabled photo sharing.
- Fotki (www.fotki.com): Another Ajax-enabled photo-sharing site.
- Google Maps (maps.google.com): One of the Ajax applications that brought the technique to the attention of developers the world over.
- Google Suggest (www.google.com/webhp?complete=1&hl=en): Probably the most famous example of a type-ahead Ajax application.

- Google's GMail (`gmail.google.com`): One of the other great examples of Ajax usage from Google.
- Google's RSS reader (`www.google.com/reader`): A web-based RSS reader from Google utilizing Ajax.
- iBiblio (`www.ibiblio.org`): iBiblio has a modest goal: to back up the entire Internet! Well, that might be exaggerating a bit, but it is billed as a public library and archives. Most important for the purposes of this book is the Maven repository (`www.ibiblio.org/maven`) they maintain, where many of the most popular open source libraries and toolkits can be downloaded automatically by Maven as well as Ant scripts.
- The JSON home page (`http://json.org`): All about JavaScript Object Notation (JSON).
- Mappr (`www.mappr.com`): An excellent example of a Flash site done well.
- MSNBC (`www.msnbc.com`): The website of the news channel MSNBC.
- Num Sum (`www.numsum.com`): An Ajax-based spreadsheet.
- OpenSymphony (`http://opensymphony.com`): An organization, along the lines of Apache, that supplies a number of open source products, including WebWork and XWork.
- PBase (`www.pbase.com`): Yes, yet another Ajax-enabled photo-sharing site.
- Prototype documentation by Sergio Pereira (`www.sergiopereira.com/articles/prototype.js.html#Enumerating`).
- Shadow Gallery (`www.shadowgallery.com`): One of the bands I have made reference to in this book. Check them out—you'll love them!
- Slashdot (`www.slashdot.org`): News for nerds, stuff that matters!
- Sun (`http://java.sun.com`): The place for all things Java.
- W3Schools (`www.w3schools.com`): An excellent all-around reference site for all things HTML. You can learn about CSS, HTML, DOM scripting, and even Ajax itself there.
- WebShots (`www.webshots.com`): Another Ajax-enabled photo-sharing site.
- Wikipedia (`www.wikipedia.com`): The free, online dictionary that everyone can help make better!
- Yahoo! (`www.yahoo.com`): One of the oldest search sites around; now they do just about everything.

Books

- *Beginning CSS Web Development: From Novice to Professional*, by Simon Collison. An excellent book to get your CSS knowledge up to snuff (Apress, 2006).

- *Beginning JavaScript with Ajax and DOM Scripting: From Novice to Professional*, by Chris Heilmann. A great book for JavaScript and Ajax novices, with a slightly different scope than Jeremy Keith's book (Apress, 2006).
- *Beginning XML with DOM and Ajax: From Novice to Professional*, by Sas Jacobs. Another great web development book, showing how XML can be used effectively for web applications, including DOM scripting and Ajax (Apress, 2006).
- *CSS Mastery*, by Andy Budd, with Simon Collison and Cameron Moll. If you're already familiar with CSS, then this book will take you up to the next level, with invaluable techniques and good practices (friends of ED, 2006).
- *DOM Scripting: Web Design with JavaScript and the Document Object Model*, by Jeremy Keith. This book will give you a good grounding in DOM scripting (friends of ED, 2005).
- *Pro Ajax and Java: From Professional to Expert*, by Nathaniel Schutta and Ryan Asleson. A great companion book to the one you're reading now, this book also looks at the fusion of Java and Ajax, but from a more technology/workflow perspective rather than looking at complete projects. It covers setting up the perfect development environment, testing and debugging, using Ajax libraries, and understanding the Ajax capabilities of Java frameworks such as Spring and JSF (Apress, 2006).

Index

B

D

H

I

X

Z